The Cambridge Companion to the Lied

Beginning several generations before Schubert, the Lied first appears
as domestic entertainment. In the century that follows it becomes one
of the primary modes of music-making. By the time German song
comes to its presumed conclusion with Richard Strauss's 1948 *Vier
letzte Lieder*, this rich repertory has moved beyond the home and
keyboard accompaniment to the symphony hall. This is the first
introductory chronicle of this fascinating genre. In essays by eminent
scholars, this Companion places the Lied in its full context – at once
musical, literary, and cultural – with chapters devoted to focal
composers as well as important issues, such as the way in which the
Lied influenced other musical genres, its use as a musical commodity,
and issues of performance. The volume is framed by a detailed
chronology of German music and poetry from the late 1730s to the
present and also contains a wide-ranging guide to suggested further
reading.

Cambridge Companions to Music

Topics

The Cambridge Companion to Blues and Gospel Music
Edited by Allan Moore

The Cambridge Companion to Conducting
Edited by José Antonio Bowen

The Cambridge Companion to Grand Opera
Edited by David Charlton

The Cambridge Companion to Jazz
Edited by Mervyn Cooke and David Horn

The Cambridge Companion to the Lied
Edited by James Parsons

The Cambridge Companion to the Musical
Edited by William Everett and Paul Laird

The Cambridge Companion to the Orchestra
Edited by Colin Lawson

The Cambridge Companion to Pop and Rock
Edited by Simon Frith, Will Straw and John Street

The Cambridge Companion to the String Quartet
Edited by Robin Stowell

Composers

The Cambridge Companion to Bach
Edited by John Butt

The Cambridge Companion to Bartók
Edited by Amanda Bayley

The Cambridge Companion to Beethoven
Edited by Glenn Stanley

The Cambridge Companion to Berg
Edited by Anthony Pople

The Cambridge Companion to Berlioz
Edited by Peter Bloom

The Cambridge Companion to Brahms
Edited by Michael Musgrave

The Cambridge Companion to Benjamin Britten
Edited by Mervyn Cooke

The Cambridge Companion to Bruckner
Edited by John Williamson

The Cambridge Companion to John Cage
Edited by David Nicholls

The Cambridge Companion to Chopin
Edited by Jim Samson

The Cambridge Companion to Debussy
Edited by Simon Trezise

The Cambridge Companion to the

Lied

· · · · · · · · · · · ·

EDITED BY
James Parsons

CAMBRIDGE
UNIVERSITY PRESS

CAMBRIDGE UNIVERSITY PRESS
Cambridge, New York, Melbourne, Madrid, Cape Town,
Singapore, São Paulo, Delhi, Tokyo, Mexico City

Cambridge University Press
The Edinburgh Building, Cambridge CB2 8RU, UK

Published in the United States of America by
Cambridge University Press, New York

www.cambridge.org
Information on this title: www.cambridge.org/9780521800273

First published 2004

A catalogue record for this publication is available from the British Library

Library of Congress cataloguing in publication data
The Cambridge companion to the Lied / edited by James Parsons.
    p. cm. – (Cambridge companions to music)
Includes bibliographical references (p. 369) and index.
ISBN 0 521 80027 7 (hardback) – ISBN 0 521 80471 X (paperback)
1. Songs – Germany – History and criticism.   2. Songs – Austria – History and criticism.
I. Parsons, James, 1956–   II. Series.
ML2829.C36   2003   2003051229

ISBN 978-0-521-80027-3 Hardback
ISBN 978-0-521-80471-4 Paperback

Contents

Part V • Reception and performance

Contributors

Ruth O. Bingham, after receiving her Ph.D. from Cornell University, moved to Honolulu, where she lectures at the University of Hawaii at Manoa, and reviews for *Opera News* and the *Honolulu Star-Bulletin*. Past projects include summer workshops on music in American history for Boise State University and a series of lecture/workshops on early childhood education for the University of Hawaii, Manoa, Childcare Center. Publications include *Topical Song Cycles of the Early Nineteenth Century* (A-R Editions, 2003), an edition of six cycles, and *Music Theory in Practice: A Companion to Fundamentals in Western Music* (Kendall-Hunt Publishing, 1995).

Jane K. Brown is Professor of Germanics and Comparative Literature at the University of Washington. A former president of the Goethe Society of North America, she works on drama, narrative, and poetry of the seventeenth through nineteenth centuries and has published extensively on Goethe, particularly *Faust*, and also on Droste-Hülshoff, Shakespeare, Schubert, and Mozart. Currently she is working on a book on allegory and the advent of neo-classicism in drama and opera from Shakespeare to Wagner.

James Deaville is Associate Professor in the School of the Arts at McMaster University in Hamilton, Canada. His 1986 dissertation from Northwestern University concerned Peter Cornelius as music critic. Since then, he has spoken and published on the music of Liszt and his circle in Weimar, Wagner, Mahler, Strauss, Reger, music criticism, music and gender, television music, and music and race. His edition of the Bayreuth memoirs of Wagner's balletmaster Richard Fricke was published as *Wagner in Rehearsal 1875–1876: The Diaries of Richard Fricke* (Pendragon Press, 1997). Essays and reviews by him have appeared in *The New Grove Dictionary of Music and Musicians*, *The New Grove Dictionary of Opera*, *Norton / New Grove Dictionary of Women Composers*, *Pipers-Enzyklopaedie des Musiktheaters*, *Studies in American Music*, *Notes*, *Canadian University Music Review*, *Journal of Musicological Research*, and *Studien zur Wertungsforschung*.

Marie-Agnes Dittrich studied history and musicology in Germany at the University of Hamburg where, in 1989, she completed her dissertation, "Harmonik und Sprachvertonung in Schuberts Liedern." She was a lecturer in Music Theory and Musicology at the Conservatory of Hamburg from 1983 until 1993 and a guest lecturer at the Universities of Ibadan, Ilorin and Nsukka in Nigeria. In 1993 she was named Professor of Formal Analysis at the Universität für Musik und darstellende Kunst Wien. Since 1995, she also has been a lecturer for the Vienna Courses of the American Heritage Association. Her research interests include music analysis, music of northern Germany, and Schubert. Publications by her have appeared in *Musica, Hamburger Jahrbuch für Musikwissenschaft* and numerous collections of essays.

Christopher H. Gibbs is James H. Ottaway, Jr. Professor of Music at Bard College and Co-Artistic Director of the Bard Music Festival. He is the author of *The Life of Schubert* (Cambridge University Press, 2000) and editor of *The Cambridge Companion to Schubert* (Cambridge University Press, 1997). He received the ASCAP-Deems Taylor Award in 1998 and has been musicological consultant and program annotator for The Philadelphia Orchestra since 2000.

Amanda Glauert joined the academic faculty of the Royal Academy of Music in 1994 where she is now Head of Research. She studied at Clare College, Cambridge, and subsequently undertook research into the aesthetics of the Lied at Cambridge and Goldsmith's College, London. She has held lecturing positions at Trinity College, Dublin, and Colchester Institute. She has contributed essays to *Wagner in Performance* (Yale University Press, 1992) and *The Cambridge Companion to Beethoven* (Cambridge University Press, 2000), and her article "'Ich singe, wie der Vogel singt': Reflections on Nature and Genre in Wolf's Setting of Goethe's Der Sänger" was published in 2000 in the *Journal of the Royal Musical Association* (vol. 125). Her book on Wolf song, *Hugo Wolf and the Wagnerian Inheritance*, came out in 1999 (Cambridge University Press). She currently is writing a book on the Lieder of Beethoven.

David Gramit teaches musicology at the University of Alberta, in Edmonton, Canada. A recipient of the Alfred Einstein Award of the American Musicological Society for his work on the aesthetic context of Franz Schubert's circle, he has published on a variety of topics including Schubert's Lieder, the social construction of musical meaning in the nineteenth century, and the social history of German musical culture. He is the author of *Cultivating Music: The Aspirations, Interests, and Limits of German Musical Culture, 1770–1848* (University of California Press, 2002).

Graham Johnson lives in London and is one of the world's most sought-after collaborative pianists. *The Songmakers' Almanac – Twenty Years of Song Recitals in London* (Thames Publishing, 1996) tells the story of the ground-breaking series of concerts which established his reputation. His complete set of Schubert Lieder for Hyperion on thirty-seven discs includes contributors from (among many others) Elly Ameling, Janet Baker, Ian Bostridge, Brigitte Fassbaender, Matthias Goerne, Thomas Hampson, Felicity Lott, Ann Murray, Peter Schreier, and Christine Schäfer. A Schumann Lieder project on twelve discs now is halfway completed; both series are issued with Mr. Johnson's own commentaries. He is Senior Professor of Accompaniment at London's Guildhall School of Music, and co-author of the comprehensive and wide-ranging *A French Song Companion* (Oxford University Press, 2000). Studies of the songs of Britten and Schubert are in preparation.

Rena Charnin Mueller is a musicologist specializing in nineteenth-century music, in particular the work of Franz Liszt and Richard Wagner. Articles on Liszt's compositional aesthetics have appeared in *19th Century Music*, the *Journal of the American Musicological Society*, the *Journal of the American Liszt Society*, *Studia Musicologica Hungarica*, *The Hungarian Quarterly*, *Magyar Zene*, *Muszika*, and *La Revue Musicale*. She has published new editions of *Les Préludes* for Editio Musica Budapest (1997), the *Trois Etudes de Concert* (1998) and the *Ballades* (1996) for Henle Verlag; and her edition of the newly discovered Liszt *Walse* was issued by Thorpe Music Publishing in 1996. With Mária Eckhardt, she is the author of the

Franz Liszt "List of Works" for the revised edition of *The New Grove Dictionary of Music and Musicians*, and they are also co-authoring the forthcoming new *Franz Liszt Thematic Catalogue* (Henle Verlag).

James Parsons is Associate Professor of Music History at Southwest Missouri State University, in Springfield, Missouri. His research centers on late eighteenth- and early nineteenth-century music, Beethoven, musical aesthetics, and the Lied. His article "'*Deine Zauber binden wieder*': Beethoven, Schiller, and the Joyous Reconciliation of Opposites" appeared in *Beethoven Forum*, vol. 9, no. 1 (2002). Other essays and reviews have been published in *Early Music*, the *Journal of the American Musicological Society*, *Musical Analysis*, and *Notes*. He is the author of the essay on the eighteenth-century Lied for the revised edition of *The New Grove Dictionary of Music and Musicians*. At present, he is at work on a book-length study of the twentieth-century Lied, for which he was awarded fellowships from the National Endowment for the Humanities and a Fulbright Research Fellowship in 2002.

Heather Platt, a native of Canberra, Australia, is Associate Professor of Music History at Ball State University, in Muncie, Indiana. A particular scholarly interest of hers is the reception of Brahms's Lieder by subsequent composers; her article "Hugo Wolf and the Reception of Brahms's Lieder" appeared in *Brahms Studies*, vol. 2, and her article "Jenner versus Wolf: The Critical Reception of Brahms's Songs" was published in the *Journal of Musicology*. She also has published articles using Schenkerian analysis to examine the relationships between text and music in Brahms's songs in such journals as *Intégral* and *Indiana Music Theory Review*. Numerous articles by her on Brahms's Lieder are included in *The Compleat Brahms*, ed. Leon Botstein (W. W. Norton, 1999). Her *Johannes Brahms: A Guide to the Research,* part of Routledge's Music Bibliographies series, was published in 2003.

Jürgen Thym is Professor Emeritus at the Eastman School of Music (University of Rochester) where he served as musicology department chair from 1982 until 2000. He has lectured, both in the United States and abroad, and published on the music of Beethoven, Schubert, Schumann, Wolf, Weill, and others (mostly on text–music relationships in German Lieder). He is the co-editor of several volumes in the *Arnold Schoenberg Gesamtausgabe* and co-translator of music theory treatises by Johann Philipp Kirnberger and Heinrich Schenker. In 1983 he received ASCAP's Deems-Taylor Award. He currently is working on a volume of essays, *Of Poetry and Music: Approaches to the German Lied in the Nineteenth Century*, and an edition of the writings by composer Luca Lombardi, *Construction of Freedom.*

Susan Youens is Professor of Musicology at the University of Notre Dame. She is the author of numerous articles in scholarly journals and of seven books: *Retracing a Winter's Journey: Schubert's Winterreise* (Cornell University Press, 1991), *Hugo Wolf: The Vocal Music* (Princeton University Press, 1992), and (all for Cambridge University Press), *Schubert: Die schöne Müllerin* (1992), *Schubert's Poets and the Making of Lieder* (1996), *Schubert, Müller, and Die schöne Müllerin* (1997), *Hugo Wolf and his Mörike Songs* (2000), and *Schubert's Late Lieder: Beyond the Song Cycles* (2002). She currently is working on a study of Heine and the Lied as well as a social history of the Lied.

James L. Zychowicz is a musicologist whose specialization is nineteenth-century music, especially the works of Gustav Mahler. His publications include *Mahler's*

Fourth Symphony, in the series Studies in Musical Genesis and Structure published by Oxford University Press, as well as articles and reviews in the *Journal of the American Musicological Society*, *Notes*, and the *Journal of Musicology*. He is the editor of the two-volume critical edition of Mahler's score for Weber's opera *Die drei Pintos*, published recently in the series of Recent Researches in the Music of the Nineteenth and Early Twentieth Centuries (A-R Editions, 2000) and given its first performance at Lincoln Center in 2002. Articles on Mahler and Strauss are forthcoming in several collections of essays devoted to those composers.

Acknowledgments

It is a pleasure to acknowledge the assistance and encouragement of many friends and colleagues during the planning and preparation of this volume. Above all, I am indebted to my contributors, none of whom grumbled even once (or at least not to me) when I allowed my attention to be diverted from this project by others. Working with all of the authors whose work appears in this book has been one of the highpoints of my professional career. From the start, Susan Youens was unstinting in her help, sagacious counsel, and formidable knowledge of the German art song. At Cambridge University Press, Victoria Cooper provided equal amounts of patience and unfailing good faith: every editor of a collection of essays should be so lucky. Nikki Burton, also at the press, cheerfully responded to an endless array of questions. Paul Watt, production editor, was a gracious guiding spirit once the volume went to press; I owe him much. I am grateful to Christopher Gibbs, Rufus Hallmark, Glenn Stanley, Susan Youens, and Neal Zaslaw for helping to identify potential contributors. For other kindnesses, I thank Tom Beghin, Mark Evan Bonds, Michael J. Budds, James S. Fritz, Denise Gallo, Duncan Large, and my dear friends in Springfield, Missouri, Michael Murray, and Joseph Schellhardt. If I have but one regret having to do with this volume, it is that Joe did not live to see it completed.

My own chapters benefited from discussions with and suggestions from Ruth Bingham, Deanna Bush, Denise Gallo, David Gramit, and my colleague at Southwest Missouri State University (in German studies) Carol Anne Costabile-Heming. I owe Michael Collins a special word of thanks as not only did he read numerous versions of my chapters, he also has been a source of support for more years than either of us would care to own up to: first as an inspiring teacher and, as of late, as a valued colleague, and always a friend. Research on my chapters was supported in part by a Study Visit Research Grant for Faculty from the Deutscher Akademischer Austauschdienst (German Academic Exchange [DAAD]) and a Summer Faculty Fellowship from Southwest Missouri State University. This funding facilitated my first visit to Berlin and the Musikabteilung of the Staatsbibliothek zu Berlin – Preußischer Kulturbesitz and the Akademie der Künste zu Berlin; being able to work at both collections has been of enormous assistance. Friends made during my now three trips to Berlin likewise have been a source of support, above all Christiane Waskowiak and Frauke Mahrt-Thomsen. Also in Berlin, I am pleased to acknowledge the gracious help of Hermann Danuser, at Humboldt Universität, and Albrecht Riethmüller, at Freie Universität. Berlin is an exciting city right now; its extraordinary archives, amazing art museums, abundant music making, and always tempting restaurants provided a heady backdrop against which to formulate many of my thoughts on the Lied. I also thank the staffs of the Goethe and Schiller Archives and Herzogin Anna Amalia Bibliothek, both in Weimar, where I was fortunate to engage in research during a lovely May visit in 2001.

Thanks also are due to Thomas Tietze at Bärenreiter-Verlag, who graciously granted permission to publish a modified version of Marie-Agnes Dittrich's essay on Schubert, which first appeared in German in *Schubert Handbuch*, ed. Walther Dürr and Andreas Krause (Kassel and Stuttgart, 1997).

Lastly, I am grateful to my family – my mother, Patricia Parker; my brother and his wife, Randy and Brenda Parsons, their vivacious and adorable children, Sarah and Aaron; and my grandmother, Louise M. Vines – for a rare gift that has enriched my life as of late and, I can only hope, theirs too.

The Lied in context: a chronology

1729	Johann Christoph Gottsched, *Versuch einer critischen Dichtkunst vor die Deutschen* (dated 1730; 4th expanded edn. 1751), provides one of the earliest definitions of modern Lied: "nothing but an agreeable and clear reading of a verse, which consequently must match the nature and content of the words."
1732	Joseph Haydn born.
1736	J. S. Sperontes, *Singende Muse an der Pleisse* (to 1745; enlarged 1747).
1737	Johann Friedrich Gräfe, *Samlung verschiedener und auserlesener Oden, zu welchen von den beruhmtesten Meistern in der Music eigene Melodeyen verfertiget worden.*
1738	Johann Adolf Scheibe devotes entire issue of his journal *Der critische Musikus* to the Lied; C. P. E. Bach appointed harpsichordist to Prussian Crown Prince Frederick.
1739	J. Mattheson, *Der vollkommene Capellmeister.*
1740	Frederick II (the Great), thirty-eight, ascends Prussian throne; Maria Theresa, twenty-three, inherits Austrian and Habsburg throne.
1741	First German translation of Shakespeare play, *Julius Caesar*, by C. W. von Borck; Frederick the Great orders construction of Royal Opera House, Berlin; Handel, *Messiah*; Telemann, *Vier und Zwanzig Oden* (Hamburg), dedicated to "renewed golden ages of notes" worthy of Homer; Vivaldi dies.
1742	Friedrich von Hagedorn, *Oden und Lieder* (Hamburg); J. V. Görner, *Sammlung Neuer Oden und Lieder* (Hamburg [vol. II 1744]).
1744	Johann Gottfried Herder, J. A. P. Schulz born.
1745	Construction begins on Frederick the Great's palace, Sanssouci, under supervision of architect Georg Wenceslaus von Knobelsdorff.
1748	Ludwig Christoph Heinrich Hölty born.
1749	Last public execution of witch in German-speaking lands; Goethe born; Maria Theresa unites Austria and Bohemia; J. P. Uz, *Lyrische Gedichte* (Berlin).
1750	J. S. Bach, G. Sammartini die.
1751	*Encyclopédie ou Dictionnaire raisonné des sciences, des arts et des métiers* (to 1772).

1752   Benjamin Franklin invents lightning rod; Johann Joachim Quantz, *Versuch einer Anweisung die Flöte traversiere zu spielen* (3rd edn. 1789); Christian Gottfried Krause, *Von der musikalischen Poesie*; J. F. Reichardt born.

1753   Founding of British Museum; C. P. E. Bach, first part of *Versuch über die wahre Art das Clavier zu spielen* (2nd edn. 1787); *Oden mit Melodien*, ed. K. W. Ramler, C. G. Krause; Krause, *Von der musikalischen Poesie* (Berlin).

1754   Hagedorn dies.

1755   Samuel Johnson, *A Dictionary of the English Language*; Johann Joachim Winckelmann, "Gedanken über die Nachahmung der griechischen Werke in Malerei und Bildhauerkunst."

1756   Seven Years War begins; Leopold Mozart, *Versuch einer gründlichen Violinschule*; W. A. Mozart born; Friedrich Gottlob Fleischer, *Oden und Lieder mit Melodien*.

1757   Johann Friedrich Agricola, *Anleitung zur Singkunst*.

1758   C. P. E. Bach, *Gellert Geistliche Oden und Lieder* (Berlin); Zelter born.

1759   A. B. V. Herbing, *Musikalischer Versuch in Fabeln und Erzählungen des Herrn Professor Gellerts*; Handel dies; Schiller born.

1760   George III ascends British throne; Zumsteeg born.

1762   Catherine II becomes Empress of Russia; James Macpherson, *Poems of Ossian*; C. P. E. Bach, second part of *Versuch über die wahre Art das Clavier zu spielen*; C. P. E. Bach, *Oden mit Melodien* (Berlin); Johann Christoph Schmügel, *Sing- und Spieloden vor musikalische Freunde componiert* (Leipzig).

1765   Joseph II crowned Emperor of Holy Roman Empire, co-regent with Maria Theresa until 1780; Bishop Thomas Percy, *Reliques of Ancient English Poetry*.

1766   Haydn named Kapellmeister at Esterházy; C. P. E. Bach, *Der Wirth und die Gäste eine Singode von Herrn Gleim*.

1767   *Lieder der Deutschen mit Melodien* (Berlin, 4 vols. –1768, 240 songs), poetry by Ramler, music by Krause; Telemann dies.

1768   Captain James Cook's first circumnavigation; Johann Michael Vogl, Austrian baritone and frequent Lied collaborator with Schubert, born.

1769   C. F. Gellert dies; Napoleon born.

1770   Friedrich Hölderlin, Ludwig van Beethoven born.

1772   Herder, *Über den Ursprung der Sprache*; Hiller, *Lieder mit Melodien*; Novalis born.

1773   Ludwig Tieck born.

1774   Discovery of oxygen; Goethe, *Die Leiden des jungen Werther*;
         Goethe moves to Weimar to tutor future Duke Karl August of
         Saxe-Weimar-Eisenach.

1775   Reichardt, *Gesänge fürs schöne Geschlecht.*

1776   American Declaration of Independence; Joseph II establishes
         Nationaltheater, Vienna; Friedrich Maximilian Klinger's play
         Wirrwarr; oder, Sturm und Drang – name taken for literary
         movement; Hölty dies.

1777   Schiller publishes first poem, "Der Eroberer."

1778   Mesmer practices "mesmerizing" in Paris; Herder, *Stimmen der
         Völker* (1778–79), a collection of folk poetry.

1780   Kirnberger, *Gesänge am Clavier*; Maria Theresa dies, succeeded
         by Joseph II; Conradin Kreutzer born.

1781   Reichardt, *Lieder für Kinder*; G. E. Lessing dies; Karl Friedrich
         Schinkel, A. Chamisso born.

1782   Goethe, ballad poem "Erlkönig"; Haydn, *XII Lieder für das
         Clavier*; Juliane Reichardt (née Benda), *Lieder und
         Klaviersonaten*; J. A. P. Schulz: Part I, *Lieder im Volkston* [parts II,
         III 1785, 1790].

1783   Montgolfier brothers, J. M. and J. E., launch first hot air lift
         balloon.

1784   First political cartoons by Thomas Rowlandson; Ernst Wratislaw
         Wilhelm von Wobeser, *Ein Roman in fünf Liedern*; Louis Spohr
         born.

1786   Frederick the Great dies, succeeded by Frederick William II;
         Goethe's Italian journey (until 1788); Schiller, "An die Freude,"
         other poems; Mozart, *Le nozze di Figaro*; Corona Schröter
         publishes *Fünf und Zwanzig Lieder* (includes first setting
         of Goethe's "Erlkönig"); Carl Maria von Weber, J. Kerner
         born.

1787   USA Constitution signed by George Washington and twelve
         states (ratified following year); Schiller moves to Weimar, writes
         Don Carlos; Immanuel Kant, 2nd edn. *Kritik der reinen Vernunft*;
         Boccherini Hofkapellmeister in Berlin; C. P. E. Bach, *Neue
         Melodien*; Mozart, *Abendempfindung an Laura*, K523; Ludwig
         Uhland born.

1788   Carl Gotthard Langhans, Berlin chief city architect, begins work
         on Brandenburg Gate; C. P. E. Bach dies; Eichendorff, Rückert,
         Arthur Schopenhauer born.

1789   French Revolution begins; first steam-driven cotton factory in
         England; D. G. Türk, *Clavierschule*; C. P. E. Bach, *Neue
         Lieder-Melodien*.

1790   Zumsteeg, *Des Pfarrers Tochter von Taubenhayn von G. A. Bürger*;
        Joseph II dies, succeeded by Leopold II.

1791   Thomas Paine, *The Rights of Man*; Goethe heads Weimar Court
        Theater; waltz becomes fashionable in England; Mozart, *Die
        Zauberflöte*, *Requiem* (incomplete), dies; Theodor Körner born.

1792   Mary Wollstonecraft, *Vindication of the Rights of Women*;
        Gustavus III, Sweden, assassinated; Leopold II dies, succeeded by
        Francis II; French monarchy dissolved; Beethoven settles in
        Vienna; Berlin Singakademie founded; Gioachino Rossini born.

1793   Louis XVI, Marie Antoinette executed – Reign of Terror; Louvre
        opens; Whitney invents cotton gin; Mackenzie crosses Canada;
        Paganini debuts; Goethe, *Römische Elegien*; Hůrka, *12 deutsche
        Lieder*.

1794   First telegraph, Paris to Lille; Goethe, Schiller meet; Wilhelm
        Müller born; Reichardt, *Göthe's lyrische Gedichte*; Haydn, *VI
        Original Canzonettas*.

1795   First horse-drawn railroad, England; Schiller, *Letters on the
        Aesthetic Education of Man*; Zelter comes to Goethe's attention;
        Goethe's *Wilhelm Meisters Lehrjahre* published with eight Lieder
        by Reichardt; Karl Müchler, *Die Farben*; Haydn's second set of
        canzonettas.

1796   Napoleon marries Josephine; Reichardt's *Musikalischer
        Almanach* cycle and *Lieder geselliger Freude*; Uz dies; J. K. G.
        Loewe born.

1797   Frederick William II dies, succeeded by Frederick William III;
        Wordsworth, *Lyrical Ballads*; Annette von Droste-Hülshoff,
        Heinrich Heine, Schubert born; Hans Georg Nägeli, *Lieder*.

1798   The brothers August Wilhelm and Friedrich von Schlegel found
        literary journal *Athenaeum*; Reichardt, *Wiegenlieder für gute
        deutsche Mütter*.

1799   Rosetta Stone found in Egypt; Napoleon becomes First Consul;
        Haydn, *Die Schöpfung*; Mozart, *Sämtliche Lieder und Gesänge
        beym Fortepiano* (posthumously published); Reichardt, *Lieder
        für die Jugend*.

1800   Postal service introduced in Berlin; Schiller, *Maria Stuart*;
        Beethoven, Symphony No. 1; Zumsteeg, *Kleine Balladen und
        Lieder* (vol. I; II–VII to 1807); Reichardt, *Lieb' und Treue*; G. F.
        Daumer born; Schulz dies.

1801   Schiller, *Die Jungfrau von Orleans*; Haydn, *Die Jahreszeiten*;
        Novalis dies.

1802   H. C. Koch, *Musikalisches Lexikon*, defines Lied as "the one
        product of music and poetry whose content today appeals to

every class of people and every individual"; Zumsteeg dies; N. Lenau born.

1803 Louisiana Purchase; Gleim, Herder, Klopstock die.

1804 World population estimated at one billion; Napoleon crowned Emperor, defeats Austria at Austerlitz; Lewis and Clark begin travels; Schiller, *Wilhelm Tell*; Immanuel Kant dies; Eduard Mörike born; Beethoven, Symphony No. 3; Reichardt, *Lieder der Liebe und der Einsamkeit*; Himmel, *Fanchon das Leyermädchen*.

1805 French occupy Vienna (until 1806); Walter Scott, *The Lay of the Last Minstrel*; Schiller dies; Fanny Mendelssohn born; Reichardt, *Romantische Gesänge*.

1806 Holy Roman Empire dissolved; Napoleon defeats Prussian army at Jena; A. von Arnim, C. Brentano, *Des Knaben Wunderhorn* (to 1808).

1807 Peace of Tilsit between France, Prussia; David paints *Coronation of Napoleon*; Britain abolishes slave trade; first voyage of Fulton's steamship, Claremont; Pleyel founds pianoforte factory in Paris.

1808 Source of Ganges River discovered; Caspar David Friedrich paints *The Cross in the Mountains*; Johann Gottlieb Fichte presents lecture *Addresses to the German Nation*; Goethe, *Faust* part I; Beethoven, Symphonies Nos. 5, 6; Himmel, *Die Blumen und der Schmetterling*.

1809 French bombard Vienna, stray shell falls on Royal Seminary where Schubert is enrolled; C. Brentano, *Romanzen vom Rosenkranz*; Haydn dies; Mendelssohn born.

1810 Peter Durand, in France, develops technique for canning food; Scott, *The Lady of the Lake*; Mme de Staël, *De l'Allemagne*; Kleist, *Kätchen von Heilbronn*; Reichardt, *Schillers lyrische Gedichte*; Chopin, Schumann born.

1811 Prince Metternich, Austrian chancellor until 1848; Jane Austen, *Sense and Sensibility*; Goethe, *Aus meinem Leben: Dichtung und Wahrheit*; Franz Liszt born; damper pedals invented for piano; Reichardt, *Göthe's Lieder, Oden, Balladen und Romanzen* (4 vols., first issued in 1809); Ries, *Sechs Lieder von Goethe*, Op. 32; Schubert's *Hagars Klage*, earliest surviving complete song.

1812 Girard invents machine for spinning flax; Napoleon defeated in Russia; war between Britain and USA; Brothers Grimm, *Märchen* (vol. II); Byron, *Childe Harold's Pilgrimage*; Tiedge, *Das Echo oder Alexis und Ida. Ein Ciclus von Liedern*; Niklas von Krufft, *Sammlung deutscher Lieder*.

1813 Wieland, T. Körner (German poet-soldier) die – his father publishes his *Leyer und Schwert* posthumously following year; Giuseppe Verdi, Richard Wagner born.

1814 Napoleon abdicates – banished to Elba; Louis XVIII assumes throne as his hereditary right; formal opening of Congress of Vienna; Maelzel invents metronome in Vienna; Schubert composes *Gretchen am Spinnrade* (D118) and nearly 150 other songs; Beethoven, final version of *Fidelio*; Gesellschaft der Musikfreunde founded in Vienna; Reichardt dies; E. T. A. Hoffmann writes that "the very nature of the Lied" is "to stir the innermost soul by means of the simplest melody and the simplest modulation, without affectation or straining for effect and originality: therein lies the mysterious power of true genius."

1815 Napoleon defeated at Waterloo, banished to St. Helena; final act of Congress of Vienna redraws map of Europe – thirty-eight German states become German Confederation; first steam warship, USS Fulton; advent of Biedermeier styles until c. 1848; Uhland, *Frühlingslieder*, *Vaterländische Gedichte*, *Wanderlieder*; Schubert composes *Erlkönig* (D328) and other songs to Goethe poems; Otto von Bismarck, Robert Franz, Josephine Lang born.

1816 Beethoven, *An die ferne Geliebte*, Op. 98, to poetry by Jeitteles; selected songs by Schubert on Goethe poems (including *Erlkönig*, *Gretchen am Spinnrade*) sent to Goethe – returned without comment.

1817 Weber, *Die Temperamente bei dem Verluste der Geliebten*.

1818 Mary Wollstonecraft Shelley, *Frankenstein*; Karl Marx born; Ludwig Berger, *Gesänge aus einem gesellschaftlichen Liederspiel*, *Die schöne Müllerin*.

1819 Maximum twelve-hour work day for children in England; Goethe, *West-östlicher Divan*; Theodor Fontane, Clara Wieck born.

1820 Revolutionary and liberal movements suppressed in Germany; George IV becomes King of Great Britain and Ireland; Venus de Milo discovered; Müller, *Die schöne Müllerin* poems; Loewe meets Goethe; Friedrich Engels born; first use of metal frames in piano construction.

1821 Napoleon dies; Mendelssohn meets Goethe; Schauspielhaus (now Konzerthaus) construction begun in Berlin, to a design by Schinkel; Weber, *Der Freischütz*; Heine, *Gedichte*; Müller, *Griechenlieder* (until 1824).

1822 E. T. A. Hoffmann dies; Pierre Erard patents piano double escapement action; Louise Reichardt, *7 romantische Gesänge*.

1823   Müller, *Die Winterreise* (first twelve poems); Schubert, song
        cycle *Die schöne Müllerin.*

1824   Leopold von Ranke, German historian, publishes *History of the
        Latin and Teutonic Nations from 1494 to 1514*; Müller completes
        poetic cycle on *Die Winterreise*; Beethoven, Symphony No. 9;
        Anton Bruckner, Peter Cornelius born. Loewe publishes Op. 1, *3
        Balladen.*

1825   First passenger railroad, Britain.

1826   A. B. Marx, *Die Kunst des Gesanges, theoretisch-praktisch*; Weber
        dies; Julius Stockhausen born.

1827   Heine, *Buch der Lieder*; Beethoven, Müller die; Schubert,
        Winterreise.

1828   Loewe, *Gesänge der Sehnsucht*; Schubert dies.

1829   Niepce, Daguerre develop photography; Schubert,
        Schwanengesang posthumously published; Mendelssohn revives
        Bach's *St. Matthew Passion.*

1830   Kingdom of Belgium founded; Hector Berlioz, *Symphonie
        fantastique.*

1831   Ross discovers magnetic North Pole; Grillparzer, *Des Meeres und
        der Liebe Wellen*; Hegel dies.

1832   First continental railway, from Budweis to Linz; Goethe, *Faust*
        part II published posthumously; Scott, Goethe, Zelter die.

1833   Wilhelm Dilthey, Johannes Brahms born.

1834   Loewe, *Bilder des Orients*, Op. 10; Carl Alexander writes: "Just as
        language . . . directly represents the development of nations, so
        the Lied is the most faithful mirror of its soul."

1835   Edict by German Federal Diet bans books of "Young German"
        writers such as Heine; first German railroad from Nuremberg
        to Fürth; Samuel Morse develops communication code bearing
        his name; Loewe, *Der Bergmann: Ein Liederkreis
        in Balladenform.*

1836   Schopenhauer, *Über den Willen in der Natur.*

1837   Victoria becomes Queen of Great Britain and Ireland; Fröbel
        opens first Kindergarten; electric telegraph invented; Loewe,
        Frauenliebe, Op. 60.

1838   Steamship *Great Western* crosses Atlantic in fifteen days;
        Chamisso dies; Droste-Hülshoff, first collection of poems; Jenny
        Lind debuts in Stockholm in Weber's *Der Freischütz.*

1839   In USA, Goodyear discovers "vulcanization" of rubber.

1840   Queen Victoria marries Prince Albert; penny postage stamps
        introduced in Britain; Frederick William III dies, succeeded by
        Frederick William IV, in Berlin; Caspar David Friedrich,

Paganini, Vogl die; Schumann marries Clara Wieck, composes over 100 Lieder, including *Dichterliebe*, *Frauenliebe und -Leben*, and two *Liederkreise*, Op. 24 and 39.

1841   Saxophone invented by Adolphe Sax; Schumann, Symphony No. 1; Schinkel dies.

1842   First surgical operation using anesthesia; Droste-Hülshoff, *Die Judenbuche*; polka becomes fashionable.

1843   First nightclub opens in Paris; Hölderlin dies; R. Franz, Op. 1 *Zwölf Gesänge*.

1844   Marx meets Engels in Paris; Friedrich Nietzsche born.

1845   Engels, *The Condition of the Working Class in England*; Wagner, *Tannhäuser*.

1846   Electric arc lighting at Paris Opéra; Irish potato crop failure; Keller, *Gedichte*.

1847   First gold rush in California; creation of Associated Press; Charlotte Brontë, *Jane Eyre*; Fanny Hensel, Felix Mendelssohn die.

1848   Year of Revolutions; Marx, Engels, *Communist Manifesto*; Droste-Hülshoff dies.

1849   German National Assembly passes constitution, elects King Frederick William IV of Prussia "Emperor of the Germans" – he refuses; revolutions in Baden and Dresden; Wagner flees to Zurich; Chopin, Kreutzer die; Schumann, *Minnespiel*, Op. 101 and *Myrthen und Rosen*, Op. 25.

1850   Levi Strauss invents blue jeans; Lenau dies; Bach Gesellschaft founded; Wagner, *Lohengrin*.

1852   First vol. of Brothers Grimm, *Deutsches Wörterbuch* (last vol. published in 1960).

1853   Tieck dies; Brahms's first published songs, *Sechs Gesänge*, Op. 3.

1854   Crimean War; Cornelius's song cycle *Vater unser*; Hanslick, *Vom Musikalisch-Schönen*.

1856   Sigmund Freud born; Heine dies; baritone Julius Stockhausen gives first public performance of Schubert's *Die schöne Müllerin*; Schumann dies.

1857   Eichendorff dies.

1859   Work begins on Suez Canal; Charles Darwin, *On the Origin of Species*; Spohr dies.

1860   Gustav Mahler, Hugo Wolf born.

1862   Bismarck prime minister of Prussia; Peter Altenberg born; Kerner, Uhland die; Wagner, *Five Wesendonck Lieder*.

1863   Hebbel dies; Dehmel born.

1864   Richard Strauss born.

1865   Assassination of Abraham Lincoln; thirteenth amendment to the American constitution outlaws slavery; Wagner, *Tristan und Isolde* first performed.

1866   Bismarck creates North German Alliance; Rückert dies; Ferruccio Busoni, Paul Lincke born.

1867   Dual Monarchy of Austria-Hungary established; Karl Marx, *Das Kapital*; Alfred Nobel invents dynamite; Johann Strauss (ii), *The Blue Danube*.

1868   Stefan George, Heinrich Schenker born.

1869   Loewe, *5 Lieder*, Op. 145; Loewe dies; Hans Pfitzner born.

1870   Franco-Prussian War (to 1871); creation of German Empire; Bismarck first German Chancellor; John D. Rockefeller founds Standard Oil Company.

1871   Chicago fire; William I proclaimed German Emperor at Versailles; Zemlinsky born.

1872   Schubert statue dedicated in Vienna.

1873   J. Rissé, *Franz Schubert und seine Lieder*; Max Reger born.

1874   Cornelius dies; Hugo von Hofmannsthal, Karl Kraus, Austrian soprano Selma Kurz, Arnold Schoenberg born.

1875   Mörike, Daumer die; Rainer Maria Rilke, Carl Jung born.

1876   Alexander Graham Bell experiments successfully with "harmonic telegraph" – the telephone; Lula Mysz-Gmeiner, German contralto, born; Wagner, *Der Ring des Nibelungen* first performed as a cycle.

1877   Karl Erb, German tenor, born.

1878   Austro-Hungarian Empire occupies the duchies of Bosnia and Herzegovina; Franz Schreker born.

1880   Julia Culp, Dutch mezzo-soprano, born – first to record Schumann's *Frauenliebe und -Leben*; Josephine Lang dies.

1882   In Berlin Robert Koch announces discovery of tuberculosis germ; Berlin Philharmonic founded; two years after her death, Josephine Lang's collection of forty Lieder issued by Breitkopf & Härtel; Joseph Marx born.

1883   Brooklyn Bridge completed; Anton Webern, German soprano and mezzo-soprano Elena Gerhardt, Franz Kafka born; Wagner dies.

1884   German Reichstag begun in Berlin to a design by Paul Wallot (completed 1894); Mark Twain, *Huckleberry Finn*; Franz, *Sechs Gesänge*, Op. 52.

1885   World's first skyscraper built in Chicago; Alban Berg born.

1886   Robert Louis Stevenson, *Dr. Jekyll and Mr. Hyde*; Liszt dies; Schoeck born.

1887   Sir Arthur Conan Doyle's first Sherlock Holmes story, *A Study in Scarlet.*

1888   Deaths of Kaiser William I and Frederick III, accession to the throne of William II; Eastman introduces Kodak camera and roll film; Wolf, *Mörike-Lieder, Eichendorff Lieder*; German soprano Elisabeth Schumann, German soprano Lotte Lehmann, German baritone Heinrich Schlusnus born.

1889   Michael Raucheisen, Lied pianist, Martin Heidegger, Ludwig Wittgenstein born; Pfitzner, *Sieben Lieder*, Op. 2.

1890   Dismissal of Bismarck; Kurt Tucholsky, Franz Werfel born; Wolf, *Spanisches Liederbuch.*

1891   Oscar Wilde, *The Picture of Dorian Gray*; Wolf, book 1, *Italienisches Liederbuch*; Reger, *Sechs Lieder*, Op. 4; Ukrainian-American bass Alexander Kipnis, Austrian tenor Richard Tauber born.

1892   First movies, lasting about fifteen minutes, created; Franz dies.

1894   Brahms, *Deutsche Volks Lieder* (7 vols.); Paul Dessau born.

1895   German physicist Wilhelm Roentgen discovers X-rays; Norwegian soprano Kirsten Flagstad, Paul Hindemith born.

1896   In Munich, the magazine *Münchner Jugend* begins publishing illustrations by German Art Nouveau artists, thereby ushering in the *Jugendstil* – in Austria, the movement is called *Sezessionsstil*; principal artists and architects in Germany and Austria include Gustav Klimt, Koloman Moser, Otto Wagner, Josef Maria Olbrich, and Egon Schiele; Freud, in "The Aetiology of Hysteria," first uses term "Psycho-Analysis"; Clara Schumann dies; Brahms's *Vier ernste Gesänge*, Op. 121; Wolf, book 2, *Italienisches Liederbuch*; Mahler, *Lieder eines fahrenden Gesellen* first performed; Friedrich Hollaender born.

1897   Bram Stoker, *Dracula*; Schubert Centennial – collected edition completed; Wolf, *Drei Gedichte von Michelangelo*; Brahms dies; Erich Wolfgang Korngold, German soprano Tiana Lemnitz born.

1898   Cornerstone laid for "Association of Visual Artists Vienna Secession" building, designed by Josef Maria Olbrich; Bismarck, Fontane die; Bertolt Brecht, Hanns Eisler, Austrian singing actress Lotte Lenya, Austrian tenor Julius Patzak, Viktor Ullmann, born; Schoenberg, Op. 1, *Zwei Gesänge.*

1899   Karl Kraus launches journal *Die Fackel* (The Torch); English collaborative and Lied pianist Gerald Moore born.

1900   Freud, *The Interpretation of Dreams*; Erna Berger, German soprano, Ernst Krenek, Kurt Weill born.

1901   Queen Victoria dies after reign of almost sixty-four years –
        succeeded by her son, Edward VII; Schoenberg composes eight
        cabaret songs, the *Brettl-Lieder*; Marlene Dietrich, German
        baritone Gerhard Hüsch born.

1902   Max Klinger's statue of Beethoven displayed at the Secession
        House, Vienna; Max Friedländer publishes *Das deutsche Lied im
        18. Jahrhundert: Quellen und Studien*; Mahler, *Rückert Lieder*;
        Reger, *Zwölf Lieder*, Op. 66; Stephan Wolpe born.

1903   First flight of the Wright Brothers; Wolf dies; Schoenberg, *Sechs
        Lieder*, Op. 3 (begun 1899).

1904   New York City subway opens; Lincke, *Berliner Luft*; Schoenberg
        completes *Six Orchestral Songs*, Op. 8.

1905   In Dresden, a group of artists called *Die Brücke* (The Bridge)
        gather and, inspired by Van Gogh, Gauguin, and Munch,
        develop Expressionism – German and Austrian practitioners
        include Ernst Ludwig Kirchner, George Grosz, Oskar Kokoschka,
        and Russian-born Wassily Kandinsky, who studies in Munich;
        Expressionism influences other artistic media, especially
        German film; Richard Strauss, *Salome*; Mahler, *Kindertotenlieder*
        first given.

1906   San Francisco earthquake; J. Stockhausen dies.

1907   Friedrich Meinecke, German historian, publishes *The Middle
        Classes of the World and the National State*.

1908   Mahler, *Das Lied von der Erde*; Berg, *Sieben frühe Lieder* (begun
        1905; orch. version 1928); Webern, *Fünf Lieder*; German tenor
        Peter Anders born.

1909   Frank Lloyd Wright, Robie House, Chicago; Schoenberg
        completes song cycle *Das Buch der hängenden Gärten*, Op. 15;
        Schreker, *Fünf Gesänge*; German bass-baritone Hans Hotter
        born.

1910   Edward VII dies, George V becomes King of Great Britain and
        Ireland; Auguste Rodin, *The Thinker*; Paul Heyse wins Nobel
        Prize in Literature; Berg, *Vier Lieder*, Op. 2.

1911   Dilthey, Mahler die; Schoenberg writes essay "Das Verhältnis
        zum Text," completes *Gurrelieder*; Strauss, *Der
        Rosenkavalier*.

1912   Edgar Rice Burroughs, *Tarzan of the Apes*; Gerhart Johann
        Robert Hauptmann wins Nobel Prize in Literature; Schoenberg,
        Pierrot lunaire, Op. 21; Joseph Marx, *Italienisches Liederbuch*
        (Heyse, 3 vols.); Berg, *Fünf Orchesterlieder nach
        Ansichtkartentexten von Peter Altenberg*, Op. 4.

1913   Henry Ford develops first assembly line; Panama Canal opens; Stravinsky, *Le Sacre du Printemps*; Korngold, *Sechs einfache Lieder*; Zemlinsky, *Sechs Gesänge* (orch. 1922).

1914   Assassination of Archduke Ferdinand, heir to Austrian throne, in Sarajevo, leads to World War I; George Bernard Shaw, *Pygmalion*; Webern, *Three Orchestral Songs* (begun 1913).

1915   Sinking of *Lusitania*; Albert Einstein's General Theory of Relativity; Franz Kafka, *The Metamorphosis*; German soprano Elisabeth Schwarzkopf born; Reger, *Fünf neue Kinderlieder*, Op. 142.

1916   Jannette Rankin first woman in US House of Representatives; James Joyce, *A Portrait of the Artist as a Young Man*; Franz Joseph, Emperor of Austria since 1848, and Reger die.

1917   Abdication of Tsar Nicholas II; USA enters World War I; Pfitzner's *Palestrina* first given, Munich; Hindemith, *Drei Gesänge*; Joseph Marx, *Lieder und Gesänge*, 3 vols.

1918   World War I ends; Austrian, German monarchies abolished; Schoenberg founds Society for Private Musical Performance, Vienna, banning critics, applause.

1919   Versailles Treaty signed – imposes heavy conditions on Germany; Election of National Assembly in Weimar, Friedrich Ebert elected Reich President; Rosa Luxemburg murdered; Lady Astor first woman in British House of Commons; RCA founded; Walter Gropius starts Bauhaus; Altenberg dies; Austrian soprano Irmgard Seefried born.

1920   Prohibition in USA, Women's suffrage (nineteenth) amendment ratified; Edith Wharton, *The Age of Innocence*; film *The Cabinet of Dr. Caligari* released in Berlin; Dehmel dies; German soprano Rita Streich born; Hindemith, *Acht Lieder*, Op. 18.

1921   Rudolph Valentino stars in *The Sheik*; Weill, *Rilkelieder*.

1922   T. S. Eliot, *The Waste Land*; James Joyce, *Ulysses*; Hindemith begins song cycle *Das Marienleben* to Rainer Maria Rilke poems (completed 1923, revised 1948); Webern, *Sechs Lieder* (Trakl), Op. 14, and *Fünf geistliche Lieder*, Op. 15 (both begun 1917); Eisler, *Sechs Lieder*, Op. 2.

1923   Germany experiences raging inflation – attempted coups by right-wing and left-wing radical groups; Rilke, *Duino Elegies*; Martin Buber, *Ich und Du*; Yehudi Menuhin, age seven, gives first concert; Cecil B. De Mille, *The Ten Commandments*; Schreker, *Zwei lyrische Gesänge* (Whitman).

1924   Lenin dies, Stalin assumes power in Soviet Union; J. Edgar Hoover becomes FBI director; Thomas Mann, *Der Zauberberg*;

George Gershwin, *Rhapsody in Blue*; Pfitzner, *Sechs Liebeslieder*, Op. 35 (Huch); Busoni, Kafka die; German mezzo-soprano Christa Ludwig born.

1925 Hindenburg elected German Reich President; Virginia Woolf, *Mrs. Dalloway*; Scopes Trial in Tennessee; Hitler, *Mein Kampf*; Kafka, *Der Prozess*; Berg, *Wozzeck*, Chamber Symphony; Webern, *Drei Volkstexte*, Op. 7 (begun 1924); German baritone Dietrich Fischer-Dieskau, Swedish tenor Nicolai Gedda born.

1926 Hirohito becomes Emperor of Japan; Baird demonstrates first television; Krenek, *Jonny spielt auf*; Eisler, *Zeitungsausschnitte*, Op. 11 (10 songs); Rilke dies; Hans Werner Henze born.

1927 World population reaches two billion; Hesse publishes *Steppenwolf*; Heidegger publishes *Being and Time*; Charles Lindbergh flies from New York to Paris; Duke Ellington performs at Cotton Club; Babe Ruth hits sixty home runs; Fritz Lang, *Metropolis*.

1928 First Academy Awards in USA; D. H. Lawrence, *Lady Chatterley's Lover*; Schoenberg's Variations, Op. 31, his first serial orchestral work; Brecht, Weill, *Die Dreigroschenoper*; German musicologist Carl Dahlhaus born.

1929 Alexander Fleming, English bacteriologist, perfects penicillin; Thomas Mann wins Nobel Prize for Literature; Hofmannsthal dies; Austrian bass-baritone Walter Berry, Australian collaborative and Lied pianist Geoffrey Parsons born; Krenek song cycle, *Reisebuch aus den österreichischen Alpen*; Schoeck, *Liederzyklus*; Zemlinsky, *Symphonische Gesänge*.

1930 Discovery of Pluto, ninth planet; Grant Wood, *American Gothic*; Marlene Dietrich stars in film *Der blaue Engel* – music, including song "Ich bin von Kopf bis Fuss" ("Falling in Love again") composed by Hollaender.

1931 Empire State Building completed; Britain abandons gold standard; Salvador Dalí paints *The Persistence of Memory*; Pfitzner, *Sechs Lieder*, Op. 40.

1932 Charles Lindbergh's son kidnapped, killed; Aldous Huxley, *Brave New World*; Duke Ellington, "It Don't Mean a Thing, If It Ain't Got That Swing."

1933 Wiley Post flies solo around the world in seven days, eighteen hours, forty-nine minutes; discovery of radioactivity; Hitler appointed German Chancellor; Nazis open first concentration camp at Dachau to jail Communist Party members; Schoenberg dismissed from Berlin post; Weill, *The Seven Deadly Sins*;

Hindemith, *Vier Lieder*; George, Kurz die; Dutch soprano Elly
Ameling, English mezzo-soprano Janet Baker born.

1934   Persecution of Jews in Germany and Austria prompts mass
exodus; Austrian Chancellor Dollfuss murdered in attempted
Nazi coup; Schreker dies; Webern, *Drei Lieder* (Jone), Op. 25.

1935   In Germany Hitler repudiates Versailles Treaty disarmament
clauses, Anti-Jewish "Nuremberg Laws," and radio broadcasts of
jazz banned; Alfred Hitchcock, *The 39 Steps*; Gershwin, *Porgy
and Bess*; Hindemith, *Sechs Lieder*; Berg, Schenker, Tucholsky
die; German tenor Peter Schreier born.

1936   Jesse Owens wins four Olympic Gold Medals in Berlin; Germany
occupies Rhineland in violation of Treaty of Versailles; George V
dies, Edward VIII becomes King of the United Kindgom – the
latter abdicates and George VI becomes King; BBC begins public
television service; Margaret Mitchell, *Gone with the Wind*;
Joseph Marx, *Verklärtes Jahr*, song cycle.

1937   Crash of *Hindenburg* in New Jersey; Amelia Earhart and co-pilot
Fred Noonan vanish over Pacific Ocean during round-the-world
flight; Golden Gate Bridge completed; Berg's *Lulu* first given.

1938   Hitler's troops march into Austria – political union of Germany
and Austria proclaimed; *Kristallnacht*, pogrom against Jews in
Germany; Orson Welles's radio program, *The War of the Worlds*.

1939   Germany invades Poland, thereby prompting Britain and France
to declare war on Germany – World War II begins; John
Steinbeck, *Grapes of Wrath*; Paul Klee, *La belle Jardinière*; Judy
Garland stars in *The Wizard of Oz*; Freud dies; American
soprano Arleen Augér, German mezzo-soprano Brigitte
Fassbaender, Austrian soprano Lucia Popp born.

1940   Nazi Germany begins aerial bombing of Great Britain; Winston
Churchill becomes British Prime Minister; Trotsky murdered in
Mexico; Cary Grant, Katharine Hepburn star in *The Philadelphia
Story;* Ernest Hemingway, *For whom the Bell Tolls.*

1941   Japanese attack on Pearl Harbor; Orson Welles, *Citizen Kane.*

1942   Wannsee Conference decides a final and permanent solution to
the "Jewish Problem"; first extermination camps in Belzec,
Poland; Manhattan Project; Humphrey Bogart, Ingrid Bergman
star in *Casablanca*; Germany occupies France; Zemlinsky dies.

1943   Goebbels declares "total war"; Germans surrender at
Stalingrad – turning point in war; Robert Oppenheimer, Los
Alamos; Rogers and Hammerstein, *Oklahoma*; Jean-Paul Sartre,
Being and Nothingness; Eisler, *Hollywooder Liederbuch* (begun
1942).

1944 Hundreds of thousands of US, British, Free French troops land in Normandy ("D-Day"); Tennessee Williams, *The Glass Menagerie;* Krenek, *The Ballad of the Railroads,* Op. 98 (songs to his own texts); Ullmann dies.

1945 World War II ends, first in Europe and, following Atomic bombs on Hiroshima, Nagasaki, in Japan; Berlin divided into four sectors; George Orwell, *Animal Farm;* Webern, Werfel die.

1946 Nazi Nuremberg trials; Churchill delivers "Iron Curtain" speech; Dr. Spock, *The Commonsense Book of Baby and Child Care;* Hesse wins Nobel Prize in Literature; Lincke dies.

1947 English soprano Felicity Lott born.

1948 State of Israel proclaimed; apartheid becomes policy in South Africa; Berlin Blockade and Air Lift; invention of Frisbee; Korngold, *Fünf Lieder,* Op. 38; Strauss, *Vier letzte Lieder;* E. Schumann publishes book *German Song;* Mysz-Gmeiner, Tauber die.

1949 Germany divided – Federal Republic of Germany (West Germany) founded first and, five months later, German Democratic Republic (East Germany); North Atlantic Treaty Organization (NATO) founded; beginning of People's Republic of China under Mao Tse-Tung; Adorno, *Philosophie der neuen Musik;* Strauss, Pfitzner die.

1950 David C. Schilling makes first nonstop transatlantic jet flight in ten hours, one minute; Korean War begins; Weill dies.

1951 Color television introduced, USA; Hannah Arendt, *The Origins of Totalitarianism;* Karlheinz Stockhausen, Olivier Messiaen, Pierre Boulez meet at Darmstadt; Schoenberg, Wittgenstein die.

1952 George VI dies – daughter becomes Elizabeth II; Agatha Christie, *The Mousetrap;* E. Schumann, Schlusnus die; Wolfgang Rihm born.

1954 Anders dies.

1955 American baritone Thomas Hampson, Swedish mezzo-soprano Anne Sofie von Otter born.

1956 Elvis Presley's first hit, "Heartbreak Hotel"; Brecht dies; American soprano Barbara Bonney, German tenor Christoph Prégardien born.

1957 Suez Canal reopens; Soviet Union launches Sputnik; H.-G. Adam creates Beacon of Dead monument, Auschwitz; Korngold, Schoeck die; German baritone Olaf Bär born.

1958 Erb dies.

1959 Alaska and Hawaii become forty-ninth and fiftieth states; first known case of AIDS traced to this year; Cuban President Batista flees – Fidel Castro assumes power; Rogers and Hammerstein, *The Sound of Music*; American soprano Renée Fleming born.

1960 World population reaches three billion; Alfred Hitchcock, *Psycho*; American soprano Dawn Upshaw born.

1961 Berlin Wall divides city; Joseph Heller, *Catch-22*; Jung, Gerhardt die.

1962 John Glenn orbits earth; Anthony Burgess, *A Clockwork Orange*; Mies van der Rohe designs New National Gallery, West Berlin; Eisler, Flagstad, Hesse die; Danish baritone Bo Skovhus born.

1963 Kennedy Berlin speech "Ich bin ein Berliner"; Dr. Martin Luther King, Jr., Washington, D.C. speech "I have a dream"; Kennedy assassinated; Hindemith dies.

1964 Joseph Marx dies; English tenor Ian Bostridge born.

1967 Thurgood Marshall, grandson of a slave, first Black-American member of Supreme Court; Dr. Christiaan Barnard performs first human heart transplant; German baritone Matthias Goerne born.

1968 More than 500,000 US troops in Vietnam – Tet Offensive; assassination of Robert Kennedy; Stanley Kubrick, *2001: A Space Odyssey*.

1969 Willy Brandt elected Chancellor of Federal Republic of Germany; Neil Armstrong and Buzz Aldrin land on moon; first flight of the Concorde; Woodstock Festival.

1970 The Beatles disband; IBM introduces floppy disk; Julia Culp dies.

1972 Mark Spitz wins seven Olympic Gold Medals; Liza Minnelli stars in *Cabaret*; Gloria Steinem founds *Ms. Magazine*; Wolpe dies.

1973 World Trade Center completed; Alexander Solzhenitsyn, *Gulag Archipelago*.

1974 Patzak dies.

1976 Heidegger, Hollaender, Lehmann die; Philip Glass, *Einstein on the Beach*.

1977 Elvis Presley dies; Krenek, *Albumblatt*, Op. 228.

1978 Cardinal Karol Wojtyła of Poland becomes Pope John Paul II; Kipnis dies.

1979 Ayatollah Ruhollah Khomeini takes power in Iran; Dessau dies.

1981 Sandra Day O'Connor first woman in Supreme Court; MTV founded; AIDS enters public consciousness as world health crisis; Lenya dies.

1984 Hüsch, Raucheisen die.

1985 Confirmation of black holes in Milky Way, other galaxies; tercentenary celebrations of births of Bach, Handel.

1986 Chernobyl nuclear power station disaster; space shuttle Challenger explodes, killing all seven aboard.

1987 Margaret Thatcher, first woman prime minister of Britain, wins third term; Moore, Streich, die.

1988 Seefried dies.

1989 Fall of Berlin Wall; Nelson Mandela released after twenty-seven years in prison; President F. W. De Klerk announces gradual abolition of apartheid, South Africa; wreck of Exxon oil tanker off Alaska; Voyager 2 passes 3,000 miles from Neptune's North Pole; Carl Dahlhaus dies.

1990 van Gogh's *Portrait of Dr. Gachet* sets record as most expensive painting at $82.5 million, New York; Helmut Kohl first Chancellor of reunited Germany; Berger dies.

1991 Soviet Union disbanded – republics form Commonwealth of Independent States; Krenek dies.

1992 Paul John Paul II revokes heresy charge against Galileo; Marlene Dietrich, Messiaen, Cage die.

1993 Wolfgang Rihm, *Abschiedsstücke für Frauenstimme und 15 Spieler*; Augér, Popp die.

1994 South Africa holds first interracial national election – Nelson Mandela elected president; Lemnitz dies.

1995 Geoffrey Parsons dies.

1998 Frank Sinatra dies; Henze song cycle, *Sechs Gesänge aus dem Arabischen.*

1999 World population reaches six billion; Günter Grass receives Nobel Prize in Literature; new dome over Berlin Reichstag to a design by Sir Norman Foster.

2000 Walter Berry dies.

2001 First artificial heart implanted in human in Louisville; terrorist attack on World Trade Center.

2002 Euro replaces national currencies in twelve participating member states of European Union.

Names and dates mentioned in this volume

Franz Abt (1819–85)
Hans Christian Andersen
  (1805–75)
Johann André (1741–99)
Anna Amalia, Duchess of
  Saxe-Weimar-Eisenach
  (1739–1807)
Ernst Moritz Arndt (1769–1860)
Achim von Arnim (1781–1831)
Bettina von Arnim (1785–1859)
Charles Pierre Baudelaire
  (1821–67)
Gabriele von Baumberg
  (1766–1839)
Ludwig van Beethoven (1770–1827)
Ludwig Berger (1777–1839)
Hans Bethge (1876–1946)
Otto Julius Bierbaum (1865–1910)
Johann Heinrich Carl Bornhardt
  (1774–1840)
Bertolt Brecht (1898–1956)
Clemens Brentano (1778–1842)
Robert Browning (1812–89)
Hans von Bülow (1830–94)
August Bungert (1845–1915)
Gottfried August Bürger (1747–94)
Robert Burns (1759–96)
George Gordon, Lord Byron
  (1788–1824)
Karl Candidus (1817–72)
Ignaz Franz Castelli (1781–1862)
Adelbert von Chamisso
  (1781–1838)
Matthias Claudius (1740–1815)
Matthias Conradi (1745–1832)
Carl Friedrich Cramer (1752–1807)

Georg Friedrich Daumer
  (1800–75)
Richard Dehmel (1863–1920)
Hermann Deiters (1833–1907)
Paul Dessau (1894–1979)
Annette von Droste-Hülshoff
  (1797–1848)
Johann Gustav Droysen (1808–84)
Traugott Maximilian Eberwein
  (1775–1831)
Joseph von Eichendorff
  (1788–1857)
Hanns Eisler (1898–1962)
August Heinrich Hoffmann von
  Fallersleben (1798–1874)
Friedrich Gottlob Fleischer
  (1722–1806)
Theodor Fontane (1819–88)
Robert Franz (1815–92)
Ferdinand Freiligrath (1810–76)
Carl Friberth (1736–1816)
Emanuel von Geibel (1815–84)
Christian Fürchtegott Gellert
  (1715–69)
Stefan George (1868–1933)
Heinrich Wilhelm von Gerstenberg
  (1737–1823)
Ludwig Theodor Giesebrecht
  (1792–1873)
Wilhelm Ludwig Gleim
  (1719–1803)
Leopold Friedrich Günther von
  Göckingk (1748–1828)
Johann Wolfgang von Goethe
  (1749–1832)
Johann Valentin Görner (1702–62)

Johann Christoph Gottsched
(1700–66)

Johann Friedrich Gräfe (1711–87)

Carl Heinrich Graun (1703/04–59)

Edvard Grieg (1843–1907)

Klaus Groth (1819–99)

Friedrich Wilhelm Gubitz
(1786–1870)

Friedrich von Hagedorn (1708–54)

Albrecht von Haller (1708–77)

Friedrich Hebbel (1813–63)

Georg Friedrich Wilhelm Hegel
(1770–1831)

Heinrich Heine (1797–1856)

Karl Henckell (1864–1929)

August Bernhard Valentin Herbing
(1735–66)

Johann Gottfried von Herder
(1744–1803)

Georg Herwegh (1817–75)

Elisabet von Herzogenberg
(1847–92)

Heinrich, Freiherr von
Herzogenberg (1843–1900)

Hermann Hesse (1877–1962)

Richard Heuberger (1850–1914)

Paul von Heyse (1830–1914)

Johann Adam Hiller (1728–1804)

Friedrich Heinrich Himmel
(1765–1814)

E. T. A. Hoffmann (1776–1822)

Leopold Hofmann (1738–93)

Hugo von Hofmannsthal
(1874–1929)

Friedrich Hölderlin (1770–1843)

Friedrich Hollaender (1896–1976)

Ludwig Christoph Heinrich Hölty
(1748–76)

Ricarda Huch (1864–1947)

Anne Hunter (1742–1821)

Friedrich Franz Hůrka
(1762–1805)

Conrad Friedrich Hurlebusch
(1691–1765)

Charles Ives (1874–1954)

Johann Georg Jacobi (1740–1814)

Alois Isidor Jeitteles (1794–1858)

Franz Kafka (1883–1924)

Immanuel Kant (1724–1804)

Gottfried Keller (1819–90)

Justinus Kerner (1786–1862)

Alfred Kerr (1867–1948)

Theodor Kirchner (1823–1903)

Heinrich von Kleist (1777–1811)

Karl Klingemann (1798–1862)

Friedrich Maximilian Klinger
(1752–1831)

Friedrich Gottlieb Klopstock
(1724–1803)

Armin Knab (1881–1951)

Heinrich Koch (1749–1816)

Theodor Körner (1791–1813)

Karl Kraus (1874–1936)

Christian Gottfried Krause
(1719–77)

Ernst Krenek (1900–91)

Hermann Kretzschmar
(1848–1924)

Andreas Kretzschmer
(1775–1839)

Conradin Kreutzer (1780–1849)

Niklas von Krufft (1779–1818)

Elisabeth Kulmann (1808–25)

Adolph Carl Kunzen (1720–81)

Friedrich Ludewig Aemilius
Kunzen (1761–1817)

Franz Paul Lachner (1803–90)

Josephine Lang (1815–80)

Eduard Lassen (1830–1904)

Luise Adolpha Le Beau
(1850–1927)

Gottfried Wilhelm Leibniz
(1646–1716)

Nikolaus Lenau (1802–42)

Jakob Michael Reinhold Lenz
  (1751–92)
Gottlieb von Leon (1757–1830)
Gotthold Ephraim Lessing
  (1729–81)
Heinrich Leuthold (1827–79)
Detlev von Liliencron (1844–1909)
Carl Loewe (1796–1869)
Rudolf Louis (1870–1914)
John Henry Mackay (1864–1933)
James Macpherson (1736–96)
Heinrich August Marschner
  (1795–1861)
Johann Mattheson (1681–1764)
Friedrich Matthisson (1761–1831)
Johann Mayrhofer (1787–1836)
Conrad Ferdinand Meyer
  (1825–98)
Giacomo Meyerbeer (1791–1864)
Johann Martin Miller (1750–1814)
Lorenz Mizler (1711–78)
Christian Morgenstern
  (1871–1914)
Eduard Mörike (1804–75)
Friedrich de la Motte-Fouqué
  (1777–1843)
Karl Müchler (1763–1857)
Wilhelm Müller (1794–1827)
Christian Gottlob Neefe
  (1748–98)
Sigismund Neukomm (1778–1858)
Christoph Friedrich Nicolai
  (1733–1811)
August Niemann (1761–1832)
Walter Niemann (1876–1953)
Friedrich Nietzsche (1844–1900)
Novalis (Friedrich von Hardenberg;
  1772–1801)
Wilhelm Osterwald (1820–87)
Christian Adolph Overbeck
  (1775–1821)
Oskar Panizza (1853–1921)

Maria Theresia Paradis
  (1759–1824)
Thomas Percy (1729–1811)
August von Platen (Karl August
  Georg Maximilian Graf von
  Platen-Hallermünde;
  1796–1835)
Joachim Raff (1822–82)
Karl Wilhelm Ramler (1725–98)
Benedikt Randhartinger (1802–93)
Max Reger (1873–1916)
Johann Friedrich Reichardt
  (1752–1814)
Luise Reichardt (1779–1826)
Carl Reinecke (1824–1910)
Robert Reinick (1805–52)
Karl Gottlieb Reissiger (1798–1859)
Samuel Richardson (1689–1761)
Hugo Riemann (1849–1919)
Ferdinand Ries (1784–1838)
Rainer Maria Rilke (1875–1926)
Alexander Ritter (1833–96)
Hermann Rollet (1819–1904)
Jean-Jacques Rousseau (1712–78)
Anton Rubinstein (1829–94)
Friedrich Rückert (1788–1866)
Joseph Viktor von Scheffel
  (1826–86)
Johann Adolf Scheibe (1708–76)
Marcellus Schiffer (1894?–1932)
Johann Christoph Friedrich von
  Schiller (1759–1805)
August Wilhelm Schlegel
  (1767–1845)
Friedrich Schlegel (1772–1829)
Klamer Eberhard Karl Schmidt
  (1746–1824)
Georg Laurenz Schneider
  (1766–1855)
Franz von Schober (1798–1882)
Othmar Schoeck (1886–1957)
Arnold Schoenberg (1874–1951)

Corona Schröter (1751–1803)

Johann Abraham Peter Schulz (1747–1800)

Sir Walter Scott (1771–1832)

Johann Chrysostomus Senn (1792–1857)

Josef von Spaun (1788–1865)

Sperontes (Johann Sigismund Scholze, 1705–50)

Louis Spohr (1784–1859)

Mischa Spoliansky (1898–1985)

Josef Antonín Stepán (1726–97)

Laurence Sterne (1713–68)

Heinrich Wilhelm August Stieglitz (1801–49)

Friedrich Leopold von Stolberg (1750–1819)

Theodor Storm (1817–88)

Theodor Streicher (1874–1940)

Georg Philipp Telemann (1681–1767)

Christian Thomasius (1655–1728)

Ludwig Tieck (1773–1853)

Christoph August Tiedge (1752–1841)

Václav Tomásek (1774–1850)

(Johann) Ludwig Uhland (1787–1862)

Johann Peter Uz (1720–96)

Johann Michael Vogl (1768–1840)

Robert Volkmann (1815–83)

Johann Heinrich Voß (1751–1826)

Carl Maria von Weber (1786–1826)

Christian Felix Weisße (1726–1804)

Mathilde Wesendonck (1822–1902)

Christoph Martin Wieland (1733–1813)

Marianne von Willemer (1784–1860)

Johann Joachim Winckelmann (1717–68)

Ernst Wratislaw Wilhelm von Wobeser (1727–95)

William Wordsworth (1770–1850)

Justus Friedrich Wilhelm Zachariae (1726–77)

Carl Friedrich Zelter (1758–1832)

Christiane Marianne von Ziegler (1695–1760)

Anton Wilhelm Florentin von Zuccalmaglio (1803–69)

Emilie Zumsteeg (1796–1857)

Johann Rudolf Zumsteeg (1760–1802)

Stefan Zweig (1881–1942)

Abbreviations

Literature

CCS	*The Cambridge Companion to Schubert*, ed. Christopher H. Gibbs (Cambridge, 1997)
D	Given that Deutsch himself believed the "Deutsch Numbers" he devised for Schubert's music were necessary only for the instrumental music, they are included for the vocal compositions only if uncertainty might otherwise occur.
DL	Max Friedländer, *Das deutsche Lied im 18. Jahrhundert: Quellen und Studien.* 2 vols. (Stuttgart and Berlin, 1902)
GLNC	*German Lieder in the Nineteenth Century*, ed. Rufus Hallmark (New York, 1996)
J	J numbers refer to cataloging numbers developed for Weber; see Friedrich Wilhelm Jähns, *Carl Maria von Weber in seinen Werken: chronologisch-thematisches Verzeichnis seiner sämmtlichen Compositionen* (Berlin, 1871; reprint, Berlin, 1967)
LMLR	Edward F. Kravitt, *The Lied: Mirror of Late Romanticism* (New Haven, 1996)
NCGL	Lorraine Gorrell, *The Nineteenth-Century German Lied* (Portland, 1993)
NCM	Carl Dahlhaus, *Nineteenth Century Music*, trans. J. Bradford Robinson (Berkeley, 1989)
New Grove	*The New Grove Dictionary of Music and Musicians*, ed. Stanley Sadie, 20 vols. (London, 1980)
New Grove2	*The New Grove Dictionary of Music and Musicians*, 2nd edn., ed. Stanley Sadie (2001)
SCAS	*Schubert: Critical and Analytical Studies*, ed. Walter Frisch (Lincoln, 1986)
SDB	*Schubert: A Documentary Biography*, trans. Eric Blom (London, 1946. The American edn. is entitled *The Schubert Reader: A Life of Franz Schubert in Letters and Documents* [New York, 1947])
SDL	*Schubert: die Dokumente seines Lebens*, ed. Otto Erich Deutsch (Kassel and New York, 1964)

| SMF | *Schubert: Memoirs by His Friends*, trans. Rosamond Ley and John Nowell (London, 1958) |
| SPML | Susan Youens, *Schubert's Poets and the Making of Lieder* (Cambridge, 1996) |

Journals

AfM	*Archiv für Musikwissenschaft*
AmZ	*Allgemeine musikalische Zeitung* (Leipzig)
CM	*Current Musicology*
JAMS	*Journal of the American Musicological Society*
JMR	*Journal of Musicological Research*
JM	*Journal of Musicology*
JRMA	*Journal of the Royal Musical Association*
MA	*Music Analysis*
ML	*Music & Letters*
MR	*Music Review*
MQ	*The Musical Quarterly*
MT	*Musical Times*
Mf	*Die Musikforschung*
NZfM	*Neue Zeitschrift für Musik* (founded by Robert Schumann, along with Friedrich Wieck, Ludwig Schunke, and Julius Knorr, in 1834)
19CM	*19th-Century Music*
ÖMz	*Österreichische Musikzeitschrift*

Note on pitch

When specific octave register has been indicated, this book follows the system stipulated by D. Kern Holoman, *Writing About Music* (Berkeley, 1998), 7.

PART ONE

Introducing a genre

Introduction: why the Lied?

JAMES PARSONS

Of the many kinds of music to which composers from German-speaking lands have turned their attention, the Lied, or art song, is surely the most paradoxical. Among those who have fallen under the genre's spell, it is easy to discern fervent if not fanatical zealousness. Among those who have not, it is just as easy to detect bemused bewilderment as to how a musical rendering of a German poem is capable of inducing so profound a response. Suffice it to say, the Lied's fortunes seldom have been static.

The paradoxes do not end here. While Lieder often are thought of as diminutive, given that a great many last but a short time when compared to sonatas, concertos, symphonies, or operas, both the history of German song and the density of expression encountered in many works comprising the genre belie that characterization. Even in some of the most evanescent examples, such as Schubert's *Über allen Gipfeln ist Ruh*, the timelessness that Goethe compresses into his poem combined with the music underscoring it yield an expansiveness precisely because the song is so short: succinct yes, diminutive no! At once the most private yet universalizing of art forms, the Lied, less than a century ago, stood at the forefront of late Romanticism. Together with orchestral and various types of instrumental music, and later the music dramas of Richard Wagner, it formed part of a Teutonic musical juggernaut widely regarded as without peer. On the eve of World War I, at the peak of the genre's popularity, song settings of German poetry were to be encountered almost everywhere. In Berlin alone, between 1900 and 1914, according to a recent tally, public song recitals, or *Liederabende*, averaged some twenty a week and invariably were sold out.[1] The Lied was equally ubiquitous in private performances, especially those sponsored by the artistic, intellectual, and economic elite. As one witness has recalled, "Lieder fitted particularly well into the atmosphere of . . . intimate social gatherings. The poem was generally read before each setting was sung. One could easily lose oneself in the mood produced."[2] Yet by 1948, when the eighty-four-year-old Richard Strauss completed his *Vier letzte Lieder*, the status quo had changed considerably, so much so that some have found it tempting to view Strauss's four songs as a requiem not only for German song but also for German culture as cultivated during the past two centuries.

While the supposition behind this last statement is fraught with greater complexity than most historians would care to admit, there can be little argument that the Lied enjoyed a special place within German musical life. And yet one wonders: what prompted the keen attentiveness shown this body of music in seemingly every household of a certain means from the northern reaches of Schleswig-Holstein to the southern regions of Bavaria or from Salzburg to Vienna? How long did this passion endure and why is one informed in most every general music history that it ended, that the Lied now lives on as a kind of museum rarity within the arena nowadays thought of as classical music? Although more complete answers to such questions appear in the chapters that follow, I would be remiss if I did not make the point here that, beginning in the middle of the eighteenth century and continuing for almost two centuries, poetry played a fundamental role in individual and collective life. More times than not, verse dressed in song was an essential means by which this rich body of literature was disseminated. Goethe succinctly summed up what I have in mind here when he asked: "Wer sichert den Olymp? vereinet Götter?" (Who secures Olympus, who unites the gods?); his answer: "Des Menschen Kraft, im Dichter offenbart!" (The power of man, revealed in the poet).[3] Mindful of such a pronouncement, it perhaps is easy to understand why a writer from more recent times has asserted that Germany is "the only country that could have taken seriously Shelley's famous sweeping dictum that 'poets are the unacknowledged legislators of the world.'"[4]

In contrast to the heights to which it would soar, the Lied began, as did so much else in an age when communication was not instantaneous, in the home: the modest pastime of a small but growing middle class. Not surprisingly, given its initial environment, German song has reflected and often shaped individual identity. At the same time, it also has played a considerable part in giving voice – literally as it happens – to a burgeoning German national identity, so much so that by the second half of the nineteenth century the Lied had become a kind of sounding manifestation of cultural hegemony. It may not be too fanciful to suggest that the Lied's development parallels that of Germany itself: from a collection of independently governed agencies bound only by language in the eighteenth century to a united country in 1871. Intriguingly, Germany's saga has provided a compelling if seldom explicitly acknowledged analogue for those who would track the Lied's history: ascent to nationhood, dominion, downfall, splintered afterlife. One can only speculate if, like reunited Germany, the Lied will experience a comparable revitalization.

If the Lied has traveled a bumpy road during the last fifty years compared to its earlier glory days, its stock shows signs of having risen recently, thanks in no small measure to the renewed interest in music of the nineteenth century – the genre's heyday. Critical editions of the works of Rossini, Donizetti, Bellini, and Verdi have been launched.[5] In the United States, an entire journal devoted to the music of what its editors call "the long century" recently marked its twenty-fifth anniversary: *19th Century Music* (University of California Press). A great many composers have been reclaimed, at least partially so, after periods of obscurity. Others, including a fair number of women, have been made known to a broad public for the first time after having been consigned to the shadows in their own day, among them Fanny Hensel, Clara Schumann, and Josephine Lang. While such figures as Beethoven, Schubert, and Brahms continue to crowd concert programs, ways of listening to their music have been tempered by new insights and interpretations, some of which have been hotly debated.[6] Historically informed performance practice – a generation ago the exclusive province of Baroque and earlier music – now has reached beyond the nineteenth century to Schoenberg's *Verklärte Nacht* and Stravinsky's *Le Sacre du printemps*. Detailed analyses of nineteenth-century music stand alongside studies devoted to its social and intellectual backgrounds.[7] Moreover, a listener can embark upon the life-altering adventure of listening to *all* of the Lieder of Franz Schubert, thanks to the Lied pianist Graham Johnson, a legion of singers, and the Hyperion label. Launched in 1987, *The Hyperion Schubert Edition* would not attain completion until 1999 with the thirty-seventh CD. On the heels of this staggering achievement, Johnson is off again, this time to record all of the Lieder of Clara and Robert Schumann, an endeavor estimated to take twelve CDs.

Mention of Schubert and the many CDs required to record his more than 600 Lieder serves as a reminder that this composer's songs as well as those who followed after him – Schumann, Brahms, Wolf – constitute for most people the sum total of the genre's history. Previous investigations to some degree have fostered this viewpoint, given that the nineteenth-century Lied has garnered the lion's share of scholarly attention. This last statement is not meant to question the usefulness of such investigations, only to point out that the complete history of the Lied remains obscured behind the lofty vistas formed by German song during its most dynamic period. Without diminishing the value of the scholarly achievement now in place for either nineteenth-century music or the Lied, in particular, from the same period, the fact remains that German song existed before the first one completed by Schubert, dated March 1811 (*Hagars Klage*, D5), and after the last finished by Hugo Wolf, on 28 March 1897 (*Fühlt meine Seele*; he destroyed one further song as unworthy). More times than not excoriated by recent criticism, the eighteenth-century Lied may be shown to have influenced the style shift from the Baroque to the Classical periods, just as the Lied in the twentieth century was taken up by those at the forefront of early modernism and also contributed to a great many of the positive developments in popular music. Problematic and controversial, such statements seem even more so because both the pre-Schubert and post-Wolf Lied have been underserved by extant scholarship. Although neither of the subjects can be covered completely in the chapters devoted to them here, it nonetheless is hoped that the information that is provided will spark greater interest in these repertories as well as additional research and an increased number of performances than heretofore has been the case.

All of which leads to the aim of this book: to document the Lied in essays starting with its birth in the 1740s to its presumed demise during World War II. The first three sections deal with the chronological unfolding of German song, its early history in the Age of Enlightenment, its halcyon days in the Age of Romanticism, its supposed fragmentation in the Age of Modernism, while a fourth addresses issues of reception and performance. Jane Brown leads off with a consideration of the Lied's relationship with German poetry from the generation before Goethe in the eighteenth century to Bertolt Brecht in the century just past. At one extreme, poets of the earlier age succeeded in creating verse that mirrored the growing fascination with subjectivity and self, while Brecht's texts set to music by such composers as Paul Dessau, Hanns Eisler, and Kurt Weill primarily were concerned not with individuals but with classes of people and their various struggles. Given that the Lied had long stood at the center of German musical life, composers and other individuals quickly realized that song provided a ready-made medium for social causes. As the title of a song by Eisler from 1930 proclaims: "Change the world, it needs it!"[8] Predictably enough, supporters of right-wing concerns looked to song for the very same reasons; this especially is to be seen in some of the more radical offshoots of the many *Wandervogel* groups in post World War I Germany. Walking through the woods or crowded around campfires, what did German youth do when brought together in companionship in the first third of the twentieth century? They sang. As the subsequent history of the twentieth century tragically affirms, what they sang about – the lyrics with their emphasis on a "reawakening of a genuine Germanness"[9] – proves all too well the power of song as well as its susceptibility to conscription.[10]

Given that I have indicated that this book covers the entire history of German song, a logical question is why has its scope been restricted to the period it has? Does the term Lied not encompass a larger time span, whether the polyphonic Lied of the fifteenth and sixteenth centuries or the Baroque continuo Lied? Limitations have had to be set and, in so doing, I have opted for an investigation of "the modern Lied," a German poem set to music, generally for solo voice and keyboard – in the nineteenth century almost always piano – from its self-effacing start in the 1740s to Strauss's empyrean paean to this tradition, the previously-mentioned *Vier letzte Lieder*.[11] The first book in English to cover the full history of German solo song as so defined, it nevertheless does not treat everything. The American Charles

Ives turned on occasion to poetry by Goethe, Heine, and other German poets, just as did the Norwegian Edvard Grieg. It is my hope that some future book will include these and other subjects not touched on here.

Following Brown's poetical overview, I provide a summary of eighteenth-century Lieder after which Amanda Glauert looks at four focal composers from the same period. Ruth O. Bingham scrutinizes the ways in which diverse composers in the first half of the nineteenth century took up the song cycle. A sub-genre within the Lied's larger history, the song cycle is important because of the magnitude and merit of music with which composers responded to its potential and the way in which it allowed the genre to expand from within. James Deaville surveys the Lied during the middle of the nineteenth century and Christopher H. Gibbs examines how German song reached beyond its own boundaries to influence other musical genres, ranging in time from Schubert to Mahler. As a glance at the table of contents confirms, most chapters treat the individual composers who have come to be regarded as the genre's most important. Marie-Agnes Dittrich turns to Schubert, not to endorse yet again his position as the "inventor" of the Lied but rather to inquire critically into the composer's ties to his predecessors, the nature of his achievement, and the ways in which composers after him responded – or did not – to that legacy. Of these later composers, Jürgen Thym turns to Schumann and, among other things, reveals that Schumann tended to underrate the composer of *Erlkönig*; for Schumann, Beethoven was the trailblazer when it came to German song. For Lied enthusiasts this volume also contains a surprise: a chapter on the Lieder of Franz Liszt, a composer better known for his virtuoso piano works and as the creator of the symphonic tone poem. As Rena Charnin Mueller argues, the Lied played a special role within this composer's compositional career, one previously overlooked. Heather Platt explores Brahms and his union of words and music, an examination based in large measure on remarks he made to his only composition student, Gustav Jenner. Susan Youens assesses the rare composer known almost exclusively for his contributions to the Lied, Hugo Wolf. Moving into the twentieth century, James L. Zychowicz takes up two composers for whom song was equally important – if for different reasons – Gustav Mahler and Richard Strauss. I follow with an appraisal of the Lied to the middle of the twentieth century; although many have claimed that German song died during this period, the work of such disparate composers as Reger, Pfitzner, Zemlinsky, Schoenberg, Berg, Webern, Eisler, Dessau, Krenek, and a host of others belies this overly facile supposition. David Gramit begins Part IV with an outline of the "double circulation" of the Lied, both as an art form and as a commercial commodity, the latter an influence largely ignored in previous accounts of the genre but one that has shaped it just as forcefully as aesthetic considerations. Graham Johnson concludes this section and ends the book at precisely the point I hope many will take as a point of departure: with performance.

The book's chronological organization notwithstanding, it may be that the reader will wish to dip in at whatever point is of immediate interest. With the exception of my own two chapters, a different author has written each and there are no overarching threads to be missed should the reader take chapters out of sequence. In whatever manner this book is utilized, a few additional words may assist by way of placing the Lied in context. In offering a précis of what the Lied has meant to composers, performers, and listeners during the past 250 years, I hope to explain here, at least in part, why the Lied and indeed all song matters.

Most people who cherish the Lied do so because it is a refuge of intimacy. An art form given over to poetry and music, song relies on the bond between the two. Depending on the period or the composer in question, one or the other component may dominate; yet it generally is assumed that the ideal relationship is one where music and words are weighted equally. Intriguingly, composers have tended to honor such a happy medium in the breach, the result being that the way in which the two halves come together frequently strikes the listener as a fascinating balancing act.

However the two ingredients are joined, it generally is agreed that the resulting union possesses a power exceeding what either words or music are capable of on their own. At its most epoch-making, the union that lies at the heart of German song may be expressed thus: "At the sound of songs all time and space recede." These words, in English translation, are by Alois Isidor Jeitteles, an obscure poet and medical student living in Vienna from about 1815 to 1820, who provided Beethoven with the literary starting point for his Op. 98 song cycle *An die ferne Geliebte* (1816). Within Jeitteles's poem and Beethoven's setting, the line quoted here launches the concluding fifth stanza of the cycle's first song. Although at first glance they seem hyperbolic, it nevertheless is a truism that those devoted to the Lied share a belief that the coupling of words and music possesses special power if not Orphic dynamism. As the eighteen-year-old Schumann put it in 1828, shortly after having absorbed Beethoven's *An die ferne Geliebte*, ballads by Loewe, and Lieder by Schubert and Marschner, "Song unites the highest, word and tone."[12] Viewed thus, the twenty-second Lied from Schubert's 1827 song cycle *Winterreise*, *Mut*, delivers much of the devastating blow it does because the now delusional wanderer claims he does not hearken to the sentiment of his own song: "When my heart speaks in my breast I sing loudly and cheerfully. I don't listen to what it says to me, I have no ears." Stricken with such affective deafness, Schubert's lamentable pilgrim loses much more than this: he is irrefutably helpless. Isolation and madness remain. Schubert's music matches the clash at the core of Wilhelm Müller's text: energetic rhythms proclaim the wayfarer's resolve to sing, yet the phrase units do not match the 2/4 meter. The key signature is G minor yet with the appearance of the voice one hears three measures in tonic minor followed by two measures of parallel major to which the piano echoes two measures more in the major, for a total of four. Müller's protagonist claims one thing and Schubert, sensitive to his internal discord, supports that assertiveness while simultaneously repudiating it. The message is clear: to be in the presence of song and not listen is risky business.

One reason why this is so is because song – along with many other modes of creative expression – came to be thought of as an essential element in that late eighteenth- and nineteenth-century German formulation of self-cultivation or self-education. Known to Germans as *Bildung*, the program it inscribed was one whereby an individual strives for self-actualization unfettered by guidance or interference from others.[13] As Goethe discloses in what is surely the most celebrated example of the *Bildungsroman*, or educational novel, his 1794 *Wilhelm Meisters Lehrjahre*, such a forging of self depends on the equilibrium of a number of components, be they head and heart or the earthly here and now and the boundless beyond.[14] The poet Justinus Kerner muses on exactly this in his 1826 poem "Sehnsucht nach der Waldgegend," set to music two years later by Schumann as one of twelve songs forming his Op. 35. Deprived of the "wondrous forest," the seat of unspoiled nature and, more importantly, the locus of spiritual harmony where "in the twilight places bird song and silver stream" inspired "many a song fresh and bright," Kerner's protagonist is now "desolate and mute." The songs of yore "seldom stir," a condition not unlike "the mere half-song of the bird parted from tree and leaf."

I daresay all of the authors represented in this volume would agree that this "Lied sensibility," as I call it, is palpably to be experienced throughout the genre's history even if it is difficult to explain. For the poet Paul von Heyse, in 1860, and Wolf, in the twenty-third song of his *Italienisches Liederbuch* (1890–91, 1896), the empathy for words coupled with music is expressed in terms of a life force whose source *is* nature. "What song can I sing that would be worthy of you?," Heyse demands. "Where can I find one? I should like best to dig it deep out of the earth, where no creature has ever sung it; a song that no man or woman, however old, has ever heard or sung to this day." Earlier, the important philosopher Friedrich Theodor Vischer, in his *Ästhetik oder Wissenschaft des Schönen* (6 vols., 1846–57), declared: "Song is something that grows from nature; it can generate itself from life."[15] Climbing from beneath the rubble of World War II a century later, the historian Friedrich Meinecke still could write in 1946 when he was eighty-four of the reciprocity between poetry – and by extension music – and nature when he sketches the means by which his country might salvage itself and in part atone for recent horrors. "In every German city or larger village" Meinecke longs for the establishment of "a community of like-minded friends of culture" who would take upon themselves "the task of conveying to the hearts of the listeners through sound the most vital evidence of the great German spirit, always offering the noblest music and poetry together." Aware that so many libraries have been destroyed, the historian argues that it is only in such societies that the young might get "their first access to the imperishable poems of Hölderlin, Mörike, C. F. Meyer, and Rilke." Within these groups, Meinecke longs for nothing less than that union of words and music that is the Lied: "lyrics of the wonderful sort, reaching their peak in Goethe and Mörike where the soul becomes nature and nature the soul."[16] In commenting on Meinecke's reflection, Peter Gay has written: "in the impressive literature of German self-accusation, I know of no passage more instructive and more pathetic than this."[17] Given the history of German song and verse, I would add that there are few others more heartrending, unless it is Adorno's statement that "To write poetry after Auschwitz is barbaric."[18]

Notwithstanding this German empathy for song, how does one explain the continuing hold that, say, Schubert's 1814 *Gretchen am Spinnrade* exerts on listeners, many of whom neither read nor speak German and who are aware of Goethe's poem only because they are following a text translation? Is the dominion that Lied composers or their champions claim real? Is a publication devoted to this music needed? This last question may be answered in the single word "yes" and for at least two reasons: firstly, the sheer quality and quantity of works making up the Lied and secondly, the role the genre has played in German culture. The inception of the Lied in the 1740s was premised on matters artistic as well as those relating to nascent nationalism. Poets and composers alike, weary of what they perceived as the Baroque predilection for extravagance, found song a ready medium for the emerging neo-classical aesthetics of naturalism and simplicity. As the literary critic Johann Christoph Gottsched asserted in his widely-read *Versuch einer critischen Dichtkunst für die Deutschen* (1st edn., 1730), not only was Italian Baroque *opera seria* artificial and lacking in reason, it was "a promoter of lust and a corrupter of upright morals."[19] In contrast, the more earnest fare of the Lied, as the influential poet Johann Friedrich von Hagedorn noted in 1747, "soothes our earthly life, allays grief, and generously augments joyfulness."[20] Georg Philipp Telemann had expressed much the same outlook six years earlier when, in the introduction to a collection of his own Lieder, he expressed the hope that his songs might spark a "renewed golden age of notes" worthy of the ancients while also showing "foreigners how more maturely we [Germans] are able to think than do you!"[21] By 1826,

Telemann's dream had become reality. As Gottfried Wilhelm Fink, editor of the music journal *Allgemeine musikalische Zeitung*, asked in January of that year: "Has there ever been an age more prolific in song than ours?"[22] During a single month of 1826, German music lovers found themselves inundated by over a hundred newly-published Lieder. The sum is altogether unheard of when one knows that during the years from 1736 to 1799 only 779 collections of songs had found their way into print (in other words, from a rate of one collection per month during the stated sixty-four years to one hundred times that by 1826). Henceforth, the periodical stated, it would be possible to review only a small portion of this ever-growing number. As the century progressed the trend continued, so much so that in 1889 Friedrich Nietzsche could intone: "The German imagines even God himself singing Lieder."[23]

From this it in part is evident that the Lied stood at the heart of German musical life beginning slightly before the middle of the eighteenth century and continuing throughout the nineteenth, and into the twentieth. At its easy-going best, it worked, as the poet Hagedorn stipulated, to ease earthly existence, assuage anxiety, and promote human happiness. At its most ambitious, like the best Rembrandt painting, the Lied seems to anticipate a quality of photography – not in the flash-bulb glare or literal reproduction of a scene but in the assurance that the whole of a character or a mood can be implied by the revelation of a single poetical-musical instant. At once frozen into a single frame yet unbounded by music's ever and ongoing future, this isolated moment has the power to suggest the continuum of a life from which it has been discerningly cropped. At their most sharply focused, such caught moments can do still more, offering links with posterity – a connection between the then of the Lied in question and the present of those who would listen.

A few words about some practical concerns may be in order. While it may appear that English translations of German titles have been capriciously included, the policy has been to include them only where the original German seemed not otherwise obvious. Titles of German poems are given within quotation marks; those of musical settings of poems in italics. Dates of individuals figuring in the history of the Lied – especially in chapters relating to broad time spans – are given on pp. xxxii–xxxv. This seemed prudent given that some chapters were in danger of becoming weighed down by long lists of names and dates. It is hoped that the reader will not mind having to turn the occasional page.

1 In the beginning was poetry

JANE K. BROWN

In the last third of the eighteenth century Germany blossomed from a marginal participant in European letters to the dynamic center of the movement now called Romanticism – the age that would encompass Kant, Hegel, Schiller, Kleist, Hölderlin, and Goethe. As the story is almost always told, the German art song begins in the next generation – 19 October 1814, to be exact – when Schubert composes the first of his great Goethe settings, *Gretchen am Spinnrade*. The logic of this narrative makes the flowering of German poetry, or even of Goethe himself, solely responsible for the emergence of the Lied. Given that there was a flourishing market in books of songs with keyboard accompaniment for domestic use by greater and lesser-known composers in the mid-eighteenth century, the conclusion does not do justice to the genre's history. Furthermore, the development of the Lied since the eighteenth century does not follow that of German lyric poetry closely: the historical relation between poetry and song is rather more complex.

Hence to begin this volume with a survey of German poetry is not to assert that the development of poetry drives the genre's development – or vice versa. Goethe is profoundly important for the Lied because he was the most original, most influential, and most representative poet of a period in which poetry and song were closely related and expressions of the same cultural concerns. Rather than ask how poetry results in the Lied or what poetry is best suited to musical treatment, it makes more sense to explore what new or changing cultural attitudes are manifest both in German song and in the poems that composers chose to set. In other words, what made this partnership suddenly thrive and become a major musical genre in the nineteenth century? Because poetry operates with language, it is simpler to chart social and cultural change in poetry than in music. In this fashion – and only in this fashion – can German poetry be understood as a "beginning" for the Lied.

This essay describes some cultural developments crucial for German song by tracing their emergence in the German lyric poetry set by Lied composers. I begin by establishing a canon of song texts, and then describe a trajectory based upon it. By tracing the practice of the art song in the eighteenth century and the style shift of the later eighteenth century, we will see how both are tied to the cultural assumptions of the Romantic period – to its new definition of simplicity, to its preoccupation with an internal voice and indeed a pre-conscious or sub-conscious self, and to the professional status of the artist. Song turns out to be one of the genres in which these assumptions persist the longest; we shall see how their breakdown changes the genre of art song.

The canon of song texts

Although by no means all-inclusive, Dietrich Fischer-Dieskau's handbook, *Texte deutscher Lieder*, enables us to formulate useful generalizations about the literary tastes of German composers.[1] The coverage is slightly biased toward twentieth-century composers, since Fischer-Dieskau has sought to foster the modern Lied, but the selection still does not obscure the basic regressive tendency of the repertory. Here are the poets whose texts were set by the largest number of different composers, listed in rank order:

Number of composers	Poet
24	Johann Wolfgang Goethe (1749–1832)
12	Heinrich Heine (1797–1856)
11	Joseph von Eichendorff (1788–1857)
9	Nikolaus Lenau (1802–50), Eduard Mörike (1804–75)
6	Friedrich Hölderlin (1770–1843), Friedrich Rückert (1788–1866)
5	Johann Gottfried Herder (1744–1803), Ludwig Uhland (1787–1862), Gottfried Keller (1819–90)
4	Friedrich Gottlieb Klopstock (1724–1803), Friedrich Schiller (1759–1805), Friedrich Hebbel (1813–63), Conrad Ferdinand Meyer (1825–98), Detlev von Liliencron (1844–1909), Christian Morgenstern (1871–1914)

Of the volume's some 140 poets and some 50 composers, 60 per cent of the composers were born after 1840 and lived into the twentieth century, but only 19 per cent of the poets were: only 2 of the 16 poets most often set were born after 1840. Evidently, song composers look overwhelmingly to the period 1770–1870 for their texts.

Goethe is easily the poet most frequently set by major German composers. He also is the most set in terms of number of texts – sixty-five, twenty more than Wilhelm Müller, author of Schubert's two extended cycles *Die schöne Müllerin* and *Winterreise*. Only Heinrich Heine comes close with about sixty. If we consider which poems were set by the largest number of composers, the result is comparable: nine composers set Goethe's "Wanderers Nachtlied II," seven his "Kennst du das Land," six his "Wonne der Wehmut," and five set each of four other of his poems. Only among the nine texts set by four composers is there finally one *not* by Goethe. Of the twenty-nine texts set by three composers, ten are by Goethe. The concentration on these texts is noteworthy because Goethe wrote far more lyric poetry than any other important German author before Rilke. It is evident that composers through the century are setting certain of Goethe's poems not only in response to the texts, but also in response to or even competition with earlier settings, especially by the prolific Schubert, who set far more poems by Goethe than by any other poet.[2]

Apart from his professional engagement with music (as librettist and theater director), his friendships and collaborations with composers (Reichardt and Zelter), and his stated belief that poetry should be sung, there are sociological reasons for Goethe's dominance.[3] His international best-seller, the novel *Die Leiden des jungen Werther* (The sorrows of the young Werther; 1774), earned him permanent fame as the great genius of a reviving German literature. While his later works generally evoked less enthusiasm and even some resentment, his reputation remained colossal until the end of his life, and his poems, particularly from the decade in which he wrote *Werther*, also remained popular through the nineteenth century. Beginning in the 1870s he was set up as the cultural father figure of Germany by the educational establishment of the Second Empire and widely read in schools. There was remarkable intellectual ferment in the Romantic period, especially in Germany, independent of Goethe, but he represented in many respects the quintessence of his age, and the importance attached to him probably was not undeserved. The art song would doubtless have come into being without him, but it might well have been a less focused genre, and – to judge by the number of Goethe settings from the twentieth century – might not have persisted so long.

The list of poets set by more than one composer and born before 1840 falls readily into two historical groups, the period of European Romanticism known to German literary history as the Age of Goethe (c. 1750 – c. 1830), and the immediate post-Romantic generation known as Biedermeier (c. 1815–50). Both groups are concerned with the relationship of the self to nature and are distinguished primarily by the different attitudes they take toward it – Romantics look for some form of mediation or reconciliation, Biedermeier poets tend to see an insuperable gap. To the first group belong the poets born before 1790, Goethe, Eichendorff, Hölderlin, Herder, Uhland, Klopstock and Schiller; to the second, those born later – Heine, Lenau, Mörike, Rückert, Keller, Hebbel and Meyer. The only anomalous figures here are Eichendorff (usually labeled Romantic) and Rückert (usually considered Biedermeier), both born in 1788 but aligned with different

literary generations by attitude and style, and Hebbel and Meyer, who sometimes are labeled "realist" rather than "Biedermeier," a distinction that rests
on no significant difference in style or tone for our purposes. The even division between the two periods (apart from the two more modern poets,
Liliencron and Morgenstern) is striking and is found already in Schubert.[4]
Since the poets of the Age of Goethe are by and large the more famous ones,
this pattern often looks like a mix of famous and ephemeral poets, or of classic poets and then the composers' friends. The further we proceed through
the nineteenth century, the more backward-looking such a mix becomes.
In order to understand the significance of German poetry for the Lied it
is therefore necessary to focus primarily on the two or three great poetic
generations from the late eighteenth and early nineteenth centuries and to
consider what distinguishes them from earlier and later generations.

Enlightenment poetry and the Lied

German poems set before about 1770 rarely figure in the later history of
song; the ways in which they differ from later poetry thus are telling for
what characterizes the Lied in the nineteenth century. The best-known
poets of the early songs comprise the group still anthologized under the
rubric Anacreontics. These sociable poems, named for the Greek poet
Anacreon, celebrated wine and love and had been cultivated throughout
Europe since the Renaissance. In eighteenth-century Germany, these poets –
Friedrich von Hagedorn, Christian Fürchtegott Gellert, Wilhelm Ludwig
Gleim, Johann Peter Uz, and Karl Wilhelm Ramler – North Germans all, are
among the most important figures in a period generally considered to lack
major poets. German songs of the mid-eighteenth century, set in quantity
by well-known composers such as Georg Philipp Telemann, C. P. E. Bach,
Christian Gottfried Krause, and many lesser-known figures as well, were
published in books of songs that often resulted from the collaboration of
poet and composer. Of this group, only Gleim and Gellert are represented in
Fischer-Dieskau's handbook, through their settings by Haydn (who also set
many English poems) and Beethoven. Perhaps more of these poets might
have remained in the canon longer had they been set by composers of a
later period. For the style shifts in music and in literature are parallel: what
comes before Haydn and Mozart seems as distant today as the poetry that
precedes Goethe. While composers at the end of the nineteenth century and
in the twentieth century constantly turned to texts written before, say, 1870
for their songs, few composers in the early nineteenth century set poems
written before 1770. Expectations about poetry had clearly changed.

The expectations from before 1770 are crystallized in the leading handbook on poetry of the time in Germany, *Versuch einer critischen Dichtkunst*

(Critical essay on the art of poetry), by Johann Christoph Gottsched, professor of rhetoric at the University of Leipzig. First published in 1730, the work was reissued in its fourth and final revised version in 1751. A late neo-classical compendium which occasionally takes issue with but mostly accumulates the ideas of predecessors going back to Horace's *Ars poetica* (first century BC) and Aristotle's *Poetics* (fourth century BC), the book represents well what educated people of the age thought about poetry.

Gottsched discusses the genre closest to song in the sense in which it is understood today as the first (because it is the oldest) of his twenty-five literary categories under the title "Von Oden oder Liedern" (on odes or songs). Typically for the period, song and ode are conflated; our modern distinction is part of the style shift at the end of the eighteenth century. The Anacreontic songs or odes Gottsched had in mind tend to be short, relatively simple, and often playful rhymed poems about wine or love, while other odes tend to be (often) long, stylistically more complex, serious poems on mythological or philosophical themes. Odes in the specifically Pindaric or Greek style were in a verse form that matched none of the standard European forms of the period and by the end of the century they would be rendered in unrhymed free verse or rhythmic prose. The two forms are connected for Gottsched and his contemporaries by their appeal to antiquity and the fact that they require musical accompaniment. It was common knowledge that Greek lyric poetry, whether serious or love poetry, was recited with musical accompaniment, usually the lyre. Echoing an argument that harks back to ancient Greece, Gottsched asserts that poetry originated in music, according, perhaps, to scenarios like the following. In a moment of excitement, even slight drunkenness, a lively wit begins to sing for joy at a feast; needing a topic for the words that accompany his spontaneous song, he praises wine in all its aspects. Or a bored shepherd, suddenly excited by the sight of a shepherdess, decides to imitate the birds, and what better topic for his words than the beauty of the shepherdess?[5] Song thus precedes poetry, and the "original" poetry is Anacreontic song.

A song thus articulates an emotion, usually pleasurable, that arises from a social situation, and melody takes precedence over words. Originally, songs, like arias in *opera seria*, expressed a single emotion; eventually they expanded to express ideas as well. In general, however, Gottsched recommends loyalty to the classical topics of praise of heroes, love, and wine.[6] His position represents a distillation of the most pragmatic tendencies of the neo-classical tradition, which followed Horace in its focus on the social context and function of poetry. The poet is a prophet and a teacher (like Orpheus and the other mythic poets with whom Gottsched begins his tradition); he is not a possessed madman but a wise and reasonable individual who embodies the highest civility and culture.[7]

This is a theory of poetry for an emerging urban middle class. Song-books were marketed as edifying home entertainment for a bourgeoisie now prosperous and ambitious enough to want to imitate the sophisticated leisure of the upper classes. Hence the Lied emerges in North Germany in the eighteenth century, for only in an old independent trading city like Hamburg, not at the court centers further south, did such a culture flourish. Wine, love, and praise do not mean, in Gottsched or in any of the Anacreon-tic poets, drunkenness or sex; it is the love of middle-class urbanites playing at being shepherds and shepherdesses, and the drinking of solid citizens who appreciate the good cheer of no more than one glass too many. All of these poets came from similar backgrounds and were employed in the typical occupations of university-trained members of their class: they were secretaries to diplomats, princes, or cathedral chapters; teachers of rhetoric and morals; or, occasionally, judges. They wrote poetry as a gentlemanly avocation, as did virtually all other belletrists in Germany during this pe-riod. It was part and parcel of their classicism for them to be, essentially, dilettantes.

Two stanzas from Hagedorn's "Der Morgen," set by C. P. E. Bach (among many others) in his *Oden mit Melodien* (Odes with melodies, 1762) offer a good example.[8]

Uns lockt die Morgenröthe	The morning's red lures us
In Busch und Wald,	into shrubbery and copse,
Wo schon der Hirten Flöte	where the shepherd's pipe early
Ins Land erschallt.	resounds through the land.
Die Lerche steigt und schwirret,	The lark ascends and trills,
Von Lust erregt;	in joyous rapture;
Die Taube lacht und girret,	the dove laughs and coos,
Die Wachtel schlägt.	the quail calls.
Die Hügel und die Weyde	Hills and meadow
Stehn aufgehellt,	stand in new light,
Und Fruchtbarkeit und Freude	and fruitfulness and joy
Beblümt das Feld.	strew flowers on the field.
Der Schmelz der grünen Flächen	The enamel of the green surfaces
Glänzt voller Pracht;	shines full of splendor,
Und von den klaren Bächen	and from the clear brooks
Entweicht die Nacht.	the night departs.

Hagedorn celebrates nature on a spring morning. But his nature is decidedly domesticated: it consists of shrubbery and thicket, meadows and fields. Moreover, it is evoked not through its qualities, but through the objects and beings that typically inhabit such a landscape. The words "Schmelz" and "Flächen" in the second stanza come from painting, and the third stanza bids the listener "see" a shepherd arriving. This is typically what "imitation," the fundamental quality of all literature for neo-classicism, means in poetry of this period: the listener / reader is called upon to see a series of familiar objects and scenes; poetry is, in a famous cliché, the sister art of painting. Gottsched did not permit poems to have a plot, and nothing happens here. The poem simply calls to mind a picture, which in turn conveys a single emotion, happiness, through the happiness of all the figures it describes. In the last stanza, the speaker invites his Phyllis to join him in a quiet nook of this idealized landscape – model behavior for innocent lovers in a model world.

Such a poetry of literal vision and ready accessibility is often labeled simple, but the term needs to be specified. First, verse of this kind requires a community that shares a conventional language, so that the shorthand list of images can in fact speak. Hagedorn assumes his audience knows what larks, doves, and quails sound like, and that it recognizes Phyllis as a code name for a shepherdess. More important, this verse depends on clarity: word-play, complex imagery, dense language all would interfere with the reader's ability to construct the picture in the mind's eye as its parts are enumerated. The poem proceeds in unvarying strophes built from parallel two-line units, each its own clause. To the end nothing disrupts the pattern; instead, the poem maintains a uniform surface. Homogeneous precision is the essence of neo-classical simplicity, which was deemed a virtue for all critics in this tradition from Horace to Gottsched, and was the eighteenth century's battle cry in music as well as literature. Partisans of Zeno's and Metastasio's reformed *opera seria* called for noble simplicity to replace the convolutions of Baroque opera plots, while some thirty years later Gluck and Calzabigi called for the same noble simplicity to counter the excesses of Metastasian singer's opera.[9] Song was another area of special simplicity, as even composers like C. P. E. Bach and Haydn wrote the simplest of melodies and accompaniments for this new form of music for home performance.[10] Such highly domesticated clarity and simplicity constituted the dignity of even a song like Hagedorn's "Der Morgen" and thereby justified the classical designation "ode."

The style-shift of the later eighteenth century

By the early 1770s the poetic landscape in Germany had changed dramatically. A new generation of writers in their twenties inspired by Goethe and Johann Gottfried Herder – the Sturm und Drang (Storm and Stress) – was rebelling against the neo-classicism of their elders. Herder, a prolific writer on literary, philosophical and historical topics, was the most important mediator and most original synthesizer of the various currents then changing

European thought: the new social philosophy associated with the name of Jean-Jacques Rousseau, the new Idealist philosophy of Immanuel Kant, and the new discipline of classical philology emerging at German universities. Herder invented the concept of folk song, was largely responsible for the enthusiasm for Shakespeare that swept Germany in the last quarter of the century, and was a major contributor to the emergence of historical method in scholarship. He met Goethe in 1770 and is widely recognized as his decisive mentor. At Goethe's behest, he settled in Weimar and spent the rest of his life supervising religious and educational life in the Duchy of Saxe-Weimar. Oriented toward England rather than toward France, the Sturm und Drang created a new poetry from the century's growing interests in the primitive, folk poetry, the depths of history (both classical and non-classical), and the cultivation of emotion or "Sensibility." The new generation's idols included Rousseau, Shakespeare, Samuel Richardson, Laurence Sterne, and the German poet Friedrich Gottlieb Klopstock. Goethe was immediately recognized as the great poet of this movement with his Shakespearean drama *Götz von Berlichingen* (1773), his sentimental novel *Werther*, and his poems both in folk tone and in the elevated free verse of Pindaric ode. Herder was the movement's theorist, and we can gain the clearest idea of how it differed from Gottsched's Enlightenment poetics by considering aspects of his influential essays *Abhandlung über den Ursprung der Sprache* (Excerpt from a correspondence on Ossian and the songs of primitive peoples, 1772) and *Auszug aus einem Briefwechsel über Ossian und die Lieder alter Völker* (Treatise on the origin of language, 1773).

The first of the two essays says more about the origins of poetry and its relation to music than the title would suggest. Herder attacks here two prevalent theories of the origins of language: the first, that it was God-given and the second, that it derived from imitation of animal sounds. Instead, in a specifically Romantic gesture, he locates the origin of language in the uniquely human capacity to reflect. However, Herder does allow a certain kind of sub-rational language that humans have in common with animals: unreflecting cries of pain, of passion, or of pleasure. He elaborates these parallels in the essay's first section by using imagery that evokes music. Repeatedly he writes of the sounding strings of our being, of feelings expressing themselves in tones, and tones as the language of feeling.[11] The less natural written human language of reason has largely displaced this more primitive form of expression, but its traces still can be found in the innate musicality of ancient languages and especially in their oldest poetry. Even in our current languages hearing is the most important sense for the reflective process that constitutes humanity's superior rational powers. Similarly, Herder's Ossian essay centers on the premise that the heroic poems supposedly translated but, as it later transpired, actually written by James Macpherson were not epic (narrative), but really song. The essence of ancient folk poetry, regardless of the culture of origin, is its affinity with music. In these two influential essays, Herder thus associates poetry with music and with the pre-rational aspects of the soul. This is both the oldest part of our mental being and the part that in each of us comes before reflective mental activity. Music and song do not simply express emotion, as they do for Gottsched and his generation; instead, they are the voice of the spontaneous self underlying all linguistic expression. Herder lays the groundwork here for expressing the widespread sense in late eighteenth-century Europe that our real selves, buried deep within, are scarcely accessible to rational analysis and that the true inner voice finds expression only in dreams, music, and poetry.[12]

Because this secret voice of the self is so deeply rooted in the past, it is open to time in a way that the more rational speaking voice of earlier German poetry is not. Compare Hagedorn's morning poem above to Goethe's most frequently set poem, the evening poem "Wanderers Nachtlied":

Über allen Gipfeln	O'er all the summits
Ist Ruh,	is rest,
In allen Wipfeln	in all the treetops
Spürest du	you sense
Kaum einen Hauch;	scarcely a breath;
Die Vögelein schweigen im Walde.	the birds fall still in the wood,
Warte nur, balde	just wait, soon
Ruhest du auch.	you too shall rest.

At first glance, Goethe seems to follow Hagedorn in evoking the time of day in apparently simple language and in a catalog of parallel descriptors – birds and woods and hills – but that soon stops. Indeed, the poem is strikingly short. It swiftly closes off both breath ("Kaum einen Hauch") and utterance ("Die Vögelein schweigen"), transforming repose into the peace of death. Instead of Hagedorn's static visualization and deliberate simplicity, Goethe fuses the human and the natural by combining the breeze and the breath of life in the one word "Hauch." Moreover, the peace and beauty of the evening landscape can barely conceal the onset of fear in the last two lines: emotion is no longer homogeneous. If Hagedorn's poem never gets beyond the same moment of the day, Goethe's extends to the end of life. Thus while C. P. E. Bach's strophic setting corresponds admirably to the placidity of Hagedorn's text, the temporalized emotions of the later poem lead to shifting swells of emotion and rhythmic pattern in Schubert's setting and extended declamation in Liszt's. The depths of the inner voice are also the abyss of time.[13]

This immediate yet mysteriously interiorized voice opens poetry to a kind of drama previously unthinkable. Hagedorn's poem is dramatic in the simple sense that a particular speaker can be characterized who addresses a community of like-minded people in the first person plural. The drama in Goethe's poem is more complex. Neither the speaker nor the community addressed is readily identifiable. At one level, this poem with its direct address to the reader is an epitaph, like a verse inscribed on a tomb to be read by passing wanderers (of which there are many in the prose and verse of the period) – in fact, Goethe first wrote it on the window frame of a hunting lodge. Here, the voice in the poem would seem to be that of nature itself. Yet unlike a classical inscription, the statement is not a general reflection, but is tied to a particular moment of experience. Furthermore, the "du" addressed in the poem senses the motionlessness of the air and, ultimately, the approach of death: "you" is not a passive listener, but actively experiences what the speaker describes. But there is only one "you" with whom any speaker could be so intimate as to know what it senses, and that is, of course, the self. Goethe's speaker is not just personified nature addressing the wanderer; the title identifies the poem as the wanderer's song, and the wanderer addresses himself.[14] There is, therefore, no context of sociability. Furthermore, this self divides into an implied "I" who speaks and a described "you," into a subject and an object. This is the reflectiveness that grounds Herder's definition of language; here it generates a self that expands to fill and simultaneously engulf the world. To the extent that we still identify the speaker with nature itself, nature and the self have merged.

Now every poem becomes an implicit drama staged within the mind, a development crucial for nineteenth-century song. Consider how many of the songs most central to the repertory derive from dramas or from narratives in which they are embedded – the songs of the harper and of Mignon from Goethe's *Wilhelm Meister*, "Gretchen am Spinnrade," the "König in Thule," and the flea song from *Faust*. Other poems stage multiple voices, like "Der Tod und das Mädchen" or "Erlkönig" – virtually all ballads fall into this category. In many other poems, the speaker addresses some absent or inanimate interlocutor – a place, nature, the dead, or someone absent (friend, relative, beloved), the past, an ideal – often suggested by the piano accompaniment. Others are declamatory, like "Ganymed."[15] It is hard to think of poems written between about 1770 and 1870 that do not open up an interior stage and thus transform song into a domesticated opera that can be performed in the privacy of the home, or in the sanctuary of the self.

The parallel with opera is significant, for song in this period becomes increasingly professionalized. Although still marketed and consumed as domestic music through the nineteenth century and by no means so difficult as most operatic music, nineteenth-century song is more demanding technically than that of the eighteenth century; the crucial difference, reflected in the new designation "art song," is that song from the age of Schubert on is no longer primarily for musical amateurs. The songs of C. P. E. Bach and even of Haydn are notably simpler than their other music. By the 1820s, the pattern had already changed. Goethe regularly held musicales in his home; performances might include settings of Goethe's own poems, often by composers connected to local circles like Zelter and Reichardt. These songs were accessible to amateur performers, but in Goethe's home they were sung by professionals from the local theater company and accompanied by the composer himself, and, occasionally, critiqued by the poet.[16] Schubert's own musicales held to the same professional level – Schubert at the piano accompanied the noted tenor Johann Michael Vogl. It is normal in English novels for the young lady of the house to entertain company by singing and playing in the drawing room after dinner; Jane Austen, writing at the turn of the nineteenth century, makes clear that the abilities of such performers could be quite variable and thus suggests that amateur performance already left something to be desired. In the novels of Theodor Fontane in the 1890s, home musical performance is either semi-professional or by a visiting virtuoso;[17] since several ballads written by Fontane had been set by Carl Loewe, who made a celebrity career of performing his own songs, Fontane is likely to have been accurate. As performance practice shifts, the material becomes more difficult. If most of Schubert and much of Schumann can be sung by untrained voices, both require considerable keyboard training; Brahms already poses challenges to voice as well as accompanist, while Wolf and, say, Mahler are only occasionally accessible to the non-professional performer.[18] By the end of the nineteenth century, art song has become a genre for the concert hall rather than for the home.

The professionalization of song runs counter not only to the conditions that created the Lied, but also to the close alliance of art song with folk song.[19] In its willed simplicity and singability, eighteenth-century song had an implicit connection to folk song that became explicit in the style shift in the last third of the century. Herder, who invented both the term and the concept of folk song, collected and published the first such compilation in German, *Volkslieder* (1778, revised and republished 1807 as *Stimmen der Völker in Liedern*), collected by himself and others (including Goethe) and based on the model of Percy's *Reliques of Ancient English Poetry* (1765). He inspired further collections, such as the great Romantic anthology *Des Knaben Wunderhorn* (Arnim and Brentano, 1805), and also poetry in the style of folk song, such as Goethe's "Heidenröslein," adapted from a song the poet himself had collected. The term was widely attached, especially in the nineteenth century, to the interest in unique national cultures and styles (such as Rückert's orientalizing poetry or the Chinese poems set by Mahler), but it always implied that the primitive, original aspects of humanity comprised its most essential and best qualities. The directness of popular style became a sine qua non for great Romantic poetry: Wordsworth in 1800 famously prefaced the second edition of his revolutionary collection of poetry, *Lyrical Ballads,* with an attack on poetic diction (further elaborated in the Appendix of 1802) and an explanation of his efforts to bring his language "near to the real language of men."[20] It is one of the ironies of European cultural development that in rediscovering the historical significance of folk poetry the Romantics raised it to the status of high art and that late Romantic settings of folk poems (e.g. Mahler's) engage the full resources of the modern orchestra. Those texts of the period that have become folk songs in their own right – Goethe's "Heidenröslein" or Wilhelm Müller's "Am Brunnen vor dem Tore" – are sung by German children not to Schubert's melodies, but to the much simpler ones by Werner and Silcher, two of the many nineteenth-century composers who wrote songs for use in schools and social organizations, while Wolf's, Mahler's and most of Brahms's settings of genuine folk texts are considered art song.[21] It is important to be aware that all folk song – verse and music – in the nineteenth century can only be historical reconstruction and its simplicity can only be willed.

A final aspect of the style change is the concept of simplicity itself. Despite the value placed on spontaneity, both it and simplicity are already clearly willed in the songs of the mid-eighteenth century; simplicity was, as we have seen, a slogan of reformers in vocal music. But it took on new resonance after Johann Joachim Winckelmann, in his essay "Gedanken über die Nachahmung der griechischen Werke in der Malerei und Bildhauerkunst" (Thoughts on the imitation of Greek works in painting and sculpture, 1755) popularized the formula "edle Einfalt und stille Größe" (noble simplicity and calm grandeur). "Noble simplicity" evokes neo-classical beauty with its homogeneous clarity. Calm grandeur, however, evokes the parallel category of sublimity. Sublimity was generally considered not exactly a contrast, but an alternative to beauty in the nascent discourse of aesthetics, where, especially after the 1750s, it was increasingly associated with awe, terror, pathos, heightened emotion, and obscurity.[22] Winckelmann's tentative linkage of simplicity and sublimity was accentuated in the 1770s as simplicity became bound to Herder's concept of the folk. The kind of simplicity associated with sublime grandeur increasingly abandons the simplicity of clarity and accessibility so essential to neo-classicism. It becomes instead the simplicity of folk song with meaningless refrains, fragmentary narrative, and supernatural themes like Goethe's "Erlkönig" or "Heidenröslein." By the 1770s sublimity was associated with the silence of awe, and thus with the feelings that persist beyond speech. This version of sublimity thus connects to the issues of feeling and speech in Herder's essay on the origins of language and in a poem like "Wanderers Nachtlied," which deals with falling into silence. Often sublime obscurity appears in the imagery of a poem. In "Erlkönig" father and son disagree about what they see in the foggy landscape; the third stanza of Mignon's song "Kennst du das Land" leads over high mountain passes wreathed in fog past dangerous dragon-filled caves to Italy, a land simultaneously associated with flourishing nature and frozen art, comparable to the doubleness of peace and death in "Wanderers Nachtlied." Shadows in these texts are often more important than the objects that cast them. But one cannot simply speak of a shift from simplicity to complexity, for the word simplicity continues to be used to describe this very phenomenon of the shadow, of the ordinary that is extraordinary.[23] It is when simplicity becomes complex that folk song becomes professional.

Biedermeier and the historicism of the nineteenth century

The issues that preoccupied the Romantics determined the course of German poetry until the advent of modernism in the last few decades of the nineteenth century. Romantic models were so pervasive that German writers suffered from the feeling that everything had already been said and written – that they had been born too late. The quandary is addressed explicitly in Karl Immermann's novel *Die Epigonen* (1836). For most of the century, the only alternatives were either the Biedermeier style or an eclectic historicism already begun by the Romantics that involved revivals of various earlier styles. Biedermeier refers in the narrow sense to the generation in German culture that came of age after the Restoration in 1815 – Schubert's generation. Heine, Lenau, Rückert, Mörike are the lyric poets who first come to mind; German literary history sometimes uses overlapping rubrics like "poetic realism" or "realism," but the basic style known as Biedermeier dominates German poetry into the 1870s. Biedermeier culture focused on domesticity, but the important issue in poetry was a heightening of the contrasting aspects of Romanticism, often characterized by pathos. Both periods worried about the dichotomy of subject and object and addressed it dialectically, but they felt differently about it. When writers take pleasure in imaginary or paradoxical resolutions of oppositions, we tend to call them Romantic (in the German context); those who suffer from their inability to make these resolutions real we call Biedermeier. Other differences follow: the Romantic view is expansive, cosmopolitan, and optimistic, while the Biedermeier attitude tends toward pessimism, fear of disorder, and withdrawal into a cultivated domesticity that can sometimes seem smug.[24] These broad generalities lead to some very specific differences for the student of the Lied.

A look at two brief examples by the best and most set poets of the period, Heinrich Heine and Eduard Mörike, will make these differences clear. Here is the opening poem of Schumann's *Dichterliebe*, based on poems from Heine's *Buch der Lieder* (1827).

Im wunderschönen Monat Mai,	In the lovely month of May,
Als alle Knospen sprangen,	as the buds all burst open,
Da ist in meinem Herzen	then in my heart
Die Liebe aufgegangen.	love arose.

Im wunderschönen Monat Mai,	In the lovely month of May,
Als alle Vögel sangen,	as all the birds sang,
Da hab' ich ihr gestanden	I confessed to her
Mein Sehnen und Verlangen.	my yearning and desire.

Heine works with the same motifs as Hagedorn and Goethe, but through repetition he exposes their conventionality and irrelevance. The real issue is not May or buds or birds, but the poet's desire – evidently unsatisfied, since it still is being talked about. Both stanzas move from nature in the first line to the poet's own self in the third: thus the self prevails over nature, subject over object. In this respect, Heine's poem resembles Hagedorn's, which focuses on the poet's joy in nature, more than Goethe's where the central issue is the balance achieved between self and nature. Yet the poem is inconceivable without Goethe's, for this landscape is subject to time. If Hagedorn catalogs everything in the present, Heine situates his poem in a landscape of memory, what Wordsworth called "emotion recollected in tranquillity."[25] The rest of *Dichterliebe* traces not only the growth and development of the emotion but, even more, the growth and development of the speaker's reaction to his remembered emotions. This drama takes place entirely within the self; unable to escape his pain, the protagonist can overcome it only by burying the poems themselves in an absurdly oversized coffin in the last song, "Die alten bösen Lieder" (The bad old songs). One need only compare the version of death at the end of this cycle with the delicate ambiguity of repose and death in "Wanderers Nachtlied" to comprehend the difference between Biedermeier and Romantic.

But not all Biedermeier poets were satirists. Mörike's "In der Frühe" (Early in the morning), set by Wolf, offers a more subtle version of the Biedermeier aesthetic:

Kein Schlaf noch kühlt das Auge mir.	No sleep yet cools my eyes.
Dort gehet schon der Tag herfür	There comes the day already
An meinem Kammerfenster.	at my chamber window.
Es wühlet mein verstörter Sinn	My shattered senses still roil
Noch zwischen Zweifeln her und hin	back and forth among doubts
Und schaffet Nachtgespenster.	and create nightmares.
Ängste, quäle	Worry, torment
Dich nicht länger, meine Seele!	Yourself no longer, my soul!
Freu dich! schon sind da und dorten	Rejoice! Here and there already
Morgenglocken wach geworden.	morning bells have wakened.

This poem too deals with a self in relation to nature at a particular moment, in this case daybreak. This self longs to be at one with the world, to rejoice with the morning bells and thereby erase the disharmony, the "shattered senses" that did not sleep when nature did and that suffered from nightmares when the rest of the world already was waking up. Even more than in Heine's poem, the self here is completely foregrounded: the poem is an unabashed address to an inner self to which the world is not lost, but distinctly secondary. At the same time, things would be better without this imbalance. As in Goethe and in Heine, this self has a strong sense of personal time and emotional change. It also depends on voice and music: Goethe's poem centers on the reduction of sound to silence; Heine's gives voice to his love; Mörike's leads to the morning bells. Not all poems of the period are quite so explicit, but Biedermeier texts, like those of the Romantic era, do share the fundamental commitment to articulation. Thus the underlying values in Heine's and Mörike's texts are the same as in Goethe's; but neither Heine nor Mörike can still believe in Goethe's metaphorical equation of poem and feeling.

Although I have been calling the style shift of the late eighteenth century Romantic, it would now be useful to refine my terminology. European Romanticism comprises a development that extends from Rousseau through the 1830s. In Germany, however, the term is traditionally reserved for two particular schools of poetry centered in Jena in the late 1790s and in Heidelberg beginning around 1805. Romanticism in German usage specifically excludes the writers of the period currently best known outside of Germany – the mature Goethe (after the early 1780s), Schiller, Hölderlin and Kleist – who are called "Classicists." The lyric poets of the 1770s and 1780s are identified with the term "Empfindsamkeit" (equivalent to the British Age of Sensibility). Germans sometimes refer to the entire assemblage, which is defined by Goethe's life-span of 1749–1832, as the "Age of Goethe."

The Biedermeier generation readily adopted Heine's generally pejorative term for the period of German Classicism/Romanticism – *Kunstperiode*, or era of art. Except for Schiller's plays and Goethe's idyll *Hermann und Dorothea* (1797), which was understood as a patriotic celebration of German domesticity, the Biedermeier had limited sympathy for Goethe's major novels and plays, including *Faust*, and for most of German Romanticism – Tieck, Novalis, the Schlegel brothers Friedrich and August Wilhelm, Arnim and Brentano. Instead, it anthologized and took its models from the Age of Sensibility – from Goethe's works of the 1770s, or from poets such as Matthisson, Hölty, and Claudius – all familiar figures to students of Lied. The same pattern prevails in the choice of poems set by German composers. Schubert set very few poems by the poets of high Romanticism, but almost equal numbers of poems from the Age of Sensibility and by poets of his own generation. Furthermore, most of the many Goethe poems set by Schubert were written before 1790, and there is a steady decline in the number of Goethe texts set by him in successive decades of the poet's oeuvre.[26] In this respect Schubert was typical. Of the major Romantic lyric poets listed above, Novalis and the Schlegel brothers are not represented in Fischer-Dieskau's collection at all. Even though Schubert set a few texts by all three, they are not frequently performed. The other three, Tieck, Arnim and Brentano, were not set until late in the century (Tieck and Brentano by Brahms) or in the twentieth century (Arnim by Strauss), when a revival of German Romanticism was underway. The same is true for Hölderlin, for whom critical terminology wavers between Romantic and Classical: he was forgotten for much of the nineteenth century and first set by Brahms, then by five composers in the twentieth century. When Schubert set two poems from Goethe's late work *West-östlicher Divan* (West-eastern anthology) of 1819, he selected the two written not by Goethe but by a friend's wife, Marianne von Willemer (not identified in early printings). Schumann also set a few poems from this collection, but it was not until Brahms and Wolf that significant numbers of these and other of Goethe's later poems were set. There was thus a striking delay in the uptake of poems into the Lied repertory from the *Kunstperiode*: the sensibility of the Lied tradition is closely allied to that of the Biedermeier.

The mature Goethe and the German Romantics appealed so little to the Biedermeier and to composers of the nineteenth century most probably because of their strategies for combating the dangers inherent in the Romantic position. In "Wanderers Nachtlied," the poet's voice and the voice of nature are identical; at the same time the speaker splits into two voices: one that speaks for a concrete objective world and one that senses things beyond the words of the poem – like the approach of death. Because Goethe's poem is so perfectly balanced, the dangers it has successfully escaped are not immediately obvious. But if the self and nature speak with the same voice, what saves the self from being swallowed up by nature and dissolving? Alternatively, what keeps the self from overpowering the voice of nature and substituting for it some construct of its own imagining? Goethe knew of these dangers: *Werther* deals with the second problem, his poem "Ganymed" (set by Schubert) with the first. Eichendorff's "Die zwei Gesellen," set by Schumann, confronts each of its protagonists with one of these complementary problems. The first of Eichendorff's two wandering youths marries and spends the rest of his life cut off from nature, which he henceforth sees only through the window of his snug Biedermeier room. The second immerses himself in nature – he succumbs to the sirens – and returns tired and old, with nothing to show for his life. Like Mörike, Eichendorff was extremely popular with composers, especially Schumann and Wolf. Although he generally is considered a Romantic in Germany, he published his poetry mostly in the 1820s and thereafter, and is really one of the great Biedermeier poets. German Classicism and Romanticism focus on the function of the imagination, of fiction, and of the ideal in bridging the gap between self and Nature, while the Biedermeier focuses on the dangers of what it considers an unbridgeable abyss.

The Romantics had four readily distinguishable techniques for mediating between subject and object that were not accepted by the Biedermeier. The first involves the supernatural: the German Romantics raised the fairy-tale to a high art that found solutions to the disorder of the world (Goethe, Novalis, Hoffmann) or worked out the complexities of the sub-conscious emotional life (Tieck, Hoffmann) in elaborate fantasies. The Biedermeier, best represented in this context by the Brothers Grimm (born 1785 and 1786), was interested in what it considered real fairy-tales: tales collected from "the folk." It liked ghosts and witches, but not extended fantasies. The second is irony: German Romanticism is famous for its special form of irony that preserves the fantastic elements of its creations by breaking the illusion before it can be attacked by reason and logic. Such irony involves irreverent humor quite unlike the Biedermeier's genre-humor, which never undermines respect for reason and social institutions. The Romantics – and the mature Goethe – sometimes playfully, sometimes grimly – questioned all limits, whether social or epistemological. The Biedermeier preferred clear distinctions between serious and comic, and responded with greater enthusiasm to pathos than to irreverence (except Heine, whose irreverence was often self-destructive and pathetic, and thus suited to the melancholy and madness that pervaded the middle third of the nineteenth century). Schumann had a fine sense for Heine's irony, and a strong taste for pathos. Brahms is so famous for his pathos that his lighter moments receive little attention. Only in Wolf does a sense for the playful emerge, although not, it should be noted, in the Eichendorff settings, which focus exclusively on his Biedermeier pathos. The third aspect is that Romanticism everywhere in Europe, including Germany (especially German Classicism), also engaged in a major Greek revival. Poets wrote on classical topics and engaged in translation, but also, particularly Goethe and Hölderlin, wrote seriously in classical meters – dactylic hexameter, elegiac couplets, Latin ode forms, Pindaric verse hymns – with a fluency rarely matched elsewhere in European poetry. While Schubert set magnificent models early on for Goethe's Pindaric verse hymns (among them "Prometheus" and "Ganymed"), they do not make for easy domestic performance. And no one ever developed a musical idiom for the other classical meters.[27] Indeed – and this is the fourth point – there is a strong element of formalism among the German Romantics. They are fascinated with arabesques, with elaborate verse forms of all sorts but especially the Baroque forms of the Latin countries (sonnet, for example), with synaesthesia, complex word play and elaborate sound effects (multiple rhymes, internal rhyme, and assonance). The Age of Sensibility and the nineteenth century – allowing for occasional exceptions like Rückert – prefer simple stanzaic forms with straightforward rhyme schemes.[28] The threat of subterranean forces lurking beneath even simple language is so great that complex language seems too much for the Biedermeier. Nineteenth-century prose can run to great syntactic complexity, and some of the verse does as well – Annette von Droste-Hülshoff in Germany, Robert Browning in England are good examples – but such language is associated with the greater challenge of making sense of the world. All four of these elements lead away from song. By avoiding them Biedermeier poets and Lied composers avoided the Romantic tendencies that might undermine authentic voice.

On the basis of these reflections we can now appreciate Georg Friedrich Wilhelm Hegel's astute and compact assessment of the relation of poetry to music, first set forth in his lectures on aesthetics in the 1820s:

> Fusion with melodies in the strict sense is really only achieved in the case of romantic [i.e. post-classical], and, above all, modern lyrics; this is what we find especially in those songs where the mood and the heart preponderate, and music has then to struggle and develop this inner note of the soul into melody. Folk-song, for example, loves and calls for a musical accompaniment. On the other hand, canzonets, elegies, epistles, etc., and even sonnets will nowadays not easily find a composer. Where ideas and reflections and even feelings are completely expounded in the poetry and thereby more and more liberated from being wholly concentrated within the mind and from the sensuous element in art, the lyric, as a communication in language, wins greater independence and does not lend itself so readily to close association with music. On the other hand, the less explicit is the inner life which seeks expression, the more it needs the help of melody.[29]

Hegel saw with remarkable clarity the special affinity of the poetry of the period for music and the tensions between the Romantic taste for complex form and the expression of inarticulable emotional content.

Post-Romantic poetry and the Lied

It is Romantic formalism, identified by Hegel as incompatible with song, that ultimately undermined the special congruence of poetic and musical voice that characterizes the nineteenth-century Lied. For this aspect of Romantic poetics attracted the interest of the early modernists and thus determined the direction European poetry was to take. Indeed, modern poetry has been characterized in a seminal book by Hugo Friedrich as "de-romanticized Romanticism,"[30] a phrase that explains why so little modern poetry has been set by Lied composers and why the genre seems no longer to be flourishing. A quick survey of the sub-headings in Friedrich's chapter on Baudelaire, first of the great modern poets, defines the relation of modern poetry to both Romantic poetry and the poetry of the eighteenth century. Many address formal categories – arabesque (of great interest to the Romantics), incantatory language (related to the Romantic fascination with sound effects), the deformation of traditional forms and language, and the general sense for poetry as mathematical calculation (derived from German Romantic theory). In effect, Baudelaire exaggerates Romantic formalism to deprive language of meaning. At the same time that fantasy (in the Romantic fairy-tale) is set completely free, the ideal toward which Romantic poetry tends to strive is declared empty. The Romantic poet might have starved in a garret, become melancholy or gone mad, but the modern poet is even more divorced from society: his poetry must cultivate ugliness, offend its audience, aspire to the satanic. Once again, the Romantic revolt against neo-classicism's social norms is pushed to the extreme and art attacks itself.

These concerns converge in Friedrich's most important category, de-personalization. Poetry no longer speaks in a personal voice, but achieves its validity in its generality, its non-individuality. Thus modernism attempts to undo the fundamental Romantic discovery that the object can never be known without taking account of the subject. Rainer Maria Rilke, the most famous German modernist poet, cultivated what he called "Dinggedichte" (thing poems), poems that attempt to focus on objects without subjects. Very occasional examples of such object-focused poetry can be found in the nineteenth century: Conrad Ferdinand Meyer's poem "Der römische Brunnen" is often discussed as a *Dinggedicht*, and there has been controversy as to whether Mörike's "Auf eine Lampe" should be considered one: neither resulted in a setting included in Fischer-Dieskau's handbook. But modernist composers have set Rilke and the other great German modernist, Stefan George. The first of George's fifteen poems from *Das Buch der hängenden Gärten*, set by Schoenberg, is a good example of *Dinggedichte*. In the work the poet assembles a mosaic-like landscape from a list of small objects that exist in no narrative relationship to one another and, more importantly, in no relationship to a particular seeing eye or subject. A conventional love relationship emerges in the succeeding poems, but any emotions other than physical desire consistently dissolve in the cloud of detail and simile. Rilke's *Das Marienleben*, famously set by Hindemith, condenses its narrative into the moments in the life of the Virgin traditionally represented in painting and speculates consistently on the emptying of Mary's individuality and subjectivity into being itself. It is typical that the first poem begins "O was muß es die Engel gekostet haben" (Oh what must it have cost the angels). The cycle furthermore speculates about the feelings of angels, not of humans, and whenever humans enter into consideration, it has to do with grasping the ungraspable inhumanity of existence. As in the poems of Hölderlin, who also was not set until the twentieth century (except for one choral setting by Brahms), the emotional energy of these poems is attached to highly abstract philosophical concerns more than to expression of an individual subject. The poetry of Bertolt Brecht represents a different kind of impersonality; he speaks for classes, not for individuals. His famous alienation effect in drama was intended to make the audience think about the characters rather than identify with them. For him – as for the modernists in general – voice was a seduction to be avoided.

The change is crucial for song, which by its nature literalizes the presence of the voice. To be sure, Romantic composers like Mendelssohn composed songs without words, but their titles in fact call attention to their Romantic idealism and to the impossibility of their attempts. Modernism denies voice – the very quality that distinguishes Romantic (in the most general sense) poetry from its predecessors and the very quality that makes song possible. The connection between song and voice – not just making human sounds, but the dramatic voice of an individual persona or of the sub-conscious of an individual person – is fundamental to the existence of the Lied as it developed from Schubert through Mahler and Strauss. Composers tended to avoid those Romantic poets who most engage in playful formalism; and the song tradition continues to look back to those poets who write, however belatedly, in the Romantic/Biedermeier style with an individual poetic voice.

Conclusion

In a certain sense, then, it is reasonable to regard the history of German song as the history of three successive genres with different cultural pre-suppositions. In the eighteenth century we have a deliberately simplified music to accompany poetry that speaks in a language of static pictures and images and which, while perhaps not truly universal, is at least felt to be so among those who understand its conventions. Both poem and song are conceived as universally accessible; hence they are clear, simple, and take a moral stance. Romantic poetry and song, which encompasses the entire sweep of what we generally think of as the German Lied from Beethoven to Strauss, constitutes a different tradition rooted in the "songfulness" of poetry. Romantic poetry expresses an individual, personal self – a subject – that exists in time and knows of its existence only in relation to its difference from a non-self (object or its own past). Such poems depend above all on the balance between the silent voice of this inner self and the music of nature, between heard and unheard melodies. Sometime in the later nineteenth century, European culture loses confidence – or perhaps just loses interest – in this synthesis and returns to a form of poetry focused again in part on the visual world, in part on the abstractions of a philosophy that tries to account for the world apart from the self. The secrets of the inner self are objectified and given voice by the science of psychoanalysis; nature embodied in singing birds gives way to the harsher realities of technology and the city. Music itself becomes more technological. At the same time, song is no longer specifically human and the voice loses authority. Where once we collected folk songs, now we document the songs of nature. European music has had a love affair dating at least back to the Renaissance with the song of birds, but only in the twentieth century could George Crumb write *Vox balaenae* (Voice of the Whale). In such an age, both poetry and song are a different kettle of fish.

PART TWO

The birth and early history of a genre in the Age of Enlightenment

2 The eighteenth-century Lied

JAMES PARSONS

"The noble simplicity of song"

Song is such an inborn, seemingly straightforward inclination that it is easy to forget it sometimes has engendered controversy. This especially is the case if the subject is the eighteenth-century Lied. That this is so is something of an anomaly, for the very qualities praised during the genre's heyday are what latter-day critics have most decried: tuneful preeminence, diatonic clarity, strophic design, unaffected simplicity, and directness of appeal. Charles Rosen, a writer who lately has done much to advance understanding of Classical and Romantic music, dispenses with the Lied before Schubert in no uncertain terms: "a despised form, unfit for serious consideration."[1] The opinion is by no means exceptional. Edward T. Cone, who has written with discernment on Schubert's Lieder, describes those from the century before as so many "tuneful trifles."[2] For Lawrence Kramer, the achievement of Schubert's predecessors adversely compares with his unrivalled success. "In Schubert's hands the German Lied became the first fully developed genre of Romanticism in music" in contrast to the "anemic chords and arpeggios" filling out the songs of a Reichardt or Zelter.[3] Nor is Kramer the first to suggest that Schubert had to vanquish the lyric efforts of his forerunners. As Eric Sams states in the 1980 *New Grove Dictionary of Music and Musicians*, Schubert's song facility was "practically without ancestry."[4] Rosen makes the point even more emphatically. After Schubert's "first tentative experiments, the principles on which most of his songs are written are almost entirely new; they are related to the Lieder of the past only by negation: they annihilate all that precedes."[5]

"Anemic," "despised," "unfit," "annihilate" – the vocabulary would have astonished the eighteenth century.[6] C. P. E. Bach, in his 1773 autobiography, reveals that his chief effort in recent years has been "playing and composing as songfully as possible," thereby rising to "the noble simplicity of song."[7] A week before Schubert composed *Gretchen am Spinnrade* in October 1814 – the one Lied repeatedly said to have revolutionized the art form (a claim that will be pondered more than once in this book) – an even more revealing account of the Lied is offered. Ostensibly a review of Wilhelm Friedrich Riem's Op. 27 *Zwölf Lieder*, the evaluation is at first disconcerting in light of recent appraisals. Surprising, too, is the author, E. T. A. Hoffmann, known to many for his enthusiastic endorsement of Beethoven's purely instrumental Fifth Symphony, especially since he praises the work as music in its truest sense given its lack of text. "The very nature of the Lied," Hoffmann asserts is "to stir the innermost soul by means of the simplest melody and the simplest modulation, without affectation or straining for effect and originality: therein lies the mysterious power of true genius." It is not enough for the musician merely to understand a poem. The composer must become the poet:

> The spark that kindled the Lied within the poet must glow again with renewed vigor within the composer and simultaneously with the words give rise to sounds that repose in the musician's soul like a wonderful, all-embracing, all-governing mystery. It is supremely in composing Lieder that nothing can be ruminated upon or artificially contrived; the best command of counterpoint is useless here; at the moment of inspiration the idea, which is all, springs forth in shining splendor like winged Minerva from the head of Jupiter.[8]

What many will find most striking is Hoffmann's insistence that song avoid artifice. How ironic, for it is the eighteenth-century Lied's forthrightness that has most strained the patience of recent writers. This notwithstanding, is an examination of song from the German-speaking lands before Schubert from the vantage point of the eighteenth century helpful? What is to be learned? To begin with, an inquiry impartially coming to terms with German song (to the extent that this is possible) from Johann André to Johann Rudolf Zumsteeg might show how the bad press beginning at the end of the nineteenth century has fostered a wealth of misinformation. The latter has concealed the genre's origins, obscured its place within musical life, and obfuscated the fact that, like the nineteenth-century Lied, that of the previous century was propelled by German poets wishing to strike out on untried paths. And all of this has shrouded Schubert's debt to his predecessors just as it has muddied the concept of popularity and artistic accessibility that played so important a role in the eighteenth century. As to why writers nowadays have disparaged the Lied before Schubert, answers are hard to come by because the issues themselves are complex. In part, one might recall that the nineteenth century worshipped at the shrine of progress. Anticipating by a quarter century Darwin's *On the Origin of Species* (1859), Raphael Georg Kiesewetter noted in his *Geschichte der europäisch-abendländischen oder unsrer heutigen Musik*, "If we now gaze backwards, it is gratifying to observe how this most beautiful of the arts has risen ... stage by stage, slowly but surely, to the perfection which ... we believe we have achieved."[9] While the passage's black or white thinking is undeniable, the outlook behind it all too often has been an unexamined article of historiographic faith. It would seem we have a lot to learn, especially if the subject is the self-effacing eighteenth-century Lied.

On the origins of a genre

As is reflected in C. P. E. Bach's remark, Hoffmann was not alone in stipulating that the Lied be uncomplicated. As to where and how the thought originated, surely the best strategy is to cast a wide net, for the call for simplicity – one the eighteenth century equated with nature and thus all things natural – enjoyed wide currency. While history credits Jean-Jacques Rousseau with having a premium on the watchwords "return to nature," it may be that he merely was mirroring the spirit of his age. That said, there can be little doubt that he spoke for many when, in his *Discours sur l'origine et les fondements de l'inégalité parmi les hommes* (1755), he declared: "The greater part of our ills are of our own making, and we might have avoided them, nearly all, by adhering to that simple, uniform, and solitary manner of life which nature has prescribed."[10] The passage is strikingly similar to one that Friedrich Schiller would pen half a century later. In his *Über naive und sentimentalische Dichtung* (1795–96) the poet of the celebrated "Ode to Joy" reflects, "With painful urgency we long to be back where we began as soon as we experience the misery of culture and hear our mother's tender voice in the distant, foreign country of art."[11] For many of Schiller's German-speaking contemporaries, that voice nowhere was to be heard with greater clarity than in the kind of song that is the subject of this chapter. Unfettered by the later nineteenth century's teleological fascination with progress, those drawn to the pre-Schubert Lied found in it, as did Hoffmann, the "power of true genius." Beethoven evidently agreed; two years later, in his *An die ferne Geliebte*, in keeping with the poetry of the third stanza of the sixth song, he was moved to create songs "without the adornments of art."

It would be convenient to place the source for this concept in eighteenth-century folk song, on the one hand in James Macpherson's *The Works of Ossian … Translated from the Galic Language* (1765), on the other in Herder's *Volkslieder* (1778–9). Both are too late, for the desire to move literature in a new direction begins in the late 1730s. Reactionary, this artistic realignment sought to break with the perceived excesses of the Baroque; to borrow a phrase from Schiller later on in the century, the aesthetic was to be one wherein "nature must contrast with art and put it to shame."[12] Leading figures at the start of this movement include Johann Christoph Gottsched, his student and disciple the critic and composer Johann Adolf Scheibe, and the poets Friedrich von Hagedorn and Johann Peter Uz.

For Gottsched, self-appointed guardian of German neo-classicism, the composer who would set a poem to music must strive for "nothing more than an agreeable and clear reading of a verse, which accordingly must match the nature and content of the words." The latter, as he explains in his influential *Versuch einer critischen Dichtkunst für die Deutschen* (first edn. 1730), must aim at an "exact observation of nature."[13] Such streamlined simplicity makes it possible for the songster to satisfy the maxim from Horace's *Ars poetica* with which Gottsched's treatise begins, "everything you write must be modest and simple."[14] Hagedorn concurred. In the preface to his 1742 *Oden und Lieder*, he provides a thumbnail sketch of the Lied as it would be cultivated for the next seventy-odd years.[15] Quoting from a 1713 essay by Ambrose Philips from the British literary journal *The Guardian* (the poet had served as private secretary to the Danish ambassador to the court of St. James), Hagedorn makes no bones as to the sort of poetry from which he is seeking to distance himself. And what he dislikes is that variety of verse whose authors "starve every Thought by endeavouring to nurse up more than one at a time" and where "one Point of Wit flashes so fast upon another that the Reader's Attention is dazled by the continual sparkling of their Imagination." In such poetry, "you find a new Design started almost in every Line, and you come to the end, without the Satisfaction of seeing any one of them executed." Far better to imbue a poem with "great Regularity, and the utmost Nicety; an exact Purity of Stile, with the most easie and flowing Numbers; an elegant and unaffected Turn of Wit, with one uniform and simple Design." The bard would best be advised to follow the poets of yore – Sappho, Anacreon, or Horace – who pursue "a single Thought in their Songs, which is driven to a Point, without . . . Interruptions and Deviations."[16] In his *Abhandlungen von den Liedern der alten Griechen* (c. 1744, first published 1747), Hagedorn distilled his poetic platform in the name of classical antiquity. Five years later Uz embarked on a similar program, as is made clear in his encomium to "gentle feelings, the likeness of nature, the noble simplicity of unadorned expressions, or the beautiful essence of long ago antiquity."[17] (Uz thus anticipates by six years Johann Joachim Winckelmann's celebrated 1755 proclamation made in his "Gedanken über die Nachahmung der griechischen Werke in Malerei und Bildhauerkunst" on the "noble simplicity and quiet grandeur" of Greco-Roman sculpture.) Repeating the credo in his poem "Die Dichtkunst," Uz implores his muse, "O poetry withhold from me your glossy demeanor! Strive not for overweening ornament, rather sound here your gentle song that it may inspire the enraptured shepherd to take up unadorned song." The invocation to nature is not gratuitous. Nor is the adoration of "unadorned song." For Hagedorn, "Happiness and enjoyment lie in the middle ground."[18] Such poetry partakes of the Horatian golden mean, that ideal balance of mind and spirit seen by writers such as Kant and Schiller as forming the basis of Enlightenment.

Gottsched's disciple Scheibe also followed nature's path in what surely are the first published guidelines on the kind of Lied that would become the norm in German-speaking lands into the next century. Transplanted from his native Leipzig to Hamburg in 1736 where he would live until 1740, the next year saw him launching his own music journal, *Der critische Musikus*, which, in its initial run, appeared fortnightly in twenty-six issues. The importance of song for Scheibe's agenda is revealed in the fact that in 1738 he devoted an entire issue of his publication to the subject. His debt to Gottsched is apparent in at least three ways, all of which relate to his thoughts on song. First, his journal's title is modeled after Gottsched's *Versuch einer critischen Dichtkunst*. Secondly, as had Gottsched, Scheibe wishes to banish barbarity from literature and criticism, to establish a systematic means of treating his subject. Lastly, in that Gottsched had sought to base his criticism on a set of rationally derived precepts, Scheibe likewise intends to show "how happy are those who pursue reason and nature with a well-schooled power of judgment."[19] Scheibe begins by invoking the ancients, who, he writes, looked to "order and nature" above all else. Accordingly, the would-be songster must start with a poem's overall form and content. Given the invariably strophic design, the composer must provide "an expressive, skillful, and affecting melody" suitable for every strophe and the poem's recurring verse pattern and meter. One must not make a cadence, repeat a word, or extend a syllable in one strophe where such would be inappropriate in another. The last task is all-important: the creation of a "natural" melody.[20] For Scheibe, such a melody should stay close to the tonic, adhere to "a moderate range," and remain "free, flowing, pure, and really natural." How does Scheibe measure "naturalness"? His answer: if a tune can "be sung at once and without particular effort by anyone inexperienced in music."[21]

Scheibe's location in Hamburg at the time his Lied discussion was published is important for a variety of reasons, not the least being that his observations found a ready reception among the city's numerous composers. This last point calls into question one of the most cherished notions having to do with German song, namely that it began in the Prussian capital as part of a First Berlin Lied School. Berlin would not play a sustained role in the history of German song until sometime after mid century. Even then, the existence of either a First or a Second Berlin School is something of an exaggeration, supported neither by publication patterns nor the presence of a sizable number of composers. First in Hamburg in the late 1730s, composers embraced Scheibe's views, among them Georg Philipp Telemann, Scheibe himself, Adolph Carl Kunzen, and Johann Valentin Görner. Independent of Scheibe, Johann Friedrich Gräfe, in Brunswick, and Lorenz

Mizler, in Leipzig, published song collections that closely relate to the kind of Lied Scheibe prescribed. Gräfe's 1737 *Samlung verschiedener und auserlesener Oden, zu welchen von den beruhmtesten Meistern in der Music eigene Melodeyen verfertiget worden* contains thirty-six songs by Gräfe himself, Conrad Friedrich Hurlebusch, Carl Heinrich Graun, and C. P. E. Bach. The significance of the phrase "eigene Melodeyen" (characteristic melodies) underscores at least one way in which the collection differs from the popular 1736 *Singende Muse* edited by Sperontes. Gräfe's volume features newly composed melodies while those in Sperontes's are settings of texts to pre-existing instrumental and vocal works. The frequently instrumental nature of much of the music in Sperontes's volume led Scheibe to fault the publication and spurred his own ideas on idiomatic vocal music. Mizler, a friend of J. S. Bach and Gottsched, brought out three Lieder collections beginning in 1740.[22] The titles of the first two reveal the lingering influence perhaps of Sperontes: "for the benefit and pleasure of amateurs of the clavier." Only with the third, after having been criticized by his erstwhile friend Johann Mattheson as well as by Scheibe for songs the latter dubbed "unspeakably disgusting and almost completely unsingable," did Mizler enlarge the title to include not only the pleasure of keyboardists but also enthusiasts of singing.[23] (The hostility of Scheibe's assessment has been put down to personal rancor: that Mizler publicly sided with Bach when Scheibe famously reproached the Leipzig cantor for the complexity of his music also may have contributed to the unfavorable review.) All three volumes, set out on two staves, are at their best when Mizler checks his fondness for the "innovations" he mentions in the preface to the second collection. Whatever their faults, the songs, with their lean tune-dominated textures and periodic phrase structures, reveal the degree to which the Lied responded to Gottsched's call for things "modest and simple" and, in the process, contributed to the burgeoning aesthetics of musical Classicism while simultaneously attaining distance from the bloated artifice many felt radiated from Baroque *opera seria*. As Telemann amusingly observed, the typical Baroque opera aria demanded "the highs of a songbird" and the "lows of a great reed warbler" to which are added "the Ha-ha-hee-heeists" of "babbling trills."[24] The type of Lied Hamburg poets and composers sought to cultivate had none of this.

Hamburg also was Hagedorn's city and it was here that his poetry, guided by the tenets of naturalness, began to influence not only literature but also music. His program was nothing less than a new poesy, one in which "overweening ornament" is eschewed in favor of nature's uncluttered path toward Enlightenment. The "wise man," Hagedorn insists, "follows nature in its beautiful works."[25] Impelled by nature's beauty, one is led to "the most agreeable virtue" and "the most agreeable domain."[26] Such agreeableness does not preclude objective scrutiny of nature's delights. We partake of them,

Hagedorn affirms, to gain knowledge of ourselves, as he writes in his poem "Der Morgen":

Erkenne dich im Bilde	Recognize yourself in the image
Von jener Flur!	Of yonder field!
Sey stets, wie diess Gefilde,	Remain constant, as does this meadow,
Schön durch Natur.[27]	Beautiful through (i.e., because of) nature.

Hagedorn wants poetry "to possess not so much the sublime," or larger-than-life subjects, as he does "the pleasing character of the ode."[28] Uz, based in Ansbach, and who brought out the first of his own two books of *Lyrische Gedichte* in 1749, shares Hagedorn's aims. An admirer of Hagedorn and his junior by twelve years, Uz also venerates nature. In his "Der Weise auf dem Lande," he extols

Ihr Wälder, ihr belaubte Gänge!	You woods, you verdant paths!
Und du, Gefilde! stille Flur!	And you mead! serene meadow!
Zu euch entflieh ich vom Gedränge,	To you, I flee from the crowd,
O Schauplatz prächtiger Natur!	Oh arena of magnificent nature!
Wo ich zu lauter Lust erwache.[29]	Where I awaken to pure pleasure.

As does Hagedorn, Uz too finds that poetry is the voice of Joy. Heartened by "magnificent nature," he hears "the sweet sound of songs" and, "with the beauty that enraptures," discovers "the abundant fountainhead of all beauty."[30] Once more, it is from nature that the poet learns self-knowledge.

A recurring word in Hagedorn's verse is "angenehm," or agreeable. The influential Swiss poet Haller praised Hagedorn's poetry for its "Heiterkeit" (cheerfulness), touched by "die leichten Schwünge des lächelnden Anacreons" (the light swaying of smiling Anacreon).[31] Refinement, lightness, buoyancy, these were the qualities Haller and other readers admired: "unausprechliche Anmut" (ineffable grace), "süsser Klang" (sweet sound), "erhabene Töne" (exalted tones). Clinging to the "middle ground" and employing language appropriate not for gods and goddesses but for mortals here on earth, a poet could accomplish much more than merely writing a poem. What is desired is a mode of lyric reflection that allows the poet to become an oracle, thereby instilling Enlightenment's synthesis in others. Accordingly, Hagedorn's "elegant and unaffected Turn of Wit" and Uz's "noble simplicity of unadorned expressions" do not lament a lost Golden Age. The purpose of such verse is to make it possible for others to learn of the privileged insights stemming from Reason, Wisdom, and Nature as well as the Joy ensuing from their proper understanding. Schiller acknowledged just this in his previously-quoted *Über naive und sentimentalische Dichtung* in the title's distinction between naïve (natural and sensuous) and modern (reflective and abstract) poetry. The former leads not "back to our childhood" but "onward to our coming of age." So impelled, one discovers that Enlightenment's "higher harmony" leads not "back to Arcadia," but forward "toward Elysium."[32]

If poetry could spark Enlightenment's "higher harmony," others argued that song could, too. Wieland, in his widely read novel *Geschichte des Agathon* (1766–67), extols the kind of music that soothes the passions and "gently moves the soul." The music that possesses this ability is the "touching joy of unadorned nature."[33] Scheibe agrees. He offers his guidelines not for the sake of prescribing rules but to make music an enlightened discipline, "a science of tones" with "a definite decisive goal." That aim is the same as all ventures aspiring to Enlightenment: "In as much as all scholarly knowledge . . . is mutually founded on the same universal and fundamental purpose – namely the happiness of mankind – so it follows that music, too, must join this ultimate aim."[34]

A comparison of two early eighteenth-century Lieder

What did composers make of the new direction in verse and music advocated by Gottsched, Hagedorn, Uz, and Scheibe? In turning to a setting of Hagedorn's "An die Freude," the first thing to be said is that Scheibe's guidelines appear to have been assiduously followed. Starting where the composer presumably did – with the poem – the song satisfies Hagedorn's dictum that a verse be "easie and flowing" while probing a "single Thought." Published in 1742, Hagedorn's "An die Freude" was first set to music in 1744 by J. V. Görner, one of Hamburg's leading composers.[35] Brief although the setting is (see Example 2.1), it is notable not so much for its brevity as for its sparse texture.

Less apparent, at least when compared to nineteenth-century Lieder, is what the song lacks: a mood-setting introduction for solo keyboard. Far from elaborating on the poem, the accompaniment provides the barest of supports. Thus, Görner's setting has but one purpose: humbly supporting the poet's words. Yet Görner's allegiance to a purely musical process causes one to question whether the presiding persona is always the poet. This especially is seen in Görner's apparent disregard for the poem's strophic form, indicated by the *da capo* indication following m. 15. On the assumption that Görner's performers are diligent enough to render all five of Hagedorn's strophes, the listener would hear the first eight measures ten times.

Measured against Scheibe's other criteria, Görner's setting emerges as potentially problematic. Notwithstanding the song's early date and the fact that Lied composers in the 1740s were still finding their way, one could argue that Görner evinces only marginal awareness of the poem's form and

Example 2.1 J. V. Görner, *An die Freude*

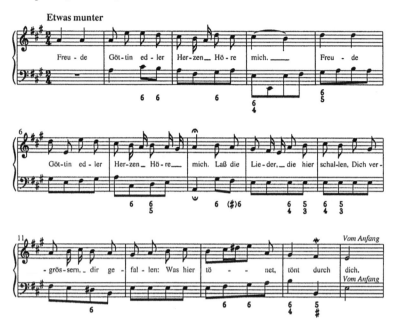

content. Still, Scheibe's other guidelines are satisfied: unaccented syllables coincide with weak beats and the melody holds to "a moderate range" and is "free flowing." The repeat of the poem's opening line in the music's second phrase, in mm. 5–7, while perhaps poetically superfluous, is effective in balancing the antecedent and consequent phrase design of the setting's first half and, following the half cadence in m. 4, in preparing for m. 8's tonic cadence. The repeat of the first text line makes good melodic sense: whereas in the antecedent phrase the voice rises a fifth from a to e, in the consequent phrase the motion is reversed. Intriguingly, it is only when turning to the coordination of harmony and phrase structure that Görner's song shows itself to be at once artless and artful. In the end, however, a poem with varying line lengths poses a challenge for the composer. The poem's opening strophe – the indention and alignment are Hagedorn's – reveals its overall organization.

	syllables	rhyme
Freude, Göttin edler Herzen!		
Höre mich.	11	a
Laß die Lieder, die hier schallen,	8	b
Dich vergrössern, dir gefallen:	8	b
Was hier tönet, tönt durch dich.	7	a

[Joy, goddess of noble hearts! hear me. Let the songs that here sound, magnify and please you: what sounds here comes from you.]

If the composer honors the poet, the next question is where to place the musical caesuras while fashioning a coherent song: should the two middle lines extend over eight measures? If yes, what of the poem's last line – ought it to stretch over eight bars? What of the first line's eleven syllables? Problematic although it at first may seem, Görner's da capo-like design may have merit. Further, the poem motivates the musical repetition of the first line. The repeat echoes the imagery of resounding song specified in the first strophe; a Joy transcending ordinary happiness in the second; a Joy greater than earthly riches in the third; the Joy that brightens reason in the fourth.

C. H. Graun, in Berlin, set Hagedorn's poem to music again almost a decade later. Two points exterior to the song are worth knowing. First, Graun's Lied is the initial item in its collection (*Oden mit Melodien*, 1753). Secondly, the collection's preface (quoted above) partially supports the claim that simple song came to be regarded as the sounding substance of Enlightenment. Immanuel Kant, one of the principal architects of eighteenth-century thought, in the second edition of his *Kritik der reinen Vernunft* (1787) noted that "the entire pursuit of reason is to bring about a union of all the ends that are aimed at by our inclinations, into one ultimate end – that of happiness."[36] Simply put, Joy is the reward granted the person who achieves Enlightenment, a process entailing a union of extremes: variously of head and heart or the worldly here and now and the boundless beyond. As has been seen, Hagedorn locates "happiness and enjoyment in the middle ground." Could it be that the self-effacing eighteenth-century Lied came to be regarded, as Wordsworth noted in a parallel context, as "an art, a music, a strain of words" so authentic that it was like life itself – "the acknowledged voice of life"?[37] During the eighteenth century this voice consistently was equated with "the noble simplicity of unadorned expressions." Interestingly, the authority of this direct utterance finds a parallel in contemporaneous ideas about the rise of human language, which, as Herder contended in 1767, in its youthful stage was synonymous with song. But, he insists, "art arrived and extinguished nature." Once this happened, poetry increasingly found itself bereft of emotional warmth, a deficiency that made it impossible to stir a reader's imagination. Thus, "poetry, which should have been the most passionate, confident daughter of the human soul, became the most insecure, weak, and hesitant, and poems turned into schoolboys' exercises for correction."[38] Small wonder that Schiller longingly would write of the "painful urgency" we have to "hear our mother's tender voice in the distant, foreign country of art." Might not eighteenth-century poetry and song be an attempt to situate that voice? In view of the esteem in which Joy – capitalized to signal its status as the reward granted the person who attains Enlightenment – then was held, the answer plausibly is yes. As Schiller reflects elsewhere, "there is no higher and no more serious undertaking" than that which "is dedicated to Joy . . . The right art is that alone which creates the highest enjoyment."[39]

The thought was dear to eighteenth-century musicians, too. Christian Gottfried Krause, one of the editors of the song collection in which Graun's *An die Freude* setting is found, observes in his *Von der musikalischen Poesie* (1752): "Joy is the primary source of music." This is so because "Joy taught the first people to sing." Moreover, "as soon as the poverty of the language of that time permitted," primordial beings "strove to combine rational words with tunes in order to make the latter all the more intelligible. Thus it happened that Lieder – the most noble offering man brought the Lord of nature – became the most agreeable pastime."[40] Viewed thus, the placement of Graun's *An die Freude* as the first item in Krause and Ramler's *Oden mit Melodien* (1753) seems part of a larger plan.[41] The titles of many eighteenth-century German song collections make the point unambiguously: August Bernhard Valentin Herbing's *Musicalische Belustigungen, in dreyßig scherzenden Liedern* (Musical Merriments, in thirty jesting songs [Leipzig, 1765]) or Reichardt's edition of *Lieder geselliger Freude* (Songs for Social Joy [Leipzig, 1796]).

As Thrasybulos Georgiades has written of another Lied, Graun's setting (see Example 2.2), like Görner's, in its no-nonsense forthrightness takes language "at its word."[42] Following Scheibe, the song aspires not to a "bombastic style" but to a "natural" one.[43] The pithy twenty measures ensure that the constantly recycling strophic music and Spartan texture serve but one purpose: to allow the words uncontested superiority.[44]

Simple though it may be, it is unfair to call the Lied simpleminded, especially since it faithfully follows Gottsched, Scheibe, Hagedorn, and Uz's guidelines. Graun's response to the potential pitfall of the poem's dissimilar line lengths provides partial corroboration for this statement. With the exception of the first two phrases, which are devoted to the poem's first line, a single verse line matches a single phrase of music. As with Görner's setting, Graun's divides into two halves. The first corresponds to the first eight measures and the second to the remainder; the two sections also project the song's twin harmonic poles – tonic and dominant. The tonic is established in the Lied's opening half before ending on the dominant. From there the second section, after a bit of harmonic piquancy on A minor (m. 9), returns to the tonic in mm. 15–16.

At first glance, it is tempting to pronounce Graun's setting more successful than Görner's. Whereas Görner does not musically observe the verbs *schallen* and *gefallen*, Graun does. He does so in two ways: by a melodic pause (punctuated by eighth rest) in tandem with the cadences on A minor (mm. 11–12), and another on the tonic (m. 16). Graun also signals the change in poetic rhyme in mm. 9–16 while advancing the song with the

Example 2.2 C. H. Graun, *An die Freude*

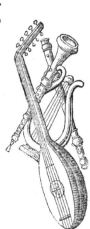

I.

Freude, Göttin munterer Jugend,
    Höre mich!
Laß die Lieder, die hier schallen,
Deinen Kindern wohlgefallen:
Was hier tönet, tönt durch dich.

Holde Schwester süßer Liebe!
    Glück der Welt!
Denn was kan in unserm Leben
Uns des Stückes Göttin geben,
Was man nicht durch dich erhält?

Stumme Hüter todter Schätze
Sind nur reich:

Denn, der keinen Schatz bewachet,
Sinnreich scherzt, und singt und lachet,
Ist kein karger König gleich.

Gib den Dichtern, die dich ehren,
    Neue Glut.
Neue Schönheit gib den Schönen,
Neuen Scherz den jungen Söhnen,
Und den Vätern junges Blut!

Aber fliehe der Bacchanten
    Unvernunft;
Fliehe, Göttin, die Gesichter
Aller finstern Splitterrichter
Und die ganze Heuchlerzunft!

echo of the voice's characteristic short–long rhythm in mm. 1–2, in mm. 9–10, and again in mm. 13–14. The rhyme shift from lines a to b is highlighted by harmonic movement away from the tonic and the sequential repetition of mm. 9–12 in mm. 13–16. Unlike Görner, who prosaically pairs lines 2–4 of the poem, Graun turns the rhyme between lines 1 and 4 into the Lied's highpoint when he dovetails the arrival of the poem's fourth line with the tonic's return. After the cadential g in the voice in m. 16, the melody signals the start of the text's last line with an octave jump. Simultaneously, for the first time in the Lied the voice quits the patterned repetition of iambs. Although one may argue that Görner's melody flows more comfortably than Graun's, it will not do to accuse him of failing to match unaccented poetical syllables with weak beats of short note values. While the accented syllable of *Göttin* coincides with an eighth note followed by a quarter in Graun's setting (line 1 of the poem, m. 2 of the song), the ostensibly shorter note is approached by a leap and left by descending stepwise motion. Modified repetitions of this figure are heard in mm. 4 (*Tu*gend), 10 (*Lie*der), and 14 (*Kin*der). Each time the shorter note values fall on a measure's strong beat. On the assumption that the singer possesses sufficient sensitivity, an interpolated breath surely ought to follow after each eighth note in keeping with the rhythmic élan of the two-bar subgroups in the first, third, and fourth musical phrases. Thus Graun devises an easily remembered tune, dresses it with "unaffected Turn of Wit," while ingeniously creating the impression that a "shorter" note is longer than the ensuing "longer" note. Concurrently, he avoids "overweening ornament" and succeeds in shaping a "little Image" in music marked by "Purity of Stile."

Performance

For many readers, even to devote a part of this chapter to performance is to yield to redundancy. Is performance truly an issue? Is not the choice of accompaniment always keyboard?[45] Although the answer to this last question usually is yes, the lack of sympathetic inquiry into this repertory has concealed the fact that options do exist. Examining the first printing of Görner's and Graun's *An die Freude*, one observes that both contain two lines, the top in treble or soprano clef, the bottom in bass. A curved bracket joins the staves; neither specifies performance medium, although the words beneath the top staff signal the vocal line. Some sources, as in the preface to *Johann Wilhelm Häßlers Clavier- und Singstücke verschiedener Art* (1782), stipulate that the keyboard should avoid doubling the voice. Others, as does Friedrich Gottlob Fleischer in the foreword of his *Oden und Lieder mit Melodien* (1756), go so far as to encourage this, especially if the keyboardist lacks basso continuo skill. In a great many eighteenth-century Lieder, if not the majority, doubling of the voice by the keyboard's uppermost line plainly is intended given that both parts are written on the same staff. While such melody-dominated textures may seem unimaginative today, the resulting *Klavierlied* ensured ease of performance, above all when singer and keyboardist are one and the same person, a concession that would have been much appreciated by the audience for whom this music was written. As to the bass, many Lieder from the century's first half include figured bass symbols, as does Görner's *An die Freude*. Since Graun's does not, the keyboardist presumably is to flesh out some harmonic realization, one in keeping with the aesthetics of naturalness. Yet, the figured bass ought not to lead one to typify the song (and others like it) as a Baroque continuo Lied; while it relates to that tradition, its unpretentiousness and frequent voice doublings highlight an affinity with the emerging neo-classical style. Additionally, a single bass line represents a practical strategy, one making it possible for the composer and her or his publisher to have the best of all possible worlds, thereby guaranteeing maximum sales: amateurs would have stayed close to the bare bass line while advanced performers would have realized the bass's harmonic implications. Aware that realizing a figured bass was a rapidly vanishing ability, C. P. E. Bach attempted to circumvent the problem by providing realizations himself. In the introduction to his *Gellerts Geistliche Oden und Lieder* (1758) he discloses: "I have added the necessary harmonies and ornaments to my melodies. In this way I have not had to relinquish them to the whimsy of bumbling figured bass players." Bach also mentions that less skilled keyboardists may find the songs useful in a strictly keyboard format. Accidentally, then, the concept of the "song without words" is anticipated in the eighteenth-century Lied, albeit motivated by didactic purposes.

While the title of the collection containing Görner's setting is performance-neutral, the one transmitting Graun's stresses melodic primacy: *Oden mit Melodien*. In that singer and keyboardist typically are one person, it must be asked if "accompaniment" is a misleading term. Support for this is to be had in the ubiquity of the title *Lieder am Clavier* (Songs at the Keyboard). The title *Auserlesene Oden zum Singen beym Clavier, vom Herrn Capellmeister Graun und einigen andern guten Meistern* (Choice Odes for singing at the keyboard . . . [1764]) plainly makes the point; so, too, does the statement from the collection's start: "in Germany one must be able not only to sing but also to perform at the keyboard." In 1786, Reichardt posits that the keyboard component could be withheld altogether. The "unity of the vocal part" is the most important thing; "the instrumental part, if not dispensable, should serve only to support the voice."[46] Song performance by a single person may have broader implications. For many, Enlightenment was a "higher harmony," which, as Kant asserted, concludes in the Joy arising from the "union of all the ends that are aimed at by our inclinations." With this in mind, it is tempting to view German song, with one performer "harmonizing" voice and keyboard, as a kind of sounding and visual embodiment of Enlightenment. Fanciful although the hypothesis may seem, a single performer as singer and keyboardist continued into the century's second half. As a guest in London of King George III, on 1 February 1795, Haydn himself sang and played keyboard in a performance of his *Der verdienstvolle Sylvius*, as he presumably had, in 1781, when performing his first Lied collection in Vienna's "best houses."[47] Even after Lied performances by two individuals became standard, the blending of singer and keyboardist as one remained an ideal. While traveling in Upper Austria with Johann Michael Vogl, leading male singer of the Vienna Kärntnerthor Theater and Hofoper, in 1825, Schubert wrote, "the manner in which Vogl sings and the way I accompany, as though we were *one* at such a moment, is something quite new and unheard-of."[48]

At a time when canonic judgments had yet to be formed, the eighteenth-century Lied strains one of the genre's subsequent chief characteristics: that the accompaniment always is for keyboard. The frontispiece of the collection containing Graun's *An die Freude* depicts a Lied performance within an idealized idyllic setting. The performers include a female singer, and, on either side, a bass string instrument playing the lowest line, and a flutist weaving a treble line (presumably beneath the voice). A number of eighteenth-century Lieder include the indication "Clavier allein," or keyboard alone, one that suggests mixed instrumental accompaniment elsewhere in the song.[49] The directive occurs at a song's structural divisions between strophes or at the end, as in the sixth number of Johann Christoph Schmügel's *Sing- und Spieloden vor musikalische Freunde componiert* (Leipzig, 1762) which contains a concluding section for solo keyboard marked "Nachspiel," or epilogue. The preface to the first issue of the Leipzig *Wöchentlicher musikalischer Zeitvertreib* (1759) states that in the interest of promoting "pleasure," a song now and then may be accompanied by "a couple of instruments." The collection's fourth song guarantees timbral variety, for it is written for voice and lute in German lute tablature.[50] In this respect, eighteenth-century German song anticipates the nineteenth-century move, however limited, toward varied accompaniments. Schubert's 1828 *Der Hirt auf dem Felsen* (D965) is an extended song for voice, piano, and clarinet obbligato. Spohr composed his *Sechs deutsche Lieder* (Op. 101; 1836–37) for voice and two pianos, four hands. The next year he brought out another collection of German songs for soprano, piano, and clarinet (Op. 103); another similarly named set appeared for baritone, violin, and piano (Op. 154; 1856, which includes an infinitely-worth-reviving *Erlkönig*). Meyerbeer's *Des Schäfers*

Lied is for tenor, clarinet, and piano (1842). Brahms's exquisite Op. 91 *Zwei Gesänge für eine Altstimme mit Bratsche und Pianoforte* adds viola to the mix of voice and piano. (The second of the two, *Geistliches Wiegenlied,* was completed in 1864 for the birth of the first child to Brahms's friends the alto Amalie Joachim and her violinist/violist husband Joseph; the first, *Gestillte Sehnsucht,* was composed in 1884.) The twentieth century moved beyond even this, as in Schoenberg's *Pierrot lunaire* (1912) for Sprechstimme voice and sundry instruments (flute or piccolo, clarinet or bass clarinet, violin, viola, violoncello, and piano) and in Wolfgang Rihm's *Abschiedsstücke für Frauenstimme und 15 Spieler* (1993).

The mention made in the 1759 *Musikalischer Zeitvertreib* of "ein Singestück" reminds one that the many names bestowed on eighteenth-century Lieder have never fully been sorted out. Although one assumes "Singestück" is used simply for the sake of variety, the surfeit of other appellations strains the current liking for generic tidiness: *Gesang, Deklamation, Lied, Musikalische Belustigung, Ode, Romanze, Spielode.* Fleischer, in 1788, brought out a *Sammlung größerer und kleinerer Singstücke mit Begleitung des Claviers.* The opening work is indeed a "big song piece," nine pages long and encompassing a tonal design beginning in A♭ major and thereafter roaming through E♭ (which features recitative), C minor, A♭, E♭, E major, and B major before ending in F major. A vocal tessitura of two octaves and melodies marked by oftentimes non-syllabic and keyboard-like turns and trills alongside declamatory directness cue to the dramatically charged images of Zachariae's poem, "Die Gewitternacht." A *Sturm und Drang Szene* in all but name, the tempestuous range of harmonies, number of tempo changes, figuration, and textures likewise inventively respond to the text's images and moods. Fleischer's label notwithstanding, the song clearly is a ballad, as its narrative content, length, through-composed design, and recourse to recitative affirm. The same year, Friedrich Ludewig Aemilius Kunzen (son of Adolph Carl) brought out a setting of one of the era's most celebrated ballads, Bürger's 256-line, 32-strophe "Lenore"(1773), to which the composer appended the subtitle "ein musikalisches Gemählde" – a musical picture. Beethoven's simple strophic setting of Christian Felix Weisße's "Der Kuß," Op. 128, was published as an "Arietta." Although Mozart called *Das Veilchen* a "Lied," Artaria published it in 1789 as one of "zwei Arien"; the same publisher issued Beethoven's Op. 46 *Adelaide* in 1797 as "eine Kantate." Did these and other labels impart anything meaningful to contemporaneous composers, musicians, and listeners? One gets the idea they were as overwhelmed as we are today. The author of an 1805 Berlin review of Beethoven's *Adelaide* describes the Lied as "a great aria da due caratere," that is "with two affections" or contrasting sections, a work that "could conclude the greatest modern theatrical scene."[51]

While at the start of this chapter it was stated that eighteenth-century writers embraced German song almost without qualification, at least one did not (another will be adduced below). Given that his objection relates to a concern expressed by many a later commentator, the disparagement needs to be met head on. Mattheson, another musician based in Hamburg, writing as early as 1722, took issue with that variety of poetry marked by "one uniform Design." For him, strophic form results in "a malady of melody" and is "a veritable scourge on the art of composition," one that confines the composer within "a cruel iron collar."[52] For the performer and listener, the incessant repetition of a strophic tune is "not at all musical." Nevertheless, to construct a different melody for each strophe is equally problematic, for to do so runs counter to the prevailing aesthetic that a movement should express only one emotional state.[53] For Mattheson, such songs "will be considered musical only by those many persons who are unaware that nothing in music will be more . . . insipid than hearing a single melody over and over to completely different words."[54] But is a constraint always constraining? Igor Stravinsky – about the last name one would associate with the eighteenth-century Lied – once remarked, "the more art is controlled, limited, worked over, the more it is free."[55] A correct understanding of how the century of Mozart dealt with strophic design shows how such freedom might apply. Johann Adam Hiller, in the "Vorbericht" of his *Lieder mit Melodien* (1772), advises the singer to introduce "eine kleine Veränderung der Noten" (a small variation of the notes) if the accent or rhythm of the words changes from one strophe to another. Two years later J. A. P. Schulz, writing in Sulzer's *Allgemeine Theorie der schönen Künste*, repeats the recommendation: "in Lieder" it often is necessary "to introduce slight variations, for it happens that words which fall on the same notes in one verse may require a little more emphasis and sensitive expression than those of another verse. In such a case, a singer may alter a melody that the composer has set the same way for all stanzas by means of appropriate variations."[56] Zelter, Goethe's indefatigable house composer, in at least one song, instructs the vocalist in how this might be done. In his *Um Mitternacht*, he sets out the vocal line so that three slightly varied versions of the same melody are superimposed over the other (see Example 2.3). Beneath is the strophic keyboard accompaniment. These vocal alterations accommodate differences in the poem's prosody from one strophe to another while also responding to the imagery of the individual words. Zelter accomplishes the latter by beginning each of the three strophes with subtly different rhythmic profiles. In strophe 1, dotted quarter, quarter, eighth, in strophe 2, dotted quarter, eighth, eighth rest, eighth, in strophe 3, dotted quarter, eighth rest, two eighth notes. In the first strophe (m. 12), he decorates the vocal line at "Vaters Haus" (Father's house). In m. 14, he engages in word painting at "Stern an Sterne" (star to star) with the

Example 2.3 Zelter, *Um Mitternacht*

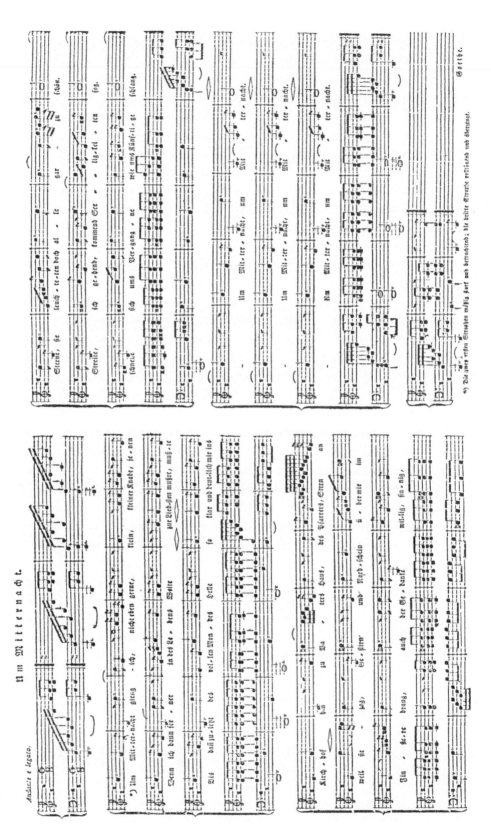

elaborate thirty-second-note turning figure, a gesture not repeated in the subsequent strophes.[57] Such *Veränderungen* were practiced well into the nineteenth century, whether in strophic or non-strophic Lieder, as is confirmed in the copies of Schubert songs made by his friend Vogl, whom the composer frequently accompanied.[58]

What of the keyboardist? Haydn, in five of his fifty-two songs, offers instruction when he modifies the accompaniment in ensuing strophes. *Pleasing Pain*, the fifth of the *VI Original Canzonettas* (1794), provides an illuminating example.[59] In setting Anne Hunter's three-strophe poem, Haydn responds with a three-part musical design in which each strophe's text is individually fitted out, an achievement that provides an object lesson that the terms strophic and modified strophic sometimes can be woefully imprecise. While each strophe relates one to the other by the process of variation, the freedom with which Haydn provides for each strophe is almost cosmic when set against the conventions then governing the Lied. The first strophe seeks to banish the "dear anxious days of pleasing pain" that often burden the protagonist's heart. At the mention of "anxious days," the G major tonality gives way to two bars of parallel minor, a poignant reminder that a person in the grip of love can suffer mercurial emotional fluctuations. In the second strophe, which calls for the return of "smiling hours," the comparable section remains in the major at the mention of the charms that such times bring. The third strophe reveals Haydn to be a keen observer of the human condition: while the text calls for a life free from "sad regrets," the music would seem to counter that unending happiness is a delusion, for G minor makes one last appearance. The keyboard provides a kind of running commentary on the textual differences between the three strophes. At the end of the first strophe, the poem calls on pleasing pain to take flight, "never to return again"; when the verb "fly" is repeated four times, Haydn assigns the keyboard an interlude marked by sextuplet and triplet figurations beginning on d^3 and plummeting to d. The fact that the keyboard descends – in conflict with the text's reference to flight – reveals the composer as someone who astutely understood the inner workings of the human heart but who also could be a musical ironist. The interlude at the end of the second strophe, on the heels of "dance in sportive rounds away," takes on an entirely different rhythmic character from what was heard in the first with an animated sixteenth-note Alberti bass in the left hand and sixteenth-note passagework in the right hand that at last is allowed to ascend. The four other Haydn songs in which the keyboard is called on to vary music in subsequent strophes are *Sailors' Song*, *The Wanderer*, *Content* (Nos. 1, 2, and 7 from the second set of canzonettas brought out in 1795; the first was published in 1794) and *Beim Schmerz der dieses Herz durchwühlet* (composed between 1765 and 1775). While the custom of the keyboard ornamenting subsequent strophes is not unknown in the North German Lied tradition (a few examples are written out in the Lieder of Reichardt), it appears to have been carried out in a comparatively more circumspect fashion.

The Lied at century's end

While the Lied continued along much the same lines in the century's second half, change nonetheless was in the air. Keyboard parts were becoming more animated, formal designs no longer exclusively strophic. The numerous modified strophic and *durchkomponiert* songs by Reichardt and Zelter in Berlin and Zumsteeg in Stuttgart demonstrate the point. *Aus Euphrosyne,* by Reichardt, to a poem by Goethe, affords a compelling illustration of the possibilities of this last formal design. The song also shows the composer anticipating a move history has preferred to bestow on Schubert: the use of the piano as an equal partner. So much for "anemic chords and arpeggios." By m. 14 the C minor tonality, en route to E♭ major, slumps toward C♭ at "entkräftender Jammer" (enervating distress). The gesture not only provides an appropriate response to the words but also offers a striking visual gloss. In the context of C minor, those C♭s not only sound doleful but also, on the page, provoke their own distress, given the number of flats the keyboardist must negotiate. Although Zelter favored strophic compositions, his *Rastlose Liebe* (also to a poem by Goethe) features an inventive through-composed construction and a piano part that could have been fashioned by the Schubert of *Gretchen am Spinnrade* given the way it comments on the protagonist's inner life.

Mention of the keyboard dictates a glimpse, however brief, at Vienna, a subject Amanda Glauert considers at greater length in the chapter that follows. At first, lacking a preexisting Lied tradition on which to draw, composers favored a conservative approach; only in the late 1770s did they begin to assert an individual style, as is demonstrated in Haydn's 1781 *XII Lieder für das Clavier* which features fairly demanding keyboard parts, evident especially in the lengthy interludes between strophes.[60] Haydn continued the trend in the next set of twelve Lieder; two are printed not with the customary two staves, but on three, thereby allowing for independence between voice and keyboard. Haydn set great store by these songs, given their "variety, naturalness, and ease of vocal execution."[61] As for variety, they include short mood-setting keyboard preludes and postludes and this despite their invariably strophic stance. In No. 3, *Der erste Kuß*, Haydn manages the seemingly impossible, combining naturalness with subtle artistry. Faithful to the text, he allows the voice and keyboard to go their separate ways in each strophe's first half. In the second half the young man finally attains union with his "beloved Chloe"; only then do voice and accompaniment unite in a heart-rending shower of parallel thirds at the words "closer came our hearts." The Viennese penchant for elaborate keyboard parts in large measure is a by-product of the fact that most of the city's Lied composers also were well known for their keyboard music. In addition to Haydn, other Viennese composers who made notable contributions to both genres include Josef Antonín Štěpán and Mozart.

Within the Lied's larger history, the increased importance given the keyboard by Viennese composers may be identified as a distinguishing characteristic in view of the continued North German fondness for simple accompaniments. Reichardt, writing from Berlin in 1796, partially confirms this when, reviewing the German edition of Haydn's first set of English canzonettas, he judges them too instrumentally conceived, a mannerism that undermines the text and degenerates into the "bizarre and affected."[62] There were, of course, exceptions; in 1793, Georg Laurenz Schneider, Kapellmeister in Coburg (in South German Upper Franconia), responded to Gerstenberg's "Phillis an das Clavier" with a near-epic keyboard part. Balancing the stirring introduction for the instrument named in the poem's title, there is a *cadenza ad libitum* at the end when the poem compares love's intensity to the keyboard's vibrating strings, this last a popular poetic conceit throughout the century (Mozart's *Komm, liebe Zither* exchanges keyboard for zither).[63] In between, Schneider obliges with a marvelously original, through-composed design, rapidly changing dynamics (from *ppp* to *ff*), and dramatically placed *sforzandi*; along the way, expressive indications accrue to a degree heretofore almost unknown in the genre: "Andante con expressione, ritardanto, a poco Recitato, con tenerezza, dolce."[64] Reichardt, if his disapproval of Haydn is any sign, would have been horrified.

In contrast to Schneider's tradition-smashing approach to Lied composition, the continued fondness for diatonicism, transparent textures, and simplicity on the part of most German song composers in the century's second half has masked other changes. Most obviously, signs of the genre's transformation are to be discerned in the sub-category of the ballad. While the ballad is associated with settings of narrative poetry in the last quarter of the century (Goethe's 1776 "Der Erlkönig," which according to Werner-Joachim Düring's count, netted 131 settings, surely is the most famous example),[65] the ballad's musical origins may be traced to A. B. V. Herbing's 1759 *Musikalischer Versuch in Fabeln und Erzählungen des Herrn Professor Gellerts.* In much the same way as has been seen in the discussion of Fleischer's *Die Gewitternacht,* also a ballad, Herbing, in his *Die Widersprecherin,* to take a representative example from the 1759 collection, shuns standard-issue strophic form for a through-composed structure of 275 measures comprising seventeen subsections. (The Lied is one of six in the collection called "a narration"; two others are labeled *Ein Fabel*, while another lacks any generic qualifier.) In the narrative sections, the voice declaims the text in recitatives in 4/4 meter with free rhythms taking their cue from the accents of the words. At the other end of the Lied's musical continuum, when the narrator tells of Ismene's rage – the "one who contradicts" identified in the song's title – the keyboard responds with right hand thirty-second notes against sixteenths in the left hand. What prompts her fury? An improperly cooked pike! Her rage likewise is suggested by the voice's disjunctive contours and demanding climb to a^2 when her anger is "swept toward heaven." Although a full account of the ballad is not possible here, it needs to be said that Herbing's Lieder, generally relegated to history's scrapheap, may have provided a far greater guiding hand on the ballad's development than previously known. (One can only ponder what his influence might have been had he lived past the age of thirty-one.) The frequently declamatory vocal lines of many of his songs, the increased importance given to the keyboard and its descriptive accompaniments, together with the multi-sectional, through-composed forms are echoed in the later ballads of F. L. A. Kunzen, Zelter, Zumsteeg, Václav Tomášek, Schubert, and Loewe.

While the ballad sometimes wrongly has been viewed as removed from the mainstream of Lied history, it provided first poets – Gellert, Gleim, Zachariae, Hölty, Stolberg, Bürger, Goethe, and Schiller – and then composers with an invitation to experiment and to move beyond prevailing strictures. Reading through Kunzen's previously mentioned *Lenore*, a setting of Bürger's poem of the same name, it is difficult to believe it was composed in 1788. A chromatically agitated, twenty-six-bar introduction for solo keyboard vividly sets the stage for the poem's populist potboiler of sin, sex, guilt, and death, all filtered through the lens of nail-biting Gothic horror. A near-record-breaking 695 measures long, Kunzen's ballad reveals its experimentalism not only in its length but also in its mixture of singing, recitative, spoken dialogue, and melodrama (the use of speech during the Lied's connecting sections), together with a keyboard part that surpasses even Viennese elaborateness and descriptive intensity. For sheer length, Johann André is the apparent winner in two of his four ballad settings of Bürger's "Lenore": the second is 954 measures long and the fourth, while only 883 bars, concludes with a rousing four-part chorus.

Literature again would present musicians with an opportunity to branch out in the 1770s with the so-called Sturm und Drang (the name comes from Friedrich Maximilian Klinger's 1775 play *Wirrarr; oder, Sturm und Drang*). In the process, the Lied once more found itself subject to change. A heterogeneous if not elusive concept, the Sturm und Drang spawned advocates who were at their most precise when pondering what the movement was not. Most conveniently, it may be seen as a reaction against the yoke of Rationalism, a dislike already encountered in Herder's 1767 invective against art's triumph over nature. Much like German song at the time, Sturm und Drang proponents revered all things lacking in artifice, particularly if the want of such bolstered nature or human feeling. A premium also was placed on "das Volk." Uncorrupted by civilization, the folk, as Jakob Michael Reinhold Lenz affirms in his play *Die kleinen* (the lower case is Lenz's), are happy because they possess "the true ardor of self-certainty!"; this is so because no dramatist or poet has corrupted them with "the dissonance of alien, unnatural feelings" – they know not culture's "poison."[66] To this, the Sturm und Drang was resolute that if culture must intrude, the resulting work should be the creation of genius unhampered by the stultifying standards of neo-classicism. Spontaneity and dynamic feeling are all-important. Creating according to rules or in imitation of something already in existence is anathema. For Goethe, only genius can accomplish this. "Genius does not imitate nature but rather itself creates like nature," he writes. "One unique source flows there equal to another, but not made in its afterimage, rather like them, born out of the cliffs!"[67] Ascending to this exhilarating summit, Schiller concurred: "Only to genius is it given to be at home beyond the accustomed and to *extend* nature."[68] Is the rule-bound eighteenth-century Lied compatible with any of this? A look at a representative Lied will prove instructive, especially since doing so shows the sometimes understated ways in which German song was changing even while retaining many of its characteristic traits.

On the face of it, Zelter's 1814 setting of Goethe's celebrated 1780 "Wanderers Nachtlied II" appears unrelated to the Sturm und Drang: Zelter's Lied surely is too late, while Goethe's poem is stamped by anything but tempestuousness and agitation. Nonetheless, the poem relates to the movement in other ways. Most striking is the way in which Goethe captures the stillness at the heart of his poem, no mean feat given that poetry relies on words and must transgress on silence – as music must, too. Simultaneously, Goethe uses art to conceal art in the service of motionless simplicity. Whereas most verse from this time compresses into the patterned space of the poem meter, rhyme, and a reliance on poetic line, Goethe explodes those concepts, yet does so in such a way that one is not at first aware that anything remarkable has taken place. While the poem marvelously projects serenity, its rhyme and internal organization are teeming with irregularities (see Example 2.4). Part of the poem's utter brilliance resides in the fact that it is held suspended without any apparent means of support between breathless calm and the screaming riot of varying line lengths all of which are formed in different ways. The achievement of this is precisely what allows Goethe to satisfy his own demand that genius "does not imitate nature but rather creates like nature" (a translation of the poem is provided in chapter 1).

Example 2.4 Rhyme scheme and structure of Goethe's "Wanderers Nachtlied II"

	rhyme	number of syllables
/ ˇ / ˇ / ˇ		
or		
ˇ ˇ / ˇ / ˇ		
1 Über allen Gipfeln	a	6
ˇ /		
2 ist ruh;	b	2
ˇ / ˇ / ˇ		
3 in allen Wipfeln	a	5
/ ˇ /		
4 spürest du	b	3
/ ˇ ˇ /		
5 kaum einen Hauch;	c	4
ˇ / ˇ ˇ / ˇ ˇ / ˇ		
6 die Vögelein schweigen im Walde.	d	9
/ ˇ ˇ / ˇ		
7 Warte nur, balde	d	5
/ ˇ ˇ /		
8 ruhest du auch.	c	4

ˇ equals an unstressed syllable; / equals a stressed syllable

Zelter's song, which he calls *Ruhe*, provides a striking complement to Goethe's poem, especially in the freedom of its design (Example 2.5). The first phrase lasts three and a half measures, yet divides into four smaller groups, a move foreshadowing the poem's injunction "Warte nur." The second phrase adds the voice and lasts one and a half measures before ending on a half cadence. The fermata over the eighth-note rest nicely suits the poem's interior asymmetry. The next phrase extends for three measures, while the voice's final phrase lasts three measures and two beats. The piano concludes with another phrase of one and a half measures. In contrast to the balanced, foursquare uniformity typical of most Lieder, and indeed most music, from this time, Zelter's song comprises five phrases of unequal length. As is well known, Goethe greatly admired Zelter's *Ruhe* as he did the composer's Lied settings of most of his poems. "The purest and highest

Example 2.5 Zelter, *Ruhe*

painting in music is the kind that you practice," the poet wrote the composer. One wonders, though, if the vocal line in m. 8 at the words "Kaum einem Hauch" (scarcely a breath) troubled Goethe: whereas Goethe demands stillness, Zelter suddenly breaks into restless thirty-second notes at these words, a move that would seem to be the antithesis of breathless calm. Not only this, but Zelter's liberty in repeating the word "balde" three times seems almost perverse when it is recalled that the one quality Goethe appreciated most about Zelter's settings of his poetry was the way in which the composer's music did not intrude on the primacy of his verse. Writing to Zelter in 1820, Goethe disclosed: "I feel that your compositions are, so to speak, identical with my verses; the music, like gas blown into a balloon, merely carries them into the heavens. With other composers, I must first observe how they have conceived my song, and what they have made of it."[69] The thirty-second notes in m. 8 plus the seemingly gratuitous text repetition hardly call to mind "gas blown into a balloon." These apparent anomalies notwithstanding, if the subordination of Zelter's music to his poetry pleased Goethe, this is what most present-day commentators have found most vexing, especially when packaged in tandem with the Lied's propensity for simplicity. Yet to see and hear in a song such as Zelter's *Ruhe* only its straightforwardness is to miss what courses beneath its surface – an unorthodox formal plan rippling with uneven phrases, held in place by the veneer of simplicity. Such extremes even now would tax the skills of performers. Perhaps the Sturm und Drang was compatible with the existing conventions of song just as it allowed the genre to change, subtly diminutive though we may find those changes today.

Legacy

Prompted by composers and publishers desirous of tapping an ever-growing public, there is no question that the eighteenth-century Lied was driven by commercialism, just as it would be in the following century. Join this commercialism with the simplicity of song at this time, and both points go far in explaining why many writers have objected to this music. Sung by amateurs at home or in literary salons,[70] German verse set to music in the eighteenth century was designed for immediate consumption and enjoyment, a point reflected in the dedication of Krause and Ramler's *Oden mit Melodien* (1753). The collection is given over not "to weighty erudition but to the science of joy and pleasure." In this way, the editors hoped their songs might afford a remedy for the excesses of Italian opera, an upper-class art form. In contrast, the Lied's simplicity promotes "the pleasure and happiness of *all* society,"[71] a view Koch upheld a half-century later when he described the genre as "the one product of music and poetry whose content today appeals to *every* class of people and *every* individual."[72] The degree to which the eighteenth-century Lied was premised on accessibility and popularity needs to be remembered if one is to understand the genre or the foundation it afforded the century that followed. Such ingenuousness extracted a price, however. A 1783 review of Haydn's first set of Lieder brings to light another rare dissenting voice: Haydn "probably did not have the intention of advancing his fame through these songs, but to create pleasure for a certain class of amateurs. No one will doubt that Haydn could have made these songs more accomplished, if he had wanted. Whether he should have is another question."[73] The matter is as unresolved today as it was 220 years ago.

A keener understanding of the eighteenth-century Lied might lead to a reappraisal of some of the innovations long ascribed only to nineteenth-century composers. As Ruth O. Bingham discusses in chapter 5, the seeds for cyclic integration in the Lied were sown in the eighteenth. The arresting effect of beginning a Lied not with its tonic but with some other harmony – what in chapter 10 Susan Youens calls "directional tonality" – which many have associated as a stock in trade devised by Schubert also may trace its roots to the eighteenth century. A song such as Schubert's 1815 *Nähe des Geliebten*, the opening harmonic gambit of which underscores the text's central message that two lovers are together no matter how physically distant they find themselves, is presaged twenty-seven years earlier by Fleischer's *An Callisten*. August Niemann's five-stanza poem is a lament on the death of Callisto; the opening sets the scene with its plea that the narrator-griever, alone at night, be permitted a tear. Fleischer responds to the text's intensity with eight bars at the start that grope toward the tonic of E minor. A♯ repeatedly is struck yet it leads to B (V of E minor) only in m. 7, as if the weeping and darkness afflicting the narrator were impeding not only the ability to see but also to plot a course through the darkness. In our haste to be done with the "tuneful trifles" of the eighteenth century, we have missed much.

For composers, performers, and listeners in German-speaking lands, the Lied also provided a sense of shared musical identity. Starting with Leibniz in the 1680s, writers increasingly expressed themselves on the "enforced blindness" of German "life, speech, writing, indeed even of think-ing" and the "slavery" to things French. As Christian Thomasius, lecturer at the University of Leipzig, observed in 1687, "if our German forefathers were to rise from the dead and come amongst us, they might think they were in a foreign land."[74] Scheibe, in the first issue of his *Critischer Musikus*, launched his critical platform with a call for German solidarity. "Let us rid ourselves of the contemptible, unnatural things we have borrowed from foreigners, which are our ruin and the ruin of music."[75] Telemann in his *Vierundzwanzig Oden* (1741), a collection of Lieder dedicated to Scheibe and marked by the new doctrine of simplicity, spoke not only of his desire for a "renewed golden age of notes," but also to "show foreigners how much richer our thoughts are than theirs."[76] In tandem with the spread of the print medium, David Gramit considers yet another way in which the Lied relates to nationalistic impulses in chapter 14. Paradoxically, the nineteenth century's move toward the veneration of purely instrumental music brought with it changes in attitude toward music set to a text. While many today will find the gendered discourse that ensued perplexing if not pointless, instrumental music began to be viewed by some as objectively confident – above all the masculine Beethoven – while the Lied, with its propensity toward self-reflection, subjectively feminine (an assessment that has spread to recent appraisals of at least one Lied composer, namely Schubert).[77] This was not how the eighteenth century saw the genre. For Gottsched, song is unequivocally masculine; in contrast, Italian opera "is a promoter of lust and a corrupter of upright morals." Listening to Italian opera, "reason must be left at home" because too "many temptations storm about all at once. Thus effeminacy is engendered in the souls of people from youth; and so it is that we are transformed into effeminate Italians before we realize we ought to be masculine Germans."[78] Unassuming and immediately intelligible, the Lied, according to Reichardt, is "truly that upon which the steadfast artist relies when he begins to suspect his art is on the wrong track" – the musician's "north star."[79] Despite Romanticism's paradigmatic aesthetic shift, such song cast a long shadow. Although Schumann would write that earlier Lied composers lacked a knowledge of "that more artistic and profound style of song" perfected in his generation,[80] it is revealing that later composers never completely lost touch with song from the previous century. Writing in Schumann's own journal, Carl Alexander reflected in 1834:

> Just as language, with respect not only to euphony, but also to characterization, richness, and capability of inflection, directly represents the development [*Bildung*] of nations, so the Lied is the most faithful mirror of its soul. . . . What the gifted, simple spirit finds instinctively, the highest cultivation finally returns to, through error and hesitation, but indeed with certainty and conviction.[81]

As will be seen in the pages that follow, German song composers would have reason to take this statement to heart time and again.

3 The Lieder of Carl Philipp Emanuel Bach, Haydn, Mozart, and Beethoven

AMANDA GLAUERT

Many song historians might hesitate before presenting C. P. E. Bach (1714–88), Haydn (1732–1809), Mozart (1756–91), or Beethoven (1770–1827) as landmark composers in the development of the German Lied. Some would argue any place for them in such a narrative would depend on their towering achievements in instrumental music or opera, rather than on the value of their songs themselves. These composers' engagement with song is often taken as a sign of the inclusive nature of their musical ambitions, rather than their interest in the genre for its own sake. In retrospect, Viennese Classicism has become parceled up with the notion of an all-embracing "style" which spread from Italian comic opera to the genres of sacred and instrumental music, a generalization that leaves little room for the Lied. Indeed theories of the Lied, as they emerged through the eighteenth century, demanded a specific stylistic justification from composers, a conscious choice of style based on their individual response to a poetic text. Some theorists reinforced this distinctiveness by denying song composers recourse to instrumental or operatic idioms at all. Yet ideals of stylistic simplicity are less significant perhaps than the broader aesthetic notion that the starting point for a composer's style should be a poem or a poet. For better or for worse, subservience to poetry seems to run counter to the achievements that these four masters of Classicism represent.

C. P. E. Bach

In view of this last point, it is revealing that the first of the four composers to be considered in this chapter – C. P. E. Bach – frequently has been credited with establishing an autonomous instrumental voice in his music. His keyboard improvisations were acclaimed for inaugurating a new narrative power that could direct the minds and feelings of listeners with an authority usually granted only to poets.[1] The early theorist of the Sturm und Drang and poet Gerstenberg sought to substantiate Bach's instrumental eloquence by adding words from Hamlet's soliloquy to the Fantasia in C minor from the *Versuch über die wahre Art das Clavier zu spielen*.[2] Yet this poetic experiment appears weak and inconclusive when compared to how Bach himself

Example 3.1 C. P. E. Bach, *An Lyda*, mm. 1–7

crystallized his improvisations through the dynamics of sonata form. In coining patterns of expectation, surprise, and fulfillment in his keyboard sonatas, Bach demanded an explicit response from his listeners in a way that paralleled the emotional claims of his well-known contemporaries in poetry Klopstock and Gellert. Klopstock wooed his readers through the metrical freedom of his poetry; this freedom has been compared to the rhythmic fluidity of Bach's music and to the composer's constant use of melodic and harmonic nuances.[3]

The possibilities of critically aligning Klopstock and C. P. E. Bach are strengthened by knowledge of their fellowship within the artistic circles of Hamburg in the 1770s and 1780s. One might anticipate their creative collaboration bringing the aspirations of Empfindsamkeit to new heights; however, Bach set only two of Klopstock's poems, "Lyda" and "Vaterlandslied." Klopstock did not like Bach's manner of claiming further metrical freedoms when setting his poetry, preferring composers to keep to a simpler musical idiom. Yet Voß, another poet of the Hamburg circle and editor of the *Göttingen Musenalmanach* in which Bach's setting of *Lyda* appeared in 1775, greeted the song as incomparably profound.[4] And it would be difficult not to admire how Bach manages to extend constantly shifting patterns of melodic appoggiaturas in his song, patterns which form and dissolve like the "sweet picture" (süßes Bild) of Lyda which hovers before the poet's eyes (see Example 3.1).[5]

In Bach's strophic setting the vocal phrases are made to contract and expand rhythmically toward points of harmonic dissonance, in ways that blur the even line lengths of the poem and intensify and interpret the effect of Klopstock's verses for his listener. Instead of merely acting as the listener's representative, capturing one response among many possible ones, the composer offers to sum up what the poet intended and to substitute his own music as the object of the listener's attention. Even Voß sometimes doubted whether Bach was not taking over too much of the lyrical process. He complained to J. A. P. Schulz that in Bach's setting of Overbeck's "Fischerlied" one

Example 3.2 C. P. E. Bach, *Nonnelied*, mm. 1–4

no longer heard the fisher singing his song but rather Bach at the keyboard.[6] The illusion of poet and composer sounding "the voice of nature," singing what anyone might sing, was pierced by the obvious individuality of Bach's approach.

The criticisms of Bach's attitude to song gain wider ground in relation to his setting of the anonymous folk text "Nonnelied," published after his death in 1789 (see Example 3.2).[7] One is struck by the simplicity of the rhythmic phrasing in this song when compared to the composer's *Lyda* (see Example 3.1).[8] But the chromatic touches that are revealed in the second bar become more extreme with each passing verse. The melodic and harmonic variations which Bach slips into the strophic repetitions allow him to introduce an explicit layer of commentary into the song, so disturbing the listener's direct identification with the girl and her lament. Voß and the poets of the Göttinger Hainbund stressed the importance of an immediate and direct appeal to the listener, and they looked to music to help veil their artistic workings.[9] Yet Bach drew attention to the artistic medium of poetic expression, and made the medium part of the message as in instrumental music.

One may take Bach's approach to song as a sign of his lack of interest in the Hainbund's aesthetic program. Charles Burney once criticized the composer for lacking the popular touch, and Bach confirmed that he was sometimes irked by having to pander to his audiences.[10] However, if one looks at the total output of his songs and their rich diversity of style and character, it is clear he was open to all sorts of poetic engagement and was quite aware of the contradictions of trying to create a lyric that might speak for one and all simultaneously. The so-called Anacreontic style of poetry, fashionable in Berlin and in other North German cities at the beginning of Bach's composing career, often used the classical imagery of shepherds and shepherdesses singing love songs to each other to create a convention that was so familiar that it established a common poetic ground. Bach's setting of Christiane Marianne von Ziegler's "Schäferlied" ("Eilt ihr Schäfer," 1742) confirms that the composer was quite at home in this carefully devised pastoral world.[11] He lays out the familiar elements of dancing triple meter,

Example 3.3 C. P. E. Bach, *Bitten*, mm. 1–8

and keyboard part doubling the voice in thirds and sixths or providing simple tonic and dominant pedals. Yet the archness of Bach's melodic writing, with its unexpected leaps and touches of syncopation, adds wit to the pastoral evocation and reminds one that the poem is dealing with a sentimental illusion; its justification lies in the feeling that comes through such a façade. Bach builds up the emotional tension in his song through the twists and turns of his melodic line, which wait for the release of the final cadence. The song's melodic shapes are directed by a small-scale tonal drama, which allows one to feel the pull between tonic and dominant keys while the whole verse is controlled with the precision of a binary dance form. This musical impetus clearly is in danger of overshadowing Ziegler's slight poetic content, and it is interesting to note the awkwardness in the vocal declamation as the words are made to fit Bach's melody.

Despite the textural simplicity of Bach's *Schäferlied*, it shows signs of being conceived as a keyboard piece, with melodic nuances that seem to respond to the touch of a clavichord rather than the words themselves. One notices an immediate difference in Bach's song writing when he came to set the poems of Gellert in 1757, a poet of much greater status. This is true even of Bach's Gellert settings that employ a similar style to *Schäferlied*. The opening bars of *Bitten* (see Example 3.3) have some of the same *galant* lilt, but the melodic emphasis on "weit" and the melismatic word-painting on "Wolken" (clouds) reveal a greater specific involvement with the text.[12]

Bach acknowledged in the preface to his Gellert Lieder that he sought to put his music entirely at the service of these poems and their high devotional purpose.[13] When the poet published his collection in 1756, he admitted that he would need a particularly skilled composer to bring home the didactic message of his poems and forge a devotional link between mind and heart.[14] Such a challenge was particularly suited to Bach's predisposition to play with the emotional and intellectual aspects of music's appeal, and his collaboration with Gellert is recognized as having brought song writing to a new level. By taking fifty-four of Gellert's poems in one collection, Bach was able to trace a series of diverse stylistic treatments, and to bring out different relationships between voice and keyboard, declamation and melody, so providing his listener with constantly new stimuli. The lilting style of *Bitten* (see Example 3.3) reemerges in several songs, for example *Die Liebe des Nächsten* and *Vom Tode*, though in the latter the keyboard's bass line enters imitatively after the upper parts, thus objectifying the vocal melody as part of a contrapuntally conceived texture. An explicit dialogue between keyboard and voice is invoked at many points in these songs. In *Bitten* the unified texture of the opening holds for four lines of the verse, but then the voice comes to a melodic standstill while the keyboard takes on a more active part, giving momentum to the voice's repeated pitches with a series of flowing eighth notes. The return to the simpler, more homophonic style for the verse's last line allows *Bitten* to keep the character of a single statement, a crucial concern given its devotional purpose.

In some of the Gellert songs, this unity seems imposed from without by a quasi-motivic frame provided by the keyboard. In *Wider der Uebermuth* Bach inserts the vocal phrases into a continuing web of chorale prelude-like keyboard elaboration. The voice thus seems to comment on what the keyboard proposes, in reversal of the usual relationship. However, it is the voice that is highlighted as articulating the cadence points in the instrumental flow and confirms the nature and goal of each musical statement. One is tempted to identify *Wider der Uebermuth* with J. S. Bach's treatment of the voice in his sacred arias, yet the simpler focus of C. P. E. Bach's dialogue between voice and keyboard keeps it firmly within the purview of the Lied. This last-mentioned song shares aspects of character with *Die Ehre Gottes aus der Natur*, one of the most interesting of the Gellert settings. The keyboard textures of this song are more varied and broken up than in *Wider der Uebermuth*, yet again there is a pattern of intimate exchange, as the listener's attention is drawn from the keyboard to the voice and back. This transference of interest is particularly noticeable in the first four bars in the passing of eighth notes between keyboard and voice.[15] In the second line of the verse the eighth notes recede further into the background as part of an accompanying texture; however, they regain their quasi-motivic status in the verse's final line. Here, as elsewhere, Bach is concerned to activate a sense of detail even in the simplest accompanying figures, so that the listener is drawn into the song's accelerating motion.

C. P. E. Bach turned his back on the use of figuring for the keyboard parts of the Gellert songs, precisely so that he could control all aspects of their texture.[16] The level of detail in songs such as *Busslied* and *Trost eines schwermüthigen Christen* is remarkable. In *Trost eines schwermüthigen Christen*, the sporadic use of motivic imitation between the parts helps order the song's textural complexity. In *Busslied*, the lower parts maintain a relatively steady tread which rhythmically separates them from the decorative turns of the vocal line, even though the melodic impulse of sighing appoggiaturas still emanates from every part of the texture. A simple parallel would be the network of shifting voices that one hears within a chorale setting. Indeed the chorale remained one of the most important models for Bach's song writing; one identifies it most strongly in his 1774 settings of Carl Friedrich Cramer's psalm translations.[17] Those in a literal chorale style contain some of Bach's most adventurous harmonic writing, though this was achieved at the cost of some of the textural freedoms and contrasts that contribute to the richness of the Gellert collection.

Bach's contemporaries recognized the significance of the Gellert songs as a landmark for the genre of the Lied in Berlin and farther afield; the collection was a huge and unexpected public success.[18] From a later perspective, the Gellert songs confirm that the musical freedoms associated with Schubert or Beethoven were actually claimed very early in the Lied's history, and by a composer who could not be accused of lacking poetic taste or conscience. Bach established song as a worthy challenge to composers at various levels, whether as a test to their powers of formal containment, or to their versatility in tracing different kinds of expressive detail. As such, one might approach the instrumentally minded settings of Beethoven or Haydn as belonging within a C. P. E. Bach heritage, as much as the more vocally responsive songs of Mozart. Each of these composers drew their own lessons from C. P. E. Bach and acknowledged his influence, even though they worked in a radically different climate.

The beginnings of the Lied in Vienna and Haydn

To be sure, Vienna had a quite different artistic culture to Bach's circles in Berlin or Hamburg. In particular, the Austrian capital was subject to stringent state censorship until 1780, which meant that literary taste was kept in a condition of relative infancy. The Anacreontic poetry that was fashionable in C. P. E. Bach's early years still held sway in Vienna in the 1780s. One can see ample evidence of this in the four collections of *Deutsche Lieder* that appeared in Vienna from 1778 to 1782, as the first collections of Lieder to be published in the city, and in the poems and songs of the *Wiener Musenalmanach*.[19] Josef Antonín Štěpán was influential in establishing the Viennese tone of the German Lied. His songs filled the first two volumes of the *Deutsche Lieder*, to be followed in 1780 by a third volume with settings by Friberth and Hofmann. Štěpán primarily was known as a keyboard composer, and his song composition is notable for his frequent use of instrumental interpolations. With these, he would span the gaps between the vocal phrases of his song and blend the whole into a smooth cantabile style. One might take as an example Štěpán's setting of Klopstock's "Lyda,"

Example 3.4 Štěpán, *An Lyda*, mm. 10–15

which could hardly be more different from Bach's approach to the text (see Example 3.1). Štěpán's balanced repetition of phrases turns Klopstock's urgent appeal to the listener into a generalized wistfulness (Example 3.4).[20]

The vogue for Anacreontic poetry had encouraged a certain neutrality to enter into these influential Štěpán settings. Carl Friedrich Cramer, the North German poet and critic, condemned their emptiness in a review of 1783,[21] a view shared by some in Vienna. Haydn published his two volumes of Lieder with Artaria in 1781 and 1782, partly prompted by what he saw as the compositional inadequacies of Štěpán, as well as those of Friberth and Hofmann. Hofmann's setting of Mariane von Ziegler's *Eilt ihr Schäfer* aroused Haydn's particular scorn, and he felt compelled to offer an alternative setting.[22] While Hofmann allowed his lilting melody to circle somewhat aimlessly between tonic and dominant,[23] Haydn picked out a much more definite melodic profile, using the keyboard prelude to establish a series of clear one- and two-measure rhythmic units for the voice to follow.[24]

The instrumental nature of Haydn's setting of Ziegler's poem is far more blatant than in C. P. E. Bach's setting of the same poem, and one might imagine that Haydn was motivated here by a wish to display his powers of thematic invention. The balance the composer achieves in tracing a miniature sonata form within the detail of a single verse is indeed exemplary. After a repetition of the Lied's first vocal phrase, a two-measure keyboard interlude on the dominant establishes a new motivic variant in the manner of a second subject. As was the case with the opening vocal phrase, the voice copies the keyboard's melodic profile, though now the declamation is awkward and one has the impression of the piano pulling the voice through four bars of instrumentally defined motivic sequences. These measures, as in a miniature sonata-form development, prepare for the return of the first melody in the tonic; the resolution of this small-scale drama is here compacted into a four-measure melodic statement, to be followed by the postlude as a summarizing coda. As in Bach's setting of Ziegler's text, every detail of Haydn's musical "drama" has its part to play in shaping the whole. However, one is tempted to find the impulse for the song's shape almost

Example 3.5 Haydn, *Der erste Kuss*, mm. 1–14

entirely in the keyboard. In a review from 1783, Cramer mentions exactly this as unworthy of the Lied and of Haydn.[25] Yet in treating the keyboard as the protagonist in his songs, Haydn is not necessarily undermining the importance of the poetic text. For Haydn, as for C. P. E. Bach, an instrument was at times the most appropriate medium for letting the text "speak," witness his string quartet meditations upon the seven last words of Christ.[26] The poems set to music in his two Lieder collections may not be felt to bear comparison with the sacred texts Haydn set there, yet Haydn believed he could use such poems to sum up the "shadow and light" of life, to quote his own words.[27] He turned to Franz von Greiner, the leader of an important artistic salon in Vienna, for help in making his poetic selections. This has been taken as evidence of Haydn's lack of confidence in literary matters, but it also showed his wish to reach beyond the personal to find a more universal approach to text setting.

Throughout his Lieder, Haydn tended to step back from his texts and offer his listeners a dispassionate summary. His setting of Jacobi's "Der erste Kuss" is one of the clearest examples.[28] The song's first vocal phrase (Example 3.5.) invokes the expressive turns of *Empfindsamkeit*, yet the composer objectifies the melody by presenting it first in the keyboard, complete with its own preludial flourish. The voice enters in m. 11 almost as an afterthought, or as a confirmation of what the keyboard has just "spoken." It seems, from Haydn's approach to the text, that the poet is looking back to the first kiss and reflecting, "this is how life goes on," rather than appealing to Chloe in the present. Yet Haydn still offers his own kind of expressive summary, as he makes the melodic semitonal leans embedded in mm. 4, 6, and 8 become more prominent in the subsequent sounding of the beloved's name. At this point, the melodic lean is transferred to the tonic and leading tone of E♭ major, so creating an expectation of melodic completion. The final cadences in the voice and the keyboard are heightened as images of a promise being completed – just as the poet highlights the kiss as sealing an everlasting bond between the lovers.

The sense of progression one traces through such a song is a clear answer to Cramer's criticism that Haydn was not engaged when he wrote his Lieder. Still, one might wonder whether his engagement was not sometimes wholly musical. Haydn's setting of Leon's "Liebeslied," for example, is a gem of expressive keyboard writing, showing the composer's ability to extend a decorative turn into larger and larger melodic arches. However, the turn fits so awkwardly with the words that it is hard to feel any point of contact between text and music. Vocal declamation and musical motif come nearer together for the enunciation of "so hold, so sanft," but without the earlier attention to the text it is hard to appreciate to whom or what these epithets apply. In other circumstances, the changes of focus between keyboard and voice in Haydn's songs offer an eloquent commentary on the poetry, as they do in the songs of C. P. E. Bach. This is true of the setting of Leon's "Cupido," where Haydn wittily changes his melodic style as the voice enters.[29] The piano prelude presents a fully fledged keyboard melody, complete with impressively decorated perfect cadence. Yet the voice responds with a much simpler version of the melodic outline that could almost belong to a different song. Haydn uses this contrast to draw attention to the condescension of the speaker as he addresses the "kleines Mägdelein" in terms he thinks she will understand. The simple façade is shown to be precarious, as the piano interjects with more touches of its elaborate rhythmic style. For the final words of the verse, "Schwänk' und List" (pranks and tricks), the voice falls in with the piano's style entirely, and one has the humorous impression that the girl knows just as much about Cupid as the speaker.

The sensitivity of Haydn's response to humorous texts is borne out by his setting of Weiße's "Eine sehr gewöhnliche Geschichte" and of Lessing's "Lob der Faulheit."[30] In both of these the composer focuses upon the simplest of verbal rhythms and bare yet graphic musical details. In *Eine sehr gewöhnliche Geschichte*, the vocal line is elaborated out of the repeated notes that depict the young man knocking at his beloved's door, eventually developing into a dance-fragment that hints at what will happen once the door is opened. In *Lob der Faulheit* Haydn uses simple stepwise movements and the descending fourth which proclaims the word "Faulheit," both to depict the idea of "laziness" and, ironically, to demonstrate his own powers of economy and invention. For all its bizarre lack of tunefulness, this song is perhaps the nearest Haydn comes to drawing his musical energies from the shape and meaning of individual words. It is significant that this should happen where the composer was hiding behind a mask of comic impersonation and so keeping an obvious distance from the text. One may note that some of Haydn's songs in a foreign language, from the English collections of 1794 and 1795, have been felt to be more successful than his Lieder in conveying an immediate response to poetry.

Despite all of his instrumental music in the popular style, Haydn seems not to respond readily to the naive immediacy of the German lyric. The triadic melodies in praise of the open-air life in his setting of Stahl's (first name[s] unknown) "Die Landlust" seem repetitive and lackluster, both compared to the wit of his setting of Leon's "Cupido" and to the arias celebrating similar joys in the *Creation* and the *Seasons*.[31] Without finding a "slant" to such poetic material, Haydn seems to have lacked a ground for his musical invention. The "slant" of humor is the one he most commonly invoked, but a couple of the poems called forth a deeper commentary bordering on the spiritual or sublime. Gleim's "Das Leben ist ein Traum" shares some of the didacticism of Gellert's odes and Haydn reserved a distinctively operatic treatment for this text.[32] The keyboard prelude suggests the expansive textures of an orchestral ritornello, with rising sequences that extend across the entry of the voice and help carry it forward to a series of declamatory climaxes. Such grandeur, causing the texture to spread over three staves as the voice is treated separately from the keyboard, is most impressive in a Lied for this time. The poetic refrain at the end of each verse – "Life is a dream" – allows the grandeur to be viewed ironically. One also notes that the song's textural scale is not substantiated tonally, for the song departs little from an immediate outline of the tonic key. The harmonic scale of *Geistliches Lied*, a song with a clear spiritual theme, is far more ambitious; here the range of modulation fully matches the setting's motivic complexity.[33] The song's motifs are laid out in the ten-measure prelude and from this we can anticipate that certain cadential gestures will act as focus points within alternating patterns of phrase expansion and contraction. Clearly, the prelude is vital in allowing Haydn to summarize his response to the text, before embarking in the verse upon a looser prayerful meditation.

With *Geistliches Lied* Haydn seemed to be chafing against the limitations of the Lied and of strophic design; in *Trost unglücklicher Liebe* he took a further step toward abandoning such containment altogether.[34] This song is a rare example of Haydn seeking to assume the mantle of Klopstock in his song writing and tracing a more personal narrative. The sense of inwardness is maintained by the continuity of the song's rocking accompanying textures and the *cantabile* prominence of the voice. Although the vocal line is prefigured in the piano prelude, for once the vocal versions of the melody seem more significant; the rhythmic and harmonic changes that are essential for the song's formal development seem to be prompted by the voice rather than the keyboard. The changes are timed to respond to individual words such as "Schmerz," "Wunden," and "tötet." These intimate links dissolve when Haydn comes to balance his harmonic departures at the end of the verse. With the wish to keep to the strophic design, Haydn introduces emphatic cadence figures in voice and keyboard that bear little relation to the prompting of individual words. Taken by itself *Trost der unglücklicher Liebe* offers a tantalizing glimpse into what might have happened if Haydn had been prepared to experiment with through-composed forms in the manner of Mozart or Beethoven. However, one must remember that this song was conceived as part of a collection, and its formal conservatism allows it to be identified with Haydn's other songs, as one extreme in his continuum of "shadow and light." The composer had clearly not reached the point of treating a single song as summarizing a whole emotional view of the world, or of gaining the distinctiveness of form and content of an instrumental movement. Nonetheless, the importance of Haydn's collective song statement should not be ignored, particularly for the concern it showed for form and motivic treatment – and for the way these might be shaped to meet the tautness of a poem's form and content.

Mozart

Mozart's reputation as a song composer has remained far higher than Haydn's and some of his songs achieve the breakthrough to musico-poetic distinctiveness that evaded the older composer. But some of the comparisons between their settings do not come out entirely in Mozart's favor. If one compares Mozart's setting of Jacobi's "An Chloe," K524, of 1787 with Haydn's *Der erste Kuss* by the same poet, one appreciates the ease of Mozart's vocal melody and its independence from the keyboard.[35] One also notices how the spinning out of vocal phrases takes place without reference to the poetic disciplines of line length and stanza. Therefore, one does not feel the challenge of containment or the sense of rhythmic and harmonic progression as strongly as in Haydn's song. In setting the first verse, Mozart moves to the dominant for the final line, timing the return to the tonic with the beginning of the second verse. One might applaud his ingenious combining of strophic repetition with sonata form-like recapitulation. But the result is that the poetic verse no longer is experienced as a syntactical unit; the verse is left open-ended on the dominant, and the moment of musical completion comes halfway through the poem's second verse. A further musical recapitulation is introduced into the last line of the second verse, followed by a coda which extends with multiple textual repetition for a further fifteen measures. The musical landmarks of recapitulation in Mozart's song turn Jacobi's two-verse poem into a three-fold sonata-rondo structure. Technically the song is through composed, yet it is hard to understand what prompted such a treatment poetically. It also is unclear how the musical form reflects upon the poem in any specific way.

Some would say Mozart treats Jacobi's poem simply as raw material for his music, much as he would a libretto for an operatic aria. Yet in stripping away the poem's formal stylization, Mozart offers his listeners a chance to retrace the spontaneous workings of a lyrical impulse, even if the lyrical impulse clearly is his rather than the poet's. In his *Über naive und sentimentalische Dichtung*, Schiller distinguished between "naïve" artists who could *be* nature, and "sentimental" artists who *sought* nature.[36] Homer, Shakespeare, and Goethe were his main examples of naïve "singers of nature," while Klopstock and Jacobi were included among those who reflected nature's impressions on them.[37] Taking an example such as the composer's setting of Overbeck's "Sehnsucht nach der Frühlinge," K596, Mozart would seem to belong firmly within the category of the "naïve." For all the notion of yearning ("Sehnsucht") in the title, Mozart's melody makes it seem as though spring had already fully arrived, as part of an eternal present.[38]

Mozart's spring song, written in 1791, relates to the kind of tunes sung by Papageno in *Die Zauberflöte*, though the operatic melodies were given a much larger frame, both musically and philosophically. Mozart seemed fascinated by the juxtaposition of the naïve and profound; one can see it reflected in the B♭ major piano concerto K595, also of 1791, where the composer used a tune very similar to the start of *Sehnsucht nach der Frühlinge* as a starting point for the developments of his impressive Rondo finale. Schiller said Goethe's "naïvety" was exposed most vividly when it was brought to bear upon "sentimental" material, as in *Die Leiden des jungen Werther*, since this could act as a foil to his challenging directness.[39] Mozart found that foil in opera and the piano concerto, but not always in the Lied. The style of some of his songs suggests he often was happy to take the genre at the relatively superficial level established in Vienna by Friberth, Hofmann, and Štěpán. Sometimes a special occasion, such as the birthday of a child as in *Des kleinen Friedrichs Geburtstag*, K529, or the opening of a freemasons' lodge as in *Lied der Freiheit*, K506, prompted the style. But sometimes Mozart's lightness of touch suggests lack of engagement with the poetry, as with his setting of J. M. Miller's "Die Zufriedenheit" (K473) or Hölty's "Das Traumbild" (K530).[40] These songs share certain stylistic aspects with *Sehnsucht nach der Frühlinge*, but they lack the verbal responsiveness displayed there as well as the melodic tautness.

Taken as a whole, Mozart's song writing does not display a consistent intention to raise the level of the Viennese Lied as manifest in Haydn's collections. Unlike Haydn's Lieder, Mozart's were published in more random fashion,[41] and the composer seemed prepared to wait for the stimulation of text or circumstances. His setting of Gabriele von Baumberg's "Als Luise die

Briefe ihres ungetreuen Liebhaber verbrannte" of 1787 (K520) reveals that he had at times an almost experimental approach to song; its recitative-like fluidity might seem to remove it from the genre of the Lied altogether.[42] The poem describes Luise consigning her beloved's songs to the flames since he sang them to someone else and, in Mozart's version, although she addresses the flames in the first person she declines to sing to them. A lingering chromaticism in the song's final section suggests her emotion might be about to surface. There is only one motif offered in summary, a dotted arpeggio figure which had rhythmically punctuated the first ten measures of the song, and this now adds its forbidding stamp to the final cadence.

Mozart's setting of *Als Luise* reveals a comparatively greater engagement with the text than many other of his songs, yet even this would hardly prepare the listener for the inspired mixing of lyrical, dramatic, and narrative traits in his three most celebrated songs, *Das Veilchen*, K476, *Das Lied der Trennung*, K519, and *Abendempfindung*, K523. Here the individual song takes on a whole new level of significance, for in each of these settings Mozart changes or develops his musical approach during the song, and plays with the lyrical expectations of the genre as part of his poetic interpretation. In his 1785 setting of *Das Veilchen*, Mozart could even claim to match Goethe's dialectical balancing of the "sentimental" and "naïve," of direct and indirect expression.[43] The poem carries significant resonance from its origins in Goethe's Singspiel *Erwin und Elmire* (Goethe completed his libretto in 1775) where the lyric is associated both with the scorned lover Erwin, who casts himself as the trampled violet of the poem, and the repentant Elmire, who sings Erwin's song as a means of reflecting on the past. In his song, Mozart outlines the poem's narrative either as stages that can be seen to unfold one after the other, or as images that exist side by side.

The first stage involves the simplest and most enclosed melodic profile, as confirmed by the piano prelude and by the emphatic close at the halfway point of the first verse. The second stage follows directly upon this with a more expansive rhythmic and melodic phrase upon the dominant, a contrast underlined by another piano interlude. Thus Mozart completes the description of the violet separately from the description of the young girl, presenting each as a self-contained picture from nature. The turn to G minor for the third phrase of the song suggests the awakening of a "sentimental" consciousness and the yearning of the violet to be united to the girl. The melodic phrases betray a more developmental tendency, as shifts between minor and major help to push the melodic line beyond its previous containment. In the song's fourth section, which coincides with the poem's third and final verse, the life of the violet is decisively broken despite the poetic hints of a sacrificial afterlife. The melodic line breaks into recitative and the return to G major is not accompanied by a return to the first melody as one might expect. Mozart's repetition of material in the concluding three measures, originally heard in mm. 12–14, appears musically tacked on, and it is an addition on Mozart's part to Goethe's poem. It is a conscious reflection on what might have been, and an appeal to the listener to remember the mood of the opening. This mood was caught decisively in mm. 12–14 and thus we might agree with Mozart that the memory can be invoked at any point, however far the song has traveled since. The composer's closing reminder of this basic quality of the lyric, of its existence in the moment, allows the listener to associate *Das Veilchen* with the unity of strophic song even while the composer's narrative interpretation seems to deny the relevance of strophic form altogether.

Responses to Mozart's *Das Veilchen* have been highly contradictory, with some critics believing it marks the beginning of the musical genre of the Lied, and others insisting it shows the composer to have little understanding of the genre.[44] The significance of *Das Veilchen* in summarizing the role of memory is enhanced by comparing it to Mozart's 1787 *Das Lied der Trennung*.[45] In this instance, the poem by K. E. K. Schmidt focuses entirely on the speaker's fear that the beloved will fail to remember him, and Mozart's strophic treatment can be seen as a specific response to this aspect of the text. One notes the intensity with which the composer brings out the appoggiatura of the minor sixth to fifth, Db to C, throughout his carefully poised vocal line, as a means of etching the melody upon the listener's mind. The further semitonal step between F and Gb in the vocal line of the refrain offers another reinforcement of the voice's pervasive figure. In the song's fifth verse, Mozart uses the refrain's Gb to prompt a tonal excursion to Db major and Bb minor. When the material of the song's first four verses returns in the tonic in verse 7, the listener is given a heightened sense of the force of such repetitions. The seventh verse still is subject to a process of variation, particularly at the point of the refrain. Yet from this more "open" interpretation of the material the appoggiatura figures emerge more strongly than ever. It is as though the speaker's anxiety for Luisa to remember has now taken over the whole narrative and brought the timelessness he dreaded.

In *Abendempfindung*, also of 1787, Mozart takes motivic treatment one stage further by presenting a continuous stream of responsive piano figuration, from which the rising sixth and the melodic fall from G to F emerge as the song's main structural landmarks.[46] The song's continuity is traced through the piano's returning eighth-note patterns and the cadence figure from mm. 11 to 13, which returns to articulate a tonal journey to the dominant and then a series of flatward keys, before Mozart introduces a large-scale tonal recapitulation for the poem's sixth verse. Such a tonal scheme bears a close relation to the dynamics of sonata form; however, the *cantabile* vocal line and steadily unfolding piano figuration allow the song also to be experienced as one single unbroken verse. This song is indeed one of the most powerful evocations of an unbroken mood or *Stimmung* in the Lieder repertory, despite its departure from conventional strophic designs.

Beethoven

It is difficult to know how aware Mozart was of the implications of his new approaches to text setting, particularly since Viennese attitudes toward poetry were so casual compared to those of North German circles – at least on the part of composers.[47] The conscious clash of wills that characterized Beethoven's attitude to poetry was born of quite different artistic circumstances. Some of Beethoven's poetic awareness stemmed from Neefe, his teacher in Bonn, who was closely associated with North German ideals of song setting, and some from his own heightened ambitions. He once stated that he envied poets their wider sphere of activity and their capacity for moral influence.[48] One can see him claiming a distinctive interpretive stance in one of his earliest songs from the Bonn years, his setting of Hölty's "Klage."[49] The rhyming patterns of Hölty's iambic quatrains are entirely subsumed by the breadth of this song's three-part structure. For the second verse, where the poet transfers his thoughts from a calm past to a tormented present, Beethoven casts off the intimate and sustained phrases of the first section for a paragraph of operatic intensity. Beethoven's song conveys a story, not a lyricist's pervasive mood, and thus he offers his own kind of criticism of the elegiac genre in which Hölty excelled. Beethoven externalizes the thoughts of the speaker and suggests they may be faced as concrete dramatic events. In his setting of Hölty's third verse, with its reference to the future, he strips away the textural richness of the first two sections as a literal depiction of the poet's death. The emphasis upon closure offered by the postlude leaves the listener with the foremost reflection that all must die, rather than personal sympathies for the poet's feelings.

It is possible from this early song to identify Beethoven's own specific attitudes to life's experiences reflected in his approach to a poetic text. His lack of ease in setting poetry is often related to his struggles with writing for the voice; as late as 1795 Beethoven was going to Salieri for lessons in vocal composition. However, his setting of *Klage* encourages one to consider also the composer's basic aesthetic disposition and his urge to dramatize emotions. Even in a simple strophic song, such as the setting (WoO 112) of Matthisson's "An Laura" from around 1792, the composer stretches out the vocal line to suggest the specific urgency of the message to be imparted.[50] In Matthisson Beethoven found a poet who matched his own desire for a consciously heightened expression. Schiller praised Matthisson's ability to point up the inner connection between images of nature, so that they became "pictures of the soul."[51] Beethoven set three other Matthisson poems – *Adelaide*, *Opferlied*, and *Andenken* (Op. 46, WoO 126, WoO 136, respectively) – and they are three of his most popular and successful songs. *Adelaide* was written in 1794 as part of Beethoven's bid to impress himself upon Viennese society.[52] One immediately is struck by the greatly enhanced role given to the piano, as though the composer wished to outstrip the instrumental writing in the Lieder of Štěpán, Haydn, and Mozart. As in Mozart's *Abendempfindung*, the keyboard establishes the through-composed continuity of the song, allowing the vocal phrases the flexibility to pause and shift in rhythmic emphasis and melodic direction. However, over the course of the song the dialogue between voice and piano becomes far more purposeful. The reiterations of the beloved's name mark the passing of time and the movement toward closure. The first utterance of "Adelaide" (mm. 14–15) occurs as a lingering echo of an already completed cadence on the tonic B♭. But the second utterance is compressed into a teasing imperfect cadence on the dominant of the dominant, which prompts a large-scale reworking of the poem's second verse before a balancing perfect cadence upon the dominant itself. In Beethoven's interpretation, the poet's search for the beloved's image, through the colors of a spring garden to the snowy Alps, finds a point of repose as he turns to images of a starry sky at the end of the second verse. The rhythmic exchange between voice and piano stabilizes during the third verse, even though the sequences of keys lead to a point farthest from the tonic. The expansive cadence for "Adelaide" at the end of the third verse articulates the tonality of G♭. The poet may have captured a poignant image, but it is far removed from daily experience. Beethoven repeats the text of the third verse as part of a call for a return to the tonic, and the fourth verse brings the desired tonal conclusion though on a scale that exceeds expectation. As in an operatic finale, the thematic material is recast in a faster tempo with many balancing repetitions. One would think that the poet's capturing of the beloved's image in death was the equivalent of Leonora leading Florestan out of prison. Some critics have indeed felt Beethoven's treatment of the text to be highly exaggerated, more fitting to the genre of the cantata than to the Lied.[53] However, despite the sense of scale that is brought into *Adelaide*'s final verse, the focus remains upon the sounding of the beloved's name itself. In the last fifteen measures a hugely expanded setting of "Adelaide" is followed by a much more intimate utterance of her name, and it is this that keeps the song's lyricism intact.

Matthisson's poem "Andenken," which Beethoven came to in 1809, also is concerned with seeing the beloved in every image of nature.[54] The setting here is on a much smaller scale than *Adelaide* as befits the clarity of the poet's statements, though the falling away of the vocal line onto a lingering imperfect cadence at the end of each verse creates a tension across the pattern of strophic repetitions. Once more, the emphasis is thrown upon Beethoven's ability to balance such harmonic tensions in his contrasting setting of the final verse, with its own much freer pattern of repetition and variation. There is indeed much evidence, both internal and external, to suggest that Beethoven found strophic forms irksome. One of the most interesting pieces of corroboration comes in the composer's four settings of Goethe's "Sehnsucht" ("Nur wer die Sehnsucht kennt") of 1807–08. In all four, he makes a point of keeping to a restricted melodic compass as well as an enclosed formal design. The settings were published even though the composer said he had not been bothered to complete them;[55] perhaps he wished to demonstrate just how hard he found it to meet Goethe's formal demands. To Goethe, the struggle to master his poetic material through form was almost more important than the content itself, hence his extreme reaction if a composer ignored any aspects of the forms he had created.[56] Beethoven was greatly drawn to the energy and tension of Goethe's poetry but was not prepared, except in the *Sehnsucht* settings, to bypass his own struggles for formal mastery. Rhythmic momentum characterizes nearly all of Beethoven's Goethe settings, as the composer sought to match the poet's verbal energy – a momentum that threatens to spill over what the voice can encompass. In the early setting of *Maigesang*, Op. 52, No. 4, from before 1796, Beethoven binds every three of Goethe's short verses into one larger musical verse, with hardly a moment for the singer to breathe.[57] A burbling piano interlude overflows at the point of cadence, so that one can imagine the line extending further still while the singer pauses, ready for the next musical verse. At no point does the piano part actually swamp the voice, although Beethoven continues to allow his textures to waver between vocal and instrumental impulses, dance and song. In Beethoven's setting of Goethe's "Neue Liebe, neues Leben," from 1798, WoO 127, some would say that dividing line is dissolved (Example 3.6).[58] The voice is challenged to the extreme by the demand to become like an instrument, the highpoint coming as the piano takes over the melodic line in m. 18, for now one knows the buildup of keyboard arpeggiated figures can be continued on as large a scale as necessary. The outcome of this *Fidelio*-like piling up of rhythmic sequences is an extended aria-like structure. And when Beethoven revised the song in 1809 as Op. 75, No. 2, he gave it even greater harmonic and textural scope.[59]

The first example of Beethoven's distinctively instrumental treatment of the voice is his setting of Bürger's "Gegenliebe" in 1794, which presents a melody that anticipates both the *Choral Fantasy* and the Ninth Symphony's *Ode to Joy*. In this instance the clumsiness of the declamation suggests the

Example 3.6 Beethoven, *Neue Liebe, neues Leben*, mm. 18–26

individual words are less important than the notion of a broad instrumental sweep, which balances the operatic contours of *Seufzer eines Ungeliebten*, the song with which it is paired. Such treatment of contrasting stylistic types might seem foreign to the intimacy of the Lied but there are other perhaps more persuasive examples of Beethoven employing conscious stylistic characterization. His six Gellert songs, Op. 48, Nos. 1–6 (1801–02), present an exaggeratedly simple hymn style as the basis for every aspect of the vocal and keyboard textures.[60] This is seen most clearly in the setting of *Vom Tode*, where the melody unfolds across a carefully measured span, from the tolling of a repeated note to the point where it stretches to a clearly defined melodic cadence and then stops. The unity of this statement even outstrips C. P. E. Bach's setting in its sense of inexorable linear progression. The melodic line of *Bitten* conveys a similarly single minded journey from dominant to tonic, as set out by the eight measures of the piano prelude. The voice's relentless intoning of the tonic for the first six measures of the second half of the verse creates one of the most graphic images of the Gellert songs, suggesting how the soul fixes itself upon God, yet it remains an essential part of the relentless abstract symmetry of Beethoven's design. Three of the other Gellert songs, *Die Liebe des Nächsten*, *Die Ehre Gottes aus der Natur*, and *Gottes Macht und Vorsehung*, share this strict alignment of melodic, harmonic, and textural details, a uniformity which makes the sixth song, *Busslied*, all the more striking. For the first three verses *Busslied* follows a much more varied sequence of phrases, as though Beethoven were asserting a musical freedom after the restrictions of the previous songs. However, at the midway point, the song's harmonic perspective shifts from openness to closure, and the last three verses present strophic repetitions of one sixteen-measure phrase. The accompanying variations in the piano confirm a sense of triumph at the return to such hymn-like simplicity, and offer a fitting conclusion to the set as a whole.[61]

The Gellert songs often are treated as an exception to the rest of Beethoven's Lieder and as his special tribute to C. P. E. Bach. Yet they offer certain crucial insights into Beethoven's means of reconciling himself to the restrictions of the Lied, both in terms of its formal parameters and the aesthetic relationships to poetry. From the Gellert songs one sees the composer embracing a self-imposed containment as a challenge to his musical invention, as well as a means of focusing his poetic interpretation. It is hard to generalize about the subsequent course of Beethoven's song writing because it continued to involve a wide range of possible styles and approaches. So that in 1815, for example, one can find the operatically expansive textures of Beethoven's setting of Tiedge's "An die Hoffnung" set alongside the intimate details of such a song as Herder's "Die laute Klage" (WoO 135). However, three of Beethoven's songs of later years, his settings of Goethe's "Was zieht mir das Herz so" (Op. 83, No. 2), "Kennst du das Land" (Op. 75, No. 1), and "Wonne der Wehmut" (Op. 83, No. 1), all bear witness to the newly conscious containment of the Gellert songs. *Was zieht mir das Herz so* invokes some of the rhythmic momentum of *Maigesang* and *Neue Liebe, neues Leben,* but on this occasion the vocal part follows a strophic design throughout, even with the change from minor to major for the song's final verse. The piano's refrains suggest a reckless energy, but this is channeled into variations within the piano part while the voice holds its line. This allows Beethoven to maintain the image of the poet flying to his beloved as a bird in its essential simplicity, even while the piano is seen to comment on the image with increasing humor.

Such layers were vital to Goethe's conception of the lyric, though he doubted composers could match his irony in any direct fashion. He objected to Beethoven's interpretive strategy in *Kennst du das Land*, for example, believing the contrasts that the composer introduced into each verse broke the unity of the strophic design too decisively.[62] However, Beethoven's dramatic contrasts centered on a simple shift of emphasis from tonic to dominant within the song's opening statement. In the first four measures, the pause upon the tonic in m. 2 is balanced by the imperfect cadence of m. 4. But with the repeat from m. 5, the first pause is elided and emphasis is directed more upon the dominant. By the end of the paragraph, the imperfect cadences have become a rhetorical landmark, summarizing the impossibility of anyone answering Mignon's mysterious question – "Do you know the land?" The release comes poetically when Mignon appeals directly to her listener to accompany her to that land, wherever it might be. Beethoven underlines such a change of thought by switching to a new swinging melody in 6/8 which circles around reiterated cadences upon the tonic. The contrast of tempo and meter is in some senses prepared by the harmonic tensions of the song's previous paragraph. The following threefold repetition of the verse imposes a kind of unity upon the song, but its musical integrity relies upon the underlying tonal balance between the two halves of each verse and the sense of one leading to the other.

In *Kennst du das Land* Beethoven linked questions of Mignon's sanity or powers of communication to questions of his own musical integrity; there could be no clearer sign perhaps of his deep involvement with the Lied. That depth is confirmed by his setting of *Wonne der Wehmut*, a song that even Goethe felt impelled to respect.[63] In this case, the poem offered no particular form to the composer, being the briefest of lyrical statements and one hardly intended for the public. In this sense, the poem demanded an active and sympathetic interpretation if it were to be at all intelligible to a wider audience. In his setting, Beethoven inserts pauses into his first vocal statement, as though waiting for responses from his listeners. Despite the linking motif from the piano, which suggests the falling of the poet's tears, there is a sense of uncertainty as one waits for the next step in the voice and piano's rising melodic line. The uncertainty increases when the subsequent repetition is introduced by the piano alone, leaving the voice to enter at the half measure. From this point Beethoven subjects the motivic shape to a series of rhythmic and harmonic explorations. It returns a third and fourth time, so tracing a periodic cycle of repetition that keeps the inviolability of the lyrical statement alive, even while the material is subject to radical variation. Some later Romantics, among them the lyricist Ludwig Tieck, condemned the complexity of Beethoven's song writing.[64] In *Wonne der Wehmut*, the patterns of motivic development and of harmonic departure and return clearly are intended to illuminate the power of the lyrical "moment," as the poet seeks to contemplate and hold the infinity of his grief. Goethe might have wished he could scorn Beethoven's help, or exclude the developments of symphonic Classicism from the lyrical movement that he epitomized. Yet such contributions were vital to the outworking of German lyricism, and they remain important to us as a warning against any tendency to limit or underestimate the scope of the German Lied.

PART THREE

The nineteenth century: issues of style and development

4 The Lieder of Schubert

MARIE-AGNES DITTRICH

Was the German Lied, as so often has been claimed, born on 19 October 1814 with the composition of *Gretchen am Spinnrade*? Did Schubert (1797–1828) – known not so much for composing as he was for a kind of channeling while in "a state of clairvoyance or somnambulism, without any conscious action," as his close friend the singer Johann Michael Vogl once observed – achieve on that day a "breakthrough in the principle of the Romantic art song"?[1] Did he create the Lied, the most important new musical genre of his century, out of a vacuum, without models and other inspirational sources save that of Goethe's "musical poet's genius"?[2] Is it true, as George Grove insisted as long ago as 1883, that Schubert had only to "read the poem, and the appropriate tune, married to immortal verse (a marriage, in his case, truly made in heaven), rushed into his mind, and to the end of his pen"?[3] Or is there nothing new under the sun: are there models and historical antecedents even for Schubert's songs?

In setting Goethe's famous poem "Gretchen am Spinnrade," the new, according to many critics, is the celebrated accompaniment that imitates the whirling motion of the spinning wheel and the foot treadle of the spinner, all of which succeeds in placing the listener in the middle of a highly realistic albeit imagined scene. But of course, the accomplishment is not as innovative as many have insisted. The *Spinnerliedchen* from the winter episode of Haydn's oratorio *The Seasons* (1801) exploits the very same means. Like Haydn, Schubert was guided by an established *topos*, or "topic" – one of numerous characteristic musical figures associated with various moods, scenes, and situations long familiar to Western Europe.[4] What is new in *Gretchen am Spinnrade*, rather, is Schubert's exploitation of the song's means: his polyrhythmic combining of an accompaniment and a quite differently structured vocal line. How felicitously he solves the compositional problem posed by the opening words "Meine Ruh ist hin" by illustrating the single word "Ruh," or peace, with a long note in opposition to the restlessness of the entire line: "My peace is gone, my heart is heavy." Then, there is the way Schubert configures Gretchen's vocal line so as to ascend in tandem with the mounting agitation of Goethe's poem; how long he withholds harmonic resolution in order to stretch the tension. Also, there is the young girl's struggle for breath and the way the spinning wheel comes to a shattering standstill and is started again only with great effort.

Finally, there is Schubert's daring to better Goethe by intensifying a barely disguised rondo form. Yet again, Gretchen repeats the words "Meine Ruh ist hin, mein Herz ist schwer," a repetition that succeeds in emphasizing the oppressed mood to which she seems destined to remain captive, not just to the end but beyond the song's limits. Schubert could create something fundamentally new precisely because he worked at a time when composers could count on listeners holding certain expectations. And because they recognized the spinning song as a *topos*, the song's extraordinary features cannot have escaped them.

In truth, the modern aspect of many a Schubert Lied is the unexpected handling of the well-known, one that affords the observer a choice: either to discover the unexpected or to recognize the known. For Schubert's contemporaries, both were easier than they are for us today, since songs of all sorts were used to accompany life's routine. One sang in the kitchen, in the spinning-room, in the field, while dragging or rowing; one sang in church, walking in the woods, dancing on holiday; and one sang at home to entertain friends, at banquets to praise brave deeds, at bedsides to comfort children. Wherever one turned, familiar sounds were to be encountered: the church liturgy of common and feast days, the fanfares and marches of wind bands, traditional dances in the country and new ones in the city, serenades from beneath the windows of pretty maidens, the hurdy-gurdy of beggars. Then, there was the musicality of the seeming natural world (not to mention the real world of babbling brooks or breezes rustling through trees), where church bells announced masses, weddings, and, with monotonous clang, funerals. One knew the posthorn signal and recognized hunting horns from afar. Attending the theater or a concert, or hearing a neighbor's child practice the piano through an open window, such sonic fallout made up part of the fabric of daily existence. Schubert listened to all of this and more and reflected it in song in sometimes obvious, sometimes subtly stylized form.

Schubert once wrote that, in the way he accompanied Vogl, his audience perceived something "new and unheard of" – namely, how in the moment of performance they seemed "as one."[5] In contrast to the keyboard treatment in most eighteenth-century Lieder, Schubert's piano parts typically are no longer structured as a simple, subordinated supplement to a more important vocal line; the piano has at least become its equal and sometimes more than that, for frequently it sets the tone for an entire Lied. This could encompass the rapid motion of the trout in the brook in *Die Forelle*; the rocking of the boat in *Gondelfahrer* or *Des Fischers Liebesglück*; the rattling chains of the dogs in *Im Dorfe* (*Winterreise*, No. 17); the serenade of the guitar or mandolin in *Ständchen* (*Schwanengesang*, No. 4); or the blowing of the wind in *Herbst*. But the keyboard part is not merely background music or sound painting: it symbolizes the poetic self. Therefore, the flowing sixteenth- or eighth-note motion of the brook in *Die schöne Müllerin* stands in for merriment (as in No. 1), gentleness (No. 4), or agitation (No. 5), thereby reflecting and commenting on the protagonist's ever-shifting feelings. And when in the sixth song he voices the crucial question, whether his love is returned, the brook falls silent. Similarly, the wanderer in *Winterreise* (No. 13) no longer hears the posthorn when he realizes that, for him, there will be no letter. A suggestion, as it were, of impressionism produced by a diminished seventh chord in *Die Stadt* (*Schwanengesang*, No. 11) is not merely to depict water rippled by the wind, but to indicate the unsettled yearning for unnamed, lost happiness. The repetition of tones in *Die liebe Farbe* (*Die schöne Müllerin*, No. 16) reminds one of a death knell, and yet it does not imitate the "real" sound of a bell as much as it symbolizes the endless mourning of the despairing lover. It is idle to argue whether the celebrated piano part in *Erlkönig* should portray the galloping of a horse. Schubert realized in all these cases a symbolism which Goethe – although he detested all tone-painting – would have allowed: "to imitate thunder with music is not artful, but the composer who gives me the feeling I would get when I heard thunder would be highly admired."[6]

Many walking songs, with their regular beat, express not only a physical motion but also indicate a path through life in the sense of a personal destiny. One cannot actually walk to the tempo of the first song in *Die schöne Müllerin* – even though it is entitled *Das Wandern* (Wandering) – since the eighth notes are too fast and the quarters too slow. Yet the song's speed seems not illogical. And in *Winterreise* one perceives, after the walking pace established at the beginning in *Gute Nacht*, that the slower tempo of the last song expresses the protagonist's weariness with life, or, perhaps more accurately, that life has beaten him down. The sarabande of *Die Nebensonnen* (No. 23) shows his step dragging, and the repeated dactyls of *Das Wirtshaus* (No. 21), marked "Sehr langsam," plainly suggest the rhythm of a funeral march. Goethe's mysterious Mignon walks a similar trail through life. Several of her songs put one in mind of the pavan or *Totentanz*, which in Schubert's hands generally points toward an inexorable fate. Such destiny speaks as well from the music of *Der Tod und das Mädchen*, and Nos. 18 and 20 from *Die schöne Müllerin*, *Trock'ne Blumen* and *Des Baches Wiegenlied*. Other songs exploiting a rhythmic ostinato in similar fashion include *Suleika I* (D720), *Abendstern*, *Fülle der Liebe*, and *Der Zwerg*. In a number of other Lieder evenly measured chords together with solemn texts evoke variously prayers or hymns, as in *Hoffnung* (D295), *Pax vobiscum*, *Heliopolis I* (D753), *Der Pilgrim*, and *Der Kreuzzug*.

Quite different are familiar rhythms occurring in an unusual context to produce an effect of alienation. Thus, the waltz, a popular dance in

Schubert's Vienna, commonly symbolized free and uncomplicated mirth. (Hearing others speak of a *Trauerwalzer*, or "Mourning Waltz," Schubert is said to have asked, "what donkey composed a Trauerwalzer?," unaware that his own *Waltz in A flat* [D365, No. 2] had been given that title.) But Schubert's *Der Atlas* (*Schwanengesang*, No. 8) presents the listener with a waltz rhythm in a surprisingly deep range to characterize ironically the unfortunate Titan's words, "proud heart, you have so desired it, you wished to be happy." In *Erlkönig*, at the words "du liebes Kind, komm, geh' mit mir" (you dear child, come, go with me), a ghostly waltz in far too fast a tempo makes the enticement of the Erlkönig seem especially sinister. Another popular dance of Schubert's day, the *Ländler*, appears markedly slower than customary in *Du liebst mich nicht*, yet another song that treats, as its title makes clear, unreturned love. Together with the exaggerated dance tempo, nothing in life, not even, as is revealed in the poem's last line, rose blooms, jasmine, and narcissus, mean anything if love is not reciprocated.[7]

When the piano part closely matches the vocal line, the result seems to be that the text is bolstered by a kind of empathetic unanimity. Thus, in *Ständchen* not only the voice but also the piano seems to plead "Liebchen, komm zu mir" – darling, come to me. *An die Musik* features a piano part that anticipates the pitches repeated by the voice: "Du holde Kunst" (you lovely art). Elsewhere, the piano is capable of placing the poetic self in an unexpected light. An independent keyboard part is used to good purpose in *Kriegers Ahnung* (Warrior's Premonition, *Schwanengesang*, No. 2) where the singer begins with a rhythm contrasting with the piano's initial statement, thus heightening the loneliness of the soldier amid sleeping comrades. In *Aufenthalt* (Resting Place, *Schwanengesang*, No. 5), a contradiction between the vocal and instrumental accompaniment proclaims a conflict between the protagonist and the world around him. Similarly, once the wayfarer of *Winterreise* reaches the village in *Im Dorfe*, the voice and piano map out separate worlds and in so doing point up the fact that the central character, although other people physically surround him, has reached a point where contact with others is impossible.

In many instances contradiction or skepticism is manifest in the accompaniment as it turns toward minor and thereby reveals the vocal line's major key to be deceptive, as in *Mut* (*Winterreise*, No. 22) and *Tränenregen* (*Die schöne Müllerin*, No. 10). Also, Schubert knew how effective it could be to silence the piano and leave the singer alone. Appropriately enough for a song given over to solitude, the piano, in *Einsamkeit*, as if struck dumb, at length abandons the singer to express the terrors of war. Commenting on the picture named in *Ihr Bild* (*Schwanengesang*, No. 9), the piano doubles the vocal line in octaves to bestow upon the latter a singularly frightening and hollow timbre: the poetic persona stands alone. At the moment the text specifies that the picture "stealthily began to come alive," accompanying chords begin anew. Similarly, in *Der Doppelgänger* (*Schwanengesang*, No. 13) spooky two-note chords are filled out with fuller harmonies at the mention of the beloved.

Melodic and harmonic conventions in songs of Schubert's time gave rise to expectations on the part of listeners. The familiar association of major and minor with the affects of joy and sadness, respectively, emerged in the sixteenth century to solidify as convention well before Schubert's time. Consequently, Schubert used these modes accordingly in the Rückert song *Lachen und Weinen*. The daily bread of composers in the Classical and Romantic eras was a reliance on the association of higher and lower chords and keys within the circle of fifths with brightness or height, on the one hand, and depth, darkness or death, on the other. In Schubert's early song *Der Taucher*, E major expresses heavenly light while in the low range of Cb major one finds an "infernal space." The words "todesschwangere Frieden" (death-prophesying peace) in *Fahrt zum Hades* (Journey to Hades) occur in Db minor. The vocal line in *Ganymed* ascends as the youth is carried on high; in *Nachthymne* the protagonist looks down from a great height, both in terms of pitch and of the circle of fifths, when B major is reached.

Schubert could, if he chose, exploit high and low sonorities, keys, and major and minor modes contrary to the above-mentioned conventions, as he does repeatedly in *Winterreise*, where departures from the norm generate powerful effects. *Letzte Hoffnung* (Last Hope), No. 16, is in Eb major, but the tonic chord is withheld and therefore all the more poignantly emphasized when the character reveals that he falls to the ground in order to "weep on the grave of my hopes." In *Mut*, No. 22, one hears the words "merrily into the world" at first in G major, but then, like a slip of the tongue, in G minor as if to reveal, unintentionally, the wanderer's true feelings. Many a Schubert song presents death as a redeeming Savior, the result being a negation of the conventional association of death and the minor mode. The word "darkness," in *Die Nebensonnen*, from the line "in darkness I shall feel better," is lit up by an arresting C♯ major chord. In *Nachthymne*, words that express yearning for death are in major, and yet this seemingly positive expression is denied by the *Totentanz* rhythm and the pianissimo dynamic marking.

Cadences, which allow for the release of melodic and harmonic tension, are perhaps the most self-evident component of tonal music, and consequently, Schubert inserts them strategically to punctuate the musico-dramatic content of his songs. A tonic chord in *Erlkönig* abruptly terminates (mm. 129–31) a chromatic passage that earlier flowed unimpeded into other keys (mm. 77ff., mm. 102ff.). This sudden end marks the death of the child well before the narrator can utter the decisive word "tot"

(m. 147). The co-creating listener thus gains prescience. Similarly, the tension of dominant chords in *Letzte Hoffnung* generates unrealistic hope that a leaf will not fall: later the falling fifth (dominant to minor tonic, m. 20) signals falling leaves and the cessation of hope. In *Ellens Gesang III* (D839) an unresolved dominant harmony lends the entreaties of the girl, "Oh mother, hear a pleading child," unusual intensity. Not before the invocation "Ave Maria" is a resolution reached to announce, through harmonic stability, the security she longs for. Indeed, Schubert can be quite economical with this simple device to express peace or death. In *Des Baches Wiegenlied* (*Die schöne Müllerin*, No. 20), the resolution of the leading tone D♯ to E is delayed to occur only once, at the very end of the vocal line (m. 20). *Der Tod und das Mädchen* shows Schubert tellingly avoiding the leading tone in the stanza sung by Death. *Nachthymne* ends with a plagal instead of the usual authentic cadence with leading tone; and in *Auflösung* a dominant seventh moves irregularly, not downwards but upwards as if to imply that the gravitational pull of such a sonority is negated – a fitting way to satisfy the song's title: Release. At the end of *Ständchen* the singer remains on the third of a chord as if questioning, although the piano postlude appears to promise a happy ending in the major mode. In *Du bist die Ruh* and in *Frühlingssehnsucht* (*Schwanengesang*, No. 3) the voice ends on the fifth of a chord. This note, in both cases, is initially the root of the dominant harmony, and thus a sign of incompletion, of anticipation – according to the poem – of hope. Transformed in the following measure into the fifth of the major (tonic chord), tension and any lingering doubt happily are released. This felicitous ending is not to be had following the last open fifth (between bass and voice) at the end of *Winterreise* in the song *Der Leiermann*: it closes on a minor chord.

Schubert's harmonic audaciousness was not lost on his contemporaries, a point perhaps in need of being emphasized given that today's listeners likely have been habituated to associate such boldness to too large a degree with the later nineteenth and much of the twentieth century (Liszt, Wagner, Mahler, Strauss, Schoenberg, and others). The critic for the *Allgemeine musikalische Zeitung*, in 1827, focusing on the first two Lieder of the composer's Op. 59 – *Du liebst mich nicht* and *Dass sie hier gewesen* – observed:

> Herr Schubert is far-fetched and artificial to an excessive degree – not in melody, but in harmony. In particular he modulates so oddly and so unexpectedly to the most remote regions as no composer on earth has done, at any rate in songs and other small vocal pieces . . . But equally true is the fact that . . . he does not seek in vain, that he really conjures up something, which, if performed with complete assurance and ease, truly speaks, and communicates something substantial, to the imagination and sensibility. Let us therefore try ourselves on them, and them on us![8]

In many of his songs, Schubert handles not only harmony in unexpected ways, but also form, a point that can only be appreciated if one understands what constitutes the norm. During his day, the word "Lied" invariably implied a strophic song in which deliberate simplicity – both textual and musical – guaranteed tuneful primacy. In support of this, the text's regular meter is matched by the music's symmetrical form, almost always major-key harmonies, and, if accompanied at all, is done so with a minimum of fuss. "As unmusical as possible" is how the Swiss composer, critic, and music publisher Hans Georg Nägeli, in 1826, described such a song, an opinion still held by many today.[9] Goethe nonetheless cherished this approach to song composition and not out of narrow-mindedness or because he was unmusical – as sometimes is still ingenuously suggested – but rather because he fully appreciated the inherently musical qualities of poetry. Accordingly, music's purpose is but to flesh out the sovereignty of a poet's words. Such a text-dominated sensibility, along with the performance tradition of these only apparently simple Lieder, would appear to be largely forgotten and poorly comprehended today.[10] Schubert himself demonstrated not only an understanding but also an appreciation of such Lieder throughout his career.

His celebrated 1815 *Heidenröslein* neatly corresponds, if not entirely, to the simple-strophic plan. Unlike Brahms's easy-going setting, Schubert's emphasizes the unusual word "morgenschön" (beautiful as the morning) by means of an unexpected note in the melody (c♯ instead of the expected c♮). Other, longer, descriptive or dramatic texts were in Schubert's day often not set strophically, but through-composed. Inspired in part by opera, composers freely mixed different styles, alternating recitative or arioso with song-like passages. The keyboard parts in these lengthier compositions also were more varied: besides clear-cut chordal accompaniments, there were passages of tone painting and virtuoso display. Reflecting this generic freedom, such works might be labeled *Gesänge, Balladen,* or *Kantaten* rather than Lieder. Schubert's *Erlkönig*, in fact, was called a cantata in a review in 1826.[11] According to his friend Josef von Spaun, as a youth Schubert would indulge himself for days in the dramatic ballads of Zumsteeg.[12] Presumably, he was fascinated not only by Zumsteeg's expressive music but also by the exciting and often sinister, blood-soaked texts to which the composer was drawn. Friedrich Schiller, a friend of Zumsteeg, was the author of many of these sensational ballads; a one-time medical student, Schiller perhaps was too deeply intrigued by dissections – or so some literary critics have speculated.[13] Moreover, Schubert was stirred by the operas of his day; one of his favorites was Luigi Cherubini's gloomy *Médée* (1797). It therefore is not surprising that some of Schubert's early works bear titles like *Leichenfantasie* (Corpse Fantasy), *Thekla, eine Geisterstimme* (Thekla, the Voice of a Ghost),

Der Vatermörder (Father's Murderer), *Totengräberlied* (The Grave-Diggers' Song), *Der Geistertanz* (Ghosts' Dance, D15, D15A, and D116), and *Die Schatten* (The Shadows).

Many of Schubert's early works respect the traditional distinction separating lengthy, dramatic *Gesänge* from short, lyrical songs. When exceptions occur, they almost always point toward the desire for bold effects. Later he experimented with numerous hybrids of both kinds of songs until around 1816 when he created a synthesis that combined the uniformity of strophic songs with the expressiveness of ballads. It is worth noting that while almost always admired now, Schubert's achievement disturbed critics of his day, some of whom were put off by the lack of generic tidiness. Thus in 1824, a critic for the AmZ, reviewing this time the four songs published as Op. 23 – *Die Liebe hat gelogen, Selige Welt, Schwanengesang,* and *Schatzgräbers Begehr –* wrote that Schubert "does not write songs, properly speaking, and has no wish to do so ... but free vocal pieces, some so free that they might possibly be called caprices or fantasies." Although he "invariably succeeds in mapping out the whole and each detail in accordance with the poetic idea," in "the execution he frequently is less successful, seeking to make up for the want of inner unity, order and regularity by eccentricities and wild goings-on which are hardly or not at all justified."[14]

The inclusion of recitative passages in some of Schubert's early songs doubtless may be traced not only to Zumsteeg but also, in one instance, perhaps to Mozart – his *Die ihr des unermesslichen Weltalls Schöpfer ehrt,* K619 – and Beethoven, at the start of his *Seufzer eines Ungeliebten,* WoO 118.[15] The traditional use of recitative generally signals the arrival of a new situation or of comparatively stronger emotions and, as such, makes possible a contrast in affect. Many such recitative passages alternate with arioso moments of reflection. Even Schubert, to begin with, used them this way, as may be observed in *Hagars Klage,* his first preserved song from 1811, but also as late as 1817, in the Ossian-setting of *Die Nacht.* Already in the fall of 1815 with *Erlkönig,* Schubert used the traditional recitative in a new way in order to gain a singular result. At the end of this Lied, it seems, the storyteller's voice fails as if moved by the tragic situation, a strategy that draws in and actively involves the listener in the moment of dramatic climax. Vivid expression is communicated by other means, too. In a song such as Schubert's *Am Meer* (*Schwanengesang,* No. 12), one hears the piano tremolo – a device surely copied from orchestral music – which allows the composer to comment on the demonic love at the heart of Heine's poem. Tremolos again are encountered in the many settings Schubert made of Goethe's *Nur wer die Sehnsucht kennt* at the words "Es schwindelt mir, es brennt mein Eingeweide" (I am dizzy, my innermost organs burn). Felicitous although such word painting now seems, Goethe would not have approved.

He criticized even Beethoven, whom he otherwise admired, for a setting because its operatic style did not suit Mignon's character.[16] In Schubert's later Lieder, recitative-like elements almost imperceptibly fuse with the lyrical, and despite the unmistakable contrast that ensues a high degree of uniformity is achieved. In the Mignon song *Heiß mich nicht reden* (D877, No. 2) the declamation is free with recitative-like inflection at the words "allein ein Schwur drückt mir die Lippen zu" (but an oath seals my lips); nevertheless, the preceding pavan rhythm, a symbol of inevitability, remains perceptible: despite her emotional outburst, Mignon is bound to her fate. Likewise, the recitative style emerges at the words "es schrien die Raben vom Dach" (the ravens shrieked from the roof) in *Frühlingstraum* (*Winterreise*, No. 11), even if, at the same time, it recalls the dotted rhythm of "merry bird calls" heard at the song's start. A declamatory recitative dominates throughout the Heine songs *Die Stadt* and *Der Doppelgänger* (*Schwanengesang*, Nos. 11 and 13). *Ihr Bild* shows a recitative-like melody with an accompaniment reduced to the barest minimum, at the time a completely new idea, and one that decisively influenced Hugo Wolf.[17]

Schubert is justly famous for his sudden major–minor changes, the juxtaposition of chords a third apart, and chromaticism. Many of the harmonies in his Lieder are so strongly wrought that they would find themselves completely at home within the realm of opera. In the songs, their effect is perhaps even more striking, since Schubert frequently relies on forceful harmonies in the context of Lieder cast according to varied strophic design. Whoever actively listens to *So laßt mich scheinen,* (D877, No. 3), another Goethe Mignon song, will be overwhelmed by the sudden shift in m. 38 from F♯ major to D minor at the word "Schmerz" (pain), because what is expected is the surprise of D major, heard in the second stanza (m. 18). Just as gripping is the often-cited switch from D major to B♭ major at the words *gegen Wind und Wetter* (mm. 51–55) in *Mut (Winterreise*, No. 22): the latter key is quite unexpected, since, at the words "against wind and weather," the listener anticipates D major or G major. At the phrase "even if my heart is split," in *Fülle der Liebe*, a wrenching from A♭ major to E minor (actually F♭ minor) takes place precisely at the word "zerspalten" (split). In this case, nothing has prepared the listener for such an unusual conjunction of harmonies.

Even more shocking for listeners during Schubert's day would have been the shifts between chords a half step apart. Such chromatic sideslipping appears already in his longer, earliest songs, as if Schiller's Sturm und Drang texts had provoked the composer to the edge of a harmonic precipice. In other words, Schiller's dramatic style might well be recognized as an influence on the development of Schubert's song, as was Goethe's poetry. (The numbers alone are compelling: after Schubert's seventy-four Goethe settings, his friend Mayrhofer follows with forty-seven, and Schiller next with forty-four.) Already in the previously mentioned *Leichenfantasie* Schubert risked highly irregular chromatic progressions and deliberately so, because the text reads "königlich wider die Zügel sich bäumen" (royally rearing up against the reins). Comparable is the connection between two chords in second inversion, F major and F♯ minor, in *Der Kampf* (The Struggle), a setting of another Schiller poem, at the words "und laß mich sündigen" (and let me sin). *Gruppe aus dem Tartarus* (D583) might reasonably be considered a study in chromaticism. Climaxing in a portrayal of the eternal torment of the damned, the poem reads in translation: "eternity circles above them, breaks in two the scythe of Saturn" (the guardian of time). The splintering of the scythe is depicted by a harmonic rupture midway through the strophe: it begins in C major but ends in D♭ major; at the word "bricht" (breaks) the two keys seem to collide. In the repeat, the vocal line doubles at the octave the conventional bass notes of a cadence in the piano: an ascending fourth followed by a falling fifth. Every listener in Schubert's time would have expected the pitches g♯/c♯ after the initial c♯/f♯. However, Schubert's cadence moves from c♯ to c♮. In the *Petrarca-Sonett*, G♭ major is abruptly confronted by G minor at the moment the poetic self discovers it will never escape the god of love. A tone in common, namely B♭, is initially the third of G♭ major but then suddenly of G minor. Thus, the foundation beneath the melodic line shifts, thereby powerfully suggesting that those chased by the deity will find the very ground snatched from beneath them. *In der Ferne* (*Schwanengesang*, No. 6) includes a jerking downwards from B minor to B♭ major in the middle of a musical phrase (mm. 17–18), at the words "Mutterhaus hassenden" (hating the mother's home), a provocation in the view of the AmZ critic, who went so far as to voice the fear that musical anarchy was but around the corner.[18] While Schubert clearly engages with and otherwise acknowledges his relationship to the traditions of German song in many other ways, in these and other bold uses of harmony he seems indebted to no one.

The composer's later songs reveal, as Paul Mies pointed out three quarters of a century ago, a tendency toward formal simplification.[19] But in rhythm, melody, texture, and harmony, as has been seen, Schubert's Lieder oftentimes are anything but simple. Thus a conflict arises between the sophistication otherwise apparent in terms of musical content and simplicity of form, one that accounts for many a strong effect.[20] Truly simple strophic songs, earlier the standard, with easily sung vocal lines, straightforward major harmonies, rhythms, and forms, are but one of many possibilities in the late works. In an otherwise complex context, simplicity can take on special meaning. In *Winterreise*, where songs are formally very different and musically multi-layered, simple stanzas sometimes symbolize tranquillity that eventually will be shown to be false. Thus Schubert's music is at odds with the words "But I have done nothing, that I should shy away from people," in *Wegweiser* (The Signpost, No. 20). The unassuming vocal line, supported by the keyboard's consoling and folk-like parallel thirds and sixths and the timeworn half cadence (mm. 25 and 39), holds out the promise of hope, yet it is cruelly crushed. Other moments of apparent solace similarly reveal themselves to be deceptive, as in the preceding No. 19, *Täuschung*, where "ein Licht tanzt freundlich vor mir her" (a light dances welcomingly before me) proves, as the title has already given away, an illusion, just as does the dream of spring in No. 11, *Frühlingstraum*, in the midst of winter. *Totengräber-Weise* (Grave-Digger's Air) illustrates how the strophic form is not always disclosed at the outset but rather emerges gradually after a complicated start. Simplicity, no longer something to be taken for granted, ensues only with effort and sometimes struggle and so takes on added meaning, symbolizing the end of conflict in the release of death.

Heine's poem "Der Doppelgänger" tells of a man standing before a house where his beloved once lived and which she left "long ago." The compositional process of Schubert's Lied recalls the "long ago" quite literally given that it harks back to the seventeenth-century chaconne with its ever-repeating bass progression of four bars, triple meter, and minor mode. Such a combination also appears at the words "Agnus Dei" in the E♭ Major Mass (D950). In the event, years earlier Heinrich Ignaz Franz von Biber (1644–1704) had used this very ostinato in masses.[21] A strange song by just about any criteria, it owes its expressive power in part to the way in which the "long ago" continues to haunt the protagonist. The vocal line's fractured and faltering character marvelously matches his disquieting turn of mind, an uneasiness at first difficult to pinpoint precisely. Yet the frequently stated F♯s, while they initially put one in mind of old-fashioned psalmody, grow increasingly ominous, for the note moves throughout the Lied almost like a modern-day stalker. Not only does the vocal line appear fixated by the F♯s, but the piano part is equally obsessed – the harmonies it provides, while richly varied, almost always contain the note. At the same time, the singer's phrases are oddly out of kilter with the piano's insistent, regular rhythms: only when the protagonist recognizes that the ghostly double named in the song's title is his own image (mm. 39–41) can the 3/4 meter in turn be recognized in the vocal line.[22] When this happens at the word "Gestalt," it has been claimed that Schubert struck as many keys on the piano as he could reach with his hands before releasing all but the pitches notated in the score: these he held into the next measure (m. 42).[23] As if such terror is empowered to rend asunder everything it touches, the chaconne is interrupted. But, without abandoning the central pitch of F♯, as frequently is the case with Schubert when he wishes to depict terror, a chromatic ascent begins in the accompaniment and thereafter cadences on D♯ minor (m. 47). The tonality was recognized by theorists of the day for its ability to suggest "the affect of anxiety, of the deepest mental distress, of brooding despair, of the blackest melancholy, and of the most sinister condition of the soul."[24] When the chaconne returns at last (mm. 56–59), it is significantly altered: the fourth pitch is now C (instead of C♯), so that the sadness of the "Neapolitan" (the chromatically altered supertonic chord) is enlisted to communicate mourning. The final cadence is heard in its plagal form, yet another antique touch that signals the forlorn character is not to be liberated from the prison of his past.

Schubert wrote music about music as an act of artistic citation in many of his late Lieder. In so doing, the achievement is not unlike some of the slow movements of Beethoven's last string quartets, the beauty of which is manifest precisely because of the bizarre, often harsh movements surrounding them. Also, in the late works of Liszt simplicity similarly is used, especially to place revision of his own early works in a new light.[25] Mahler, too, shows the lyrically simple transformed into something very special, a point abundantly evident in his Ninth Symphony.[26]

Despite the fact that many of Schubert's songs are now almost two hundred years old, few have lost their ability to move us, no matter how difficult many undeniably still are. In truth, the apparent peculiarity of some of the Lieder surely stems from the fact that we no longer understand what their poems address. That which nowadays sounds tamely simple may have struck listeners in Schubert's day as wildly revolutionary. Also, the large forms typical of Sturm und Drang poetry, while they likely will seem exaggerated to today's readers, encouraged the Viennese public of the 1820s – the aristocracy and middle class alike – not only to experience strong passions but to act accordingly, even if this meant flouting social mores. Many songs take issue with the Restoration politics of Metternich. Schubert's friend the poet and patriot Johann Chrysostomus Senn wrote in his memoirs that the struggles for freedom against Napoleon during the years 1813–15 "left behind in Austria a significant intellectual uplifting," and that it brought together "a splendid social circle of young literati, poets, artists and well-educated persons . . . Within this circle, Franz Schubert composed his songs."[27] Because he was suspected by the authorities, Senn's residence was searched in March 1820 and four friends there, including Schubert, hurled "opprobrious language" at the intruding officer. Senn was arrested and banned from Vienna; Schubert was "summoned and severely reprimanded."[28] That Schubert not only set Senn's poems "Selige Welt" and "Schwanengesang" (D744, not to be confused with the posthumously published fourteen songs popularly known as *Schwanengesang*, D957, settings of poems by Rellstab, Heine, and Seidl), but also published them – as Op. 23 together with Platen's "Die Liebe hat gelogen" and Schober's "Schatzgräbers Begehr" – demonstrates solidarity with his friend.[29] Because the Metternich administration viewed every intellectual activity with suspicion, even Lieder were subjected to stringent censorship.[30] Schubert's friend Johann Mayrhofer, who was forced to earn his living as a censor, and who because of this pressure later committed suicide, disguised many of his poems' topical references beneath the guise of antiquity. *Heliopolis I* (D753) depicts "the city of the sun," a place full of hope, whereas *Heliopolis II* (D754) exhorts "let your arms embrace the world. Dare to remain devoted only to the great and the worthy." Self-assured resistance to authority is sounded in *Der zürnenden Diana* (To the Angry Diana), a topic also alluded to in *Prometheus* (Goethe). *Orest auf Tauris* treats the subjects of exile in conjunction with the yearning for deliverance.[31] The enthusiasm for the ancient world was shared by Schubert's friend the singer Vogl, whom the composer dubbed "der griechische Vogel" (the Greek bird),[32] and by the poet of *Die Schöne Müllerin* and *Winterreise*, the "Griechenmüller" (Greek miller) – Wilhelm Müller, who enthusiastically supported the ongoing struggle for freedom in Greece.

Social criticism of a similar sort is disclosed by medieval themes celebrating an idealized past where art is prized, as in *Der Sänger*, set to a poem by Goethe, and by songs of great deeds and ancient heroes such as the "Ossian" songs.[33] All of these Lieder show a sense of life that Schubert missed: in his own poem "Klage an das Volk" he viewed the social climate of his day as one that impeded a person attaining greatness.[34] The same message is to be discerned in the lyric dramatization of art as redeemer in *An die Musik*. Following the first line, which has been given above, the text goes on to reveal (in translation), "when life's wild tumult wraps me round, have you [art] kindled my heart to loving warmth, and transported me to a better world." Thus Schubert described his own condition in July 1824 in a letter to his brother Ferdinand as "that fateful recognition of a miserable reality, which thanks to my own imagination (God be praised), I attempt as much as possible to make more attractive."[35] Shortly thereafter, on 14 August 1824, his brother Ignaz wrote him: "The newest here is a rash of suicides, quite as if people knew for sure that upon arriving over there, they would be able to jump straightaway into heaven."[36] Alas, in many a Schubert Lied, death is the only escape. Unlike the poem on which it is modeled, Claudius's "Der Tod und das Mädchen" (Death and the Maiden), set by Schubert as D531 and where death is something to be dreaded, the setting of Spaun's "Der Jüngling und der Tod" (The Youth and Death), D545, tells of one that is longed for. (The two songs are separated by only one month: the first was composed in February 1817, the second in March.) Prompted by the Restoration, this essentially *Weltschmerz* point of view shows how much things have changed from the sunny optimism that had characterized so much of the Enlightenment. In many ways related to this is the fact that the protagonists in most of the composer's numerous *Wanderlieder* are home-less. The most famous, after the piteous wayfarer of *Winterreise*, must be *Der Wanderer* (D489), a setting of a poem by the otherwise little-known Georg Philipp Schmidt von Lübeck, given the heartrending revelation that even though the protagonist hears the speech of other men he still feels as if he is "a stranger everywhere." Likewise, Friedrich von Schlegel's poem "Der Wanderer" (D649) treats a wayfarer who is alone and homeless, and perceives the world as good only in darkness.

The saber-rattling in Körner's "Schwertlied" (Song of the Sword) and Klopstock's "Vaterlandslied" today are no longer very palatable – Schubert made more of Körner's love poems.[37] Yet texts such as these did not always connote the chauvinistic and militaristic sentiments we find in them to-day. Klopstock and Körner were in no way reactionaries. Klopstock had embraced the French Revolution enthusiastically; and the patriotism and nationalism that animated Körner's poetry were at that time equivalent to political self-determination – freedom from foreign domination as well as local absolutism. Not surprisingly, either too much or too little love for one's country could prompt misgivings in Metternich's reactionary regime.

As a student, Schubert presumably received guidance toward his later choice of Lieder texts: besides Latin and Greek classics, he came into contact with the poetry of the Enlightenment and Empfindsamkeit, in-cluding many works by Schiller and Goethe. Later, his circle of friends helped to shape his literary interests. Two groups, the so-called "Linzer" or "Oberösterreichischer Kreis" (Upper Austrian group) and the "Wiener Kreis" (Vienna Group), thanks to their concern for social and educational problems and their influence on Schubert, have become the focus of mu-sicological research.[38] Under the sway of the ancients but also of Herder, Goethe, and Schiller, the Upper Austrian group of friends debated the ben-eficial influence of art and the ways in which it might incite greater pro-ductivity and human happiness. The political Restoration following the Congress of Vienna in 1815 dampened much of this idealism, and so it is no coincidence that for a time Schubert belonged to Vienna's "Unsinns-gesellschaft" (Nonsense Society), where much sentimental and idealistic poetry was parodied.[39] Inspired by his Viennese friends, Schubert turned to contemporary Romantic poetry. Whether from the various groups he frequented or through his many individual friendships, the lively exchange that clearly ensued stimulated him to expand upon his choices in texts and thereby sharpen his tastes. To this, there also is the composer's own in-nate literary sensibilities, which, despite the old but inaccurate cliché that he would set willy-nilly any poem that came into his hands, reveal a num-ber of shared traits despite the many and different subjects, some unique to him, others the result of living at the time he did. Establishing absolutes clearly is foolhardy in a composer as prolific as Schubert, yet recurring topics nonetheless are to be observed: social and artistic freedom, the joys of friendship, an absorption with nature, earthy delight in life, a fascination with death, a sympathetic bonding with social outcasts and misfits, love in all of its multifarious permutations. But even when initially attracted to the subject of a poem, he rejected it if it did not seem musically suitable. Only a portion of what he composed was released for publication after performance and discussion within his circle of intimates.

Schubert's influence on later composers is impossible to ignore. Liszt surely was not alone in admiring the older composer's "ability," as he put it, "to dramatize to the greatest degree his lyrical inspirations."[40] The poetical piano introductions and conclusions that Schumann composed for many of his songs seem not too far removed from what Schubert fashioned for his *Der Lindenbaum* (*Winterreise*, No. 5) or *Die junge Nonne*. Moreover, Schubert's characteristic scenarios re-echo in the bell sounds and waltzes of Schumann's *Dichterliebe*. Brahms's raindrops in *Regenlied* and *Abendregen* fall in a way very similar to the leaves in Schubert's *Letzte Hoffnung*, the sixteenth song of *Winterreise*. The bird in Brahms's *Auf dem Schiffe* flies much as does *Die Krähe* in *Winterreise*, No. 15. The rhythm of Brahms's *Es liebt sich so lieblich im Lenze* is adjusted to the changing moods of the female protagonist in ways that recall many a Schubert Lied. Veiled chords in Liszt's *Blume und Duft* remind us of Schubert's *Daß sie hier gewesen* just as the beginning of the *Faust Symphony* suggests the start of Schubert's *Szene aus Faust*. The tone repetition in Wolf's setting of the Michelangelo poem "Alles endet, was entstehet" symbolizes death much as in *Die liebe Farbe*, the sixteenth song from *Schöne Müllerin*, or *Der Wegweiser* from *Winterreise*. Moreover, Wolf's recitative-like shaping of melody and his modulations could be rooted, at least in large part, in Schubert's earlier experiments. Whoever knows Schubert's songs will find them reverberating again in almost every Lied of these and other composers from the nineteenth century. But that Schubert directly influenced a specific composition can reasonably be claimed only where an unequivocal quotation is uncovered. In his *Herbstgefühl*, Op. 48, No. 7, Brahms refers to the concluding pitches of Schubert's *Doppelgänger*, and in his canon *Einförmig ist der Liebe Gram*, Op. 113, No. 13, harks back to the hurdy-gurdy man of the last song of *Winterreise*. That we hear so much of Schubert in later songs – even though, for example, Wolf undoubtedly learned as much from Schumann or Wagner – is probably because, of all the songs composed in the nineteenth century, we know Schubert's best. The Lieder of his contemporaries, like Lachner or Randhartinger, or somewhat older composers like Krufft, only now are beginning to interest performers; presumably because of their comparatively greater length, the ballads of Reichardt and Loewe have yet to return to fashion. One need not restrict this scenario to the longer songs of these composers. The same could be said for countless later composers, among them some discussed or otherwise mentioned in the pages of this book, such as Cornelius, Franz, and Kirchner.

Only when we know the Lieder of these and other composers better will we be able to judge what was common in Schubert's day as well as what he alone could have written in just his own way. But we should not limit ourselves to the repertory of song in searching for influences upon Schubert and those who came after him. Schubert gained stimulation from all genres: from Mozart's D minor Fantasia, K397, quoted in the *Leichenfantasie,* Beethoven's keyboard tremolos mentioned above, the harmonic language of Cherubini's operas, and more. Not only did Schubert develop something new by exploring the unusual in music that has come down to us as important and worth knowing. Just as significantly, what he and other composers of his day thought was new and from whence it came are questions as yet far from answered.

Translated by Sven Hansell, revised by the editor

5 The early nineteenth-century song cycle

RUTH O. BINGHAM

Origins and forerunners of song cycles probably cannot be determined with any finality. Cycles and circles predate history and continue to permeate our lives in an unbroken tradition: seasonal rites and holidays, gathering around a fire, round table discussions, circular dances, ecological circles of life, wedding rings, halos . . . Even within our comparatively brief musical history, examples of cyclic forms abound, from cyclic Masses and madrigal cycles to cyclic symphonies and record albums.[1] Song cycles are yet another example in an ancient history of cyclic art forms mirroring patterns in our lives. As the nineteenth century approached, however, cyclic forms in all the arts acquired greater significance, blossoming primarily in Germany after the turn of the century into the quintessentially Romantic song cycle, markedly different in style and structure from earlier cycles. Why Germany, why the nineteenth century, and why the Romantic song cycle require explanation: they were not mere coincidence.

Around the turn of the nineteenth century, primary sponsorship for composers began to shift from aristocratic classes to ambitious upper middle classes, who displayed their acquisition of culture in their piano parlors, creating an almost insatiable market for songs.[2] Songs that combined bourgeois pleasures with at least the appearance of high art were in particular demand. As the market grew, so of course did the need for composers to distinguish their songs from the rest, prompting ever more fanciful titles. Terms now associated with song cycles arose haphazardly out of vague associations, intentions, and meanings: whimsical titles such as *Liederkreis* (Lied-circle), *Blumenkranz* (Flower-wreath), *Liederroman* (Lied-novel), or *Liedercyklus* (Lied-cycle) sometimes indicated something new in the music, but sometimes did not, and a fair number of cycles held no characterizing title at all.[3] Distinguishing between collections and cycles remains enigmatic, owing in large part to an almost complete absence of studies on the history and principles of song collections. In the early years of the century, any generic contract, or generally accepted set of expectations, for song cycles was at most a play of connotations or ambiguous understanding; later composers and writers did not alter a contract so much as they created one to suit their historical perspective.[4]

The appearance of the Romantic song cycle coincided precisely with a crucial aesthetic shift, the first cycles appearing in the 1790s and the mature genre established by 1840. Although Classical and Romantic traits mingled throughout the eighteenth and nineteenth centuries, nineteenth-century Romanticism turned from linear logic, balance, and resolution to emphasize mystical circles, conundrums, the stretching and crossing of boundaries, and sublimely inexpressible extremes.[5] As aesthetics shifted, the song cycle offered appealing anomalies: dramatic lyricism, miniatures in an infinite whole, open-ended closed pieces, unity in variety, circular forms, and inexplicit meanings. Not surprisingly, where and when the song cycle flourished reflected the where and when of Romantic aesthetics: that is to say, in the latter half of the eighteenth century among the English poets and only much later in France and Italy, where neo-classicism remained strong. Poets and composers in Germany embraced Romantic aesthetics with special passion: romanticized nature aptly described their darker ultramontane world; medieval, mystical, and supernatural topics resonated with German folk culture; and the cragginess of Romantic aesthetics gave credence to a people who often suffered from feeling second best to the culturally powerful Italian and French models.

During the eighteenth century, German countries and especially those further north developed a strong tradition of song self-consciously distinct from French, Italian, or English: the Lied was not just in the German language but connected to German culture through its artfully folk-like (*volkstümlich*) ideal and was promoted as a symbol of nationalist sentiment, evidence of a shared culture. The Lied's folk-like ideal accorded poetry unchallenged primacy: music was to support the words, to provide correct scansion and mood without getting in the way. Cycles composed in the Lied tradition almost exclusively were poetic cycles accompanied by music, and the simplicity of their keyboard accompaniments reflected music's subsidiary role. As aesthetics shifted, however, music gained stature as the most Romantic, i.e., least concrete or explicit, of arts and began to rival poetry's dominance in songs: the folk-like ideal slowly yielded to one of parity between music and words, allowing settings and their accompaniments to become increasingly complex. Music began to provide competing structures that altered both individual poems and relationships between poems. The songs of Schubert, with their compelling accompaniments, were a revelation.[6] These two ideals – folk-like settings or a parity between words and music – actually coexisted for almost fifty years, even though later historians chose to focus on parity.

The poets themselves contributed to a shift toward parity, experimenting with mixing lyric, epic, and dramatic elements, and writing poetic cycles and novels infused with lyric episodes.[7] Friedrich Schlegel, for example, found the Romantic novel, which he defined as a type of poetry, especially well adapted to the mixing of genres:

All classical poetic arts are now laughable in their strict purity . . . [The] novel is entirely poetic poesy . . . [The] novel [is] an enduringly useful genre for us . . .

[The] character of the novel 1) A mix of the dramatic, epic, lyric 2) Opposition to the didactic 3) Return to mythology and even to classical mythology.[8]

At the same time, Goethe, Germany's cultural colossus, transformed German into a wellspring of lyric expression, creating a language that Germans everywhere could point to with pride.[9] Although Goethe himself preferred folk-like settings that did not impinge upon his poetry, he and his contemporaries inspired composers to convey more than just the surface meaning of words, thereby moving beyond the traditional boundaries between words, music, and meaning. Composers turned from providing background support to incorporating the poetry's drama into their settings, and music began to assume the role of expressing the inexplicit symbolism so important to Romantic poetry.

Vocal melody remained tied to the poetry, but piano accompaniments allowed composers freer rein and reflected most clearly changes in music's stature. Beginning in spurts and starts during the last quarter of the eighteenth century, accompaniments became ever more complex and harmonically rich, spurring heated debates about Lied aesthetics and what constituted *volkstümlich*. The Lied's primary aesthetic goal remained unchanged: to support the poetry and to convey its inexpressible emotions. Increasingly, however, the responsibility of conveying those emotions shifted to the harmony, long a strength of German music but of particular importance to German Romanticism. As accompaniments became more prominent, the music – that most Romantic of Romantic arts – began to challenge poetry's hegemony.

Significantly, German music theories of the time often espoused organicism, a theory derived from the sciences that described the relationship between whole and constituent parts, and that inclined composers toward trying to cohere individual songs into a unified whole.[10] However much organicist thought may have contributed to nationalist sentiments, it would probably be going too far to suggest that the song cycle offered Germany a cultural symbol, that of a revolutionary art crossing traditional boundaries by tying together disparate entities that shared an underlying unity.

These changes between 1790 and 1840 – an expanding song market, the ascendance of Romantic aesthetics, the identification of the Lied with German nationalism, the emergence of music as the most Romantic of arts, the shift to an ideal of parity between words and music, an emphasis on symbolism, a preference for cyclic forms and structural anomalies, the privileging of harmonic structures, and the influence of organicism – created a climate ripe for song cycles. Early cycles, that is those from c. 1790 to 1830, tended to focus on relating the parts to the whole and on achieving "unity and diversity" (*Einheit und Vielfältigkeit*); later cycles, from after the 1830s, tended to focus on the work as a whole, its harmonic process and formal coherence. Through it all, there was a trend away from conveying the poetry through vocal melody to interpreting the poetry through harmony and musical structure. No surprise then that Beethoven's only contribution to song cycles, his setting of *An die ferne Geliebte* (Op. 98, 1816), was not only built upon an unusually strong harmonic structure, but was also the most acclaimed by late nineteenth-century writers, who admired its unity and organic structure. Once the song cycle was defined as a tonally unified structure, competing models disappeared into the past.

Definitions and categories

Defining song cycle as a distinct genre has long been a sticking point for research: for each of a wide variety of distinguishing characteristics there seems to be an exception in the literature, but without distinguishing characteristics, the definition sounds uncomfortably like a collection of songs. The only unqualified characteristics are multiplicity – three or more poems – and coherence – achieved through the poetry, the music, or the interaction between them. Inevitably, collections approach cycles, particularly if the collector possesses some skill. The definition dictates only that the songs cohere, not that they cohere to any particular degree, yielding an unbroken continuum where carefully arranged collections neighbor loosely constructed cycles. Focusing on how song cycles and collections were constructed and on the ways in which they created coherence proves to be a more productive line of inquiry.

In the first half of the nineteenth century, three types of cycles dominated: "topical cycles," or cycles based on poems connected by a theme; "external-plot cycles," or cycles of poems excerpted from a narrative context; and "internal-plot cycles," or those whose poetry entailed a narrative. A fourth type began with Beethoven and became typical in the latter half of the century: "musically constructed cycles," or those whose coherence relied equally, sometimes even primarily, on the music rather than on the poetry. Perhaps the most striking difference between earlier and later song cycles was the shift from poetry as primary to music as primary.

Topical cycles

Topical cycles followed the prevailing aesthetic of balanced unity and variety and in their structures reflected three conceptual shapes delineated in contemporary definitions of *circle* or *cycle*. The first shape, and perhaps most familiar to us, is the circumference of a circle, including topics such as the seasons or the calendar of months. These circular themes were very popular in the eighteenth century: note, for example, Vivaldi's *Four Seasons* of 1725, in which each season is preceded by a sonnet, or James Thomson's *The Seasons* published in 1730 and set most famously by Haydn in 1801 as an oratorio. As these themes were carried into the nineteenth century, their more circular aspects were emphasized, and four contrasting seasons often expanded into twelve months that ended with a return to winter, as in *Musikalischer Almanach* of 1796 by Reichardt and various poets, including Johann Heinrich Voss, Goethe, and Herder; *Zwölf Monate* (undated) by Johann Heinrich Karl Bornhardt and Ignaz Franz Castelli; and *Die Jahreszeiten* from c. 1820 by (Johann Christian) Friedrich Schneider and T. L. A. Heinroth. In these cycles, the poetry provided the primary coherence: music's role was to support the poetry, to portray its mood as simply as possible, to set it correctly according to rules of scansion, and to balance poetry's coherence with variety. Consequently, the music offers an unpatterned variety of keys, meters, and tempos as well as an array of different styles (lullabies, marches, Lieder, drinking songs, and so on). In general, there were no obvious motivic returns and some cycles even required a variety of forces, from solos and duos to full choirs. This type of topical cycle gradually declined in popularity, virtually disappearing by mid-century.

A second conceptual shape resembled a spoked wheel, in which each point of the circle was defined by its relationship to the central point, yielding a versatile form that provided both unity (to the central point) and variety (to the other points). Like the points of a circle, the number of possible poems or songs was infinite and the order unrestricted, especially appealing possibilities for early Romantics; not surprisingly, this became the most popular and influential type of cycle as Romanticism bloomed. One of the earliest of this type was *Die Farben*, published in Berlin in 1795 in a section of Karl Müchler's book of poetry, with songs composed by Friedrich Franz Hůrka and Friedrich Heinrich Himmel. Examples of cycles built in this shape abounded and almost every composer of Lieder published sets entitled *Blumensträuße* (Flower Bouquets), *Lieder der Liebe* (Lieder of Love), *Frühlingskränze* (Wreaths of Spring), *Wanderlieder* (Wandering Lieder), or something similar, the most popular topic at first being flowers, a particularly pliant and rich source of allegory and one that was deeply rooted in eighteenth-century culture.

By the 1810s, however, flower cycles were eclipsed by more Romantic topics such as wandering, love, and tragic death, vogues inspired in part by Theodor Körner's *Leyer und Schwert* (published posthumously, 1814) and especially by (Johann) Ludwig Uhland's *Frühlingslieder* and *Wanderlieder* (both 1815). Contemporaneous critics claimed Uhland's cycles marked a new stage in German lyric poetry, and composers flocked to set them or imitations of them. On the subject of Uhland's *Wanderlieder*, for example, Wilhelm Müller commented, "Justly so, we remember above all the outstanding *Wanderlieder*, which drew a long line of imitations along behind itself. Because now, hardly an almanac appears in which a pair of such 'Wanderlieder' are not given as a treat."[11] The settings which remained the most acclaimed for decades were those published in 1818 by Conradin Kreutzer, one of the most prominent Lied composers of the time. Like most topical cycles, Kreutzer's used no motivic returns, no structuring of keys, and no preludes or postludes to connect songs, but in context, the songs nevertheless gave the impression of a symbolic voyage through a variety of stages. The critics should have been aghast at Kreutzer's departures from traditional Lied aesthetics; instead, they hailed his works, claiming the text and music were so unified that they seemed to spring from the same mind, and used such words as *Kreis* or *Cyclus* to describe them.[12] Kreutzer's cycles confirmed that a new aesthetic was emerging; only nine years later, Schubert composed a similar cycle of wandering songs, a cycle that shared its title with one of the Uhland/Kreutzer songs: *Winterreise*.

Other influential cycles of this type included works by Traugott Maximilian Eberwein/Matthias Conradi, *Amor Proteus, oder Liebeserklärungen verschiedener Stände und Temperamente* (Protean Love, or Declarations of Love by Different Classes and Temperaments, Op. 13, 1810–11); Reichardt/ (various poets), *Lieder der Liebe und der Einsamkeit* (Lieder of Love and of Loneliness, 1798 and 1804); Christian Gottlob Neefe/Johann Gottfried von Herder, *Bilder und Träume* (Images and Dreams, 1798); Ferdinand Ries/(various), *Verschiedene Empfindungen an einem Platze* (Different Sensibilities in One Place); Carl Maria von Weber/Körner, *Leyer und Schwert* (Lyre and Sword, J174–77 1815); and several works by Heinrich August Marschner: *Sechs Wanderlieder* (with W. Marsano, Op. 35, 1820s), *Lieder der Liebe* (various, Op. 44, 1820s), two sets of *Bilder des Orients* (Heinrich Wilhelm August Stieglitz, Opp. 90 and 140, 1830s and 1840s), two sets of *Frühlingsliebe* (Friedrich Rückert, Opp. 106 and 113, before 1843), and *Liebeslieder* (August Heinrich Hoffmann von Fallersleben, Op. 155, c. 1850).

The third conceptual shape, a three-dimensional sprung circle or spiral that ends elsewhere than where it began, appeared only rarely in the first half of the century but proved to be a more compelling model that eventually merged with the musically constructed cycle. There was still a central point or idea, but the individual units were no longer random; internal progressions and relationships set a definite order with a beginning, middle, and end. The structure that emerged created a conceptual paradox: a circle that did not close. An early example of this type was Müchler's *Die Blumen und der Schmetterling* (The Flowers and the Butterfly), composed in 1808 by one of the foremost composers of early song cycles, Himmel. The cycle opened with "Zueignung an Deutschlands Töchter" (Dedication to Germany's Daughters); the next seven songs described individual flowers and apparently were written for a variety of singers; the ninth song, "Wechselgesang der Blumen" (Alternating Song of the Flowers), provided climax and close with reprised solos and choral verses, presumably performed by the "flower girls"; and the final song, "Der Schmetterling" (The Butterfly), commented on what came before, closing the performance by "flitting from bud to bud." As with virtually all topical cycles, the music provided simple but careful conveyance of the poetry and a wide variety of keys, meters, and tempi. Functional key relationships between songs was apparently not an issue: Songs 7, 8, and 9 and the reprises within Song 9 juxtaposed keys a tritone apart, a fact that disturbed neither composer nor critic.

One of the finest examples of this type, and a greatly underrated cycle, was Weber's setting of Friedrich Wilhelm Gubitz's *Die Temperamente bei dem Verluste der Geliebten* (The Temperaments upon the Loss of Loved Ones, J200–203, published 1817), a comic play on an older type of cycle and one in which Weber uses contrast as a unifying feature.

Reichardt and the Liederspiel

The next two types of cycles – external-plot and internal-plot cycles – derived less from eighteenth-century cycles than from early Romantic experiments in combining lyric and dramatic genres. One of the earliest of these and certainly the most publicized was the Liederspiel – literally, a drama including or consisting of Lieder. The first work so subtitled, the popular *Lieb' und Treue*, was composed by Reichardt and produced for Berlin's Royal Opera House in 1800. Reichardt promoted himself and his new genre in a well-known article in the Leipzig *Allgemeine musikalische Zeitung* of 1801.[13] According to Reichardt, the Liederspiel served two purposes: it restored the aesthetic ideal of simplicity in music, delivery, and staging, and it adapted French vaudeville to the German stage. His timing was impeccable: the Liederspiel rode both the receding wave of Francophile fashion and the advancing wave of German nationalism. Furthermore, Liederspiele offered a few hours of nostalgic escape back into simplicity in the midst of increasingly complex and unstable times, responding to a longing by both elite and bourgeoisie. The Liederspiel's initial success was ample proof that Reichardt struck a chord on cue; unfortunately, it was a chord that could not be sustained. The distinctive character of the Liederspiel hinged on that of the Lied, a stylized folk simplicity embodying German nationalist sentiment. Simplicity in the name of nostalgia can be refreshing, but it can also be boring: complexities and chromaticisms gradually encroached until the Liederspiel was indistinguishable from other, more established genres of musical theater, to which the Liederspiel eventually yielded.

When Reichardt published his Liederspiele, he brought out only the songs and not even all the verses of those, pointing out that because the Lieder (i.e., poems) were well known, reprinting all those verses was a costly waste of space. Instead, consumers should apply directly to him for the complete edition of music and to the publisher for the text of the play. Such incomplete publications were both financially expedient and common: all or some of the arias from an opera, of Lieder from a Liederspiel, of Gesänge from a Singspiel, and so on, were often published separately from the complete book.[14] Such publications were probably never intended as independent works, but as vehicles to disseminate music for popular consumption and as supplements to the play: amateur groups could then perform the entire work, supplying the material in between from another source, by composing, or simply through memory. Both text and music were simple, so that anyone with a general idea of the plot could whip up a performance with just the published melodies. In and of themselves, however, the songs from a Liederspiel did not constitute a dramatic or musical whole; without the intervening text, the songs related a jumbled and confusing tale. While the play could be read and even performed without the songs, the reverse was not coherent.

External-plot cycles

Liederspiel's awkward relationship between published songs and complete work pertained to a large number of early nineteenth-century works that have been virtually ignored: sets of songs excerpted from a narrative context, i.e., external-plot cycles. Titles such as *Gesänge aus Goethes "Faust," Zwölf Gesänge aus "Frithof's Sage," Sechs Lieder aus "Sintram und seine Gefährten," Gesänge aus "Wilhelm Meister,"* and so on, proliferated, referring consumers to the original source; contemporary reviews often cited the importance of the literary source for the cycle's maximum impact. These cycles helped reveal the dramatic possibilities in juxtaposed poems, but they also reflected the turbulent times and remain difficult to analyze. Their structures vary widely, from quasi-dramatic settings of every poem in the novel to a few lyric moments excerpted haphazardly. Their text–music relationships also run the gamut: some are independent works whose coherence relies on connections enhanced or created by the composer; others adhere closely to the original, relying on its coherence to reconcile disjunctions. In general, however, the weaker the literary connections, the stronger the musical ones, which relates back to the unity and diversity aesthetic: music does not mirror the text, but balances it. External-plot cycles present difficulties in performance as well, because not infrequently they require forces out of balance with their size – two soloists, a men's chorus, and a women's chorus, all for seven short Lieder, as in Schubert's Op. 52, for example – and they demand of the audience a homogeneous literary background quite rare today.

Even how these cycles were used remains unclear: perhaps the songs were enjoyed individually, as from a collection; perhaps the sets were companions to the novel, intended to be read and sung in alternation; perhaps they provided music for amateur performances of the drama; or perhaps they were cycles that relied on the audience's familiarity with the source for context and coherence. Relying on an audience's literary knowledge is always risky: the more complex and diverse the culture, the less assured the connection. Also, the coherence in such a presentation relies almost entirely on the audience's imagination; the music is only a catalyst. If either imagination or memory falters, coherence is lost. Not surprisingly, works chosen for such treatment were exceptionally well known, such as the most popular novels by Goethe, Sir Walter Scott, and Friedrich de la Motte-Fouqué.

Evaluation of these works depends largely on an intimate understanding of the original source because each work was primarily a response to that source and only secondarily a song cycle. As varied as external-plot cycles were, they nonetheless shared some characteristics. First, whether including all or only some of the songs from the original source, external-plot cycles were generally complete as published, in the sense that they were performable as a work, unlike Lieder from Liederspiele from which verses were sometimes omitted. Second, external-plot cycles usually exhibited a coherent linear order of some type, usually based on the original plot. Third, the primary coherence was literary, not musical: even in fairly independent cycles, musical connections were subsidiary to literary ones. Finally, readily evident disjunctions between songs were an integral part of these cycles, cuing audiences to recall the original.

External-plot cycles flourished in the first half of the century but then virtually disappeared in favor of internal-plot and musically constructed cycles. Nowhere is the fundamental disjunction between literary and musical structures more evident than in these works, and external-plot cycles were quickly eclipsed by cycles that conformed more readily to the ideals of unity and of organicism. Their popularity at the time, however, is understandable: they achieved the Romantic ideal of merging art forms, and they exploited the vogue for *artiste* characters who spouted poetry and song at every turn. Furthermore, they represented a lucrative marketing ploy, capitalizing on the proven success of their literary counterparts. The challenge today is to address these works without resorting to teleology: external-plot cycles were not experimental, transitional works that led to later types but a type that arose concurrently and that exhibited different but equally valid characteristics.

Partly because external-plot cycles present analytic difficulties, some worthwhile cycles have passed unnoticed into history: to name just a few, Schubert's *Don Gayseros* cycle (from de la Motte-Fouqué; D93, composed 1815), *Sieben Gesänge* (from Scott's epic poem *The Lady of the Lake*; D837, 838, 835, 836, 846, 839, and 843, published as Op. 52 in 1826), and *Gesänge aus "Wilhelm Meister"* (from Goethe; D877, published as Op. 62 in 1827); Kreutzer's *Gesänge aus Goethe's "Faust"* (early 1820s); and Schumann's *Lieder und Gesänge aus "Wilhelm Meister"* (Op. 98a, published 1851).[15] External-plot cycles remain a sub-genre in search of research.

Internal-plot cycles

Internal-plot cycles – that is, cycles in which the poetry relates a narrative – began to appear shortly after the Liederspiel, developing concurrently with external-plot cycles. The idea of conveying a drama through a series of lyric poems, another newly Romantic conundrum, was advanced by the poets first: in 1777, for example, Leopold Friedrich Günther von Göckingk published *Lieder zweier Liebenden*, a series of songs exchanged between two lovers like an epistolary novel. And when Ernst Wratislaw Wilhelm von Wobeser published his *Ein Roman in fünf Liedern* of 1784, he stated that, except for Göckingk's work, "the idea of producing an entire novel without narrative, just through a series of Lieder . . . is new."[16] Such experiments undoubtedly influenced narrative song cycles, but probably the most direct influence was Reichardt's Liederspiel: not only are their structures and styles similar, but their earliest advocates created both genres and knew each other and each other's works well. Himmel, Reichardt's friend first and then rival Kapellmeister in Berlin, composed not only the most successful Liederspiel ever, *Fanchon das Leyermädchen* (Berlin, 1804), but also numerous early cycles, including topical cycles (*Die Blumen und der Schmetterling*, see above), external-plot cycles (*Gesänge aus "Tiedges Urania"*, Op. 18, c. 1800), and internal-plot cycles (*Alexis und Ida*, 1813, below). Himmel composed and published sets of songs long before 1803, his earliest dating from the 1790s, but his most strongly coherent cycles coincide rather remarkably with his foray into Liederspiel.

Internal-plot cycles most likely took shape from a variety of influences, and their early appearance in Himmel's works is owed in large part to his being in the right place at the right time: early nineteenth-century Berlin was a cultural and political flashpoint.[17] The Prussian capital, under political threat from France, was a center for German nationalism while paradoxically remaining enamored of things French; it was a center for philosophy and for theorizing new, modern approaches to all fields; it had a long and celebrated tradition of Lied composition; it was a center for German Singspiele; and it was a stronghold of the cultured and culture-acquiring bourgeoisie. Perhaps most importantly, Berlin society revolved around intellectual and cultural salons, which not only brought together craftspeople from different arts, but also fostered the exchange of ideas, collaboration, and experimentation. Little evidence about what took place in these Berlin salons survives, but two events significantly impacted song cycle history: the collaboration between Himmel and the poet Christoph August Tiedge, both associated with the same salon; and the creation of *Die schöne Müllerin* in the Stägemann salon.

Tiedge was as familiar with Göckingk and his *Lieder zweier Liebenden* as Himmel was with Reichardt and his Liederspiele, and both published new types of cycles almost simultaneously and ahead of the curve. The narrative poetic cycle did not become widespread until after 1815, but Tiedge published *Das Echo oder Alexis und Ida. Ein Ciclus von Liedern* (The Echo, or Alexis and Ida. A Cycle of Lieder) in 1812; similarly, the internal-plot musical cycle did not become widespread until the 1820s, but Himmel published *Alexis und Ida, ein Schäfferroman in 46 Liedern von Tiedge* (Alexis and Ida, a Pastoral Novel in 46 Lieder by Tiedge) in 1813. That Tiedge was consciously creating a cycle is clear from his foreword: "[Virgil's] example inspired the following cycle of small, idyllic Lieder . . . Although a subtle thread of alternating connections runs through the cycle, each individual Lied nonetheless can be extracted and stand on its own as a minute whole."[18] Himmel's setting remained remarkably faithful to Tiedge's text, suggesting artistic agreement.

One of the hurdles to creating narrative song cycles was how to relate a narrative in music, which vastly stretches performance time, without losing the intimacy and scale associated with Lieder. Referring to *Alexis und Ida*, which requires roughly the same time as a full-length opera, one reviewer commented, "To whom, for example, would it occur to want to sing the forty-six pieces one right after the other; and who could do it as well? But if one chooses individual pieces each time, one also relinquishes and no longer [even] misses how the collection should constitute a true whole . . ."[19] It is indeed difficult to imagine sitting around a piano and singing the same work for over three hours, particularly when only two characters sing all but three of the songs. It is also difficult to imagine that Royal Kapellmeister Himmel, successful composer of operas, Liederspiele, and Singspiele, regular patron of salons, frequent guest of royalty and the elite, did not know this. The assumption that Tiedge and Himmel had some other purpose in mind seems as obvious as the fact that such a purpose could not have been usual, at least outside Berlin, because it so clearly escaped the reviewer. Viewed as a parlor version of the Liederspiel, however, *Alexis und Ida* could work: once everyone was involved in creating a scene or living picture for each song, including support characters, rudimentary props, and staging, the work could be an evening's entertainment and thus performable as a staged, dramatic work, although not in the usual sense of that phrase.

Despite the work's popularity, its musical links drew criticism from reviewers, who seemed to think that Himmel's thematic and harmonic recurrences indicated a lack of imagination. Such recurrences revealed the cycle's origins in staged dramatic works and helped infuse a lyric genre with dramatic connections. Although there were imitations, such as Sigismund Neukomm's *Aennchen und Robert* (1815), the significance of Tiedge and Himmel's experiment remains primarily historical as an early but flawed attempt to create a coherent narrative cycle of Lieder. Before music could assume the role of providing coherence, the cycle had to become more of a musical genre.

The second event from Berlin salons that significantly influenced song cycle history was the creation of *Die schöne Müllerin*, the only known example whose transition from Liederspiel to internal-plot cycle can be tracked.[20] The work itself was not unique, but its history is remarkable because the people involved were well known and influential, its transition was exceptionally well documented, and the final piece remains a mainstay of the vocal repertory.

Die schöne Müllerin began as an informal play with songs created and enacted in the Stägemann salon in the fall and winter of 1816–17. The salon was hosted by Elisabeth Stägemann, a friend of Reichardt's and lead actress in his *Lieb' und Treue*, and included among others her daughter Hedwig Stägemann, who played the first miller-maid and recorded the events of the salon in her memoirs, and the poet Wilhelm Müller, who was of course the young miller. *Rose, die Müllerin* was inspired by Reichardt's Liederspiele (Rose was the female lead in *Lieb' und Treue*, as well) and based on miller/miller-maid/nature *topoi* of the early nineteenth century. Typically, this Liederspiel had multiple characters, action and staging directions, and a dramatic tension that focused on relationships between several characters, not just on one in particular. The Stägemann group then enlisted a composer, Ludwig Berger, to complete the Liederspiel by setting it to music. Berger set only ten of the poems, thirty-eight of which are extant, and titled his version *Gesänge aus einem gesellschaftlichen Liederspiel, Die schöne Müllerin* (Songs from a Social Liederspiel [Berlin, 1818]).[21] In the process, he virtually recreated the work: he narrowed the tale's focus to the miller's inner turmoil and death; he highlighted the tension between miller and hunter; he rearranged, revised, and juxtaposed the poetry into a clear dramatic structure; and he employed numerous musical techniques to connect disparate lyric moments. Working within traditional Lied aesthetics, Berger nonetheless included some musical connections, including melodic and harmonic recall; rudimentary tonal planning; preludes, interludes, and postludes; characterization through tessitura; and an overall structure based on tempos and pacing.

Müller created yet another version in 1818 when he published twelve poems under the title *Müller-Lieder,* a dual reference to subject and poet. Differences between Berger's and Müller's cycles stem mainly from the fact that Berger was writing a Liederspiel and working with the poetry of numerous characters while Müller was assembling a cycle of his own poetry, which necessarily yielded a focus on his character. In 1820, Müller again revised his poems for publication, expanding the work to include a prologue, twenty-three songs, and an epilogue. This final version of the poetry was a true recasting of the tale, incorporating the Liederspiel's dramatic framework while removing almost all traces of true drama. The result was an amalgam, a narrative lyric cycle, as his title reflected: *Die schöne Müllerin* (*Im Winter zu lesen*). The work's subtitle, "to be read in winter," ensured intellectual and emotional distance, which heightened Romantic longing – of age for youth, of cynicism for sentimentality. Müller reinforced that distance through the prologue's and epilogue's unmistakable irony. Also, the poems were not a topical cycle of miller-Lieder but a tale that circled the miller around the focus of his life, i.e., the miller-maid. Finally, Müller created the impression of a drama by substituting disjunction and juxtaposition for progression, internal emotions for action, recall for characterization, and recurring themes in new contexts for development. With these techniques, new only to song cycles, Müller created events and characters that were purely subjective, a development critical to the narrative cycle because it redefined conflict in a static context. At the time, the intertextual reference was probably Giovanni Paisiello's popular opera *La molinara* (The Miller-Maid [1788]), a story that was old and worn enough to serve as an unvoiced foundation; today, the foundation is more often a mentally fabricated or reconstructed drama based on the timeless topic of a young man falling in love, only to discover that the young woman loves another. Part of the strength of the cycle lies in its flexibility in supporting a wide variety of readings and in its solo viewpoint that speaks to and expresses each listener's experience.

Schubert set Müller's 1820 cycle to music in 1824, creating arguably the most popular and accessible song cycle ever, *Die schöne Müllerin*, D795. In his five-part publication, Schubert omitted Müller's ironic framework, which ever since has been included or omitted in performances according to the prevailing fashion for either irony or earnestness, as well as three internal poems, which remain virtually unknown, leaving a total of twenty songs. Without those three poems, the structure of the poetic cycle became less clear, but Schubert compensated with a stronger musical coherence. What he created was a musical work, not the setting for a poetic work. Schubert's songs seriously challenged poetry's hegemony, accomplishing so much more than merely embodying the poetry perfectly. That "more" became an integral part of Lied aesthetics.

Schubert's cycles actually exhibit few of the techniques later hailed as cyclic: his preludes and postludes are usually brief; breaks between songs remain clear; and thematic recall is rare. One particularly thorny issue is Schubert's key choices and overall tonal structure, which remain controversial. Schubert's *Die schöne Müllerin*, for instance, highlights a glaring conflict between an intuitive perception of rightness and a late-Romantic conviction about how keys in song cycles should work. What is most obviously wrong is that the work begins and ends in keys a tritone apart, a fact that analysts have gone to great lengths to explain away, using keys as symbolic representations of the text (the brook as G major, for example), key characterizations (D major as "lively" or G minor as "uneasy"), and functional analysis (the G major of Song 2, *Wohin?* for example, suggesting a dominant for the miller's tonic C major arrival in Song 3, *Halt!*).[22] Schubert's choice of keys was not immutable; he transposed at least three, his concern being apparently less for large-scale tonal planning than for singers' vocal ranges and songs' tessituras. The songs' tessituras, incidentally, seem to mirror the plot's progression, rising with the tension of the first six songs; ranging widely in the next eight as the miller becomes increasingly unstable emotionally; dropping dramatically between Songs 13 and 14 as the miller's fantasy world comes crashing down; and finally remaining constant, almost monotonous, in the final six in an extended lullaby of minor–major fluctuations playing out the miller's despair unto death.

Schubert composed only one other large song cycle, *Winterreise*, D911, published in 1828 with twenty-four songs in two books. The poems were once again by Müller, this time created as a lyric cycle independent of any Liederspiel associations. *Die schöne Müllerin* and *Winterreise* were similar in topic and structure, but *Winterreise*, more homogeneous in style and reflecting the darker trends that were emerging in German Romanticism, melded narrative aspects of internal-plot cycles with the non-linear structure of topical cycles. Once again a lover mourned a failed love affair, but rather than relating a plot, the lover drifted in a fog of numbing despair. Where distance was an optional framework in *Die schöne Müllerin*, it was integral to *Winterreise*: a haunting winter reminiscence of a summertime affair and the epitome of Romantic longing for the impossible – for the distant beloved. Schubert's two cycles mark the arrival of internal-plot cycles as a musical genre and remain at the core of cycle repertory.

Beethoven and musically constructed cycles

When nineteenth-century German musicologists began documenting the history of song cycles, they inevitably began with Beethoven and *An die ferne Geliebte*. They hailed the work as the first true cycle, a decision that has proven difficult to overturn despite a century and a half to reconsider overwhelming evidence to the contrary.[23] But there were, and remain, good reasons for that decision. First and foremost was Beethoven's stature as the preeminent Romantic genius. The desire to view the "great German masters," and especially Beethoven, as the beginning of all great music grew during the nineteenth century so that by the 1870s, Beethoven and Mozart headed the lists of great Lied composers. Reichardt, Himmel, Kreutzer, Marschner, Carl Loewe, Robert Franz, those who had headed the lists in the earlier part of the century and who had composed the vast majority of high-quality Lieder, were either relegated to the ends of lists or were left off altogether, and Ferdinand Ries's *Sechs Lieder von Goethe* Op. 32 (1811), which may have been a model for Beethoven's cycle, was virtually forgotten.[24] The campaign was successful: when the French school (Franck, d'Indy, etc.) "invented" cyclic form, they attributed it to their studies of Beethoven rather than of Berlioz, whose works were prime examples of cyclic form.

Second, Beethoven's cycle epitomized the genre as it came to be defined in the latter half of the nineteenth century, a definition that was based on Beethoven's cycle: *Liederkreis* or *Liedercyclus* in the title; central theme; lyric cycle as text (preferably exhibiting a progression); tonal key scheme; thematic return; musical connections between songs; and so on.[25] It was an inspired example of Romantic irony, using a circular argument to define cyclic form. Beethoven's was not the first song cycle, but it was the first "musically constructed" cycle, in which musical coherence relied on techniques formerly associated with instrumental and dramatic genres. Not surprisingly, musicians and musicologists alike celebrated the cycle's emancipation from textual mimesis, a subservient role that had shackled music's Romantic freedom.[26]

Musically constructed cycles may have resolved some of the increasing tensions between poets and composers but they offered no panacea for analysis. Musical analysis became easier (compare analyses of Beethoven's cycle with those of Schubert's cycles), but text–music relationships became, if anything, even more complex, the independent musical coherence introducing competition as often as cooperation.

The relationship between music and poetry relies on aesthetic judgments that unavoidably reflect respective valuations of composers and poets, their work, and their historical impact. In the case of *An die ferne Geliebte*, Beethoven's innovations have almost completely overshadowed those of the poet, Alois Isidor Jeitteles. A greater mismatch between composer and poet is difficult to imagine: we know how many beans Beethoven ground for his morning coffee, but little is known of Jeitteles other than that he was a medical student in Vienna between 1815 and 1820. The poems of *An die ferne Geliebte*, apparently never published separately, exist only within the context of Beethoven's work.[27] Jeitteles's authorship, however, has never been in question, in spite of an intriguing and unusual comment by the reviewer for the Leipzig *Allgemeine musikalische Zeitung*: "The author, whether or not his name is as given . . ."[28]

Beethoven's oft-cited innovations continue to exemplify cyclic technique: the music is continuous, without breaks between songs; the succession of keys (E♭–G–A♭–A♭–C–E♭) is planned and rounded; inner songs are tonally and perceptually dependent on the outer ones; the final melody recalls the opening; the piano effects a truncated recapitulation in the intermezzo of the last song; and the piano assumes an active, prominent role. Without diminishing the importance of those innovations, even a cursory assessment reveals that Beethoven did not invent his cycle in a vacuum: his setting adhered closely to a strongly coherent poetic cycle with a rounded form and careful progression. The poetry is admittedly not stellar, but it does reveal a structure quite remarkable for its time and is one of the earliest examples of a psychological cycle: the protagonist does not embark on the typical *Wanderung* – only his fantasy wanders. The songs themselves are the journey, which is then not related but recreated and re-experienced in performance.

Beethoven's setting admits none of the ambiguity typical of early cycles (the six songs are unquestionably a single work, concluded by a single cadence) and there are remarkably few similar works in cycle literature from any era. As a defining model, *An die ferne Geliebte* was a poor choice: Kreutzer's *Wanderlieder* and *Frühlingslieder* were both more typical and had greater impact on contemporary Lied composers.[29] Later historians were mystified that the 1817 reviewer could have failed to recognize Beethoven's creation of a new genre, but the achievement for which it was later acclaimed, use of a form and techniques borrowed from instrumental and narrative genres to connect discrete lyric poems, was neither new nor particularly influential. In fact, the reviewer pointed out Beethoven's techniques for coherence in some detail. By the 1830s, perceptions had changed: technical aspects of the cycle were less important than the composer's name, and negative comments disappeared in favor of effusive praise. After mid-century, Beethoven's eminence effectively dampened criticism and promoted it as the genre's first masterpiece.

Nevertheless, *An die ferne Geliebte* remains significant for two reasons other than its perennially precarious position as an historical first of its kind. First, it represents something new in Beethoven, composed during a personally and professionally lean time when his style was undergoing significant change – a new genre, a new type of poetry, a new form. Whatever the inspiration for turning to a vocal genre, his focus remained on instrumental style, where music dominated, and the result is a hybrid that lies on the edges of vocal and instrumental traditions, expanding their possibilities. Beethoven composed no more song cycles, but he did repeat that experiment, most notably in his Ninth Symphony, where he used many of the same techniques for ensuring musical coherence.

Second, Beethoven's impact on the song cycle was to channel the emerging genre toward a coherence that relied more heavily on instrumental, as opposed to verbal, constructs. As a result, musical coherence began to take precedence over textual and Beethoven's stature lent the cycle validity as a serious musical genre. Disposed to believe in him as the great innovator, later generations chose to overlook both competing examples and generic context. In the history of song cycles, Beethoven and his cycle served as a pivot between an earlier aesthetic, in which poetic coherence dominated and music's job was to convey the text as faithfully as possible, and a later, still current, aesthetic, in which the ideal was a perfect union but in which musical coherence dominated, at least in analysis if not always in fact.

The ballad

The works from the first half of the nineteenth century that most closely resembled Beethoven's *An die ferne Geliebte* were not cycles at all. Schubert's 1823 setting of Franz von Schober's *Viola*, D786 (published as Op. 123 in 1830), for example, also had a single final cadence, included musical and textual returns, and began and ended in the same key, using transitions and modulations to connect sections. Schubert's piece, however, was subtitled a ballad. The remarkable similarity between these two works underscores the close, mutually influential relationship between ballad and cycle in the 1820s and 1830s and suggests that ballads and cycles were different sides of the same coin.

In the early nineteenth century, the distinction between ballad and cycle was based on poetic criteria: *Viola* was a ballad primarily because Schober wrote a single narrative poem and *An die ferne Geliebte* was a cycle primarily because Jeitteles wrote six related lyric poems. Musical genres analogous to, but separate from, poetic ones began to emerge in the second quarter of the century, notably in the 1830s, only gradually acquiring distinguishing characteristics. At the time, the musical structure of *An die ferne Geliebte* resembled a ballad, and Loewe's multipartite ballad *Der Kaiserjagd im Wiener Wald*, Op. 108, No. 1, resembled a cycle.

Loewe knew both cycles and ballads well: his cycles *Bilder des Orients* (Op. 10, 1833–34) and *Frauenliebe* (Op. 60, 1836–37) are still discussed in cycle histories, and he remains Germany's foremost nineteenth-century balladist. In the years 1834–35, shortly after he began experimenting with multipartite ballads, he composed two works that meshed the genres in startling ways: *Der Bergmann: Ein Liederkreis in Balladenform* (The Miner, A Liederkreis in Ballad Form), Op. 39, a setting of Ludwig Theodor Giese-brecht's 1833 cycle, and *Esther: Ein Liederkreis in Balladenform*, Op. 52, text also by Giesebrecht. Loewe retained clear breaks marked by unambiguous cadences between songs, but he linked the ballads' often contrasting dramatic sections using the same techniques as Beethoven – harmonic connections and recurring motives. In *Der Bergmann*, for example, Loewe presented his own musical cycle, distinct from the poetry: main motives in each song derive from an idea in the first song, and the cycle's opening descent into the mine ends with a retrograde climbing back out into the light, neatly returning the end to the cycle's beginning. Loewe was by no means the first to use such connections, but his works reveal most clearly the interaction between ballad and cycle. Few composers of the later nineteenth century chose to imitate Loewe's ballad cycles; such works were apparently a parting as well as meeting of the ways.

Schumann

Robert Schumann's outpouring of song in 1840 marked a turning point in song cycle history akin to that of *An die ferne Geliebte*.[30] Unlike Schubert, Schumann was not a contemporary of Beethoven; he was a conscious admirer who strove to carry on Beethoven's legacy, a legacy founded largely on instrumental works, and his writings reveal that he was familiar with not only *An die ferne Geliebte* but also Loewe's *Esther*. Schumann developed his concept of a cycle during the 1830s while experimenting with cyclic musical forms in his piano works, such as *Papillons*, *Carnaval*, and *Davidsbündlertänze*, and while writing for the *Neue Zeitschrift für Musik*. Tellingly, Schumann relegated the role of providing contrast to the poetry, a reversal of the earlier poetry-to-music relationship, and stressed that musical coherence relied on harmonic connections and recurring motives.

In 1840, pressured to make enough money to marry, he discovered a way to make his innovative but relatively unsuccessful cycles more accessible to the public: song cycles rather than piano cycles.[31] Schumann used nearly identical techniques to foster coherence in both: thematic recall, tonal structuring, weak or incomplete closure between songs, melodies derived from basic motives, delayed resolutions, and so on. Musical connections such as these compensated for and thus allowed Schumann's rapid shifts in mood without losing coherence; they also may explain why his piano accompaniments carry greater weight than those of other Lied composers. Schumann's concept of a cycle, often assumed to have been generally accepted, was in fact unusual for its time and came to be accepted in part because Schumann and his colleagues diligently promoted it through essays and reviews in the *Neue Zeitschrift für Musik*.[32]

Once Schumann turned to song, he preferred to compose and publish in distinctive sets. In the course of his short life, he produced a wide variety of song cycles exhibiting virtually a compendium of styles and techniques. His works, all from 1840 except as noted, include some of the most loved and analyzed cycles – *Dichterliebe* by Heine, Op. 48; *Frauenliebe und -leben* by Chamisso, Op. 42, which owed much to Loewe's setting; *Liederreihe* by Kerner, Op. 35; and the two *Liederkreise*, Op. 24 by Heine and Op. 39 by Eichendorff – as well as numerous little-known cycles such as *Spanisches Liederspiel* by Geibel, after Spanish poets, Op. 74, and *Spanisches Liebeslieder*, also by Geibel, Op. 138 (both 1849). Few of his topical and external-plot cycles have been studied, such as *Minnespiel* by Rückert, Op. 101 (1849); *Myrthen und Rosen* by various poets, Op. 25; and *Lieder und Gesänge aus "Wilhelm Meister"* by Goethe, Op. 98a (1849). Many more have yet even to be categorized, including *Zwölf Gesänge aus "Liebesfrühling"* by Rückert, Op. 37, which he composed with Clara Wieck Schumann; *Vier Husarenlieder* by Lenau, Op. 117 (1851); and *Mädchenlieder* by E. Kulmann, Op. 103 (1851).

Although *An die ferne Geliebte* offered both model and inspiration, the musically constructed cycle began in earnest only with Schumann and his contemporaries, and it is this type of cycle that continues to provide the generic contract today. After Schumann, the song cycle became a recognized genre that followed Romanticism's flow, spreading to other countries, adopting a loftier, more serious approach, and expanding into orchestral song cycles near the end of the century.[33] Musically constructed cycles varied widely in style and structure, but their composers remained focused on that tantalizingly unattainable ideal of a perfect melding between words, music, and meaning.

6 Schumann: reconfiguring the Lied

JÜRGEN THYM

A widely held stereotype sees the Romantic artist as a vessel of divine and largely uncontrolled inspiration. But Robert Schumann (1810–56) – an ardent Romantic in so many other ways – pursued an almost eerily systematic path in channeling his creativity. One by one, he conquered the important genres of instrumental and vocal music of his day. These ranged from the piano character piece in the 1830s, often grouped in large cycles, to songs, again grouped into cycles or collections, to symphonies, chamber music, and secular oratorio during the early 1840s, all of which gave him confidence in his last years to try his hand at opera and sacred music. During an unusually rich creative career, which lasted more than twenty-five years from the late 1820s to 1854, Schumann, at three different times and always at crucial crossroads, took up the composition of Lieder. The first of these occurred during the years 1827–28 and coincides with his first significant attempts at composing. The second dates from 1840 and overlaps with a period of crisis, both personal and professional, from which he emerged victorious and strengthened. The last came after 1847 when he attempted to renew himself as an artist in the face of demons both within and without; while the former doubtless will elude historical exactitude, the latter were egged on by the political turmoil that swept all of Europe in the late 1840s. As will be seen, there are specific reasons why the Lied, and not some other musical genre, became the catalyst for self-discovery, salvation, and renewal at each of these junctures.

First stabs: 1827–1828

It was by no means certain that Schumann would become a composer. Literary rather than musical endeavors mark his adolescence. After the death of his father, in 1826, he found support and guidance a year later in the friendship of a music-loving couple in his hometown. The wife, Agnes Carus, introduced Schumann to the Lieder of Schubert and spurred him on to composition. There is some evidence that the highly susceptible young man fell in love with her and that he vented his feelings in more than half a dozen songs of unfulfilled longing, unrequited love, erotic reminiscence, and seduction.

By and large, performers and critics alike have neglected these early songs, if for no other reason than that they are not easy to track down. The composer himself seems to have taken a dim view of these Lieder, since they remained unpublished during his life.[1] Yet Schumann must have recognized some strength in these songs, for he cannibalized three of them for material in as many piano works of the early 1830s.[2] The songs – or at least some of them – reveal a skilled imitator of Schubert and deserve scrutiny as the composer's first statements as a budding artist and his first utterances in a genre for which he would become so famous in later years.

Schumann is surprisingly surefooted in his choice of texts, featuring several poets to whom he would again turn in subsequent decades, including Goethe, Byron, and especially Kerner, who is represented by five songs. Not surprisingly, many of these early songs are strophic; the Goethe era, with its aesthetic premises about what a Lied ought to be, still made its impact felt.[3] But in other Lieder Schumann sets the last stanza to different music, as in *Kurzes Erwachen, Gesanges Erwachen,* repeats the first stanza at the end to arrive at an ABA form, as in *An Anna I,* or even adopts through-composition with minimal repetitive elements, as in *Die Weinende, Erinnerung, An Anna II,* and the Goethe setting, *Der Fischer.* Without exception, the textures are of the voice-plus-accompaniment category, whereby the chordal accompaniment occasionally is rendered flexible through arpeggios, as is the case with *Sehnsucht,* or tremolos, in order to capture the water imagery of *Der Fischer.* Schumann still has some distance to cover before reaching the imaginative pianistic textures or the polyphonic interweaving of vocal and instrumental parts so characteristic of his more mature songs, but sometimes vocal phrases are anticipated or echoed in the piano – *Gesanges Erwachen, An Anna I* – resulting in a give-and-take relationship that becomes a Schumannian fingerprint in the celebrated 1840 *Liederjahr.* The piano preludes and postludes almost always are brief. There is no trace yet of the extensive instrumental commentaries, but noticeable is the frequency of non-tonic beginnings. Thus *Sehnsucht* and *Die Weinende* begin with a secondary dominant, *Kurzes Erwachen* with the dominant, and *An Anna II* with the subdominant; *Erinnerung* enters with an appoggiatura upbeat leading to a diminished seventh chord of the relative minor. The short postludes sometimes echo, albeit faintly, the voice's last phrase, as in *Sehnsucht* (where it is supplied by the editor) and *Die Weinende,* but more often they rearticulate introductory material as cadential, as in *Erinnerung, Kurzes Erwachen,* and *Gesanges Erwachen.* In *Im Herbste* Schumann provides a closing commentary in the piano – a tantalizing anticipation of things to come. Schumann revels in mediant relationships, juxtaposing F and Db major in *An Anna I,* and in colorful, vagrant harmonies in *Der Fischer* and *An Anna II.* As in some of Schubert's songs, the centrifugal forces of harmony appear unchecked, reinforcing the impression of mannerism for expression's sake by a youthful follower.

In the summer of 1828, Schumann, with some anxiety, sent three of his Kerner settings to Gottlob Wiedebein, Kapellmeister and composer in Braunschweig. While Wiedebein faulted some aspects of the compositions, he excused them in view of the composer's young age. In a subsequent letter Schumann concurred, attributing the shortcomings to the fact that he had not had at that time any formal training in harmony, thoroughbass, or counterpoint. Still, Wiedebein concluded his letter with a prophetic statement: "You have received much, indeed very much, from nature; use your gifts, and the respect of the world will not escape you."[4] Schumann took the statement to heart. His first encounter with the Lied proved to be fateful; from this point on, he wanted to become a composer.

Spring harvest: 1840–1841

The rich yield of Schumann's *Liederjahr* of 1840 comes as a surprise, and many commentators have reacted to the amazing display of creativity with puzzlement. This especially is the case in view of Schumann's confession to his friend Hermann Hirschbach, as late as the summer of 1839, that "he always considered music for the human voice inferior to instrumental music and never thought of it as great art."[5] Even though he added a request for confidentiality – "Please do not pass this on to anybody" – his bias could not have escaped the attentive readers of the *Neue Zeitschrift für Musik*. Throughout much of the 1830s, he delegated the review of Lieder to his second-in-command at the journal, Oswald Lorenz, preferring instead to focus his own critical writing on instrumental music.

The *Liederjahr* can be explained in part by biographical circumstances in which Schumann and his bride found themselves in 1839–40. After several years of personal upheavals and legal struggles, Schumann and Clara Wieck, another muse, like Agnes Carus, albeit on a higher plane, married against the wishes of Clara's father, Friedrich Wieck (1785–1873). The emotionally charged circumstances may have contributed to Schumann's sudden outburst of creativity, which found an outlet in songs, most of them dealing with love in its many-faceted aspects and covering the entire range of possible emotional response from the agony of rejection to the bliss of fulfillment. Certainly there are statements in Schumann's correspondence with his bride that link his ultimately successful courtship with his uncannily rapid and fecund creativity. "The cycle is my most Romantic ever," he wrote to Clara in May 1840, referring to his Eichendorff *Liederkreis*, Op. 39, "and it contains much of you in it."[6]

For all of this, it is possible to connect the composition of Lieder with Schumann's impending marriage in a less metaphorical way. In 1839, Schumann and Clara Wieck had started collecting poems – mostly by contemporaneous poets – and entering them into a book titled, in Robert's handwriting, *Abschriften von Gedichten zur Composition* (Copies of Poems for Composing).[7] Many of the poems would, at some later stage, serve as texts to be set to music. Even though one or the other Schumann would continue to add poems to the book on an individual basis well into the early 1850s, the collection was begun as a joint project of two artists who, during their time of courtship, wanted to be linked by artistic and spiritual bonds, even when they were physically separated. Schumann set to music the lion's share of the poems gathered in the collection, but Clara contributed with a number of Rückert songs, which, together with others by Robert, were published as *Liebesfrühling*, Op. 37.[8]

The early months of 1840 were fraught by emotional turmoil for the young couple because of the stubborn refusal of Friedrich Wieck to consent to their marriage. The turbulence set in motion by suits and counter-suits, contrived stalling techniques, and plain procrastination turned the courtship of the two lovers into a court battle.[9] One of the reasons for Wieck's reticence in accepting his future son-in-law was his perhaps justifiable concern that Schumann's income would not be sufficient to ensure a worry-free future for his daughter. In a sense, Wieck had a point. Until 1839, Schumann had published little more than esoteric and difficult piano works, compositions that hardly qualified as financial bestsellers. (Well, not for several decades, anyway; they remain today among the standard items in a music publisher's active "backlist.") Schumann himself was aware of the difficulties of comprehension, and that meant problems of marketability, which his keyboard works caused for audiences because of the sometimes bizarre juxtaposition of contrasting miniatures. "I was again delighted about your remarks about my piano works," he wrote to W. H. Rieffel in June of 1840. "I wish I would find more people who understood my meaning; I hope to succeed more easily with vocal compositions."[10]

Schumann's statement, of course, is more than an expression of commercial concern. In his letter to Rieffel, he draws a connection between the piano works and his songs – implying to some degree that the aesthetic difference between the music he composed in the 1830s and that which burst forth in the *Liederjahr* was not as large as the trope of the completely new Schumann of 1840 suggests. It was Franz Brendel (1811–68), Schumann's successor as editor of the *Neue Zeitschrift für Musik*, who pointed out, as early as 1845, that Schumann's songs really were a continuation of his character pieces for piano.[11] And Wilhelm Josef von Wasielewski (1822–96), the composer's first biographer, extended this view by interpreting Schumann's turn to song to be the result of Schumann's striving for clarification of expression.[12] Arnfried Edler, and later John Daverio in a more symbolic way, have maintained that the core of Schumann's artistic creativity, no matter whether it took the form of vocal or instrumental music, was the conception of translating poetry into music, of imbuing musical artworks with a poetic spirit.[13] Schumann's letter to Rieffel, which probably was known to Wasielewski, certainly allows such an interpretation: the poetic text, rather than being a skeleton or cantus firmus along which a composer writes music, makes explicit the meaning of the artwork conceived in musico-poetic terms.[14]

After 1840, Schumann himself occasionally put pen to paper to review Lieder for his journal, and his writings provide a glimpse of the composer's point of view on the art of setting poetry. One particularly poignant example is his well-known and often-quoted review from 1843, in which he considers Lieder by Robert Franz.[15] As is typical of almost all of Schumann's song reviews, he considers both historical and aesthetic concerns. In so doing, he proudly proclaims the arrival of a new era of Lied composition, going so far as to suggest that this genre is perhaps the only one in which progress has been made since Beethoven. Curiously, in view of Schubert's unrivalled standing as a Lied composer nowadays, Schumann, while acknowledging the composer of *Gretchen am Spinnrade*, assigns him a somewhat perfunctory role in the genre's development, in marked contrast to the esteem in which he holds him as a composer of instrumental music.[16] As Schumann would have it, Schubert simply appears as someone who, generally inspired by Beethoven's manner, prepared the way in song composition. Whereas Schumann does not criticize Schubert's accomplishments directly, he claims that the real breakthrough occurred after Schubert's death. The songs that Schumann reviewed – Theodor Kirchner's Op. 1 and Robert Franz's Op. 1, among others – to critics today no longer seem weighty enough to lend themselves to grand historical perspectives. Thus one wonders whether or not Schumann was really thinking of – perhaps even hinting at – his own songs and song cycles from 1840, only some of which had been published by the time he wrote this particular review.[17]

Several strands leading to a "new era in song composition" may be discerned in Schumann reviews. The reaction against shallow virtuosity and formulaic composition, in Schumann's perspective, already had led to first results in the 1830s when more thoughtful and substantial piano music began to appear, and Schumann mentions Bach and Beethoven as guideposts inspiring the contemporary music scene in Germany. Schumann felt that the advances made in recent piano music, by necessity, also were felt in the Lied, pointing the way toward a new relationship and balance between voice and instrumental support. Developments in piano design notwithstanding, the central pillar for Schumann's new age of Lieder rested on a new school of poetry. Schumann himself mentions Eichendorff, Rückert, Heine, and Uhland as the main representatives, and he scolds those composers who squandered their talents on inferior or mediocre poetry in order to respond to market demands with the mass production of songs.

When Schumann returned to the Lied in 1840, he drew his texts from a wide variety of sources. Being the son of a book dealer and possessing a keen and lively lifelong interest in literature, he showed considerable discrimination in his selection of poetry. In view of this, it is surprising to realize that Goethe, the poet-laureate of German literary classicism, whose poems Schubert set with such frequency a generation before, does not figure all that prominently in the younger composer's songs from 1840. In all, he is represented with only five settings, all of them in *Myrthen* – myrtles, the traditional German wedding flower, Schumann's name for the Lieder collection he dedicated to his "beloved bride." (Schumann again would turn to Goethe for more substantial settings later in his life, partly in response to the national celebration of the Goethe centennial in 1849.) Schiller, Goethe's colleague and counterpart in Weimar, is missing altogether. In 1840, Schumann was attracted to a different type of poetry. On the one hand, he captured with his settings of more than a dozen Eichendorff poems a lovely late blossom of literary Romanticism (Eichendorff's collected poems were not published until 1837). On the other hand, he turned to poets whose poems, in one way or another, represent transformations of the Romantic spirit. Heine, who distanced himself from Romantic imagery and sentiment with irony and urbane wit, found a most congenial musical interpreter and commentator in more than forty Schumann settings. Chamisso, Reinick, Rückert, and, to a certain extent, Kerner, to whom Schumann turned during the *Liederjahr*, capture in their poems the Biedermeier sensibilities of the *Vormärz* (the period preceding the March 1848 revolution): domestic bliss, friendship, patriotism, regional pride, and consolation in religion. Of these four poets, Rückert stands out given the musicality and virtuosity of his poetic language which, no doubt, was an important factor in attracting the attention of composers such as Schumann and, two generations later, Mahler. While still drawing strength and inspiration from literary Romanticism for his musical settings, Schumann's poetical choices show him to have been an adherent of the cultural values typical of German middle-class society in the decades before the 1848–49 revolution.

The range of Schumann's literary taste also is evident in the many poems he set by non-German poets in 1840. The first setting of the *Liederjahr*, as far as his songs can be dated, seems to have been *Schlußlied des Narren* from Shakespeare's *Twelfth Night*. Other English-language poets set in German translation include Burns, Moore, and Byron; in like manner, translations by Chamisso yielded Hans Christian Andersen from Denmark and Pierre

Béranger from France. Schumann's catholic choice in poetry belies to some extent the impression of a narrow German provincial who, as music critic, often singled out Italian and French artists for biting criticism in order to promote his artistic ideals.

A quick glance at Schumann's texts reveals that the majority are strophic and that their stanzas are organized in quatrains, favor trimeter and tetrameter lines, and rhyme schemes such as a-b-a-b or a-a-b-b. The folk song, or what was considered a folk song in the aftermath of the publication of Clemens Brentano and Achim von Arnim's *Des Knaben Wunderhorn* (1806–08), made itself felt in the structures in which poets couched their lyrics, and it is remarkable to witness how long the mold proved useful for the contents poured into it. To be sure, poets of the nineteenth century often wrote in more sophisticated poetic forms, such as those borrowed from classical antiquity, the Petrarchan sonnet, the Persian ghazel, or even free verse. But from the beginning of what may be termed the modern Lied, composers gravitated toward the simpler poetic structures associated with or redolent of folk song. For one thing, they wished to capture the *Volkston* – popular or even rustic tone – in their settings; many of Schumann's songs, especially the Heine, Kerner, and Reinick settings, can be adduced as examples. Over and above this, Lieder composers throughout the nineteenth century were drawn to simple and repetitive poetic forms because they provided a skeleton to rein in the centrifugal forces associated with through-composition and the emancipation of the instrumental accompaniment that had entered the genre because of Schubert's break with the aesthetics of the Goethe era. Whereas occasionally more complex poetic structures (such as five- or six-line stanzas, a-b-b-a rhymes, or the sonnet form with its pentameter lines) make their appearance in Schumann's Lieder, they clearly are the exception. In that respect, Schumann was conservative in his choice of poetry.

Despite Schumann's literary sensibilities, he often was not faithful to the letter of his texts when setting them. In contrast to Hugo Wolf who, almost without exception, meticulously adhered to the poetic text, Schumann subjected his poems to considerable changes, often at the expense of their quality as works of literary art. Repeating lines or an entire stanza of poetry to highlight a touching statement or to reinforce a cadential point was by this time a long-established stratagem of Lied composers, and Schumann utilized it frequently. Composers also were in the habit of repeating a poem's first stanza at the end of a song to round off a setting, a move that yields a kind of recapitulation. But Schumann goes beyond this: he sometimes omits an entire stanza, as in *Die Stille*, Op. 39, No. 4, and adds, omits, or contracts syllables or otherwise changes the wording of a line. Sometimes, it seems as if Schumann may have incorrectly memorized the poem; in most instances, however, the changes have to do with compositional process or practical considerations.[18] A case in point is his setting of Eichendorff's "In der Fremde," which in the second edition of the *Liederkreis*, Op. 39, replaced another song in first position. As the autograph shows, Schumann initially composed the text pretty much as published by Eichendorff; dissatisfied with the harmonic disposition and a rather jerky return to the tonic, he felt the need for additional verbal material and, in turn, repeated segments of the text, wreaking havoc on the line and rhyme structure – but not on the syntactical structure.[19]

According to Schumann's views on the Lied's historical position, it was not only the blossoming of a new school of German poetry that raised song composition to a higher level but also a new style of piano writing, expressive and substantial rather than formulaic and striving for superficial effects. Schumann had ample opportunity to hone his skills as a composer of piano works during the 1830s – all his compositions with opus numbers up to Op. 23 are keyboard compositions – and his experiences with different pianistic textures bear fruit in the works of his *Liederjahr* in various ways. But beyond increasing the piano's role in settings of poetry, Schumann's significance as a song composer rests largely on establishing a new interdependence of voice and piano. Even though Schubert already had made the keyboard the voice's equal at least fifteen years earlier, Schumann integrates both parts to a degree heretofore unknown so that one cannot exist without the other; indeed, the one relies on the other in a collaborative and complementary relationship.

Granted, the traditional voice-plus-accompaniment texture can be found in many Schumann songs, especially those in which the composer is striving for a popular tone, or *Volkston*, as is the case with his *Wanderlieder*: the Goethe setting *Freisinn* from *Myrthen*, the Kerner song *Wanderlied* or the Eichendorff setting *Der frohe Wandersmann*. (The latter originally was published as Op. 39, No. 1 in the 1842 edition of the Eichendorff *Liederkreis*, and republished in 1851 as Op. 77, No. 1.) In these songs the piano functions largely as support to the vocal part, even though it occasionally gains prominence of its own in the form of short preludes, interludes, or postludes. "Accompanimental" in the strict sense of the word are the "oompah-oompah" textures that Schumann employs frequently, as in the first and fourth songs of the Heine *Liederkreis*, Op. 24, or in the patter song *Die Rose, die Lilie* from *Dichterliebe*. Similarly, the piano restricts itself at times to syncopated doublings of the vocal part in the middle section of *Intermezzo* from the Eichendorff *Liederkreis*, of *Ein Jüngling liebt ein Mädchen* from *Dichterliebe*, or the fourth song of the Heine *Liederkreis*. Sometimes the keyboard is entrusted with repeated chord textures that support the singer, as in *Der Himmel hat eine Träne geweint* from *Liebesfrühling* and the Kerner song *Stille Tränen*, Op. 35, No. 10. Elsewhere, Schumann assigns the piano arpeggiated

Example 6.1a *Hör' ich das Liedchen klingen*, Op. 48, No. 10, mm. 4–12

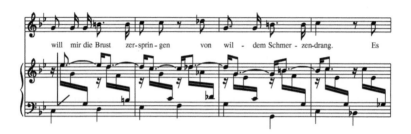

filigree, as in *In der Fremde*, Op. 39, No. 1, and *Hör' ich das Liedchen klingen* and *Am leuchtenden Sommermorgen*, both from *Dichterliebe*.

What at first glance appears to be a traditional accompaniment reveals itself upon closer inspection to be an artful interweaving of voices. A horn-call motive of ascending and descending fourths and fifths emerges in vocal and instrumental parts in the middle section of *In der Fremde*, enriching the texture and intensifying the expression of longing at a crucial moment in the poem. And the melody which at one time "was sung by the beloved" ("das einst die Liebste sang") returns several times in *Hör' ich das Liedchen klingen* in the piano texture as a painful and haunting reminder of former bliss. The last statement at "übergroßes Weh" (colossal woe) initiates a postlude which presents the poignant reminiscence three times in canon (the last time incomplete) hidden and interwoven in the broken-chord filigree (see Examples 6.1a and 6.1b).

The extent to which voice and piano become collaborators in articulating a song's texture can be seen in the first song from *Dichterliebe*, an artful polyphony of arpeggiated suspensions and resolutions, in which vocal and instrumental parts are inversionally related (see Example 6.2; the respective segments in the texture are bracketed). In the event, counterpoint plays a major role in determining the texture of Schumann's songs. It is evident in the archaic modal evocation of a medieval landscape in *Auf einer Burg* from the Eichendorff *Liederkreis*, or the equally old-fashioned depiction of Cologne Cathedral in *Im Rhein, im heil'gen Strome* from *Dichterliebe* – a

Example 6.1b *Hör' ich das Liedchen klingen,* Op. 48, No. 10, mm. 19–26

Example 6.2 *Im wunderschönen Monat Mai,* Op. 48, No. 1, mm. 1–6

veritable exercise in Fuxian species-counterpoint with the cantus firmus changing octave registers – or the transposition of Bach's fugal writing in *Zwielicht,* also from the Eichendorff *Liederkreis.*[20] Counterpoint of a very Schumannian kind, replete with arpeggios and implied voices (even in accompanimental figures) appears in settings with a less historicizing style in songs ranging from *In der Fremde* [I], *Schöne Fremde* and *Frühlingsnacht* from the Eichendorff *Liederkreis* to *Im wunderschönen Monat Mai, Hör' ich das Liedchen klingen* and *Am leuchtenden Sommermorgen* from *Dichterliebe.*

An unusual relationship between voice and piano is established in *Ich hab im Traum geweinet,* from *Dichterliebe.* During the poem's first two stanzas, voice and piano are completely separated, that is, the one is silent when the other sounds. Throughout the song, the keyboard punctuates the various phrases of the recitative-like vocal part with lugubrious chords in the low register, imbuing the song with a funereal quality. It is not until the third and final stanza that pianist and singer join forces: the monotone vocal statement now is supported with jarring dissonant chords which do not find resolution until the voice is finished.

Elsewhere, Schumann sees fit to reverse the texture of voice-plus-accompaniment. *Das ist ein Flöten und Geigen,* a ballroom scene from *Dichterliebe,* comes across as a waltz in the piano onto which the vocal part is grafted to deliver the poetic text – in essence a character piece for piano with obbligato vocal part. While this kind of texture maintained for an entire song is a rare occurrence – and Schumann warned Lieder composers about this kind of mannerism[21] – such role reversals between voice and piano, especially short ones, occur frequently. In *Waldesgespräch,* from the Eichendorff *Liederkreis,* the breathless statements of the hunter are superimposed on a self-sufficient piano part, capturing the poem's forest landscape with a hunting horn texture. For much of the last song of *Dichterliebe,* the voice accompanies while the piano provides the overall coherence of the musical discourse. The opposite can happen, too: the piano interjecting into what is essentially an independent passage for the voice alone, as for much of *Ich hab' im Traum geweinet.*

When Schumann began composing Lieder early in 1840, he immediately seized on the possibility of ordering individual songs into groups or cycles. More than half of his output from the *Liederjahr* was published in collections, comprising six, eight, nine, twelve, sixteen, or more settings connected by a common thread, both poetic or musical, or often both. Sometimes the thread unifying a song at best is only vague and general; at other times it is quite specific. Still used by performers today, the Peters volumes are confusing in that they distort and disassemble some of the original groupings. Only *Myrthen,* Op. 25, *Liederkreis,* Op. 39, *Frauenliebe und -leben,* Op. 42, and *Dichterliebe,* Op. 48 are kept together, whereas the other "cycles" of the *Liederjahr* – *Liederkreis,* Op. 24, the Kerner Songs, Op. 35, and the Reinick Songs, Op. 36 – are separated. The most popular songs appear in the first volume, whereas settings that did not reach evergreen status are relegated to volumes 2 and 3. Even more complicated is the dispersal of the twelve

Rückert songs, Op. 37, published under the title *Liebesfrühling*, since they also contain three settings by Clara Schumann as well as a couple of duets that are disregarded in the Peters edition.[22]

Of the eight 1840 collections, *Myrthen* is the furthest from being a coherent cycle. Its twenty-six settings use poems from seven different poets, including Burns, Goethe, and Rückert, and they share no common poetic theme. Schumann intended the songs to be a gift for Clara, a bouquet – a *Myrthen* or "myrtle of flowers" – to be presented to his bride on their wedding; traces of this purpose can be found in some of the songs. *Myrthen* is framed by the Rückert settings *Widmung*, a paean to a beloved and clearly a kind of introduction, and *Zum Schluß*, which closes the series of songs with the dedication: "Here . . . I have woven for you an imperfect garland, sister, bride!" *Myrthen* also contains two paired songs, also on Rückert texts, both entitled *Lied der Braut* (Song of the Bride), as well as two Venetian gondola songs, of barely disguised eroticism, and quite a few imply a dialogue between male and female personae. Still, even if we ascertain a coherent succession of keys in the sequence of songs, progressing mostly by closely related keys, there can be no doubt that *Myrthen* is only a loosely unified collection – a gallery of beautiful vocal miniatures to be sampled and revisited by performers and listeners following no particular logic.

Other collections cohere by poetic theme, narrative thread, shared motives and imagery, and these commonalities in the poetry often are reinforced by musical elements of repetition and progression. *Liederkreis*, Op. 24, *Frauenliebe und -leben*, and *Dichterliebe*, fall into this category, and our notion of what a song cycle is often has been, perhaps one-sidedly, derived from these works. All three works are based on poems from a single poet, and in all three instances the poems are taken from a preexisting cycle of poems. All nine poems entitled "Lieder" in the "Junge Leiden" section of Heine's *Buch der Lieder* furnished Schumann with texts for the Op. 24 *Liederkreis*. Likewise, *Frauenliebe und -leben* is based on a lyric cycle by Chamisso (Schumann dropped the last of the cycle's nine poems), and in *Dichterliebe* Schumann used sixteen of the sixty-five poems of "Lyrisches Intermezzo," again from Heine's *Buch der Lieder*.[23] Even though Schumann curtails the poetic cycle drastically, he by and large preserves Heine's ordering of the poems and thereby the narrative thread. The three cycles establish through the succession of poems a narrative logic that very much imbues them with coherence and unity.

Op. 24 follows the emotional path of a lyric subject in an unhappy love relationship, from despair and restlessness in songs 1–3, separation from the beloved in songs 4–6, to overcoming bitterness and finding recovery in songs 7–9. In its way, *Dichterliebe* is an expanded version of a similar narrative sequence. In songs 1–6, the lyric protagonist dwells on love's blissful

Table 6.1 *Key structures of Schumann's Op. 42, 24, 48, and 39 song cycles*

Frauenliebe und -leben, Op. 42
Bb, Eb, C minor, Eb, Bb // G, D, D minor (Bb)

Liederkreis, Op. 24
D, B minor, B // E minor, E, E // A, D minor, D

Dichterliebe, Op. 48
F♯ minor (or A), A, D, G, B minor, E minor, C, A minor // G minor (or D minor), G minor, Eb, Bb, Eb minor, B, E, C♯ minor (Db)

Liederkreis, Op. 39
F♯ minor (or D*), A, E, G, E, B // A minor (or E minor), A minor, E, E minor, A, F♯

* In the 1842 edition of the cycle.

moments tinged not infrequently with doubt and pain. In songs 7–8 the subject is the barely suppressed anger at the discovery of treachery. In songs 9–14 he vents his disappointment in memories of bitterness, sentimentality, and self-mockery. Finally, in songs 15–16 consolation is found in envisioning an imaginary utopia whereupon bitter memories at last are laid to rest. *Frauenliebe und -leben* presents excerpts from a woman's life in eight vignettes, ranging from secret adoration of her future husband, engagement and wedding, in songs 1–5, to pregnancy and childbirth, in songs 6–7, to the death of her husband, in song 8. Chamisso's – and Schumann's – portrayal of female fulfillment in subservience to a male is problematic in today's gender-conscious world for performers and listeners alike, especially since the poetry lacks the distancing effects of Heine's verse. However passé and questionable the cycle now seems, it nonetheless documents the domestic culture of its time like a series of old photographic snapshots.[24]

Schumann reinforces the coherence of each of these cycles by musical means. (See Table 6.1 for an overview of the tonal designs pursued in the Op. 42, 24, 48, and 39 song cycles.) *Frauenliebe und -leben* is perhaps the most straightforward in terms of forging the individual settings into a larger unit. The cycle's eight songs follow a well-calculated plan in which the first five – wherein the protagonist's unfolding emotional state up to the wedding is revealed – harmonically move from one key to another according to keys closely related to the first song's Bb major. What ensues is a symmetrically arranged arch form. The three post-wedding Lieder explore keys of a different tonal world, yet they also are closely related: G major, D major, D minor (and Bb). Material from the first song, together with its key of Bb, returns at the end, concluding the cycle with a piano postlude in which the protagonist remembers the start of the relationship with her now dead husband. The only time a distantly related key is used is the juncture between songs 5 and 6, one that allows Schumann to demarcate the boundaries between the heroine's old and new life. Mindful of this, performers might consider articulating this new beginning with a long pause between these songs. In addition to key scheme and piano postlude, Schumann also achieves unity through the repetition or varied repetition of melodic material that allows for cross-references among individual numbers.[25] The Heine *Liederkreis* also proceeds through closely related keys, grouped three by three in accordance with the three stages of the cycle's narrative: the pains of love, farewell, and recovery. The songs are related to each other mainly by descending fifths (B–E–A–D), relative major/minor, or explore major/minor modes of the same key. As in *Frauenliebe*, the last song brings back the key of the first.

Like *Frauenliebe und -leben, Dichterliebe* falls into two sections, a division determined by both narrative content and key structure. The cycle's sixteen songs advance initially by thirds and fifths in the first section, then move from keys with sharps to two climactic songs with no accidentals in the key-signature (Nos. 7–8). In the second section, the songs explore a rather adventurous path, wending their way through various bittersweet memories, touching on flat regions and enharmonic relations, until they arrive at the cathartic conclusion in both C♯ minor and D♭ major – two keys standing in a sort of fifth relationship to F♯ minor, one of two keys implied in the first song. *Frauenliebe und -leben* and the Heine *Liederkreis*, and, to some extent, also the Eichendorff *Liederkreis*, as we will see, are tonally closed and anchored around B and D, respectively. In contrast, *Dichterliebe* is tonally open-ended, and, at the same time, more adventurous, a point evident not only in the individual songs but also throughout the entire cycle. The first song, whose interweaving of vocal and instrumental parts already has been commented on (Example 6.2), is tonally ambiguous; the piano part implies F♯ minor even though this tonic is never sounded, whereas the voice cadences in A major (confirmed by the piano); the conflict never is resolved as the song concludes with a dominant seventh chord of F♯ minor. A different kind of tonal ambiguity pervades the ninth song, with which the cycle's second half begins. D minor and G minor alternate, with the former seeming to gain the upper hand, a preliminary conclusion thwarted by the piano postlude, which ends after a slithering chromatic descent in D major. It is unclear how the last sound is to be understood. Is it the tonic major or the dominant of G minor, the key of the next song? The last song of the cycle provides closure, but it is open-ended, a conclusion typical of Schumann and of this cycle: in terms of tonality the cycle does not return to an earlier key but moves to C♯ minor, which in the piano postlude appears enharmonically as D♭ major. In a different sense, however, the postlude constitutes a return, similar to that achieved in *Frauenliebe und -leben*. This is so because the material which is elaborated in the concluding instrumental commentary seems to take its point of departure, on first hearing, from the poem's penultimate line: "Ich senkt' auch *meine Liebe*."[26] Yet it really harks back to something heard before, the consoling conclusion of an earlier song ("Hör' ich das Liedchen klingen"), by bringing back the postlude of that song and now expanding it as the epilogue for the entire cycle.

Somewhere between the looseness of a flower bouquet such as *Myrthen* and the cyclic coherence of *Frauenliebe und -leben* and *Dichterliebe* lie the few other cycles composed in the *Liederjahr*, from February 1840 to January 1841: the Kerner *Liederreihe*, Op. 35, the Reinick songs, Op. 36, *Liebesfrühling* (after Rückert), Op. 37, and the Eichendorff *Liederkreis*, Op. 39. Here, too, each work gathers poems from the same poet, in the case of the *Liebesfrühling* poems already published by the poet as a cycle. But, in most cases, a clear narrative thread is lacking – although we may see the Kerner songs as a descendant of the *Wanderlieder* cycles with a protagonist wending his way through life after an unhappy love experience.[27] Accordingly, the poems appear as a kind of tableau grouped and ordered by the composer around a poetic idea or common theme. *Liebesfrühling* clearly is a celebration of love, to which both Robert and Clara Schumann contributed in a collaborative effort, engaging both male and female personae in dialogue form and in the form of duets.[28] The subjects of requited love and conjugal bliss loosely link the Reinick songs.

The Op. 39 *Liederkreis* gathers twelve Eichendorff poems, some of which existed as lyric insertions in several of the poet's novels and novellas and thus have their origin in entirely disparate contexts. Many of the poems are paeans to nature, evocations of mysterious landscapes suffused with nature's imagery; they range from painful recollections about love lost to jubilant affirmation of love's blissful moments. As most commentators agree, the cycle falls into two halves: songs 1–6 concern subjects largely of an upbeat nature, while songs 7–12 deal with topics of a darker hue. The concluding songs of each half, *Schöne Fremde* and *Frühlingsnacht*, unmistakably are articulated as climactic statements, providing closure to their respective sections; in both poetry and music they are shaped as corresponding or related units. The promise of future happiness ("wie von künftigem grossen Glück") and the fulfillment of love ("sie ist deine, sie ist dein") are highlighted through similar music. One factor contributing to the cyclic nature of Op. 39 is the rather uncomplicated key sequence (see Table 6.1). Keys with sharps prevail in the first half, and the number of sharps in the key-signature increases as one moves toward the end. More subdued emotional states are captured in the second half, in part, through less "exuberant" keys, but the last song tops the key sequence pursued in the first half with an ecstatic F♯ major, rounding off the cycle through a return to the tonic of the first song, at least that published in the second edition. The logic of the key sequence – as well as other musical correspondences between adjacent songs – is not thwarted by the fact that Schumann originally published Op. 39 with a happy-go-lucky song of Wanderlust (*Der frohe Wandersmann*) in D major in first place rather than the melancholy *In der Fremde* (which replaced *Der frohe Wandersmann* in the second edition of 1849). But it is clear that either song imparts a different emotional trajectory to what follows. While Schumann's ordering principles, both textual and musical, imbue the Lieder with latent cyclicism, the ambiguity about how to begin the cycle puts into question various assumptions about motivic recall usually identified, unproblematically, as contributing to cyclic coherence. Rather than forcing constructs of unity on Schumann's cycles – this one as well as others – it may be more appropriate to recognize, and find aesthetic pleasure in, the discontinuities and rapid mood shifts and view these features as reverberations of Romantic modes of narrative.[29]

"A poem should rest like a bride in the arms of the singer, freely, happily, and wholly. Then it will sound as if from heaven."[30] Schumann made this proclamation in one of his Lieder reviews. There are many instances of perfect text–music unions within Schumann's own Lieder. *Im wunderschönen Monat Mai* in *Dichterliebe* and *Mondnacht* and *Zwielicht* in the Eichendorff *Liederkreis* immediately come to mind as examples of such perfect unions. To paraphrase the old adage, they are like a marriage made in a heaven where poets and composers live in perfect harmony. But those instances may be the exception among his Lieder, some of which offer quite idiosyncratic (albeit plausible) readings of the poems he set. Without question, word and tone are different artistic media with vastly different principles and elements establishing meaning, expression, and coherence. The many debates about the proper relationship between both, from the time of the belligerent musings of the Florentine Camerata to the consoling artistic rendition of the issue in Richard Strauss's *Capriccio*, afford ample evidence for the tension-filled coexistence of music and poetry. The history of the Lied – Schumann's contributions very much included – is no exception. It is clear from the discussion provided thus far that Schumann injects himself in various ways into the interpretations of the poems he sets to music, often prompting raised eyebrows or downright condemnation, with literarily inclined critics.[31] Without question, Schumann appropriates his poets, most notably by inserting extensive commentaries in the piano and by ordering the poems into cycles that seem to have little to do with the original poetical context.[32] In fact, Schumann may be likened to a stage director who, through his production, renders an interpretation of another artist's work.

Most intriguing is the skill of his Heine settings, apparent above all in *Dichterliebe*. Schumann's responses to Heine are quite varied, leading to interesting and, at times, surprisingly idiosyncratic readings. *Ich will meine*

Seele tauchen, Op. 48, No. 5, is based on a poem with an openly erotic subject, rippling with barely concealed sexual imagery. As Lawrence Kramer has remarked, in a process he calls "expressive revision,"[33] Schumann suppresses the text's undisguised eroticism by setting its two stanzas to an almost mechanical keyboard accompaniment, not unlike that of a toy piano. The text's sensual quality is not musically admitted until the piano postlude (only briefly mentioned by Kramer) which, through a more exuberant melody and chromaticism in various voices, finally captures the blissful moment in the love relationship remembered in the poem. The next song, *Im Rhein, im heiligen Strome*, Op. 48, No. 6, takes the image of Cologne Cathedral perhaps more seriously than it needs to. The solemn evocation of the cathedral's majestic architecture in the guise of the already-noted species counterpoint maintained throughout the song – although "bending" just a little for the third stanza – stands in expressive dissonance with the almost blasphemous comparison of the painting of the Madonna with the image of the beloved. But the effect is striking: the poem's persona conceals his uncouth thoughts and continues his mock-pious procession through the cathedral in the concluding piano postlude. The setting of *Ich grolle nicht*, Op. 48, No. 7, seems to contradict the denial expressed in the poem's first line (which Schumann reinforces through repeats); the piano's pounding eighth notes over a strong bass motion in half notes intensify the discrepancy between surface words and the barely concealed strong passion.[34] Often Schumann finds musical equivalents for Heine's distancing effects by citing stylistic *topoi*: the chivalric style in *Aus alten Märchen winkt es*,[35] or the previously-mentioned archaic counterpoint in *Im Rhein, im heiligen Strome*. The ninth and eleventh Lieder of *Dichterliebe*, respectively, are a waltz parody and a narrative operetta song casually presented to render a heart-breaking story about a love triangle; the eighth song from the Op. 24 song cycle, *Anfangs wollt ich fast verzagen*, is set to the chorale melody *Wer nur den lieben Gott läßt walten*. From this, there is no evidence that Schumann misunderstood Heine's wit and irony. On the contrary, he relishes the multiple meanings of the poems and finds imaginative and multiple ways to capture their essence.

New impulses: 1849–1852

Schumann's third phase in Lieder composition is less easy to define than the earlier outpourings. After the *Liederjahr* (which did not come to an end until January 1841 with *Liebesfrühling*), Schumann set out over the next several years to conquer other musical genres. Only a handful of songs were written between the time of the *Liederjahr* and 1849, but then the Lieder composer suddenly burst forth again in what Schumann himself characterized in a letter to Hiller as his "most fruitful year."[36] If there had not been so many other works during that year,[37] one might be tempted to speak of a second *Liederjahr*, given that nearly fifty settings originated in 1849 alone. The unbounded creativity continued to the following years almost unabated up to the *Maria Stuart* cycle composed in December 1852, Schumann's last essay in Lied composition.

The incredible surge of productivity in Schumann's last years is puzzling on two counts: the political upheaval that swept Europe in 1848–49, and that reached also Dresden, where Schumann lived at that time, and the gradual weakening of Schumann's mental health. Schumann himself commented on the revolutionary events in the aforementioned April 1849 letter to Hiller: "It seems as if the outer stresses impelled people to turn inward and only therein did I find a countermeasure against the forces breaking in so frightfully from without."[38] Schumann was an artist very much interested in the contemporary political scene (and there can be no doubt about his republican sympathies), but the chaos and violence were threatening to him and his family in May 1849 and forced him to retreat to the countryside and a nearby spa to wait out the storms from a distance. It is tempting to connect Schumann's withdrawal from worldly events with his preference for composing in more intimate musical genres, including songs – a reaction not uncommon among artists. This notwithstanding, it needs to be stressed that Schumann's compositional projects during 1849 also can be characterized as a form of reaching out to his middle-class audiences, the *Bildungsbürgertum* of the *Vormärz*. The *Liederspiele* of 1849, Op. 74 and Op. 138 after Geibel, and Op. 101 after Rückert, are representative of Biedermeier conviviality. The *Liederalbum für die Jugend*, Op. 79, is a collection with a clear pedagogical purpose, and the turn to Goethe in the *Wilhelm Meister* settings and the *Scenes from Faust* stands in close relationship to the centenary of the poet's birth in 1849.

Schumann's mental health declined gradually, especially after the move from Dresden to Düsseldorf in 1850. Whatever its origin, it is difficult to ascertain exactly what effect such problems had on his composition. Bouts of depression had haunted the composer throughout much of his life, and he had learned to cope with them, even in stressful periods, keeping his professional and personal life intact more often than not. It has become fashionable to view Schumann's later works as being overshadowed by his health problems and to explain their alleged shortcomings with reference to his mental decline.[39] Reinhard Kapp and Ulrich Mahlert, among others, have spoken out against this rush to judgment and analyzed many of Schumann's last works as conscious essays in resolving compositional and aesthetic issues that are representative of the state of music around 1850.[40] Schumann's unchecked creativity, even when demons from within threatened, is no small miracle, and his last songs and song cycles, the Lenau settings, Op. 90, the *Wilhelm Meister* settings, the Kulmann songs, Op. 104, and the *Maria Stuart* cycle, Op. 135, deserve to be studied as works of art rather than pathological documents. The choice of poems with their pessimistic, death-bound imagery may have been influenced by Schumann's premonitions of his own demise, but in setting such texts he found a way to extend his artistic life and creativity.

Who are the poets whose lyrics inspired Schumann to his third wave of Lieder composition? Here the absences are as revealing as those who made the list: Heine, Kerner, and Chamisso, the chief poets from the *Liederjahr*, now are missing altogether. There is only a faint echo of Eichendorff's myste-rious forest landscapes, captured with such subtlety in the earlier *Liederkreis*, in the chorale-like setting of *Der Einsiedler*. Byron is represented with a few songs, perhaps a spin-off of the renewed encounter with that poet during the composition of *Manfred*. Rückert and Geibel also reappear as poets of several *Liederspiele*, and Goethe, who was represented in the *Liederjahr* with less than a handful of songs, is celebrated with an entire cycle, the *Wilhelm Meister* settings as well as a few other songs. The choice of Hoffmann von Fallersleben for many of the songs from the *Liederalbum für die Jugend* perhaps derives from the simplicity, intimacy, and singability of the poet's output, which make it appropriate for the youthful audience specified in the title. Schumann's choice of poetry is perhaps not as felicitous as in the *Liederjahr* 1840, and some authors have adduced this observation as evi-dence for the composer's declining literary sensitivity. Granted, the poems of Wilfried von der Neun, Emanuel Geibel, Gustav Pfarrius, and Elisabeth Kulmann (the latter a gifted German-Russian poet who died at seventeen) fall short of being great literature, but Schumann also grasped the signifi-cance of Mörike, whom he sampled with a few settings, and Lenau, whose passionate and elegiac utterances inspired Schumann to what arguably is his finest song cycle of the later years. And one should not underestimate the quality of those poems attributed to Mary Queen of Scots, even in trans-lation, which became the basis for Schumann's last song cycle.[41]

Most of the poems Schumann selected for his later settings are in the lyric vein. Nonetheless, in comparison with the *Liederjahr*, there is a noticeable drop in the number of narrative poems, or ballads, and an increase in the number of dramatic poems, or *Rollengedichte*. The latter may be attributed to Schumann's interest and expertise in dramatic composition – including opera – in his later years; indeed the first settings anticipating the third wave of song composition are two Mörike songs of 1847, *Das verlassene Mägdlein* and *Die Soldatenbraut*, based on *Rollengedichte*, in which the protagonists characterize themselves through their lyric statements.

In many ways, Schumann's later songs revisit topics and textures from the *Liederjahr*. The kinship of *Freisinn* from the *Myrthen* collection of 1840 and *Die Hütte*, Op. 119, No. 1, after a poem by Pfarrius, or of the *Wanderlied* from the Kerner *Liederreihe* and the later *Ins Freie*, Op. 85, No. 5, after a poem by von der Neun, is obvious, and several other songs capturing the *topos* of the *Wanderlieder* can be cited as evidence. Both *Lied der Suleika*, again from *Myrthen*, and the Platen setting *Ihre Stimme*, Op. 96, No. 3, are linked topically and musically.[42] The Lenau song *Der schwere Abend*, Op. 90, No. 6, with its separation and coming-together of vocal and instrumental parts, dotted rhythmic motive and lugubrious sonorities in the low register, to some degree can be considered a recomposition of *Ich hab' im Traum geweinet*, from *Dichterliebe*.[43] The links to the *Liederjahr* could even be extended to entire cycles. The idea of a multi-voice song cycle manifest in *Liebesfrühling*, Op. 37, of 1841, and, to some extent, hidden rather than revealed in the Eichendorff *Liederkreis*, is picked up again in the late 1840s in the *Spanisches Liederspiel*, Op. 74, and *Spanische Liebeslieder*, Op. 138 (both after Geibel) and the *Minnespiel*, Op. 101 (after Rückert).[44] The *Wilhelm Meister* settings, Op. 98a, alternating female and male personae, perhaps could be mentioned here as well. The Lenau cycle, Op. 90, gathering poignant poems of lost love and concluding with a "Requiem" – to a text thought to be written by Héloise after the death of Abélard – for the poet (Schumann believed mistakenly that Lenau had died in a mental asylum before the event actually took place) is, in a way, a revisiting of the subject matter of *Dichterliebe*, albeit without Heine's wit and irony as distancing effects. The Kulmann songs, Op. 104, and the *Maria Stuart* cycle, Op. 135, may be thought of as distantly analogous to the earlier *Frauenliebe und -leben*.[45]

While there are many links between the later song production and that of the *Liederjahr*, the differences should not be underestimated. By the end of the 1840s Schumann had nearly completed his "conquest" of musical genres, including opera, and was revisiting the Lied in full awareness of aesthetic and compositional challenges that had emerged for himself and other thoughtful musicians in the 1840s. Two contradictory strands can be discerned in his third flowering of Lieder composition, and both have been misunderstood as manifestations of the composer's waning creative faculties.

On the one hand, a trend toward simplification is most noticeable in the songs of the *Liederalbum für die Jugend*, Op. 79, conceived together with the *Album für die Jugend*, Op. 68, the *Musikalische Haus- und Lebensregeln*, and the *Zwölf vierhändige Klavierstücke*, Op. 85, as a substantial pedagogical project that would reaffirm the value of *Hausmusik* as the foundation of a solid musical education. The twenty-nine solo songs and duets gathered in the *Liederalbum* progress from the simple *Frühlingsbotschaft*, No. 3, and *Sonntag*, No. 6, to the intermediate *Der Sandmann*, No. 13, to the playfully sophisticated *Schneeglöckchen*, No. 27, and the elegiac *Mignon*, No. 29; the latter also was published as Op. 98a, No. 1, thereby making it clear that the path from simple to artistic had been completed. Most of the songs in the *Liederalbum* are strophic – even the concluding Mignon setting *Kennst du das Land* – and, by and large, they exhibit easily singable melodies and simple piano textures, as appropriate for performance by budding musicians, as well as four-plus-four-measure phrase structures. In no way are the settings of the *Liederalbum* evidence of a compositional decline. On the contrary, it is surprising to see and hear how much artfulness Schumann was able to muster in a largely modest format. The artful simplicity and straightforwardness of the *Liederalbum* reverberates in other songs composed around 1850, for example, the Kulmann settings, Op. 104, and the *Fünf heitere Lieder*, Op. 125.[46]

On the other hand, Schumann's later songs exhibit a trend toward increasing differentiation, reflecting his experience as a composer of dramatic music during the late 1840s, namely the opera *Genoveva*, *Scenes from Goethe's Faust*, and Byron's *Manfred*, as well as his reactions to a debate over proper declamation in German vocal music, including song. The debate, conducted in various music journals during the middle of the century, occasionally exhibited a nationalistic bent in denouncing Italian opera and *bel canto* singing as inappropriate for setting texts in the German language.[47] A more realistic, even dramatic, declamation is by no means absent in Schumann's songs of the *Liederjahr*. Note the conclusion of *Zwielicht* from the Eichendorff *Liederkreis* or the recitative-like settings of *Wenn ich in deine Augen seh* or *Ich hab' im Traum geweinet* from *Dichterliebe*. Yet such features as these are encountered with greater frequency in the later songs, a fact that gives to some of Schumann's works from this period a proto-Wagnerian sound. (Schumann and Wagner were colleagues in Dresden, before the latter was forced into exile because of his participation in the Dresden uprising, and may have had discussions about the subject of text–music relations.) While only a few of Schumann's late songs could be categorized as declamatory Lieder – *Melancholie*, Op. 74, No. 6, cited by both Mahlert and Hallmark, may be a particularly convincing sample in Schumann's output[48] – a freer approach to declamation which, in turn, had an impact on piano textures and phrase-structure informs several of Schumann's later songs. *Kommen und Scheiden* and *Der schwere Abend* from the Op. 90 Lenau cycle and the two sonnet settings from the *Maria Stuart* cycle, *An die Königin Elisabeth* and *Abschied von der Welt*, are cases in point. The declamatory vocal part is supported and delineated in these songs by sparse motives contributing to a texture entirely appropriate to the oppressive emotional situations captured in the verses.

The picture that emerges from studying Schumann's later songs is ambivalent. Folk-like simplicity, partly necessitated by the pedagogical project the composer had embarked upon around 1850, and simplicity of a different kind achieved through declamatory vocal parts and stark keyboard textures alternate with lush revisitations of earlier *topoi*. Many of the composer's later songs bear characteristics of a *Spätstil* whose blossom and full engagement was cut short by the composer's mental illness and death. When Schumann's demons finally overtook him, it was left to others, among them Brahms, Cornelius, and Liszt, to draw conclusions from the state of the art as left by him and to forge a synthesis, albeit different from the one Schumann may have envisioned, of the various stylistic strands and approaches to the composition of Lieder.

7 A multitude of voices: the Lied at mid century

JAMES DEAVILLE

To many observers at mid century, the Lied was in decline.[1] Despite the activity of Liszt, there was a period between early (Schubert and Schumann) and late (Brahms and Wolf) progenitors when no one figure was seen as leading the way. August Reißmann, in 1861, highlighted one of the dilemmas then facing the Lied – whether it had a future beyond the works of Schubert, Mendelssohn, and Schumann:

> Generally speaking, the development of the sung Lied appears to be completed in those three masters [Schubert, Mendelssohn, and Schumann], both in idea and form . . . If the Lied is not to disappear in subjective caprice, it will have to hold itself within the limits established by those masters.[2]

Twelve years later, Reißmann – as edited by Hermann Mendel – is more sanguine about the Lied's prospects, which he sees as "having grown to a broad stream, which also does not lack depth" (although he considers the "destructive frenzy of the innovators" as jeopardizing the fixed form of the Lied).[3] This said, the ever-growing number of Lieder had become a recurring concern, especially as they were seen as contributing toward the "spreading dilettantism and fashionableness in this compositional genre."[4] As Wolfgang Joseph von Wasielewski wrote in 1858, "we are by no means poor in lyrical productions in recent times – at least according to quantity. It has almost become a fashion that young composers put forward a volume of Lieder as Opus 1."[5] Wasielewski would prove accurate on both counts. The number of Lieder would swell past the point of counting just as many a composer would attempt to launch a career with an Opus 1 Lied or set of Lieder. Schubert presumably inaugurated the custom in 1821 with his Op. 1 *Erlkönig*; others who did likewise include Carl Loewe, Fanny Hensel, Robert Franz, Peter Cornelius, and Arnold Schoenberg. While many an unskilled or under-prepared composer may have found unbidden access into the professional world of music through the Lied, the genre nonetheless presented important opportunities for young composers to show their abilities in a medium that did not require large resources and was readily marketable. This is to be discerned in the Lieder of Cornelius and Adolf Jensen as well as those by women composers like Fanny Hensel, Clara Schumann, and Josephine Lang, who otherwise were unable to enter the public arena with operatic and symphonic scores. (The Lied's relationship with gender issues of the time remains to be thoroughly examined. Above and beyond its suitability as a vehicle for women composers, the Lied appears to have been positioned as inherently female, in comparison with the various transcendental categories of instrumental music.)

The present chapter is intended to highlight the diversity of approaches to the Lied at mid century; thus no one composer's name stands at its head. It also is my intention to bring to the surface the many challenges then facing the Lied. The proliferation of songs weakened any single composer's claim to superiority just as the canonic command of Schubert and Schumann cast a long shadow engendering responses ranging from epigonism to revolution. At the same time, the Lieder of Liszt – despite their quality – appear to have had little impact. The same holds true for Felix Mendelssohn, Loewe, and Franz, none of whom were able to challenge the preeminence of Schubert and Schumann.[6]

Over and above this, at least three other factors account for the Lied's unsettled standing at this time. First, the genre was pulled to the concert hall (while remaining a fixture of the salon), thereby gradually establishing itself as a vital part of musical life in the century's second half. Secondly, while Goethe and Heine still were leading poets for song composers, such figures as Nikolaus Lenau, August Heinrich Hoffmann von Fallersleben, and Emanuel von Geibel provided new directions in German lyric poetry. Lastly, for a variety of (mostly pragmatic) reasons Lied publications moved away from individual songs to small non-cyclical collections that exploited a diversity of poets and styles. An additional tension was the conflict between advancing musical style and the conservatism of the Lied itself: Reißmann's previously cited comments on Schubert, Loewe, and Mendelssohn reflect the era's expectations. As Jürgen Thym has written, "the aesthetic requirements of the genre during the Goethe era – simplicity, singability, popularity – repeatedly were invoked throughout the century."[7] The art song was defined by a set of expectations more than a century old, as this 1849 comment by Ferdinand Simon Gaßner reveals:

> Lied . . . Music and poetry are so blended in and with each other, as in
> virtually no other notable type of vocal music . . . The music of a Lied
> naturally orients itself exactly in accordance with the mood of the poem,
> and if it is to be successful, it is to merge fully with the same, so that it is
> impossible to conceive another melody of the same value for that text. No
> composition demands so much exactness of expression as the modest,
> simple song . . . The Lied must be easily singable, readily comprehensible
> and of no substantial dimensions.[8]

Similar criteria were voiced by Hans Michel Schletterer more than twenty years later, in a historical assessment of Louis Spohr. Invoking standards for German song familiar for more than a century, Schletterer begins by demanding that the Lied possess simplicity, tunefulness, and singability, to which the composer must oblige with individuality and originality. The composer's starting point must always be the poem, for it is this that sets "the narrowly delimited form of the Lied." This notwithstanding, "writing Lieder requires a special talent on the part of the composer, and even when this is present, a certain penchant and love for the subject."[9] As Schletterer continues, the composer's challenge is to find an individual path within the Lied's circumscribed parameters. Each of the composers surveyed in this chapter attempted that in her or his own way. In the countless journal reviews of Lieder, however, the most successful composer was the one who blended the elements of song into an organic entity, a prominent musical paradigm of the time.[10] In describing the works by Beethoven and Schubert in 1852, Julius Schucht provides insights into this important concept. "Words of the text are most beautifully fashioned into musical shapes," he observes. "Music and word here are so organically united that they together make up a whole . . . Every part depends on the other through the most highly organic interrelation." The process was widely seen as itself natural. As Schucht continues: "Just write every note from the holiest depths of your heart and the proper unity as well as the most attractive variety will appear on their own."[11]

Text choice was seen as key to the creation of the organically conceived Lied. The poets preferred by Schumann in 1840 remained popular beyond mid century, but in the sober climate of the 1850s, after the failed revolution, tastes were changing. The enduring popularity of such Romantic poets as Heine and Eichendorff was grounded on the aesthetics propounded by Edouard Schuré and his contemporaries, that certain poets and styles of poetry were more eminently "musical."[12] "We ever perceive in Heine that inner music of the soul, which is the true heartbeat of life."[13] If one surveys the choices of poets by mid-century composers such as Franz, Fanny Hensel, and Clara Schumann, the continuing reliance on Heine and, of course, Goethe – whose popularity would not waver throughout the century – is to be observed. Given the Lied's relative conservativeness at mid century, when originality was permitted only within firmly demarcated boundaries, it stands to reason that composers would be attracted to poems that already had yielded musical fruits in the hands of previous composers, whether in the multiple settings of Goethe's "Erlkönig" or "Mignons Lied" ("Kennst du das Land") or Heine's "Du bist wie eine Blume." Still, poetic taste varied considerably among composers. While Clara Schumann might share the literary predilections of her husband, Cornelius preferred to set his own texts. Also, a certain critique of Romantic poets, especially Heine, became observable as literary style evolved, so that Schucht could postulate, "if you ... now consider how the frivolous and blasé poems by Heine have been composed so many times, you have to wonder even more over the neglect of Lenau."[14] In the works of a Lied composer like Adolf Jensen, it is possible to detect a progression over time, from such Romantic poets as Heine and Eichendorff in his earliest works to an assortment of contemporary poets in later years, including Heyse and Geibel, Georg Friedrich Daumer and Joseph Viktor von Scheffel.

It was the text that drove all other components of the organically conceived song. Yet if poetic choice ranged widely, musical style (including textual declamation) varied so significantly in its details as to preclude any overall assessment, other than to reintroduce the elements of continuity and unity already identified: simplicity, singability, popularity. Even within one composer's oeuvre, the working out of these details differed or changed substantially, at times within the same collection, as for example Felix Mendelssohn's Op. 19, which ranges from the utter simplicity of No. 5, *Gruß*, to the subtly varying details of phrase length and accompaniment in No. 2, *Das erste Veilchen*. This is what makes the study of the Lied at mid century so interesting: observing how composers achieved variety while preserving the genre's time-honored constraints.

The latter also impinged on matters relating to the setting in which the Lied was cultivated, for, by and large, this was not virtuoso music that exceeded the technical reach of the amateur singer and pianist almost always available within a family or intimate social circle. Reviewers reinforced song's domesticity by assessing its performance demands, as they did for contemporaneous piano works. This is not to say that Lieder did not figure in public concerts at mid century – indeed, beyond Liszt's solo piano recitals, concerts that juxtaposed orchestral music, chamber music, solo works for piano and song remained the rule – but the Lied recital as practiced today only gradually became popular during the century's second half.[15] It also was rare that entire song cycles would be performed at this time, although we know that Liszt accompanied a full performance of *An die ferne Geliebte* sung by Ludwig Titze in 1839, in the concert hall of the Gesellschaft der Musikfreunde.[16] It would not be until after mid century that the Lied began to establish itself in the recital hall, an accomplishment associated preeminently with the celebrated baritone Julius Stockhausen, the first singer to perform in their entirety the song cycles *Die schöne Müllerin* (1856) and *Dichterliebe* (1861).

Long before mid century, however, the case can be made that the Lied came to be regarded as a "revered national treasure," an achievement Kravitt defers to the 1870s.[17] The date seems a bit late. In comparison with the extensive study devoted to the German "ideologizing" of instrumental music during the nineteenth century, very little has been written about the national politics of the Lied during the same period.[18] The problem, of course, was the tying of music to text, but the importance attached to organicism, as has been seen, came to the rescue. Since the Lied as poem ideally arose from the depths of the German soul and soil (unlike the operatic text), and the music of the organically conceived song arose from that text, the Lied as poetic-musical entity was a manifestation of the German spirit. Throughout the nineteenth century the Lied enshrined the legacy of the German poetic muse. Maintaining its purity became of paramount importance, as is evident in the previously mentioned definitions and descriptions of the Lied. In a very real sense, Lied composers were contributing to a national resource by providing an integrated vehicle for the display of German lyricism. The resulting "treasure" would play a not unsubstantial role in the escalating fervor over German identity. (I shall return to this point at the end of this essay.)

In examining this crucial segment of Lied history, a brief explanation may be helpful. To the extent that most investigations of the mid-century Lied focus on the high points rather than a broad survey, the one that follows will take something of a middle-of-the road approach wherein well-known figures are juxtaposed with those who are nowadays relegated to secondary or even tertiary rank, but whose music may be worthy of reevaluation or is otherwise historically important. Included will be a look at the Lieder of two women composers, whose high-quality work was neglected during their lifetimes. These composers reflect a diversity of approaches to Lied composition at mid century, with stylistic influences ranging from the so-called Berlin School (Loewe, Fanny Hensel, Felix Mendelssohn), Robert Schumann (Clara Schumann, Jensen), and "neo-Baroque" (Franz) to the New German School (Cornelius, Jensen). (*Die Neudeutsche Schule*, or New German School, is an important concept for this chapter and one that often will be mentioned. Franz Brendel coined the name at the first conference of German musicians, or *Tonkünstler-Versammlung*, held in Leipzig in 1859 as an alternative to the ubiquitous "music [or musician] of the future" – *Zukunftsmusik* or *Zukunftsmusiker*.[19] Many of the innovations associated with the school were prompted by poetic ideas. In addition to Brendel, the most active participants were disciples of Liszt from his Weimar years, including Hans von Bülow, Joachim Raff, and Cornelius.) The earliest of our composers, Loewe, made his mark on the genre with the composition of ballads, which served as models for succeeding generations. For his part, Felix Mendelssohn maintained a conservative approach to Lied composition in a style reminiscent of Reichardt and Zelter; as a result, Mendelssohn the song composer generally has attracted little attention, for he appears not to have significantly or originally contributed to the genre's development. His talented sister Fanny Hensel typically wrote in a similar style – in fact, she published several songs under his name and collaborated with him on other Lieder, even though she was a gifted composer in her own right. The highly respected Franz excelled as a musical miniaturist who focused on the nature and mood of his texts and whose better efforts bear comparison with Robert Schumann. Clara Schumann did not write many songs, but the best of them certainly stand on the same level as those of husband, Robert. Cornelius was the New German most successful in merging the aesthetics of the Lied with "progressive" musical ideals. Finally, brief consideration will be given to a more marginal figure, Adolf Jensen, whose songs were written under the influence of Wagner, yet who never entered the pantheon of nineteenth-century song composition. This still omits such notable mid-century composers as Spohr, Karl Gottlieb Reissiger, Josephine Lang, Franz Abt, Heinrich Marschner, Carl Reinecke, Ferdinand Hiller, Theodor Kirchner, Robert Volkmann, Joachim Raff, Eduard Lassen, Alexander Ritter, Luise Adolpha Le Beau, Anton Rubinstein and Edvard Grieg. The comprehensive history of the Lied in the nineteenth century clearly still is to be written.

Carl Loewe

Loewe (1796–1869), the earliest of the composers examined here, is actually a contemporary of Schubert by year of birth (born a year before), but his contributions to the Lied, or more accurately the ballad, extend beyond mid century. The author of a valuable autobiography, Loewe recently has become a topic of serious scholarship.[20] More importantly, he is recognized as a significant influence on and contemporary of Schubert and Schumann (in fact, he was compared to Schubert during his lifetime). This notwithstanding, Loewe customarily has been relegated to the sidelines of nineteenth-century musical history; in view of his contributions to the Lied and the quality displayed in his very best work, the time perhaps is at hand to reconsider his standing. Raised by a mother who entertained the youth with fairy tales, and growing up with a sister who would declaim ballads to him, Loewe's tendency toward dramatic composition was established early on, and had its first public manifestation in a collection of ballads published as Op. 1 in 1824.[21] The collection's third setting, of Goethe's *Der Erlkönig* (composed 1818), greatly contributed to Loewe's reputation as the "North German Schubert."[22] In 1820, Loewe received an appointment as music director in Stettin, where he would remain for the rest of his life, notwithstanding summer trips through Europe during the 1830s and 1840s when he would sing his ballads (to his own accompaniment) to select audiences.[23] In all, he composed seventeen oratorios, six operas, approximately 350 Lieder and 200 ballads. Thus his song output is numerically comparable to that of Schubert, although the ballad accounts for a comparatively greater percentage.

As a ballad composer, Loewe initially showed a taste for leading poets, one likely inherited from Zumsteeg, whose influence he acknowledged.[24] In his early works Loewe set texts by noted ballad poets Goethe, Herder, and Uhland into the late 1830s, often on topics of the supernatural, whereas in later years – when poets largely had ceased writing ballads – he turned to less significant poets, including Johann Nepomuk Vogl and Ferdinand Freiligrath, whose tales center on historical figures. That his later ballads by and large did not attain the artistic level of the 1820s and 1830s may well confirm Martin Plüddemann's assessment of Loewe's strengths (and weaknesses): "His music always achieved the same heights to which the poet rose."[25] In the event, a commentator such as Max Friedländer did not believe Loewe again attained the level of his Op. 1 ballads.[26] The best works from this collection impress by their sure assimilation of the existing ballad tradition. At the century's start, the sub-genre tended toward simple strophic musical setting or else complex through-composition, as is to be seen in the works of Zumsteeg.[27] Like Schubert, Loewe negotiated a middle path that both preserved or at least worked within the stanzaic formal design of the poetry while satisfying the dramatic requirements of the narrative. The results are relatively short ballads (usually between three and five minutes – his *Erlkönig* clocks in at almost a minute under Schubert's) that nevertheless often present unified dramatic scenes, with close attention to character portrayal and advancing of the storyline. Melodies are motivic, fragmentary, and filled with dramatic touches; accompaniments are often descriptive, with the piano on an equal plane with the voice.

A comparison of Loewe's setting of the noted Goethe ballad "Der Erlkönig" with Schubert's illustrates the former's ability as a song composer. Schubert composed his setting in 1815, Loewe his in 1818, and the compositions are remarkably similar; Walther Dürr attributes the correspondence to a common model, in Zumsteeg.[28] Like Schubert, Loewe was fascinated by the poem's requirement that three different characters be delineated by means of music. Again much like Schubert, Loewe accomplishes this through vocal style and range; unity is maintained by a recurring, menacing trill (see Examples 7.1a and 7.1b for a comparison of Loewe and Schubert's opening measures). The two settings even share key dramatic gestures: at the Erlkönig's final statement, the music abruptly changes character as he threatens to take the child by force, and the agitated accompaniments only cease at the end, at the words "das Kind war tot." Loewe's Op. 1, No. 1 setting of Herder's "Edward" likewise is a tribute to the ability of the twenty-two-year-old; here he establishes a dialogue between mother and son that reveals the gruesome details of the son's murder of his father. For dramatic effectiveness, the impassioned exclamations of "O!" are a masterstroke unsurpassed in his later works; the unusual key of E♭ minor contributes to the

Example 7.1a Schubert, *Erlkönig*, mm. 1–3 and 15–24

prevailing darkness of mood. Similarly compelling ballads are *Herr Oluf,* Op. 2 (1821), *Heinrich der Vogler,* Op. 56 (1836), and *Tom der Reimer,* Op. 135 (1867). Some of the longer ballads take on characteristics of the cantata, given their proportions and sectionality. The much-lauded *Archibald Douglas,* Op. 128 (1858) extends to almost 275 measures and goes through no less than ten tempo changes and seven key changes as the protagonist

Example 7.1b Loewe, *Erlkönig*, mm. 1–7

voices his pleas for reconciliation and repatriation with growing desperation. Other extended ballad settings include *Die verfallene Mühle*, Op. 109, *Der gefangene Admiral*, Op. 115, and *Der Nöck*, Op. 129, No. 2, all relatively late works.

While the longer ballads tend to be sectional, Loewe did compose a ballad cycle – *Gregor auf dem Stein*, Op. 38 (1836) – an Oedipal story divided into five interrelated scenes.[29] But this work reveals Loewe's problematic position within the history of the Lied. Although arguably the last great ballad composer (despite the activity of Martin Plüddemann),[30] he cultivated the genre at a time when, on the one hand, "simplicity" was the governing guideline for the successful Lied, and, on the other, genres like the melodrama (Liszt's *Der traurige Mönch*) and the instrumental ballad (piano and orchestral) began steadily to usurp the sung ballad.[31] It is not without nostalgia for the composer and his characteristic genre that New-German song critic Emanuel Klitzsch, in 1850, reviewed Loewe's Op. 114, *Der Mönch zu Pisa*, in the pages of the *Neue Zeitschrift*: "this work is the fruit of a beautiful 'Indian summer' which we consider with a melancholy gaze."[32]

Fanny Hensel

Heartening signs are at hand that Fanny Hensel (1805–47) at last is being accorded the status of a composer in her own right, one not in need of the deprecating (whether intended or not) prefatory remark, "sister of Felix Mendelssohn." Recent studies of her life, works, and publications of her music have established her position as one of the most significant Lied composers in the period from Schubert's death in 1828 to Schumann's *Liederjahr* in 1840, even though Hensel's Lieder largely were unknown at the time.[33] In fact, her more than 275 songs – the backbone of her compositional output – can be said to surpass in quality and diversity those of her brother (to be discussed below), for whom the Lied by and large was tangential in comparison with compositions for piano and those for larger orchestral and vocal forces. (One reason for this is that Hensel was not granted the same opportunity for gaining familiarity with large performing forces or for drawing upon their resources in performance.) Although her training was by no means inferior to Felix's – they both received first-rate instruction from Zelter and Ludwig Berger in Berlin – her father and brother strongly discouraged Hensel from publishing her music in the belief that doing so was inappropriate for a woman from their family. And yet she persisted; as she wrote to Felix in 1846: "I hope I won't disgrace all of you through my publishing."[34] That rebellious act came almost too late as her life was cut tragically short at the age of forty-two. In all, only about thirty songs appeared in print before or shortly after her death. Many more were performed in the salon of the Mendelssohn home, especially after 1831, when Hensel assumed responsibility for the *Sonntagsmusiken*, where the intellectual elite of Berlin gathered. She would find greater self-assurance as a composer only after her marriage to the open-minded court painter Wilhelm Hensel in 1829 and after the death of her father in 1835.[35] Given this succession of obstacles, Hensel was only as successful as she was thanks to her social status; the many opportunities she enjoyed were unavailable to women of lower rank.[36]

Fanny and Felix grew up surrounded by some of the finest minds of their day. At one time or another they brushed shoulders with the likes of Goethe, Humboldt, Heine, and Eichendorff, a grandfather recognized as one of Germany's foremost philosophers (Moses Mendelssohn), an aunt (Dorothea Veit) who lived with the writer and poet Friedrich Schlegel, and another aunt (Henriette) a school principal in Paris. (The models of such obviously strong-willed aunts no doubt encouraged Hensel's lifelong assertiveness.) All of this fostered intellectual curiosity and wide familiarity with the literature of past and present. Goethe, a remarkable influence in the lives of both Fanny and Felix, was the poet Hensel most often set to music, followed by Eichendorff, Heine, Lenau, Uhland, and Tieck, as well as a fair number from the eighteenth century including Klopstock and Hölty.[37] Having literally grown up surrounded by the leading literary figures of her time, like many a Lied composer, Hensel appears to have intuitively understood that to set a poem to music is not an act of translation.[38] Slight changes sometimes are necessary, such as successively repeated lines or the creation of a textual refrain for the purpose of musical expression or formal unity (*Bergeslust*, Op. 10, No. 5); in others, she undertakes more significant alterations in order to leave a personal mark on the poetry. This was less the case with her earliest songs from the 1820s, which in their literal, strophic settings of Goethe followed in the footsteps of Zelter.

After those early songs, her musical style came to contrast significantly with the relative simplicity that mark the Lieder of composers then active in Berlin; in the event, the sophistication of many of her songs warrants comparison with the best of Robert Schumann's songs. Her Lieder moved from the realm of objective, light-hearted compositions (the Op. 1 *Morgenständchen*), well suited for consumption within the *Sonntagsmusiken*, to the subjective interpretation of texts through wide-ranging melodies, varied harmonic resources, through-composed forms, and an equal partnership of voice and piano.[39]

All of these characteristics converge in *Im Herbste*, Op. 10, one of many works composed in the 1840s which, as Thym has written, show Hensel "finding her voice – one which, when necessary, is capable of skillfully fusing complex formal designs and textural variety."[40] The poem, by Geibel, features a single eleven-line stanza with a-b-a-b-c-c-d-e-e-e-d rhyme scheme. In setting it, Hensel freely treats the poem to internal repetition, as when lines 5 through 7 are climactically repeated to different music. Here the piano accompaniment takes on structural importance, for while the vocal melody is arguably through-composed, the piano's right hand, in alternation with a rising arpeggio figure, holds the song together through constant ornamentation of the vocal line. At key points in the text such as the word "ach," the piano stops altogether, in this case through caesuras on the high notes gb^3 and g^3. Numerous other touches reveal the composer's sensitivity to the poem: the Neapolitan chords at the words "die dumpfe Klage" that all but stop the rhythmic motion or the fully diminished seventh chord at "schmerzlich." The harmonic and tonal instability throughout the song underscores the pain expressed in the text, whether the fully diminished seventh chords on accented beats, descending chromatic lines in the voice, or the unorthodox final cadence (diminished ninth chord on F♯ resolving to a G major chord). Rarely settling onto a stable key, the song moves through G minor, B♭ major, C♭ minor, C minor, and A♭ major, with a remarkable descending sequence of dominant chords a few measures before the end.

In such a work, Hensel reveals that hers was a voice of individuality, especially in the years before her untimely death. Yet the full range of that voice even now is insufficiently appreciated, as it typically was during her lifetime. Hensel at one point witnessed six of her Lieder published not under her name but her brother's. Her songs *Das Heimweh, Italien, Suleika und Hatem* (duet), *Sehnsucht, Verlust,* and *Die Nonne* were published under Felix's name as part of his 1827 Op. 8 (Nos. 2, 3, 12) and 1830 Op. 9 (Nos. 7, 10, and 12), respectively. Nancy Reich suggests that these songs came out under Felix's name, "not to deceive the public or because he could not compose songs, but because her 'modesty' would have been at stake."[41] Whatever the explanation, it effectively diminished Hensel's voice. Her Lieder nevertheless merit greater scrutiny both by performers and public.

Felix Mendelssohn

Having spent his formative years in Berlin, it is natural that Felix Mendelssohn (1809–47) would be influenced by the song ideal of Reichardt and Zelter. In his parents' salon, Mendelssohn also came to enjoy the friendship and support of Goethe and other leading poets of the day. Historians of the genre often overlook his Lieder,[42] since he remained largely untouched by the songs of Schubert and Schumann[43] – his songs in fact hark back to an earlier aesthetic. For Mendelssohn, his unpretentious lyric efforts often served as gifts to friends, as a form of sociability, and not necessarily an expression of deeper subjectivity. Whatever their ultimate inspiration, Mendelssohn's some one hundred songs span a period of about twenty-five years, beginning in the early 1820s. Nevertheless, at no time did the Lied ever serve as a central point of his creative activity. Forty-eight Lieder appeared in seven collections during his lifetime, another seventeen under four posthumous opus numbers, and the remainder – largely early works – have been published only recently. Stylistically and formally, the songs can be grouped chronologically: an early phase until about 1833 (Opp. 8, 9, 19a), one of maturity between 1834 and 1845, and a late period in the last two years of his life (the last songs stand out by virtue of their depth of feeling and "characteristic" tone).[44]

A survey of the texts Mendelssohn set yields unexpected, paradoxical insights: despite Loewe's presence in the Mendelssohn household, Felix set only lyrical poetry (no ballads), and despite Goethe's close acquaintance with the family and Hensel's predilection for composing his poems, Goethe is author of only four song texts by Mendelssohn. Both observations reflect a Lied aesthetic that eschewed close interpretation of a text.[45] As he wrote to his friend the poet Karl Klingemann, "in other poets, namely Goethe, the words turn away from music and want to maintain themselves on their own."[46] Mendelssohn's poetic texts divide into three categories: (1) those by dilettante friends such as Klingemann and Johann Gustav Droysen; (2) *Lieder im Volkston* (by and large anonymous); and (3) poems by noted figures of the past and present. This latter group falls into further categories of older and newer, Hölty and Voß on the one hand, Goethe, Heine, Uhland, Geibel, Byron, and Lenau on the other. Relative proportions are important, however: not only is Goethe all but missing, but Heine and Uhland are little represented (especially in comparison with Hensel).

Musically, Mendelssohn's Lieder embody the principles of simplicity and popularity, tending toward strophic form, modest accompaniments (which nevertheless may be illustrative, as is *Venezianisches Gondellied*, Op. 57, No. 5), and tuneful melodies, although some reflect an instrumental conception. This latter tendency is seen in such instrumental devices as melodic sequences (*Andres Maienlied*, Op. 8, No. 8) and melodies that function independently of the words (such as the strophic *Wenn sich zwei Herzen scheiden*, Op. 99, No. 5). Both lead to his keyboard "songs without words," a hybrid genre that is arguably his most significant contribution to the Lied. Even though he seems uninterested in entering into the details of poetry, Mendelssohn nonetheless constructed beautiful melodies that satisfied the needs of a public enamored of tunefulness. More than Schubert and other leading song composers of his day, he used strophic form for *volkstümlich* settings, such as in *Gruß* from Op. 19, *Sonntagslied* from Op. 34, *Volkslied* from Op. 47, and *Lieblingsplätzchen* from Op. 99. Meters and rhythms remained simple until Mendelssohn's last period, despite his frequent reliance on 6/8. The harmonic elements are not particularly adventurous, especially in comparison with Schubert and Schumann, even though Mendelssohn occasionally uses augmented triads in transitional contexts (m. 35 of *Nachtlied*, Op. 71, No. 6) and will settle into the subdominant region to darken the sound of a song (*Jagdlied*, Op. 84, No. 3). Accompaniments almost always are subordinate to the vocal part, and preludes and postludes serve no real poetic purpose. When all of these features come together in one and the same song, Mendelssohn's Lieder stand apart from those of Schubert, Schumann, Loewe, and even his sister Fanny. Gisela Müller has compared settings of the same Heine poems by Felix and Fanny, and determined that rather than allowing the text to shape his songs, "he conceived his Lieder according to pre-formed musical models that strongly neglected the texts."[47] Still, it would be wrong to characterize Mendelssohn's songs as musically unsophisticated or lacking resonance with the culture of his times.[48]

Considered by some commentators to be one of his best, Mendelssohn's setting of the Goethe sonnet "Die Liebende schreibt" (composed in 1831, published posthumously as Op. 86, No. 3) provides an absorbing example of the degree of sophistication he was capable of investing in a song.[49] (Schubert, Schumann, Brahms, and August Bungert also set the text.) Goethe has furnished a classical sonnet, consisting of fourteen lines, organized into four stanzas with the rhyme scheme abba-abba-cde-cde. The internal scheme of individual lines poses particular problems to composers, since each begins and ends on a weak syllable with five stresses in between; Mendelssohn himself reported: "it is too insane to compose that; it is not suited for music at all."[50] At first glance, Mendelssohn's solution to the poetic structure seems simple: the two quatrains are accompanied by repeated eighth-note motion, while for the two tercets, he changes to a sixteenth-note broken arpeggio figuration in the piano, ascending for the first three lines, descending for the second three. However, the composer elides the transition between the quatrains and the tercets by introducing the new accompaniment figure three measures before the end of the last quatrain. Furthermore, and more importantly, Mendelssohn lets the text direct the tonal structure of the song. The first quatrain that describes the relationship of the lovers is squarely in E♭ major, with a modulation to the subdominant and return to the tonic. When Goethe's second stanza questions that which was established in the first, Mendelssohn moves through E♭ minor to G♭ major, a key not closely related to the tonic that represents the break in the relationship. The third stanza begins in G♭ major, but as the writer anticipates the response of her lover, the key returns to the tonic by settling on the subdominant, given that the emotional uncertainty is yet unresolved. Even though Goethe leaves the resolution open-ended, Mendelssohn settles the outcome by introducing a new 'Espressivo' theme in the left hand in E♭ major at the point where the poet asks for a sign from his beloved. Here we see Mendelssohn not only entering into the spirit of the poem, but also affecting its outcome through music.

Although he did not contribute to the mainstream of nineteenth-century song, Mendelssohn did establish a model for a conservative successor such as Carl Reinecke, whose substantial Lieder production, while lacking in individuality, nonetheless was successful in finding a public.[51]

Clara Schumann

Few women composers have attracted as much scholarly attention as has Clara Schumann (1819–96), starting with a series of biographies, many popular or fictional (including several films), culminating in the definitive life-work study by Nancy Reich.[52] In light of her activity as a virtuoso pianist, it is not surprising that her substantial body of piano and chamber music should have initially attracted more scholarly attention than her twenty-five songs, fifteen of which were published during her lifetime.[53] Her Lieder range in date from 1841 to 1853, and their origins are closely tied to her husband. Thus, upon Robert's encouragement, Clara wrote three songs that she presented to him as a Christmas gift in 1840. He approved of the results, encouraging her to undertake a joint composition of Rückert's "Liebesfrühling," which she completed in time for his birthday in 1841 (8 June). The resulting twelve songs featured three by Clara (Op. 12) and nine by Robert.[54] In 1842 and 1843, she again gave gifts of Lieder (respectively two and three) to Robert on his birthday. In turn, he arranged for Breitkopf & Härtel to publish a collection of six of her songs (Op. 13 in 1844). The six songs of Op. 23 (1853) also owe their origins to Robert, to the extent that he was reading the poems of Hermann Rollet and appears to have recommended them to his wife.[55]

Clara did not write much about her songs, but her attitude toward her other works is surely suggestive, as is revealed in a letter to Robert from 14 March 1840. "I cannot compose," she discloses. "It makes me at times quite unhappy, but it really is not possible, I have no talent for it. Don't think that it is laziness. And moreover now a song – that I can't do *at all*. It takes inspiration to compose a song, to comprehend a text in its full meaning."[56] In response to the Lieder from late 1840, she remarked that "while Robert is out" she spent the time "trying to compose a song (which always has been his wish), and then I in the end succeeded in creating *three*, which I will give to him for Christmas. Even if they are of no value at all, only a *really weak attempt*, I am counting on Robert's indulgence."[57] She deferred to Robert as well for the choice of poets. In her published songs she set Rückert, Heine, Geibel, and Rollet, noted Romantic poets all except for Rollet, a minor Austrian poet whose *Jucunde* Robert was reading in 1853. The extensive poetry reading in the Schumann household ensured mutual discussions of poems for musical setting.[58] However, unlike Robert, she avoided setting ballads or more complex poetic forms. As Reich has observed, she "generally chose poems of two to three stanzas on such subjects as love, parting and rejection, springtime and nature . . . Most are in varied strophic form."[59]

The quality of Clara Schumann's songs is quite high; typically, they feature richly varied harmonies and idiomatically conceived piano parts. For example, *Die stille Lotosblume*, Op. 13, No. 6, ends on an unresolved dominant seventh chord in A♭ major and explores the flat keys in a harmonically roving middle section. In general, the piano works well with the voice to establish moods, yet sometimes requires virtuoso performing abilities, as in *Er ist gekommen in Sturm und Regen*, Op. 12, No. 2. Her best Lieder compare favorably with Robert's, such as her three contributions to Op. 12 that for contemporary reviewers were all but indistinguishable from his works in the same set.[60]

The high achievement of the six Rollet Lieder, Op. 23, merits separate consideration. Even though the poetry is below the standard usually identified with the Schumann household, Clara shows her literary acumen by selecting the strongest of Rollet's works and introducing qualitative improvements (omission of strophes). Here she prefers strophic or modified strophic forms, but everything is diverse, depending on the text. The accompaniments range from simple to demanding, the generally diatonic harmonic palette effectively incorporates expressive dissonances, and the melodies closely reflect the character of the individual poems. What we see in Op. 23 is a composer sure of her craft, one who need not resort to length or hyperbole to make a statement. Neither Op. 23 nor her earlier collections can be considered to be cyclical, in terms of textual narrative, key scheme or thematic material (in this regard, her Lieder resemble those by Robert Franz or her husband in his later years). Twelve songs remained unpublished during her lifetime. By and large, these date from the 1840s and served as birthday and Christmas gifts to Robert. As such, they are less substantial than the published songs, even though some – such as *Am Strande* or *Das Veilchen* – are entirely effective.

Er ist gekommen is considered one of Clara's best songs. Following Rückert's poem, the music divides into three strophes. The restlessness, passion, and uncertainty of the first two strophes are expressed in the rushing accompaniment (Example 7.2), the prominent half-step in the fragmented melody, the surging dynamics, and the F minor tonality. As the text in each of the first two strophes moves from the literal depiction of the storm to the emotional states of the man and woman, the music lyrically settles into A♭ major. After the second strophe, repeated to the music of the first, there occurs one final return of the stormy opening material, and then the mood changes to the calm after the protagonist's affirmation of love (marked 'Ruhig'). A♭ major prevails, the voice moves in large rising arches, and the piano is less active. This section also draws on melodic material previously heard in the B phrases. The piano postlude adds a significant commentary: references to the opening attempt to establish themselves and thus introduce uncertainty at the moment of resolution, a move thwarted by the song's lyrical ending. The overall form reveals an inventive type of modified strophic form with a scheme of A B A B A C, C being a distant version of B.

Critical reaction to Clara's Lieder was mixed, depending on the source. Not surprisingly, the AmZ, with its "conservative song ideal,"[61] embraced a song such as *Er ist gekommen*,[62] while Robert's NZfM wrote more favorably about her lyrical work.[63] Writing about Op. 12, Robert himself, in a letter dated 23 June 1841, declared: "Together we have composed a number of Rückert's songs, which relate to each other like questions and answers . . . I

Example 7.2 Clara Schumann, *Er ist gekommen in Sturm und Regen*, Op. 12, No. 2, mm. 1–13

think the songs will have to arouse interest. They are almost all in a light and easy style and written with real heart."[64] And her songs did spark interest, given that they were greeted with a degree of commercial success during Clara's lifetime – they remained in publishers' catalogues throughout the century. In 1872, Franz Liszt published three in transcription (Op. 12, No. 11; Op. 13, No. 5; and Op. 23, No. 3), long after their original publication.

Although Liszt's important article about Clara does not specifically mention her songs, he identifies her talent in "continuous, mystical reflection on that which is sublime, beautiful, ideal."[65] As is the case with today's scholars and performers, Liszt recognized the value of her contributions. With the valorization of her piano music, it is hoped that her songs will find a similar position both in performance and study.[66]

Robert Franz

Esteemed by Schumann and Liszt in his day, Franz (1815–92) remained little known even in his native country until the Halle Händel-Haus began promoting his music in the 1980s.[67] This continued with the centenary of his death in 1992, which inspired a comprehensive *Festschrift* with articles about his music and its reception.[68] It has been argued that his almost exclusive dedication to the Lied is one reason why listeners are unaware of his music; the point makes sense, especially since, in contrast to the symphony and opera, the Lied generally has been considered a lightweight genre. A few of his Lieder nevertheless have survived in the repertories of a handful of singers, such as *Widmung* (Op. 14, No. 1) or *Gute Nacht!* (Op. 36, No. 5), but the majority await revival. Whether or not this occurs is an open question, given that recent commentators have faulted his textual "literal-mindedness," overall "sameness," and "lack of passion."[69] Yet if for no other reason than that he offers an alternative to Schubert and Schumann at mid century, Franz is deserving of another look. As the composer himself noted in 1871, "my music generally has its basis less in Schubert and Schumann than in Bach and Händel."[70] The remark nevertheless pinpoints another possible weakness; it seems that Franz venerated a bit too thoroughly the music of the past, one in turn inspiring a conservative approach seen as out of touch with the times in which Franz lived.

Largely self-taught, Franz did study music in Dessau with Friedrich Schneider (1835–37). Early acquaintance with the music of Bach, Handel, Haydn, and Mozart, folk music, and the Protestant chorale resulted in life-long influences.[71] Franz spent most of his relatively uneventful life in Halle, occupying positions as organist, director of the *Singakademie*, and finally music director at Halle University (where he received an honorary doctorate in 1861). An important milestone was Robert Schumann's favorable review of his Op. 1 in the *Neue Zeitschrift* of 1843, which helped bring Franz's name before a wider public.[72] Thus began his career. Unfortunately, Franz already had begun to lose his hearing in 1848; by 1867 he was completely deaf, which forced him to give up performing a year later. He continued to compose until at least 1884; in later years, he also suffered from a nervous disorder. Throughout his life, Liszt – who recognized Franz's talent and always treated him with respect – helped at key moments, including publishing a laudatory article in 1855, republishing it in book format in 1872 (upon Franz's request), and making generous donations to the Robert Franz Fund.[73] In 1848, Liszt transcribed thirteen of his Lieder for piano.[74] Franz valued this support, telling Liszt's associate August Göllerich in 1885, "I have him to thank for everything."[75] Thym argues that Franz "was unwilling to take sides" in the battle between the New German School and the conservative camp.[76] This may be true publicly, where he did not want to besmirch his benefactor Liszt, but privately, with Joseph Joachim and Clara Schumann, Franz took a stand against the music of the New German movement.[77] It is indicative that in his conversations with Waldmann, Franz does not mention Liszt's music, but rather his noble spirit.[78]

In all, Franz published over 280 Lieder between 1843 and 1884, usually in groups of six. Despite a creative life lasting more than forty years, his songs resist division into stylistic periods, even though the earliest tend to be more innovative and adventurous (Opp. 1, 2, 5, and 10).[79] Characteristically, he avoided anything that could be called "pathos," "sentimentality," or "sensuality." Instead, as Franz declared, he favored "chasteness."[80] Songs were not to awaken a listener's passions, but rather to promote "peace" and "reconciliation" through what Thym identifies as "warm, gently passionate sentiments, often tinged with feelings of nostalgia and melancholy."[81] Exceptions exist, above all such earlier songs as the dramatic *Ja, du bist elend* (Op. 7, No. 6, a Wagner favorite) or *Gewitternacht* (Op. 8, No. 6). Noted as "the lyricist and master of miniature painting," Franz may be said to represent the flipside of the coin from Loewe.[82] Thus he avoids the ballad and other dramatic forms, his songs are brief, and he rarely uses piano preludes or postludes. While his taste in poets was wide-ranging, he preferred such figures as Heine (more than sixty settings), Goethe, Mörike, Rückert, Eichendorff, Lenau, Geibel, and Burns, or befriended poets such as Wilhelm Osterwald (fifty-two). Despite the number of musical settings of one poet, Franz only published eight collections of songs to poems by the same author, and among them only the *Schilflieder* (Op. 2) is truly cyclical.

Franz himself best summarized his word–music relationship: "I have composed feelings, not words."[83] Moreover, "musical content is essential [to a Lied], not the emphasis on this or that word."[84] It could be said that he engaged in "mood painting" rather than "tone painting." For Franz, a mystical relationship exists between a poem and the music: "the text not only inspires the composition, but the latter already mysteriously resides hidden in it. It goes without saying that I am only speaking of poems that really long for music, consequently roam the world as a 'half being' until they have found their completion in notes."[85] While Franz suggests a Romantic unity of word and tone in this statement, the belief that each text had an ideal musical setting led both to a "literal-mindedness" in his musical settings of poetry and to a failure to understand the paradoxes of word–music relationships in Schubert and Schumann.[86] As already suggested, the composer's "basic mood" ruled out the possibility of his being able to set more complex texts – unity and clarity were key. Commenting on his own Lieder, Franz stresses how a generating motive at a song's start prepares for all that follows. Given this privileging of melodic unity, it is not surprising that Franz would prefer strophic or ternary forms. "I do not compose the text as it gradually unfolds," he noted. "Rather I illuminate it from [its] essential point. Once that has been discovered and has found its musical formula, presented as a motive, everything else will then take care of itself."[87]

Franz's aversion to heterogeneity and his investment in the organicist metaphor carry over into all aspects of his songs. A work's harmonic structure should function as a "skeleton" rather than as a collection of unrelated juxtaposed harmonies.[88] While most of his Lieder stick close to the tonic (in part because of their brevity), he does introduce touches of harmonic color. Thus a song like *Aus meinen großen Schmerzen*, Op. 5, No. 2, which begins in F major, passes through A major, and ends in D minor, all within twenty measures. The notion of interrelationships applies as well to language and music, voice and accompaniment, for "the parts, from which a song is put together as an independent artistic whole, must determine each other, that words and music, voice and piano complete . . . each other in such a manner that one cannot exist without the other."[89] As the scholarly literature frequently has emphasized, the accompaniments can take on the character of a chorale setting, which may reinforce religious imagery (*Widmung*, Op. 14, No. 1) or may archaicize (*Bitte*, Op. 9, No. 3). In such cases his interest in past music, particularly Bach and Handel, comes more obviously to mind. Other Baroque influences include polyphonic textures (*Kommt Feinsliebchen heut?*, Op. 25, No. 4), imitation (*Ein Stündlein wohl vor Tag*, Op. 28, No. 2), and sequence (*Für Musik*, Op. 10, No. 1).

In rounding out this section, it will repay our effort to briefly consider the five *Schilflieder*, Op. 2, dedicated to Schumann and considered by many to be his best songs.[90] The only set of Franz's songs that is a true cycle (by narrative, key, and mood) and one of only eight of his opus numbers devoted to one poet, the *Schilflieder* occupy a unique position within Franz's work. Franz even changed the order of Lenau's poems to lend the whole greater dramatic shape. He moved *Auf geheimem Waldespfade* to the beginning because, as he noted, it gave the cycle a "swelling" and diminishing of sounds from nature.[91] Emotionally, "the lyrical I" increases in despair, only to diminish in intensity, attaining what Franz called "quiet resignation" at

Table 7.1

Incipit	Form	Tempo	Meter and key
Auf geheimem Waldespfade	a b a¹	Andantino	2/4 E♭ minor
Drüben geht	a b c	Andante con moto	4/4 G minor / B♭ major
Trübe wird's	a a¹	Allegro maestoso	4/4 C♯ minor
Sonnenuntergang	a a a¹	Allegro agitato	2/4 F♯ minor
Auf dem Teich	a b b¹	Andantino	2/4 C minor / E♭ major

Example 7.3a Robert Franz, *Schilflieder*, Op. 2, No. 1, *Auf geheimem Waldespfade*, mm. 1–6

the end.[92] Table 7.1, adapted from Waldura, shows the collection's overall unity and cyclic structure.

Example 7.3 compares the beginnings of Nos. 1 and 5, to reveal the similarities in *Grundbestimmung*; in the former the "softest whisper of tearful lament," in the latter "quiet resignation." The way Franz establishes this mood at the start of *Auf geheimem Waldespfade* is ingenious: a gently undulating melodic line alternates with triplets and duplets, supported by an elliptical harmony (A♭ minor – G♭ major – B♭ minor – E♭ minor, the tonic) mitigated by suspensions (7–6, 9–8, 6–5). His Lieder are filled with this type of subtle detail, although most not as pronounced as Op. 2. Even so, they depend on "individuality of invention, care of execution, and close adherence to the sense of the poet," as Gustav Engel wrote of Franz's style in 1856.[93] His is a voice that deserves to be heard.

Example 7.3b Robert Franz, *Schilflieder*, Op. 2, No. 5, *Auf dem Teich*, mm. 1–10

Peter Cornelius

Curiously, the "progressive" Liszt circle in Weimar in the 1850s brought forth no significant composers of symphonic music (other than Liszt himself and Joachim Raff, who left Weimar in 1856), but rather composers of Lieder, operas and, as might be expected, piano works. The most talented song composer among the New Germans, Cornelius (1824–74), was well prepared for a career in writing for the voice, growing up in a family of stage actors.[94] Like other young people of his era (e.g., Robert Schumann), Cornelius immersed himself in German literature at an early age, including novels and short stories by Jean Paul and E. T. A. Hoffmann and the poetry and plays of Goethe and Schiller. His primary activity as song composer took place between 1852 and 1856, a period that brought forth more than half of his total production of approximately eighty Lieder. After the composition of his comic opera *Der Barbier von Bagdad* (1855–58), Cornelius had several more good years of Lied composition (1859, 1861–62), but after that, he all but discontinued song, favoring instead works for choir and small vocal ensemble.

Cornelius set an assortment of older and newer poets in a selection that gives him an individual profile: Goethe, Schiller, Hölderlin, Bürger, Platen, Hebbel, his friend Heyse all inspired musical composition, whereas Eichendorff and Heine barely appear. Moreover, unlike other Lied composers of his day, Cornelius developed a strong talent as poet, and often set his own poems to music.[95] What is remarkable is the high quality of poetry set by Cornelius, whoever the poet. His selection of texts and forms also stands apart. As has been recognized, Cornelius departed from Romantic traditions of nature lyrics, at least in their darker or more mysterious aspects.[96] His songs tend toward introspective portraits (as in the cycle *Trauer und Trost*, Op. 3) or religious reveries (the cycle *Vater Unser*, Op. 2 and *Weihnachtslieder*, Op. 8). He avoided longer structures like the ballad in favor of shorter lyric poetry or older forms like the ode and sonnet, and introduced irregular metrical patterns and rhyme schemes.

In his Lieder, Cornelius folds features inherited from Schumann and the New Germans into a personal interpretation. Most of his songs are short, unified settings cast according to modified strophic design, although beneath their apparent simplicity lies a deeper motivic, harmonic, and formal complexity. Chromatic lines and harmonies reveal Lisztian and Wagnerian harmonic practices (*Auftrag*, Op. 5, No. 6). The melodic line – essentially lyrical – flows in short phrases that closely match the text's declamation (*An den Traum*, Op. 3, No. 4). Working to unify a song, the accompaniment also supports the text's changing modes while introducing harmonic fullness (*Ein Ton*, Op. 2, No. 3). As Thym has observed, Cornelius's advanced musical (and poetic) language presages the practices of Wolf and Schoenberg.[97] In his union of word and music, Cornelius ranks among the finest of nineteenth-century Lied composers, a reality that makes his current neglect inexplicable. Cornelius, unlike Franz or Liszt, followed in Schumann's footsteps in grouping songs into thematically unified cycles. The cycles are: *Vater Unser* (Op. 2), *Trauer und Trost* (Op. 3), *Rheinische Lieder, Brautlieder, Weihnachtslieder* (Op. 8), *An Bertha* (Op. 15). Based on the available evidence, it appears that Cornelius wrote a cycle's poetry before turning to the music.

At least one of Cornelius's cycles deservers a closer look. *Trauer und Trost*, composed in late 1854, sets six poems written earlier that year. The poetry describes the emotional journey of a man whose beloved has died, moving from grief in the real world to solace in a realm of dreams that assure her immortality. The sequence of poems establishes this narrative,[98] one Cornelius underscores through the cycle's key scheme: E minor (Phrygian-inflected) – D major – E minor – B minor – G major – E minor (Phrygian-inflected). The lament of *Trauer* is noteworthy for its expressive yet unorthodox harmonies. The first song also presents two harmonic/melodic ideas that connect the cycle. The first is the recurrence of the pitch B, the second the tension between the key of E minor (or simply the pitch E) and its Phrygian neighbor F, a tonal relationship that takes on significance in the first and last songs, where it creates a "frame."[99] The arpeggiated four-note descending melody of *Angedenken* evokes the memory process, but even more striking is the

Example 7.4 Peter Cornelius, *Trauer und Trost*, Op. 3, No. 3, *Ein Ton*, mm. 1–15

song's tonal instability: six of its twenty-nine measures are rooted in D major and it begins on an E minor chord. Perhaps the most noted (and notorious) song by Cornelius is No. 3, *Ein Ton*, in which the voice intones its text throughout on the single pitch B. This idiosyncratic gesture allows for hope to enter through the piano accompaniment, which creates melodic and harmonic interest (Example 7.4) while representing the external sounds to which the voice refers (the voice internalizes the tone by the end of the song). The right hand of the piano picks up the B in *An den Traum*, where the roles are reversed as the voice requests release through dreaming. The grieving one discovers that his beloved takes substance through Lieder in *Treue*. *Trost* brings the various musical elements together: as the dream takes on certainty in eternity, Cornelius provides a simple, chorale-like accompaniment. The B is much less prominent and, even though the key returns to the Phrygian-inflected E minor of the first song, the message of solace and hope is tonally affirmed in the last measures by a final cadence on E major.

The care Cornelius paid to poetic and musical elements in his cycles recalls the work of Robert Schumann. However, Cornelius applied the advances of the New German School to the Lied, above all in the realm of harmony, where he pointed the way to later developments. Liszt's Lieder may have surpassed those of Cornelius in formal and harmonic innovation (the "Tristan" chord in *Ich möchte hingehn*), but Cornelius was more successful in integrating the New-German advances into the traditional Lied, whereby his songs retained at their core the simplicity and singability that characterized the best works in the genre throughout the century.

Adolf Jensen

Adolf Jensen (1837–79) is emblematic of the mid-century Lied composer who recognized Robert Schumann as *spiritus rector*,[100] although Liszt and Wagner tempered the older composer's influence. Of the works to which the composer assigned an opus number, more than half are Lieder – a count yielding 175 songs. Jensen's poets were mainly Eichendorff, Geibel, Heyse, Scheffel, and Roquette, a selection that reflects a shift from his earlier preferences for Goethe and Heine.[101] While his settings of eleven songs from the Hafis (Persian) and fourteen songs from the *Spanisches Liederbuch* of Heyse and Geibel may reflect the late nineteenth-century fascination with exotic material, Jensen's thirty-five songs to texts by English-language poets (Shelley, Burns, Moore, Scott, Tennyson) are unique among German composers.

Jensen's style combines several different directions of Lied composition at mid century. His subtle timbral effects (bordering on the Impressionistic), preference for details of tone painting, and adoption of Wagnerian harmonic devices (including ninth and half-diminished seventh chords) create a bridge between Schumann and Wolf. Independent chromatic lines, imitative devices, and generally polyphonic textures bring him closer to Brahms. It was above all his "cloying" vocal lines and "sweetly" chromatic harmonies, in support of the texts, that caused some contemporaries to dismiss Jensen for sentimentality bordering on the effeminate. As Riemann observed: "his numerous collections include a fullness of musically poetic expression, its sensitivity often is elevated to the level of the feminine, the salon."[102]

Other Lied composers during the third quarter of the nineteenth century who followed in the footsteps of Robert Schumann include Theodor Kirchner (1823–1903) and Robert Volkmann (1815–83), neither of whom are much remembered for their songs. Whereas Jensen attempted to reconcile New-German and conservative approaches in his Lieder, these successors of Schumann did not really advance beyond his ideals and style. Among the New Germans during the same period, it was Eduard Lassen (1830–1904) and Alexander Ritter (1833–96) who – after Liszt and Cornelius – cultivated the Lied most prominently, even though their songs did not have the same influence.

Conclusion

As this survey of selected song composers at mid century has sought to establish, the genre was not in imminent danger of disappearing, despite contemporaneous predictions to the contrary. In many ways this is ironic, as there existed no single voice to carry on after Schubert and Schumann, and their increasing ascendancy made it all but impossible to fill such a role. Each composer followed her or his own voice, shaped by a variety of approaches to Lied composition, whether that of Schumann, the Berlin School, the New German School, or some other set of influences (such as Bach and Handel in the case of Franz). Despite the principles of simplicity and singability (and each composer's attempt to satisfy those requirements), this diversity reflected a time of change. While the majority of newly composed Lieder remained intended for domestic consumption, the continuing canonization of works by Schubert and Schumann fostered the genre's move into the concert hall. As mentioned above, baritone Julius Stockhausen would not sing a complete song cycle in public until 1856, first with *Die schöne Müllerin* and again in 1861 with *Dichterliebe*. Not everyone greeted this development with praise and it was not until the 1870s that the Lied became a staple of concert life. By that time, what determined the genre's triumph may have been not so much a matter of aesthetics as it was an issue of politics. With the establishment of the German Empire in 1871, the need to flaunt national pride sometimes came at the expense of musical concerns. At times such pride could turn ugly. As Wolf would discover, a performance of his *Heimweh* during which he was serving as pianist "was made the occasion of a pan-German demonstration." At the song's concluding line – "Grüß dich, Deutschland, aus Herzensgrund" (I greet thee Germany, with all my heart) – mayhem broke out at Vienna's Wagner Verein, much to the composer's outrage.[103] This was not the last time the Lied would be conscripted for such purposes. This, too, is another story – one yet to be completely told.

8 The Lieder of Liszt

RENA CHARNIN MUELLER

Although the name Franz Liszt (1811–86) is associated mainly with key-board and symphonic compositions, in the writing of Lieder one finds some of his most progressive and finely wrought expressions. Within song's inti-mate setting, Liszt was able to convey musical thoughts and gestures often found to be problematic in his larger works: here he was not always the public figure leading the New German School and devoting himself to the "Music of the Future," champion of often unpopular compatriots, such as Richard Wagner. The Lieder were a compositional testing ground, not un-like the way in which Beethoven treated his piano sonatas as harmonic and formal experiments for other genres. More tellingly, in Lieder, Liszt found it possible to convey the very complex soul of the devoted but absent father, impatient lover, often tortured and unhappy but generous man of the world, and, finally, resigned mystic.

There are eighty-seven songs for voice and piano, and sixteen for voice and orchestra,[1] and he perhaps was the first nineteenth-century composer to conceive of orchestral Lieder for the concert hall:[2] his orchestration of *Die Vätergruft* was the last composition on which he worked in the days before his death on 31 July 1886. But in reality, there are many more songs, because he was an artist who continually rethought his compositions, re-vising them several times after their initial state had been achieved, yielding multiple readings of the same musical text.[3] This is a constant throughout his oeuvre: as with many artists, musical as well as visual (for example, Monet's famous *Haystacks*), for Liszt, repetition was not a stylistic tic but an article of faith – he could return to previously composed works and see fresh possibilities at every juncture. Some of these Lieder revisions have yet to be published because they are extant only in manuscript copies, offering fasci-nating insight into the composer's creative process throughout the decades of his compositional maturity.[4] Yet even taking into account these multiple versions, Liszt's vocal output is not as large as that of Schumann, Brahms, or Wolf. His choice of texts was frequently dictated by the personal situation in which he found himself, and may thus appear haphazard: he often set poetry that was sub-standard even by the arguably saccharine, sentimental tastes of the era in which he worked, and some of the errors in language setting (his early Lieder suffer from imperfect Italian syllabification, as well as incorrect stresses in German) that he allowed to go to print did not always

serve the music or the performers well.[5] But overall, from a qualitative perspective, the Lieder stand as perhaps the most consistent part of his oeuvre,
free of many of the issues associated with the sometimes problematic piano
music.[6]

The young composer's first encounters with the newly popular Romantic
Lied came in the early 1830s as a result of his transcriptions of the works
of Beethoven and Schubert as solo piano compositions.[7] Living in Paris,
and anxious to increase his personal repertory for the concert stage, he
undertook several projects involving the transcription of famous Schubert
Lieder for keyboard, single-handedly opening up a vast new platform for
the new concert virtuoso. Among the earliest transferences of the two-
person performing genre to the soloist venue, his transcribing efforts met
with considerable success with the newly emergent musical public and the
publishers who sought to satisfy it (especially Maurice Schlesinger in Paris,
Friedrich Hofmeister in Leipzig, and Theodore Haslinger and Anton Diabelli
in Vienna). And always faithful to his original, Liszt invariably insisted that
a song's poetical text be printed on a page preceding the piano transcription,
or beneath the musical text.[8]

Liszt struck out on his own in Lieder only after he had left Paris in 1835,
moving to Switzerland with the Countess d'Agoult. The composition of his
original Lieder fall into three distinct periods: the earliest (1839–47) immediately followed the several Schubert cycles for the publishers mentioned
above (among them selections from *Winterreise*, *Die schöne Müllerin*, and
Schwanengesang). The second period (1848–61) coincides with his tenure in
Weimar as the leader of the *Hofkapelle*; and the third covers the final third of
his life (1862–86). While this is a convenient subdivision, it is not intended
to suggest anything more than a chronological breakdown, for as we shall
see, the sophisticated qualities usually singled out in the late music are to be
found throughout all phases of his career and especially in the Lieder.[9]

Liszt's first solo song was written in Italy in 1839, where he was traveling with the Countess d'Agoult – a lullaby for his three-year-old daughter,
Blandine, entitled *Angiolin dal biondo crin*, with a text by a favorite traveling companion of Liszt and Marie, the Marchese Cesare Bocella.[10] By this
time, Liszt was chafing at the strictures of his life with Marie, and about
to set off on an eight-year period as traveling virtuoso, returning only in
the summer to reunite and vacation with her and their children on the
island of Nonnenwerth in the Rhine near Cologne.[11] It was during these
German travels that he encountered first-hand the Lieder compositions of
Schumann and Mendelssohn, and began to collect a variety of texts for
composition from the same literary sources – among them the popular
poetry of Heine, Goethe, Rückert, Georg Herwegh, Heinrich Hoffmann
von Fallersleben, Friedrich Hebbel, and Emanuel von Geibel. While Liszt's

approach to Lieder composition closely resembles that of Schumann, like Schumann Liszt not only sought to link the works through content but also to develop a freer approach to form, infrequently obeying the strictures of the strophic settings he encountered and often relying on modified strophic or through-composed constructions, which better suited his adventurous tonal palette. His initial sets differed immediately from those of his contemporaries: all the cycles published in the early 1840s contain fewer numbers, with texts loosely linked in terms of content.[12] This is in line with his attitude in contemporaneous works such as the *Etudes d'exécution transcendantes* or the *Album d'un Voyageur/Années de pèlerinage*, original collections much larger in concept than anything he had previously attempted. Few if any of Liszt's Lieder are *volkstümlich* in character, or contain substantial folk-like elements, save for the material in *Die Loreley* (to which I shall return below).

The first Heine text he set – and by far one of the most important – is *Die Loreley*, written in Nonnenwerth in 1841 and published by Schlesinger in Paris as one of six songs joined loosely by Liszt with the common thread of the Rhine river,[13] a reflection of the preoccupation with the still fresh "Rhine Crisis" of 1840.[14] Liszt subsequently ventured forcefully into song settings in languages other than German, as has been noted above: his interest in the French *Romance* and *Mélodie* tradition is exemplified during this period in settings of such pieces as Delphine Gay's *Il m'aimait tant* (c. 1840), various Hugo texts, the French version of the 1841 *Die Zelle in Nonnenwerth* (*En ces lieux tout me parle d'elle*, Lichnowsky [trans. E. Monnier], 1844), as well as the 1845 Béranger *Jeanne d'Arc*, which he subtitled "scène dramatique" to distinguish it from the other French works.

Drawing inspiration from the musically inflected title of Heine's poetic collections (*Buch der Lieder*, 1827; 2nd edn., 1837), he appropriated Heine's wording for two sets of songs published by Schlesinger in Paris. The first set, entitled *Buch der Lieder* I (1843), contained settings of Goethe, Heine, and Lichnowsky;[15] for the second set, he selected six Hugo texts he called *Poésies lyriques*, which he proposed to Schlesinger in 1843, and which became *Buch der Lieder* II (published in 1844).[16]

Liszt's setting of three Petrarch Sonnets (Nos. 47, "Benedetto sia 'l giorno," 104, "Pace non trovo," and 123, "I' vidi in terra angelici costumi") came about as a result of his encounter with Petrarch's Laura as she was invoked in Hugo's poetry.[17] When in 1842 Marie d'Agoult brought Hugo's *Poésies choisis* to his attention, Liszt wrote: "I would also like to send you a song of Victor Hugo [that I have written]. 'Oh! Quand je dors viens auprès de ma couche, Comme à Petrarque, etc.' . . . Thanks for the volumes of Hugo. I will read them."[18] Always susceptible to the immediate inspiration of the written word, as he was working on the Hugo songs, Liszt sketched untexted melodies for the three Petrarch sonnets into the Lichnowsky Sketchbook in 1843–44 while in Germany (not, as reported by Ramann, in 1838–39),[19] first bringing them out as piano pieces in 1846; the versions for voice followed later in the same year.[20] Because of the proximity of publication between the readings for voice and piano and for keyboard alone, it has always been difficult to determine which version came first in Liszt's musical consciousness, the vocal or the piano, a situation replicated by countless other examples (see below). However, we can be sure of one thing: Liszt never lost interest in his musical interpretations of this poetry, penning no fewer than nine complete versions of the *Benedetto sia 'l giorno* melody alone over some fifty years. The precision of the text declamation in the song versions attests to the fact that, just as with the texts that sit beneath the piano parts in the Schubert song transcriptions, Petrarch's texts were embedded in Liszt's musical subconscious: the underlay is so adroit that the song versions may indeed have come first. This conceptual duality continued throughout his career: Liszt was torn between genres – the piano versus any other medium or choral versus instrumental, but we find the majority of cross-overs between song and piano – "songs with imagined texts," as it was so elegantly put by Wolfgang Dömling.[21] And in the truest sense many of the piano solo versions are indeed "Songs Without Words."

One of Liszt's most popular piano works, the famous third *Liebestraum* (*O Lieb, O Lieb, so lang du lieben kannst*), actually began life as a song, although the first edition of this work, and its two companion pieces, were issued almost simultaneously in 1850 in versions for both voice and solo piano by Kistner in Leipzig. *O Lieb* had been conceived in 1843, with a text by Ferdinand Freiligrath: but two unpublished letters from Liszt to his publisher Eck & Lefèbvre in Cologne, one dated 25 December 1843, the other 9 January 1844, show clearly that the song had been intended for the 1844 Eck publication of a collection of Liszt's Lieder.[22] The manuscript apparently was lost in transit, along with some other works, and the vocal *O Lieb* did not appear until 1847, and then with Kistner. In 1850, Liszt revised the 1847 song, reworked a solo piano piece dating from some five years earlier and set it to the text "Gestorben war ich" by Uhland, adding a new third song entitled *Hohe Liebe* to another text by Uhland. All three songs then were published simply as *Drei Lieder für eine Tenor oder Sopranstimme*, while the piano works were retitled *Liebesträume: Drei Notturnos*. The conceptual duality referred to above becomes fully operative in this set. Liszt composes a song (*O Lieb*), and then later adds two companion pieces with texts of similar sentiments by Uhland: the first song (*Hohe Liebe* – "In Liebesarmen") is a freshly composed work; the second (*Gestorben war ich*) is drawn from the keyboard genre and a text also by Uhland is grafted on. All three songs then are published as a set, after which the composer returned to the compositions, altering them slightly, and issued them for keyboard alone, creating among the most popular of all Liszt's piano works.[23]

It is clear that almost one-half of Liszt's Lieder were initiated by 1850. Many of the revisions from the mid-1850s should really be viewed as "new" works, since the reworkings were so thorough as to render the original versions all but unrecognizable.[24] In 1843–44 Liszt had published a dozen songs in two sets with Schlesinger (the *Buch der Lieder* I and II mentioned above), and another six songs with Eck & Lefèbvre in Cologne in 1844 (see n. 9). These publications were followed by the versions of the *Petrarch Sonnets* in 1846 (Haslinger), and a few miscellaneous publications continued to come out under the auspices of various French and German houses – mainly Kistner, Schott, Ricordi (though mainly as an agent), Hofmeister, Troupenas, and Schuberth. It was not until the 1850s that Liszt firmly established himself with Breitkopf & Härtel and Kahnt, who became two of his most important later publishers. After Kistner published the song versions of the *Liebesträume* in 1850, it was thought that song composition ceased, for no more were issued until 1856. But while Liszt does seem to have set aside the genre briefly in the early 1850s,[25] the reality was quite different, for between 1849 and 1860 he wrote more than twenty new songs, and thoroughly revised many more, sometimes producing several versions of a single text. While he had fair copies prepared of nearly all this material, he still kept most of the music to himself, not submitting it to the publishers until many years after the initial conception, reworking the manuscripts in several stages over the years.[26] For his Lieder we are faced with the challenge of evaluating compositions that originated in the late 1840s, were amended several times in the 1850s, and were finally published in 1859–60.

This mature phase of Liszt's career as a song-writer coincides with his years as *Hofkapellmeister* at the court in Weimar to Grand Duke Carl Alexander von Saxe-Coburg-Eisenach, and encompasses the creation of some of his most enduring works. From this period on, the poets he chose to set were mostly German: indeed, there are only three Hungarian, one English, and one Russian setting among his works.[27] Many songs written in the early and mid 1840s were thoroughly revised between 1849 and 1860 specifically for the singers of the Weimar Hofkapelle. Feodor and Rosa von Milde, the husband and wife duo who created the roles of Elsa and Telramund for Wagner in the 1850 premiere of *Lohengrin*, were often the principals in Lieder evenings held at the palace in Weimar; Liszt himself would accompany them in some of his newest compositions. Another singer, Emilie Merian-Genast, seems to have acted the muse for many of Liszt's Lieder during the later 1850s. In an extended correspondence, much of it still unpublished, and once inscribed on the manuscript of the song *Die Zelle in Nonnenwerth*, Liszt referred to Genast as the "savior of my first and last Lieder, for which you [Genast] should not expect a civil-service medal from whatever conservatory (or even less the gang of critics)."[28] Much of Heft VII of the *Gesammelte Lieder* (Kahnt 1860) is tailored to the superior vocal qualities of another Weimar singer, the tenor Franz Götze, like Genast a member of the ensemble whose brilliant renditions of songs such as *Ich liebe dich, Ich scheide, Jugendglück* ("O süßer Zauber im Jugendmut"), *Blume und Duft* ("In Frühlings Heiligtume"), and *Die stille Wasserrose* demand a singer with *bel canto* training and an uncommon ease in changing registers, an ability to summon subtle gradations in tone color within a phrase, and a fearless top register. Yet more is required than this, for Liszt intended these songs for an interpreter of uncommon talent in savoring the text and delivering the sense of the word, albeit within a small vehicle, as if this were part of an operatic continuum.[29] The emotional sense is not too large for these songs: but the executant must craft them as if the music straddles the operatic and chamber genres.

In 1855 Liszt began to contemplate a collected edition of his Lieder. The scale of his perception broadened, and he recognized the acceptability of including multiple settings of the same text. This thinking is evident from a preliminary inventory inscribed on the last page of the copyist manuscript of *Ich möchte hingehn* (Herwegh), a work that originated in 1844 but which Liszt revised for the *Gesammelte Lieder* in the mid-1850s after entering into an agreement with Schlesinger in Berlin on the project. Included in this inventory are nineteen items, among them two versions of *Ein Fichtenbaum steht einsam* (Heine), which joined several revised songs and a number of new compositions.[30] When he first conceptualized this project, Liszt easily broke up earlier sets of works – for instance, he anticipated taking only two of the six published Hugo songs for the volume, and he selected several but not all of the previously published Heine and Goethe settings. Liszt called into question how he perceived these collections: at first they were loosely joined by subject matter, but subsequently the works reflect his judgment about which songs were successful and which were better left in his portfolio. This inventory, and many others like it in all genres, demonstrates his continuing tendency towards anthologizing, the gathering of previously composed works into groups for publication, an approach which was so prevalent in the piano sets written in the Weimar period and thereafter.[31] So often it is here where the mixing of genres is most evident. Six volumes of the *Gesammelte Lieder* were issued by Schlesinger between 1856 and 1859;[32] then the project was taken over by Kahnt in Leipzig, who began by publishing Heft VII in 1860. But no further volumes appeared until Heft VIII was issued by Kahnt in 1879, although from the number of revised printed copies extant in Weimar and elsewhere, it is clear that Liszt was considering a substantial revision of the entire set of eight volumes.[33] Yet

Example 8.1 Liszt, *Wie singt die Lerche schön*, mm. 1–8

even with Liszt's own misgivings about his abilities within the genre, and his preoccupation with anthologizing, there is one miniature that never ceases to amaze. Many associate Liszt's late compositional rhetoric with the last years of his life, a time that has come to be regarded as the one in which he became one of the startling precursors of modernism. But the Lieder repertory, his compositional testing ground, as noted above, indicates just how early his far-reaching tonal thinking had been established. In the 1855 *Wie singt die Lerche schön* (Hoffmann von Fallersleben), first published a year later in the *Deutscher Musen-Almanach*,[34] Liszt provides an arresting opening with an ear for sonority that prefigures the Impressionists by some fifty years. While some find Liszt's *Les Jeux d'eaux à la Villa d'Este* (1877) to be a model for Ravel's *Jeux d'eau* (1901), the opening of *Wie singt die Lerche schön*, composed more than twenty years before, attests to Liszt's marvelous ear for sonority (Example 8.1).

Now that we have traveled some distance from the music and poetry of Liszt's Lieder themselves, a few specifics are in order.

In *Die Loreley* (1841; rev. 1854–56), Liszt reads Heine's poem as a dramatic monologue in much the same way as Schubert read Goethe's ballad "Erlkönig": while clearly maintaining Heine's strophic formula for all six

Example 8.2 Liszt, *Die Loreley*, mm. 1–44

verses, Liszt's music does not repeat in each verse (Example 8.2). In fact, the narration begins in semi-recitative, and the composer retained the stanzaic integrity only through the fourth verse. In the last two stanzas, the narrative flow demands that the fifth stanza join with the first two lines of the sixth, a move that leaves a single couplet hanging – a potential pitfall the composer turns to an advantage given that he uses it to great effect. Liszt frames the

Example 8.2 (*cont.*)

question that is posed ("Ich weiss nicht, was soll's bedeuten"), together with the remainder of the first stanza, in a double-tonic complex of E and G, both of which are modally inflected.[35] E finally is settled upon in the second stanza when the text moves to a description of the Rhine Valley, where-upon Liszt obliges with a spectacular musical rendition of "Die Luft ist kühl" (m. 31).[36] Heine's insouciant Loreley sits in stark contrast to her surroundings; painted by Liszt in the key of Bb (the key an augmented fourth away), her alluring gestures and her continuing lament in the fourth stanza are in the beguiling if simply complementary key of Db (m. 60). The hapless boatman and his watery end are depicted in the fifth strophe and the first two lines of strophe 6 (mm. 73–98). The anxiety suffusing this dramatic moment is reflected in the transitory modulations that rise chromatically from F♯ to Bb (the "Loreley" key), all of which effects a return to the final hanging couplet, which Liszt sets in G (mm. 107 ff.). While it is easy to trace this tonal point back to the recitative and the unstable tonality of strophe 1, Liszt needed time to underscore his final tonic. He accentuates the profligacy of Heine's ingenuous maiden with the return to G major, and we too are left incredulous: the unknowing sailor once more appeases her appetite. But this was a problem: of the 130 measures in the song, sixty-eight are transitional, as Liszt quickly moves in and out of keys, never remaining in one area too long (sixteen measures in E, eleven in Bb, seven in Db). (This is typical of his rhetoric in pieces such as *Orpheus* and *Les Préludes*, constructs in which thematic areas are dwarfed by the dimensions of transitory sections.) In order to secure his final tonic, Liszt *had* to repeat the last lines because no more text remained to be set, and the effect is stunning. Liszt's setting intensifies what is only hinted at in Heine's little drama: fully cognizant of what she has done, the Loreley is tonally indifferent, almost callous to the havoc she has wrought. The concluding tonal center on G needs all the time Liszt can give it, especially after the preceding thirty-eight measures of harmonic transition; thus the final twenty-five measures in G major constitute the most protracted tonal center in the entire song. This in itself is vital; for as the poem's pacing increases, Liszt spends less time in each successive tonal center; in place of this, he accelerates the tempo, the speed of declamation and text delivery, the surface and harmonic rhythm, to say nothing of his old trick – the speed of chromatic change. Notwithstanding the importance of the tonal dimension, other details also demand consideration: Liszt endows Heine's wanton siren with a sinuous, chromatically inflected melodic line, one replete with enchanting upward-bending inflections on "sitzet" (m. 56) and "blitzet" (m. 60). The full-blown warmth of the setting of "Abendsonnenschein" (mm. 46–50), and her delight in a *Ländler*-like figuration, a folk ethic invoked at "Und singt ein Lied dabei" (mm. 64–65), only serve to illustrate further how finely crafted this little *scena* is. The accompaniment is a joy; the piano transcription, performed by Liszt as early as 1840 but not written down and published until 1862, differs only slightly from the song text itself.

Liszt's setting of *Du bist wie eine Blume*, undertaken at exactly the same time as Schumann's, is deceptively simple. In the 1860 revised edition, which is best known today, the song explores the process of semitone voice-leading. The two-strophe Heine text is a reverential paean to the beauty of the beloved, who is compared to a wondrous flower – with the inevitable twist in attitude when the lover voices the fear that grips him when he contemplates the aging of such beauty. Liszt sets the first half straightforwardly, moving from the initial A major tonality up to B minor for the second couplet (with the half-note formerly set to the first syllable of "Blume" now stressing the first syllable of "Wehmut" in m. 15, a small gem of word-painting and the first real chromaticism in the piece), pausing only momentarily on F♯ major, the relative key area, on the way to D major for the second half of the song. As he restates the opening theme in mm. 23–24, Liszt goes on to reinforce the D tonality at the *dolcissimo* marking, with interesting spacing in the accompaniment, focusing on the sustained Ds in the bass and the middle voice, and Schumannesque dove-tailing of the voice and the piano in mm. 25–31. The entire range of the piano is exploited now, from the deep *un poco marcato* bass octaves at mm. 31–32 which precede the elegantly fashioned, semitone diversion in m. 32 to an implied F♯ major on a 6/4 chord at m. 33. But it is the vocal part, left to pivot alone on C♯ in mm. 35 and 36, that effects the effortless transition back to the A major 6/4 chord, through to the winning postlude of five measures, that reinforces this return and seals the song's beauty. Yes, Liszt does repeat the same material at an octave transposition, material taken directly from the incipit of the vocal line; but the placement and spacing of the triads reveal his uncommon touch in handling the simplest of chordal progressions. It is this artist's ability to copy himself, yet do it differently each time, that makes such a work an obvious jewel.

But Liszt was ever mindful of the psychological effects of tonality, and in his 1857 setting of Rückert's "Ich liebe dich," we find him exploring chromatically stacked tonal plateau for emotional impact. In the poem's eight lines one encounters eight ways in which the poet loves his lover. Liszt describes these various states by exploring the many enharmonic resolutions possible for chords altered through the simplest step-wise chromatic motion. After the first statement of the premise in A♭ major ("Ich liebe dich, weil ich dich lieben muß" [I love you because I must love you]), the thought "ich liebe dich weil ich nicht anders kann" (I love you because I cannot do otherwise) is negated by a smooth transition to the relative minor, F, at m. 14. Ascending to the heights of heaven with "ich liebe dich nach einem Himmelsschluß" (I love you until the end of heaven) Liszt initially deflects the progression, heading toward E♭ major to C♭ major instead (m. 20) and then returns to A♭ major on "Zauberbann" (magic spell) for the end of the first stanza at m. 29. On the manuscript of the solo piano version (Example 8.3) of this song in the Library of Congress (US-Wlc ML.96.L58), it is interesting

Example 8.3 Liszt, manuscript, vocal-piano version, *Ich liebe dich*, mm. 23–30

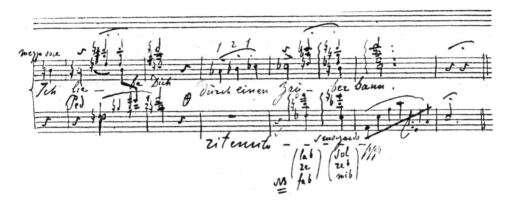

to note that even Liszt kept track of these enharmonic changes to remind himself and his scribes where he was going (the key signature is A♭). He labeled the components of the chord vertically and in parentheses beneath the staff in m. 27, so that the copyist would not think the unusual notation a mistake: "NB: la b[♭]/re/fa b[♭] moving to sol/re b[♭]/mi b[♭]." In the second stanza, he moves to C major for the first couplet ("Dich lieb' ich, wie die Rose ihren Strauch," mm. 32–38), immediately diverting to D♭/C♯ on the way to A major at m. 46. Again, the voice alone turns the last two lines enharmonically back to A♭ on the pivot tone C♯/D♭ for the final cadence on a high A♭.

It is interesting that the piano introduction is missing from the first version of the song, only added later after Liszt had worked through the various modulations of the piece in the piano solo manuscript – it is clear he thought the firm grounding of the A♭ major triads were required to begin this journey. The voice in the first stanza always points the way for the ensuing modulation, as each time the antepenultimate pitch in the vocal line serves as the pivotal sonority that deceptively propels the modulation away from the expected tonality. In the second stanza, the accompaniment takes the lead, while achieving each new tonal point of rest simultaneously with the voice. The vocal demands increase as the piece progresses, while the exquisite voice-leading and the gradual heightening of tessitura, especially the last sixteen measures, prove a test for any singer (and indeed Emilie Genast and Franz Götze must have been superb singers). Liszt leaves us with no fewer than three endings, in the same way he often did in the solo piano music.[37] The two *ossia* versions confirm the vocal prowess of the members of his ensemble: two of the variants for the last phrase finish on the top A♭ *ff*, and held, the highest note in the entire piece.

Blume und Duft ([Flower and fragrance] Hebbel, 1862), while novel in many ways, is an extension of ideas already established in *Die Loreley*, only here they are taken to an extreme with a predominance of chromatically transitional material. In the simple two strophes of the work one is caught in a web of tonal ambiguity: at m. 9, the ear gladly accepts F♯ major as a tonal center, one that Liszt affirms with a classic I$_4^6$–V^7 construct. But his predilection for chromatic voice-leading immediately leads the music beyond the realm of F♯ in mm. 9–13, and the tonality evanesces at the beginning of the second strophe at m. 15, serving the symbolism evoked by the text "Der Duft lässt Ew'ges ahnen" (Fragrance permits us a premonition of eternity). For the year 1862, Liszt demands much of his listener: as the second strophe continues, not only does he prolong the sense of delayed tonal punctuation, but the texture is continually reduced as he minimizes every musical perspective, extracting the sighing half-step descent from the vocal line and giving it over to the piano (mm. 22–25). Not until the text is finished does the piano postlude finally close in A♭, a point of repose so desperately needed and, despite the change of key signature to four flats in the last four bars, a tonality still left hanging with the final 6/4 sonority. The song's delicate, nearly impressionistic fabric suits the poem's aphoristic imagery: Hebbel, like Heine, adds a bitter twist to his words, warning that one should not seek the source of the perfume from the flower that produced it: the flower is bound to have decayed and will thus destroy the promise of eternity that emanates from the scent. Liszt's ephemeral setting does much to intensify these images, and even the momentary repetition of the final line ("wie schnell sie welken soll" [how quickly it will wilt]) does little to destroy the mood.

With such musical experiments as these from his Weimar years, it is hardly surprising to note that Liszt's later efforts in the genre contain many fascinating elements as well, and it is to the *Petrarch Sonnets* that we now must turn. As has been noted, the early versions (published 1846) are much indebted to stylistic elements from *bel canto* opera. All are in A♭ major: No. 104, *Pace non trovo*, has an obvious recitative–aria structure, in which the tortuous tessitura looks forward to the declamatory style of *verismo* opera (Example 8.4).

Of additional interest is the piano introduction, which outlines what we know as an octatonic progression beginning on E♮ in the bass, preceding the text "Pace non trovo," surely one of the most arresting instances of word-painting in the period. The early version of No. 47, *Benedetto*, adumbrates Strauss's *Cäcilie*, with its octave leaps and generous melody; while No. 123, *I' vidi in terra angelici costumi*, begins *in medias res*, as if it is simply prolonging the A♭ major cadence in *Benedetto* which precedes it. In the later

Example 8.4 Liszt, *Erstes Sonett von Petrarca, Pace non trovo,* mm. 1–6

versions (undertaken in 1865 but not published until 1883), the tonalities, and therefore the syntactical connections, have been altered and filtered through the intermediate compositional stage of the 1858 versions of the piano solos written for the *Années de pèlerinage II (Italie)*. *Benedetto* has moved to the front of the set and shifted to Db major. While some might be struck by the simplification of the piano accompaniment, it has changed much less than the vocal line, which has lost most of its Romantic flight and bloom. *Benedetto* is now more like a song by Wolf, controlled in range and tessitura, balanced between accompaniment and voice, concentrated more on the words rather than the vocal style. But with the next two settings Liszt moves his earlier conceptions beyond what a contemporaneous audience might have expected. To be sure, the later version of *Pace non trovo* now is moved to second place, and transposed to E major, but Liszt now fashions a melodic line and accompaniment possessing so great a degree of flexibility that both function like recitative. The effect continues the thrust of the piano introduction, as if Liszt had realized that it was the word rather than the tone that would enliven the listener's emotion. The piano postlude ends on the single pitch B, which is then picked up at the beginning of *I' vidi in terra angelici costumi,* now transposed to F major; thus a semblance of continuity is retained from the earlier sequence. No. 123 also has become more like a melodrama,[38] with a section of recitative punctuating the return to the tonic near the end, underscoring the meaning of the text ("Ed era 'l cielo all'armonia s'intento"). In the later songs, some vestiges of the original versions do remain, for instance, the openings of Sonnets 104 and 123 – the result of the sonority possible from the 1862 Erard piano on which these works were written in Rome, with its iron frame and sylvan sound, an instrument which did not need the constant reiteration of arpeggiated sonorities to maintain the harmonic background. The tenths at the bottom of the accompaniment in the early version are no longer necessary because the sonority of the Erard carries through with an octave alone. The later version is more reliant on tremolandos and widely spaced static harmonies, having more points of contact with the late piano works – notably the "Threnodies" in *Années III* (Nos. 2 and 3) and pieces such as *Nuages gris*.

Over and above all that has been written thus far, Lieder allowed Liszt catharsis and immediate relief from the demands of his busy life and personal turmoil. And, just as *Wie singt die Lerche schön* was used to encapsulate his sonic visions, so one song can exemplify his inner strife. In *Tristesse: J'ai perdu ma force et ma vie*, one is presented with one of Liszt's most poignant utterances, his only setting of the poetry of Alfred de Musset (one of his high-living compatriots in the Paris of his youth),[39] written just days after mending the long rift with Richard Wagner and his only surviving child, Cosima. Liszt had not spoken to either for nearly five years (1867–72), maintaining an unhappy distance from the couple who in so many ways had betrayed him and what he held dear. Cosima had abandoned her husband of ten years, Hans von Bülow,[40] permanently in 1868, after four years of an illicit relationship that produced two children with Wagner.[41] Then, after renouncing Catholicism, she divorced Bülow on 18 July 1870 and married Wagner just thirty-eight days later. Even in this long period, Liszt was conflicted: he never ceased promoting Wagner's aesthetic ideals and music and avoided openly reproaching his only surviving child.[42] Needing Liszt's weighty approbation in 1872 as the push to subsidize Bayreuth gained momentum, Cosima wrote to her father in an attempt to heal the breach. But Liszt only relented after Wagner wrote to him personally on 18 May 1872, inviting him to the laying of the Festspielhaus Foundation Stone four days later (22 May 1872, Wagner's birthday). Though Liszt did not attend the event, he wrote with characteristic magnanimity:

> Sublime, dear friend, Profoundly moved by your letter, I am unable to thank you in words. But it is my ardent hope that all shadows and considerations which bind me at a distance will disappear – and that we shall soon see one another again. Then it will become clear to you, too, how inseparable my soul remains from *both of you* – living again in your 'second higher life,' in which you can achieve what you could not have achieved alone. Therein I see Heaven's amnesty! God's blessing be with both of you, as all my love. FL [P.S.] I am more than reluctant to send these lines by post.

They will be handed to you on 22 May by a woman [Baroness Olga von Meyendorff] who has known my thoughts and feelings for several years.[43]

The emotional effort that went into this acquiescence was never outwardly acknowledged, but Liszt retreated to Musset's *Tristesse* to voice his feelings: only the tortured, bitter words lamenting the plight of the artist in the face of overwhelming personal obstacles and the stark music of this song remain to document his anguish. From the very first bar it is clear the piece is to be autobiographical, for what is heard first is the augmented triad F A C♯ (FrAnCIScus), a musical signature found often in the late music.[44] Liszt's personal search for truth is reflected in the chromatic non-resolution of the augmented sonority in the first four measures. The voice enters innocently enough with an extended recitative outlining a diminished seventh chord (mm. 7 ff.); the song proper starts with a strong affirmation in G♭ major (m. 13), so strong that even the transient modulations at the words "J'ai cru" (mm. 22–23) do little to destabilize the sense of tonality. But at the words "Quand je l'ai comprise" (mm. 30–32) the piece starts to become unhinged as the song ascends through a series of fleeting modulations through G minor and A♭ major, landing at A major (albeit in second inversion) at the double bar (m. 51). Here Liszt reintroduces the opening material, music that successfully and resoundingly coalesces into D major at the words "Dieu parle" (m. 61). In the subsequent seventeen measures, Liszt focuses on D as a final point of repose. But what happens in the final four measures is nothing short of shocking: could our ear have been satisfied if he had stopped at the antepenultimate measure that rests on the relative minor? Perhaps it could. The final two measures, however, with the sonority E♯–G♯–D – a pitch collection that rends the tonal fabric asunder – reflects his negation of self in the service of his own motto "Génie oblige."

In conclusion, Liszt's Lieder are an unjustly overlooked part of the song repertory in the nineteenth century, a kind of missing link which in some ways provides a more natural transition between Schumann and Wolf than do the Lieder of Brahms. While the early settings of Liszt's Lieder do owe their inspiration more to the generation of Schumann and Loewe, his middle and later compositions are as innovative and forward-looking as his late keyboard music, presenting a highly chromatic tonal palette that owes much to the precepts that he and Wagner espoused from the early 1850s on. On the centenary of Liszt's birth in 1911, no lesser an authority on what was then "new" in music than Arnold Schoenberg published a brief critical essay on Liszt that is too often ignored, considering the depth of its insight. He wrote:

Was he not after all one of those who started the battle against tonality, both through themes which point to no absolutely definite tonal center, and through many harmonic details whose musical exploitation has been looked after by his successors? Altogether his effect has perhaps been greater, through the many stimuli he left behind for his successors, than Wagner's has been – Wagner, who provided a work too perfect for anyone coming later to be able to add anything to it . . . It may well be assumed that Liszt's works will not achieve the kind of popularity ascribed to the works of the classics. It is not impossible, even, that his work will be quite forgotten: the works of great men, too, can be forgotten. *But their name remains!*[45]

9 The Lieder of Brahms

HEATHER PLATT

In a letter to Johannes Brahms (1833–97) from May 1885, Elisabet von Herzogenberg singled out for special praise the composer's *Wir wandelten*, Op. 96, No. 2, set to a poem translated from the Magyar by Georg Friedrich Daumer. In so doing, she remarked:

> How perfectly the words and music are blended in their deep emotion, their lovely animation! Such loving care has been lavished on every detail, and each tiny variant has its calculated effect in rendering the particular part more impressive.[1]

Herzogenberg, wife of the composer Heinrich von Herzogenberg and herself a highly talented musician and former student of Brahms, easily could have been writing about any number of the composer's some 200 Lieder.[2] Depth of feeling and seeming spontaneity are prized just as much as calculated craft together with the myriad fine points that go into any Lied. In this, she was in good company, for many of the composer's closest friends and admirers enthusiastically commented on the union of music and words to be found in his vocal music. Of these reactions, one of the most revealing and certainly one of the most concise comes from Brahms's only composition student, Gustav Jenner (1865–1920).[3] First published in 1903, Jenner's remarks emphasize that the music must reflect the structure and meaning of the original poem, and he notes that such relations between the text and music include form, musical and verbal syntax, declamation, word painting, and harmony. In view of the depth of insight Jenner offers, together with his association with Brahms, his discussion will serve as the jumping-off point for the present introduction into the expressive world of the composer's Lieder.[4]

Poems, form, and syntax

Jenner begins by emphasizing the necessity of thoroughly knowing the text before beginning to compose a Lied, and he recalls that Brahms specified familiarity with all of the intricacies of a poem including being able to recite it correctly. He mentions Brahms's vast store of poems, and the composer's library further attests to his broad literary interests.[5] Like Schubert and many other nineteenth-century composers, Brahms used a wide array of texts including not only those by first-class poets, such as Eichendorff, Heine, Goethe, Mörike, Rückert, and Tieck, but also those by less well-known writers, some of whom, like Klaus Groth, were personal friends. Brahms also frequently set to music folksong texts, many of which were drawn from such anthologies or editions as the well-known *Des Knaben Wunderhorn*, the volumes published by Anton Wilhelm Florentin von Zuccalmaglio,[6] as well as poems translated from other languages. Many of Brahms's selections, however, have been criticized, especially when compared with the consistently higher literary quality of the texts set to music by Wolf. Writing in 1971, Jack Stein baldly concluded: "well over half of" Brahms's Lieder "use mediocre-to-bad poems."[7] Even his friends, including Clara Schumann, criticized the quality of some of his texts, as well as some of their morbid and bawdy topics.[8] Nevertheless, Brahms defended his choices of such poets as Ludwig Hölty, famous for the emotional ambiguity of much of his poetry, and he was not pleased when Groth attempted to improve on the poem by Hermann Allmers that he used in *Feldeinsamkeit*, Op. 86, No. 2.[9] Although Brahms admitted to his friend the composer and music critic Richard Heuberger that he did select some difficult texts, Brahms insisted that he did not use impractical ones, and in his somewhat defensive description of Brahms's texts, Hermann Deiters, another of the composer's friends and his first biographer, declares that Brahms chose texts that "vibrate in the heart."[10]

The first aspect of the text–music relationship Jenner discusses is form, and he reports that Brahms believed the musical structure of a Lied should correspond to its text; thus, in examining a poem for possible setting to music, form was the first thing Brahms considered. Although his own Lieder feature a number of formal strategies, Brahms strongly recommended strophic design and, in particular, the study of Schubert's strophic songs as an essential starting point. Nevertheless, as is the case with Schubert, most of Brahms's songs are not strictly strophic; rather, they vary the opening strophe of music in ensuing stanzas. Brahms employs a wide variety of techniques to modify an initial strophe of music, from slight melodic variations to extending or rewriting phrases. Jenner notes that *Wie Melodien*, Op. 105, No. 1, *Feldeinsamkeit, Liebestreu*, Op. 3, No. 1, and *Das Lied vom Herrn von Falkenstein*, Op. 43, No. 4 exemplify contrasting types of strophic settings. Although he does not go into additional detail, scrutiny of these pieces demonstrates that Brahms often alters an initial strophe of music to better match the subsequent stanzas of text.[11] Spanning almost his entire compositional career, these songs likewise reveal Brahms's ability to handle diverse subject matters and styles and at the same time document his abiding commitment to sympathetically exploring real human emotions.[12]

Brahms's contemporaries widely praised *Liebestreu*, composed in 1853 to a poem by Robert Reinick, and it was with this song that the composer chose to open his first set of Lieder. For his friend the great violinist Joseph Joachim (1831–1907), for whom Brahms composed his Violin Concerto in 1878, the song was "like a revelation."[13] Divided into three stanzas, each one features two lines sung by a mother followed by two for her daughter. While the second stanza includes a small number of changes pertaining to the expressive markings, the daughter's concluding section in the third stanza is entirely rewritten. In these last phrases, the girl strongly rejects her mother's advice and promises undying love to a man who already has caused her sorrow. Unlike the girl's earlier phrases, this section begins loudly and assertively, and it uses the mother's melody, her fuller accompaniment, and continues the agitated tempo. Yet just as the girl does not accept her mother's advice, so too she does not simply repeat her mother's music, rather she transforms it in a seemingly defiant manner. Aside from the louder dynamics, new harmonies move through the tonic major, the melody climaxes on its highest note – ab^2 – and word repetitions and longer notes draw out this section to almost twice the length of the second phrases of the other stanzas. Nevertheless, this is far from a triumphal ending – such love is not without pain – and throughout this climactic phrase, as well as during the subsequent conclusion, the dissonant three-note bass motive that has pervaded all of the mother's phrases recurs and negates the seeming confidence of the girl's rising melody. Moreover the drawn-out conclusion, with its fading dynamics, slowing tempo, and descending melodic line, suggests the girl's strength is ultimately sapped by this misplaced devotion.

One of Brahms's most popular songs, *Feldeinsamkeit* demonstrates that even subtle modifications to the initial strophe can be effective. Written between 1879 and 1881, this song quickly gained widespread popularity and was included on numerous concert programs. Many, including Elisabet von Herzogenberg, who was particularly fond of Julius Stockhausen's performance of the work, praised its beauty and expressiveness. The critic Richard Specht wrote of the song's creation of a "feeling of dissolution in the universe through the mystery of a melodic inspiration that actually seems to carry us into eternity."[14] The Lied's two stanzas are almost identical in length, and in the second Brahms reuses the music from the first and last lines of stanza 1. Although a wistful mood pervades both stanzas, the second takes on a change in atmosphere as the protagonist gazes upwards at the clouds and imagines a peaceful union with nature at the moment of his death. Measures 21–28 vary the material from the first strophe, in F major, by moving through Db major, a subtle turn to the bVI that serves to intensify the words, "Die schönen weißen Wolken zieh'n dahin / Durch's tiefe Blau, wie schöne stille Träume" (the beautiful white clouds pass by through the deep blue, like beautiful quiet dreams). While the melody retains the same general contour and both phrases end on the dominant of the home key of F, the second strophe has a more elegiac mood, in part achieved by the one-measure phrase expansion with its pensive appoggiatura on "Träume" (m. 23). Similarly, the next phrase (mm. 26–28) at once preserves the contours of the opening stanza while it also provides contrast by virtue of the sudden change to austere, bare octaves. This starker accompaniment, devoid of the eighth-note motion that pervades most of the song, along with the halting effect of the half note at the end of the phrase, dramatically disrupt the rhythmic flow of the dreamy mood, suggesting the anguish of death.[15] Furthermore, although this phrase emphasizes D♭ major, the last note is a surprising B♮, which facilitates the return to the tonic of F.

Although *Das Lied vom Herrn von Falkenstein* rarely is performed nowadays let alone discussed, in Brahms's own time it was widely admired. The composer's friend the surgeon Theodor Billroth (1829–94) praised the intensity of the song, comparing it to a drawing by Michelangelo.[16] A ballad anticipating the style of *Entführung*, Op. 97, No. 3, and *Verrat*, Op. 105, No. 5, the Lied features three characters – the narrator, Lord Falkenstein, and a maiden whose man is held prisoner by Lord Falkenstein. Unlike the other songs in the group cited by Jenner, this one combines elements of ternary and modified strophic forms; while the outer stanzas are based on the first strophe of music, the fifth and sixth stanzas are set to new music motivically and tonally linked to the main strophe. In his book *Brahms's Lieder*, Max Friedländer positively comments on the song for the richness of its melodic development. This is evident not only in the transformations of motives in the central section, but also in the melodic and accompanimental variations of the original strophe, particularly in stanza 4 where the melody is placed in the bass while the voice is given a new countermelody. Brahms's modifications to the initial strophe of music, as well as his use of the central contrasting section, take into account the slightly differing structural features of each stanza's text. Although the poem consistently uses four-line strophes, there are small differences in the length and metrical patterns of some of the stanzas, and Brahms follows these by inserting extra notes. He also alters the dynamics and reinforces the accompaniment figuration to convey the girl's devotion to her beloved and her defiance of Falkenstein. Both stanzas of the central section begin with the same line, which is longer than the first line of the other stanzas. They are the only stanzas in which both the narrator and the girl speak, and they describe the girl walking around the tower, calling to her loved one. Brahms sets these stanzas to the same music, and the new bass figure – a transformation of the syncopated, rhythmic pattern of the piano's interludes – suggests the girl's repeated circling within the tower's confines. The new melody is based on an inversion of the falling third motive first used when the girl is introduced in m. 8 of the opening stanza, and, similarly, the Ab tonality used for the first two phrases of each of these central stanzas also is anticipated in this earlier measure.

While modified strophic settings dominate his output, Brahms does employ other forms. He uses simple and expanded ternary designs, as in *Parole*, Op. 7, No. 2, *Vom verwundeten Knaben*, Op. 14, No. 2, and *So willst du des Armen*, Op. 33, No. 5. Less frequently he writes through-composed Lieder, as for example *Von ewiger Liebe*, Op. 43, No. 1. Lieder comprising one stanza, such as *Nachklang*, Op. 59, No. 4, and *Es schauen die Blumen*, Op. 96, No. 3, also use these forms, and, as with the modified strophic pieces, their structures take their cue from the organization and drama of the poem in question.[17]

After form, Jenner moves on to consider a text's punctuation, going so far as to remark that the ability to correctly attend to this was considered by Brahms to be the mark of a true artist. According to Jenner, Brahms recommended reciting the poem, pausing in all the right places; indeed, in his handwritten notebooks of poems, Brahms sometimes marked the punctuation points with slashes. Jenner offers *Von ewiger Liebe* as an example of the way in which Brahms observes the matter of punctuation, and he specifically refers to the interlude that separates the two sentences of the first stanza (mm. 12–13). Although a straightforward example, the overriding point nevertheless is significant: many of the most poignant moments in Brahms's Lieder are characterized by attention to pauses in the text. The third stanza of the early song *An eine Aeolsharfe*, Op. 19, No. 5, offers an especially sensitive example. Mörike wrote his poem in 1837, some thirteen years after the death of his seventeen-year-old brother. When he published it, he included a quotation from Horace's Ode II, No. 9, which criticizes the inordinately long and intense mourning of the character Flavius. Most commentators have inferred that this quotation, as well as the poem, relate to Mörike's grief for his own brother.[18] The poem comprises three stanzas: the first introduces the mournful strains of the Aeolian harp, which long has been associated with death or intense sadness.[19] The strings of this instrument freely vibrate with the wind and these unpremeditated sounds poignantly parallel Mörike's character's alternating moods of hope and despair, and his "süßem Erschrecken" (sweet terror). In the concluding stanza the winds blow even stronger, ripping to shreds a ripe rose just as the protagonist's peace of mind has been undone by heartache. Brahms's sensitivity is impressive: at the spot that the poem's penultimate line reads "Und hier – die volle Rose" (and here, the full rose), he responds to the dash as well as the character's emotional hesitation with almost a full measure's rest between "hier" and "die" while at the same time slowing the tempo. Moreover, he encloses the subsequent words "streut, geschüttelt" (strews, shaken) with rests that realistically depict the rose's destruction.

In other instances, a dramatic reading of a poem gives way to pauses otherwise not indicated by the poet. In *Nicht mehr zu dir zu gehen*, Op. 32, No. 2, Brahms fragments the melodic line to portray the faltering speech of the heartbroken protagonist. The realism of this opening has captured the attention of numerous commentators. For Friedländer, Brahms's Lied is not so much a song in the usual sense but rather "a declamation hesitating between a recitative and an aria."[20] For Kalbeck, Brahms vividly captures the plight of the ensnared, ill-fated lover depicted by Daumer: "on each syllable hangs a drop of blood," he writes.[21]

Jenner also connects a text's punctuation to the music's cadences:

> just as the poet, in his purposeful construction, ties his sentences more or less closely together using commas, semicolons, periods, etc., as his external signs, so the musician, similarly, has at his disposal perfect and imperfect cadences in a variety of forms to indicate the greater or lesser degree of coherence of his musical phrases. (p. 198)

Although Jenner does not offer specific examples, a number of songs illustrate the point. In the long stanzas of *Vom Strande*, Op. 69, No. 6, Brahms marks the text's periods with authentic cadences and the commas with half-cadences (compare m. 12 with m. 15). Similarly, questions in a text, as in *Das Mädchen spricht*, Op. 107, No. 3, or *Der Strom, der neben mir verrauschte*, Op. 32, No. 4, are often associated with incomplete cadences. In the latter, as well as in some less turbulent works, such as *In Waldeseinsamkeit*, Op. 85, No. 6, concluding plagal cadences, accompanied by ascending melodies that move away from the tonic convey the yearning of a poem's leading character.[22] But Jenner is not concerned merely with individual cadence points; the close of his remark suggests that he also is aware that the way in which cadences connect phrases can be determined by the text. Changes in piano figuration or different types of links between phrases, including motivic repetitions and voice leading, may be connected with either the meaning or the structure of the text.

Brahms's Op. 33, No. 9 setting of Tieck's "Ruhe, Süßliebchen, im Schatten" (Rest, my darling, in the shade) highlights many of Jenner's observations as they pertain to punctuation. Each of the poem's three stanzas is subdivided into three sections, containing lines 1–2, 3–5, and 6–8. Tieck's poem is provided here in its entirety:

1. Ruhe, Süßliebchen, im Schatten
2. Der grünen, dämmernden Nacht;
3. Es säuselt das Gras auf den Matten,
4. Es fächelt und kühlt dich der Schatten,

5. Und treue Liebe wacht.
6. Schlafe, schlaf ein,
7. Leiser rauscht der Hain,
8. Ewig bin ich dein.

1. Schweigt, ihr versteckten Gesänge,
2. Und stört nicht die süßeste Ruh'!
3. Es lauscht der Vögel Gedränge,
4. Es ruhen die lauten Gesänge,
5. Schließ, Liebchen, dein Auge zu.
6. Schlafe, schlaf ein,
7. Im dämmernden Schein,
8. Ich will dein Wächter sein.

1. Murmelt fort, ihr Melodien,
2. Rausche nur, du stiller Bach.
3. Schöne Liebesphantasien
4. Sprechen in den Melodien,
5. Zarte Träume schwimmen nach.
6. Durch den flüsternden Hain,
7. Schwärmen goldene Bienelein,
8. Und summen zum Schlummer dich ein.

Lines 2 and 3 usually are separated by a period or semicolon, but the division between lines 5 and 6 is more clearly marked. Aside from the period at the end of the fifth lines, the sixth lines are shorter than any other; stanzas 1 and 2 have the identical sixth line; and lines 6 through 8 of each stanza have the same rhyming syllable. Brahms follows these subdivisions by separating the three sections with rests in the vocal line, and by using the same melody and harmony for lines 6–8 of each stanza – the refrain. However, he makes sure that lines 6 through 8 still are heard as belonging to the preceding lines of the respective stanzas: each refrain continues the type of piano figuration used in the preceding phrases, and the piano's introductions to the refrains overlap with the conclusion of the main body of each stanza.

There are slight differences in the syntactical structure of the main sections – lines 1 through 5 of each stanza – and Brahms adapts the music to fit the new structures. A comparison of the settings of the first two lines of each stanza illustrates these kinds of changes, while also demonstrating some of the ways Brahms links phrases of music. The first two lines of stanza 1 are enjambed, and are separated from the other three by a semicolon. Brahms preserves this enjambment: he does not pause at the end of the first line; rather he unites the two lines by using a dominant pedal throughout while alternating five-three and six-four chords. Furthermore, he follows the commas and creates three melodic segments, each lasting two measures. By contrast, a comma separates the first two lines of the second stanza and

Example 9.1 *Ruhe, Süßliebchen,* Op. 33, No. 9, mm. 93–100

Brahms consequently alters the phrase structure. Instead of a six-measure group all over a dominant pedal, he uses two groups of four measures (mm. 49–52 and 53–56) separated by rests in the vocal line. Tieck linked these two lines by the word "und" and Brahms keeps the respective phrases together as the second is a sequential repetition of the first, and the melody of the second begins just one note higher than the first ended. Harmonically there is not a break between the two as their seventh chords briefly resolve to a Gb chord only on the last eighth note of the second phrase (in m. 56, which is also the beginning of the next phrase). A comma also separates the first two lines of the third stanza and Brahms separates the respective melodies with even more rests (Example 9.1). These two phrases are linked by a pedal point (but unlike the first stanza the harmonies above the pedal change with line 2): they use the same accompanying figuration and are connected by a motivic repetition. During the brief interlude between the two phrases (mm. 95–96), the piano repeats and extends the last four notes of the first phrase's melody so that it overlaps with the next entry of the voice. Motivic links and overlaps of this kind become something of a norm in this song and, as the voice ends the second phrase (m. 100), the piano anticipates the melody of the third. In line 2, Brahms repeats the words "du stiller" and he breaks the melody into three segments, following the text's subdivisions. At the start of this stanza, Tieck introduces an extra foot into each line of text, and Brahms captures this new, more animated mood by an accompaniment marked by greater rhythmic activity, louder dynamics, as well as by the Animato indication. This change in mood, along with the text's idea of going forth, also is conveyed by the change in emphasis at the beginning of line 1. Instead of starting strongly on the first measure, as do the other stanzas, a crescendo, a melodic leap, and the harmonies emphasize the second measure (m. 94). A somewhat similar, though weaker, affect is created by the upbeat at the beginning of the next phrase.[23]

Although Jenner discusses only the relationship of punctuation to pauses and cadences, Brahms also writes melodies that underscore grammatical structures. Lines using repeated words or that are constructed in similar ways often are set to related melodies. For example, the melody of the first two lines of both stanzas of *Kein Haus, keine Heimat*, Op. 94, No. 5, emphasizes their two-part structure and word repetitions by leaps beginning on d^1. The opening of the second stanza of *Du sprichst, daß ich mich täuschte*, Op. 32, No. 6, reads: "Dein schönes Auge brannte, die Küsse brannten sehr" (Your beautiful eyes burned, your kisses burned intensely). Brahms sets "brannte" to a descending leap, c^2–f^1, and then, in order to illustrate the intensification, he inverts this dyad for the words "brannten sehr."

Declamation

While Jenner mentions that Brahms emphasized the importance of correct declamation, he nonetheless does not explore the way in which the composer went about this. Some of Brahms's other friends, however, offer more advice. In his recollections, Heuberger states that Brahms recommends that an inexperienced songwriter should first place the text in empty measures, so that the words fall in the metrically correct positions. Brahms's handwritten copies of poems as well as the few remaining sketches of his Lieder reveal that he studied the metrical properties of his texts. In some of his copies of poems, Brahms marked the accentuation, and some of the sketches reveal that initially he did align bar lines with accented syllables.[24] Twentieth-century music scholars, including Helmut Federhofer and Siegfried Kross, also have demonstrated Brahms's concern for correct declamation, and they have shown that he emphasized accented syllables through pitch height, as well as by metrical placement, and that he relied on durations and harmonic structures to emphasize especially important words.[25]

Aside from the many songs, such as *Sapphische Ode*, Op. 94, No. 4, where Brahms's music accurately follows the poem's metrical structure, there are some instances in which his declamation helps to clarify a text's meaning. *Wie rafft' ich mich auf in der Nacht*, Op. 32, No. 1, offers one such example. It is a setting of a text by the self-critical August von Platen, whose poems Schubert used in two songs;[26] Platen, a homosexual, saw himself as an outsider – a type of self-view that, for differing reasons, also reverberates through some of Brahms's most dispirited letters to his friends. The anguish of the isolation that both Platen and Brahms claimed to experience is portrayed with great realism not only in the first of the Op. 32 songs, but also in Nos. 3 and 4, as well as in the songs of the somewhat more resigned rebuffed lover in Nos. 5 and 6 – all of which also use texts by Platen. In the first stanza of No. 1, Brahms's melody, with its dotted rhythms, leaps, and pauses, emphasizes the appropriate syllables while also communicating the mystery of the protagonist waking in the middle of the night. His word repetitions – along with the related rising pitches and chromatic harmonies – create the image of the character being drawn outside, almost against his will.[27] During the second and third stanzas, which are marked by comparatively more lyrical melodic lines describing the flowing waves and tranquil sky, short ornaments are strategically placed on such words as "wallten" (flowed) and "funkelten" (beamed).

Despite these examples of Brahms's sensitivity to text declamation, criticisms of precisely this aspect of his song composition date back to the reviews of his first Lieder collections. To be sure, Op. 3 and *Wie bist du, meine Königin*, Op. 32, No. 9, with its clearly misplaced accents on "König*in*" and "wonne*voll*" (among other errors), repeatedly have been singled out in both the nineteenth and the twentieth centuries as obviously flawed. Brahms's friends and professional critics mention other problematic passages. Some of the most conspicuous mistakes in accentuation are found in Brahms's early songs, up to and including Op. 32. Nevertheless, occasional errors occur even in his later works. In *Sind es Schmerzen*, Op. 33, No. 3, m. 10, the word "sind" (the present indicative of "to be") is ornamented, and thereby given undue emphasis; in m. 23, and elsewhere, a rest separates the syllables of a single word. The first passage exemplifies perhaps the most common type of misjudgment in Brahms's Lieder: a repeated rhythmic pattern, including an ornament or a long note, is effective for some lines of text but not for others. Nineteenth-century writers fiercely criticized this problem, and Wolf was fond of ridiculing Brahms for what he viewed as his mundane, insensitive repeated rhythms.[28] Similar problems sometimes occur in strictly strophic songs, as in *Ständchen*, Op. 14, No. 7, where the melody and rhythm fit the text's first stanza but not the second; or in *An die Stolze*, Op. 107, No. 1, where pairs of notes separated by rests suit the first stanza but break up individual words in the second. In other songs, particularly middle-period works with expansive, lyrical melodies, texts seem unnecessarily drawn out. In *Nachklang*, Op. 59, No. 4, the words "aus den" and "in das" are set to uncommonly long notes, and, furthermore, the first pair are ornamented.[29] Although in most of these sorts of passages the words are usually placed in the correct metrical position, there are examples in which unaccented syllables are misplaced. For example in mm. 9–10 of *In der Gasse*, Op. 58, No. 6, the word "Gasse" is spread across two measures with both syllables falling on downbeats, and a similar problem occurs in the settings of "Betrübter" and "schwinden" in *Frühlingstrost*, Op. 63, No. 1.

In the view of some commentators, declamation is the most important aspect of a Lied's text–music relationship. This emphasis largely is due to the influence of post-Wagnerian composers, particularly Wolf, who aimed at a realistic, speech-like style of declamation. During Brahms's lifetime, some of the strongest criticisms on the subject of his declamation came from supporters of Wagner and Wolf, many of whom complained that Brahms's rhythmic patterns were too repetitive and did not follow speech inflections. Twentieth-century commentators who support this type of realistic declamation offer similar critiques.[30] It would seem, however, that Brahms himself adhered to the earlier style of Lied, in which the declamation was closer to the style found in folk song: accentuated syllables are placed in metrically strong positions while more involved relationships between speech patterns and musical rhythms are not pursued. Moreover, the recollections of Jenner, as well as the written observations of Brahms's other friends and supporters in the press – including Deiters – demonstrate that declamation was just one aspect of Lieder: there were many other ways in which music could be fitted to a text. Thus, while Wolf complained about *Vergebliches Ständchen*, Op. 84, No. 4, and particularly its declamation, many of Brahms's admirers, including Kalbeck, praised its dramatic and comic nuances.[31]

Word painting

Many of the topics that Jenner discusses concern the manner in which Brahms dealt with a text's structure. Additionally, Jenner is concerned with techniques for conveying a text's meaning, including Brahms's attitude toward word painting. According to Jenner, Brahms was not interested in "atmospheric" accompaniments; rather, he used melodic contour to convey the meaning of particularly important phrases or words (p. 200). For example, the composer often used altered intervals to portray a character's extreme state of mind. In *Es träumte mir*, Op. 57, No. 3, leaps involving augmented fourths, diminished fifths, and diminished fourths convey the agony of unrequited love. Similarly, Elisabet von Herzogenberg, in a letter of 21–22 May 1885, suggested that the augmented fourths in *Nachtigall*, Op. 97, No. 1, imitate the bittersweetness of a real nightingale's song. In the second section of *In Waldeseinsamkeit*, the lines "und meine bebenden Hände um deine Knie ich schloß" (and I closed my trembling hands around your knee) are given a particularly realistic setting with the shaking hands depicted by the melody's shorter notes and the embrace of the character's knees suggested by its circling motion.

Despite Jenner's description and the wealth of such examples, few critics have appreciated the extent of Brahms's word painting. Textbook discussions of Lieder typically claim that Brahms cared little for word painting. By and large, such publications are concerned with the type of illustrative figures in the piano part in which Jenner reports that Brahms had little interest. Nevertheless, specialized studies document that Brahms did employ even this type of word painting.[32] In such songs as *Regenlied*, Op. 59, No. 3, *Während des Regens*, Op. 58, No. 2, and *Vom Strande*, Op. 69, No. 6, the figuration clearly is meant to depict the rain or flowing water. In *Parole*, the huntsman is brought to life by many a traditional word-painting technique, including ascending arpeggios, 6/8 meter, and dotted, repeated-note figures. In *Wir wandelten*, Op. 96, No. 2, oscillating octaves imitate the sound of tinkling bells; in *Blinde Kuh*, Op. 58, No. 1, a two-part invention portrays a chase; in *Liebe und Frühling*, Op. 3, No. 2, a canon depicts the wind encircling a rosebush. In these songs, Brahms utilizes keyboard and melodic figurations not unlike those used by earlier composers, such as Schubert, and, like Schubert, he often uses one musical figure throughout most of a song. In contrast, some later composers, above all Wolf, changed their figurations with each new image in a poem. Perhaps Brahms was cautioning Jenner against such an approach because it can jeopardize the continuity of a relatively short composition.

Harmony

Jenner's discussion of cadences also includes the topic of modulation and the establishment of the tonic. Here he is principally concerned with the importance of tonal unity, but he also indicates that harmonies can be expressive. He observes: "precisely the lack of clear identification of a key, even the tonic, can serve as an excellent means of expression" (pp. 198–99). Obscuring the tonic is of course an important element of nineteenth-century music in general, and there are a number of Brahms's compositions – including the last movement of the Third Symphony – that reach an unequivocal root-position tonic chord only in their concluding measures. His Lieder demonstrate a wide variety of ways in which the tonic can be obscured, and many begin without clearly stating the tonic chord. Some songs begin deceptively, implying one key, but then establishing another; others mask the tonic chord with embellishments; still others merely imply the key rather than giving a conspicuous root-position tonic chord.

Vom Strande, Op. 69, No. 6, is an example of a song that begins deceptively while also illustrating one of the ways in which this harmonic device can be

Example 9.2 Harmonic reduction of *Vom Strande*, Op. 69, No. 6, mm. 1–11

used to accentuate the psychological and dramatic issues stemming from the text. It uses an expanded ternary form in which the repeated A section functions as a refrain. Eichendorff's translation of a Spanish poem, found in his 1843 *Gedichte*, portrays a forlorn young girl whose sweetheart has returned to his ship and sailed away. During the refrains she addresses her absent beloved, but during the stanzas she appears to be addressing her mother. As Ira Braus has pointed out, the refrain and stanzas also are distinguished by assonance, with the repeated "u" of the refrain being less prominent in the stanzas.[33] Brahms conveys these differences in a number of ways. The declamation rate of the refrain is twice as slow as that of the stanzas, the piano has contrasting figurations – though both sections use sixteenth notes and appoggiaturas in the bass – and, perhaps most importantly, the two sections have different tonal designs. Whereas the refrain begins away from the tonic of A minor, the stanza firmly asserts the tonic from its initial measures. The refrain begins on an F major chord, but already in m. 3 the upper voices move to form a six-four chord above the F (Example 9.2). This suggests a cadence in B♭ major, a notion supported by the introduction of the seventh over the F in m. 5. At the same time, the piano introduces new figuration, the dynamic level drops, and the seventh resolves to B♭ minor. This progression is repeated, and when the seventh chord is restated in m. 7, a cadence in B♭ minor might be expected. Instead, the seventh chord is transformed into an augmented sixth, which resolves to a six-four on E. This cadential chord moves directly, without resolving to the dominant, to the tonic at the beginning of the stanza (m. 11). This progression from F major to A minor, along with the associated changes in the accompaniment and dynamics, underscores the poem's change in focus from the distant ship to the shore on which the girl stands. The tonal deception also may be a metaphor for the girl's misplaced emotional attachment to the sailor. She believes her future happiness depends on the sailor, but his departure suggests that this is unfounded. The girl herself implies that, on some level, she understands her error when, during stanza 2, she sings: "Such fleeting castles [the ships], who could trust them and joyfully build upon them a love that would last?" Her unease and perhaps the faintness of the sounds of the faraway ship likewise are suggested by the unusually weak cadence that ends the refrain. Here, the rising melody, the continual dissonances introduced by the piano's oscillating motion in the right hand, the syncopated bass line, as well as the withholding of a dominant chord, all weaken the resolution to the A minor tonic.

A number of Brahms's other songs begin deceptively, including *Parole*, *Botschaft*, Op. 47, No. 1, and *Meine Liebe ist grün*, Op. 63, No. 5. Additionally a smaller number of pieces move between tonal centers, as does *Klage*, Op. 105, No. 3: although in F major, much of the song, including the voice's concluding phrase, is in D minor. This Lied uses the text of a Niederrheinisch folksong; Werner Morik, in his study of Brahms and German folksong, has posited that this sort of tonal ambivalence is typical of songs from this northwestern region of Germany.[34]

Brahms also creates tonal unrest by coloring the initial tonic chords of a Lied with non-tonic tones. During the first half of each stanza of *Sommerfäden*, Op. 72, No. 2, the melodic notes that one might expect to be harmonized by the tonic are set to IV or VI chords, and sometimes distinguishing between these two chords is difficult. The poem, by Karl Candidus, describes gossamer threads, representing dreams of love, streaming down from heaven, and the piano's texture, which weaves a two-part invention around the voice, as well as the harmonies, all evoke the lightly flowing threads. Brahms summons similar sonic dreaminess in a number of other songs by deploying the tonic chord in first or second inversion, rather than the stronger root position. Examples of this are to be found in *Es träumte mir* and *Die Schnur, die Perl an Perle*, Op. 57, nos. 3 and 7, both of which employ six-four chords where one might expect tonic root-position chords. In *Die Schnur, die Perl an Perle*, the root-position tonic chord appears only at the final cadence.

Jenner mentions as well the expressive quality of modulations to remote keys, and although he does not illustrate this idea, numerous suggestive modulations abound in Brahms's Lieder. *Schwermut*, Op. 58, No. 5, includes perhaps one of Brahms's most striking and unexpected modulations. The text, once again by Candidus, consists of one stanza of six uneven lines, which Brahms divides into three sections: a plaintive alla breve first section characterized by short vocal segments and a repeated dotted-note, dirge-like figure in the piano; a transition including a startling harmonic shift; and a comparatively more lyrical, flowing conclusion in 4/2. The text portrays an intensely dispirited character who yearns for the peace of death. (While Brahms was fond of depicting such dejected men, their despondency drew considerable criticism from his contemporaries.) Throughout the first section of *Schwermut*, as well as the transition, a dotted figure in tenths or octaves in the lower register obsessively shadows the main character. As the piano finally reaches the tonic root-position chord of E♭ minor to close the first section, the voice enters on G♭; this note is repeated, after which the piano enharmonically reinterprets it as F♯, facilitating a move to B minor which quickly is followed by a move to G minor. These unusual, sudden harmonic shifts capture the disorientation of the protagonist, as he confesses to being tired of living. The last section gradually reestablishes the tonic, but final rest is achieved only in the last measure of the piano's postlude, after an inner voice chromatically descends from E♭ to B♭.[35]

Aside from modulations to remote keys, there are numerous other types of harmonic progressions meant to capture the emotional situations described in the songs' texts, and Brahms's friends, including Deiters as well as early critics such as Paul Mies, acknowledged many of these.[36] The animated central section of *Meerfahrt*, Op. 96, No. 4, offers a good example of Brahms's expressive chromaticism (mm. 34–50). Diminished sevenths, augmented sixths, chromatic passing chords, and an enharmonic detour by way of A♭ major, a remote key from the A minor tonic, all characterize this tonally unstable section. This arsenal of harmonies combined with appoggiaturas and unyielding syncopations seems a rather perverse accompaniment to Heine's description of a couple in a boat, listening to a beautiful waltz from the far-off shore. Only with the last line of text is it clear that this couple is far from happy, and that Brahms's setting underscores more their turbulent emotions than the joyful music in the distance. The recurring motive in this song begins with a prolonged suspension, which is harmonized in a number of different ways. At the climax, in mm. 54–55, when the true relationship of the principal characters is revealed, a sustained F♯ appoggiatura clashes against the A-minor tonic. Although these harmonies are used in the song's prelude, they are especially effective in this later passage as they prevent any sense of closure or release that the tonic chord – which comes after the chromatic passage – should have offered. On 21–22 May 1885, Elisabet von Herzogenberg wrote to Brahms praising the intense emotional impression made by this song, above all the entirely original harmonies and harsh appoggiaturas.

Motives

Although Jenner describes most of Brahms's important compositional techniques, he does not discuss the use of motives. However, George Henschel (1850–1934), conductor, composer, and baritone, who in 1875 sang in a performance of Bach's *St. Matthew Passion* under Brahms's baton and later would become closely acquainted with him, recalled the composer's description of his working method. According to Henschel's well-known account, this began with a small motive or a seed-corn, and he cites the opening of the composer's setting of Hölty's "Mainacht," published as Op. 43, No. 2, as an example. Many writers have explored this further, analyzing the motivic content of this song, as well as others.[37] Schoenberg praises Brahms's manipulation of motives, and he credited this technique as having aided his own development as a composer. In his article "Brahms the Progressive," Schoenberg describes some of the manipulations of a motive built on the interval of a third in *O Tod, wie bitter bist du*, Op. 121, No. 3, the third of the composer's *Vier ernste Gesänge* (Four Serious Songs), composed in 1896.[38] Walter Frisch, in an extended study, explains this analysis and further explores how the motivic structure relates to the song's metrical fluidity as well as to its harmonies. Ultimately, he relates all these features to the two contrasting views of death at the heart of the text, drawn from Ecclesiasticus 41: 1–2. In the first stanza death is dreaded, while in the second it is viewed as a release.[39] The Lied is characterized by a descending cycle of thirds that many commentators have interpreted as symbolizing death given that Brahms had used similar descending motives as a symbol for death in other songs, including *Steig' auf, geliebter Schatten*, Op. 94, No. 2, and *Feldeinsamkeit*. Frisch demonstrates that Brahms's motives as well as their manipulations are not entirely abstract structures, but instead are often bound to a text's imagery and its drama.

The richness of Brahms's motivic manipulations is evident even in his first published songs. The mother–daughter dialogue in *Liebestreu* discussed above, for example, is pervaded by a three-note motive, comprising two eighth notes followed by a quarter. Aside from the literal repetitions, transpositions, and intervallic variations in the bass, the mother's melody uses a variant of the motive, whose repetitions trail after those in the bass. This quasi-canonic effect perhaps suggests the sorrow and pain that plagues the girl, and that also afflicts her mother. Additionally, much of the melody, including the girl's phrases, is characterized by rising and falling third motion. Even the climax on the word "Treue" is set to a falling third, and its ab^2 also is the last note of one of the transformations of the original bass motive. The motivic saturation of the entire song was inspired perhaps by the original poem's word repetitions, which are a particularly strong feature of the first stanza.

Über die Heide, Op. 86, No. 4, composed almost thirty years after *Liebestreu*, sets a poem by Brahms's fellow North German Theodor Storm, and is another good example of how motives can permeate an entire song and at the same time serve the text. The bass repeats a four-note motive in almost every measure. The deep sounds portray the monotonous echoing of the tragic character's plodding onwards across the heath. Versions of this motive also appear in the vocal line and in the upper part of the piano part, in imitation, and in contrary motion. These repetitions and variations are particularly prominent in the central section, where the character describes mist encircling him like ghosts. The motives are harmonized in a number of ways: some are accompanied by seventh chords, while others form dissonances against consonant triads. All of these discords, along with the song's numerous syncopations, convey the character's frustrations with such force that the listener has little recourse but to share in them. Although Brahms's contemporaries were often put off by the intense bitterness and isolation of the characters in songs such as this, these works are an important part of the composer's oeuvre, not only because of their psychological impact but also because, as Billroth recognized in *Ein Wanderer*, Op. 106, No. 5, they reflect Brahms's own world view and experiences.

Not all of Brahms's Lieder are characterized by such intricate motivic structures, yet many include motivic manipulations that are linked to the text. This is the case with one of Brahms's most popular songs, *Vergebliches Ständchen*, Op. 84, No. 4, completed by 1879 to a poem drawn from one of Zuccalmaglio's anthologies. In this light-hearted work, a suitor tries to persuade his sweetheart to let him into her house and Brahms combines the folksong style with artful motivic manipulations to produce a comic scene. The song, widely performed in the 1880s, was greatly prized by Hanslick – to whom it was dedicated – and Kalbeck thought so highly of it that in his Brahms biography he included a three-page effusion of the work's masterful irony.[40] The prelude introduces an ascending motive of two eighths and a half note, and variations of this motive, as well as rhythmic patterns that also emphasize a pair of eighths, recur throughout the piece. Brahms's exploitation of this initial motive is especially effective during the lead-in to the final stanza, where the girl wittily rejects her suitor's entreaties, ending with "Gute Nacht, mein Knab'!" (Good night, my boy!) in response to his "Guten Abend, mein Schatz" (Good evening, my treasure). From m. 51 (Example 9.3), the rhythmic tension begins to increase, with the melody emphasizing the second beat of each two-measure segment with an ascending leap, while the piano, using a variation of the opening motive, accents the second beat of every second measure. During the final phrase of the stanza (m. 57), the piano imitates the voice's rising eighth-note pattern, and excitement is further heightened as the tempo picks up (m. 60). Although the piano begins the following brief interlude with the ascending arpeggio, it leads to a new, full, loud chord on the downbeat of m. 61. Then the motive is repeated in a manner that Kalbeck describes as resembling a stretto. These repetitions not only create additional tension by heightening the pitch, they also shift the accent from the first beat, to the third, and then in m. 62 to the

Example 9.3 *Vergebliches Ständchen, mm. 52–67*

second beat. Here, for the first time, the motive ends on an accented high A, and the girl enters in the following measure. This interlude is then repeated for the postlude, but the last motivic repetition is varied. Now the high A (m. 82) is marked with a *sforzando* and is harmonized with a half-diminished chord that resolves to the final authentic cadence. This phrase is the only time the opening ascending gestures lead to a conclusive authentic cadence, and this further conveys the finality of the girl's negative response. Furthermore, chords using the raised fourth (D♯) had been featured prominently in the third and fourth phrases of each stanza, and here, in the fourth stanza, this note occurs on the words "Knab'" (m. 76) and "gute" (m. 79), before appearing in the bass for the last, resounding high A (m. 82).

Vergebliches Ständchen, like the other songs discussed in this section and elsewhere in this chapter, clearly demonstrates the importance of the bass line. In many cases the bass line is essential to a song's motivic development and it almost always provides a strong, contrapuntal framework for the melody. Henschel, Max Graf, and the little-known composer Eduard Behm, all of whom recall that Brahms strongly emphasized the contrapuntal role of the bass when composing songs, further attest to the prominence of these lines. Graf and Behm both relate that when Brahms examined their songs he covered the middle voices so he could inspect the outer ones, and Graf also notes that in accompanying singers on the piano, Brahms brought out the bass. Further evidence of this feature is to be found in Brahms's sketches for such songs as *Vorüber*, Op. 58, No. 7, which show that he began to compose with the outer voices.[41] Although this emphasis on the outer voices was surely strengthened by Brahms's study of eighteenth-century theorists and thorough bass, the prominence of the bass is already evident in some of his earliest songs, including *Liebestreu*.

Whether through motivic manipulations, harmonic progressions, rhythms, or melodic contour, Brahms's Lieder reveal a composer energetically engaged in bringing a text to life by musical means. Brahms's friends and colleagues, including Billroth and Kalbeck, repeatedly praise the emotional affect of these psychological portraits. Furthermore, their critiques reinforce Jenner's report that the relationship between music and text draws on numerous parameters, and not primarily on correct declamation. In her 28 October 1888 discussion of *Auf dem Kirchhofe*, Elisabet von Herzogenberg notes the emotional impact of the harmony, melodic line, declamation, and the imagery of the opening measures of the piano. Similarly, in his discussion of *Die Mainacht*, Friedländer refers to the way in which the harmonies profoundly convey the changing moods of the poem, as well as the effectiveness of the pauses and the piano part.[42] Although the exploration offered here of Brahms's text-setting techniques has taken each compositional element in turn, in any one song these techniques function together, as Herzogenberg and Friedländer demonstrate. It is this multifaceted approach to text setting that makes Brahms's Lieder so rich and his characterizations of the protagonists that populate the poems he set to music so compelling. Moreover, it is these features that justify Brahms's inclusion with Schubert, Schumann, and Wolf as one of the true masters of the nineteenth-century Lied.

10 Tradition and innovation: the Lieder of Hugo Wolf

SUSAN YOUENS

By the time that the fiery, fifteen-year-old Wolf (1860–1903) from the town of Windischgraz in what was then Lower Styria (now Slovenjgradec in Slovenia) arrived in Vienna in 1875 to study at the Conservatory, the Lied had a rich history and an immense repertory, with more songs rolling off the presses each year. The question of how to compose Lieder in an original manner – and originality was a constant desideratum of late Romanticism – when so much German lyric poetry had been colonized many times over was complicated in this instance by a young composer's Wagner-mania. Comparing his predicament to that of a seedling tree trying to grow in the shadow of a mighty oak, the young Wolf struggled to assimilate the music of Schumann and Schubert, Wagner and Liszt, in the formation of "Wölfer's own howl," as he dubbed his unique compositional voice.[1]

The successful outcome of those struggles was a Lied aesthetic whose true originality we are only beginning to appreciate. In his brief compositional maturity, Wolf made complicated use of Lied traditions in order to forge a style in which late Romanticism's extensions of tonality were applied to nuanced, multivalent interpretations of older poetry.[2] Not for him the poetic avant-garde: there is a revealing anecdote about Wolf reading rhapsodic effusions hot off the press and hopping up and down in rage at the pretentiousness of the poems.[3] Instead, he gravitated to earlier generations of nineteenth-century poets, including three of the century's greatest masters of German lyric poetry: Goethe, Eichendorff, Mörike. Wolf once stated defiantly – he was challenging Schubert with this assertion – that certain poems had to await the creation of a post-Wagnerian tonal language before they could find full realization in music.[4] This idiosyncratic melding of older verse and modern tonal adventures is not Wolf's only achievement: he was the first to call attention to one of Germany's greatest poets, he refashioned comedy in the Lied, and he even pointed the way toward atonality at the end of his life without, however, stepping over the threshold. "Auch kleine Dinge können uns entzücken" (small things can also enchant us), Wolf proclaims at the beginning of his *Italienisches Liederbuch*, and one understands the pride of place given this song as tantamount to an artistic credo. In song's restriction, containment, and finitude, he found new depths. "Small things," Wolf asserts, can be as significant as the elephantine genres, used to commanding attention on the basis of size – better a great Lied by Wolf than many a late nineteenth-century imitator of Beethoven's symphonies or Wagner's music dramas.

Wolf made his way to compositional mastery slowly and painfully: it was not until he was almost twenty-eight years old that the promise evident in sporadic earlier works became an outpouring of consistently superb songs. His father Philipp, a tanner by trade, loved music, if only as an avocation, and saw to it that his fourth-born son was given music lessons at home and in the schools the teenage Wolf attended in Graz, Carinthia, and Marburg. He was anything but an ideal student, his multiple failures in his academic subjects being one means of blackmailing his father into sending him to the Conservatory in Vienna. Philipp Wolf, nervous about a future in music for his son, finally relented when his sister offered to give Hugo a place in her own household in Vienna, where the budding composer experimented with novel chord progressions on his aunt's parlor piano and gave full vent to his passion for opera – most of all, the operas of Wagner. To say that the young Wolf, already prone to all-consuming passions for whatever music was most important to him at the moment, was an enthusiastic Wagnerite is an understatement. Wagner even appeared to him in a dream in which Wolf sang the "Venusberg" scene to its composer (seduction of another sort), and Wolf moved heaven and earth to arrange a personal meeting at which he showed "the Master" his Piano Sonata, Op. 1, and Variations for Piano, Op. 2.[5] It is only to be expected that Wolf too would set his sights on operatic composition, beginning with the bloodthirsty melodrama *König Alboin*, of which only twenty-one bars survive; he would struggle with operatic projects for the rest of his life. But his compositional studies were seriously affected, first by a pedantic teacher who, Wolf asserted, actually impeded his progress and then by expulsion from the Conservatory in early 1877 "for offences against discipline." For eight months, he was back home in Windischgraz before Philipp, at wit's end about what to do with his errant son (that father and son loved one another dearly was never in doubt, however), consented to his return as a free artist to Vienna. Thereafter, Wolf would be an autodidact for whom the exercise of actual composition, at first in imitation of others and then increasingly in his own manner, took the place of formal training.

Wolf's earliest completed songs are settings of poems by Goethe, Heinrich Zschokke, and Nikolaus Lenau in 1875–76, followed in December 1876 by his first songs on texts from Heinrich Heine's *Buch der Lieder*. His foremost models as a song composer were Liszt and Schumann, especially the latter; indeed, Wolf's settings of *Du bist wie eine Blume* and *Wenn ich in deine*

Augen seh' bear the unmistakable imprint of their models in Schumann's *Dichterliebe*. Revealingly, Wolf was unable to finish his setting of Adelbert von Chamisso's (the poet of *Frauenliebe- und Leben*) *Was soll ich sagen?* because it was, in Wolf's own scrawled comment on the manuscript, "too much like Schumann." Undaunted, Wolf in 1878 planned an entire *Liederstrauß*, or garland of songs, of Heine settings, a foreshadowing of Wolf's later practice of composing "not poems, but entire poets," as the Viennese critic Eduard Hanslick once complained. Of the eight Heine songs composed in May and June of 1878, the first, *Sie haben heut' Abend Gesellschaft*, is a considerable achievement in the Schumannian manner – including a lengthy piano postlude – but with a significant glimpse of a later Wolfian trait. Music from the external world is progressively transformed by the poetic persona's perceptions, as in this example of dinner-party music consumed at the end by the rage of the betrayed, lovelorn outcast who speaks in this poem. Other examples of this separation of voice and piano into distinct presences which merge or separate as the persona's psychological experience dictates include the early Eichendorff song *Rückkehr* of 1883 and two mature masterpieces, the Eichendorff song *Das Ständchen* and *Mein Liebster singt am Haus im Mondenscheine* from the *Italienisches Liederbuch*. In all three instances, it is lovers' serenades the personae hear, but elsewhere, it is military marches – Mahler was not the only fin-de-siècle composer to concoct march-songs. The 1878 setting of Heine's "Es blasen die blauen Husaren" sets the stage for two later songs with military music as their backdrop: *Sie blasen zum Abmarsch* from the *Spanisches Liederbuch* and the comic song *Ihr jungen Leute* from the *Italienisches Liederbuch*. That Heine's poem treats of sexual betrayal from a man's point of view and that Wolf may have contracted the syphilis that would eventually cause his insanity around this time (we do not know the circumstances) are worth noting. Choices of poetry for musical setting are never disinterested and were perhaps particularly not so in this instance, although this is a poetic strain Wolf would soon reject. Heine's bleak view of humanity and his pose of subjectivity were not congruent with Wolf's mature taste for greater objectivity, generosity, and variety.

Songs on texts by Eichendorff, another Schumann poet, followed the early Heine songs, as well as settings of Robert Reinick, Friedrich Rückert, Friedrich Hebbel, and, most important of all, Eduard Mörike (1804–75). Mörike, who died in poverty the year Wolf went to Vienna, wrote only one volume of poems, revised and augmented through four editions in his lifetime, but these poems and his novella *Mozart auf der Reise nach Prag* (Mozart on the Journey to Prague) are more than enough to establish his greatness. Schumann in later life had found his way to Mörike's poetry for five songs, but Mörike was never Schumann's man in the same way that Heine and Eichendorff were. Wolf, who made it a practice not to set poetry already made into song by his great predecessors unless he felt they had fallen short of the mark, professed great respect for Schumann's setting of Mörike's *Das verlassene Mägdlein*. Nevertheless, he composed his own versions both of this poem and *Der Gärtner*, another Mörike text which Schumann had set, in 1888.[6] The first Wolf–Mörike songs were settings of *Suschens Vogel* in 1880, *Mausfallensprüchlein* in 1882, and the ballad *Die Tochter der Heide* in 1884. *Mausfallensprüchlein* is arguably Wolf's first masterpiece, and his first example of what one might call tendentious humor in the Lied. One way of coping with anger, violence, malevolence, and aggression, Freud would subsequently write, is by converting it into humor. Wolf, whose fluent swearing had earned him the nickname "Fluchu" (Fluch = curse) among his friends, would make just such jests into works of art.

During the years from 1880 to 1887, Wolf experienced, first, a painful love affair with a young woman named Vally Franck and then a liaison, probably beginning in 1884, with a married woman named Melanie Köchert that was to last for the rest of his life. From 1884 to 1887, he worked as an often outspoken music critic for the *Wiener Salonblatt*, hence his appellation by the Viennese as "the wild Wolf," and suffered painful artistic rejections of his symphonic tone poem *Penthesilea* and his one string quartet (completed in 1884 and eventually published in 1903). This series of tribulations in early manhood was capped by the death of his beloved father in May 1887, shortly before Wolf finally achieved, through the auspices of a friend, the long-sought miracle of first publication. The Viennese firm of Emil Wetzler agreed in late 1887 to bring out the *Sechs Lieder für eine Frauenstimme* and the *Sechs Gedichte von Scheffel, Mörike, Goethe und Kerner* the following year, in 1888, the latter collection including the 1883 setting of Justinus Kerner's *Zur Ruh', zur Ruh', ihr müden Glieder* that later would be sung in choral arrangement at Wolf's funeral. *Zur Ruh', zur Ruh'* forecasts Wolf's mature manner in its string quartet texture (thereafter a mannerism of this composer), its chromatic voice-leading, carefully disposed prosody, and its close attention to poetic reading, while the lovely Reinick songs, *Wiegenlied im Sommer* and *Wiegenlied im Winter*, from the set of women's Lieder anticipate Wolf's practice in maturity of pairing songs on occasion. Wolf, ecstatic over his impending first appearance in print and determined to compose still more songs, journeyed in January 1888 to a borrowed house in the village of Perchtoldsdorf near Vienna. There, one of the three "miracle years" in German song began (Schubert in 1815, Schumann in 1840, and Wolf in 1888).

The renewed contact with Mörike's poetry was the catalyst for an explosion of creativity. The first two songs composed at Perchtoldsdorf were not Mörike Lieder, however, but Wolf's last Heine song (a listless affair) and a setting of Reinick's comic *Gesellenlied* about a cheeky, charming apprentice who longs for mastery. One imagines that Wolf both saw Wagner's apprentice David from *Die Meistersinger von Nürnberg* in the poem and sensed that his own mastery was just around the corner. Three weeks later, on 16 February 1888, he composed *Der Tambour*, the first of the fifty-three *Gedichte von Eduard Mörike*; with uncanny appropriateness, this is a song about a lad on the threshold of adulthood who imagines metamorphoses. If the boy's fantasies are comic (he longs to turn his saber into a sausage and his drum into a bowl of hot sauerkraut), Wolf's transformation into a mature composer in full possession of his powers was both a serious, mysterious matter and cause for exultation. From February through May of 1888, and again from September through November of that same year, Wolf composed song after song: fifty-three Mörike settings and thirteen new Eichendorff songs to add to the seven earlier Eichendorff Lieder awaiting publication. After years of struggle, Wolf was dazed, amazed, filled with enormous pride. "'Erstes Liebeslied eines Mädchens' is of such intensity that it would lacerate the nervous system of a block of marble," he wrote to a friend, adding, "What I write now, dear friend, I write for posterity too."[7]

Wolf was drawn to Mörike's poetry for many reasons, some identifiable, some not. Mörike's slipperiness of categorization, his shape-shifting ability to be Romantic, neo-classical, idyllic, or folkish, to write in many forms, and the sheer profundity of his poems surely were reasons. So too was Wolf's singular opportunity to be the herald of a major poet still little known at the time. "The good Swabians [Mörike spent his life near or in Stuttgart, in the German region of Swabia] shall yet come to know their poet!," Wolf declared, and he was one of the most influential early proselytizers on Mörike's behalf. It is obvious from Wolf's letters that he loved Mörike's Baroque-influenced trafficking in oxymorons, the poet's gift for fantasy, and the psychological depths of this body of poetry "written with blood" (Wolf's term), but without the confessional tone of Heine.[8] That Wolf did not set out to compose a song anthology of this size seems obvious from his amazement as song after song came into being, but the massed anthology of poems by a single poet became the model for most of his subsequent song collections and was possibly his replacement for the song cycles he may have identified too closely with Schubert and Schumann to wish to compose himself. (The late eighteenth-century composers Reichardt and Zumsteeg had brought forth even larger compendia of Goethe and Schiller songs a century earlier, but Wolf's volumes were differently calibrated.) Surveying Wolf's choices of texts for this first large songbook, one is impressed by his discernment of what is finest in Mörike and by the variety of these songs. Wolf's operatic ambitions are implicated in his attraction to Mörike's many *Rollenlieder* ("role poems," or poems in which archetypal figures – hunters, old women, village maidens, drummer boys, love-sick boys – speak), and the composer's love of flights of the imagination drew him to Mörike's supernatural worlds. While a reluctant theology student in Tübingen in the early 1820s, Mörike had invented a new mythology about the fictive island-kingdom of Orplid, populated by rustic mortals, elves, fairies, a cursed king, and a goddess named Weyla. Weyla hails her island kingdom in a noble acclamation, the "Gesang Weylas," and Wolf's setting of it is rightly among his best-loved Lieder. Both for Weyla's solemn invocation and the poet's reverent acclamation of Christ at the beginning of *Schlafendes Jesuskind*, Wolf uses a similar progression (I–V–IV, with IV a substitute for the submediant, VI) to similar beautiful effect.

It is not possible to summarize fifty-three songs here, but one *can* cite examples representing important aspects of Wolf's art. Mörike's "Das verlassene Mägdlein" was probably inspired by a Baroque emblem book which included the image of a solitary servant-girl who lights the kitchen fire at dawn.[9] It is a recurring element of Mörike's poetry that sad truths fended off in the light of day appear suddenly, shockingly, to his poetic personae in the darkness just before dawn ("the Mörike hour," some German scholars call it).[10] The hour is even named in the title of another lament by another abandoned maiden, *Ein Stündlein wohl vor Tag*, which Wolf also set to music and paired with another song, *Der Knabe und das Immlein*.[11] In "Das verlassene Mägdlein," a servant girl whose lover has abandoned her lights the hearth fire at cock-crow, and its sparks are the catalyst for the revelation that she has dreamed of the faithless boy that night. Struck anew by sorrow, she begins to weep. Mörike loved folk poetry and knew from its example how to pare a poem to the bone, as these four austere quatrains demonstrate. The few words are dense with emotional meanings, as Wolf tells us in his setting. The composer's fondness for tonally ambiguous beginnings is manifest here throughout the four bars of the piano introduction; we hear harmonic intervals of thirds and seconds in the treble, nothing else. The key from which these isolated, incomplete intervals – like fragments of unanchored consciousness – issue is a mystery. We may realize later that these tones coalesce, piece by piece, into a dominant eleventh chord in A minor (a key which Wolf would have associated with mourning, loss, and sexual betrayal in such Schubert songs as *Du liebst mich nicht, Der Zwerg, Die Götter Griechenlands, Atys*, and others), but Wolf is in no hurry to clarify the matter. The harmony in m. 9 at the words "Muß ich am [Herde stehn, / muß Feuer zünden]" (I must stand at the hearth, must light the fire) is the first "tonic," but is it the tonic chord with an added sixth degree (A–C–E + F) or a tonic substitute with the added seventh degree (F–A–C–E)? The confusion of awaking at dawn after a difficult night finds a musical corollary in the harmonic ambiguity of the moment, indeed, of most of the song. Wolf does not, for example, present us with a dominant seventh harmony immediately audible as such until just after the maiden's moment of revelation. Not until uncertainty gives way to grief-stricken understanding is the tonality made clear. Even then, it "resolves" back to the musically ambiguous strains of her first words. This anguish, both Mörike and Wolf tell us, is a tape loop, a condition the girl will relive over and over.[12] One notices Wolf's insistence throughout the song on the dactylic rhythmic pattern of a quarter note and two eighth notes. He would have known to associate this pattern with matters cosmic and supernal, as in the Schubert–Leitner song *Die Sterne*, and with fated loss of love, as in the Schubert–Platen Lied, *Die Liebe hat gelogen*.[13] Schubert would, of course, have gotten the rhythm from the Allegretto second movement of Beethoven's Seventh Symphony.

One cannot leave the Mörike songbook without mentioning two categories of the Lied in which Wolf took a particular interest. It is evident from his music criticism that he was a "fan" of Loewe, whose 1830 setting of *Erlkönig* he liked better than Schubert's, according to anecdotes by his friends.[14] It was only to be expected that Wolf would try his hand at ballad composition in the wake of Loewe's achievement as the *Balladenmeister* par excellence.[15] Ballads are narrative poems – sometimes quite lengthy – in which the culmination of a historic or legendary event appears almost without context; we are given only the sketchiest preliminaries to the dénouement. From the eighteenth century on, ballad texts were set to music as episodic or sectional formal structures, often with quasi-orchestral piano accompaniments. Wolf's preference was for ballads in which events are experienced right then and there, or so goes the poetic feint, rather than recounted later by an unknown narrating voice. Mörike, who lived during the heyday of the fashion for balladry, wrote comic, tragic, and supernatural specimens of the genre, and Wolf chose the finest specimens that were composable of each type. In accord with the long tradition of *Schauerballaden*, that is, horror ballads, or necromantic imaginings to make the flesh creep, Wolf set Mörike's "Die Geister am Mummelsee" (The Ghosts at Mummel Lake, a lake in the Black Forest reputed to be haunted) and "Der Feuerreiter" (The Fire-Rider) in 1888, and these two ballads are among his most brilliant homages to and modernizations of Loewe's art. The enigmatic fire-rider who burns to death in a mill is a symbol of anarchy, its flames consuming both the anarchist himself and the mill where grain is ground to make life-sustaining bread for innocent folk. All suffer when anarchy rides the countryside, Mörike states. In Wolf's mad ride, we also hear a distant homage to Carl Maria von Weber, who made the extended composing out of a diminished seventh chord in *Der Freischütz* the foremost musical symbol of the demonic in the nineteenth century. Wolf was justly proud of *Der Feuerreiter*, and even Hanslick had to concede its power in Wolf's 1892 choral-solo-orchestral arrangement of the Lied.[16]

"Leave 'em laughing," the pundits say, and Wolf evidently agreed. The Mörike songbook ends with a group of six comic songs, three of them ballads (*Storchenbotschaft*, *Zur Warnung*, and *Abschied*) and three of them small songs (*Auftrag*, *Bei einer Trauung*, and *Selbstgeständniss*). These, and Wolf's other comic songs to follow, are a considerable achievement. Before him, humor in nineteenth-century music was to be found primarily in operettas, waltz songs, or children's songs, that is, music in more conservative harmonic and tonal styles than those of serious music. Wolf, who was drawn to comedy with a psychological slant, endowed his comic songs with the entire arsenal of late-Romantic tonal devices, reinventing humor in music for the world after Bayreuth. For example, in *Zur Warnung*, Mörike tells the tale of a hung-over poet who in post-alcoholic grandiosity peremptorily bids his Muse bring him a song. Inspiration is not to be summoned in this way, and his mocking Muse dictates nonsense until the poet banishes her with the hair of the dog that bit him. Wolf turns the rueful joke about recalcitrant creativity into a musical joke about the predicament of modern song-composers. His hung-over composer hiccups in enharmonic confusion, undecided whether to turn to the sharp side or the flat side, while his Muse dictates a nonsensical parody of Beethoven's Ninth, Wolf thus taking a jab at the Beethovenian aspirations of Brahms and other symphonic composers (Example 10.1). In the initial section, Wolf parodies his own justly famous vocal declamation, his care for matters of prosody and accentuation, by mimicking in music the overly precise, finicky speech of someone who has to compensate mightily for liquored laxity of tongue.

Example 10.1 *Zur Warnung* (from *Gedichte von Eduard Mörike*), mm. 15–26

When at the end of *Abschied* (appropriately, the volume's last song), Wolf's persona kicks a critic down the stairs to the strains of a rambunctious Viennese waltz, the listener in stitches realizes just how funny Wolf could be.

Wolf took a brief break from the Mörike floodtide in the autumn of 1888 to complete a smaller-scale collection of songs (twenty in all) on texts by Eichendorff. Many of them fall into one or the other of two categories: the first is this poet's characteristic strain of Catholic mysticism, in which one is impelled either away from or toward the highest transcendent love, the poet's inner world painted in symbolic pictures from nature. The many nocturnal poems are among Eichendorff's most beautiful, and Wolf set four of them to music: *Nachtzauber, Die Nacht, Das Ständchen,* and *Verschwiegene Liebe.* However, Wolf was particularly proud of his discovery for music of the second category, or Eichendorff's *Rollenlieder,* poems whose personae include an itinerant scholar, a sailor, a despairing lover, soldiers, and a wandering minstrel. One of the Eichendorff songs, *Das Ständchen,* mingles the *Rollenlied* and night magic strains, and it also exemplifies Wolf's propensity to structure some of his songs tonally as a chain of thirds, in this case rising major third root-relationships which return us to the opening key at the end. In Eichendorff's poem, an elderly man hears a student serenading his beloved by night and remembers when he too wooed and won a beloved woman with songs of a summer night, remembers too when "they" carried her "across the still threshold." In this poet's symbolic language, we understand the "still threshold" as the boundary between life and death. At the end of the song, the old man wistfully bids the youth "sing on"; some listeners will remember Schubert's miller-lad in *Der Müller und der Bach* from *Die schöne Müllerin* telling the brook, "So singe nur zu" (Sing on then) in another, much sadder, death-haunted context. The witty introduction of *Das Ständchen* depicts the student tuning his mandolin and plucking an introductory strain before he begins his serenade in D major. The sound of the rustling fountains and the trees issues from another tonal realm, F♯ major, which then cedes to B♭ major at the invocation of the "bygone, beautiful time." As the old man turns from thoughts of the past back to awareness of the happy serenader in the present, B♭ gives way to D major yet again. The shift to F♯ major in m. 21 ("and the fountains rustle") seems an abrupt contrast but actually is carefully prepared by the F♯s of the preliminary "tuning" in the introduction and the B♭s that tinge D major with a passing cloud of darkness at the word "Wolken" (clouds) in the initial D major section. Two of the most affecting details of this chain-of-thirds formal design are: (1) the moment of the enharmonic shift from F♯ to B♭ as the old man summons the "bygone, beautiful [time]" and (2) the fact that Wolf returns to D major as a recognizable recapitulation, just before the persona sings "But across the still threshold, they bore my love to rest." At the thought of his beloved's death, the old man returns from the past to the present and hears again the young man's sweet strains. Life, love, and song are now youth's prerogative.

In late October of 1888, Wolf began duplicating the Herculean feats of Mörike composition with another poet, this time the most revered figure in all of German literature: Goethe. In the year between 27 October 1888 and 21 October 1889, Wolf composed fifty-one Goethe songs, beginning with the mad Harper's songs from *Wilhelm Meisters Lehrjahre* (William Master's Apprenticeship, the protagonist's name a doffing of Goethe's cap to Shakespeare). Given a body of poetry that attracted more composers than any other poet except Heine, Wolf chose for his Goethe anthology both poems famously set to music by his great predecessors and a much larger selection of poems other composers had passed by, such as *Anakreons Grab*. In a gesture of mingled defiance and pride, Wolf placed groups of familiar texts as frames around his songbook, with the ten *Wilhelm Meister* songs placed at the beginning and three of Goethe's poetic meditations on Greek mythology – *Ganymed* (the beautiful youth kidnapped by Zeus in the form of an eagle), *Prometheus*, and *Grenzen der Menschheit* – at the end. The latter is one of Wolf's masterpieces, a Lied of suitable sublimity to conclude an array of Goethe songs. The poem, written in 1781 when the poet was immersed in studies of Pindar and Homer, tells of awe before the gods and warns mere mortals against the temerity of measuring themselves against them.

"Grenzen der Menschheit" (stanzas 2, 4, and 5 of 5)	Limits of Humanity
Denn mit Göttern	For with gods
Soll sich nicht messen	no mortal should
Irgend ein Mensch.	dare be measured.
Hebt er sich aufwärts	If he lifts himself up,
Und berührt	and bestirs
Mit dem Scheitel die Sterne,	the stars with the crown of his head,
Nirgends haften dann	nowhere then can his uncertain feet
Die unsichern Sohlen,	find anchor,
Und mit ihm spielen	and the clouds and winds
Wolken und Winde.	play with him.
. . . .	. . . .
Was unterscheidet	What distinguishes
Götter von Menschen?	gods from men?
Daß viele Wellen	That many waves
Vor jenen wandeln,	move before them,
Ein ewiger Strom:	an eternal stream:
Uns hebt die Welle,	the wave lifts us up,

Verschlingt die Welle,	the wave swallows us up,
Und wir versinken.	and we sink.
Ein kleiner Ring	A little ring
Begrenzt unser Leben,	bounds our life,
Und viele Geschlechter	and many peoples
Reihen sich dauernd	are arrayed, enduring
An ihres Daseins	on their existence's
Unendliche Kette.[17]	endless chain.

Awing himself into ever-sparer utterance (the stanzas above are ten, eight, and six lines), the persona contemplates unknowable divinity and the insignificance of individual human life, except as a link in the chain of being. Among those things which make Wolf's setting of this hushed immensity so powerful is his use of augmented triads en masse, beginning with an isolated instance to make still more emphatic the word "irgend" (never) in the phrase, "Denn mit Göttern soll sich nicht messen irgend ein Mensch." Thereafter, these chords consume the song in wave after wave. Wolf, a long-time admirer of Liszt's music, would have associated enchained, broken-chordal augmented triads with the first movement of Liszt's Faust Symphony, and the encoded reference for the cognoscenti has profound meaning. In Liszt's *Charakterbild* of Goethe's Faust, the descending sequence of outlined augmented triads, including all twelve tones, is a bold symbol of Faust's striving for the omniscience denied human beings but sought anyway. Moreover, Liszt also had used successions of augmented chords in his Dante Symphony to suggest immensity, apropos because augmented chords consist of equal intervals (major thirds), the root thus being difficult to ascertain. Both the Faustian and the cosmic associations seem beautifully apt to Wolf's reading of Goethe's neo-classical ode.

Wolf, who had learned from Schumann the art of long piano postludes in which the composer rewrites the ending of the poem, fashioned what is arguably the most majestic such passage in all of his songs at the end of *Grenzen der Menschheit*. One finds in this postlude an example of a Lied composer engaged in confrontation with his chosen text, wrestling with it, not just agreeing but arguing with its premises as only the best song composers can do. Just as at the beginning, we hear solemn block chords, their pitches distributed over a wide range in inexorable half-note rhythms. These are not, however, the pure triads in unusual progressions (Wolf's frequent musical symbol for the supernatural and divine) from the introduction. Rather, Wolf incorporates struggle into the descent (Example 10.2). The inevitable goal is the D major associated earlier with the verb "versinken," "to go under, to drown," and indeed, Wolf anchors most of the postlude to a low bass D undertow from which there is no escape.

Example 10.2 *Grenzen der Menschheit* (from *Gedichte von Goethe*), mm. 94–126

But Wolf's persona resists the inevitable, and his resistance is made audible in dissonant, *forte*, accented chords at mid-measure. If the loud dissonances also are pinned to the low bass D and are forced to cede each time to D major resolution, they nonetheless tell us that *this* speaker does not go compliantly into the still darker D minor oblivion at the bottom of the keyboard. It is significant that minor mode is kept at bay until the last moment and that the singer stops short of tonic closure in the vocal line. If the latter detail (characteristic of Wolf) tells us that Goethe's "unendliche Kette" is thereby open to continuation, it is also part and parcel of the musical persona's refusal to accept obliteration by the cosmos. Wolf knew from *Faust* and many other works by Goethe that this poet found grandeur in human striving, against whatever odds, and the composer incorporates this understanding into a poem which seems to state the opposite: that we are significant only as links in a biological chain. "No," Wolf insists, and writes music to prove it.

For his next songbook, Wolf turned to one of the most popular poetic sources for song composition in the second half of the century: the *Spanisches Liederbuch* of 1852, translations of Spanish poetry by the poets Emanuel Geibel (1815–84) and Paul Heyse (1830–1914). Given the allure of Spanish exoticism in colder German climes, poems from this collection already had been set to music by Fanny Hensel and Felix Mendelssohn, Schumann, Franz, Brahms, and many others. Wolf, however, managed to find poems relatively neglected by previous composers, with certain exceptions. Schumann's duets for his *Spanisches Liederspiel* are lovely, and yet one can imagine Wolf's objection to setting *In der Nacht* for two voices when the poetic persona of this text speaks in the singular. Given Wolf's dislike of Brahms, it is unlikely that the younger composer paid much heed to Brahms's early setting of *In dem Schatten meiner Locken*, and he had little respect for the minor composers who set the same texts he chose. Geibel and Heyse were not field ethnographers, and they relied on printed sources from five European countries, from which they chose thirteen "geistliche Lieder" (spiritual songs) and ninety-nine "weltliche Lieder" (worldly songs). Most are the anonymous products of popular lyrical art, with a sprinkling of poems by famous writers such as Lope de Vega, Cervantes, Luis de Camoes – and Geibel and Heyse themselves, masquerading under the pseudonyms Don Manuel del Rio and Don Luis el Chico. Wolf set ten of the spiritual poems and thirty-four of the secular texts between 28 October 1889 and 27 April 1890 as the astonishing roll-call of one Lied after another continued.

One month after completing the *Spanisches Liederbuch*, Wolf turned once again to a single writer: Gottfried Keller (1819–90), best known for a novel entitled *Der grüne Heinrich* which Wolf loved and whose creator he had planned to honor in 1889 with songs in celebration of Keller's seventieth birthday. The six songs from Keller's poetic cycle *Alte Weisen* were delayed until 1890 by the composition of the Goethe songs and include two poems set to music earlier by Brahms (*Du milchjunger Knabe* and *Singt mein Schatz wie ein Fink*; Brahms used an earlier edition of Keller's poems in which those two poems are given the women's names *Therese* and *Salome* respectively). Wolf had already demonstrated his liking for *Rollenlieder*, and Keller gave him another opportunity to exercise the predilection in the virtuoso portrayal – the pianist has a work-out – of a drunken charcoal-burner's wife howling in delirium tremens in the forest (*Das Köhlerweib ist trunken*). The set ends with homage to Wagner at the close of one of Wolf's loveliest lyric gems: *Wie glänzt der helle Mond*. Both in this song and in *St. Nepomuks Vorabend* from the Goethe songbook, Wolf makes much use of descending chromatic vocal lines accompanied by an alternation between triadic harmonies and sweetly dissonant added-note chords (an evocation of bell-chimes), the sweetness due in some measure to the ethereal treble tessitura. One model for such music was surely Liszt's song *Ihr Glocken von Marling*, and Britten must have remembered them all when he set Goethe's *Um Mitternacht* to music. The poetic persona of the Keller poem is an old peasant woman who looks at the moon and imagines her arrival in heaven. There, she will wear a silver veil and look in wonder at her white fingers, no longer reddened, old, and worn with toil, while God the Father will sit on his throne and feed the Holy Ghost with grain from His own hand. Outside the gates, St. Peter is given no rest but instead "squats in front of the door and mends old shoes" to transformed treble echoes of Hans Sachs's cobbling music in act 2, scene 2 of *Die Meistersinger*. (One remembers that both Keller's and Wolf's fathers were leather workers.)

Beginning in late September of 1890, Wolf began setting poems from the *Italienisches Liederbuch*, a compilation of Italian folk poetry translated by Paul Heyse and published in 1860. As in the *Spanisches Liederbuch*, the Italian peasant maidens and men of these poems are transformed into Germans with larger vocabularies and greater intensity of expression than their models. The genesis of the musical settings makes a painful tale, even if it ends in triumph. After composing seven songs, compositional block intervened for a year; when it released him from its grip in December 1891, Wolf composed another fourteen songs and then fell silent again, this time for much longer. Not until March of 1895 was he able to compose, and the agony of the interim years was excruciating. "I would just as soon suddenly be able to speak Chinese as to compose a note," he told a friend.[18] Reasons both psychological and physical – his all-consuming desire to compose an opera, the inability to find a libretto he liked, and possibly the inroads of syphilis – all may have combined to cause his creative impasse. Once he had embarked on the composition of his only completed opera *Der Corregidor*, he was able to return to Heyse's anthology in March and April of 1896 to compose the remaining twenty-four songs of his Italian songbook.

The anonymous folk poets of the *Italienisches Liederbuch* are preoccupied almost entirely with love in its many manifestations. Wolf's forty-six poems vacillate between texts clearly emanating from a male speaker, others in a female voice, and still others applicable to both sexes when in the grip of passion. The men's songs are mostly tender and worshipful, while many (not all) of the women's songs are comic – here, the descendants of Mozart's Susanna and Zerlina scold lovers for their stupidity or bad manners, flirt outrageously, and, at the end, call imprecations down on the head of an unsatisfactory ex-sweetheart. Most of the poems were originally *rispetti*, an Italian verse-form in which the same basic idea is expressed several times in succession, and Wolf clearly found it an apt vehicle for the exploration of tonal ambiguity. One also finds in the *Italienisches Liederbuch* examples of a recurring Wolfian phenomenon, one with roots (if the pun is pardonable) earlier in the century which Wolf made his own: directional tonality. Schubert had experimented c. 1817 with songs such as *Ganymed* and *Auf der Donau* which begin in one key and end in another, and both Mahler and Wolf in their different ways also explored the possibilities of directional tonality in the Lied. One especially beautiful example in the Italian songbook is the nineteenth song, *Wir haben Beide lange Zeit geschwiegen* (Example 10.3), in which a lover, either male or female, tells of a quarrel healed by God's angels, who brought peace down from heaven. The poet sums up the tale in the first two lines ("Wir haben Beide lange Zeit geschwiegen, / Auf einmal kam uns nun die Sprache wieder," or "We have both been silent for a long time. Suddenly speech came back to us again"), followed by the threefold statement of celestial intervention on behalf of peace: (1) Angels, who fly down from heaven, bring peace again after war; (2) God's angels have flown down, bringing peace with them; and (3) The angels of love came by night and have brought peace to my breast. The transformation from anger to love, silence to speech, happens in the first five bars of a small but intense song (twenty-one measures in total). The beginning is shrouded in dissonance and harmonic uncertainty, the tonality impossible to identify until we hear the dominant seventh of D♭ major in m. 5 and its resolution in m. 6. In typical tonal wit, Wolf begins the transformation in the lovers' hearts by respelling the G♭ pitch of "[ge]-schwiegen" of m. 2 as F♯ in m. 3, but he does not clarify what the emphasis on B♮ in these first five measures means until later in the song when it becomes the meltingly expressive flatted sixth degree of E♭. As the poetic persona repeats that angels were the agents of peace, the brief D♭ tonality is transformed from being the tonic key to being the dominant of G♭ major, and G♭ in turn gives way to Wolf's favorite third

Example 10.3 *Wir haben Beide lange Zeit geschwiegen* (from *Italienisches Liederbuch*), mm. 1–6

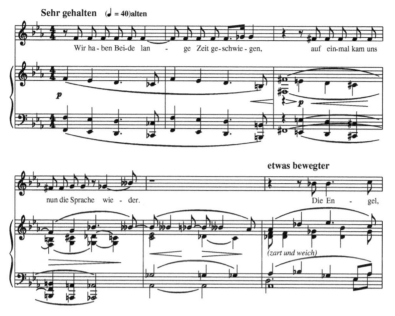

relations for the end of the song in E♭ major. *Wir haben Beide lange Zeit geschwiegen* thus presents an idiosyncratic tonal structure in which the key of a work must be understood as undergoing continual evolution rather than establishing and sustaining Classical tonal stability. That this is a concept beautifully apt for the love hymned in the poem will occur to many who study this Lied.

Despite his obsession with finding the text for a second opera, Wolf composed several remarkable songs in late 1896. In October, he returned to the poetry of Robert Reinick to compose *Morgenstimmung*, and in late December, he completed two settings of poems by Byron in German translations by Otto Gildemeister, *Keine gleicht von allen Schönen* and *Sonne der Schlummerlosen*. As Wolf was working on the Byron songs, a friend gave him a volume of German translations of Michelangelo's poetry as a Christmas present, and the composer immediately conceived the notion of an "imposing volume of songs" that would constitute a portrait in music of the great artist. "Naturally the sculptor must sing bass," Wolf told another friend, the sculptor who would later create Wolf's tomb monument in Vienna's Central Cemetery.[19] In early 1897, Wolf set four of the poems to music, although he destroyed the fourth and last as "unworthy." The three remaining works – *Wohl denk' ich oft, Alles endet, was entstehet,* and *Fühlt meine Seele* – would be his last songs, although not his last music: his unfinished second opera *Manuel Venegas* has that tragic honor. The second of the Michelangelo songs, an implacable "vision of dry bones" singing, struck its own creator as extraordinary.[20] In a much-quoted letter, he declared:

> More significant, however, seems to me the second poem, which I consider to be the best I have thus far knocked off . . . If in your emotion over it, you don't lose your reason, you cannot ever have possessed any. It is truly enough to drive one mad and moreover of a staggering, genuinely antique simplicity. Your eyes will pop! I am awestruck by it and frightened, for I fear losing my reason over it. Such dangerous things I am now creating to the public danger.[21]

This text is a setting of most of a *barzelleta* (an epigrammatic verse-form deemed particularly suitable in the Renaissance for moral instruction, here a *memento mori*) beginning "Chiunche nasce a morte arriva" (Whatever's born must come to death). The death-haunted artist was only eighteen years old when he wrote this unfinished poem, breaking it off after words invoking the hollow eye-sockets of skulls vacated by those once living. It is no wonder he frightened himself. In this poem, the dead speak to the living in chilled, passionless tones, confronting us with that we would rather not see and cannot escape.

Alles endet, was entstehet.	All that is created ends,
Alles, alles, rings vergehet,	all, all must perish
Denn die Zeit flieht,	as Time flies on.
Und die Sonne sieht,	And the sun sees
Dass alles rings vergehet.	that all must perish:
Denken, Reden, Schmerz und Wonne;	thought, speech, pain and rapture.
Und die wir zu Enkeln hatten	And those who were our descendants
Schwanden wie bei Tag die Schatten,	vanished as day banishes shadows,
Wie ein Dunst im Windeshaus.	like mist in a breath of wind.
Menschen waren wir ja auch,	We too once were human beings,
Froh und traurig, so wie ihr,	happy and sad, just like you.
Und nun sind wir leblos hier,	And now we are lifeless here,
Sind nur Erde, wie ihr sehet.	are only earth, as you see.
Alles endet, was entstehet.	All that is created ends,
Alles, alles, rings vergehet.	all, all must perish.

Wolf's setting of *Alles endet, was entstehet* is remarkable for its austerity, the music distilled to skeletal essence. Every note in the song is derived from the bleak, unharmonized, four-bar piano introduction, in particular two figures that permeate the song: a descending tetrachord that first appears at the words "Alles endet" in m. 5 and the cambiata-like figure in the piano

Example 10.4 *Alles endet, was entstehet* (from *Drei Gedichte von Michelangelo*), mm. 1–8

in mm. 5–6, 7–8, made up of an ascending and a descending semitone at the distance of either a major or a minor third (Example 10.4). Both the descending tetrachord and the semitone "sighing figure" have traditional connotations of grief, but Wolf, who twists and turns them inside out, makes them point to a future beyond tonality. If this is undeniably a tonal composition, or more accurately, a tonal nether region between E major and C♯ minor in which now one, now the other is predominant for brief periods of time, the words "Und nun sind wir leblos hier, sind nur Erde, wie ihr sehet" (mm. 30–33) issue from a mysterious, unidentifiable realm. And yet, the brief passage consists of clearly recognizable manifestations of the familiar tetrachord and cambiata figures. The implications of this are immense: the death of tonality is contained within tonality itself, as death is contained within life. Like an intricately carved Chinese *objet d'art* in which proportionately smaller components fit within a larger identical structure, the form of the whole and the form of the individual elements of *Alles endet, was entstehet* are the same, and both are ultimately circular. "From dust are we created and to dust we return," Wolf says as a matter of musical architecture, bringing us at the end back to the microcosm from which the song's macrocosm was created. From Michelangelo's mingling of life and death, of past and present and future, Wolf created a complex abstraction in which original, retrograde, transposed, and varied forms of the same minimal material constitute a larger entity. The implications for twentieth-century music are obvious.

Wolf's music, some say, is a "hard sell." If Lieder as an entire category are considered an esoteric taste shared only by the minute percentage of the population who revel both in German poetry and in classical music contained in small packages (here, I am echoing Graham Johnson in chapter 15), then Wolf's Lieder are among the most esoteric of all, according to the myth of this man and his music. Those who repeat this oft-heard shibboleth point to Wolf's cultivation of late Romantic chromaticism and the conceptual difficulties his songs pose for performers and listeners who might prefer less taxing strains. Certainly the song with which I have ended this chapter, *Alles endet, was entstehet*, is not charming, not pretty, not comfortable, nor is its power of the heaven-storming variety which attracts by virtue of forcefulness, sweeping the listener along in a deluge of sound. Like Rembrandt's portraits of old age, *Alles endet, was entstehet* plumbs the depths of what it is to be human, and its artificer knew how to make every aspect of his tonal language jump through hoops to that end. "The first principle of art for me is inexorable, harsh, strong truth, truth to the point of terror [Wahrheit bis zur Grausamkeit]," Wolf wrote to Emil Kauffmann in a famous letter, and he meant it: this is his artistic credo.[22] One can imagine his agreement with Goethe, who said in an epigram, "Works of the mind and of art do not exist for the mob."[23] Indeed, Wolf himself said similar things on occasion.

But at the same time, he wanted every listener he could possibly convert to his cause, and the body of songs he created is by no means wholly a confrontation with what is grim in life and death. Wolf could seduce with the best of them and laugh with the best of them. The sheer loveliness – apparent on first hearing – of such songs as *Verschwiegene Liebe*, *Der Gärtner*, *Komm, Liebchen, komm*, and many others should entice listeners initially shy of "the wild Wolf" to explore further. Once embarked on that exploration, one finds a dazzling variety of characters, forms, moods, styles, and thoughts, the encyclopedic range truly staggering. As few things in life can do, these songs repay long acquaintance because they are so dense with nuance, with riches both subterranean and on the surface. If poetry is language at its most incandescent because a minimum of words is made to convey maximum content, then song, as Wolf understood it, must raise the stakes. Music too is to be made maximal, not by crowding more performers onto the stage or enlarging the dimensions of Classical forms, but by compressing into a contained space a cluster of highly sophisticated musical elements. The multiple allusiveness, the ambiguities, the chromaticism of Wolf's tonal language constitute his answers to the many meanings of poetry.

11 Beyond song: instrumental transformations and adaptations of the Lied from Schubert to Mahler

CHRISTOPHER H. GIBBS

The presence and significance of the nineteenth-century Lied extend well beyond solo vocal settings with piano accompaniment of German poetry. Composers often wrote songs for other instrumental partners (such as guitar), in multi-voice combinations (duets, for example), and in languages other than German (as did Grieg in Norwegian and Dvořák in Czech). A broad definition of the Lied therefore must take into account the diversity of instrumentations, vocalists, and languages that fits somewhat uneasily within a category exemplified by works of Schubert, Schumann, Brahms, Wolf, Mahler, and others. Ultimately, the domain of the Lied stretches even farther, into the non-vocal, into purely instrumental compositions, which is our concern in this chapter.

A song, in short, is not always sung. Prominent examples that frame the period under discussion here begin with Schubert's "Wanderer" Fantasy, "Trout" Piano Quintet, and "Death and the Maiden" String Quartet, and extend through Mahler's so-called *Wunderhorn* symphonies and beyond. Such well-known instances of songs subsumed into keyboard, chamber, and orchestral compositions represent only a small part of a practice with broad musical, aesthetic, and cultural manifestations and implications. The phenomenon encompasses far more than the works of Schubert and Mahler, and in various ways affects most significant nineteenth-century composers, in Germany and elsewhere.

A transmuted vocal presence was hardly a nineteenth-century innovation. For hundreds of years, sung works were used as the basis for new compositions. The earliest notated Western polyphonic music built upon monophonic plainchants. Medieval and Renaissance secular songs were often recast in sacred works, such as parody Masses, or were played in some purely instrumental fashion. Lutheran chorales – descendants of plainchant and cousins to secular German Lieder – appeared in cantatas, oratorios, and passions, as well as in organ preludes and in various other instrumental guises during the Baroque era. (Chorales would later make new kinds of instrumental appearances in countless nineteenth-century compositions.) Bach ingeniously made a quodlibet of two German folk songs in the last variation of his Goldberg Variations. Composers of the Classical era

sometimes incorporated German song (as well as those from other countries) into symphonies, chamber music, and works in other genres. The
twentieth century continued this tradition in countless compositions, from
Schoenberg's thorny Second String Quartet, Op. 10, to rebellious Beatles
tunes tamed as elevator Muzak.

It would seem that the practice of taking something vocal and rendering
it instrumental is nearly as old as Western music itself. If so, what distinguishes the nineteenth-century transformations of German Lieder from
those drawing upon other vocal sources, such as sacred music or operas?[1]
I would like to approach this vast topic by considering some representative
compositions, especially ones by Schubert and Mahler. To overstate the case
somewhat, Schubert "created" the genre of the *Kunstlied* near the beginning
of the nineteenth century and Mahler re-created it in extraordinary ways less
than a century later. Many of the most pressing compositional and aesthetic
issues relating to subsumed songs are connected to their accomplishments.
For, even if it is an exaggeration to say Schubert is the "Father of the Lied"
(in fact he is usually called the "Prince of Song"), his elevation of its artistic status had profound impact not only on that particular genre, but also
more generally on matters relating to instrumental lyricism, compositional
technique, folk-like simplicity, naturalness, expression, and hermeneutic
associations allied with words.[2] This chapter touches on a variety of related
musical, aesthetic, and socio-historical concerns, of which I will concen-
trate on four: (1) unsung song; (2) subsumed song; (3) meaning, messages,
memory in song; and (4) transfigured song.

Unsung songs: literal and figurative *Lieder ohne Worte*

The simplest way for a song to become purely instrumental is to eliminate the text (and usually the voice as well), to create a *Lied ohne Worte*
(song without words). Although the label immediately brings to mind
Mendelssohn's four dozen keyboard pieces, his works constitute figurative, not actual, song transformations. For Mendelssohn, as for many other
composers who used this and similar titles, the designation "Lied" signifies
an approach to melody, phrasing, and figuration, rather than the real trans-
ferral of a musical line originally bound to a specific literary text. Yet there
also exist countless examples of songs from which the words have been
removed – literally. Sometimes the original vocal line was simply played
by a solo instrument, such as the cello, violin, or flute, although the far
more common nineteenth-century practice was to incorporate it into the
keyboard accompaniment. Many nineteenth-century composers, arrangers,
and publishers produced such textless Lied transformations, which point

to realities of everyday musical life. In an age before recordings, arrangements provided access to music otherwise heard rarely, if at all. Publishers released arrangements of Schubert's most famous songs, just as they did of Beethoven's enormously popular *Adelaide*, Rossini opera arias, and so much else, because they addressed practical needs and because they sold extremely well.

Among the earliest transformers of Schubert Lieder, and certainly the foremost figure, was Liszt. At least one contemporaneous review called his Schubert transcriptions *Gesangsstücke ohne Text* (sung pieces without text).[3] His arrangements, beginning in the mid 1830s, proved to be astonishing commercial successes and provided favorite repertoire for his concert tours.[4] In this way, the simple, domestic Lied fueled Liszt's virtuoso needs and entered the concert hall. Nonetheless, Liszt's treatments of songs by Schubert, Beethoven, Schumann, and others, as well as a few of his own, offered more than just satisfying fare for performers, publishers, and the public. Here we find one great artist musically interpreting his predecessors, his contemporaries, and himself. We do not possess any recordings of Liszt playing, but at least we have some specific musical access to his interpretations through his arrangements, which reveal many facets of his interpretive powers.

Contemporaries viewed those powers as exceptional. Responding to 1839 performances of a Schubert Lied transcription in Vienna, a critic using the name "Carlo" remarked in the *Wiener Zeitschrift für Kunst, Literatur, Theater und Mode* that Liszt had "created a new genre." Continuing, he noted:

> It is a successful attempt to reproduce the melodic and harmonic beauty of the new classical song as a lyrical whole for the piano *alone*, and to perfect it with the power of singing and declamation without the sacrifice of any of his keyboard richness. The composer's skillful, characteristic, and tasteful treatment [of the material] has made these pieces favorites nearly everywhere. Schubert's immortal songs will be the property not only of cultured singers, but also of cultured pianists.[5]

Although Liszt was undoubtedly the principal popularizer of Lied transcriptions, to say, as this critic does, that he invented the genre is akin to saying Schubert invented the Lied. This, of course, is exactly the point. Both claims register historical truths that supersede strict chronology. When the critic writes of "the new classical song," he draws attention to the crucial role Schubert's songs had in elevating the Lied from a domestic genre to one that assumed major artistic importance in the nineteenth century. In sum, although songs had been arranged for piano before Liszt, the Lied transcription became a viable subgenre only later, in large measure because Schubert's Lieder invited such treatment.

Beyond the artistic prestige Schubert eventually brought to the Lied, the musical innovations in his songs facilitated the effectiveness of textless arrangements. One of the most significant breakthroughs was a new relationship between vocal line and keyboard. The Lied tradition Schubert inherited, and from which he clearly learned so much, tended toward rather simple vocal melodies and keyboard accompaniments. (In many cases the latter were so straightforward that the vocal and piano parts might easily be performed by the same person.) Mechanical improvements in the construction of pianos during the first decades of the nineteenth century well served Schubert's interpretive goals: the possibilities for thrilling keyboard parts of unprecedented intensity, extraordinary difficulty, sustained lyricism, and rich textures all were enhanced. Indeed, Schubert's piano parts could sometimes even stand on their own as pieces with genuine musical interest, almost character pieces themselves. Into this elaborate keyboard fabric, Liszt found the most ingenious ways of weaving the vocal melody.

Schumann observed that Liszt's treatments of Schubert Lieder introduced "a new style in the school of piano playing."[6] As in many of his early compositions, such as the reworkings of Paganini's music, Liszt was concerned with expanding keyboard technique. Although Schumann found the Schubert Lied arrangements "perhaps the most difficult pieces ever written for the piano,"[7] other works of the so-called transcendental period (many of which were probably unknown to him) make comparable demands on the pianist, and often exceed them. A pioneering aspect of the Lied transcriptions, something Liszt may have wished to "learn" from Schubert, is lyricism.[8] The pyrotechnics in most of Liszt's own music from the 1830s are daunting, but none requires such a sustained melodic line. One of Liszt's primary objectives was to make the piano a more lyrical instrument and an indication of his success is that critics consistently remarked on his ability to have Lied arrangements "sing" in his playing of them.[9]

While the structure of a few of Liszt's reworkings of Schubert Lieder departs significantly from that of the original, most are "transcriptions" that retain the same number of measures and tonality.[10] They are, literally, Schubert's song without words or voice. The critic Heinrich Adami, who wrote detailed reviews of Liszt's trailblazing Vienna concerts in 1838, 1839, and 1840 for the *Wiener Theaterzeitung*, initially reacted to the "original" pieces by stating "they are not so much brilliant concert pieces, as one usually encounters today, but rather musical impromptus."[11] Adami thus recognized the similarities between Liszt's transcriptions and the lyric piano piece, a hallmark of burgeoning Romanticism.

Mendelssohn's *Songs without Words* often approach melody and accompaniment in ways comparable to those found in Liszt's Lied transcriptions.[12] Fanny Mendelssohn first mentioned her brother's pieces in 1828 in connection with small *Albumblätter.* "Felix gave me three things," she writes: "a piece for my album – a *Song without Words*, of which he has written some very lovely ones recently."[13] Schumann likewise was enchanted by his friend's creations: "Who of us in the twilight hour has not sat at his upright piano (a grand piano would serve a statelier occasion), and in the midst of improvising has not unconsciously begun to sing a quiet melody? Should one happen to be able to play the cantilena along with the accompaniment, above all, should one happen to be a Mendelssohn, the loveliest *Song without Words* would result."[14] The enhanced lyricism of song and advances in accompanimental textures, as well as the ascendance of the miniature and of the Romantic fragment, share basic features with the lyric or character keyboard piece. Slow movements of some of Beethoven's piano sonatas, his bagatelles, and later the nocturnes of John Field and Chopin likewise deploy song-like melodies and accompaniments. The Bohemian composers Václav Tomášek, Jan Voříšek, and Leopold Eustache Czapek composed small keyboard works with designations such as "Eclogues," "Rhapsodies," "Dithyrambs," and "Impromptus." And Schubert wrote his own two sets of Impromptus, Opp. 90 and 142 (D899 and 935; 1827), and his Moments Musicaux, Op. 94 (D780; 1823–24), some of which are closely related to songs from around the same time. John Reed calls the Impromptu in C minor, Op. 90, No. 1, "a kind of keyboard paraphrase of *Der Wegweiser*" (D911/20; 1827).[15] These lyric keyboard pieces by early Romantic composers typically offer a subsumed vocal line that is neither operatic, like much of Chopin's music, nor dramatic, as are the ballads of Chopin, Brahms, and others,[16] but rather is primarily song-like. Liszt's literal "songs without words" and Mendelssohn's figurative ones explicitly make this connection between song and the lyric keyboard composition.

It also should be noted that the phenomenon of unsung songs occurred in a wide variety of ways that extended well beyond the keyboard. For example, Heinrich Wilhelm Ernst's spectacular transcription of *Erlkönig* for solo violin, Op. 26 (1842) reduced the work to a lone instrument in an even starker manner.[17] Other transformations increased the number of musicians. One observes the adaptation of songs for string quartets, small ensembles, and, even more frequently, enlarged for full orchestra. Once again, the conventions of nineteenth-century musical life account for these practices. As the century progressed, composers began to expand their conception of the Lied so as to reach larger audiences, to utilize the greater weight of operatically trained voices, and to exploit the instrumental possibilities of big ensembles. The orchestral Lied emerged as a prominent subgenre, one that reached its height late in the century with Wolf, Mahler, and Richard Strauss, and continued to attract Reger, Pfitzner, and the composers of the Second Viennese School.[18] The histories of the early nineteenth-century piano Lied and the later orchestral Lied merge in the many mid-century orchestrations of Schubert songs by Berlioz, Liszt, Brahms, and others. Singers who wished to perform Lieder for large audiences attending symphonic concerts commissioned such orchestrations from noted composers and conductors.[19] That so many accepted the challenge suggests an incipient awareness of the potential of the orchestral Lied and its possibilities for expanded expressiveness, a potential that finds its supreme expression with Mahler. The instrumental transformation of song, accomplished either through a reduction or through an enlargement of the instrumentation, sung or unsung, pointed in new generic directions.

Some of the musical and aesthetic issues raised by the wholesale instrumentation of songs can be extended with respect to the use of only selected materials drawn from song – a melody, accompaniment, and so forth – within instrumental compositions. Unlike Liszt's transcriptions, which in essence transform entire songs into new pieces, composers elsewhere extracted particular elements of a Lied. This subsuming of specific melodic, rhythmic, and accompanimental materials within larger instrumental works is the issue to which we now turn.

Subsumed song: Lied materials within instrumental works

Although the stature of instrumental music reached new heights during the early nineteenth century, the prestige of vocal music continued in opera, oratorio, and more intimate genres such as the newly prominent *Kunstlied*. At the same time, the presence of vocal music found other outlets by means of its being subsumed within purely instrumental compositions, as may be seen in a number of string quartets by Beethoven. For example, there are Russian folk songs in the "Rasumovsky" Quartets, Op. 59, and a figurative "Heiliger Dankgesang" – a holy song of thanksgiving – in the A minor Quartet, Op. 132. In many of his works, Beethoven includes distinctly vocal and rhetorical passages, most famously the "Ode to Joy" in the last movement of the Ninth Symphony. Joseph Kerman has remarked on a "vocal impulse" especially noteworthy in Beethoven's late works, which constitute a "crowning monument to lyricism."[20] Maynard Solomon extends this observation: "Not only lyricism, but rhetoric, declamation, and recitative as well: speech and song together press to fulfill Beethoven's drive toward immediacy of communication."[21]

What became ever more significant for Beethoven near the end of his compositional career was crucial for Schubert from the outset. Perhaps this is not surprising given that their vocal impulses occurred simultaneously, from the mid 1810s to their respective deaths a little more than a decade later. This

Example 11.1a Schubert, *Die Forelle* (D550), mm. 1–8

vocal impulse left its mark on many genres, from the keyboard miniature to the lyrical symphony.[22] The merging of the vocal and instrumental led, as Reed has observed, to compositions that "adapt the expressive freedom and 'inwardness' of Romantic song to the formal patterns of instrumental music in such a way that, as [Schubert's close friend Moritz von] Schwind put it, these instrumental works 'stay in the mind, as songs do, fully sensuous and expressive'."[23]

Despite the long history of vocal elements within instrumental works, nineteenth-century developments relating to German Lieder are distinctive. Not only melodic, accompanimental, formal, and harmonic properties were drawn from song, but one also finds the incorporation of a wide range of characteristic moods, methods, and other materials specific to the Lied. Let us first consider some of the cultural and musical manifestations of these infiltrations before turning to hermeneutic implications in the next section.

We might begin by looking at a relatively early, straightforward, and well-known example of a nineteenth-century Lied subsumed within an instrumental work. *Die Forelle* (D550; 1817) quickly became one of Schubert's most famous works, and it is hardly surprising that he chose to incorporate it into his "Trout" Quintet for piano, violin, viola, cello, and double bass (D667; 1819), apparently after being asked to do so by Sylvester Paumgartner, a wealthy music patron and amateur cellist (Examples 11.1a and 11.1b). In the fourth movement Schubert constructs a set of five variations on the

Example 11.1b Schubert "Trout" Quintet (D667), mvt. 4, mm. 1–8

song's melody, accompaniment, and harmony. He changes the key from D♭ to the more string-friendly D major, slows the tempo from *Etwas lebhaft* to Andantino, and subtly modifies the principal vocal melody in a variety of ways: the rhythm is altered, grace notes added, the first half is repeated, and the middle section omitted altogether. Initially Schubert uses the singer's charming tune and harmony, not the figuration of the rippling keyboard accompaniment, but at the end of the movement, when the tempo is also quickened, melody and accompaniment are reunited.

That Schubert employs variation technique in the "Trout" Quintet, and in other instrumental compositions, allies them with myriad variation sets on popular melodies drawn from a wide range of sources, usually from operas and songs. Haydn's "Emperor" Quartet, Op. 76, No. 3 (1797) is a notable example of a rather uncommon practice during the Classical era wherein a song (Haydn's own *Gott erhalte*) is folded into a slow variation movement of a chamber composition.[24] Other well-known Schubert works that recast Lieder, typically as theme and variations, include the "Death and the Maiden" Quartet (D810; 1824), the "Wanderer" Fantasy (D760; 1822), the Fantasy for Violin in C (D934; 1827, which uses *Sei mir gegrüsst*), and the "Trockne Blumen" Variations for Flute and Piano (D802; 1824). In addition to the ways Lieder helped Schubert build instrumental compositions, these transformations also reflect cultural practice: Schubert's fame and success in "popular" genres – songs, dances, modest keyboard compositions – helped prepare the public for his "great" instrumental works. We should not underestimate a shrewd career element at play in some of these pieces: an audible connection between Schubert's initial fame as a Lied composer and his mature ambitions as a composer of large-scale instrumental works is the incorporation of his songs into his instrumental music.

What is obvious and familiar in works like the "Trout" Quintet is more obscure elsewhere in Schubert's oeuvre. Perhaps no composer since the Baroque so consistently recycled musical ideas as did Schubert; there is a vast network of interconnections, relationships between and among works so varied and complex that they offer a key to his compositional technique.[25] Reed notes that Schubert's first completed song, *Hagars Klage* (D5; 1811), uses a tonal sequence, familiar in Baroque music for its association with laments, that reappears in other early songs and instrumental works.[26] Although songs most frequently provided the raw material that Schubert recycled and transformed, dances and other types of music also served as sources. Alert Schubertians have spotted an enormous number of such transformations, some more convincing than others, and a few of which Schubert may not have been consciously aware.[27]

These myriad interrelationships reveal a compositional mind forever transforming the vocal and the instrumental to generate new compositions. In fact, the migrations cannot easily be separated, as in some cases the progression is from instrumental to instrumental. The last movement of the late Piano Sonata in A major (D959; 1828) recasts the slow movement of the Sonata in A minor (D537; 1817), written eleven years earlier; both are song-like. Schubert used the melody of the entr'acte in B♭ from his incidental music for *Rosamunde* (D797; 1823) in the second movement of the String Quartet in A minor (D804; 1824), written the following year. He returned to this melody again in the Impromptu in B♭, Op. 142, No. 3 (D935). None is a vocal work, yet these orchestral, chamber, and keyboard compositions all share the same melody, one which ultimately is similar to ideas in two late songs, *Wiegenlied* (D867; 1828?) and *Der Winterabend* (D938; 1828).[28]

For Schubert's purposes, the melodic content of a Lied was not its only transformable feature. Accompaniments also might form the sole or principal foundation for a later instrumental work, as in the "Death and the Maiden" Quartet, or the basic motive of *Der Doppelgänger* (D957/13; 1828) that Schubert uses in the Agnus Dei of his Mass in E♭ (D950; 1828). The mood of the glorious *Im Frühling* (D882; 1826) seems to breathe the same air as the rondo finale of the A major Piano Sonata (D959), even if we might be hard pressed to call this a conscious reference. In the end, it is a rich combination of musical elements that provided models and points of transference from a Schubert Lied to an independent instrumental composition. Sometimes the most general types of song procedures – melody and accompaniment – influenced Schubert, even when he was not apparently drawing on a specific song. At the start of the "Unfinished" Symphony (D759; 1822), after the eight-measure cello and bass introduction, the strings continue with what sounds like a keyboard accompaniment: a rapidly moving right-hand figuration in the first and second violins and pizzicato punctuation

Example 11.2a Schubert, "Unfinished" Symphony (D759), mvt 1, mm. 1–14 (reduction)

beneath in the lower strings. Once this accompaniment is established for four measures, the "singer" enters with the melody (in this case oboe and clarinet). What makes this famous opening even more fascinating are the similarities to one of Schubert's greatest songs, written around the same time: *Der Zwerg* (D771 [1822]; Examples 11.2a and 11.2b).

These interrelationships and infiltrations helped Schubert develop as a composer. His early instrumental works are clearly based on, yet rarely went much further than, Classical models by Haydn, Mozart, and early Beethoven. Yet from the start, Schubert experimented in smaller domestic genres, even if here too he benefited from his predecessors. Whereas Beethoven sought new paths in endless sketching, especially as he matured and his hearing worsened, Schubert broke ground in song and then learned from himself by applying these innovations to instrumental works. Schubert explored his characteristic major/minor shifts and unconventional tonal progressions in song (and sometimes dance), before transferring them to sonatas, quartets, and symphonies. This represents an essential aspect of his artistic growth.

Schubert's lyricism permeates all the genres in which he composed and is, of course, a distinguishing feature in many of his instrumental works. But it would be a mistake to limit the importance of song to Schubert's sovereign lyric sensibility, as accompanimental, harmonic, formal, and other musical parameters also derived from song. The Romantic Lied, in the hands of a master like Schubert, is more than a tune. As the genre deepened, so did its constituent musical and literary elements, which offered new extra-musical possibilities beyond song.

Example 11.2b Schubert, *Der Zwerg* (D771), mm. 1–12

Meaning, messages, and memory: the hermeneutics of instrumental song

We have seen in the discussion both of unsung and of subsumed songs that instrumental works sometimes derive from Lieder from which the words have been removed. What traces do these banished texts leave on composers, performers, and listeners?[29] What meanings, messages, and memories might the original words retain as their associated melodies go on to assume new instrumental guises? Are allusions to song used mainly to make something new, are they a recollection of something known in another form, or do they constitute some kind of commentary?

To explore these issues, I should like briefly to return to the example of Liszt's unsung songs – his Lied transcriptions. Liszt insisted that the words be printed over the music so that the performer would be aware of the specific literary origins.[30] But what of listeners who do not have score or poem at hand? Many of Liszt's Viennese audiences knew Schubert songs "by heart," and therefore a listener could silently supply the words during a performance. We might still call this a "Lied" in which the listener assumes an unusually active role, almost as a silent vocal partner with the pianist. The phenomenon is familiar: when one hears a textless arrangement of a known vocal composition, an inevitable, although often unconscious, mental process is triggered that supplies the missing textual dimension. One silently sings along. Composers frequently exploit this psychological mechanism to great effect, especially in opera. For listeners intimately familiar with a particular Lied, an instrumental arrangement is not really a "song without words," but, more accurately, a "song performed without words."[31]

For mid-nineteenth-century audiences outside Vienna, often unfamiliar with Schubert Lieder, the matter was rather different. Reviews indicate that these listeners were just as captivated by Liszt's virtuoso transcriptions as were listeners elsewhere. Even when audiences did not have recourse to the lyric poem or dramatic ballad, they found that his arrangements succeeded on their musical merits alone. That Lied transcriptions could prove so effective as "absolute music," reveals something about the purely musical qualities of Schubert's songs, over and above his powers to interpret a specific text.

No doubt there also were listeners who, while they did not exactly know the words of a particular Schubert song, were at least aware of its title and general content. For them, a Lied transcription was "program music" in a more traditional sense. A listener might know that a song was a love serenade, just as he or she might know that a symphonic work depicted a lovers' encounter. Similar issues arise with subsumed songs. Because of the association with established literary texts, musical quotations and allusions encountered in instrumental works carry special expressive weight. In some cases a composer may not even be aware of the meaning such passages impart, but more often private associations are directed to a particular person or group. In any event, a listener who knows the words to Schubert's *Der Wanderer, Der Tod und das Mädchen,* and *Die Götter Griechenlands* may find meaning in the later instrumental compositions that recast those songs. What autobiographical implications might there be, for example, in the "Death and the Maiden" Quartet in D minor (D810), which Schubert wrote not long after contracting syphilis, when he believed that his life was changed forever?[32] One cannot help but read a deeper significance into his return in 1824 to Matthias Claudius's poem "Death and the Maiden" (D531; 1817), in which the solemn figure of death confronts an innocent youth with an offer impossible to refuse:[33]

> Maiden:
> Pass me by, ah, pass by!
> Away cruel Death!
> I am still young, away, dear one.
> And do not touch me.
>
> Death:
> Give me your hand, you beautiful, delicate creature.
> I am your friend, and come not to chastise.
> Be of good courage. I am not cruel;
> You shall sleep softly in my arms.

In both the A minor String Quartet (D804; 1824) and the Octet (D803; 1824) Schubert quotes from *Die Götter Griechenlands* (D677; 1819), where the melody originally carried the words "Beautiful world, where are you?"

Although Schubert most often quotes his own songs, he occasionally employed foreign material.[34] A particularly significant, and I have argued secretly meaningful, encoding is found in his Piano Trio in E♭, Op. 100 (D929; 1827). For more than a century it was known that he used a Swedish song in the second movement, but the music was only located in 1978.[35] Schubert took three melodic fragments from *Se solen sjunker* ("See, the sun is setting"), as well as some material from the accompaniment, and used them in the haunting cello and piano duet that opens the movement. Especially prominent is a falling octave motive attached to the words "Farewell! Farewell!" The specific hermeneutic importance of the Swedish song, particularly of the "farewell" motive, which closes the movement as well, emerges when other evidence is considered: the entire Trio is modeled on, and the second movement specifically quotes the funeral march of, Beethoven's *Eroica* Symphony; the public premiere of the Trio was given on 26 March 1828, the first anniversary of Beethoven's death in a performance featuring Beethoven's own musicians; and another work written specifically for that concert, *Auf dem Strom* (D943; 1828), likewise alludes to the funeral march of the *Eroica*.[36] In these and in other late works as well, Schubert paid homage to Beethoven, the composer he revered above all others. He may not have divulged his "secret program" to anyone, but it shows another significant side of the composer that goes well beyond his well-known self-quotations.[37]

Later Romantic composers similarly drew upon their own songs, as well as those of others, to convey messages both public and private. In fact, Mendelssohn also appears to have employed song to mourn Beethoven's death in a chamber composition. His A minor String Quartet, Op. 13 (1827), owes a strong debt to a number of Beethoven's quartets, especially that in A minor, Op. 132. Mendelssohn unifies his quartet by ingenious cyclical use of his song *Frage*, Op. 9, No. 1, which opens with the question "Ist es wahr?" (Is it true?).[38]

Brahms made use of his own Lieder, as well as folksongs, in a wide variety of pieces, such as the Second Piano Concerto, the Piano Sonatas, Opp. 1 and 5, the Violin Sonata in G, Op. 78, and the Piano Trio in B, Op. 8.[39] He reportedly told composer Albert Dietrich that "when composing, he liked to recall folksongs, and that melodies then spontaneously presented themselves." As it happens, some specific songs can be connected with a number of slow movements.[40] Schumann incorporated the French anthem the "Marseillaise" in *Faschingsschwank aus Wien*, Op. 26, *Die beiden Grenadiere*, Op. 49, No. 1, and the *Hermann und Dorothea* Overture, Op. 136; and used the seventeenth-century *Grossvater-Tanz* in *Papillons*, Op. 2, and *Carnaval*, Op. 9.[41] He, and later Brahms, apparently hid references in their works that were intended for Clara Wieck Schumann.[42] In some instances, composers' intentions and public reception become complicated and difficult to unravel. There is a quotation of Beethoven's *An die ferne Geliebte* in Schumann's Piano Fantasy, Op. 17, and more recently Nicholas Marston's suggestion that the same work alludes to Schubert's *An die Musik* (D547).[43] The boundaries between quotation, allusion, and resemblance begin to blur, as do the meanings composers intend and that listeners impute.

Clearly one reason for certain composers' fascination with Lied allusions was the chance to send messages, hide secrets, and encrypt codes, such as those noted in the Beethoven homages by Schubert and Mendelssohn, and the references to and for Clara by Schumann and Brahms. Just as pervasive and illuminating, although less familiar, is the case of Dvořák. My choice here is strategic in that it also addresses the issue of language. Dvořák was fluent in German, and composed Lieder in that language, although he wrote more often in his native Czech. He put songs in both German and Czech to instrumental use, and echoes of his very first songs resonated uncannily throughout his life.

In 1865, Dvořák quickly composed his *Cypřiše* (Cypresses), a cycle of eighteen songs set to Czech poems by Gustav Pfleger-Moravský. They deal with the theme of a disappointed romantic love in turn sublimated into love of country. Although evidently neither published during his lifetime nor performed in public, the cycle clearly haunted Dvořák. Two of the original eighteen songs (Nos. 10 and 14) reappear in his operas *Král a uhlíř* (The

King and the Charcoal Burner; 1871) and *Vanda* (1875), and in his piano cycle *Silhouety* (c. 1870). Twelve were revised and published in two Lied collections – Four Songs, Op. 2 (1881–82) and *Písně milostné*, Op. 83 (Love Songs; 1888). Finally, twelve of them, including some he had not returned to previously, were recast for string quartet and originally given the telling title *Ohlas písní* (Echo of Songs; 1887). Twenty-two years after composing the initial song cycle, Dvořák kept most of the music intact, with only modest expansion in a couple of instances.[44]

Not surprisingly, as Dvořák himself conceded, some inexperience is evident in these, his first surviving attempt at vocal composition, not only in matters of harmony, but also of text declamation. (Some of the songs use German rather than Czech emphasis.[45]) Yet Dvořák kept returning to these songs for decades. One usually thinks of a composer "working through" themes in a strictly musical sense, and in some respects Dvořák does just that with these songs. But far more importantly – and this perhaps best explains his continued interest in such youthful pieces – Dvořák "worked through," in a psychoanalytical sense, pressing psychological themes.[46] Some meanings in a musical work may be purely autobiographical and its messages entirely self-directed.

What was the lingering appeal of songs that Dvořák penned in a matter of days at age twenty-four? Apparently he associated the *Cypresses* with his first love, a young singer named Josefina Čermáková at Prague's Provisional Theater, where Dvořák played viola in the orchestra. Little is known of their romance, but in 1873, at age thirty-two, Dvořák married her younger sister, Anna. He remained close to his sister-in-law for the rest of her life, and may have continued to harbor romantic feelings. The possibility that unrequited love might be channeled into emotions connected to country casts a somewhat different and fascinating light on Dvořák's "nationalism," as well as on his eternal return to the *Cypress* songs.[47]

The fourteenth of the *Cypresses*, *Zde v lese u potoka* (Here in the forest by the brook), is similar in some respects to one of Dvořák's German Lieder *Lasst mich allein* (Leave me alone!), Op. 82, No. 1.[48] Written in 1888, that song was a particular favorite of Josefina's according to Dvořák's biographer Otakar Šourek, and in December 1894 he incorporated its melody in the slow movement of the celebrated Cello Concerto in B minor, Op. 104. After completing the concerto the following February, and returning from the United States in April, Dvořák recast the triumphant coda in the finale to include another reference to the song, this time in a funereal manner. The revision is dated 6 June 1895. Josefina had died ten days earlier.[49]

Like the better-known examples in Schubert, Schumann, Mendelssohn, and Brahms, Dvořák's use of Lied materials in instrumental works served a variety of musical and personal ends. We may not always be sure to whom these messages were addressed. Nor is it clear that composers were in every case aware of what they were doing. The traces of absent words, however, powerfully can convey meaning, send messages, and haunt the memories of composers and listeners alike.

Song transfigured: Mahler's ultimate synthesis

The instrumental implosion and explosion of the nineteenth-century German *Kunstlied* ultimately stretched the genre's bounds far beyond its humble origins, reaching a notable peak with Mahler at the dawn of the new century. The symphony, as Mahler famously remarked to Sibelius in 1907, "must be like the world, it must embrace everything."[50] Not surprisingly, the relationship between songs and symphonies in Mahler touches on many of the musical, aesthetic, and cultural issues raised in this chapter thus far. Mahler composed Lieder for voice and piano, as well as for voice and orchestra, and at some point usually orchestrated the former or reduced the latter, so that most of his mature songs exist in dual versions. Three songs relate to the literal "song without words," as in 1905 Mahler himself made piano rolls (a type of early recording) of *Ging heut' morgens übers Feld*, *Ich ging mit Lust durch einen grünen Wald*, and *Das himmlische Leben*. Brief passages from Mahler's songs are incorporated within his symphonies and entire Lieder deployed as orchestral movements. Once again, the meanings, messages, and memories that emerge are remarkable and poignant. Ultimately, however, the significance of song for Mahler goes far beyond his use of melodies and accompaniments, and extends to form, content, and overall conception of new compositions. From these song "seeds" (*Keime*, Mahler's word) grew the longest and largest symphonies ever written by a major composer.[51] We should resist the cliché of speaking of the song/symphony and rather talk of dialectical and synthetic relationships that enriched both genres, while also creating new ones.

Mahler's first significant completed works were Lieder and the cantata *Das klagende Lied* (1878–80), compositions that paved the way to the First Symphony (c. 1885–88), a work that incorporates his own, as well as imported, song materials. Mahler's next three symphonies are traditionally referred to as the *Wunderhorn* trilogy because they feature melodies or complete songs associated with the folksong anthology *Des Knaben Wunderhorn* (The Youth's Magic Horn), assembled in the early 1800s by Achim von Arnim and Clemens Brentano.[52] Mahler's trilogy of purely instrumental middle symphonies (Nos. 5, 6, and 7) contains neither vocal movements nor references to songs that are as obvious as in the earlier symphonies (although some can be found, especially to the later Rückert Lieder), and yet Lieder continued to be central to their musical conception. The Eighth Symphony stretches the genre of the symphony toward the direction of Mass and oratorio, while the instrumental Ninth once again keeps its explicit connections to song more hidden. (A poignant reference at the end of the work [fourth movement; mm. 163–71] to the fourth of the *Kindertotenlieder* [mm. 62–69] is representative of Mahler's late subtlety.) *Das Lied von der Erde* marks the ultimate synthesis of song and symphony.

Beginning with his First Symphony, Mahler drew upon songs to construct large, often lyrical, works and to take advantage of the associative power of words that could advance his programmatic conceptions. The opening movement of the symphony draws upon extended sections from *Ging heut' morgens übers Feld*, the second Lied in Mahler's orchestral song cycle *Lieder eines fahrenden Gesellen*. Later movements use *Die zwei blauen Augen* from the same cycle, and *Hans und Grethe*, Mahler's first published song. Mahler also employs foreign material, a minor-key version of the folk song *Bruder Martin* (*Frère Jacques*), to open the third movement.

In 1888, the year he completed the initial version of his First Symphony, the full force of *Des Knaben Wunderhorn* struck Mahler. For more than a dozen years thereafter he set nothing but these poems, save one text from Nietzsche's *Also sprach Zarathustra* for the fourth movement of the Third Symphony. The Second and Third Symphonies make both orchestral and vocal use of *Wunderhorn* songs. The third movement of the former instrumentally incorporates most of *Des Antonius von Padua Fischpredigt* and the fourth is a sung setting of *Urlicht*; the latter uses *Ablösung im Sommer* instrumentally in the third movement, and *Es sungen drei Engel* is sung by alto, women's and children's chorus in the fifth movement. Mahler originally planned to end the Third Symphony – already the longest ever composed – with a seventh-movement setting of *Das himmlische Leben*, but opted instead to divert that song to the finale of his next symphony.

Das himmlische Leben provides an especially rich opportunity to scrutinize just how important song could be to Mahler's symphonic conceptions. He first set the poem, which relates a child's innocent idea of heaven, for voice and piano in February 1892 and orchestrated it the following month. Although Mahler chose not to conclude the Third Symphony with it, the decision came late in the process, by which time he already had anticipated its use in earlier movements, most noticeably the fifth (mm. 39–44). He initially planned for the Fourth Symphony to have six movements, three of them songs, leading to *Das himmlische Leben* at the end. While he ultimately decided to eliminate the other songs, and suppressed the programmatic elements he had envisioned, the last *Wunderhorn* song remained and in fact generated the entire symphony.[53] Mahler called attention to this on a number of occasions, as when he informed critic Georg Göhler that his analysis of the work was missing one thing: "Did you overlook the thematic connections that figure so prominently in the work's design? Or did you want to spare the audience some technical explanations? In any case, I ask that that aspect of my work be specially observed. Each of the three movements is connected thematically with the last one in the most intimate and meaningful way."[54]

Das himmlische Leben breeds other elements of the Fourth Symphony as well. Mahler retained the rather modest orchestration of the original 1892 song, which omitted trombones and tuba, even though he regretted not having recourse to lower brass for the climax of the slow movement.[55] The unusual instrumental sound of sleigh bells that opens the first movement is derived from those that separate the strophes in the final movement (mm. 40f., 76f., 115f.). Even the large-scale key scheme of the symphony, the progressive tonality so rare in symphonies before Mahler, comes from the song, where G major ultimately leads to an ethereal E major. From melody and rhythm, to orchestration and tonal planning, *Das himmlische Leben* was the source of the Fourth Symphony, ultimately providing the spiritual vision for the work as well. Mahler decided not to divulge its program, telling his friend and confidant Natalie Bauer-Lechner, "I know the most wonderful names for the movements, but I will not betray them to the rabble of critics and listeners so they can subject them to banal misunderstandings and distortions."[56] Yet the presence of this song as heavenly apotheosis inevitably invites programmatic interpretations. Bauer-Lechner also reports Mahler remarking that "At first glance one does not see all that is hidden in this inconspicuous little thing. Yet one recognizes the worth of such a seed by testing whether it holds within itself a manifold life, just as in the case of *Das himmlische Leben*."[57] The rich image of the "seed" from which an enormous work grows is useful in understanding the importance of this particular song and its hold on Mahler for nearly a decade.

It is no coincidence that Mahler began to compose his middle symphonies around the time when he so adamantly rejected programs. Mahler in the end withheld information about the Fourth Symphony, and withdrew, as best he could, the descriptive programs and some of the titles he had already bestowed on his earlier symphonies. And although Mahler now stopped the patent use of song, either for sung movements or as large-scale instrumentations, he did not turn away from this genre so integral to his compositional method. Instead, song became ever more subtly enmeshed with his symphonies. After a life-threatening medical crisis in February 1901, Mahler's compositional focus changed in two intimately related respects: he turned from the folk poetry of *Des Knaben Wunderhorn* to the art poetry of Friedrich Rückert; and he abandoned programmatic symphonies so closely and obviously connected with his *Wunderhorn* songs for purely instrumental ones ingeniously related to his Rückert Lieder. The Fifth Symphony marks a turning point. The funeral opening movement resembles *Der Tambourg'sell*, the last of the *Wunderhorn* settings, which also dates from the summer of 1901.[58] The famous fourth movement, the Adagietto, is a lyrical song without words scored for harp and strings alone that is reminiscent of the Rückert song *Ich bin der Welt abhanden gekommen*. Not only does the Rückert world increasingly inform the middle-period symphonies, but as Donald Mitchell has remarked, the songs themselves are conceived symphonically, as with the *Kindertotenlieder* cycle.[59] Mahler's ultimate fusion of song and symphony, indeed the creation of a joint genre, is *Das Lied von der Erde*, subtitled "Symphony for Tenor and Alto Voice and Orchestra." The stupendous final movement, *Abschied*, which lasts nearly as long as the preceding five combined, shows how far the composer had come in combining the modest Lied and the monumental symphony, for this movement is neither song nor symphony, but both at once.[60]

Conclusion

As noted at the outset, the migration of vocal melody into instrumental works was not new to the nineteenth century. Yet this chapter has tried to show that the Romantic Lied had an impact far beyond the newly prominent genre of modest-scale works sung in German with piano accompaniment. The infiltration of song into instrumental compositions, the ability of song to convey meanings both private and public, its alliance with new genres (for example, the lyric keyboard piece and the song/symphony), testify to a far greater significance. For some composers from Schubert to Mahler (but for those two especially), song was central to their conception of instrumental music. Why this happened exactly at this time in music history is more difficult to explain, although clearly once such great and substantial pieces, however small, began to issue forth from Schubert and later Romantics, the Lied could not help but leave its mark on the instrumental music of the time.

The literary culture of Romanticism also helped to generate, and then to sustain, these developments. In so far as many of the accomplishments stem from Schubert, it may be possible to speak of a parallel track of Romanticism, one running alongside Beethoven, if less prominently and prestigiously. The authority of Beethoven and of the musical values his works established in that most elevated genre – the symphony – overshadowed what may initially seem lesser accomplishments and more humble models. Yet traces of pure melody, of words and their semantic associations, and perhaps even of the mother's voice, of the human body, and of the urge to sing, powerfully affected song's potential to mark, even to subvert, instrumental genres. Surely these factors account in various ways for the profound influence exerted by Romantic songs. To the extent that Schubert himself learned from his own Lieder, we may recognize a model of considerable consequence for later composers. While Beethoven's towering legacy has obscured the significance of some of this lyric inspiration, the discernible effects on Schumann, Mendelssohn, Brahms, Dvořák, Mahler, and others ultimately are the most eloquent testimony to the impact of Schubert's songs far beyond song.

PART FOUR

Into the twentieth century

12 The Lieder of Mahler and Richard Strauss

JAMES L. ZYCHOWICZ

If one can describe the first half of the nineteenth century as a golden age of Lieder, it is understandable that composers in the century's second half found the inevitable comparisons with that period to be challenging. For once, it was not the long shadow of Beethoven that overawed, given that the feelings of inadequacy he engendered mostly affected instrumental music. As Brahms revealed during the long gestation of his First Symphony, completed in 1876 at the age of forty-three, "never compose a symphony! You have no idea how it feels ... when one always hears such a giant marching along behind."[1] In the area of song, the source of anxiety stemmed from an altogether different source. As Brahms remarked a decade later in 1887,

> The true successor to Beethoven is not Mendelssohn . . . nor is it Schumann, but Schubert. It is unbelievable, the quality of music contained in these songs. No composer understands as he does how to set words properly. With him perfection is always so naturally the outcome that it seems as if nothing could be otherwise . . . In comparison to Schubert everything is botching.[2]

Brahms himself risked such comparison in his own Lieder, none of which could fairly be described as botched. This aside, there can be little doubt that the second half of the nineteenth century was so influenced by the past that it raises the question of the impact that increasing historicism had on creativity. Such a perspective comes to bear in a chapter devoted to the Lieder of Gustav Mahler (1860–1911) and Richard Strauss (1864–1949), since both composers seem to sum up their historical positions while simultaneously moving beyond them. The young Mahler, in turning to the Lied in the 1880s through the agency of his beloved *Des Knaben Wunderhorn* (The Youth's Magic Horn), looks beyond Schubert to some earlier idea of German folk song, just as the elderly Strauss, in his *Vier letzte Lieder*, with the rubble of World War II around him, invokes a sound world impossible to describe adequately: tempered by the times he had survived, steeped in the traditions of the Romanticism that shaped him, but not truly part of either. One wonders whether either composer was aware of August Reißmann's comment in 1861 that the Lied may have already run its course by then, a remark made within three years of Strauss's birth and one year after Mahler's.[3] By the time they began composing, there would have been not only just Schubert – and Schumann – but also Brahms. In composing Lieder Mahler and Strauss no doubt experienced the kind of "Angst" described by the literary critic Harold Bloom when he writes that the "anxiety of influence" can bring with it the fear of being "flooded" by the achievement of an exemplary precursor.[4] In taking up the genre of Schubert, Schumann, and Brahms, Mahler and Strauss certainly risked the inevitable comparison that would sometimes favor those earlier composers of Lieder.

In Mahler's case, the Lied and symphony constitute the two genres to which he contributed the most, and he was continually combining the two. As is generally understood, song indeed provided Mahler with springboards for many of his symphonies. For Strauss, the situation is different, since he did not allow Lieder to filter into his symphonic poems and operas. On the other hand, Mahler consciously used orchestral Lieder as concert material to counter the tendency in his day to program arias and other opera excerpts in symphony concerts. Just as he restored cuts in the operas he conducted so as to preserve their integrity, he had no desire to present operatic music out of context. By composing Lieder for voice and orchestra, Mahler created a repertory that he could use as a conductor. Although not the first to move what previously had been an intimate mode of domestic music into the concert hall – as discussed in chapter 8, Liszt began doing precisely this in the 1850s – Mahler in his orchestral songs, especially his orchestral song cycles, formed an essentially new Lied sub-genre. As such, the orchestral songs marked the first time the genre had expanded from within since the song cycle for voice and piano earlier in the century. At the same time, Mahler composed Lieder with piano for both the traditional venues of the home and recital hall while investing the orchestral song with the comparatively broader gestures of symphonic music. Strauss moved in similar directions, since he had performed Lieder with his wife, Pauline (De Ahna), a talented soprano during her early years, and also included his orchestral songs in the symphony concerts that he conducted. Notwithstanding their interest in the orchestral Lied, neither composer can claim to have had a monopoly on it.

Whereas piano Lieder had been a staple of symphony concerts for many years, in the period 1870–80 the practice witnessed a decline. Yet songs in orchestral settings had secured a place in the ever-burgeoning institution of the public concert, and it was not long before orchestral songs found their own place in the repertory. So successful were Felix Mottl's scorings of Wagner's *Wesendonck Lieder* that listeners soon forgot Wagner had orchestrated only one of the five (*Träume*).[5] Following in Mottl's path, the composer-conductor Felix Weingartner brought out what appear to be the first true orchestral songs in 1887, his *Wallfahrt nach Kevlaar*, Op. 12, with Pfitzner following in 1891 with his *Herr Oluf*, Op. 12. Whatever the reasons for turning to orchestral songs, by the final two decades of the nineteenth century such music allowed composers to reach a larger audience than had been the case with Lieder for voice and piano, a reality with potential economic repercussions both for composers and also for the Lied as a reflection of German cultural values. While some reactionary critics might have bemoaned the practice, a new type of Lied had come into its own.[6]

Mahler

Mahler's Lieder comprise approximately fifty individual songs in several major sets, including the early cycle *Lieder eines fahrenden Gesellen* (Songs of a Wayfarer), the settings from *Des Knaben Wunderhorn*, settings of Rückert poetry, and his final major vocal work, *Das Lied von der Erde* (The Song of the Earth). For a full listing, including references to textual sources, Lieder used in symphonies, and quotations of Lieder in symphonic works, see Table 12.1, pp. 248–51 below.

Mahler's output is relatively small when compared to other Lied composers, but this should not be taken to mean that his songs are insignificant. An integral part of his total creative output worthy of consideration in their own right, his Lieder are essential to comprehending his symphonies. In the words of his younger contemporary, the composer and conductor Georg Göhler (1874–1954):

> [just] as Beethoven's sonatas and quartets prepare us for his symphonies, so do Mahler's songs for his. Here are the seeds, the new, fresh shoots from which grow the tree-giants of the symphonies, of whose obscure shadows and mighty roaring in the storm so many music lovers still are afraid today. It is through his songs that even the least sophisticated friend of the arts can come to know and love Mahler.[7]

While later commentators might resist the judgment implicit in Göhler's statement, it is difficult to deny the rich harvest that the songs made possible.

Guided to the degree that he was by literature, Mahler allowed the style of the poetry he set to inform his Lieder. In the early works, while under the spell of Achim von Arnim and Clemens Brentano's famous anthology of German folk poetry *Des Knaben Wunderhorn*, Mahler himself revealed that the attraction he felt for the collection's poems lay in the fact that "rather than art, they are about nature and life (the source of all poetry)."[8] While folk-like elements are indisputable, the *Volkston* is but a part of the total musical landscape. To insist otherwise is misleading, since the musical content invariably is more complex than the many folk-inspired Lieder of the period by other composers. Whereas an essential feature of Mahler's early songs is his use of an expansive vocal tessitura, which includes arpeggiated

Table 12.1 *The Lieder of Gustav Mahler*

Title	Text source	Composition date(s)	Accompaniment		Lieder used in symphonies	Quotations of Lieder	Comments
			Piano	Orchestra			
Lieder (1880)							
1. Im Lenz	Mahler	1880	piano				Three Lieder exist from a projected set of five
2. Winterlied	Mahler	1880	piano				
3. Maitanz im Grünen	Mahler	1880	piano				
Lieder und Gesänge, vol. I (1880–87)							
1. Frühlingsmorgen	Leander	1880–87	piano				
2. Erinnerung	Leander	1880–87	piano				Reworking of Maitanz im Grünen
3. Hans und Grethe	Mahler	1880–87	piano				
4. Serenade aus *Don Juan*	Tirso de Molina	1880–87	piano				
5. Phantasie aus *Don Juan*	Tirso de Molina	1880–87	piano				
Lieder und Gesänge, vol. II (1887–90)							
1. Um schlimme Kinder artig zu machen	*Des Knaben Wunderhorn*	1887–90	piano				
2. Ich ging mit Lust durch einen grünen Wald	*Des Knaben Wunderhorn*	1887–90	piano				
3. Aus! Aus!	*Des Knaben Wunderhorn*	1887–90	piano				
4. Starke Einbildungskraft	*Des Knaben Wunderhorn*	1887–90	piano				
Lieder und Gesänge, vol. III (1887–90)							
1. Zu Strassburg auf der Schanz	*Des Knaben Wunderhorn*	1887–90	piano				
2. Ablösung im Sommer	*Des Knaben Wunderhorn*	1887–90	piano			Symphony no. 3 movement 3	Fragment of an orchestration by Mahler exists

3. Scheiden und Meiden	Des Knaben Wunderhorn	1887–90	piano		Mahler adapted the Wunderhorn text
4. Nicht wiedersehen!	Des Knaben Wunderhorn	1887–90	piano		
5. Selbstgefühl	Des Knaben Wunderhorn	1887–90	piano		
Lieder eines fahrenden Gesellen (1883–85; later revised)					
1. Wenn mein Schatz Hochzeit macht	Des Knaben Wunderhorn	(1883–85; later revised)	piano	orchestra	Symphony no. 1, first movement
2. Ging heut' morgens übers Feld	Mahler	(1883–85; later revised)	piano	orchestra	
3. Ich hab' ein glühend Messer	Mahler	(1883–85; later revised)	piano	orchestra	
4. Die zwei blauen Augen	Mahler	(1883–85; later revised)	piano	orchestra	Symphony no. 1, fourth movement (Finale)
Des Knaben Wunderhorn (Brentano and Arnim)					Texts from Des Knaben Wunderhorn
1. Der Schildwache Nachtlied	Des Knaben Wunderhorn	1892	piano	orchestra	
2. Verlor'ne Müh	Des Knaben Wunderhorn	1892	piano	orchestra	
3. Trost im Unglück	Des Knaben Wunderhorn	1892	piano	orchestra	
4. Wer hat dies Liedlein erdacht?	Des Knaben Wunderhorn	1892	piano	orchestra	
5. Das irdische Leben	Des Knaben Wunderhorn	1893	piano	orchestra	Symphony no. 10, "Purgatorio" (sketches)
6. Des Antonius von Padua Fischpredigt	Des Knaben Wunderhorn	1893	piano	orchestra	Symphony no. 2, third movement

(cont.)

Table 12.1 (*cont.*)

Title	Text source	Composition date(s)	Accompaniment		Lieder used in symphonies	Quotations of Lieder	Comments
			Piano	Orchestra			
7. Rheinlegendchen	*Des Knaben Wunderhorn*	1893	piano	orchestra			
8. Lied des Verfolgten im Turm	*Des Knaben Wunderhorn*	1898	piano	orchestra			
9. Wo die schönen Trompeten blasen	*Des Knaben Wunderhorn*	1898	piano	orchestra			
10. Lob des hohen Verstandes	*Des Knaben Wunderhorn*	1896	piano	orchestra			
11. Es sungen drei Engel	*Des Knaben Wunderhorn*	1895 (draft)	piano	orchestra	Symphony no. 3, fifth movement		
12. Urlicht	*Des Knaben Wunderhorn*	1895	piano	orchestra	Symphony no. 2, fourth movement		
Das himmlische Leben	*Des Knaben Wunderhorn*	1892	piano	orchestra	Symphony no. 4, fourth movement		
Kindertotenlieder							
1. Nun will die Sonn' so hell aufgeh'n	Rückert	1901–04	piano	orchestra			
2. Nun seh' ich wohl, warum so dunkle Flammen	Rückert	1901	piano	orchestra			
3. Wenn dein Mütterlein	Rückert	1901	piano	orchestra			
4. Oft denk' ich, sie sind nur ausgegangen	Rückert	1901	piano	orchestra			
5. In diesem Wetter, in diesem Braus	Rückert	1901	piano	orchestra			

7 Letzte Lieder					
1. Revelge	*Des Knaben Wunderhorn*	1901	piano	orchestra	
2. Der Tamboursg'sell	*Des Knaben Wunderhorn*	1901	piano	orchestra	
3. Blicke mir nicht in die Lieder	Rückert	1901	piano	orchestra	
4. Ich atmet' einen linden Duft	Rückert	1901	piano	orchestra	
5. Ich bin der Welt abhanden gekommen	Rückert	1901	piano	orchestra	"Rückert-Lieder" (nos. 3–7)
6. Um Mitternacht	Rückert	1901	piano	orchestra	
7. Liebst du um Schönheit	Rückert	1902	piano	orchestra	
Das Lied von der Erde					
1. Das Trinklied vom Jammer der Erde	Bethge	1907–09	piano	orchestra	Bethge's *Chinesische Flöte*
2. Der Einsame im Herbst	Bethge	1907–09	piano	orchestra	
3. Von der Jugend	Bethge	1907–09	piano	orchestra	
4. Von der Schönheit	Bethge	1907–09	piano	orchestra	
5. Der Trunkene im Frühling	Bethge	1907–09	piano	orchestra	
6. Der Abschied	Bethge	1907–09	piano	orchestra	

figures and other devices related to the folk idiom, in the later Rückert songs a narrower range is in keeping with the different ethos. For the most part, the vocal writing inclines toward the syllabic, although melismas are used to excellent effect in pieces such as *Wer hat dies Liedlein erdacht?!*[9] (Who invented this little song?!) and *Des Antonius Fischpredigt* (of St. Anthony [of Padua's] Sermon to the Fish). Mahler's harmonic vocabulary likewise resists hard and fast classification. While one at first would be tempted to describe his harmonies as conventional, particularly when compared to younger composers at work during his day (among them Arnold Schoenberg), a song such as *Das irdische Leben* (Earthly life) affords a striking case study while at the same time revealing itself as the outstanding work among the mature *Wunderhorn* songs. The Lied's intensity is matched in every way by its harmonic ambiguity. While some have interpreted the song as being in B♭ minor, just as others have suggested B♭ Phrygian, the key signature of six flats and the frequent D♮s imply E♭ minor.[10] Although Mahler frequently seems to be evoking an earlier Romantic age, a great many of his Lieder challenge tradition, given the way they freely move between major and minor modes while making use of other modal inflections. In *Die zwei blauen Augen* (The Two Blue Eyes), the final song of *Lieder eines fahrenden Gesellen,* Mahler avoids conventional harmonic resolution in favor of a second-inversion tonic chord. *Das himmlische Leben* (Heavenly life) does not end in the same key in which it begins; the modulation from G major to E major foreshadows Mahler's approach to tonality in the Fourth Symphony (1900), an altogether unexpected turn of events in that the 1892 song provides the kernel from which not only the finale but the entire work grows. (As has frequently been noted, Beethoven's Ninth Symphony inspired Mahler to end his Fourth Symphony with a movement similarly informed by the vocal impulse, here no longer a vocal quartet and chorus but rather a soprano solo. Notwithstanding each symphony's differing performing forces, both finales are indebted to the Lied. In Beethoven's case, the so-called *Freude* tune harks back to the composer's Lied *Gegenliebe,* WoO 118, composed in 1794 or 1795, just as material from the finale of Mahler's Fourth derives from an earlier song.[11])

Despite Mahler's sometimes adventurous harmonic usage, he never deflects attention from a Lied's melodic line. At times he uses relatively simple larger structures supported by carefully constructed details including variation episodes and interludes in which various motifs are developed. This compositional strategy is part of his symphonic style, but it is also integrated into some of his Lieder. The resulting fusion is a distinctive feature of Mahler songs, one that reveals the ostensibly simple as infinitely more involved. Throughout Mahler's music, the mundane is shown to be anything but commonplace, as the network of references to dance rhythms, military motives, and chorale-like passages attest. Although Mahler chose to call attention to this point in his often-cited 1907 comment that "the symphony must be like the world" by embracing "everything,"[12] it would appear that the reality lying behind it influenced not only his orchestral music but also his Lieder. A text that on first inspection typifies childlike innocence, such as the *Wunderhorn* setting "Um schlimme Kinder artig zu machen" (How to Make Naughty Children Good), has profound implications within the adult world. Similarly, the *Kindertotenlieder* involve texts that function on multiple levels, with the implied occasion of the deaths of children being but one layer within multifaceted meanings, both textual and musical.

Mahler's texts

In his earliest songs, Mahler used texts that he himself wrote or else adapted from the collection *Des Knaben Wunderhorn*.[13] A milepost of literary Romanticism, the *Wunderhorn* anthology attracted the attention of many a nineteenth- and indeed twentieth-century composer, including, among the first rank, Schumann and Brahms, and, among the lesser known, Armin Knab and Theodor Streicher. That this was so is small wonder given the volume's wide range of subjects, including religious reflections, popular ballads, love songs, as well as children's verse. Subtitled *Alte deutsche Lieder* (Old German Songs), the work's more than 700 lyrics were published in three volumes between 1806 and 1808. Encountering the collection in the mid-1880s, Mahler undertook a series of settings for voice and piano and continued to use it well into the next decade. In many of these, however, Mahler treated the poetry less strictly than other composers who used the same texts. As with several composers before and after him, Mahler's artful, sometimes extensive alterations of the poems he set to music provide evidence of a deep-seated literary disposition. While he sometimes changed a few words or lines, in other settings he went so far as to conflate texts from entirely different poems. Moreover, the influence of *Des Knaben Wunderhorn* extends to the Second, Third, and Fourth symphonies, and the continuing influence of the anthology is apparent later in his career, when he considered using children's poetry in his Eighth Symphony.

Around 1901, Mahler turned to the poetry of Friedrich Rückert, composing ten songs: a cycle of five Lieder on the poet's 1872 *Kindertotenlieder* and five other settings known as the *Rückert-Lieder*. In the former, Mahler's generalized evocation on the death of children should not be confused with specifically tragic events in his own life. Here and in *Das Lied von der Erde* (1908), a partial setting of Hans Bethge's German adaptations of Chinese poetry, *Die chinesische Flöte* (1907), the pervading world-weariness is unmistakable. Bethge's orientalism is not a direct translation from Chinese, but an interpretation of poetry from the East, including verse by Li-Tai Po, Wang-Wei, and others.[14] Moreover, in composing this last work Mahler adapted Bethge's verses, just as he had altered poetry from *Des Knaben Wunderhorn*.[15] As it had been in his earlier settings, the urge to revise texts is essential to understanding Mahler's creative process. At the same time, the poetry he chose for this cycle is consistent with his evolving exploration of other, existential concerns. The overtly oriental atmosphere is not far removed from some of Rückert's poetry, which, in turn, is related to the spiritual sentiments he began to explore in his Second and Fourth Symphonies. Attempting to express the grand, cosmic themes of his symphonies, Mahler at first relied on explicit programs but later forswore such accompanying texts. In a work like the Fourth Symphony, he let the sung text stand on its own, in lieu of any other expressed interpretation. Such is the case with *Das Lied von der Erde*, where the texts exist without additional explanation.

To turn to other poets set by Mahler, it is seen that he evinced a decidedly German disposition. In his Second Symphony, the first verse of Klopstock's "Auferstehung" (Resurrection) provides the basis of the concluding fifth movement (after which Mahler continues with words of his own invention). In the fourth movement of the Third Symphony, he draws on the third part of Nietzsche's *Also sprach Zarathustra* (the section "Das andere Tanzlied"), one the composer once called "Was mir die Nacht erzählt" (What the night tells me). Years later in the first part of the Eighth Symphony, he set the Latin hymn "Veni creator spiritus," written probably by the ninth-century theologian Hrabanus Maurus. While such settings are obviously not Lieder, they nonetheless show a composer with a strong literary bent.

Mahler's early Lieder and *Lieder eines fahrenden Gesellen*

Mahler's interest in song dates from his earliest compositions, among them the youthful fragments that survive for two Heine settings ("Es fiel ein Reif" and "Im wunderschönen Monat Mai") and plans for a Lieder cycle dedicated to Josephine Poisl, a young woman with whom the nineteen-year-old composer fell in love. Of the five settings planned for this cycle, Mahler composed three in 1880, *Im Lenz*, *Winterlied*, and *Maitanz am Grünen*. The last of these is an early version of the song *Hans und Grethe*, part of Mahler's published *Lieder und Gesänge*. Relatively short pieces, these three songs anticipate the folk-like world Mahler would explore later. Also worth noting is the fact that music from the introduction to *Hans und Grethe* was subsequently incorporated into the First Symphony at the opening of the Scherzo.

Dating from Mahler's earliest days as a composer, the cycle *Lieder eines fahrenden Gesellen* is a significant accomplishment for a composer in his twenties. Originally intended to include six Lieder, the finished four songs in the completed work were composed between 1883 and 1885.[16] The texts treat a topic of enduring appeal within the history of song: a young man's expressions of love in the first two and the loss of that love in the final two. While the protagonist at first is heartbroken when his beloved marries someone else, he eventually finds solace in the memory of his love, a state of affairs that, like so much in Mahler, reflects aspects of his own life. On another level, the implicit narrative shows another influence, one stretching back more than half a century to Schubert and his *Winterreise*.[17] Having composed the cycle first for voice with piano, Mahler later created a version for voice and orchestra. Just as it is difficult to establish a precise date for the cycle's composition, so too is it difficult to determine when Mahler orchestrated the songs. The two versions differ in detail and the later orchestration in part reflects Mahler's rethinking of certain passages without substantially altering the music's content.

More importantly, Mahler used thematic material from this cycle in the First Symphony (1888), particularly in the first movement and funeral march. (In the early five-movement version of the Symphony, the funeral march is the fourth movement, whereas in the final four-movement version it is the third.) Mahler did not simply quote a theme or a motive, as other composers might have done, but rather used the substance of *Ging heut' morgens übers Feld* (I walked across the field this morning) in the first movement. Reworking his own ideas in this manner, Mahler established a new context for his music when he transformed his vocal music into the symphonic idiom and brought along with it the additional layers of meaning that stem from the original poetical texts. Mahler left it to the listener to make the connections between symphony and song.

Wunderhorn Lieder

The many and varied folk elements pervading Arnim and Brentano's *Des Knaben Wunderhorn* would suggest that Mahler responded to the anthology exclusively in terms of the self-consciously simplistic. In the first volume of Mahler's *Lieder und Gesänge*, it is possible to find such songs as the *Serenade aus Don Juan* and *Phantasie aus Don Juan* (both settings of Tirso de Molina), with their relative brevity and direct appeal, as an indication of the composer's dedication to a revitalized *Volkstümlichkeit*. This would appear to be the case, especially if one places such songs against the maelstrom of Wagnerian chromaticism then resounding throughout the German-speaking lands; compared to the progressiveness of *Tristan*, many a Mahler song composed in the 1880s strikes an undeniably retrogressive note. In the early songs the accompaniment is largely homophonic, with the voice doubled most of the time, but this begins to change with the orchestral *Wunderhorn* settings, where the doubling of the vocal line gives way to a quasi-heterophonic relationship between voice and orchestra. A song such as *Wo die schönen Trompeten blasen* (Where the beautiful trumpets blow, *Lieder aus "Des Knaben Wunderhorn"*), represents an apparent advance given Mahler's use of so many varied instrumental timbres. Elsewhere, the voice and the accompaniment – unsatisfactory as this last term is for many a Lied – exhibit a degree of equality absent from the traditional folk aesthetic.

Many of the works included in the *Lieder aus "Des Knaben Wunderhorn"* comprise some of Mahler's more familiar songs. Of these, the 5 *Humoresken* for voice and piano – *Der Schildwache Nachtlied, Verlor'ne Müh', Trost im Unglück, Das himmlische Leben,* and *Wer hat dies Liedlein erdacht?!* – written during January–February 1892, yield an intriguing group. Just as Mahler had distinguished between *Lieder* and *Gesänge*, one cannot help but wonder if the designation *Humoreske* has significance. Although no hard and fast rules apply, it seems that the word *Lied*, at least to composers in the latter part of the nineteenth century, implied simplicity and strophic designs while *Gesang* connoted through-composed forms and comparatively greater in-dependence on the part of the instrumental component. Similarly, the fact that Mahler himself referred to Loewe's famous *Humoresken*[18] suggests that he understood the term as possessing more than mere generic meaning.[19] Such distinctions notwithstanding, Mahler ultimately abandoned them, a move that perhaps relates to the fact that he ultimately turned away from programmatic associations in his symphonies. In both his orchestral music and Lieder, he relinquished basic taxonomy in an effort to let the music speak for itself.

Such is the case with the final *Wunderhorn* settings, *Revelge* (Reveille) and *Der Tamboursg'sell* (The drummer boy). In keeping with their large-scale designs both songs have more in common with the dramatic *scena* than with traditional Lieder. Moreover, the way in which Mahler uses the orchestra is closely related to the instrumental style of the Fifth Symphony he was then composing. Both settings are fully realized orchestral Lieder, not just songs rewritten for voice and piano. Mahler esteemed *Revelge*, announcing on the day he finished it that it was the most successful and beautiful of his *Wunderhorn Lieder*, even "the most important of all his Lieder." Contrary to the normal procedure of a song serving as the basis of a purely orchestral work, the composer likewise drew attention to the fact that the first movement of the Third Symphony had been just a "study in rhythm" for *Revelge*.[20]

Rückert settings

Although few nowadays would include Friedrich Rückert in the upper eche-lon of German poets, Mahler's attraction to him was productive. By contrast with the *Wunderhorn Lieder*, which occupied him from the early 1880s until 1901, the fascination with Rückert was a comparatively more concentrated and short-lived affair, lasting from 1901 until 1904. According to Anton Webern, Mahler once stated that "after *Des Knaben Wunderhorn* I could not compose anything but Rückert – this is lyric poetry from the source, all else is lyric poetry of a derivative sort."[21] Mahler took on a new direction in his settings of Rückert. As Donald Mitchell states, "gone are the fanfares, the military signals, the dance and march rhythms and the quasi-folk style of the *Wunderhorn* songs. Gone are those songs' satirical excursions, with their accompanying instrumental pungencies and sarcasms."[22] The Rückert set-ting *Ich atmet' einen linden Duft* (I breathed a sweet scent), with its delicate, otherworldly imagery anticipating the ethereal atmosphere suffusing much of *Das Lied von der Erde*, provides a revealing example. In commenting on this song Theodor W. Adorno observed the way in which melody passes ef-fortlessly between voice and orchestra and, in so doing, "lifts Mahler's Lieder composition as a whole far above those of his time." Voice and orchestra "blend into one another perfectly, so that emotional intensity finds an outlet in extreme tenderness."[23] Such profound lyricism also lies at the heart of *Ich bin der Welt abhanden gekommen* (I have become lost to the world), another Rückert setting. The use of harp triplet arpeggios, and the overall sense of timelessness suggested by the sixth added to the tonic chord as well as the fact that each phrase begins on the weak part of the measure, are retained in the reworking of this song in the Adagietto of the Fifth Symphony.

The second phase of Mahler's Rückert settings, the *Kindertotenlieder*, coincided with his efforts after the completion of the Fourth Symphony and through work on the Sixth, that is, from 1901 until 1904. (The specific dating of the individual songs has never been established conclusively.)[24] As a true cycle, the coherence of the *Kindertotenlieder* is revealed on one level by musical means, specifically through key choices; unlike earlier Mahler cycles, this one begins and ends in the same key, D (minor and major). In an effort to ensure the cycle's integrity Mahler included the following injunction on the first page of the version with piano that "these five songs form a complete and indivisible whole, and for this reason their continuity must be preserved (by preventing interruption, such as for example applause at the end of each song)." Mahler's selections of the poet's texts likewise contribute to the work's unity. This especially is to be seen in the cycle's many references to light. Established in the first, the metaphor of the rising sun is echoed in the second song's dark flames, the third's candlelight that is "too soon extinguished," and the fourth's sunshine from on high, all of which attains eventual resolution when it is revealed that the children in question now are "sheltered by God's hands," as if they were in their mother's house.

To turn to other aspects of musical style at this time in Mahler's career, it will be seen that his harmonic usage is endlessly supple and evocative, one in which virtually any passage could illustrate his assured ability to match music with text.[25] The second of the *Kindertotenlieder, Nun seh' ich wohl, warum so dunkle Flammen* (Now I well see why with such dark flames), is an unusually concentrated example. At the same time, it provides the rare example of the composer in Wagnerian mode – "Tristan-style *Sehnsucht*" as La Grange phrases it.[26] Though clear tonal centers emerge here and there, the overall harmonic character is determined by chains of chromatic appoggiaturas, both prepared and unprepared, and through the absence of the ubiquitous Mahlerian pedal point.[27]

That any of the *Kindertotenlieder* fit the technical and musico-poetic confines of a small vocal idiom only with effort suggests that with this cycle Mahler reached the limits of the Lied as it had been practiced for almost a century. The depth of psychological perception, projected through an intimate union of poetry and music; the immediacy of communication between poet, composer, and listener; the natural hierarchy of the relationship between voice and accompaniment – these were some of the ways in which intimacy presided over the early and high Romantic German art song. Predictably enough, when the Lied began to move to the concert hall, the internal dynamics of an art form seemed to many to be disintegrating. Even though composers, including many to be considered in the following chapter (Reger, Pfitzner, Schoenberg, Webern, and Eisler), continued to write Lieder for voice and piano, the genre was changing. Exchanging the piano for orchestra and involving performance in increasingly larger halls, such modifications brought with them new challenges. On the surface, it could be argued that Mahler had little concern for a genre that had had its glory days in the salon and was in need of transformation, especially since he took such a leading role in the development of the orchestral Lied. In truth, Mahler's dedication to unencumbered lyricism and the equality he sought between voice and orchestra contradict the notion that he was insensitive to the pressures then closing in on the Lied. Yet it seems inevitable that the orchestral song should have burst its seams, especially where latent symphonic features were consolidated into large-scale cyclic structures, as occurred with the orchestral *Kindertotenlieder*, and, later, in *Das Lied von der Erde*.

Das Lied von der Erde

Mahler seems destined to have been the composer of *Das Lied von der Erde*, since in this work he achieved the ultimate fusion of song and symphony, a fusion that had occupied him since the days of his First Symphony and the orchestral version of *Lieder eines fahrenden Gesellen*.[28] In fashioning such a synthesis he drew on the strengths of both genres to compose a symphonic work with vocal elements throughout. For a composer who had often relied on programmatic ideas to enrich his symphonies, the use of a sung text within the context of a song-symphony may be regarded as a fitting culmination. The result surprised even the composer. As he wrote to Bruno Walter in September 1908, when the work was completed although not as yet named, "I myself do not know how to express what the whole thing might be called. A beautiful time was granted me, and I believe it is the most personal thing I have yet created."[29]

Das Lied von der Erde comprises six songs alternating between two vocal soloists.[30] The six are: (1) *Das Trinklied vom Jammer der Erde* (Drinking song of the earth's sorrows); (2) *Der Einsame im Herbst* (The lonely one in autumn); (3) *Von der Jugend* (Of youth); (4) *Von der Schönheit* (Of beauty); (5) *Der Trunkene im Frühling* (The drunkard in spring); and (6) *Der Abschied* (The farewell). The first five Lieder taken together last almost the same amount of time as the final sixth song, just one of the many characteristics that reveal the work's exceptional nature. (In most song cycles, even orchestral ones, the durations of individual movements tend to be more evenly proportioned.) This disparity draws attention to the work's large-scale partition into two sections, one harking back to the division into parts in the composer's First, Third, and Fifth Symphonies. The first and fifth songs are in A minor and A major respectively, a construction paralleled in the final song's movement from C minor to C major. Drawing on all that had come before, Mahler joins these two tonal centers in the highly charged sonority with which the last song concludes – appropriately enough on the words "ewig, ewig" (forever, forever).[31] Textual considerations also support the large two-part structure; the first five movements all pertain to earthly life, while the last, with its images of the sun setting behind the mountain, the moon floating upwards, and the distant horizon's gleaming blue, looks beyond the earth while at the same time singing its praises.

When one compares *Das Lied von der Erde* to the monumental Eighth Symphony (1906–08) that precedes it, a greater study in contrast is difficult to imagine. One work storms the heavens with sheer sound, while in the other the justly renowned ending seems to be the musical equivalent of a willing slipping away into nothingness – as Benjamin Britten has written, the "final chord is printed on the atmosphere."[32] In a certain sense, Mahler drew on the disparities between the Eighth Symphony and *Das Lied von der Erde* and made them the ultimate subject of the latter work, albeit in compressed form. Mahler relies on a large orchestra, but uses the full forces of the ensemble only sparingly. For the most part, especially in the final song, chamber-like textures predominate. Elsewhere, Mahler juxtaposed other dualities: youth with death, night with day, autumn with spring – binary oppositions inform the work on any number of levels. The first and second, and fifth and sixth movements anchor the work in their paired reflections on the subject of death. Other ways in which opposites are played out are to be experienced in the music assigned the vocalists: the drunken excesses of the fifth movement are countered by Apollonian acquiescence in the concluding sixth. However such contrasts are articulated, they all add up to the same thing: a study of the human condition, one that Mahler had been probing and pondering for most of his life.

In combining that which had previously been thought impossible to unite – the intimate Lied and the more public symphony – Mahler's *Das Lied von der Erde* may be seen as the fulfillment of a lifetime ambition, one he had anticipated in many of his earlier works. Song had been a critical element in his first four symphonies, and the composer himself referred to those works as a tetralogy. Thus the *Wunderhorn* Lieder turn up in his symphonies, including *Urlicht* (Primeval light) in the second movement of the Second; *Es sungen drei Engel* (Three angels were singing) in the fifth movement of the Third; and *Das himmlische Leben* in the finale of the Fourth. In each of these works the Lied as a generating force is incorporated into the larger structural design. In the Second Symphony, *Urlicht* is a relatively short movement that precedes the Finale with soloists and chorus, and it serves as the introduction to the large-scale choral tableau of the final movement. In the Third Symphony, the voice has a different role. After the fourth movement, with its Nietzsche setting, Mahler proceeds to another vocal movement standing in sharp contrast to it. Whereas the fourth movement is concerned with "Was mir die Nacht erzählt" (What the night tells me), the fifth movement, with its text "Was mir die Engel erzählen" (What the angels tell me), sparks a musical response given over to the portrayal of a higher realm of existence. Inspired by the final movement's eventually withdrawn programmatic title, "Was mir die Liebe erzählt" (What love tells me), he abandons the voice, presumably because divine love cannot be circumscribed by mundane words.

In the Fourth Symphony Mahler appears to have had second thoughts about the inexpressible. If one interprets the symphony as a reflection on heavenly life, then it can be said that he provides a clue about the fourth movement's function, a view confirmed by the composer himself when he told Bauer-Lechner that the words of the finale are the key to the entire work.

Song was the seed from which the entire Symphony grew, and thematic ideas from *Das himmlische Leben* occur throughout the first three movements. Prepared for in this way, the song's function in the finale – one indicated by Mahler's description of the movement as the Symphony's "tapering apex"[33] – is one of coalescence. Tellingly, even the overtly instrumental Fifth Symphony is not without references to Lieder, especially in the reworking of *Ich bin der Welt abhanden gekommen* in the celebrated Adagietto. Yet in the middle-period symphonies, Mahler's use of song changed. The extensive quotation of Lieder as found in the *Wunderhorn* symphonies no longer is a part of the Fifth Symphony, nor is it in the Sixth and Seventh. Instead of the lengthy Lied quotations that occur in the earlier works, Mahler uses comparatively shorter motives and ideas drawn from the *Rückert Lieder* in these three middle symphonies. Given that he absorbed the existing Lied traditions of Schubert, Schumann, and Brahms while simultaneously pointing toward new ones, Mahler's importance to German song is impossible to deny.

Strauss

Strauss composed over 200 Lieder for voice and piano and approximately forty for voice and orchestra, and, of the latter, around twenty-five are reworkings of songs originally for voice and piano.[34] (For a summary, see Table 12.2, pp. 262–65.) Strauss wrote significantly more songs than did Mahler, although comparing their Lieder from the standpoint of quantity alone reveals little. For a more meaningful understanding of song in their respective careers, one needs to ask why each composer turned to the medium. Unlike Mahler, Strauss did not make explicit connections with compositions in other genres. (A rare exception occurs in 1898 when the Lieder *Befreit* [Released], composed that year, and *Traum durch die Dämmerung* [The Dream in Twilight], composed in 1895, are quoted in the tone poem *Ein Heldenleben*.) Yet Strauss did not compose songs in a vacuum, since the Lied was precisely the medium that possessed the capacity to capture his complex personality over his long career. To suggest that Lieder did not influence Strauss's instrumental compositions is also disputable. In a recent study, Suzanne Marie Lodato argues that the Lied, and Strauss's work with German naturalistic poetry and prose from the late nineteenth century, brought about changes in his compositional style, one ultimately leading to his operas *Salome* (1905) and *Elektra* (1908).[35]

Strauss's Lieder span most of his life, beginning in 1870 with *Weihnachtslied* and continuing to 1948 with *Malven*.[36] Taking into account the considerable gap between the *Sechs Lieder*, Op. 56, in 1906, and *Krämerspiegel*

Table 12.2 *The Lieder of Richard Strauss*

AV[a]	Op.	For voice and piano	For voice and orchestra[b]
2	–	Weihnachtslied (C. F. D. Schubart), 1870	
3	–	Einkehr (J. L. Uhland), 1871	
4	–	Winterreise (Uhland), 1871	
5	–	Waldkonzert (J. N. Vogel), ?1871	
7	–	Der böhmische Musikant (O. Pletzsch), ?1871	
8	–	Herz, mein Herz (E. Geibel), 1871	
10	–	Gute Nacht (Geibel), 1871, inc.	
13	–	Das Alpenhirten Abschied (F. von Schiller) 1872?	
16	–	Der müde Wanderer (A. H. Hoffmann von Fallersleben), ?1873	
42	–	Husarenlied (Hoffmann von Fallersleben), 1873?	
48	–	Der Fischer (J. W. von Goethe), 1877	
49	–	Die Drossel (Uhland), 1877	
50	–	Lass ruhn die Toten (A. von Chamisso), 1877	
51	–	Lust und Qual (Goethe), 1877	
58	–	Spielmann und Zither (T. Körner), 1878	
59	–	Wiegenlied (Hoffmann von Fallersleben), 1878	
60	–	Abend- und Morgenrot (Hoffmann von Fallersleben), 1878	
62	–	Im Walde (Geibel), 1878	
63	–	Der Spielmann und sein Kind (Hoffmann von Fallersleben), 1878	Der Spielmann und sein Kind (1878)
–	–		Arie der Almaide (Goethe: *Lila*), orchestrated, 1878
65	–	Nebel (N. Lenau), 1878	
66	–	Soldatenlied (Hoffmann von Fallersleben), 1878	
67	–	Ein Röslein zog ich mir im Garten (Hoffmann von Fallersleben), 1878	
74	–	Für Musik (Geibel), 1879	
75	–	Drei Lieder (Geibel), 1879: Waldgesang, O schneller mein Ross, Die Lilien glühn in Düften	
77	–	Frühlingsanfang (Geibel), 1879	
78	–	Das rote Laub (Geibel), 1879	
87	–	Die drei Lieder (Uhland), 1879	
88	–	Im Vaters Garten heimlich steht ein Blümlein (H. Heine), 1879	
89	–	Der Morgen (F. von Sallet), 1880	
90	–	Die erwachte Rose (Sallet), 1880	
98	–	Begegnung (O. E. Gruppe), 1880	
100	–	Mutter, o sing mir zur Ruh (F. von Hemans), 1880	
101	–	John Anderson, mein Lieb (R. Burns, trans. F. Freiligrath), 1880	
107	–	Geheiligte Stätte (Fischer), 1881	
112	–	Waldesgang (K. Stieler), 1882	
113	–	Ballade (A. Becker), 1882	
119	–	Rote Rosen (Stieler), 1883	
128	–	Mein Geist ist trüb (Byron), 1884	
129	–	Der Dorn ist Zeichen der Verneinung (F. Bodenstedt), 1884	
141	10	Acht Gedichte aus Letzte Blätter (H. von Gilm), 1885: Zueignung, Nichts, Die Nacht, Die Georgine, Geduld, Die Verschwiegenen, Die Zeitlose, Allerseelen	Zueignung (1940)
142	–	Wer hat's gethan? (Gilm), 1885	

Table 12.2 (*cont.*)

AV[a]	Op.	For voice and piano	For voice and orchestra[b]
148	15	Fünf Lieder, 1884–86: Madrigal (Michelangelo), Winternacht (A. F. von Schack), Lob des Leidens (Schack), Aus den Liedern der Trauer (Dem Herzen ähnlich) (Schack), Heimkehr (Schack)	
149	17	Sechs Lieder (Schack), 1885–87: Seitdem dein Aug' in meines schaute, Ständchen, Das Geheimnis, Aus den Liedern der Trauer (Von dunklem Schleier umsponnen), Nur Muth!, Barkarole	
152	19	Sechs Lieder aus Lotosblätter (Schack), 1885–88: Wozu noch, Mädchen, soll es Frommen; Breit über mein Haupt dein schwarzes Haar; Schön sind, doch kalt die Himmelssterne; Wie sollten wir geheim sie halten; Hoffen und wieder verzagen; Mein Herz ist stumm, mein Herz ist kalt	
153	22	Mädchenblumen (F. Dahn): Kornblumen, 1888; Mohnblumen, 1888; Efeu, 1886–88; Wasserrose, 1886–88	
160	21	Schlichte Weisen (Dahn), 1887–88: All' mein Gedanken, mein Herz und mein Sinn; Du meines Herzens Krönelein; Ach Lieb, ich muss nun scheiden; Ach weh, mir unglückhaften Mann; Die Frauen sind oft fromm und still	
166	26	Zwei Lieder (Lenau), 1891: Frühlingsgedränge, O wärst du mein	
170	27	Vier Lieder, 1894: Ruhe, meine Seele (K. Henckell); Cäcilie (H. Hart); Heimliche Aufforderung (J. H. Mackay); Morgen (Mackay)	Ruhe, meine Seele (1948); Cäcilie (1897); Morgen (1897)
172	29	Drei Lieder (O. J. Bierbaum), 1895: Traum durch die Dämmerung, Schlagende Herzen, Nachtgang	
173	31	Drei Lieder: Blauer Sommer (C. Busse), 1896; Wenn (Busse), 1895; Weisser Jasmin (Busse), 1895; Stiller Gang (R. Dehmel) [added no.], with va, 1895	
174	32	Fünf Lieder, 1896: Ich trage meine Minne (Henckell), Sehnsucht (D. von Liliencron), Liebeshymnus (Henckell), O süsser Mai (Henckell), Himmelsboten zu Liebchens Himmelbett (Des Knaben Wunderhorn)	Liebeshymnus (1897)
175	–	Wir beide wollen springen (Bierbaum), 1896	
178	–	Vorüber ist der Grau der Nacht (anon.), ?1896	
179	–		Ganymed (Goethe) Strauss's arrangement of Schubert's song), 1897
180	33		Vier Gesänge: Verführung (Mackay), 1896; Gesang der Apollopriesterin (E. von Bodmann), 1896; Hymnus, 1896; Pilgers Morgenlied (Goethe), 1897
185	–		Zwei Lieder von Beethoven, orchestrated by Strauss, 1898: Ich liebe dich (K. F. Herrosee), Wonne der Wehmut (Goethe)
186	36	Vier Lieder: Das Rosenband (F. G. Klopstock), 1897; Für funfzehn Pfennige (Des Knaben Wunderhorn), 1897; Hat gesagt – bleibt's nicht dabei (Des Knaben Wunderhorn), 1898; Anbetung (F. Rückert), 1898	Das Rosenband (1897)
187	37	Sechs Lieder: Glückes genug (Liliencron), 1898; Ich liebe dich (Liliencron), 1898; Meinem Kinde (G. Falke), 1897; Mein Auge (Dehmel), 1898; Herr Lenz (E. von Bodman), 1896; Hochzeitlich Lied (A. Lindner), 1898	Ich liebe dich (1943); Meinem Kinde (1897); Mein Auge (1933)

(*cont.*)

Table 12.2 (*cont.*)

AV[a]	Op.	For voice and piano	For voice and orchestra[b]
189	39	Fünf Lieder, 1898: Leises Lied (Dehmel), Junghexenlied (Bierbaum), Der Arbeitsmann (Dehmel), Befreit (Dehmel), Lied an meinen Sohn (Dehmel	Der Arbeitsmann (1918); Befreit (1898)
195	41	Fünf Lieder, 1899: Wiegenlied (Dehmel), In der Campagna (Mackay), Am Ufer (Dehmel), Bruder Liederlich (Liliencron), Leise Lieder (C. Morgenstern)	Wiegenlied (1900)
196	43	Drei Gesänge älterer deutscher Dichter, 1899: An Sie (Klopstock), Muttertändelei (G. A. Bürger), Die Ulme zu Hirsau (Uhland)	Muttertändelei (1900)
197	44		Zwei grössere Gesänge, orchestrated, 1899: Notturno (Dehmel), Nächtlicher Gang (Rückert)
198	–	Weihnachtsgefühl (M. Greif), 1899	
199	46	Fünf Gedichte (Rückert): Ein Obdach gegen Sturm und Regen, 1900; Gestern war ich Atlas, 1899; Die sieben Siegel, 1899; Morgenrot, 1900; Ich sehe wie in einem Spiegel, 1900	
200	47	Fünf Lieder (Uhland), 1900: Auf ein Kind, Des Dichters Abendgang, Rückleben, Einkehr, Von den sieben Zechbrüdern	Des Dichters Abendgang (1918)
202	48	Fünf Lieder, 1900: Freundliche Vision (Bierbaum), Ich schwebe (Henckell), Kling! (Henckell), Winterweihe (Henckell), Winterliebe (Henckell)	Freundliche Vision (1918); Winterweihe (1918); Winterliebe (1918)
204	49	Acht Lieder: Waldseligkeit (Dehmel), 1901; In goldener Fülle (P. Remer), 1901; Wiegenliedchen (Dehmel), 1901; Das Lied des Steinklopfers (Henckell), 1901; Sie wissen's nicht (O. Panizza), 1901; Junggesellenschwur (Des Knaben Wunderhorn), 1900; Wer lieben will, muss leiden (C. Mundel: *Elsässische Volkslieder*), 1901; Ach, was Kummer, Qual und Schmerzen (Mundel: *Elsässiche Volkslieder*), 1901	Waldseligkeit (1918)
206	51	Der Einsame (Heine), 1906 (arranged for piano)	Zwei Gesänge: Das Thal (Uhland), orchestrated, 1902, Der Einsame (Heine), orchestrated, 1906
218	–	Der Graf von Rom (textless), 2 versions, 1906	
220	56	Sechs Lieder: Gefunden (Goethe), 1903; Blindenklage (Henckell), 1903–06; Im Spätboot (C. F. Meyer), 1903–06; Mit deinen blauen Augen (Heine), 1903–06, Frühlingsfeier (Heine), 1903–06, Die heiligen drei Könige aus Morgenland (Heine), 1903–06	Frühlingsfeier (1933), Die heiligen drei Könige aus Morgenland (1906)
226	–	Herbstabend, before 1910 (unfinished)	
235	68	Sechs Lieder (C. Brentano), 1918: An die Nacht; Ich wollt' ein Sträusslein binden; Säusle, liebe Myrthe; Als mir dein Lied erklang; Amor; Lied der Frauen	An die Nacht (1940); Ich wollt' ein Sträusslein binden (1940); Säusle, liebe Myrthe (1940); Als mir dein Lied erklang (1940); Amor (1940); Lied der Frauen (1933)
236	66	Krämerspiegel (A. Kerr), 1918: Es war einmal ein Bock; Einst kam der Bock als Bote; Es liebte einst ein Hase; Drei Masken sah ich am Himmel stehn; Hast du ein Tongedicht vollbracht; O lieber Künstler sei ermahnt; Unser Feind ist, grosser Gott; Von Händlern wird die Kunst bedroht; Es war mal eine Wanze; Die Künstler sind die Schöpfer; Die Händler und die Macher; O Schöpferschwarm, O Händlerkreis	

Table 12.2 (*cont.*)

AV[a]	Op.	For voice and piano	For voice and orchestra[b]
237	69	Fünf kleine Lieder, 1918: Der Stern (A. von Arnim), Der Pokal (Arnim), Einerlei (Arnim), Waldesfahrt (Heine), Schlechtes Wetter (Heine)	
238	67	Sechs Lieder, 1918: I Drei Lieder der Ophelia (W. Shakespeare, trans. K. Simrock): Wie erkenn' ich mein Treulieb vor andern nun?; Guten Morgen, 's ist Sankt Valentinstag; Sie trugen ihn auf der Bahre bloss; II Aus den Büchern des Unmuts der Rendsch Nameh (Goethe): Wer wird von der Welt verlangen; Hab' ich euch denn je geraten; Wanderers Gemütsruhe	
239	–	Sinnspruch (Goethe), 1919	
240	71		Drei Hymnen von Friedrich Hölderlin, orchestrated, 1921: Hymne an die Liebe, Rückkehr in die Heimat, Liebe
241	–		Walzerlied zu einer Operette von Maximiliano Niederberger, 1921 (unfinished).
244	87	Erschaffen und Beleben (Goethe), 1922	
251	–	Durch allen Schall und Klang (Goethe), 1925	
257	77	Gesänge des Orients (trans. H. Bethge), 1928: Ihre Augen (Hafiz), Schwung (Hafiz), Liebesgeschenke (Die chinesische Flöte), Die Allmächtige (Hafiz), Huldigung (Hafiz)	
	–	Wie etwas sei leicht (Goethe), 1930	
258	87	Und dann nicht mehr (Rückert), 1929	
260	87	Vom künftigen Alter (Rückert), 1929	
261	–	Spruch (Goethe), 1930	
264	88	Das Bächlein (attrib. Goethe), 1933	Das Bächlein (1935)
268	87	Im Sonnenschein (Rückert), 1935	
269	–	Zugemessne Rhythmen (Goethe), 1935	
280	88	Sankt Michael (J. Weinheber), 1942	
281	88	Blick vom oberen Belvedere (Weinheber), 1942	
282	–	Xenion (Goethe), 1942	
296	–		Vier letzte Lieder, orchestrated, 1948; Frühling (Hesse), September (Hesse), Beim Schlafengehen (Hesse), Im Abendrot (Eichendorff)
297	–	Malven (B. Knobel), 1948	

[a] E. H. Mueller von Asow, *Richard Strauss: Thematisches Verzeichnis* (Vienna, 1955–74).
[b] Dates in parentheses refer to the year Strauss completed the orchestration of Lieder originally for voice and piano.

(The shopkeeper's mirror), Op. 66, in 1918, there are songs from every creative period, with three quarters of them having been written by 1906. Although many of the Lieder stem from relatively early on, most were written between 1894 and 1906 and thus are contemporaneous with his modernist tone poems and the provocative opera *Salome*. Although the Lieder seem at first to be more traditional when compared to other music by Strauss written at the same time, they stand out as a vehicle for him to demonstrate his extraordinary talent for sustained, soaring melody. A song such as *Zueignung* (Dedication), the opening number of the *Acht Gedichte aus "Letzte Blätter"* von Hermann von Gilm, Op. 10, owes its status in the modern song recital to its appealing and straightforward tunefulness, unambiguous harmonies and formal design, along with its exciting vocal climax near the end. With his energy diverted by operas between 1906 and 1917 – Salome, Elektra, Der Rosenkavalier (1910), Ariadne auf Naxos (1912; revised 1916), and Die Frau ohne Schatten (1917) – Strauss found almost no time for songs. (Yet another reason Lieder were not composed during this period concerns the fact that the singing career of his wife, Pauline, was winding down.) In a return to the genre after World War I in 1918, the next phase extends to 1929 and is noteworthy for the attention Strauss devotes to many older poets, including Brentano and Hölderlin. Another period of falling off occurs between 1929 and 1942, before the final burst of song that yields the Vier letzte Lieder, a set of songs that have come to be viewed as the composer's paean to a bygone Romanticism and also to the Lied itself.

Strauss's poets

In contrast to the relatively few sources Mahler used for his texts, Strauss turned to more than sixty poets ranging from Michelangelo and Shakespeare (in translation), to Bürger, Klopstock, Goethe, and Heine, as well as folk texts such as Des Knaben Wunderhorn. While Mahler revised his texts, Strauss tended to set texts unaltered, and never set to music a poem of his own invention. Strauss occasionally was also drawn to a number of contemporary poets, including some who were capable of raising the eyebrows of turn of the century audiences, among them Richard Dehmel, Oskar Panizza, and John Henry Mackay.[37]

Lieder for voice and piano

Beyond reflecting his preference for such poets as Uhland, Goethe, Chamisso, and Heine, Strauss's earliest Lieder – including some now lost – reveal a composer testing his mettle against such figures from the past as Schubert, Schumann, and Brahms. Of the approximately forty songs finished by 1883, a great many were written for immediate use within the context of family music making, a point reflected in the number dedicated to his aunt, Johanna Pschorr. Another, isolated piece is the orchestral song from 1878, Der Spielmann und sein Kind (The minstrel and his child), with a text by Hoffmann von Fallersleben. Along with the previously mentioned Zueignung, another song from the Op. 10 collection that has retained its popularity is Allerseelen (All Souls' Day). Whereas Zueignung features a modified strophic design allowing for sometimes striking changes in each of its three stanzas, *Allerseelen* is fitted out with a through-composed form, one well suited to the text's mounting passion, and which Strauss enhances by ending each strophe with the same words: "Wie einst im Mai" (As once we did in May). Although *Allerseelen* displays obvious ties with the tradition of the nineteenth-century Lied – apparent above all in the piano's subordination to the entirely syllabic vocal line – other details are unique to Strauss. The accompaniment involves lush, widely spaced harmonies that anticipate the kind of ecstatic expression found in later works and also, in their gathering intensity, seem to bring the departed lover back to life before the eyes of the grief-stricken protagonist. Poignant, too, is the last repetition of the line "Wie einst im Mai," at the very end, after the piano has embarked on its concluding postlude.

While the other songs making up the Op. 10 set have not enjoyed the popularity of these two, all the individual pieces in the *Vier Lieder* Op. 27 have fared better. A wedding gift for Pauline (the couple married 10 September 1894), *Ruhe, meine Seele!* (Rest, my soul!), *Cäcilie* (Cecilia), *Heimliche Aufforderung* (Secret invitation), and *Morgen!* (Tomorrow!), served a dual purpose, since she also performed them in concerts. *Ruhe, meine Seele!* is a touching, exhortatory song, although its weightiness, Wagnerian declamation, and complex harmonies exceed the limitations of a keyboard accompaniment. In fact, Strauss orchestrated the song in 1948, and a case has been made for including it among the songs gathered in his *Vier letzte Lieder*.[38] While the first Op. 27 song had to wait more than half a century to be orchestrated, *Cäcilie* and *Morgen!* were scored in 1897. While it captures its overall musico-poetic character flawlessly yet unassertively, the composer's scoring of the latter does not necessarily enhance what is present in its original form. The question remains as to why Strauss would orchestrate three of the four songs at different times. Along with other factors, this inconsistency has led some to postulate that the grouping was not intended as an integrated whole, a charge leveled at other sets of Strauss songs as well. Arguing against this view, Marie Rolf and Elizabeth West Marvin, in a close reading of the Op. 27 Lieder, have concluded that the first and last songs of the collection form the outer pillars of a closely knit work bound by numerous musical and textual considerations.[39]

Given that he epitomizes for most people the arch-bourgeois (the 1924 domestic opera *Intermezzo* would seem to support such a view, not to mention the 1903 *Sinfonia domestica*, described by the composer himself as "a day in my family life"), some of the poets whom Strauss set ought to shock more than they do. Richard Dehmel, a poet associated perhaps more with Schoenberg (in eight songs written between 1897 and 1905 as well as *Verklärte Nacht*, Op. 4) and later Webern (in five Dehmel songs from 1906–08), is one of these.

In Strauss's ten Dehmel settings (including one orchestral Lied), composed between 1895 and 1901, one senses the poet sparked something previously untapped. *Wiegenlied*, Op. 41, No. 1, is a lullaby with, perhaps, greater appeal for adults than for children; despite its no doubt deliberate naiveté, the soaring cantilena celebrates the pleasures of conception as much as it does those of motherhood. *Befreit*, Op. 39, No. 4, often praised as one of the composer's finest songs, disappointed Dehmel, who voiced his displeasure, calling it "soft-grained." Yet it is difficult to comprehend the poet's objection in the context of the song's slowly mounting intensity. *Der Arbeitsmann* (The Workman), Op. 39, No. 3, is surprising for a different reason, since it reveals the composer sympathizing with the plight of a common laborer. A bitter protest song, it relies more on motives rather than the long musical lines more characteristic of Strauss's Lieder.

Among Strauss's other works for voice and piano dating from around the turn of the century are two melodramas, the first the well-known setting of Alfred Lord Tennyson's "Enoch Arden" (in German translation by Adolf Strodtmann), the second, perhaps less well known, a setting of Uhland's "Das Schloss am Meere" (The Castle by the Sea). Both works were written for Ernst von Possart, intendant of the Munich Court Opera and a former actor, who helped Strauss secure the prestigious post of principal conductor of that company in 1896. Composed respectively in 1897 and 1899, each features piano parts which, in their difficulty, belie the description "accompaniment." Supporting the spoken line, the keyboard provides a continuous commentary on the texts. In composing these two melodramas, Strauss by no means can be said to have invented the genre – Schubert, Liszt, and Wagner contributed to it long before he did.[40] This notwithstanding, it seems entirely plausible that the two by Strauss, especially the second, which is awash with chromatic adventurousness, anticipate Schoenberg's *Pierrot lunaire*, a work that, in its use of Sprechstimme, bridges the domains of speaking and singing.

For those who would make comparisons with Mahler, it is intriguing to be reminded that it was Strauss who first turned to the poetry of Rückert, in the *Fünf Gedichte*, Op. 46 (1899–1900). Although Strauss's Rückert settings appear a bit more traditional in nature when compared to Mahler's, they nonetheless go far in revealing Strauss's characteristic Lied style and suggest as well that his songs may have provided him with a way to test compositional strategies that he would later take up in the operas *Ariadne auf Naxos* and *Die Frau ohne Schatten*. In the event, some of the Rückert texts Strauss used are even more erotic than those by Dehmel or other poets from his day. *Die sieben Siegel* (The Seven Seals), Op. 46, No. 3, is provocative for the description of the seals as seven kisses left on various parts of the beloved's body to protect her virtue during the night, ending with the promise that, by morning, the two lovers together will release the seals. The shock appeal of the poem stands in contrast to Strauss's setting in which his usually complex harmonies give way to music that is light-hearted in the extreme.

Occupied with operatic projects during the years 1906 and 1917, Strauss returned to Lieder around 1918. When one surveys the Op. 66 *Krämerspiegel*, the composer's only true song cycle, it may be that one is unprepared for its stinging cynicism, yet the scornful tone is in the service of a definite goal.[41] In the hope of being released from his contract with the music publisher Bote & Bock, Strauss collaborated with the poet, publicist, and Berlin theater critic Alfred Kerr on this highly topical song cycle. Given that he was an individual who campaigned for fair treatment in music copyright issues, the subject was clearly dear to Strauss's heart and he responded to Kerr's text with a variety of musical quotations from his own works as well as those by other composers in a vicious satire of the German music publishing industry. Despite the topic and intent, the musical inspiration is earnest and involves effective piano writing, wide-ranging vocal lines, and a concluding postlude of such beauty that the composer reused it twenty-three years later in the "Moonlight" music of his last opera, *Capriccio*. Outraged, the music firm took Strauss to court, and, in losing the case, he was forced to write "proper songs." What followed was a subtle form of retribution, the *Sechs Lieder*, Op. 67, which contain the three songs of the mad Ophelia along with the three impertinent poems from Goethe's *West-östlicher Divan*. A decade later, in 1928, having put his travails with publishers behind him, Strauss took up, as had many before him, the allure of the East in the five songs he called *Gesänge des Orients*, Op. 77. Just as Mahler had in his *Das Lied von der Erde*, Strauss drew in part on Bethge's *Die chinesische Flöte*. While he continued to compose Lieder after these, the Op. 77 set was the last to which he would assign an opus number.

Lieder for voice and orchestra

While orchestral Lieder may be found at various points throughout Strauss's career, the majority were produced during two periods: the first around the last decade of the nineteenth century, the second comprising the last years of his life. Of these, only fifteen were written expressly for voice and orchestra, such as the *Vier Gesänge*, Op. 33, and the *Brentano Lieder*, Op. 68; the rest are reworkings of music originally conceived for voice and piano. The immediate inspiration for orchestral expansion, aside from the obvious challenge, was a practical one – singers, such as his wife or, later on, Elisabeth Schumann, in need of rewarding material for orchestral concerts. Although Strauss appears seldom to have hesitated to modify a voice and keyboard song into one for voice and orchestra, the opposite procedure, that is transforming an orchestral song into one for voice and piano, evidently held no interest for him, since none exist. In view of the fact that Strauss was a composer who relished the resources of the orchestra and who furthermore provides one of the most arresting musical portrayals of metamorphism in his opera *Daphne* (1936–37), the changes to be observed in the Lieder reworked into songs with orchestra are of continuing interest. A similar process may be found in the orchestral transcriptions Strauss made of the songs by Beethoven and Schubert: his 1897 scoring of Schubert's *Ganymed* and his 1898 orchestration of *Zwei Lieder von Beethoven*.

Strauss's own orchestral Lieder are no less engaging, above all the second of the *Zwei Gesänge für eine tiefe Bassstimme mit Orchesterbegleitung*, Op. 51, *Der Einsame* (The lonely one). A fine example of musico-literary synthesis, the work is both intimate and stirring. Strauss matches Heine's brooding poetry with a vocal line at once passionate, splendidly unpredictable, and marked by frequent leaps. It relies on a large orchestra, and the attention to detail is everywhere apparent: the densely voiced string ensemble calls on a remarkable quartet of unmuted soloists – violin, viola, violoncello, and double bass – within a full but muted string tutti, while the rich winds include two basset horns, a contrabassoon, and bass tuba. As is frequently the case in late Mahler, Strauss employs the large group sparingly – in only nine of the fifty measures, mainly in block chords deployed in the lowest register of the instruments to underscore the poem's central ideas of "Abgrund" (abyss) and "uralte Nacht" (Primeval night). Supporting all of this, the harmonies are rich and functional, yet encompass the strong modal hues of F Phrygian and A♭ Mixolydian, an intentional archaic touch that well serves the imagery of primeval night.

Vier letzte Lieder

Strauss's last songs are also his best known, as the *Vier letzte Lieder*, a fact at first slightly curious given that neither the title nor the ordering stems from the composer. Rather, the designation appears to have been the invention of Ernst Roth, who oversaw publication of the songs shortly after the composer's death. Completed between May and September 1948, the four are: *Frühling* (Spring), *September*, *Beim Schlafengehen* (While going to sleep), and *Im Abendrot* (At twilight). The first three songs are settings of poems by Hermann Hesse; the last one turns to Eichendorff. The retrospective sound world includes the composer's favorite musical "instrument," the soprano voice, a vocal type associated with his wife as well as a long and distinguished list of other singers. Moreover, the horn is called upon so often as to establish links between all four songs. An instrument with a venerable and illustrious history throughout German Romanticism, the horn would have had wide-ranging associations for Strauss. Inspired in part by the fact that his father, Franz, served as principal horn at the Bavarian Court Orchestra for more than four decades, the composer wrote gloriously for the instrument all his life. (In addition to the two horn concertos, the first from 1883, the second from 1942, the beginning of *Till Eulenspiegel* provides one of the most memorable examples.) In *Beim Schlafengehen*, the horn resembles the lone call first heard at the conclusion of *September;* at the beginning and end of *Im Abendrot* the horn is also prominent. These and other backward glances have led some to search out other connections with Strauss's earlier works. Timothy Jackson has argued that all four songs are an outgrowth of a generating idea that has its origin in the 1894 song *Ruhe, meine Seele!* As will be recalled, Strauss orchestrated the latter song in June 1948; elsewhere, Jackson observes that the song traditionally performed last in the set, *Im Abendrot,* resolves an otherwise unresolved motive in the 1894 Lied.[42]

As is well known, Strauss renders *Im Abendrot* even more moving by quoting from an earlier work, his youthful tone poem *Tod und Verklärung* (Death and Transfiguration). Strauss engaged in such self-reference before when, in two songs from his *Krämerspiegel,* he quoted material from his symphonic work. In *Die Künstler und die Schöpfer* he returns to motives from his *Ein Heldenleben* (1898), and *Sinfonia domestica* (1903), and in *O Schöpferschwarm* he alludes to *Till Eulenspiegels lustige Streiche* (1895). In *Im Abendrot,* the quotations assume a much more intimate and elegiac tone. Eichendorff's poem depicts a couple walking side by side, who, after life's long journey, are ready to take leave of the world, a sentiment Strauss plainly understood at the time he composed the song. In his late *Die Liebe der Danae* (1940), Strauss already had suggested his own leave-taking from opera in the departure of the character Jupiter.[43] Yet in *Im Abendrot,* the quotation from the earlier work draws attention to a mood of acceptance given that the tone poem concerns death and apotheosis. The self-reference is not self-promotion, but rather expresses his awareness of mortality.

After a survey of a life as long as Strauss's, one filled with arguably more than its share of mistakes, misjudgments, and sometimes unpardonable blunders, it is instructive to ponder the paradoxes so strikingly evident when his late creative efforts are placed alongside Mahler's. The long farewell that lies at the heart of the conclusion of Mahler's *Das Lied von der Erde* is not unlike that in Strauss's *Vier letzte Lieder,* despite the abundance of stylistic dissimilarities between the two works. Beneath their differences, the two are related spiritually, since both may be regarded as grand leave-takings, moving and masterful summaries of the respective emotional and musical worlds of each composer.[44] Thus, it is possible to return finally to the question raised at the start of this essay – whether Mahler and Strauss succeeded in dealing with the tuneful anxiety of influence of the nineteenth-century Lied. Using song for different purposes, each met the traditions of the Lied in the century of Schubert, Schumann, and Brahms head-on, absorbing, enlarging, and ultimately renewing them.

13 The Lied in the modern age: to mid century

JAMES PARSONS

"Revolutionary upheaval and conservative retrenchment both move in the same direction"

For those who would concern themselves with music's meaning, the ending of Strauss's *Im Abendrot*, from his *Vier letzte Lieder*, prompts any number of questions. Many stem from Eichendorff's text. The poem tells of two individuals walking hand in hand at twilight's glow; the last line asks, "ist dies etwa der Tod?" (is this perhaps death?).[1] Intentionally equivocal – the clause restlessly hinges on the word "etwa" (perhaps) – the poet leaves the matter open-ended. Strauss's music seems less ambiguous. Once the poetical question is sounded, the eighty-four-year-old composer quotes from a work of his written a half century earlier, *Tod und Verklärung* (Death and Transfiguration, 1889). A literal echo of Strauss's own past, the gesture provides compelling evidence of a person facing mortality with undiminished faith in the tenets of Romanticism. The song's retrospective sound world, a quality it shares with the three others with which it traditionally is grouped, has incited many to speculate that Strauss intended the set as a farewell to the Lied.[2] For Paul Griffiths, "Strauss could reasonably have thought his *Vier letzte Lieder . . .* bore their epithet for the genre."[3] Or, as Edward F. Kravitt would have it, "Strauss's return late in life to the Lied – when it was of minor importance in the modern world – is further evidence of his conservative nostalgia for things past." Moreover, "this yearning reminds one also of the past significance of the Lied."[4] But does Strauss really intend *Im Abendrot* as a panegyric to an art form that had had its day and expired? Playing off the title of the composer's youthful symphonic poem, this essay asks: did the Lied succumb to the vicissitudes of the century's upheavals or was it transfigured?

In searching for answers, a few frames of reference are helpful. If nineteenth-century Lieder provided a kind of two-way mirror – reflecting and shaping life's concerns – one might reasonably expect that the same holds true for German song in the twentieth century, too. A case can be made that the genre's history is in large measure the saga of music and words at the crossroads of nature, however idealized. It is not within the madding crowd of the city that one gains self-knowledge or learns of the joys and pains of love, but in untrammeled Arcadia.[5] For the poet and Lied composer, nature provided a vast wellspring of symbolic meanings with potential for subjective significance. As Goethe poeticizes (in verse set by Zelter, Franz, Wolf, Schoenberg, and Zemlinsky), the beloved is to be found not on the market road but wandering "happy and free, at the cliffs by the river, where she bestowed the kiss."[6] Even after nature found itself in the shadow of the Industrial Revolution, old habits changed slowly. As the nineteenth century unfolded, "progress" was the word on almost every lip; while things new were all the rage, things old were discarded without care. This was as true of the arts as it was of the cares of day-to-day living. For some, the race toward the new was not fast enough. In 1858, the French novelist and journalist Maxime Du Camp (1822–94) bemoaned:

> Everything advances, expands, and increases around us . . . Science
> produces marvels, industry accomplishes miracles, and we remain
> impassive, insensitive, disdainful, scratching the false chords of our lyres,
> closing our eyes in order not to see, or persisting in looking towards a past
> that nothing ought to make us regret. Steam is discovered, and we sing to
> Venus, daughter of the briny main; electricity is discovered, and we sing to
> Bacchus, friend of the rosy grape. It's absurd![7]

Songs to the gods did not continue indefinitely. Technology, hand in hand with the rise of the modern metropolis, would see to that, as Leo Marx, among others, persuasively has shown in his book *The Machine in the Garden*.[8] In the wake of Europe's rush toward industrialization, the existing expressive universe disappeared with ever-vanishing nature.[9]

Concurrently, traditional concepts of space gave way to a vision of the city prophesied by George Grosz in his painting "Großstadt" (Large City [1916–17]), a canvas awash in shrieking reds and teeming with riotous movement. Walther Ruttmann's silent film "Berlin, Die Sinfonie der Großstadt" (1927) depicts the city as the seat of competing activities, motivations, and forces, many of which are propelled by machines and locomotives; in a climactic moment toward the end, one individual, unable to withstand the never-ending bustle, seeks sanctuary in the comparatively motionless river Spree by jumping off a bridge. The shift from largely rural to urban life brought with it changes in social interaction and human consciousness, the result of urban centers being linked together, first by train and then by other mechanical modes of conveyance. Whereas the regular rhythms of the seasons order nature, the surfeit of pulses encountered in the city frequently result in sensory overload. As Ernst Krenek observes in a crucial moment in his 1926 opera *Jonny spielt auf* (Johnny strikes up), the key to urban living is to embrace every moment of this existence of endless movement yet not lose one's self.[10] What has gone largely unasked is how such changes influenced or were reflected in the Lied. Three years later in his *Reisebuch aus den österreichischen Alpen* (Travel Book from the Austrian Alps [1929]), Krenek, now in nature's preserve, launches his song cycle with these words: "I set out . . . looking for self and homeland." Could it be that composers continued to turn to the Lied in the twentieth century because the genre aided in the formation of individual identity? And does it follow that a point made by Jane K. Brown in chapter 1 – that poetry in the modern era "no longer speaks in a personal voice, but achieves its validity in its generality, its non-individuality" (see above, p. 30) – is inaccurate? Answers prove difficult, if for no other reason than that the role played by German song in the twentieth century has figured so little in the era's larger history. Perhaps the key to understanding such song is the way in which individuality continues to be a source of importance in an age that has found it easier to devalue and in turn distance itself from individuality.

The question of when modernism began is crucial if one is to appreciate what the twentieth-century Lied became. Others have examined how the century's "patterned energies" have been absorbed both in science and in poetry, how the radically altered "quality of city life" compelled a "change in artistic means." The author of these words, Hugh Kenner, has discussed how the James Joyce of *Ulysses* and other writers then at work were influenced by modernism in terms not only of subject matter but also of structure. "The deep connections between modernism and modern urban rhythms," Kenner observes, are to be detected not only in Joyce but also in John Dos Passos's *Manhattan Transfer* (1925) and Alfred Döblin's *Berlin Alexander-platz* (1929).[11] But who has examined the Lied for comparable structural or substantive changes? Given that most have assumed the genre expired sometime before the Indian Summer of Strauss's *Vier letzte Lieder*, no one has bothered inquiring. And why should they? The Lied in the age of the automobile, Hiroshima, Sputnik, and an ever-ascendant popular culture, even if a handful of composers in the twentieth century clung to it, surely is at odds with the spirit of the times now, a revenant with little or no relevance. This especially appears to be the case when the Lied's supposedly starched traditions are placed next to this exhaustingly energetic definition of modernism made by Marshall Berman in his study *All that is Solid Melts into Air*. The sheer density of all that he crowds into this passage, itself a reflection of modernity, warrants quotation in full:

> The maelstrom of modern life has been fed from many sources: great
> discoveries in the physical sciences, changing our images of the universe and
> our place in it; the industrialization of production, which transforms
> scientific knowledge into technology, creates new human environments and
> destroys old ones, speeds up the whole tempo of life, generates new forms
> of corporate power and class struggles; immense demographic upheavals,
> severing millions of people from their ancestral habitats, hurtling them

halfway across the world into new lives; rapid and often cataclysmic urban growth; systems of mass communication, dynamic in their development, enveloping and binding together the most diverse people and societies; increasingly powerful national states, bureaucratically structured and operated, constantly striving to expand their powers; mass social movement of people, and peoples, challenging their political and economic rulers, striving to gain some control over their lives; finally, bearing and driving all these people and institutions along, an ever-expanding, drastically fluctuating capitalist world market. In the twentieth century, the social processes that bring this maelstrom into being, and keep it in a state of perpetual becoming, have come to be called "modernization."[12]

Has the twentieth-century Lied kept pace with any of this? If it has, where does one plot the start of a "Modern Lied"? Is one justified at all in calling a Lied Modern? For Kravitt, the modern age starts after World War I, a conflict that "shattered the dominance of the old tradition" and prompted an abiding friction "between innovators and traditionalists."[13] A case could be made that such either/or thinking misses the mark. In contrast, for Carl Dahlhaus modernism begins in 1889 with Mahler's First Symphony and Strauss's *Don Juan*, a position that allows for the dialectic: "revolutionary upheaval and conservative retrenchment both move in the same direction."[14] (One might add that Wolf completed fifty-one Goethe settings as well as much of his *Spanisches Liederbuch* the same year.) Schoenberg's *Das Buch der hängenden Gärten* (1908–09), set to the poetry of Stefan George, partially supports Dahlhaus's claim. Described by the composer as the work in which he broke "through every restriction of a bygone aesthetic," the cycle's bracing atonality, sparse textures, anti-lyrical treatment of the vocal part, and incongruity between voice and piano deflect attention from at least two conservative features.[15] The composition is, after all, a song cycle, a Romantic construct *par excellence*, and it calls for that most quintessential of Lied performing forces: voice and piano. While we do modernist composers an injustice in failing to recognize their innovations, it is equally erroneous to insist on those innovations while ignoring their ties to tradition. Schoenberg again provides an example. In a Beethovenian gesture if ever there was one, his Second String Quartet (also from 1908), for the first time adds the human voice to that most Classical of genres. Once more to words by George, the soprano sings of feeling "a breath from other planets" while throughout the music juxtaposes key-centered and non-tonal passages while simultaneously reversing the accustomed associations of tonality/consonance with stability and atonality/dissonance with instability.[16]

If one can pinpoint a twentieth-century Lied, was it a Janus-faced genre simultaneously traveling the paths of "revolutionary upheaval and conservative retrenchment"? If yes, what elements from the Lied's characteristic union of music and words were retained from the nineteenth century and what were discarded? How did the Lied reflect the fundamental changes in society attending the shift from a rural world to one dominated by the city? While this chapter will attempt to provide answers to these questions, it is clear that a comprehensive examination of German song in the century just past is beyond the scope of a single essay. What is attempted, then, is a highly selective snapshot gallery.

Issues and challenges

As a genre with a glorious past and presumably promising future, the Lied found itself, as did the arts in general, at the center of controversy at the start of the last century. Was tonality – that shared musical language of Western Europe that had endured for almost three centuries – exhausted? If so, what should replace it? Should music or poetry be accorded top billing? This last question proved difficult to answer, one the age dubbed the *Wort-Ton Problem*, the problem of unifying words and music. In opera, the query occupied Richard Strauss for the greater part of his career. First broaching it in the prologue of *Ariadne auf Naxos* (1918), he returned to it in his last opera *Capriccio* (1942), where, notably, the matter is unresolved. Krenek responded by writing not only the music but also the texts of many of his Lieder, as he did in the aforementioned *Reisebuch*, *The Ballad of the Railroads* (1944), and *Albumblatt* (Album Leaf [1977]), thereby presumably insuring that neither music nor text would gain the upper hand. The second work of Krenek's mentioned here highlights another concern. When is a Lied a Lied and must it always be a musical setting of a German poem? The question goes far in focusing attention on the way in which the genre changes during the century both from within and from without, as may be seen in Hanns Eisler's *Hollywooder Liederbuch* (1942–43). A collection otherwise of musical settings of German texts, in four songs Eisler turns to the English language to heighten the sense of dislocation in a song collection mainly devoted to exile.

Other composers rethought what a Lied was altogether, as when Schoenberg abandoned vocal lyricism in favor of Sprechstimme, or speech song, in his *Pierrot lunaire* (1912). In other quarters, critics sounded the question of generic integrity. Hermann Kretzschmar, in 1911, worried that the Wagnerian music drama was unduly influencing the Lied, a trend that could only upset the balance between words and music, for the music drama encouraged Lieder composers to write intricate piano parts that obscured the vocal line and desiccated declamation that dispossessed living song.[17] And was the symphony not overwhelming the Lied as well? For many, Mahler's

Das Lied von der Erde (1909) provided the archetypal example. For others, the work showed the Lied influencing a non-Lied genre, a tradition stretching back to the song-like melody at the heart of the choral finale of Beethoven's Ninth Symphony.[18] Whether Mahler's *Das Lied von der Erde* is a Lied (or more accurately a song cycle) or a symphony misses the point. It is both, clinging to tradition while embracing innovation in a variety of ways, including formal design, harmonic vocabulary, tone color, and text itself. Moreover, the work influenced subsequent composers, among them Zemlinsky, in his *Lyrische Sinfonie* (1922) and Franz Waxman, in his *Das Lied von Terezín* (The Song of Terezin [1965]).[19]

Max Reger and the modern Lied

Mention of the word–tone relationship as well as controversy will signal to many that a look at Max Reger is at hand. Walter Niemann, five years after the composer's death, summarized Reger the song composer. "If one knows a half dozen of his Lieder, in general completely unsingable, imitating the words of the text with pedantic tone painting, formally shaky and crumbly in structure, whose texts of unbelievably unequal value betray Reger's lack of literary culture in a painful way, then one knows all of them."[20] Unpromising although Niemann's words are, they provide a provocative starting point for an examination of the Lied at this time because he articulates so many of the themes then current. He isolates (or implies) musical absolutism versus the programmatic, craft versus spontaneity, a composer's understanding of literature, as well as text painting and vocal declamation. What remains to be seen is whether Niemann is laying down procrustean expectations or if he has done Reger justice.

From the start, Reger has elicited critical extremes. In contrast to Schoenberg's and Webern's progressiveness, Reger's ostensible respect for Germany's musical past – specifically that centering on instrumental music (fugue, passacaglia, sonata) – has struck many as incompatible with a genuine Lied sensibility. Yet a composer who wrote almost three hundred songs cannot be ignored, especially one who turned to the genre almost continuously throughout his life: from the six songs of Op. 4 published when he was seventeen to his last issued a year before his death.

Whereas Wolf gravitated toward Goethe, Eichendorff, and Mörike, Reger looked to poets closer to his own time. "Goethe has been set enough," he once quipped.[21] The composer's allegiance to the poets of his day in part explains why Niemann reproached him for lack of literary discernment. There is yet a larger agenda lurking here. Kravitt helpfully has assembled a symposium of contemporaneous views on the "Modern Lied." Consensus had it that Wolf was the primary offender if not ringleader. For Rudolf Louis, in 1909, the type of Lied that Wolf composed "is poetry in the eminent sense of the word." This is problematic because "this is the first time in the history of the Lied that the musician has merged completely with the poet," the outcome being that poetry dominates music. One may forgive Louis for being less than completely informed on the history of the Lied. Although what resulted was a far cry from the tune-drenched simplicity admired in the age of Goethe, poetry's preeminence did not constitute anything new. What was seen as a threat at the start of the twentieth century was very different from what the Lied faced a hundred years earlier. If declamation is the prime consideration, it can only obliterate melody and "dissolves poetry into prose."[22] This in turn spawns other extremes. Niemann and other critics denounced Wolf and those who followed him for having "destroyed the traditional Lied," the purely "lyrical genre" conceived for "performance in the home."[23] Instead, what performers and listeners increasingly were subjected to was an "unsingable pianoforte song meant for the concert hall." Even worse, the Lied perfected by Schubert, Schumann, and Brahms increasingly found itself disfigured by "rich, radiantly colored, and symphonically conceived instrumental" parts, by which "the natural balance between voice and piano suffered dire consequences." To call a Lied modern at century's start was not to commend it. For a critic such as Niemann, such a song could possess only "false pathos, exaggerated emotional and dramatic perception."[24]

For many an early listener, Reger's 1906 setting of Stefan Zweig's "Ein Drängen" (A Yearning), Op. 97, No. 3, embodied all these and a great many more faults. Even Reger's erstwhile composition teacher Hugo Riemann criticized the Lied. From the Bach stronghold of Leipzig, Riemann inclined toward an interest in past music, one that surely colored his perceptions of the work of a younger generation. In the concluding pages of the 1913 third volume of his *Große Kompositionslehre*, Riemann singled out *Ein Drängen* for its "meaningless hodgepodge of right and wrong notes," in which he discerned the "renunciation of our way of thinking about and writing music."[25] Endeavoring to find a way through Reger's labyrinthine harmonies (Example 13.1a), Riemann declared the entire song to be in E major and to prove the point he corrected the opening measures in the hope of making them less complicated (Example 13.1b).

Such assistance obscures one of the song's cardinal events, one that allows Reger to underline the all-consuming longing of Zweig's poem. Voice and piano, as in many a Wolf Lied, go their separate directions; Reger's notation visually reinforces this, as does the rhythmically differentiated voice and piano in the Lied's first section. The improvement conceals something else. Throughout, the interval of the ascending minor third continually expands

Example 13.1a Reger, *Ein Drängen*, Op. 97, No. 3, mm. 1–3

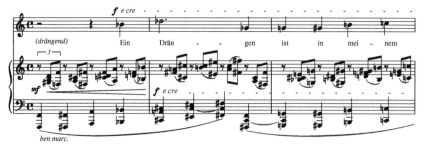

Example 13.1b Riemann, *Große Kompositionslehre*, III: 325 (*Ein Drängen* as notated by Riemann)

to a perfect fourth while simultaneously the piano's left hand plots permutations of the ascending half step. Tellingly, the semitones almost never resolve upward as traditional tonality demands. Both suggest the ever-expanding love desired by the protagonist – "Nach einer Liebe, die die Seele weitet," which ends in tears that are swallowed up by enervating hot nights ("und heiße Nächte trinken meine Tränen"). Taking his cue from Zweig's poem, Reger at length reveals two Wagnerian allegiances: the symphonically conceived piano part and the chromatically side-slipping harmonies that ensue when the poem's second strophe mentions the long wait for love. Yearning may render the poetic persona mute, yet Reger's music breaks out in harmonies that speak volumes and might well be thought of as a resuscitation of *Tristan und Isolde* in miniature, another work that treats love's desire (Example 13.2).

It has been argued that Reger always needed a "point" when setting a poem to music, "a single moving external or internal factor that would release the musical inspiration."[26] In *Ein Drängen*, this is seen in the minor third constantly expanding to the perfect fourth. Reger is not so much concerned with musically attending to a poem's every word as he is in extracting

Example 13.2 Reger, *Ein Drängen*, mm. 24–48

Example 13.2 (*cont.*)

a musical process that sums up the whole. In doing so, something else is achieved as well. For Reinhold Brinkmann, one definition of modernism is a "critical, almost enigmatic relationship between allegorical (nonrepresentational) and symbolic (representational) language."[27] Reger, in his *Ein Drängen*, anticipates this to a large degree in striking this balance. Schoenberg achieved this equipoise too; small wonder that he esteemed Reger's music.[28]

An anti-Modernist? Hans Pfitzner

If Reger heralded the future, Hans Pfitzner (1869–1949) has been portrayed as a composer who rejected modernity. To characterize either so simplistically is to paint history with too broad a brush. The complex keyboard parts of Reger's Lieder owe as much to Brahms (as Reger admitted) as they do to Wagner.[29] While Pfitzner presents the curious figure of a composer clinging to tradition, his dedication to the past tells only part of the story. Werner Diez, in his study of Pfitzner's Lieder, asserts that in contrast to Mahler, Strauss, and Reger, it is only with Pfitzner that the Lied "unequivocally occupies a central position."[30] The comment is meant not to question the importance of song for these other composers but to highlight the genre's significance in other areas of Pfitzner's creativity. As the Pfitzner Lied scholar Hans Rectanus reminds one, the composer frequently quotes his own songs in instrumental and stage works.[31] (One could argue that both Diez and Rectanus underestimate a comparable generating role for the genre for Mahler.) Pfitzner himself, in a passage worthy of Schumann, formulates his Lied aesthetic thus: "The same spirit comes forth from two different sources and flows into one configuration, in which word and tone become one, and the mood harmonizes with all this as a pure consonance."[32] As with all generalizations, the statement cannot do justice to all of Pfitzner's 115 songs. Nor is it possible to provide sweeping pronouncements about the composer's text choices. While Eichendorff leads with nineteen settings (not counting the twenty poems of the Eichendorff cantata *Von deutscher Seele*), poems by Bürger, Dehmel, Huch, Heine, Goethe, Keller, and Mörike, together with those by a variety of friends, reflect a wide-ranging literary taste. Unlike Reger, who found inspiration in the Lied until the end of his life, Pfitzner abandoned it in 1931; perhaps this is just as well. As Alex Ross has observed, the music Pfitzner wrote during the Third Reich degenerated into dullness: "Carl Maria von Weber in a shopping mall."[33]

Das verlassene Mägdlein, Op. 30, No. 2 (1922), is Pfitzner's second setting of Mörike's poem; the first dates from around 1887 and, it is generally agreed, lacks the depth of the second. The latter holds its own against Wolf's

Example 13.3 Pfitzner, *Das verlassene Mägdlein*, Op. 30, No. 2, mm. 1–13

masterful 1888 response to the same text while outwardly recalling the older composer's setting. (Susan Youens discusses Wolf's Lied in chapter 10.) The similarities between Pfitzner's setting and Wolf's include his reliance on a slow dactylic rhythm (modified in every ensuing bar by one comprising dotted eighth, sixteenth, and quarter notes), a pattern continually heard in the first thirteen measures (Example 13.3). Another is the placement of the piano's right hand in a high treble register, one that lends the song an obsessive quality. Whereas Wolf begins with the piano's two hands in divided duty, Pfitzner starts with stark chords in which hollow octaves predominate and the opening high C♯ is sounded in thirty-one of the song's forty-eight bars. In the concluding three measures, when the treble drone at last gives way, the C♯ is transferred to the lowest voice of the piano's left hand, a move that, in the context of the F♯ minor tonic, confirms the maiden's unresolved plight. The drone, syllabic text setting, expressive indication *Einfach* (simple), and outward lack of complication show Pfitzner a master of the folk idiom.

Although the folk style was by no means a Pfitzner specialty, the fact that he calls on it in 1922 is significant, for it highlights an enduring influence on the Lied, one stretching back almost two centuries. For Kretzschmar, in 1911, the idiom offered Lied composers one way of escaping the thick piano accompaniments redolent of Wagnerian music dramas or late nineteenth-century symphonic composition. In many ways, to call a song a folk Lied

was to hark back to the simplicity of the eighteenth-century Lied, a style
Reichardt described in 1781 as the musician's "north star." Almost a century
later, Brahms still found much to recommend in the aesthetic. Writing to
Clara Schumann in 1860, he noted: "The Lied is now sailing so false a course
that one cannot hold fast enough to the ideal," he declared. "And for me that
is folk song."[34] (Schoenberg's four arrangements of fifteenth- and sixteenth-
century folk songs from 1929, which he insisted were "art songs," go in the
opposite direction with their densely contrapuntal piano parts.)

Beneath the seeming simplicity of Pfitzner's *Das verlassene Mägdlein* lies
a substratum of sophistication in the service of Mörike's poem. The third
strophe reveals that it is only after having gone about her chores – ones
that recall another abandoned girl, the Gretchen of Goethe's "Gretchen am
Spinnrade" – that the maiden realizes she has dreamed of the "faithless
boy" the night before. That awareness prompts the fourth strophe's shower
of tears – "Träne auf Träne." Before those words, the music passes in m. 31
through the key of B♭ minor, one tonally distant from the F♯ minor tonic.
The third of the B♭ minor triad is doubled in the outer voices, yet that D♭
is C♯ respelled, the same note that launched the song. In m. 32 the voice
descends D♭–A♭–G♭ in tandem with the girl's tears. Those same notes first
are heard as C♯–G♯–F♯ at the Lied's beginning, when the voice enters in
m. 3, and again in mm. 5, 7, 9, 11, and 13 – at the start of strophe 2.
The enharmonic equivalence in m. 32 links with these earlier incarnations
and economically announces grief's unyieldingness. The maiden's sorrow
is present even when she is not consciously aware of it and will continue
long after the day she wishes would end has passed. T. S. Eliot declared, "in
my beginning is my end." Pfitzner conceives Mörike's protagonist in such
a way that in her beginning there is no end. Never once is there a true V–i
cadence; F♯ minor is the song's putative key, but only because we count the
key signature's sharps and tell ourselves F♯ *is* the tonic. So, too, "the glow of
the flames is pretty" because the girl lights them daily and convinces herself
they are attractive. But the fire's glow sparks her dream, the memory of
which triggers despair, a state that, while she wishes it away, Pfitzner's music
announces will not budge. The final chord sinks to the tonic, but it is not
the lowest tone. Once more it is C♯, the same note that began the Lied and
which has haunted it throughout.

Between World Wars: the *Neue Sachlichkeit*

When Pfitzner's Op. 30 was published in 1922, Germany had had almost
four years to grapple with the outcome of World War I. The ensuing conditions were a far cry from the optimism and economic boom that had greeted

the establishment of the German Empire a half century earlier in 1871. In the face of the successive indignities of military defeat, foreign occupation, and out-of-control inflation, the Germany of the Weimar (First German) Republic began to regard post-Romanticism and Expressionism as symbols of a bygone era. Although this last artistic movement was not all that old, it nonetheless was felt by many to have run its course; its artificiality and penchant for hysteria were no longer felt to be in keeping with the prevailing mood. "No more about war, revolution and the salvation of the world," Paul Kornfeld declared in 1924, himself a leading Expressionist. "Let us be modest and turn our attention to other and smaller things."[35] The resulting aesthetic, a *Neue Sachlichkeit*, or New Objectivity, sought broad appeal through its treatment of contemporary life, especially technology's effect on humanity and the various fads it spawned.[36]

The quest for "smaller things" notwithstanding, it soon became clear that even those could take on surprisingly substantial proportions. As Berlin audiences discovered in May of 1928, the latter was subjected to good-hearted lampoon in the musical revue *Es liegt in der Luft* (There's Something in the Air), featuring a then little-known Marlene Dietrich in her stage debut. With words by Marcellus Schiffer and music by Mischa Spoliansky, the theme song treats not only the potential for anything newfangled to be satirized, but also the "new objectivity" and soberness in the face of so much patent yet fleeting silliness:

Es liegt in der Luft eine Sachlichkeit.	There blows in the air a certain objectivity.
Es liegt in der Luft eine Stachlichkeit.	There blows in the air a certain practicality.
Es liegt in der Luft, es liegt in der Luft, in der Luft.	There's something in the air, there's something in the air, in the air.
Es liegt in der Luft was Idiotisches.	There's something in the air a bit idiotic.
Es liegt in der Luft was Hypnotisches!	There's something in the air a bit hypnotic!
Es liegt in der Luft, es liegt in der Luft.	There's something in the air . . .
Und es geht nicht mehr raus aus der Luft!	And what blows in the air no longer is propelled by the air!
Alles rennt, hetzt sich zu Tode.	Everything darts about, works itself to death.
Täglich ändert sich die Mode.	Daily the fashion changes.
. . . .	. . . .
Durch die Luft geht alles drahtlos.	Through the air everything goes wireless.

Und die Luft wird schon ganz	And the air thus becomes
ratlos:	completely helpless:
Flugzeug, Luftschiff – alles schon!	airplane, zeppelin, everything
	already!
Hört, wie's in den Lüften schwillt![37]	Hear how the whole lot swells up in
	the air!

Above all opera, specifically *Zeitopern*, or operas of the time, such as Krenek's *Jonny spielt auf* and Max Brand's *Maschinist Hopkins* (1928), established meaningful ties with the movement.[38] Both Krenek's and Brand's works treat the tried and true operatic subjects of crime and passion together with class issues and technology's "brand new crazes" in a progressive, up-to-date world. Just as significantly, both ask if technology liberates or enslaves.

Although usually not a genre associated with the New Objectivity, the Lied nonetheless began to attract a younger generation of composers who found it a ready-made medium with which to examine social issues. Precisely this radiates from a 1933 drawing (the year is hard to ignore) by Bruno Voigt (1912–88) entitled "Cultivate the Music of the German Home." Conscripting the nineteenth-century image par excellence of wholesomeness – the piano in the parlor – the artist portrays four women and a man gathered around a piano in song. Yet the "home" is a brothel, the women prostitutes, the man their pimp. The values of the entire society, not merely its music, are called into question, and so, too, is song as an agency of high culture. At the same time as Voigt's drawing, composers began turning to the Lied to effect social and political change. This especially is the case with composers such as Eisler and Paul Dessau. Thus Dessau, in setting François Villon's "Ballade vom guten und schlechten Lebenswandel" (Ballad of the good and bad way of life [in Paul Zech's German translation]), employs jaundiced cynicism to support a presumably optimistic outcome. The Lied mixes a biting, accusatory speech-song style, the mordant commonplaces of street music, and a refrain that continuously intones, "none of it matters much." Writing this song in 1936, Dessau did know what mattered, for he then was three years into an exile (first in Paris, later the USA) prompted by the National Socialists' seizure of power in Germany. As a Jew who composed socially engaged music, his departure was a necessity. Eisler, whose work as a song composer straddled the domains of both popular and high art, time and again succeeded in bridging those realms. This is true whether the song in question was composed for a Brecht play, for factory workers, or for the recital hall. In songs aimed at people from all walks of life, Eisler combines heterogeneous musical resources from jazz, church music, and other vernacular idioms with techniques inspired by cinema's *montage*. Eisler's

Kuppellied (Panderer's Song), composed for Brecht's play *Die Rundköpfe und die Spitzköpfe* (Eisler completed his music in 1936), provides a telling illustration. As is the case with Voigt's drawing, Eisler's goal is to provoke strong reaction. The song, sung by "a fat, sodden old hag," quotes the Tristan chord from Wagner's *Tristan und Isolde*. The socially charged meaning is unequivocal. As the quotation is sounded, Brecht's text reveals: "money makes one sensuous." In appropriating the symbol of all things progressive in Wagner's music drama, given that the chord seemingly abandons traditional tonality, Eisler's setting utterly undermines that forward-looking association. No longer meant to convey advancement, the chord now exemplifies an enervated world. Not only is the old order bankrupt; whores overrun it.

For all this, does the Lied truly figure in the history of twentieth-century music or was this the age, as many have insisted, that saw the "death of song"? Answers prove difficult, not for lack of musical evidence but because the usual responses have become such entrenched clichés. For many, the temptation will be strong to file Dessau or Eisler's Lieder in the category of popular song, a genre at odds with German art song. In this way, one can point to a falling off in Lied composition and an eventual demise. Admittedly, which side of the fence one comes down on depends on how one defines the word Lied. I incline to a socially informed meaning, one in which song by Austro-German composers beginning in the eighteenth century and continuing to the present has inscribed and reflected individual and societal concerns through a medium of words mediated by solo voice and some type of instrumental partner(s). Clearly, such a definition takes into account the function and purpose of song, yet it leads to another question, one some will deem imprudent. Is it time to drop the word *art* from the English translation of the word Lied as "art song," at least in discussing twentieth-century Lieder? If we did, a more inclusive understanding of the way in which song has figured in the lives of composers from German-speaking lands and their listeners (from whatever country) might be possible.

Krenek's *Reisebuch*

Krenek's *Reisebuch*, while reflecting an "enthusiasm for the immediate,"[39] also explores topics of longstanding interest to arts and letters within the German-speaking lands. The cycle's twenty songs, as in *Jonny spielt auf*, again find the composer in charge not only of music but also of text. This double talent – starting with *Jonny* a near-lifelong feature of Krenek's vocal music – is just one of the ways he reveals his singularity within the course of twentieth-century music. The composition intrigues on a variety of levels.

First, it relates to the venerable *Bildungsroman*, a genre harking back to the eighteenth century. In one of the most celebrated examples, Goethe's 1794 *Wilhelm Meister's Apprenticeship*, the protagonist proclaims his most enduring ambition to be "the harmonious development of my personality," in short, self-synthesis, or Enlightenment.[40] (The process itself proceeds along a *Bildungsweg* or path to self-cultivation.) In the first movement, *Motiv*, expressing his desire to know himself and his homeland, Krenek stakes his *Reisebuch* to this tradition, for to know one's homeland *is* to know one's self. Krenek's word for homeland is *Heimat*, one heavy with history in German verse and song. Interestingly, the idea of *Heimat* is experienced almost never in the here and now but as something toward which one strives. As the early nineteenth-century arch-Romantic Tieck, in his "Ferne" (Distance), asks: "O alte Heimat süß! wo find' ich wieder dich?" (O ancient homeland sweet! Where will I find you again?). Krenek saturates *Motiv* with pedal points and a steady quarter-note rhythm that satisfy the opening line "I now set out." The song also recalls the start of Schubert's *Winterreise*, a work depicting a central character striking out on a journey of outward and inward discovery which, in its opening *Gute Nacht*, discloses a constantly reiterated eighth-note journeying motive. Intentional Schubertisms abound in Krenek's cycle, some musical, others symbolic. The eighth song, *Unser Wein*, bears the dedication "to the memory of Franz Schubert." The entire collection was published in four volumes in oblong *Querformat*, as were Schubert's song cycles *Die schöne Müllerin* and *Winterreise*, reissued in facsimile the year before (1928), the centenary of Schubert's death.

It has been asserted that all of this is Krenek's way of tapping the Schubert mania then sweeping Austria. Certainly, critics at the time found the cycle along with other recent Krenek works to be "unequivocal high treason" against the New-Music revolution.[41] Both assessments miss as much as they illuminate. Krenek revisits the past in order to ponder it, to learn its lessons and thereby make ready for the future. As Krenek admitted almost a quarter century later, his *Reisebuch* "contained just enough dynamite in the form of skepticism, critical innuendo, and unexpected dissonance to make the keepers of the traditional *Gemüthlichkeit* feel uncomfortable."[42] *Gemüthlichkeit*, easy going, is the tip-off that Krenek intends his bows to the past not to be self-indulgently cozy but rather to provoke. A central tenet of the Enlightenment *Bildungsroman* is that art, and by extension the artist, aids in self-synthesis. Art "almost alone," Schiller noted in 1791, is capable of reuniting "the separated powers of the soul, that occupies head and heart, acumen and wit, reason and imagination in a harmonious cooperation that, as it were, restores in us *human wholeness*."[43] This Krenek achieves by bringing together multifarious musical styles. Following the Schubertian *Motiv*, *Verkehr* follows with biting dissonance and percussive rhythms suggestive of the various modes of modern transport that conduct one ever higher into the mountains. The "critical innuendo" comes in a variety of ways. In the middle of *Verkehr*, after having switched from train to bus, Krenek's music breaks out into prosaic salon music once it is clear the bus will make it safely up the incline. In the eighth song, *Unser Wein*, Krenek critiques the commercial image of Schubert then being perpetrated by parodying the type of music to be heard in Austrian wine taverns – *Heurige*. Only the unwary would take the song as a tribute to Austrian geniality. While the song gives the appearance of being strophic, the far-flung harmonies that support the continuous return of the opening phrase move increasingly away from the E♭ major tonic. The strategy reaches a climax at the words "The foreign visitors know little of our wine because it's unassuming, offered without ostentation." In tandem with this, the music veers to the remote key of A major. The text continues, "It's lovely, though, for those who take their pains to seek it out," and Krenek's harmonies spin in searching uncertainty. Wine, the referent to the "it's" in Krenek's text, clearly is being used as a metaphor for Austrian culture in general. In association with Schubert, the appearance of easy familiarity may have another meaning. Beginning with Heinrich Kreissle von Hellborn's 1865 biography, it had become a commonplace that Schubert possessed "childish naiveté" as well as a "delight in a glass of wine."[44] Krenek takes issue with both stereotypes, insisting that understanding either Schubert or Austria is predicated on transcending the superficial.

The trek terminates in the nineteenth song, *Heimkehr*. The three-note figure heard in the first song at the word "Vaterland" returns, as does the opening tonal region of E♭ major which brings with it circular unity. For all this, Krenek's *Reisebuch* does not end here. There follows an *Epilog*, which, while it brings new questions, directs composer and listener toward the possibility of a more rewarding conclusion. As Schiller reflected, the "higher harmony" of self-cultivation is "never completely concluded . . . Strive for unity, but seek it not in uniformity; strive for repose, but by means of the equilibrium and not of the cessation of your activity."[45] In *Epilog*, Krenek symbolizes the open-endedness of such an endeavor in the most arresting of ways. After a song cycle anchored largely on discernible tonal centers peppered with liberal doses of atonality, Krenek adopts for the first time in his career Schoenberg's twelve-tone method. Justification for this only partly is to be had in the text, "Marching on, I know I'm alive." Turning to twelve-tone composition allows Krenek another means of effecting Enlightenment's "higher harmony" in the guise of uniting tradition and innovation.

The move toward dodecaphonism also provides a prophetic intimation of Krenek's own future musical journey. It is tempting, too, to speculate that this also relates to the *Bildungsweg*. For the architects of the Enlightenment such as Kant, Goethe, Schiller, and Hegel – all of whom Krenek would have read growing up in Vienna – the path to self-understanding, while an ongoing process, is meant to be difficult. As Hegel reflected in his *Phenomenology of Spirit* (1807), the spirit "must travel a long way and work its passage" if it is "to become genuine knowledge." Such an undertaking is accomplished not "like the shot from a pistol," but "as stages on a way that has been made level with toil." The latter is imperative just as is "the length of this path"; it "has to be endured, because each moment is necessary" in order that the whole might be pieced together.[46] After numerous antagonisms with Schoenberg, Krenek's adoption of the twelve-tone method – understood to be Schoenberg's intellectual property – doubtless was more difficult than it might otherwise have been.[47] Krenek continued his embrace of the twelve-tone method, albeit unsystematically, in his next song cycle, *Durch die Nacht* (Through the Night [1931]), a setting of seven poems by the acerbic Viennese satirist Karl Kraus. In exile in the United States, he persevered with the twelve-tone technique with virtuoso flair and wit in his *Fünf Lieder nach Worten von Franz Kafka*, Op. 82 (1937–38). By way of illustrating both characteristics, in the second song, *Kämpfte er nicht genug?* (Did he not struggle enough?), Krenek responds to the protagonist's existential plight with an economy of means in every way Kafka's equal. If one takes action, is anything truly gained? If one does not, is anything lost? Kafka's one-word answer is "Kaum" (hardly). Krenek reacts to the word with two forms of the twelve-tone row simultaneously in the piano's left and right hand, as if to say that in either action there is "hardly" any difference. Go in this or go in that direction: it all is the same.

Throughout this essay, the ways in which twentieth-century Lied composers turned to the genre to express human concerns continually have been stressed. "Song leads us home to where we have not yet been," George Steiner asserts.[48] Although written about song in general, Steiner's words are especially apt in characterizing the Lied. But do they describe twentieth-century Lieder? Moreover, can it be that a song from Krenek's *Reisebuch* relying on twelve-note technique even remotely appertains to leading a person home toward Enlightenment's self-synthesis? Are not a great many of the styles associated with twentieth-century music antithetical to the Lied, much less the ideas associated with *Heimat*?

The Lied in Switzerland: Othmar Schoeck

By way of moving in the direction of an answer to this last question, a brief look at the Op. 44 *Zehn Lieder nach Gedichten von Hermann Hesse* (1929) by the Swiss Othmar Schoeck proves instructive. This said, those with even passing familiarity with this composer's music may wonder whether his Lieder are compatible with such questions. At the start of his career, Schoeck frequently was compared to Wolf; some critics, in fact, dispensed with him as little more than the older composer's acolyte. Nonetheless, an argument can be made that his true measure is to be had more accurately by understanding his dual allegiance to the old and new. On the one hand, Schoeck continually was drawn to vocal composition with six operas (the *New Grove's* count) and some 300 Lieder written over sixty years.[49] On the other, despite his nationality, until his later years he evinced a preference for setting German poets. In contrast to Krenek, who, when not setting his own texts, preferred those by his contemporaries, Schoeck felt most at home with poets from the late eighteenth- and nineteenth-century lyric tradition, among them Claudius, Goethe, Heine, Eichendorff, and Mörike. With the chief exception of his ten Lieder on poems by his friend and fellow Swiss Hermann Hesse, only in his late fifties did Schoeck turn to poets from his own country with any sustained enthusiasm. Schoeck completed *Unter Sternen*, Op. 55, a cycle of twenty-three songs on poems by Gottfried Keller in 1943, while the Zurich poet Heinrich Leuthold, several of whose poems had been sent to him by Hesse, inspired the song cycle for voice and harp (or piano) *Spielmannsweisen* as well as *Der Sänger*, both of which date from 1944; in 1946, Schoeck composed *Das stille Leuchten* to poems by Conrad Ferdinand Meyer.[50]

Schoeck looks longingly toward the past and sometimes seems enmeshed in it to the point of not being a true member of his age, a trait he evidently shares with Richard Strauss. Schoeck does, after all, end his Op. 20 *Lieder nach Gedichten von Uhland und Eichendorff* (1910) with a setting of Eichendorff's *Nachruf* (Obituary), the central strophe of which states: "What now is the point of singing here and in solitude, when all have departed from us who took pleasure in our song?"[51] Of course, Schoeck did continue to sing and, despite his veneration of the past, there is another side to this easily misunderstood composer, one that calls into question the usefulness of the summation made by his friend and first biographer Hans Corrodi, who labeled him the "last Romantic."[52] Like many who lived in the twentieth century, Schoeck may have found the plethora of stylistic possibilities overwhelming; if so, he only rarely was creatively overwhelmed. Moreover, he does not hide the fact that he is searching for a place within the tide of eclecticism then enveloping composers. Instead, he makes his search a part of his aesthetic, not at the expense of artistic coherence or command of his craft, but rather in such a way that the listener is caught up in the music's unfolding process.

Like Krenek in his *Reisebuch*, Schoeck in his ten Hesse songs is impelled by something more than what is at hand in the here and now. The texts call variously for the coming together of heaven and earth, of two lovers, of the lone individual and humanity, of the child with its mother. The union of such extremes in part explains why Hesse's poetry juxtaposes the presumably prosaic and professedly profound. Schoeck's music contains polarities, too, given that he conjoins the Lied's archetypal lyricism with free ranging post-Romantic tonality and twentieth-century atonality. At the conclusion of the fourth song, *Abends* (Evenings), Hesse's poem tells of weaving "from past afflictions a playful poem," of divining the sense of moon and stars, of going "with them, no matter where." Throughout the Lied, the piano engages in episodes of canonic exchange between the left and right hands at the rate of only an eighth-note; the episodes regularly recur, yet at continuously changing pitch levels from the time before, a move that gives them a dual sense of reassuring predictability and unsettling randomness in keeping with Hesse's text. By the final song, *Vergänglichkeit* (Passing), Hesse's ultimate goal is clear: release in death, a topic with a venerable history in German literature.[53] Happily, neither poet nor composer gives in to distressing sentimentality. Just as the leaf falls to the ground and replenishes the earth, so death effects a circular return to origins. In seeming agreement with the text, the Lied – at least in the piano part – three times seduces the listener into believing that it is cast according to tried and true strophic design. But just as death's journey does not lead one back to infancy, Schoeck's music eschews the literal return of strophic form in favor of an ever-continuing expansion of motives given to the piano at the start – a vivid encapsulation of the process expressed in the Lied's title "Passing." In a world of constant volatility where everything eventually drifts away, the poet's last image is of "die ewige Mutter" (the faithful mother) whose "finger writes our names in the fleeting sky." With this, the music at last abandons its agitated chromaticism, coming to rest in the final measure on the one unalloyed concord in the entire song, a D major triad.

Schoeck, in pursuing moon and stars "no matter where," and Krenek, in his journey over the Austrian Alps, are by no means haphazardly drawn to lofty destinations. From on high one can see further not only literally but also metaphorically. To ascend to the summit is to commune with the divine. Only on high can a person see into her or his own inner self. Anton Webern was particularly drawn to mountaintops, a fact not without significance for the Lied as well as the Lied's compatibility with the many stylistic sea changes wrought in the twentieth century. For Krenek, Schoeck, and Webern, musical modernism and the Lied are compatible. The fact that all three composers provide evidence for this unanimity while setting texts that deal with extremes of verticality once more would appear to relate to the Enlightenment *Bildungsweg.* As will be recalled, Schiller declared his allegiance to a "*higher* harmony." So, too, does Krenek in the ninth song of his *Reisebuch, Rückblick* (Looking Back). "Living in days of unrest is our lot as city dwellers," Krenek's text reads, and the music breaks into knotty canon. Thereafter the text reveals that "Life as we find it in the mountains fully reveals the intangible sources of being," whereupon Krenek restores his music to homophonic clarity.

Diverse paths

In a recent study, Julian Johnson brilliantly demonstrates the importance of mountains as a locus of inspiration for Webern in general, his work as a Lied composer, and his move away from the means of musical expression associated with late Romanticism. Krenek, who knew Webern well, noted: "If a listener is inclined towards associative ideas, he might easily find that Webern's music evokes the clear, thin air and the formidable, tense silence of the very high mountain summits."[54] Space does not allow for a full exegesis on Johnson's explication. Suffice it to say, Webern was a passionate mountain climber and his fondness for "da oben," or up there, may be thought of literally as a heightened form of nature, one that Webern reflected in his own music. Most pertinent is a remark Webern made in his *The Path to the New Music* (1932–33). Commenting on the passage to atonality in such works as Schoenberg's Three Piano Pieces Op. 11, the younger composer revealed: "When one moved from the white to the black keys, one wondered, 'Do I really have to come down again?' "[55] As Johnson observes, "atonality, it seems, was for Weber also a kind of 'up there.' "[56] That Webern discloses this in a study called *The Path to the New Music* is triply fascinating and, in the event, suggests a possible refinement of Johnson's impressive interpretation. Not only does the path relate to a person making their way through an arduous mountain landscape, it also may be seen as a symbolic representation of the path "made level with toil" that, as Hegel describes it, is the *Bildungsweg*. The "length of this path has to be endured" if the harmony of Enlightenment is to ensue, Hegel insists. As is now well known, Webern's own path to new music was equally arduous. Yet the journey was more than this. It was a quest for self-actualization repeatedly made through the medium of song. With Lieder, Webern launched both the atonal and the twelve-tone phases of his career. While composing his *Fünf geistliche Lieder* (1921–22), Op. 15, Webern wrote out and used a twelve-note row, his first surviving twelve-note sketch. Is it coincidence that the song in question is entitled *Mein Weg geht jetzt vorüber*, my path now crosses over? The fact that Webern abandoned the twelve-tone version is significant; as Anne Chatoney Shreffler has observed, Webern's move to the twelve-note method was anything but effortless or instantaneous.[57] In keeping with

Hegel's *Weg*, it was accomplished by exertion and took time. Revealingly, Webern eventually crossed over within the medium of song in the Op. 17 Lieder (1924–25).

Like Krenek and Schoeck, Webern does not turn his back on nature; he seeks an intensified form of nature. Rising to the challenge of Krenek's *Jonny spielt auf* – of how to live in the modern world yet not lose one's self – Webern participates in that world by blending old and new. By means of the former he continues yet distills ideas harking back to the late eighteenth and nineteenth centuries. This Webern attempted not through the imitation of nature by musical means but through "genuine aesthetic mediation."[58] Inspired by his mountain wanderings, Webern's move toward atonality and serialism brought with it a new sense of time – one taking on the appearance of boundlessness – while breaking the constraints of musical gravity, that is to say tonality. As Webern wrote to Alban Berg in 1925, he wanted his music to "grasp the ungraspable," although he admits this is a "vain struggle."[59] And so, the Lied continues to meet at the crossroads of nature, even if that crossroads has been placed at a higher level. The sonic result is that Webern rethinks what a Lied is from the inside out: it is transfigured.

The Lied was transformed in other ways, too. While this story remains to be told in fuller detail elsewhere, it can be hinted at here. In the hands of a number of composers coming to maturity in the 1920s, the Lied begins to intersect with popular culture in a way that too long has been swept under the musicological carpet. Not alone in this, Eisler provides a convenient focal point. Following his Op. 2 *Sechs Lieder* (1922), which he sent to his teacher Schoenberg along with thanks to Webern from whom Eisler sometimes received instruction, Eisler begins to chart different compositional waters. This especially is to be seen in his choice of texts. In Op. 2, which is dedicated to Webern and indebted to the Second Viennese School, Eisler sets the eighteenth-century poet Matthias Claudius and Hans Bethge, whose German translations of Chinese poems, *Die chinesische Flöte*, Mahler turned to in *Das Lied von der Erde*. Eisler's next set of songs is his Op. 11 *Zeitungsausschnitte* (1925–27), which, as its title makes clear, derives from newspaper scraps: lonely-hearts ads, children's songs, school surveys, a supplement to a novel. The deceptive triteness of the texts provokes a tug of war with Eisler's music, still largely in the style of Op. 2. It may be that Eisler intends this as a distancing stratagem from Schoenberg, with whom he famously broke in March 1926. The motivation for both may be related: Eisler's growing Marxist leanings, which in due course saw him taking up the Communist cause in earnest. A 1927 article by Eisler in the Communist party newspaper, *Die rote Fahne* (The Red Flag), provides a glimpse of how his politics influenced his views on music. "Modern music has no audience; no one wants it," he affirms. "The proletariat views it with indifference as the private concern of well-bred persons . . . In spite of all its technical refinement, it is

Example 13.4 Eisler, *Liebeslied eines Grundbesitzers* (from *Zeitungsausschnitte*, Op. 11), mm. 8–17

redundant, since it is lacking in ideas as well as a community."[60] Eisler uses the Lied to scrutinize not only German culture but also German song itself. The piano part in the second personal ad (song 8) contains a quotation from Wagner's *Tristan und Isolde* anticipating the quotation from the same work in *Die Rundköpfe* by a decade (see above, p. 288); lest one miss the reference, Eisler explicitly draws attention to his Wagner reference in his score. Not the "Tristan chord" this time but rather the chromatically rising figure that follows it, the quotation prefaces the ad's imploration: "I am looking for understanding, inner spiritual life" (Ex. 13.4). Eisler's ironical appropriation annuls the possibility of either. His message? "Turn to the monuments of yesterday's high art if you will. You will not find there what you are searching for."

Eisler's commitment to the proletariat reached its apex in the 1930s in his so-called *Massenlieder*, or workers' songs, composed for solo voice or chorus in a deliberately accessible style. A sampling of some of the titles of these songs proves instructive: *Solidaritätslied* (Solidarity Song, 1931), *Lied der Arbeitslosen* (Song of the Unemployed, 1929–31), *Lied der deutschen Rotarmisten* (Song of the German Red Army Soldiers, 1932), *Das Einheitsfrontlied* (United Front Song, 1934). Such directly appealing tunefulness and unencumbered rhythmic élan bore future fruit in the songs composed for the many plays on which he collaborated with Brecht. Both characteristics left their mark on the composer's *Hollywooder Liederbuch*, arguably the most extraordinary if poorly known song collection of the twentieth century. Eisler's work in all three of these categories – music for the masses, songs for plays, and high-art Lieder – is significant because it reveals the inventive way he fuses high and low art. Other composers who worked along similar lines include the young Hindemith, Krenek, Kurt Weill, and Dessau. It remains to be seen to what degree the Lied influenced or was influenced by the type of song familiar in revues and cabaret. The latter, especially, was a medium famous for biting satire in support of social causes and one that allowed star performers such as Marlene Dietrich to use song to experiment with sexual roles and female self-determination. This, too, is a story for another time.

In the meantime, it is worth recalling that in one way or another all of the Lieder examined in this chapter mirror a kind of musical melting pot while at the same time they bear witness to a melding of tradition and innovation. The cynic might concede that it is this dual direction that allowed the Lied to endure to the extent it did in the face of less elitist modes of artistic expression. But the Lied did not simply endure. Here the past yields a model. Beethoven emerged from a compositionally lean period with his path-breaking song cycle *An die ferne Geliebte* in 1816. Schumann broke through personal and artistic crises with a flood-tide of more than 100 Lieder in 1840. In like manner, in the twentieth century Schoenberg, Webern, Krenek, Eisler, and others took up German song when striking out in untried ways. Such a view stands to alter fundamentally the Lied's status within the history of twentieth-century music. Many have claimed that the genre expired beneath the ashes of World War II. Others, noting Classical music's ebbing fortunes throughout the century, have ignored the Lied altogether. Brief although this chapter has been, it nonetheless has demonstrated that in the twentieth century the Lied was not forgotten. Until the story of the Lied's participation in twentieth-century music – only partially recounted here – is told in greater detail, an understanding of music during this uneasy yet exhilarating age will remain incomplete. As long as that is so, knowledge of twentieth-century life will remain fragmentary, too, for the Lied everywhere reflects human concerns.

PART FIVE

Reception and performance

14 The circulation of the Lied: the double life of an artwork and a commodity

DAVID GRAMIT

The Lied has a kind of double nature, born of the interaction of poetry and music. This is scarcely an original observation; indeed, it is a truism so familiar that it would not bear repeating if not for its relevance to another sort of double life, one that has far less frequently received consideration: throughout its history, the Lied has existed both as an artistic genre and as a class of commodity, an object for sale in the marketplace. To be sure, this does not by itself set the Lied apart from many other forms of art within capitalist societies – and as we will see, the Lied's existence is closely bound up with a specific phase of capitalist production. That double life, however, is particularly revealing in the case of the Lied, whose status as a genuinely artistic genre long was contested precisely because its status as an all-too-viable commodity appeared to threaten its standing as art. Because of the Lied's location on the border between high art and popular music, a consideration of the ways in which it has circulated can reveal much, not only about the Lied per se, but also about the shifting nature of that border, which is less certain at the beginning of the twenty-first century than it has been since the boundary between high and low came into existence in the minds of the advocates of high art.[1]

To begin to explore the ramifications of the Lied's mode of circulation for its history, consider the moment that music history has traditionally identified as its origin. That moment, of course, is the act of creation that elevated the genre to art, conventionally symbolized by Schubert's composition of *Gretchen am Spinnrade* (D118) on 19 October 1814. John Reed succinctly summarizes the view: "the establishment of the Lied as an autonomous musical form was by far the greatest achievement of Schubert's early years."[2] Neither Schubert nor his friends, however, seem to have been particularly aware of the significance of that achievement. On the contrary, in 1816, when Schubert's friend Josef von Spaun composed a letter to Goethe to accompany a selection of Schubert's settings of Goethe's poems, his description of an ambitious and never realized publication plan for eight volumes of Lieder singled out the last two, settings of the songs of Ossian, as "excelling all others."[3] As Elizabeth Norman McKay notes, this observation was "rather tactless in the circumstances";[4] more than that, however, it flies in the face of what is by now nearly two centuries of critical judgment. The rarely performed Ossian settings are dominated by sprawling, cantata-like compositions in which passages of recitative and arioso alternate and which seem to defy expectations of concision and unity – they are precisely what "the Lied as an autonomous musical form" was not. But while one might easily be tempted to add to Spaun's diplomatic blunder an equally embarrassing aesthetic one, his judgment cannot simply be ascribed to the inferior artistic insight of Schubert's friends, for the composer himself seems to have felt similarly. One of the few early statements in which he evaluates one of his own songs provides what has struck most later authors as an equally wayward assessment. On 3 August 1818, he wrote to his friends from Zseliz (where he was temporarily employed as a music teacher to a branch of the Esterházy family) that "Mayrhofer's 'Solitude' [*Einsamkeit*, D620] is ready, and I believe it to be the best I have done, for I was without a care."[5] Again, few have agreed with Schubert's assessment. Weighing in at over four hundred measures, *Einsamkeit* is a meandering, episodic effort that is rarely mentioned except to point out the lapse in Schubert's judgment it represents.[6]

While it is true that a witness's apparent unawareness of an epochal event – or even that of the event's originator – does not necessarily undermine the significance of that event, it is surely disquieting that the few sources from Schubert's own circle that rank his efforts in song point with such conviction toward what are nearly unanimously regarded as also-rans. Here, I would argue, is precisely where a consideration of modes of circulation can provide insight. Although Spaun's letter to Goethe envisioned a whole series of publications, Schubert had in fact not published a single Lied when the letter was written. Even by the time of Schubert's later letter just one of his songs – he had by that time written well over three hundred – had appeared in print, and that in the unassuming form of a musical supplement to a travel almanac.[7] With that single exception, then, Schubert's songs did not yet exist in the print medium that was the basis of the Lied's public, economic life. Rather, they circulated in far more limited form among a circle of friends for whom they formed part of a convivial, literary-aesthetic cultivation. Under those circumstances, a sprawling but vividly illustrative setting by one of their own of an interesting text (in the case of *Einsamkeit*, also by one of the circle) could evoke as much enthusiasm as the numerous strophic songs or the retrospectively elevated lyric gems that he also had written, including, of course, *Gretchen am Spinnrade* – or, as these documents suggest, even more.

But Schubert's entry into the public musical world changed this situation dramatically. A report printed in a Dresden periodical early in 1821 attested to Schubert's growing reputation, although it noted that his songs still circulated only in (manuscript) copies.[8] The attention produced by a series of successful public performances of *Erlkönig*, however, created an opportunity to enter the realm of print, and by the end of 1821, Schubert had published 20 songs in seven separate opus numbers – but neither any of the Ossian settings nor *Einsamkeit* was among them, nor would those songs appear during Schubert's lifetime. Schubert's first independent publications – and by far the bulk of songs published during his lifetime – were far more in keeping with the aesthetic of "the Lied as an autonomous musical form." By those standards, pieces like *Einsamkeit* or the Ossian settings were simply deficient. As a Berlin reviewer of the posthumously published Ossian settings put it in 1830: "not a one of the pieces has a shape; we have a few lines of recitative, then a few lines of arioso, finally a section that can be called almost completely melodic but which does not shape itself into a clear form – in short, an accumulation of thoughts and details that do not form a whole."[9] Curiously, then, while Schubert's early song compositions ranged widely, the broadened exposure of publication would appear to have narrowed his preferences and moved them in the direction of the form he is said to have invented. Serious poetry dominates Schubert's early publications, just as it did the abortive plan Spaun described, but the musical forms of those settings are considerably more conventional by the standards of the early nineteenth-century Lied than the songs he and Spaun singled out before publication was a real possibility.[10]

This episode merits attention not only because it serves as a salutary warning against the illusions of simplistic developmental clichés, but also because it suggests something essential about print as a mode of circulation. Publication, like concert performance, creates a *work* identified with a composer's name, excising it from the circumstances in which it originated and bringing with it expectations of wholeness, of closure – precisely what the Berlin reviewer found lacking in the Ossian settings. And in the case of Lieder, a large, preexisting discourse (to be sure, not primarily of Viennese origin, but nonetheless circulating throughout German-speaking Europe) ensured that standards of relative simplicity and compactness would further discipline the aspiring composer entering the public musical sphere (see the discussion of these issues in chapter 2).

If that Lied discourse stressed the poetic aspect of the genre through its demands for faithful representation and lack of musical ostentation, the demands of wholeness and coherence brought by public exposure had musical consequences as well – both aspects of the Lied's *other* double nature interact with the demands of broadened circulation. Joseph Kerman long ago noted the significance of Schubert's piano introductions, observing that Schubert's later songs invariably included one, and that after 1821, when Schubert published an earlier song that had begun without such an introduction, he composed one for it.[11] Kerman further noted that Schubert's earlier songs without introductions represented "an economy that he lived to avoid studiously, and to regret," and while the former is demonstrably true, the latter oversimplifies the matter by failing to consider the changing modes of existence of the songs.[12] For if removal from the immediacy of informal social gatherings effectively doomed songs like *Einsamkeit*, it also had a significant, if less drastic, effect on the perception of the more compact, often strophic songs that remained viable: a song sung among one's friends can be introduced informally, perhaps emerging from the surrounding activities with the informal advance sounding of a singer's pitch, but when time came to publish some of those same songs, Schubert felt the need to establish a clearer boundary, to mark the opening of the work that would establish his name as an author.[13] With publication, what had originated as an informal, albeit written, activity was redefined as a claim to the permanence of a composed work.[14] From this perspective, the creation of the autonomous Lied-as-artwork appears not simply as an ahistorical stroke of individual genius, but as the product of the interaction of an individual aspiring to distinguish himself as a composer with both the generic conventions and the altered circulatory potential of what was for him a newly available medium. Viewing Schubert's activity in this way in no way denies his unique musical-poetic sensitivity, but rather places it in the context of the larger developments through which it found expression and which rendered it intelligible.[15]

Schubert, however, was a relative latecomer to the printed Lied, not only biographically but also historically; the expectations of print could exercise so powerful an impact because a long history of Lied publication stood before him. As Rolf Wilhelm Brednich has argued, the Lied became a print commodity as soon as print became an available medium in the late fifteenth century.[16] And the history of the more direct predecessor of Schubert's Lieder, the eighteenth-century solo song, is inseparably connected with the development of print capitalism as its medium of production. Ann Le Bar has described what she terms "the domestication of vocal music" in early-to-mid-eighteenth-century Hamburg, through which Italian opera lost its place first to cantatas for bourgeois domestic use and later to Lieder, as an "early, strong signal of the emerging national-cultural awareness of the *Aufklärung*."[17] That development occurred through a conscious appeal to middle-class patronage and a reconceptualization of vocal music as a product for domestic consumption rather than a public or aristocratic spectacle. The economic viability of that new use depended on printed media and an audience receptive to and capable of purchasing the products of those media, whether the periodicals in which the aesthetic nuances of a new art could be debated or the collections of songs produced in such profusion in the later eighteenth century. The national character of that development is also worth recalling; as Benedict Anderson observes in tracing the origins of nationalism, print capitalism not only "created unified fields of exchange and communication below Latin and above the spoken vernaculars," it also elevated one dialect within a language to the status of printed standard.[18] The Lied, adopting the new explosion of High German lyric poetry as its starting point, could thus become a national and nation-defining genre, circulating well beyond the local owing to its participation in print culture, but limited by the bounds of its language to the German-speaking realm. This at least was the case until the elevation of the Lied's music above its poetry, an elevation for which Liszt's Schubert transcriptions are both vehicle and evidence, transformed the Lied yet again, into a genre capable of transnational circulation.

In its earlier existence, however, the Lied's advocates held that it could meet the needs of a broad national populace while simultaneously benefiting its composers. I have elsewhere discussed how the North German composer J. A. P. Schulz's evocation of the *Lied im Volkston*, of songs conceived "more in the manner of the folk than in the manner of art," as well as his advocacy of popular music education, align him with the Enlightenment project of popular cultivation and position him as composer analogously to the beneficent enlightened ruler.[19] Schulz was also, however, keenly aware of the practical, print-based side of his efforts; the well-known programmatic statement of the second edition of the *Lieder im Volkston* (1785) is preceded by a far less familiar paragraph that serves as a reminder of the material basis of the Lied's existence:

> The approval with which the public has taken up my previous
> Lied-compositions has encouraged me in a pleasing way to give this new
> edition of my complete *Lieder im Volkston* all the perfection that I am
> capable of providing. Accordingly it will consist of several parts ... The
> theater-songs omitted [from this first part of the new edition] will make up
> the second part, expanded with many new songs, along with the best
> *Volkslieder* from my [earlier collection,] *Gesänge am Clavier*, after which I
> intend to have follow gradually several parts of the same size, as soon as a
> sufficient quantity of good song texts allows me to set them with such
> melodies as I believe I can offer to the public.[20]

The matter-of-factness of this passage can easily mask its significance: not only is it liberally sprinkled with language calculated to entice buyers with claims of novelty, scope, and quality, but it also begins and ends with the public, an anonymous but crucial entity whose approval motivates Schulz's efforts and for which his subsequent publications are intended. The print medium both brings about the separation that creates that generalized entity and enforces the composer's dependence on it.[21]

Of course, both the accessibility that Schulz sought and the public approval that he alludes to could become liabilities, as a long tradition of ambivalence reveals. In 1782, for instance, Johann Friedrich Reichardt, who shared Schulz's hope for a simple, widely circulated Lied, criticized the commercialization of art that publication seemed to require in the same article in which he outlined those hopes. The conflict was straightforwardly one between artistic value and commercial viability; "a single written page many a true artist gave me from his hidden store during my travels was often infinitely more valuable than twenty engraved and printed works of the same man, prepared for the constricted heart of his gracious buyer and the iron-mongering of his music printer."[22] Schubert, whose early reputation was built largely on Lieder and who by the end of his life received invitations from prestigious German publishers that identified Lieder prominently among the genres they most eagerly sought from him, famously wrote of a turn from song composition to instrumental genres and ultimately to the most prestigious of them. "In fact I intend to pave my way towards grand symphony in that manner," he remarked.[23] The hope of enhanced status implicit in this plan is reinforced by the memoirs of Schubert's friends, which are peppered with anecdotes of Schubert's being dismissed as a mere song composer and with nervous attempts to enhance their late friend's standing.[24] An echo of generic dismissal also surfaces in an equally familiar statement from Robert Schumann; in 1839, the year before his famous *Liederjahr*, he inquired of another composer whether "you are perhaps like me, who have never considered song-composition [*Gesangkomposition*] to be great art?"[25]

Schumann's question is pertinent precisely because of the Lied's ideal suitability to print circulation, a problem that scholars of German literature long have recognized when considering the vast expansion of the reading public in the eighteenth and nineteenth centuries.[26] If unrestricted, the public to whom Schulz had unselfconsciously appealed in the 1780s could, by the mid-nineteenth century, indeed jeopardize the artistic credibility of the genre. Brief and at least potentially widely accessible, the Lied threatened to melt into the sea of printed ephemera that a cultivated reader/listener could only see as failing to meet the standards of art. As Carl Dahlhaus, both a chronicler and defender of those cultivated standards, insisted, a difference in kind that did not exist in the case of genres like the string quartet or the symphony distinguished Lieder with claims to the status of art from "the vast output of nineteenth-century works which served an estimable social function but leave us under no compunction to include them in a history of music as art."[27] But musicology has been reluctant to recognize that such art itself served a social function – that of distinguishing those sensitive to its nuances from the growing and troublingly disordered masses of urbanized life. This is by no means to suggest that art, including a serious interest in

Lieder, was pursued merely as a superficial status symbol. On the contrary, at least in the ideology of the German bourgeoisie, a class dominated by civil servants and officials, depth and seriousness of cultivation were explicitly prized qualities, as Wilhelm von Humboldt, reformer of the Prussian civil service, made clear:

> Nothing is so important in a high-level official of the state as the complete conception he has of mankind and as the degree of intellectual clarity with which he ponders these questions and responds to them emotionally . . . There is nothing so important as his interpretation of the idea of *Bildung* [cultivation].[28]

In this context, the Lied could thrive as a concentrated example of and exercise in appreciating the intellectual and emotional depth required of the ideal official. Uniting the lyric exploration of subjectivity with what conventionally had come to be understood as the ability of music to speak directly to the soul beyond the mediation of words, the Lied could contribute to cultivation with a comprehensiveness that no other domestic genre could match.[29]

Such an ideology could assure a meaningful (if limited) circulation for the genre as art, even if it would never completely lose its associations with simplicity and popularity – indeed, they became institutionalized in the sub-genre of the *volkstümliches Lied*.[30] Both aspects of this generic situation are apparent in the 1877 memoirs of Maria Mitterbacher, the daughter of a Viennese lawyer and notary; she recalled in old age her introduction to Schubert's songs in her youth. Particularly noteworthy are Mitterbacher's oscillations between exclusivity and popularity and between serious quality and accessibility. She begins by describing early performances "before a small circle of true music lovers," but proceeds to note that Schubert's songs made an overwhelming impression "on the whole world at that time." This is difficult to comprehend now, she continued, because "in addition to the songs of Schubert, we also know those of Schumann, Mendelssohn, Brahms, Franz, etc., and are accustomed to the more or less beautiful renderings of the finest poems" – a clear evocation of the genre's artistic standing. And yet her account of the power of Schubert's songs is given in terms that hardly seem calculated to suggest high-minded seriousness. "Such music made an absolutely overwhelming impression on a lively girl in her teens," she writes, "who was accustomed to music and had a passion for poetry (I had just reached the age of fifteen and first love had awakened my heart)."[31]

These tensions reveal another, gendered facet of the Lied's circulation. Mitterbacher's account of the by-then-established value of the genre evokes the discourse of seriousness that guaranteed the Lied's cultural value; that discourse was based on an ideal of cultivation unambiguously intended to prepare men (like her father) for their public lives. By contrast, her description of the impact of Schubert's songs is couched in the conventionalized language of sentiment deemed appropriate to women, and especially to young girls – that is, precisely the most devalued segment of the literate public, the insufficiently rational consumers of ephemera and fashionable literature whose putatively indiscriminate voracity threatened the existence of serious art.[32] Once again, the Lied inhabits a border zone, and its domestic associations, small scale, and commercial accessibility ensured that it could not easily escape that zone. Association with the devalued feminine long kept it as a superficial counterpart to more serious genres, as, for instance, when the music critic Louis Ehlert used the contrast to elevate the instrumental Adagio by comparison with the Andante: "we require of an Adagio greater depth, grander proportions, and a broader outlook than we do of an Andante, which, it must be said, does not call forth and resolve a conflict, but rather is simply a 'Lied,' an instrumental song [*Gesang*]."[33]

If association with the feminine threatened the Lied's status, however, it also made it one of the genres in which activity by women composers was most visible and acceptable. As a result, a succession of women achieved public visibility as composers in whose output Lieder played a dominant role, among them Maria Theresia Paradis, Luise Reichardt, Emilie Zumsteeg, and Josephine Lang, in addition to the more familiar figures of Fanny Mendelssohn Hensel and Clara Wieck Schumann. Moreover, women whose principal activities lay in other areas could participate relatively freely in the composition of Lieder (as, of course, did numerous male amateurs) – among the most prominent examples are Anna Amalia, Duchess of Saxe-Weimar-Eisenach; the actress, Romantic author, and friend of Goethe Corona Schröter; Bettina von Arnim; and the poet Annette von Droste-Hülshoff. And so the Lied played a role in yet another ambivalent situation: it provided a creative outlet for women, who were strongly discouraged from other public creative activity, even while its position within the hierarchy of musical genres reinforced the ideologies that justified their exclusion.[34]

By the later nineteenth century, however, signs of the Lied's seriousness and canonic status are unmistakable, heralded by a weighty new mode of circulation: critical editions of the works of the great composers. Not surprisingly, the movement that began in 1851 with the Bach Gesellschaft edition initially had little to do with the composers most closely associated with Lieder. Instead, the editions initiated by Breitkopf & Härtel centered on the leading figures in the pantheon of official, public art, both sacred and secular – the first two decades of publication included only Bach, Handel, Palestrina, and Beethoven. Mendelssohn followed in 1874, and Schumann in 1880 (after Mozart and Chopin). The Schubert edition began only in 1884 (the same year as Grétry's). Once launched, however, the critical edition was

Example 14.1a Schubert, *Der König in Thule* (D367), mm. 21–24

er leert' ihn je - den Schmaus;

a powerful and highly visible certification of the prestige of those composers' Lieder and their distinction from those of their uncanonized contemporaries. If the recognition such editions accord is in large part retrospective – the acceptance of a composer's status must precede and justify the edition – their prestige and authority nonetheless verify and preserve the judgment they represent.

The monumentalization of the canonized Lied is apparent in a variety of other developments. Most familiar, perhaps, are Hugo Wolf's large collections of Lieder devoted to a single poet; not only do they draw weight from the authority of canonized literature (as suggested by his title *Gedichte* as opposed to the more ambiguous *Lieder*) but they also situate themselves as part of an established heritage through Wolf's scrupulous avoidance of texts he felt had already been set definitively by an earlier composer. Brahms could use the genre for the weightiest of texts (although the title *Ernste Gesänge* again avoids the lighter associations of the more common generic label) as well as more conventional Lieder, but distinguished both from his numerous folksong settings. A reflexive sense of participating in a genre with a distinguished past informs the songs of Richard Strauss, as for instance when in *Zueignung* he refers subtly but unambiguously to a textually related passage in Schubert's setting of Goethe's "Der König in Thule" (D367). (The text of Schubert's Lied [Example 14.1a] reads in translation: "he emptied it [the cup given him by his late lover] at every feast." The text of Strauss's [Example 14.1b] reads: "and you blessed the drink" [from the preceding line's "amethyst cup"].) And finally the Lied, originally, of course, a domestic and chamber genre, became a more visible presence in concert performance than it had ever been.[35]

The most revealing indication of the position of the Lied within high musical culture, however, may be that provided by Arnold Schoenberg early in the new century. In a 1912 essay on music–text relationships, he insisted

Example 14.1b Richard Strauss, *Zueignung*, Op. 10, No. 1, mm. 16–17

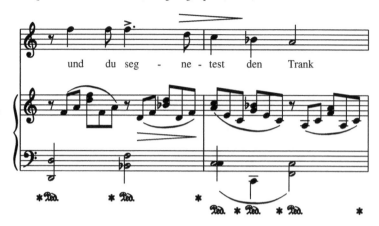

that the meaning of vocal music was fully conveyed through its musical structure despite (and in explicit opposition to) a long tradition of viewing such music as illustrating the text in a sometimes painfully literal manner. Schoenberg's final example is particularly relevant here:

> A few years ago I was deeply ashamed when I discovered in several Schubert songs, well-known to me, that I had absolutely no idea what was going on in the poems on which they were based. But when I had read the poems it became clear to me that I had gained absolutely nothing for the understanding of the songs thereby, since the poems did not make it necessary for me to change my conception of the musical interpretation in the slightest degree. On the contrary, it appeared that, without knowing the poem, I had grasped the content, the real content, perhaps even more profoundly than if I had clung to the surface of the mere thoughts expressed in words.[36]

Schoenberg's insistence on interpretive depth and on grasping the whole is not in itself a novelty, nor is his limitation of real insight to a select few ("The capacity of pure perception is extremely rare and only to be met with in men of high calibre" [142]). The superficiality that Schoenberg criticized, however, was symptomatic for him of an overly comfortable, self-satisfied bourgeois culture – precisely the audience that might revel in the recognition of such details as the link between Strauss's intimate effusion and Schubert's strophic setting of one of Goethe's most familiar ballads.[37] Over against that comfortable reception within literate culture, Schoenberg advanced the ideal of a deep, structural, and essentially *musical* hearing that grasped the whole as the ultimate validation of a genre whose status as art he never questions. Schoenberg, in fact, makes no distinction whatsoever between listening to Lieder and listening to Wagner's music dramas or Beethoven's symphonies, and this flattening out of generic differentiation finds its way into Schoenberg's own output as well. One searches in vain for signs of the tension between the popular and the elevated that had been pivotal to the Lied's history in such works as his settings from Stefan George's *Buch des hängenden Gärtens*, Op. 15. When Schoenberg sought to evoke vocal forms with popular associations, he would turn, as in *Pierrot lunaire*, to a very different tradition, that of the cabaret song.[38] For Schoenberg, the Lied had found its way irrevocably into the canon of the great and serious.

Still, despite Schoenberg's deliberately provocative stance, his insistence on the profundity of canonized Lieder aligned him at least to that extent with the "official" literary-musical culture that had canonized them. Both the modernist avant-garde and the conservative culture of classical music, however, would face in the twentieth century modes of circulation that challenged the very basis of their claims to authority: recording and the electronic media. And the Lied, more closely linked to the medium of print than any other classical genre, would have the basis of its existence more fundamentally shaken than at any time in its history.

Although the phonograph was invented in 1877, not until the early decades of the next century did recorded music begin to circulate widely. When it did, Lieder must have seemed a natural candidate for recording, suitable both in their modest performing forces and in their brevity to the limits of early recording technology. And yet the greater public visibility and broader popularity of opera meant that the latter offered a larger potential market for commercial recordings, and operatic excerpts indeed dominate early recordings.[39] Still, recording could provide a vehicle for continuing the monumentalization of the Lied that the critical edition had begun, and the Hugo Wolf Society recordings of 1931–38, Dietrich Fischer-Dieskau's near-complete recordings of the Lieder of composers like Schubert, Schumann, and Wolf, and more recent projects like the Hyperion Schubert Edition all testify to the longevity of that project.[40]

But it was not through monumentalizing the canon that recording had its greatest impact. To consider its other effects, though, I must draw attention to characteristics of recording that may seem transparently obvious, but that merit closer consideration than they conventionally have been given. Like print, recording changes music from a transitory phenomenon to a repeatable one, but unlike a printed work requiring the realization of performers, a recorded one preserves and makes repeatable not only "the music itself" but also the nuances of a particular performance. Consequently, recording, despite numerous attempts to use it to disseminate the classical canon, is a format whose primary medium of exchange aligns itself with performers and performances rather than works.[41] It is therefore most likely no coincidence that the final freezing of the classical canon – including the Lied repertory – occurred simultaneously with the rise of recording, because the performer's nuances are far more apparent when one can compare innumerable recordings of, say, Schumann's familiar *Mondnacht* than when one is faced with the challenge of coming to terms with an unfamiliar new song. In the case of the Lied this same priority of the performance severed the link between the Lied's prestige and the bourgeois literary culture that Schoenberg saw as outworn and complacent more effectively than Schoenberg's own protests could have hoped to do, even if he would hardly have approved of the authority of the star performer of received repertory that replaced it. But replace it it did, and such publications as the 1936 "Concert Edition of Schubert's Songs," selected and edited by Richard Tauber and featuring a full-page photo of the singer on its cover, only anticipate the innumerable later recordings of Lieder graced with full color cover photographs of the performer.[42] In this context, it is not surprising that one of the Lied's rare moments of visibility in the post-World War II critical canon comes about by means of a discussion of the nuances of performance, in the comparison of the singing of Charles Panzéra and Fischer-Dieskau with which Roland Barthes exemplified his concept of "the grain of the voice."[43]

In another, less familiar essay, Barthes characterized the status of the Lied (especially of the canonic repertory "of Schumann and Schubert . . . the incandescent core of romantic song") as "by nature uncertain: out of date without being repressed, marginal without being eccentric."[44] The antiquarian marginality that Barthes presents as an essential characteristic of the genre, however, can better be understood as a result of its historical place in a society in which multinational media conglomerates have replaced national print industries. To an extent, the Lied shares its marginal standing with the entire classical canon. Although recording has vastly broadened the available variety of such music and made that repertory more widely accessible than ever before, the medium cannot change – and indeed has helped to bring about – a situation that Robert Fink has persuasively identified: "for the first time in a century, classical music has lost even its symbolic or ritualistic power to define hierarchies of taste within the larger culture."[45] To explore the origins and implications of this development is far beyond the scope of this essay, but its relevance to the Lied and its prospects motivate my final considerations.

First, it seems likely that, owing to its traditional location at the border between the popular and the serious, the Lied was particularly vulnerable in this redefinition of musical culture. I have already suggested that recording undermined the genre's link to authoritative print culture, but, as Simon Frith has argued, recording also fundamentally altered the nature of the popular. It "enabled previously unreproducible aspects of performance – spontaneity, improvisation, etc. – to be reproduced exactly and so enabled

Afro-American music to replace European art and folk musics at the heart of western popular culture."[46] The Lied is thus doubly cast adrift, its validation through the authority of literary culture obscured by a medium that elevates instead star performers, and its ties to the popular rendered incomprehensible by a fundamental transformation of listeners' stylistic points of reference. The genre can apparently hope for little but the recognition that Barthes accords it as quaintly marginal.[47]

But recording alone did not create the cultural landscape in which we and the Lied currently find ourselves. I have argued that nationally based market capitalism, paradoxically coupled with an often anti-capitalist ethic of service and personal cultivation, provided the context in which the Lied developed and thrived. But the multinational capitalism and globalization of the more recent past have given rise to a very different culture, characterized by an ideology of unbounded desire and consumption (at least among the minority of the world's population that reaps its material benefits), and that ideology is inimical, if not to the Lied's survival – for a tiny niche market is still a market – then certainly to its cultural relevance. For the aesthetic concomitant of *this* socio-economic order is what Fink, drawing on Frederic Jameson, has summarized as "the repudiation of depth," a willed flatness and banishment of hierarchy and concealed significance.[48] There could hardly be a genre more ill-suited to this aesthetic than one so bound up with interiorized subjectivity and revelation of the depth and inner meaning of poetic texts.

On what appeal, then, can the Lied draw, in a culture that would apparently deny the basis of its existence? Barthes's "grain of the voice" points in the direction of a kind of connoisseurship of the surface, of vocal quality, that at least would align the use of the genre with the tendencies of the medium through which it primarily circulates, even if it is not without a nostalgia that recognizes that the moment of both the genre and its artists is past.[49] That nostalgia becomes the entire justification for the Lied's survival in this remarkable statement by Fischer-Dieskau:

> Today's artist, it seems, has lost the inclination to feel responsible for
> humanity. The singer's voice, however, will remain responsible, and
> symbolically so, by representing the most direct expression of the harmony
> of form and content, of husk and kernel . . . The interpreter as a kind of
> builder of bridges to the new that is to come – whatever name it may go
> under – is left with the glorious task of preserving, by means of immaculate
> performance, the existing creations of the masters.[50]

A comparison of such retrospective appreciations with the roles accorded the Lied in the past reveals how fully it has been transformed by the current conditions of its existence. A genre that many in eighteenth-century

Germany hoped might be the key to the cultivation of an enlightened, aesthetically sophisticated populace, and that many in the nineteenth held to be an indispensable part of the cultivation of a well-developed human being and citizen, has by the beginning of the twenty-first century become something very different. Although it continues to exercise a peculiar fascination for its devotees (among whom I do not hesitate to count myself), it forms a relatively arcane part even of the already marginal field of classical music. At present, then, the Lied is distant both from the vanguard of contemporary art and from the interests of the multinational music industry, just as the vision of the sensitive, individualized, and national bourgeois subjectivity that it supported is remote from the internationalized consumer culture of late capitalism.

15 The Lied in performance

GRAHAM JOHNSON

Perhaps the editor of this volume expects a different article from me than the one that I have written. (Some years ago, an English professor of music informed me that asking performers to contribute to books such as this always resulted in headaches.) But one can read elsewhere about the history of Lied reception, and how important singers – Schubert's friends Johann Michael Vogl and Karl Freiherr von Schönstein (1797–1876), Brahms's Julius Stockhausen (1826–1906), Adolphe Nourrit (1802–39) in France – carried forward the torch of an art form that began as a domestic phenomenon and went on to conquer the world. A glance at Ernst Challier's 1885 *Großer Lieder-Katalog* is enough to show that the Lied was big business at the end of the nineteenth century. Names now long forgotten rub shoulders with the immortals in astonishingly lengthy lists of settings that have vanished without a trace. In consulting Challier we are, after all, scanning a catalogue where great Lieder and pop songs of the time jostle with each other for attention. At this stage the Lied was still all-encompassing, still nominally something for everyone. Once popular music achieved its own momentum and was hived off to its own discographies and discotheques, we are left with the songs that really matter, the songs that survived. But to whom do these songs matter, and how much? In my case, the question is not merely rhetorical: my living as a concert accompanist depends on that continuing interest.

I daresay that even the greatest Lied enthusiast, when divested of her or his rose-colored Schubertian Brille, is aware that many people view the art form as a formidably highbrow category (German) of an esoteric sub-section (song) of an embarrassingly emotional corner (vocal music) of an already doomed species (classical music). In these times, when even mainstream symphonic repertoire is under economic siege, it is cause for some optimism that there is a market for a symposium of this kind; enough people still seem to want to listen to Lieder. It is heartening that the university presses remain supportive; but piano-accompanied song needs a broader base in order to survive, and commentators almost certainly enjoy a false sense of security about its future. We have come to accept the Lied's Cinderella status as inevitable (in contrast to its rich sister Op'ra who has a standing invitation to the bawl). More dangerously, we even may have begun to enjoy the fact that its seeming inaccessibility to the common listener has given it the glamor of a minority cult. There are countless artistic disciplines, after all, which are unconnected with the realities of everyday life, and the university publications devoted to these are increasingly arcane manifestos of power-politics within academia more concerned with internal point-scoring and scholarly one-upmanship than with communicating with the outside world.

Music, however, by its very nature, encourages more vital, less marginal, attitudes. And those who write about music should surely aspire to connect with both performer and public in a way that makes a practical difference to how the music *sounds.* Fortunately Lieder performance remains a living thing, but by no great or comfortable edge. It does not help that the German Lied of today is no longer a real force to be reckoned with, at least not in the way it influenced the world of music during its apogee. This contemporary area is another sub-section of a field of study which, by the very nature of the quality of music written by Schubert, Schumann, Brahms, and Wolf, remains a phenomenon of the nineteenth century, certainly in the consumer's mind. From the point of view of commerce alone, we should perhaps be grateful that these masterworks are more likely to retain public favor precisely because they are part of the beloved German Classic-Romantic tradition. But can we be sure of this? Almost all of my musical life I have thought of myself as being devoted to the music of the "last century"; that the Lied has overnight become music from "the century before last" lends a different perspective, as if watching something fading away into the distance. I was born a year after the death of Richard Strauss, and now my students are born a year after the death of Benjamin Britten, a composer whom I knew but who seems to them to be an equally mythical figure. In this way, European art song is brushed with the fairy-tale magic of the past. These *märchenhaft* qualities are just what make the Lied appealing to its admirers but they appear increasingly irrelevant to the majority.

As always, economics plays a crucial part in determining the future. Most universities are a long way from concert halls where enough customers pay to hear art songs. Ardent student recitals fade into nostalgic memories as graduates go into the outside world and find that Lieder singing, for all its beauties, pays very few of the bills. Recital dates are rare because audiences are scarce; there is little sign that the abundance of commentary about German song is reflected by a growth industry in actual performance. The authors of this book can only hope that somehow and somewhere their discoveries and observations will filter through to the lucky few who are permitted to sing Lieder on a regular basis, and that the vitality of the interchange will be like a blood transfusion to the patient whose actual state of health is difficult to determine. It would be marvelous if we could simply believe that the power and greatness of the music itself would insure the art song's survival. But in the light of the dwindling number of live recitals, even in the bigger metropolitan centers, it is the recording industry which is now mainly responsible for dissemination and revitalization: the power of commerce insures that it is the human voice, linked to a marketable personality, which is best placed to make new friends for the Lied. It seems that the only people with the ability to save it from extinction in practical terms are those with attractively vibrating vocal cords.

The possessors of these instruments are a fascinating but motley bunch; some of the most gifted singers I know are utterly uninterested in any books of a theoretical or musicological nature. Their curiosity about music journals is limited to the possibility of a review of one of their performances or recordings therein. Those who think a lot about the Lied (academics, some performers, and informed listeners) want to hear it sung with knowledge and understanding, and with an awareness of its historical context. The general public, as always, wants to hear vocal music sung *beautifully* (whatever that means, and however many spectra of personal taste that adverb covers), where Lieder must take its chances with all the other genres jostling for the buyer's attention in a dumbed-down musical environment. The triangle made up of town, gown, and performer – between the money to buy (and thus support) the Lied, the knowledge to explicate its subtleties, and the hands-on ability to sing and play it – seems to me to mark out the battle lines for survival in the modern world. Is this a covered-wagon laager to defend song from its detractors, or is there a temptation to turn the guns inwards? The danger in pursuing an interest in Lieder is that an ever smaller number of people will find themselves going round in song-singing circles of ever-decreasing circumference. Even German-speaking lands are no longer the special case they once were: the *Liederabend*, once an inviolable tradition, is also under threat, and the lack of a language barrier (once cited as the main reason why German song could never become very popular in English-speaking lands) seems to make little difference to the size of audiences, or the enthusiasm of reception. Loving the Lied (or not) is a state of mind that seems increasingly independent of national boundaries. Age, however, is a more powerful factor: the majority of the faces that one sees in song-recital audiences are not in the first flush of youth; most young people in the audience are either aspiring performers or connected in some way with the business.

So far in this book we have heard from the think-tank, the intellectual elite who devote a great deal of thought to the subject: my job, on the other hand, is to face audiences on a daily basis peddling the wares that have been exquisitely discussed in these pages. This is not to say that performances, and some good ones, have not been given by the distinguished scholars who are this companion's authors. But they do not have to rely more or less solely, as I do, on the precarious wages of itinerant music-making to pay the bills; the fickle nature of my business is that the discovery of a Lieder-singing tenor is difficult enough, but Lieder-performing tenure for a pianist (in my country at least – the United States is kinder in this regard) is a hopeless dream. The observations that follow are thus those of a blue *colla voce* worker rather than a properly accredited scholar. I have been privileged, however, to teach fleetingly at various universities (I am writing this essay during a master-class stint at Bloomington, Indiana) and I think I understand the reason for the gap between the scholastic and performing cultures: I have seldom encountered a *first-class* singer who cares much about musicology, and I have seldom encountered a musicologist who understands much about the way a singer's mind works. Each may think they do, but there is a real communication problem between university life (where earnest and well-meaning student performances are the yardsticks by which excellence is measured) and the hard world outside the cloisters where the battle-scarred professional struggles to make her or his mark. Vocal students, the divas of tomorrow, may well obediently work on end-of-term projects with their music professors, but when they become world-famous singers outside the academy their attitudes change dramatically. (Many an American singer begins his or her career in the music department of a university, but most European singers attend conservatories with an unashamed emphasis on practical music making at the expense of theoretical studies.) Yes, singers can be lazy and self-centered and incurious, luxuriating in their vocal gifts; but musicologists can be remote and impractical, more concerned with their papers and conferences than with reaching out to touch the lives of those they might help to perform more vividly.

The singer is a very special case in the world of music. Song accompanists, always trained in the first instance as pianists, and musically disciplined from an early age, lean more toward a respect for musicology. The link between academia and the singer of the concert stage has often been the pianist or coach. It would be too obsequious an image to cast my profession as a group of roving ambassadors and plenipotentiaries accredited to the courts of assorted vocal monarchs, but in some instances this is near the truth. The first myth to be disposed of, however, is that of the "stupid singer." I had to learn from the beginning of my professional life that singers are made differently from instrumentalists, certainly, but they are seldom stupid. On the contrary, they are wise in ways undreamed of by their listeners. To be in their company on a daily basis is to learn much, not always directly about music, but about life. In many instances singing is merely the second string to their bow. In Europe, singers who have taken a music degree are the exception rather than the rule. Most of them, if they go to university at all, study subjects that have nothing to do with music, before taking up the singing option as older postgraduates. Among my own regular colleagues degrees are to be found in modern languages (Dame Felicity Lott, for one) as well as biochemistry (Christopher Maltman), zoology and ornithology (Simon Keenlyside), or a doctorate in history (Ian Bostridge). Singers have already established a wide range of outside interests before they make their names as artists. To have discussed painting with Sir Thomas Allen is to realize his passion for the subject, and his ability on canvas (Dietrich Fischer-Dieskau, Gérard Souzay, and Brigitte Fassbaender also are painters, as was Lotte Lehmann); and Robert Tear is a leading authority on British watercolors. The most penetrating discussion I have ever had about English–Irish politics (of all things!) was with the late Lucia Popp, a woman of dazzling intelligence and intellectual insight. Other examples abound. To hear Anthony Rolfe Johnson – engaged with animal husbandry until the age of twenty-eight – talk about cows is to encounter real expertise, something matched by Bryn Terfel who is a proud landowner in Wales, and conversant with all the techniques of modern farming. Among the singers of today sporting distinctions are relatively common – singing is after all a very physical profession – and the image of the hopelessly large soprano or tenor is a stereotype encountered less and less, certainly in the world of song.

Singers can be remarkable people intellectually, and their musical gifts often seem to come as an "extra." But the "clever" singer should not be postulated as the truth to correct the myth of the stupid one. It is a sad fact that the singer who is *too* clever often lacks the necessary voice or vocal instincts to go to the top. The majority are decent, normally intelligent, hard-working musicians, grounded and earthed in the physical demands of their profession. (Show me a highly-strung singer and I will show you someone – however talented an interpreter – who struggles technically, his or her temperament in constant conflict with the physical demands of the job.) While some of the greatest musicological and instrumental work is done by older musicians in their seventies, a singer's span is a great deal shorter: by the time he or she has become established, a thirty-year career is an optimistic ambition rarely exceeded and often unattained. This places singing, of all the musical arts, in a category of its own. Like the dancer and the sportsman, the singer has to rely on his or her own body as an instrument, a body that is poignantly fallible and constantly degenerating. That the singing voice, even a healthily deployed one, will only be up to the demands of the job for a finite time concentrates the mind wonderfully: as Shakespeare might have said, "In the lay there lies no plenty / If one sings the Lied from twenty / Cords are stuff may not endure." The ability to live in the present, to celebrate the here-and-now and rejoice in a paean to nature, as long as it is permitted to last, is built into the temperament of the singing animal. As Goethe (who knew something about performers) says in

"Der Sänger": "Ich singe wie der Vogel singt, / Der in den Zweigen wohnet" (I sing as the bird sings / Who lives among the branches).

The last sentence may also be applied to certain great composers, Schubert among them. Vogl's famous remark about Schubert's "somnambulism," however patronizing, might be interpreted as a description of someone composing unselfconsciously, seemingly unburdened by technical considerations, having access to a mastery of form and content via a different route from other mortals. Benjamin Britten once told me that he read Hans Keller's technical analysis of the opera *Billy Budd* with genuine astonishment: "I had no idea of how clever I was supposed to have been." And I have lost count of the number of times I have heard singers complimented for all sorts of intellectual insights for which admirers of their performances have given them credit, while nothing of the sort was in their heads. Granted, the performance has been deep and profoundly felt, as well as wonderfully sung, but it is amazing how many different projections and diagnoses of *why* it was so successful might be imagined and described by the commentators. There are as many pathways to the Vienna of the *Liederfürst* Franz Schubert as there are to the Rome of the emperors.

In the case of many a singer, knowledge is replaced by something more visceral: instinct in bucketloads, instinct for what *sounds* and *feels* right. Experience has taught me to respect this in my colleagues, and even in myself. And Schubert's well-known patience with Vogl (who was a law unto himself in terms of his old-fashioned love of ornamentation) shows that the composer too respected the magic that only an imaginative and experienced singer can bring to a song. Many composers have been forced to sit back and listen in grateful astonishment as the experienced performer tackles their works. Of course the singer's instinct has to be schooled and refined by teaching and coaching, encouraged to grow and then cut down to size when necessary. But the miracle of being "musical" and of being at one with one's instrument and oneself, and thus with music that fits one's emotional and technical resources, is not to be underestimated. I have come across some dazzling cases where a singer can scarcely claim to have read a book from cover to cover – any serious book, not just a book about music – and still will be endlessly revealing and moving through an inherent ability to marry word with tone with conviction and honesty. Such singers need to be strong personalities: intellectually, they easily can be pulverized, and the "diva" persona often arises out of intellectual insecurity and a need to protect the center of individuality which must remain impervious to other people's well-intentioned tampering. The enlightened accompanist soon learns to respect something beyond book learning in such artists.

Such *artists*? Of course they are, but it would not be insulting to say that singers also are craftsmen, and that decisions which seem to be taken as a result of artistic deliberation often are arrived at as a result of more down-to-earth considerations than high art. When I first met Dame Janet Baker to rehearse Schumann's *Liederkreis* Op. 39 she insisted on a much slower and deliberate tempo for *Waldesgespräch* than the one to which I was accustomed. "I understand your tempo," I said. "You find the mood darker, more menacing at this speed." "Not at all," she replied. "It's just that I find it quite impossible to spit out the words "Es ist schon spät' at your faster tempo!" At the time I thought this was said to deflate, in the most polite way, any tendency on my part for wordy metaphysical discussion in mid-rehearsal; but now I see it as a simple reminder from a no-nonsense professional that singing is the art of the possible. And what is possible for one singer is not possible for another. Because no performance is ever definitive, I was quite free to play the song faster (it is marked *Ziemlich rasch* after all) for other people who felt comfortable with it. Another example of singing being the art of the possible is slightly more humorous because it has to do with human nature. I have never encountered a tenor (or baritone, come to that) with an impressive top A who declines to sing that note at the climax of Schumann's *Ich grolle nicht* and opts instead for the lower F. And I have met countless baritones with only an F at their disposal for that passage who assure me that the middle note of the chord is infinitely preferable from the musical point of view. Perhaps one day I will meet a singer with a ringing and exciting top A who declines to use that note in *Ich grolle nicht* on the grounds of interpretation, or because the F was probably Schumann's first thought as opposed to the later, higher *ossia*. But I am not holding my breath.

The moot point of transposition lies very much at the heart of the battle between musicology and practical music making. Much has been written about the significance of the composer's choice of key in any song, and no one can deny that this has played a crucial role in the work's creation. Of course it is pleasant and gratifying to hear songs in the composers' original keys, but in a milieu dominated by baritones we have to resign ourselves to transposition. (Those with absolute pitch admittedly find this more difficult.) Fischer-Dieskau would not have had a Lieder-singing career without his having shifted keys, and it is better, surely, to hear songs sung by a great singer in transposed keys than by uninteresting singers in the original ones. But I will now describe an instance when the musicologists imply that it is better for a singer *not* to sing a song in the original key. Having grown up with the Peters Edition versions of *Winterreise*, I initially reacted by welcoming the *Neue Schubert Ausgabe* version for middle voice, which transposes all twenty-four songs consistently one tone lower. As interesting as it might be to have a sequence of keys that follows Schubert's original, the fact is that this leaves a song like *Erstarrung* uncomfortably high for most baritones (Bb minor in the middle-voice transposition in the *Neue Schubert Ausgabe*, A minor in Peters) and more, importantly, *Der Lindenbaum* too low (D major in the NSA, E major in Peters). The august editors of the new edition have considered everything apart from the practical considerations that only working with singers over a long period can teach. *Der Lindenbaum* in its original key of E major is low for tenors; in D major higher baritones are digging for the bottom notes and there is not much possibility of rarefied heady magic in the floated higher passages. A baritone with a good control of *mezza voce* in the *passaggio* can make something unforgettable of this song in the key in which Schubert wrote it.

Because he understood this latter point that underestimated Schubertian Max Friedländer in the Peters Edition (of which he was editor) leaves the song in the original key in the volume for middle voice. If a good high baritone sings *Der Lindenbaum* in E major the audience will remember the radiance of the performance long after forgetting the more pedantic point that the singer has failed to preserve the original key-sequence of Schubert's cycle (that is if they ever realized it in the first place, a most debatable point). Keeping the key sequence the same in a transposed performance is a worthy academic consideration, but it is the singer's first responsibility to his public, and to himself, to create musical magic. Because the placement of each voice is subtly different, as is each singer's lung capacity and musical sensibility, there are many aspects of interpretation that must remain open and flexible as the singer and his or her pianist prepare for performance. "I can sadly see," Brigitte Fassbaender once said to me when I challenged her over some point in the printed score, "that you are an academic and a purist." Not at all, dear Brigitte, just attempting to tread the middle line between fanatical *Werktreue* (of which you do not approve) and living in the real world (where you have taught me much). All an accompanist can do, to adapt what Wilfred Owen wrote about being a poet, is warn.

We have all, at one time or another in our careers, opted for the excitement of chasing extremes and in the process forgotten the elusive golden mean. Schubert also went through phases of extravagant exploration "on the wild side," but these always were countered by another still, small voice that kept ever present a wider vision, a sense of proportion. Artists must always explore their artistic and personal limits but their aim must be to become centered, the only way to remain sane and functional in a world of artistic fantasy and unreality. It is the old contest between Dionysus and Apollo. Heaven knows how glamorous singers manage to placate both gods, but speaking as an accompanist I know that too much of the former and the pianist is a hot-head, little caring for the needs of his partners; too much of the latter and he is a cold fish, efficient but uninvolved.

Thinking about the problem of balance between voice and piano is a good starting point for an understanding of musical balance in general. *Am I too Loud?* Gerald Moore asked in his autobiography, but that is only half the question. I remember him coming backstage in the middle of a Queen Elizabeth Hall recital to tell me I was too *soft*. ("Looking forward to the start of your recital!" was his acid remark in the intermission.) If the pianist swamps his fellow artist with a barrage of sound the dangers are obvious; but too little sound and the singer feels under-supported, and the music lacks character and focus. Most student accompanists could afford, on almost any page of music, to play both more assertively *and* more softly, as they move between the valleys and hills of the song's terrain. It takes courage and experience to make these seismographical judgments. It is even possible, believe it or not, for the singer to sing too loudly for the pianist: there are delicate passages in certain piano parts which the composer meant momentarily to occupy the high ground of the listener's attention.

This particular definition of balance is only the beginning of rivalries between one viewpoint and another that require constant inner arbitration. What of that age-old conflict between words and music, for example? It seems to me an obvious thing to say that a Lieder singer must care for words and clear enunciation, but I well remember an English singer (an astute and distinguished one) who asked Sir Peter Pears for an honest opinion of his work. The kindly but frank reply (and the younger singer himself told me this, having come to agree with the verdict) could be reduced to the phrase: "Too many words, too much diction." Knowing when to throw words away in favor of a sensuous musical line, knowing when the ear will hear things without extra-pedantic insistence from tongue and teeth, is as much a part of the art of singing as spitting out the text ferociously when need be. (English-speaking singers, however, are apt to throw foreign words away in rather the wrong way, and need no further encouragement to do so!)

There also is constant controversy between atmosphere-painting with a broad brush across the whole canvas of the song, and word-painting relying less on pure voice than on the use of tiny touches of local color and effect (the latter is said by some critics to be a post-war phenomenon invented by Dietrich Fischer-Dieskau and Elisabeth Schwarzkopf, but it actually goes back to Schubert's favorite singer Vogl, whom some admired, and some deplored for this very reason). It is true that affectation and mannerism are a danger in Lieder singing (at what point, for example, does comic projection become arch?). But carry the admiration of unaffected simplicity too far and it can become a rationalization for a lack of imagination, and even insensitivity. It is all too easy for the stolid and unimaginative to castigate their rivals for "too much" interpretation. The ultra-manliness of many German male singers in the immediate pre-war years is sometimes held up to be a golden example of unaffected singing (it also happened to be the period best documented by the gramophone up to that time), but there is a lot of singing on record from this epoch which reflects the less attractive aspects of the time and is smug, dull, and boorish. I believe that Fischer-Dieskau's advocacy of a volatile (and arguably at times too fervent) reaction to words reflected his need to break with the traditions of his country's immediate past. His was a younger generation that needed to remind the world of German sensibility and flexibility rather than the grandiose and marmoreal (to say the very least) aspirations of Germany in the 1930s and 1940s. The Third Reich had hijacked Lieder and a lot of other German cultural traditions that had largely been based on tolerance and consensus. We are still feeling the after-effects of this in the question of Lieder's present-day popularity: and the English-speaking world, still enamored of war-films with Nazi villains, needs to be reminded that our Victorian forefathers looked to Germany as a paradigm of culture and civilization. It is a twentieth-century tragedy that the modern-day visitor may view Goethe's house and Buchenwald in a single day, while George Eliot could visit Weimar and write of it with unreserved rapture. And Germany is not the only country whose politics have been mirrored by its singing. The complacency, snobbery, and insularity of "little Britain" comes flooding from the shellac in certain pre-war records of English song, not to mention our performances of Lieder in English translation, or perhaps worse, atrociously enunciated German. The fascination of song interpretation is that it is not exempt from the influence of history and of *Zeitgeist*.

The battle between so-called vocal honesty and so-called artifice is almost an impossible one to referee accurately when some singers by nature are as direct, up-front, and immobile as John Wayne, and others have the mercurial reactions and passions for disguises of Alec Guinness. The fact is that Lieder's cowboys, in order to sing more than just an OK chorale, have to work hard at adding sensitivity to their manly presences, and the Guinness types have to add a touch of earthy reality to give red blood and metallic weight to their kind hearts and coronets. It is quite a battle this, between earthiness and refinement. With the average Italian singer one may reasonably bet on the presence of the former, and in English song and French *mélodie*, the latter is a prime requisite, all too frequently exaggerated, however. In Lieder it is necessary to have both, just as both were found in equal measure in Schubert's personality. The poetry of the Lied is almost always too subtle and complex to be given a generalized treatment, but on the other hand the fundamental humanity and immediacy of a great song's message is trivialized by pussyfooting and beating about the bush. Every artist will attempt to solve these problems in his or her own way and every member of the audience will have a different sense of priorities. It is this that makes the task difficult. There always will be people who regard singing as an athletic skill where the object of the exercise is to thrill and arouse with sound; then there are those who regard singing as a higher form of declamation and recitation, those who would argue with Whitman, as he reflects in his poem "That music always around me" (*Leaves of Grass*), that

> I hear not the volumes of sound merely,
> I am moved by the exquisite meanings.

Both are wrong, and both are right. The talented Lieder singer is aware of both these seemingly conflicting demands and finds a balance. There are some singers who are faithful to the printed music to a punctilious degree of accuracy, and others who treat the composer's demands on paper as inferior to their instincts in actual performance. (Here is the ongoing controversy of *Werktreue* all over again.) Both are wrong, and both are right. Music on paper has to be released into life by the performer, and sometimes the best way of doing this is to follow the composer's directions faithfully, and sometimes the only way is to take the law into your own hands. But when and how, and with which composers, that is the question, and in that question alone lies the work of a lifetime. Does the head rule the heart, or the heart the head? (Shakespeare in "Tell me where is fancy bred?" asked something of the same question.) The most moving and touching thing in singing is the sound of an open heart, but in Lieder singing this is not enough in itself; the brain has to be heard to work too. It is a hierarchical art where tradition plays a large part, but there have been great innovators who have defied tradition to create new ways of doing old things. The energy of the young Lieder singer with the power of youth on her or his side is a contrast to the old singer, vocally depleted perhaps, who coasts his way through a song. It is a contest which youth does not automatically win, but neither do the laurels automatically go to the famous singer when compared with the humbler initiate, unspoiled by the fruits of success. An accompanist in his early fifties, such as myself, who has worked with distinguished older singers, must retain the ability to keep himself open to new ideas and viewpoints – in short, to be ever-prepared to learn.

A rehearsal with Matthias Goerne

We meet for a quick rehearsal in London before a concert in Portugal which is to feature the *Schwanengesang* preceded by a group of Schiller settings. We have done most of the songs on this program before. But among the Schiller Lieder that need to be rehearsed for the first time is *Gruppe aus dem Tartarus* D583. In this song the poet, like a latter-day Dante, describes souls gripped with anguish during their terrible transit to the portals of hell. I have just been writing notes for a reissue of a recording from 1972 where Benjamin Britten accompanies Fischer-Dieskau in this song, among others. This is a magnificent performance, recorded live, and full of the electricity and dynamism generated by two great artists, Titans who seem not entirely comfortable in each other's musical company and who, as a result, brew up a formidable musical storm. But this reading stays with me strongly because I have heard it very recently. I have played this song many times with many singers. The decisions I took, for example, with Thomas Hampson when I recorded the song with him in 1991 are no longer in my head, and do not form the basis of my expectations with Goerne. (Very few artists are interested in re-listening to their own records past the editing stage.) The great thing about this repertory is that every time one approaches a great song, one can – indeed *must* – do so with a clean slate. It is impossible to erase the palimpsest of one's own experience hidden beneath the surface of each score, but this should be the most subtle and enlightened of background guides, not a blueprint for the future. It is for this reason that when I work on a song for the first time with a singer I do so from my printed scores which are as clean and unmarked as the day that they were issued. As the collaboration proceeds I take photocopies which are then marked accordingly and taken on tour. In this way, decisions taken with a particular singer at a particular time of our lives never seem to be permanent or binding.

Goerne and I work from the Peters Edition which remains the most singer- and pianist-friendly of the Schubert editions: this song, for example, occupies seven pages in the *Neue Schubert Ausgabe* and a much more manageable four in Peters. (The old Mandyczewski *Gesamtausgabe* remains a joy. I recently found a second-hand copy of the extremely rare hard-backed Dover reprint for Matthias, as he had often envied mine, but these heavy tomes are for home consultation rather than everyday use.) The smaller format of the *Neue Schubert Ausgabe* seems, on first acquaintance, more compact, but has it occurred to the musicologists, I wonder, that artists actually need to use volumes of music in performance, and that the spacious spread of the new edition is mightily inconvenient with a turn of the page every forty seconds? In any case, one has learned to look past the anomalies of Peters which are the result of Friedländer's reprinting first editions rather than going back to the manuscripts when extant. In m. 3 the hairpin after the *fortissimo* is not a diminuendo (as performed by Britten as late as 1972) but an accent. (Schubert's handwriting makes the differentiation between the sign of the accent and that of the *diminuendo* difficult, but this point is now mostly understood.) If one keeps the volume up until m. 6, the beginning of the following bar (on the peremptory word "Horch") is a sudden and dramatic return to *pianissimo*.

I am surprised that Goerne, still in his early thirties and a man of strong impulses, wants the tempo steadier than I had envisaged – perhaps my head is too full of the impetuous onslaught of Britten's accompaniment. But as he now points out, the marking is only "Etwas geschwind" and the 12/8 time signature indicates four-in-the-bar, not two. In practical terms, the difference we are talking about is a small one, but such minute adjustments are at the heart of interpretation. The appoggiaturas on the words "Meeres" and "Bach" (two equal quarter notes in each case) are faultlessly done. Most singers of the younger generation have got the hang of this, not always the case twenty years ago when an incorrect use of the appoggiatura was frequently to be found in performances of Schubert's songs. The long *crescendo* through "ein schweres, leeres / Qualerpresstes Ach!" is most exciting. And here the singer gives a color and a weight to these desperate words which is as impossible to describe as it is to notate on the printed score. I realize that the slightly slower tempo makes of the accompaniment's sextuplets something more like water-music, lapping at the music's edges and ominously rising with each phrase; this is a new idea for me, as I had always imagined that these figurations depicted the frisson of a dreadful shudder from the very beginning. At a slower speed the Styx is more sluggish, but that too is tenable. During the song's first pages each of us is making countless tiny decisions: Matthias with the phrasing, the weight and duration of consonants, the managing of a hint of portamento (on "emp*ö*rten" and "weint" for example); I with piano color and dynamics and arm weight (bearing in mind that there are passages which lie low for the singer and one has to calculate the amount of piano sound accordingly) as well as voicing between the hands – where to slightly favor the left hand's triplets over the churning right-hand sextuplets.

In the middle of this, the fact that Goerne can sing to a world standard and that I can play the piano adequately is taken for granted. Of course, a rehearsal is not a performance. There might be wrong notes in rehearsal from the pianist, and the singer, no matter how good, has to watch his intonation. In this case discussions about diction do not arise as they might with an English-speaking singer. Goerne asks me to repeat certain phrases, searching for a sound he has in his head, or an expressive quality, or simply solving a technical problem, without explaining what he is searching for. I can usually guess what he is after, but not always. "Nein, das ist nicht gut!" he says, half to himself, half to me. And we try it again until the key turns in the lock. The creation of a true legato is a priority. One day he will be a fine teacher; indeed, I have already seen him teach a young friend of mine, and he has a passion for technical discussion. Compliments between singer and pianist are rare and spontaneous – on these occasions, the result of genuine surprise and delight. At this stage we are like potters searching for a shape on the wheel and enjoying the feel of the pliable raw material under the fingers; one must also be prepared for a bit of a mess, to be allowed to throw away one's first efforts and begin again.

The music suddenly changes to a martial Allegro in held accents and exciting dotted rhythms. I set off a very brisk pace in response to the idea of "Verzweiflung" – the desperation and pain of the damned souls. The singer comes with me at my tempo, and we both enjoy bellicose excitement generated by this passage, as well as all the remarkable suspensions at the passage beginning "Hohl sind ihre Augen." Then, as the music shifts into F♯ minor, and where the composer most unusually places a *pianissimo* in the vocal line, it is clear that Goerne needs more time. To my disappointment he adopts a slower more lachrymose speed; my inclination, more Toscanini-like, would have been to keep the same tempo as the souls progress ever onward to their doom. I do not feel that there should be extra time given to their weeping; after all, the composer marks no change of speed. All right, I think (and all this happens in a trice), let's take that tempo, but I bet he will want to go back to a faster tempo when the eighth notes resume. But not a bit of it. Once having settled in that more spacious tempo, it seems the singer is happy to stay there. I have to admit to myself that he is courageous in not merely relying on speed to generate the sense of drama in those remarkable mounting sequences which lead the song to its climax (mm. 48–64, from "Fragen sich einander ängstlich leise").

We stop to speak about it. It seems he went along with my tempo at the initial Allegro just to try it on for size, but that it too was faster than he wanted it. Such a challenge from a colleague can generate defensiveness, but I admire Goerne's instincts, and it is clear that he is feeling rushed and unable to make the most of the expressive potential of the words. So, going back to first principles, I calculate the speed of my quarter notes and realize that I had adopted a tempo which, in comparison with many tempi in other Schubert songs, is more *Schnell* than Allegro, and certainly more *alla breve* than the marked four-in-a-bar ¢. (Anybody who has worked any length of time with Schubert will know that the difference between four- and two-in-a-bar is an absolutely crucial one, and that the composer knows what he is doing when he asks for one rather than the other.) If I had started the Allegro at a tempo that was in four, rather than a clipped two, there would have been no need to slow down at the F♯ minor phrase ("Folgend tränend seinem Trauerlauf") to accommodate the singer. Whatever the speed, I am certain that the composer envisaged one that was all of a piece.

The crowning glory of the song (if so terrible a subject can be glorious) is the two implacable outbursts of "Ewigkeit" in the final section. Like a life sentence pronounced from on high, a faster tempo gives to this section an imperious almost fist-brandishing grandeur. But a slightly slower tempo – in four rather than two – emphasizes the very meaning of the word "Ewigkeit," as the musical image is made to last longer, stretching into a terrible and broad perception of infinity. The effect is grander and more somber, less exciting perhaps, less of a dash across the keyboard between bass and treble than usual, but conveying hopelessness more effectively. The fact that Schubert has written two-bar phrases at this point, punctuated by rests, also indicates that he had a broader tempo in mind – each of the phrases seems designed to use the complete span of a single breath. One remembers that Vogl almost certainly was the first to sing this song, and that the extent of the older man's breath control apparently left something to be desired. How clever and practical Schubert was, his feet ever on the ground as his gaze embraced the infinite.

My way of playing and thinking about this song, developed over the course of a professional lifetime, has thus been challenged in a few minutes. It is all in a day's work, and I have no idea whether this new vision will be a permanent one, either for him or for me. Long before working on the song we have both listened to many of the important recorded performances, not in order to copy them but in a sense to be liberated from them. One must have the courage to think afresh. I cannot relinquish my admiration for the sheer animal energy of the recorded performance of Fischer-Dieskau and Britten that I have heard recently, but I remember that for all my admiration of Britten, he was apt to be a speed-merchant: his febrile tempi for performances of songs like *Wohin* from *Die schöne Müllerin* (marked *Mässig*) and *Auflösung* (marked *Nicht zu geschwind*) go against the composer's own moderating advice. "What the hell!" Britten admirers will say, and it is true that there comes a time when even the Koran-like pronouncements of the text must yield to the racing pulses of the here and now. But I admire Goerne for placing his confidence in what the composer has asked for, and arguing his viewpoint from the text. His requirements in this case are not based on vanity or a desire to show off; pointing to the markings in the music, he has had every right to challenge my automatic pilot. We shall see how the song works in performance in a few days' time.

It would be difficult to describe the mood of this rehearsal, so lively, so humorous it is, so enlivened by scurrilous (but harmless) story-telling and gossip, so full of trust for each other's musicality, and our mutual attempt to do our level best for dear old Schubert. We are down to earth in every sense; I fear that an eavesdropping listener would be disappointed in our lack of musical colloquy, for when it comes to the serious matters in hand we work silently, throwing musical suggestions at each other without verbal analysis. I do not attempt to lecture Goerne on the significance of Greek mythology (he would merely yawn, or laugh at me), nor do I show him Blake's illustrations for Dante's *Divina Commedia*, begun only seven years after the song was composed. The Viennese Schiller Edition of Anton Döll (1810) which was possibly Schubert's source for the text remains unconsulted on the shelf. Nevertheless I am happy to know about these things and they have stimulated me in a way that is impossible to define. It occurs to me that I reach for these artifacts with students when there is a problem, when some imaginative faculty stubbornly refuses to kick-start. No, this rehearsal is not a master class, and I have no idea if Matthias has seen, or whether he knows about, the background reading that has helped me find my way. His performance, bristling with awareness, suggests he does, but I do not inquire as to how and where he has acquired such understanding. Some artists inherit these things as if from another life, or are born with something that others have to fight long and hard to acquire. All this higher thought, however, sounds far too solemn and pompous for the mood of the day. We behave like a pair of engineers brought in on site to mend a telephone cable underneath the road. There is in our work a similar sense of camaraderie, sleeves rolled up, and getting our hands dirty in the process. The manual of how to do it "by the book" is never consulted; the correct way of connecting wire to wire has been moderated by much experience, and we take shortcuts that would make the supervisor raise his eyebrows. But we get the job done quickly, and go on to the next.

In this analogy the "supervisors" and the "manual" are the scholars of the Lied and the books they write about the subject. Their discoveries and perceptions are fed into the bloodstream of musical life and eventually come the way of performers (what a contrast this is, for example, with the world of early music, where the transfer between the two worlds is virtually instantaneous). But I wonder whether many of the musicologists are *au courant* with our working methods where, in a day's work, any number of decisions are taken on the hoof, and it is these which are offered to the paying public. In every preparation of a performance such as this there is an unwritten essay, an unpublished theory, a new hypothesis – in short, an ever-improvised do-it-yourself musicology without footnotes and bibliography, which is how music is made in the real world. It strikes me that there is a similar difference between the Apollonian perfection of an architect's plans and the Dionysian upheaval of the building site. It is no surprise that so few practicing musicians write about interpretation because it is the hardest thing in the world adequately to chart in words the tiny, yet ongoing, decisions of a performer, changing calibration every second. As the two of us work on our "connections" we do not flatter ourselves that we are making decisions for all time – we merely insure that the power is turned on for another day and that the public (in this case in Oporto, Portugal, hardly the Lied's most natural milieu) will have its recital.

A word here about singing from memory, something which Goerne always does in Lieder recitals. He heartily disapproves of anything else, and I have heard him castigate his German-speaking colleagues for having "let down the side" when a music stand appears in their recitals. This is an instance where the purity of the German *Liederabend* has been compromised by the real world. Dame Margaret Price, among many other singers, usually not of German origin, gave wonderful recitals with the music stand, and I have seen a number of artists, tortured by the fear of memory blanks, who have communicated with greater ease when they have the book with them. The trouble is that making exceptions for great artists (like Dame Myra Hess who played piano concerti from the scores) encourages everybody, including students, to claim the right. There is no doubt in my mind that communication between the singer and his or her public is better when the song is known "by heart" in every sense – this frees the singer from the tyranny of the bar line as much as anything else, and the great amount of work necessary to memorize the song is part of the process of truly "owning" it. A recent tendency for accompanists to work without the score is less convincing. I can understand that it makes a statement about accompanists' lib (that political movement which has as much chance of success as a call for the burning of Brahms), but it is only for those geniuses who know the score well enough to jump in the same direction as the potentially erring singer who may miss out a line or even a verse, and expects instantaneous rescue. These new-age accompanists must also be able to sing the entire text in German were the singer suddenly to stop, in other words to have as complete a command of the vocal line as of the piano's two staves. Without this complete and continuing identification with the text in front of one's eyes – experiencing each word and image not as the singer sings it, but before, the better to mirror the verbal imagery, and experience the song from within – the accompanist is merely a solo pianist doing the singer a favor.

Twenty-five years ago, at the beginning of my friendship with the great accompanist Gerald Moore (then in his late seventies) we discussed over the telephone a Mendelssohn and Schumann song program for a London South Bank Festival of which he was director. "What about a group of Giebel settings?" he said. (He had no doubt accompanied at some point the distinguished German mezzo Agnes Giebel, but he meant, of course, the poet Emanuel Geibel.) In the manner of a silly know-it-all, I mischievously recounted this story to Eric Sams. "What does it matter" this great expert of song replied, "whether he says Giebel or Geibel? He has all those songs deep in his heart and fingers, and he knows them better than either of us." I have never forgotten that rap on the knuckles from a man who, like Kipling, admires the fighting capacities of the British Tommy, grammatical slips and all, rather more than the pronouncements of the generals. Now, much later in my own life I too am a pedal foot soldier, entrenched at my keyboard, muddy but proud of my hands-on status, even if I am all too likely to say *Fallersleben* when I mean *Feuchtersleben.* The onset of one's own forgetfulness is the greatest reproof to the youthful know-it-all that was once oneself. Many of us performers do our best to keep up with the decisions and discussions by musical thinkers, but it is not our natural milieu. Perhaps there is a certain amount of fear of musicology (just as musicologists would often be terrified of being made to perform in the loftier public arenas). We gather together not at conferences but in green rooms, and there is a strong camaraderie among those of us who stand in the firing line. But it is we who have to face the music, as well as give it a face.

Fortunately song recitals are not wars or football matches. One cannot *win* a song recital and everyone has a different version of the score. What matters is not only the state of the body and vocal musculature, but also the state of mind and, dare one say, the soul. It all could not have been better put than by Robert Louis Stevenson (who knew his Schubert, incidentally), when, in his *Songs of Travel,* he wrote:

> Bright is the ring of words
> When the right man rings them.

We performers all long to be that *right* man or woman; words must be made to ring with beautiful sound, and sounds must be circled by poetic magic. At the highest level, only the strongest conjunction of these two aspects of the Lieder singer's art will do. We have to fight aspects of imbalance in our own personalities that threaten to cut us off from the full and rounded understanding that the art demands. Perhaps this struggle to be a worthy instrument in terms of one's own being is what separates the performing world from the academic to the greatest degree. But like performers, there are smug scholars who know it all (or think they do) and those who are still on a quest. Performers who are convinced that they have got it right once and for all may well be remarkable singers or pianists, but do we really wish to spend an evening in their company as they display their prowess? At a convivial dinner we expect conversation and rapport rather than a narcissistic monologue, and at a recital the audience expects the sharing of humanity and involvement in a journey which it is also undertaking. (The same is true of people who write or talk about music for a living and how they relate to their readers.) We must measure out equal quantities of Prometheus's fire, the miller boy's stream, Suleika's breezes and the gravedigger's earth to find the mix that contains the multitude of contradictions which is life itself. It gives the duty of practicing with one's scales an entirely new meaning. The great singer whom we all long to discover, hear, and accompany is one with heart and intelligence, who gives voice to joy and happiness in song, but who also has the imaginative capacity to speak consolingly for those without voices, love, or happiness.

In this humane and most civilized of arts, composers and performers have aspired not only to mirror the extremes of the major and minor key, but also the vast terrain in between which can only be charted by travelers of patience and understanding. Of all the brave singers and accompanists who set out on this exacting journey, only a few will endure the winding pathways of search and self-search, and stay the course. It is good to know that a lot of scholars, people often more clever than ourselves, are also involved in the same work. As our careers progress we may become less diffident in seeking their advice. In return they should respect our contribution, and there are heartening signs that a younger generation of musicologists is less inclined to disdain performers, and their thoughts, than was the case when I was a beginner. After all, we have one grand thing in common: a love of the Lied which has nothing to do with material success and fame. True, it is a passion in which expertise is increasingly regarded as eccentric and arcane, and it is relatively poorly rewarded – in material terms at least. But who among our number can adequately describe the elation experienced when word and music come together with knowledge and understanding, imagination, skill, compassion? When these coordinates converge (with luck for at least a few times in each of our lifetimes) we look forward to a state of reflective inner fulfillment married to something like wild exaltation. We expect that it will bring another century back to life. And even if that century is the one before last, such a resurrection is surely better late than never.

Notes

Introduction: why the Lied?

1. LMLR, 20, according to a personal interview with the well-known accompanist Michael Raucheisen.

2. LMLR, 20–21; this reminiscence by Emilie Bittner, a singer and widow of the composer Julius Bittner.

3. Quoted from *Johann Wolfgang Goethe, Gedenkausgabe der Werke, Briefe und Gespräche*, ed. Ernst Beutler (Zurich: Artemis, 1950) V: 146. The passage is from the *Vorspiel auf dem Theater* to *Faust*.

4. Peter Gay, *Weimar Culture: The Outsider as Insider* (New York and London, 1968), 67.

5. *The Critical Edition of the Works of Gioachino Rossini*, under the aegis of the Fondazione Gioachino Rossini, in Pesaro, Italy, and the Center for Italian Opera Studies (CIAO) at the University of Chicago, began publishing this composer's works in 1979. *The Works of Giuseppe Verdi*, published by the University of Chicago Press (and also directed at CIAO), issued its first volume in 1983. The Donizetti Society in London began a series of Donizetti's collected works in the 1970s. A critical edition of Vicenzo Belllini's works, a joint effort between the City of Catania, Italy, and Ricordi BMG, is in the planning stages.

6. Of the three, Schubert has been the subject of greatest controversy in the wake of the suggestion that he may have explored homoeroticism through musical means. For a recent overview of this subject, see my review of Lawrence Kramer's *Franz Schubert: Sexuality, Subjectivity, Song* (Cambridge, 1998) and Brian Newbould, ed., *Schubert Studies* (Aldershot, 1998) in JAMS 54 (2001), 651–61.

7. Although both volumes are in need of updating, the listing of studies devoted to nineteenth-century music in the two following books amply document the explosion of interest in this music: Arthur Bampton Wenk, *Analyses of Nineteenth and Twentieth-Century Music: 1940–1985* (Boston, 1987) and Harold J. Diamond, *Music Analyses: An Annotated Guide to the Literature* (New York, 1991).

8. This is the title, in translation, of Eisler's "Ändere die Welt, sie braucht es," composed for Brecht's play *Die Massnahme*, first performed Berlin, 13 December 1930.

9. The phrase is quoted from Ernst Buske, "Jugend und Volk," in Werner Kindt, *Grundschriften der deutschen Jugendbewegung* (Düsseldorf, 1963), 198.

10. One indication of the role song played in the *Wandervogel* movement is provided by Hans Breuer's compilation of German folk songs, gathered under the title *Der Zupfgeigenhansl*. A runaway best-seller, the song collection attained its tenth edition by 1913.

11. I am not the first to refer to "the modern Lied." As it happens, August Reißmann, *Das deutsche Lied in seiner historischen Entwicklung* (Kassel, 1861), 208, uses exactly this phrase – "das moderne Lied" – to refer to almost the same body of music, extending the boundaries back to "the Lied in the age of Goethe" and up to his own day. In using the phrase here, I do so with the understanding that it begins in the 1740s and continues until at least World War II.

12. Georg Eismann, *Robert Schumann: Ein Quellenwerk über sein Leben und Schaffen*, 2 vols. (Leipzig, 1956), I: 18; my translation.

13. Kant's definition of *Bildung* within the program of Enlightenment is perhaps the most to the point. In his well-known essay "What is Enlightenment?" (1784), he answers the question asked in his title as follows: "Enlightenment is man's release from his self-incurred tutelage. Tutelage is the inability to make use of one's understanding without direction from another. Self-incurred is this tutelage when its origin lies not in lack of courage but in lack of resolution to use it without direction from another. *Sapere aude!* Have the courage to use your own reason! – this is the motto of Enlightenment." Quoted after *Kants Werke: Akademie-Textausgabe*, vol. VIII, *Abhandlungen nach 1781* (Berlin, 1968), 35. The centrality of *Bildung* in the history of European and particularly German culture is reflected in a bibliography of ever-growing proportion. A short list of such investigations includes W. H. Bruford, *The German Tradition of Self-Cultivation: Bildung from Humboldt to Thomas Mann* (London and New York, 1975), Franco Moretti, *The Way of the World: the Bildungsroman in European Culture*, new edn. trans. Albert Sbragia (London and New York, 2000), Rolf Selbmann, *Der deutsche*

Bildungsroman, 2nd edn. (Stuttgart, 1994), and Martin Swales, *The German Bildungsroman from Wieland to Hesse* (Princeton, 1978). Oddly, given the concept's significance, its correlation with music has received little sustained attention.

14. As the central character avers in Book V, chapter 3, his life's ambition is "the harmonious development of my personality." *Wilhelm Meister's Apprenticeship,* ed. and trans. Eric A. Blackall, *Goethe's Collected Works,* vol. IX (Princeton, 1995), 175. The importance of *Bildung* for German culture as it intersects with German song is considered again in chapters 2, 13, and 14.

15. Cited in Walter Wiora, *Das deutsche Lied: Zur Geschichte und Ästhetik einer musikalischen Gattung* (Wolfenbüttel and Zurich, 1971), 15.

16. Meinecke, *The German Catastrophe: Reflections and Recollections,* trans. Sidney B. Fay (Cambridge, MA, 1950 [originally pub. 1946 as *Die deutsche Katastrophe*]), 119–20.

17. Gay, *Weimar Culture,* 68.

18. Quoted from Theodor W. Adorno's "Kulturkritik und Gesellschaft," *in Prisms [Prismen],* trans. Samuel and Shierry Weber (Cambridge, MA, 1992), 34.

19. *Versuch einer critischen Dichtkunst für die Deutschen,* 3rd edn. (Leipzig, 1742), 760 and 759.

20. Hagedorn, *Oden und Lieder in fünf Büchern,* book I (Hamburg, 1747), 1.

21. "Zuschrift" to *Vier und zwanzig, theils ernsthafte, theils scherzende, Oden, mit leichten und fast für alle Hälse bequehmen Melodien versehen* (Hamburg, 1741).

22. AmZ (25 January 1826), 28. Jahrgang, No. 4, column 56.

23. *Götzen-Dämmerung,* "Sprüche und Pfeile," §33, in *Nietzsche Werke Kritische Gesamtausgabe,* ed. Giorgio Colli and Mazzino Montinari (Berlin, 1969) VI/3: 58 – "Der Deutsche denkt sich selbst Gott liedersingend." Nietzsche's aphorism in turn is an intentional misreading of a line from Ernst Moritz Arndt's 1813 poem, "Des Deutschen Vaterland." The latter was written at a time when the German-speaking lands were smarting under Napoleon. Divided into nine strophes, the poem begins with the question "Was ist des Deutschen Vaterland?" (What is the German fatherland?). In the sixth strophe, Arndt answers it is the realm that extends from where one hears the sound of German tongues to where "God in heaven sings Lieder": "So weit die deutsche Zunge klingt / Und Gott im Himmel Lieder singt." For Arndt's poem in full, see *Gedichte von Ernst Moritz Arndt,* ed. Heinrich Meisner (Leipzig, 1894): I: 18–21.

1 In the beginning was poetry

1. Dietrich Fischer-Dieskau, *Texte deutscher Lieder: Ein Handbuch* (Munich, 1968).

2. Schubert set seventy poems by Goethe; the next largest number derives from his friend Johann Mayrhofer and totals forty-seven. Schubert's two song cycles to poems by Müller resulted in forty-five individual Lieder. For a convenient listing of Schubert, his poets, and the names and numbers of poems he set, see John Reed, *The Schubert Song Companion* (Manchester, 1985), 461–81.

3. For a discussion of Goethe's centrality to the history of the Lied, see Harry Seelig, "The Literary Context," GLNC, 1–30.

4. For an extended analysis of this issue in Schubert, see my "The Poetry of Schubert's Songs" in *Schubert's Vienna,* ed. Raymond Erickson (New Haven and London, 1997), 183–213.

5. Gottsched, *Versuch,* 82.

6. Ibid., 428.

7. In this respect, Gottsched follows Horace closely. His views on the nature and character of the poet are elaborated at length in chapter 2 of the *Versuch.*

8. This and all subsequent translations are mine except as noted.

9. For a thorough assessment of this issue, see Reinhard Strohm, *Dramma per Musica: Italian Opera Seria of the Eighteenth Century* (New Haven and London, 1997), 23–29.

10. For an extended discussion of simplicity as an ideal in eighteenth-century song, see J. W. Smeed, *German Song and its Poetry, 1740–1900* (London and New York, 1987), 66–81, and chapter 2 below.

11. *Abhandlung über den Ursprung der Sprache* (Berlin, 1770); quoted from *Sturm und Drang: Kritische Schriften,* ed. Erich Loewenthal (Heidelberg, 1963), 404.

12. I describe here the roots in the period for what Lawrence Kramer so compellingly has analyzed as the "convergence" of music and poetry in the Romantic period; see Kramer, *Music and Poetry: The Nineteenth Century and After* (Berkeley and Los Angeles, 1984), 18–24.

13. As Max Kommerell tellingly puts it, every Goethe poem has its "moment of the heart." Quoted from "Das Volkslied und das deutsche Lied," in Kommerell, *Dame Dichterin und andere Essays* (Munich, 1967), 7–64.

14. Although Schubert (and Fischer-Dieskau) use the common title, "Wanderers Nachtlied," the actual title in Goethe's collected poems, where it follows the poem entitled "Wanderers Nachtlied," is "Ein Gleiches" (Another), which nevertheless implies that its speaker is a wanderer.

15. As one moves outside the central repertory the proportion of declamation increases. Reichardt's Goethe settings include not only declamatory poems, but also settings of passages from dramas. Some of Liszt's songs are so declamatory as to verge on melodrama, a popular genre in the nineteenth century. His settings of the songs from Schiller's *Wilhelm Tell,* for example, contrast markedly with the lyricism of Schubert's settings of the same texts.

16. See Eduard Genast, *Aus Weimars klassischer und nachklassischer Zeit: Erinnerungen eines alten Schauspielers,* ed. Robert Kohlrausch (Stuttgart, n.d.), 126–27.

17. *Die Poggenpuhls* (1896) contains a semi-professional performance, *Effi Briest* (1894) a virtuoso one.

18. The tendency to write at least in part for the professional is implicit from the 1790s. In the songs of Reichardt, for example, there is often a strong *Singspiel* influence, a form of north German operetta to be performed by actors who also sang but were not normally trained opera singers.

19. Compare, for example, Smeed, *German Song,* 20–37, Seelig, "The Literary Context," 1–2.

20. Wordsworth, *Selected Poems and Prefaces,* ed. Jack Stillinger (Boston, 1965), 461.

21. For a useful compendium of German folk-songs with melody, author and composer where known, see Ernst Klusen, ed., *Deutsche Lieder: Texte und Melodien* (Frankfurt am Main, 1980).

22. Discussions of sublimity all go back to Longinus's treatise on the sublime of (probably) the first century AD. It is concerned primarily with the rhetorical devices that enhance the grandeur of conception and emotion in literature. Although he was read with considerable sympathy and interest by neo-classical commentators, in the course of the eighteenth century he was adopted as a figure of classical authority in the accelerating attack on neo-classicism. For a thorough history of this shift in England, see Samuel Holt Monk, *The Sublime: a Study of Critical Theories in Eighteenth-Century England* (Ann Arbor, 1960).

23. This underlying complementarity of the natural and the supernatural constitutes for Meyer H. Abrams the defining quality of Romanticism in his general study of the period, *Natural Supernaturalism: Tradition and Revolution in Romantic Literature* (New York, 1971).

24. The most influential analysis of the Biedermeier period and concept is Friedrich Sengle's monumental three-volume study *Biedermeierzeit: Deutsche Literatur im*

Spannungsfeld zwischen Restauration und Revolution, 1815–1848 (Stuttgart, 1971–1980). For an excellent analysis of the relation of Biedermeier to Romanticism, see Virgil Nemoianu's *The Taming of Romanticism: European Literature and the Age of Biedermeier* (Cambridge, MA, 1984), 1–40.

25. Wordsworth, *Selected Poems,* 460.

26. See again my "The Poetry of Schubert's Songs," 188.

27. Wolf, for example, set "Anakreons Grab," one of Goethe's earliest, and relatively loose, attempts at elegiac form, as lyrical declamation; Reichardt set passages from two of Goethe's elegies, "Alexis und Dora" and "Euphrosyne," as declamations, grouped with other declamatory songs and passages from dramas. See Reichardt, *Göthes Lieder, Oden, Balladen und Romanzen mit Musik von J. F. Reichardt* [1809], ed. Walter Salmen (Munich, 1964), vol. LVIII, *Das Erbe deutscher Musik,* 86–93. In the settings of both composers, the particular rhythms of the language are lost in the freer rhythms of the declamation.

28. Settings of German sonnets are rare; Seelig, "The Literary Context," 18–19, lists eighteen in the entire repertory. Even frequently set poets otherwise known for their sonnets, such as Rückert, tend not to be represented by sonnets in the song repertory.

29. Hegel, *Aesthetics: Lectures on Fine Art* [1835], tr. T. M. Knox (Oxford, 1975), II: 1138.

30. Hugo Friedrich, *Die Struktur der modernen Lyrik von Baudelaire bis zur Gegenwart* (Hamburg, 1956), 22.

2 The eighteenth-century Lied

1. Charles Rosen, *The Romantic Generation* (Cambridge, MA, 1995), 124.

2. Edward T. Cone, "Words and Music: The Composer's Approach to the Text," in *Music: A View from Delft, Selected Essays,* ed. Robert P. Morgan (Chicago, 1989), 115.

3. Lawrence Kramer, "The Schubert Lied: Romantic Form and Romantic Consciousness," in SCAS, 200.

4. Eric Sams, "Schubert," *New Grove,* XVI: 774.

5. Charles Rosen, *The Classical Style* (New York, 1972), 454.

6. The secondary literature on the eighteenth-century Lied, although not vast, is too extensive to acknowledge here. Nevertheless, mention must be made of a study, that, while a century old, remains the starting point for anyone interested in the subject: Max Friedländer's *Das deutsche Lied im 18. Jahrhundert: Quellen und Studien* (Stuttgart and Berlin, 1902). Vol. I is devoted to a

checklist of 798 song collections published between 1736 and 1799. Vol. II is given over to a survey of the most significant songs arranged according to poets. Other studies include Heinrich W. Schwab's *Sangbarkeit, Popularität und Kunstlied: Studien zu Lied und Liedästhetik der mittleren Goethezeit, 1770–1814* (Regensburg, 1965) and Hans Joachim Moser's *Goethe und die Musik* (Leipzig, 1949). For an overview, see James Parsons, "Lied. § III. c. 1740 – c. 1800," New Grove 2, XIV: 668–71.

7. C. P. E. Bach, from the autobiographical sketch first published in German in Charles Burney's *Tagebuch einer musikalischen Reisen*, trans. J. J. C. Bode (Hamburg, 1773), III: 199–209. The relevant passage appears on p. 209.

8. AmZ, 16 (12 October 1814), cols. 680–92; quoted from *E. T. A. Hoffmann's Musical Writings*, ed. David Charlton, trans. Martyn Clarke (Cambridge, 1989), 379.

9. (Leipzig, 1834), 98–99.

10. *Discourse on the Origin of Inequality*, in *The Social Contract and Discourses*, trans. G. D. H. Cole (New York, 1950), 157.

11. Trans. Daniel O. Dahlstrom in *Friedrich Schiller Essays*, ed. Walter Hinderer, *The German Library* 17 (New York, 1998), 192.

12. *Schiller Essays*, 180; the remark is from *Über naive und sentimentalische Dichtung*.

13. *Versuch einer critischen Dichtkunst*, 4th edn. (Leipzig, 1751), 144 and 466. My translation; unless otherwise noted, all translations are mine. For a recent assessment of Gottsched and his place in the history of German literature, see P. M. Mitchell, *Johann Christoph Gottsched (1700–1766): the Harbinger of German Classicism* (Columbia, 1995).

14. *Versuch einer critischen Dichtkunst*, 13.

15. For more on Hagedorn see Reinhold Münster, *Friedrich von Hagedorn: Dichter und Philosoph der fröhlichen Aufklärung* (Munich, 1999) and Steffen Martus, *Friedrich von Hagedorn: Konstellationen der Aufklärung* (Berlin, 1999).

16. Hagedorn, *Oden und Lieder*, xiv, xii–xiii; quoted from *Des Herrn Friedrichs von Hagedorn Sämmtliche poetische Werke*, Dritter Teil (Hamburg, 1757). *The Guardian*, No. 16, 30 March 1713; quoted in *The Guardian*, ed. John Calhoun Stephens (Lexington, 1982), 88–89.

17. Newell E. Warde discusses Uz in greater detail in *Johann Peter Uz and German Anacreonticism: the Emancipation of the Aesthetic* (Frankfurt am Main, 1978); also Helena Rosa Zeltner, *Johann Peter Uz: von der "Lyrischen Muse" zur "Dichtkunst"* (Zurich, 1973).

18. "Horaz," line 125, *Sämmtliche poetische Werke*, 72.

19. Scheibe, *Critischer Musikus* 1 (5 March 1737), 3.

20. Thirty years later Hiller would echo Scheibe in the "Vorbericht des Componisten" of his *Lieder für Kinder* (Leipzig, 1769), I: "I have preferred the simple and naturally singable to the bombastic and artistic."

21. Scheibe, *Critischer Musikus* 64 (17 November 1739), 295, 299, and 302. Half a lifetime later, Reichardt repeated the concept almost verbatim. For him, a melody is genuine if it "leaves an impression on one who is not a connoisseur and remains in his memory, this is an unfailing proof it is *natural* and *unforced*." Reichardt's *Briefe eines aufmerksamen Reisenden* (1774), in *Source Readings in Music History*, ed. and trans. Oliver Strunk (New York: 1950), 701; the emphasis is Reichardt's.

22. The first two are *Sammlung auserlesener moralischer Oden, zum Nutzen und Vergnügen der Liebhaber des Claviers* and were published by the author in Leipzig in 1740 and 1741; the third, brought out in 1743, retains the start of the title of the first two volumes yet adds: *und des Singen*. An announced fourth volume never was published. For a facsimile, see *Lorenz Mizler Sammlungen auserlesener moralischer Oden*, with afterword by Dragan Plamenac (Leipzig, 1971).

23. Quoted from Plamenac's facsimile edn., 110.

24. Telemann, *Vierundzwanzig, theils ernsthafte, theils scherzende, Oden, mit leichten und fast für alle Hälse bequemen Melodien versehen* (Hamburg, 1741), 3.

25. Quoted from *Des Herrn Friedrichs von Hagedorn poetische Werke in drei Theilen* (Hamburg: Johann Carl Bohn, 1769), I: 34.

26. "Die Schönheit" (lines 22–24), *Sämmtliche poetische Werke* (1757), part III, book IV, 82.

27. "Der Morgen" (lines 41–44), *Oden und Lieder*, III: 164.

28. *Oden und Lieder*, III, quoted from *Sämmtliche poetische Werke*.

29. "Der Weise auf dem Lande," lines 1–5, *Sämtliche poetische Werke*, 47–48.

30. From the poem "Gott im Frühling," lines 38, 13, 37, and 39, *Sämtliche poetische Werke*, 203–04.

31. *Albrecht von Hallers Gedichte*, ed. Ludwig Hirzel (Frauenfeld, 1882), *Bibliothek älterer Schriftwerke der Deutschen Schweiz und ihres Grenzgebietes* 3, 405; letter of March 1772.

32. *Schillers Werke: Nationalausgabe* [hereafter NA], vol. XX: *Philosophische Schriften*, ed. Benno von Wiese (Weimar, 1962), 472.

33. *Geschichte des Agathon* (Frankfurt and Leipzig, 1766–67), I: 57–58 and 52.

34. Scheibe, *Critischer Musikus* (1745 reprint), 722–23.

35. First published in 1742; quoted from Hagedorn's *Oden und Lieder in fünf Büchern* (Hamburg, 1747), book II, 41–42. Görner's setting was published in the *Sammlung neuer Oden und Lieder* (Hamburg, 1744); vol. I appeared in 1742.

36. Immanuel Kant, *Werke: Akademie-Textausgabe* (Berlin, 1968), III: 520.

37. Wordsworth, *The Recluse, Part First, Book First – Home At Grasmere*, lines 402–03.

38. Herder, *Auszug aus einem Briefwechsel über Ossian und die Lieder alter Völker*, trans. Joyce P. Crick in *Eighteenth-Century German Criticism*, ed. Timothy J. Chamberlain, *The German Library* 11 (New York, 1992), 138; the emphasis is Herder's.

39. Preface to *Die Braut von Messina*, entitled "Über den Gebrauch des Chors in der Tragödie," NA, X: 8.

40. Krause, *Von der musikalischen Poesie* (Berlin, 1753), 92, 2.

41. Although the collection was issued without attributions to either poets or composers, Friedrich Wilhelm Marpurg identified both in his *Historische-Kritische Beyträge zur Aufnahme der Musik* (Berlin, 1754), I: 55–57.

42. Thrasybulos Georgiades, "Lyric as Musical Structure: Schubert's Wandrers Nachtlied ('Über allen Gipfeln,' D. 768)," trans. Marie Louise Göllner, in SCAS, 93: "Musical structure is created when language is captured as something real, when it is taken 'at its word.' "

43. Scheibe, *Critischer Musikus* 64 (1738), 295.

44. For reasons presently impossible to determine, either Ramler – the same Ramler who supplied Graun with the libretto for *Der Tod Jesu* – or Graun himself made certain changes in Hagedorn's poem for the *Oden mit Melodien*. Compare the text as included in Example 2.2 with the text given above at the start of the discussion of Hagedorn's *An die Freude*. In stanza 1 Ramler changes "edler Herzen" to "muntrer Tugend" (bright virtue); "dich vergrößen, dir" to "deinen Kindern wohl" ([let the songs that here resound please] thy children). Other changes occur in the second, fourth, and fifth stanzas, while the third is preserved intact.

45. Just what keyboard instrument eighteenth-century Lied composers had in mind is not always an easy question to answer. In an attempt to disentangle this matter, perhaps the first thing to bear in mind is practicality; performers surely would have used whatever instrument – clavichord, harpsichord, and later early piano – they had at hand. This said, in some works it seems certain that a specific instrument is implied. See also below, n. 63.

46. Quoted in Ernst Bücken, *Das deutsche Lied* (Hamburg, 1939), 43.

47. Cited in H. C. Robbins Landon, *The Collected Correspondence and London Notebooks of Joseph Haydn* (London, 1959; hereafter CCLN), 31 and 305.

48. 12 September 1825. SDB, 587; my emphasis.

49. See, for example: *Sing- und Spieloden vor Musikalische Freunde* (1762); the previously mentioned *Musicalische Belustigungen* (1774); *Sammlung größerer und kleiner Singstücke mit Begleitung des Claviers* (1788); and *Melodien zum Milheimischen Liederbuche für das Piano-Forte oder Clavier* (1799).

50. Issue of 24 October 1759, 16. The song in question is *Der Freundschaftsdienst*.

51. *Berlinische musikalische Zeitung* 1 (1805), 9, trans. *The Critical Reception of Beethoven's Compositions by his German Contemporaries* [hereafter CRBC], ed. Wayne M. Senner (Lincoln, NE, 1999), 220.

52. Mattheson, *Critica musica* (reprint edn., Amsterdam, 1964), II: 311.

53. Ibid., II: 309.

54. Ibid., I: 100.

55. *Poetics of Music* (Cambridge, MA, 1942), 63.

56. Quoting respectively from Hiller, *Lieder mit Melodien* (Leipzig, 1772) preface (unpaginated) and J. A. P. Schulz, "Veränderungen; Variationen," in Johann Georg Sulzer, *Allgemeine Theorie der schönen Künste* [1774]; quoted from rev. edn. (Leipzig, 1793), IV: 637.

57. Heinrich Schwab documents other examples of such variations in his "Die Liednorm 'Strophigkeit' zur Zeit von Joseph Martin Kraus," in *Joseph Martin Kraus in seiner Zeit*, ed. Friedrich W. Riedel (Munich and Salzburg, 1982), 83–100.

58. For an overview see David Montgomery, "Franz Schubert's Music in Performance: A Brief History of People, Events and Issues" in CCS, 272–74. Fn. 6 contains a number of useful references on this subject as it applies to Schubert Lieder.

59. A. Peter Brown, "Musical Settings of Anne Hunter's Poetry: From National Song to Canzonetta," JAMS 47 (1994), 52, fn. 26, reminds us that "Haydn's canzonettas should not be mistaken for English Lieder." Their detailed keyboard parts, length, and expressive depth, he insists, relate to the Viennese Lied tradition.

60. On Viennese Lieder, see Vera Vyslouzilova, "Bei den Anfangen des Wiener Kunstliedes: Josef Antonin Stepan und seine *Sammlung deutscher Lieder*," in *Wort und Ton im europaischen Raum: Gedenkschrift für Robert Schollum* (Vienna,

1989), 69–77. The most complete treatment of song in Vienna in its early phase remains Irene Pollak-Schlaffenberg's "Die Wiener Liedmusik von 1778–1789," *Studien zur Musikwissenschaft. Beihefte zu Denkmäler der Tonkunst in Deutschland* 5 (1918), 97–139. Another important study is A. Peter Brown's "Joseph Haydn and Leopold Hofmann's 'Street Songs,'" JAMS 33 (1980), 356–83. See also Editha Alberti-Radanowicz, "Das Wiener Lied von 1789–1815," *Studien zur Musikwissenschaft* 10 (1923), 37–76.

61. Haydn to his publisher Artaria, 27 May 1781, trans. CCLN, 27–28.

62. *Musikalischer Almanach* (Berlin, 1796), unpaginated.

63. Zachariae's 1754 poem "An mein Clavier" – "You, echo of my laments, my faithful lyre" – was set to music at least ten times during the century. See DL, II: 48–49. The subject is considered in detail in John William Smeed's "*Süssertönendes Klavier:* Tributes to the Early Piano in Poetry and Song," ML 66 (1985), 228–40. Notwithstanding the completeness of Smeed's article in other details, the thought that Zachariae's poem is a tribute to the early piano needs to be modified in favor of the clavichord; see Annette Richards, *The Free Fantasia and the Musical Picturesque* (Cambridge and New York, 2001), 156–57.

64. The Lied is from Schneider's 1793 collection *Lieder zum Singen am Clavier und Forte Piano* (Mannheim), 2–7. As late as 1837, Schneider's Lieder, according to Gustav Schilling's *Universal-Lexicon der Tonkunst* (Stuttgart, 1837), still were lauded as "true masterpieces of their sort." Quoted in DL, II: 448. The publishing house of Simrock erroneously brought out Schneider's Lied under Mozart's name, a mistake in authorship corrected in the AmZ 1 (1795), col. 745.

65. Werner-Joachim Düring, *Erlkönig-Vertonungen: Eine historische und systematische Untersuchung* (Regensburg, 1972), 115–40.

66. Lenz, *Die kleinen*, in *Gesammelte Schriften*, ed. Franz Blei, 5 vols. (Munich, 1909–13), III: 327–28.

67. Johann Wolfgang Goethe, *Münchener-Ausgabe*, I/2, 363.

68. Schiller, NA, XX: 424; the emphasis is Schiller's.

69. Max Hecker, ed., *Der Briefwechsel zwischen Goethe und Zelter* (Leipzig, 1913), II: 59; letter of 20 May 1820.

70. This would remain the venue for Lieder performances until the middle of the nineteenth century. Exceptions to this rule caused surprise. In 1813 a Viennese critic, in response to a public performance of Beethoven's *Adelaide*, noted: "As unusual as the appearance of a German vocal piece is at a concert, this nevertheless did not fail to have an effect upon a public that, not prejudiced in favor of particular forms, possesses a general receptivity to everything that is truly beautiful. Text, music, and performance combined to guarantee a splendid artistic enjoyment." The singer was Franz Wild, who, in 1815, was the last performer with whom Beethoven collaborated in a public performance before the latter's deafness prohibited further such appearances, this before the Russian empress, again in *Adelaide*. As the Vienna critic goes on to note about the 1813 performance, "*Mr. Wild* correctly understood the spirit of the simple, expressive, tenderly nuanced singing. The attempt made thereby to promote German national singing is particularly praiseworthy, although it can be foreseen that *Mr. Wild* will find few imitators in this matter, for such songs presuppose a full, powerful, resonate voice, which only extremely few of today's singers possess, and the lack of which they try to hide through excessive ornamentations, which, however are not compatible with German national singing at all." *Wiener allgemeine musikalische Zeitung* 1 (1813), 300–01, trans. in CRBC, 222.

71. *Oden mit Melodien*, part I (Berlin, 1753).

72. Heinrich Christoph Koch, "Lied," *Musikalisches Lexikon* (Frankfurt am Main, 1802), col. 901; emphasis added.

73. Cramer's *Magazin der Music* 1 (1783), 456–57.

74. Quoted from Eric A. Blackall, *The Emergence of German as a Literary Language: 1700–1775*, 2nd edn. (Ithaca, 1978), 3–4, 13.

75. *Critischer Musikus*, 1745 reprint, 9.

76. Dedication, Telemann, *24 Oden.*

77. Although I have yet to come across a reference that makes this point unequivocally, the era consistently viewed the public realm as masculine, the private feminine – the latter the Lied's longstanding locale. This bifurcation of male and female spheres is the subject of an extended discussion in the *Conversations-Lexicon oder Handwörterbuch für die gebildeten Stände*, 3rd edn. (Leipzig and Altenburg, 1815), IV: 211. See also Karin Hausen, "Family and Role-Division: The Polarisation of Sexual Stereotypes in the Nineteenth Century – an Aspect of the Dissociation of Work and Family Life," in *The German Family: Essays on the Social History of the Family in Nineteenth- and Twentieth-Century Germany*, ed. Richard J. Evans and W. R. Lee (London, 1981), 51–83.

78. *Versuch einer Critischen Dichtkunst*, 4th edn., 760 and 759.
79. Quoted in DL, I: 196.
80. "Lieder (Schluß)," NZfM (31 July 1843), 33–35; trans. in *Robert Schumann on Music and Musicians*, 242. Schumann attributes this advancement to developments in German poetry, specifically those by Eichendorff, Rückert, Uhland, and Heine.
81. NZfM 1 (23 October 1834), 234.

3 The Lieder of Carl Philipp Emanuel Bach, Haydn, Mozart, and Beethoven

1. See Johann Friedrich Reichardt, *Briefe eines aufmerksamen Reisenden die Musik betreffend* (Frankfurt and Leipzig, 1774), I: 124 and *Schreiben über die Berlinische Musik* (Hamburg, 1775), 8, as quoted in Hans-Günter Ottenberg, *C. P. E. Bach*, trans. Philip J. Whitmore (Oxford, 1987), 152. See also Charles Burney, *An Eighteenth-Century Musical Tour in Central Europe and the Netherlands*, ed. Percy A. Scholes (Oxford, 1959), 219.
2. See Friedrich Chrysander, "Eine Klavier-Phantasie von K. P. E. Bach mit nachträglich von Gerstenberg eingefügten Gesangsmelodien zu zwei verschiedenen Texten" in *C. P. E. Bach: Beiträge zu Leben und Werk*, ed. Heinrich Poos (Mainz, 1993), 329–53. Also Ernst F. Schmid, *C. P. E. Bach und seine Kammermusik* (Kassel, 1931), 51–53.
3. For a comparison of C. P. E. Bach with Klopstock see the review of Bach's fantasies and sonatas in AmZ 3 (1801), 299, as quoted in Schmid, *C. P. E. Bach und seine Kammermusik*, 60.
4. See letter of 14 August 1774 from Johann Heinrich Voß to Ernestine Boie, as quoted in Gudrun Busch, *C. Ph. E. Bach und seine Lieder* (Regensburg, 1957), I: 125, and in Ottenberg, *C. P. E. Bach*, 155.
5. See C. P. E. Bach, *Kantaten und Lieder*, ed. Otto Vrieslander (Munich, 1922), 25–26.
6. See letter of October 1780 from Voß to Schulz, as quoted in Busch, *C. Ph. E. Bach und seine Lieder*, I: 136–37.
7. See the review in *Allgemeine deutsche Bibliothek*, ed. Christoph Friedrich Nicolai (Kiel, 1792), I: 113, as quoted in Busch, *C. Ph. E. Bach und seine Lieder*, I: 203.
8. DL, II: 128–32.
9. The "Göttingen Grove" was a group of poets from that city noted for their allegiance to the poetry of Klopstock as well as to all things German. For a brief discussion of the group, see Nicholas Boyle, *Goethe: the Poet and the Age* (Oxford, 1992), I: 153.

10. See the discussion in David P. Schroeder, *Haydn and the Enlightenment* (Oxford, 1990), 91 and 114; also C. P. E. Bach's *Selbstbiographie* as included in Burney, *Tagebuch seiner musikalischen Reisen*, III: 199–209.
11. See DL, II: 49.
12. Ibid., I: 242–43.
13. See the preface to C. P. E. Bach, *Herrn Professor Gellerts geistlichen Oden und Lieder mit Melodien* (Berlin, 1758).
14. See Busch, *C. Ph. E. Bach und seine Lieder*, I: 60–61.
15. See C. P. E. Bach, *Geistliche Lieder*, ed. C. H. Bitter (Berlin, 1880), I: 8. In this edition the title of the song is given as *Grüsse Gottes in der Natur*.
16. See the preface to C. P. E. Bach, *Herrn Professor Gellerts geistlichen Oden und Lieder*. Bach's abandonment of figured bass in this collection also is discussed in chapter 2.
17. C. P. E. Bach, *Herrn Doctor Cramers übersetzte Psalmen mit Melodien zum Singen bey dem Claviere* (Leipzig, 1774).
18. See Busch, *C. Ph. E. Bach und seine Lieder*, I: 58f.
19. See Ewan West, "The *Musenalmanach* and Viennese Song 1770–1830," ML 67 (1986), 37–49.
20. Example taken from *Denkmäler der Tonkunst in Österreich*, vol. LIV, ed. Margarete Ansion and Irene Schlaffenberg (Vienna, 1920), 9.
21. See Cramer's *Magazin der Musik*, 1 (1783), 453, as quoted in DL, I: 245.
22. See Haydn's letter to Artaria of 20 July 1781, as quoted in DL, I: 270–71 and in H. C. Robbins Landon, *Haydn: Chronicle and Works* (Bloomington, 1976), II: 448–49.
23. The text of Hofmann's *Eilt ihr Schäfer* is given in DL, I: 271–72.
24. The music for both Hofmann and Haydn's setting of Ziegler's poem appears in full in Brown, "Joseph Haydn and Leopold Hofmann's 'Street Songs,'" JAMS 33 (1980). Hofmann's is given on pp. 373–74 and Haydn's on pp. 374–75; in this source Hofmann's Lied is labeled *Pastorella: An Thyrsis* and Haydn's is called *An Thyrsis*. Haydn's Lied also is available in *Joseph Haydn Lieder für eine Singstimme mit Begleitung des Klavier* (Munich, 1982), 10–11.
25. See Cramer, *Magazin der Musik*, I (1783), 456, as quoted in DL, I: 288. See also Robbins Landon, *Haydn: Chronicle and Works*, II: 456–57.
26. See Theodor Göllner, "Vokal und instrumental bei Haydn," *Bericht über den Internationalen Joseph Haydn Kongress*, ed. Eva Badura-Skoda (Munich, 1986), 104–10.

27. See Haydn's letter to Artaria of 18 October 1781, as quoted in Robbins Landon, *Haydn: Chronicle and Works*, II: 453.

28. *Joseph Haydn Lieder*, 5.

29. Ibid., 4.

30. Ibid., 6 and 28 respectively.

31. Ibid., 14.

32. Ibid., 26–27.

33. Ibid., 21–23.

34. Ibid., 11–13.

35. I derive my examples of Mozart songs from *Lieder für Singstimme und Klavier*, ed. Paul Klengel (Wiesbaden, n.d.). For the reader wishing to collate my discussion with an easily obtainable source, I provide references to the Dover reprint of the Breitkopf & Härtel publication of songs originally published in *Mozart's Werke*, Serie 7, "Lieder und Gesänge mit Begleitung des Pianoforte" (Leipzig, 1881); this source is available as Wolfgang Amadeus Mozart, *Songs for Solo Voice and Piano* (New York, 1993), hereafter cited as Mozart *Songs*. In this source *An Chloe* is given on pp. 44–47.

36. Friedrich Schiller, *Über naive und sentimentalische Dichtung* (Stuttgart, 1978), 30.

37. Ibid., 53 and 57.

38. Ibid., 36. Schiller describes the impression given by "naïve" poetry as "immer fröhlich, immer rein, immer ruhig." Mozart *Songs*, 53.

39. *Über naive und sentimentalische Dichtung*, 57–58.

40. Mozart *Songs*, 22–23 and 50–51, respectively.

41. See Maurice J. E. Brown, "Mozart's Songs for Voice and Piano," *MR* 17 (1956), 19–28.

42. Mozart *Songs*, 38–39.

43. Ibid., 26–27.

44. See Paul Nettl, "Das Lied" in *Mozart Aspekte*, ed. Paul Schaller and Hans Kühner (Olten and Freiburg im Breisgau, 1956), 205–27.

45. Mozart *Songs*, 34–37.

46. Ibid., 40–43.

47. For example, Štěpán's setting of *Das Veilchen* as published in the first *Sammlung deutscher Lieder* (Vienna, 1778) erroneously attributed the poem to Gleim. Friberth's setting in the third *Sammlung* of 1780, which was in Mozart's possession, did not give the name of the poet though it seems from the "vom Göthe" written onto Mozart's manuscript that he knew who the true author was. See John Arthur and Carl Schachter, "Mozart's *Das Veilchen*," *MT* 130 (1989), 149–55.

48. See *Beethoven: Letters, Journals and Conversations*, ed. Michael Hamburger (London, 1951), 268.

49. I direct the reader to the following edition of Beethoven's Lieder: *Sämtliche Lieder, Beethoven Werke*, part XII, vols. I and II, ed. Helga Lühning (Munich, 1990). Hereafter cited as Beethoven *Lieder*. For Beethoven's *Klage*, see II: 180–81.

50. Beethoven *Lieder*, II: 187–88.

51. See Friedrich Schiller, "Über Matthissons Gedichte," *Sämtliche Werke*, ed. J. Perfahl (Munich, 1968), 702.

52. Beethoven *Lieder*, I: 25–31.

53. NCGL, 97.

54. Beethoven *Lieder*, I: 83–85.

55. See William Kinderman, *Beethoven* (Berkeley, 1995), 139–40.

56. See Jack Stein, *Poem and Music in the German Lied from Gluck to Hugo Wolf* (Cambridge, MA, 1971), 53–54.

57. Beethoven *Lieder*, I: 14–16.

58. Ibid., I: 38–41.

59. Ibid., I: 100–03.

60. Ibid., I: 46–60.

61. Questions about Beethoven's conception of the ordering of the Gellert songs are raised in the preface to ibid., ix.

62. Ibid., I: 96–99.

63. See Rellstab's account of Goethe giving the manuscript of *Wonne der Wehmut* to Mendelssohn for him to play, as recorded in Romain Rolland, *Goethe and Beethoven*, trans. G. A. Pfister and E. S. Kemp (New York, 1968), 61. For the music, see Beethoven *Lieder*, I: 124–25.

64. See Tieck's views on Beethoven's songs as transmitted in his novella *Musical Sorrows and Joys*, as translated by Linda Siegel, *German Romantic Literature* (Novato, CA, 1983), 113.

4 The Lieder of Schubert

1. Edith Schnapper, *Die Gesänge des jungen Schubert bis zum Durchbruch des romantischen Liedprinzipes* (Bern and Leipzig, 1937). The full text of Vogl's diary passage is given in Andreas Liess, *Johann Michael Vogl: Hofoperist und Schubert-Sänger* (Graz and Cologne, 1954), 153.

2. From Schubert's diary, 14 June 1816; quoted from SDB, 60.

3. Quoted from George Grove, rev. W. H. Hadow, "Franz Schubert," in *Grove's Dictionary of Music and Musicians*, 2nd edn. (London, 1908), V: 330a.

4. Although recognized by contemporaneous listeners, the aesthetics of musical absolutism shaping musical understanding in the second half of the nineteenth century worked to obscure the degree to which composers relied on *topoi*. Not totally forgotten, their authority was minimized until the second half of the twentieth century. Scholars who have worked to restore a proper understanding of the various *topoi* include: Leonard G. Ratner, *Classic Music: Expression, Form, and Style* (New York, 1980),

see especially Chapter 2, "Topics"; Wye Jamison Allanbrook, *Rhythmic Gesture in Mozart: Le Nozze di Figaro and Don Giovanni* (Chicago, 1983); and V. Kofi Agawu, *Playing with Signs: A Semiotic Interpretation of Classic Music* (Princeton, 1991).

5. 12 September 1825; quoted from SDB, 458.

6. Goethe made this pronouncement in a letter to Adalbert Schöpke, 16 February 1818; quoted from *Goethes Briefe* (Weimar, 1904), XXIX: 53–54. The letter also is quoted in *Goethes Leben von Tag zu Tag. Eine dokumentarische Chronik*, ed. Robert Steiger und Angelika Reimann (Zurich and Munich, 1993), VI: 545.

7. For more detailed examinations, see V. Kofi Agawu, "Schubert's Harmony Revisited: The Songs 'Du liebst mich nicht' and 'Dass Sie hier gewesen,'" JMR 9 (1989), 23–42; Susan Youens, "Schubert and the Poetry of Graf August von Platen-Hallermünde," MR 46 (1985), 19–34; and Kristina Muxfeldt, "Schubert, Platen, and the Myth of Narcissus," JAMS 49 (1996), 480–527.

8. AmZ, 25 April 1827; quoted from SDB, 636; trans. amended.

9. Hans Georg Nägeli, *Vorlesungen über Musik mit besonderer Berücksichtigung der Dilettanten* ([1826] Darmstadt, 1983), 61–62.

10. For more on the type of Lied composed in the nearly eighty years before Schubert, see Heinrich W. Schwab, *Sangbarkeit, Popularität und Kunstlied: Studien zu Lied und Liedästhetik der mittleren Goethezeit 1770–1814* (Regensburg, 1965) as well as chapter 2 of this book.

11. So called by the Viennese reporter for the London music periodical, *The Harmonicon*, April 1826; quoted from SDB, 518.

12. SDB, 877.

13. Karl Goedeke, *Schillers Sämmtliche Werke* (Stuttgart, 1879), I: viii.

14. SDB, 353, quoting from the AmZ, 24 June 1824; trans. amended.

15. Gunter Maier, *Die Lieder Johann Rudolf Zumsteegs und ihr Verhältnis zu Schubert* (Göppingen, 1971). In Mozart's own personal thematic catalogue he indicates that *Die ihr des unermesslichen Weltalls Schöpfer ehrt* was composed in July of 1791 and describes it as "eine kleine teutsche kantata für eine Stim[m]e am klavier" (a little German cantata for voice at the keyboard). See *Mozart's Thematic Catalogue: A Facsimile. British Library Stefan Zweig MS 63*, introduction and transcription by Albi Rosenthal and Alan Tyson (Ithaca, 1990), 56 and fol. 27v.

16. See Jack M. Stein, *Poem and Music in the German Lied from Gluck to Hugo Wolf* (Cambridge, MA, 1971), 53–54.

17. See further Albrecht Riethmüller, "Heine, Schubert und Wolf: 'Ich stand in dunkeln Träumen,'" *Muzikoloski zbornik* 34 (1998), 69–87.

18. AmZ, 7 October 1829, col. 660.

19. Paul Mies, *Schubert, der Meister des Liedes. Die Entwicklung von Form und Inhalt im Schubertschen Lied* (Bern, 1928).

20. Marie-Agnes Dittrich, *Harmonik und Sprachvertonung in Schuberts Liedern* (Hamburg, 1991).

21. Hans-Joachim Moser, *Das deutsche Lied seit Mozart* (Berlin and Zurich, 1937), 125.

22. Werner Thomas, "Der Doppelgänger von Franz Schubert," in *Schubert-Studien* (Frankfurt am Main, 1990), 115–35.

23. Moser, *Das deutsche Lied*, 125.

24. Gustav Schilling, "Dis-Moll," in *Encyclopädie der gesammten musikalischen Wissenschaften, oder Universal-Lexicon der Tonkunst*, ed. Schilling (Stuttgart, 1835–), II: 422–23.

25. Dorothea Redepenning, *Das Spätwerk Franz Liszts: Bearbeitungen eigener Kompositionen* (Hamburg, 1984).

26. Diether de la Motte, "Das komplizierte Einfache. Zum ersten Satz der 9. Symphonie von Gustav Mahler," *Musik und Bildung* 10 (1978), 145–51.

27. Quoted from Harry Goldschmidt, *Franz Schubert. Ein Lebensbild* (Leipzig, 1964), 180; see also SMF, 334. For a more detailed account of Schubert's circle and the influence they had on his taste in literature and poetry, see David Gramit, "The Intellectual and Aesthetic Tenets of Franz Schubert's Circle" (Ph.D. dissertation, Duke University, 1987). See also the same author's "'The Passion for Friendship': Music, Cultivation, and Identity in Schubert's Circle," in CCS, 56–71.

28. SDB, 128–30.

29. Walther Dürr, "Lieder für den verbannten Freund. Franz Schubert und sein Freundeskreis in Opposition zum Metternich-Regime," in *Zeichen-Setzung. Aufsätze zur musikalischen Poetik*, ed. Werner Aderhold and Walburga Litschauer (Kassel, 1992), 135–40.

30. On the subject of censorship in general in Vienna during the first half of the nineteenth century, see Walter Obermaier, "Zensur im Vormärz," in *Bürgersinn und Aufbegehren. Biedermeier und Vormärz in Wien 1815–1848*, ed. Selma Trosa (Vienna, 1988), 622–27; see also the same author's "Schubert und die Zensur," in *Schubert-Kongress Wien 1978. Bericht* (Graz, 1979), 117–25. On censorship and the Schubert Lied, see Walther Dürr, "Schuberts Lied *An den Tod* (D.518) – zensiert?," ÖMz 38 (1983), 9–17.

31. For more on Schubert's settings of Mayrhofer, see SPML, chapter 3, "Chromatic

Melancholy: Johann Mayrhofer and Schubert," 151–227.

32. The reference to "the Greek bird" is a pun on the name Vogl, as the word *Vogel* in German means bird. Quoted from SDB, 134.

33. For an examination of the latter, see Barbara Kinsey, "Schubert and the Poems of Ossian," MR 34 (1973), 22–29.

34. SDB, 375.

35. Ibid., 250.

36. Ibid., 254.

37. See further SPML, chapter 2, "The Lyre and the Sword: Theodor Körner and the Lied," 51–150.

38. Walther Dürr, "Die Freundeskreise," in *Schubert-Handbuch*, ed. Walther Dürr and Andreas Krause (Kassel and Basel, 1997), 19–45. Also Eva Badura-Skoda, Gerold W. Gruber, Walburga Litschauer, Carmen Ottner, eds. *Schubert und seine Freunde* (Vienna, 1999) and Ilija Dürhammer, *Schuberts literarische Heimat. Dichtung und Literaturrezeption der Schubert-Freunde* (Vienna, 1999).

39. Rita Steblin, *Die Unsinnsgesellschaft. Franz Schubert, Leopold Kupelwieser und ihr Freundeskreis* (Vienna, 1998).

40. NZfM 41 (1854), 104.

5 The early nineteenth-century song cycle

1. Note Peter Kaminsky's "The Popular Album as Song Cycle: Paul Simon's *Still Crazy After All These Years*," *College Music Symposium* 32 (1992), 38–54.

2. See further David Gramit's "Lied, Listeners, and Ideology: Schubert's 'Alinde' and Opus 81," CM 58 (1995), 28–60.

3. Throughout this chapter, titles translated into English reflect the German distinction between *Gesang* (song) and *Lied* (Lied).

4. For the concept of a generic contract, I am indebted to Jeffrey Kallberg's "The Rhetoric of Genre: Chopin's Nocturne in G Minor," 19CM 11(1988), 238–61. John Daverio discusses early nineteenth-century attitudes toward genre and the song cycle in his chapter "The Song Cycle: Journeys Through a Romantic Landscape," in GLNC, 279–312. Although a list of titles relating to genre from the field of literary criticism would be impractical to provide here, those interested may profit from consulting David Duff's collection of essays, *Modern Genre Theory* (London, 2000); Walter Gobel's "The State of Genre Theory; or, Towards an Anthropological Approach to Genre," *Symbolism: An International Journal of Critical Aesthetics* 1 (2000), 327–48; Johan Hoorn's "How Is a Genre Created? Five Combinatory Hypotheses," *Comparative Literature and Culture: A WWWeb*

Journal 2, No. 2 (June 2000); and Walter Bernhart's "Some Reflections on Literary Genres and Music," in *Word and Music Studies: Defining the Field. Proceedings of the First International Conference on Word and Music Studies at Graz, 1997*, ed. Walter Bernhart, Werner Wolf, and Steven Paul Scher (Amsterdam, 1999).

5. Surely related is the Romantic interest in ruins, a subject frequently at the heart of Caspar David Friedrich's paintings; his 1825 *Ruine Eldena* affords a well-known example.

6. Susan Youens summarizes Schubert's contributions in "Franz Schubert: The Prince of Song," in GLNC, 31–74.

7. Helen Mustard, *The Lyric Cycle in German Literature*, Columbia University Germanic Studies No. 17 (Morningside Heights, 1946); and Harry Seelig, "The Literary Context: Goethe as Source and Catalyst," GLNC, 1–30.

8. Friedrich Schlegel, *Kritische Schriften und Fragmente*, ed. Ernst Behler and Hans Eichner, 6 vols. (Munich, 1988), I: 244 ("Kritische Fragmente 1797"), No. 60; VI: 3 ("Zur Poesie. II. Paris. 1802. December."), No. 19; VI: 11 ("Zur Poesie und Litteratur 1807. I."), No. 50; and V: 255 ("Zum Roman. Notizen bei der Lektüre 1799."), No. 237.

9. Goethe's impact on the German language has been so widely acknowledged and remains so fundamental to studies of the German language and its literature that the idea cannot be attributed to any individual author or authors. The following sources summarize that impact and provide a starting point for those interested: Eric Blackall, *The Emergence of German as a Literary Language 1700–1775*, 2nd edn. (Ithaca, 1978); Nicholas Boyle, *Goethe: The Poet and the Age* (Oxford, 1991); and Seelig, "The Literary Context: Goethe as Source and Catalyst."

10. Discussions of the history of organicism and its impact on early Romanticism include Giordano Orsini's "The Ancient Roots of a Modern Idea," in *Organic Form: The Life of an Idea*, ed. G. S. Rousseau (London, 1972), 7–24; Ruth Solie's "The Living Work: Organicism and Musical Analysis," 19CM 4 (1980), 147–56; Brian Primmer's "Unity and Ensemble: Contrasting Ideals in Romantic Music," 19CM 6 (1982), 97–140; Lotte Thaler's *Organische Form in der Musiktheorie des 19. und beginnenden 20. Jahrhunderts* (Munich, 1984); Lothar Schmidt's *Organische Form in der Musik: Stationen eines Begriffs 1795–1850* (Kassel and Basel, 1990); and David Montgomery's "The Myth of Organicism: From Bad Science to Great Art," MQ 76 (1992), 17–66.

11. Wilhelm Müller, *Vermischte Schriften*, ed. Gustav Schwab (Leipzig, 1830), IV: 118. The

comment originally was published in *Hermes*, 1827.

12. Barbara P. Turchin, "Robert Schumann's Song Cycles in the Context of the Early Nineteenth-Century Liederkreis" (Ph.D. dissertation, Columbia University, 1981), 69–96.

13. Reichardt's essay appeared three times between 1801 and 1804: Reichardt, "Etwas über das Liederspiel," Leipzig AmZ 43 (22 July 1801): 709–17; Heinrich Christoph Koch, *Musikalisches Lexikon* (Frankfurt am Main, 1802), "Liederspiel"; and Reichardt, *Liederspiele* (Tübingen, 1804), Introduction. The text and a translation of all three versions appears in Ruth O. Bingham, "The Song Cycle in German-Speaking Countries 1790–1840: Approaches to a Changing Genre" (Ph.D. dissertation, Cornell University, 1993), 251–64.

14. Daverio, "The Song Cycle," 280, found this to be equally the case in performance: "Complete or near-complete renditions of cycles were not unknown in the first half of the century . . . But the practice of selecting and presenting individual songs was the norm, in both public and private circles." Perhaps related to this was the concert practice of performing selected opera arias and movements from symphonies or concertos. The early nineteenth-century relationship between the publication or performance of selections and perceptions of the whole needs further study.

15. Schubert's Opp. 52 and 62 remain popular as individual songs; it is only as cycles they are neglected in both performance and study.

16. "Die Idee, einen ganzen Roman ohne Erzählung, blos durch eine Reyhe Lieder . . . zu liefern ist neu." Quoted in Turchin, "Robert Schumann's Song Cycles," 45 and fn. 2, quoting Meredith Lee, *Studies in Goethe's Lyric Cycles* (Chapel Hill, 1978), 86. Turchin, 44–47, discusses Göckingk, Wobeser, Schlegel, and the rise of the Liederroman; Mustard, *The Lyric Cycle*, 18–22, discusses Göckingk and his cycle in depth.

17. I am indebted to Ludwig Kraus's "Das Liederspiel in den Jahren 1800 bis 1830: Ein Beitrag zur Geschichte des deutschen Singspiele" (Ph.D. dissertation, Vereinigte Friedrichs-Universität Halle-Wittenberg, 1921), 6–7, for the particularly apt "Brennpunkt" (flashpoint).

18. "[Vergils] Beispiel veranlasste folgenden Zyklus kleiner idyllischer Lieder . . . Wenn gleich ein leichtes Band von Wechselbeziehungen durch den Zyklus hinläuft: so kann doch jedes einzelne Lied, als ein kleines Ganze, für sich bestehen und ausgehoben werden," Christoph August Tiedge, *Sämmtliche Werke*, 4th edn.,

10 vols. in 3 (Leipzig, 1841), foreword to *Alexis und Ida*.

19. "Wem z.B. könnte es einfallen, die 46 Stücke nach einander weg singen zu wollen; und wer könnte es auch? Wählt man aber für jedes Mal einzelne Stücke, so giebt man ohnehin auf, und vermisst nicht mehr, was die Sammlung zu einem wahren Ganzen machen sollte . . ." Leipzig AmZ 17 (1815), 162.

20. A more complete history and discussion of this cycle is in Bingham, "The Song Cycle in German-Speaking Countries," 134–212; Susan Youens, "Behind the Scenes: *Die schöne Müllerin* before Schubert," 19CM 15 (1991), 3–22; and Youens, *Schubert: Die schöne Müllerin* (Cambridge, 1992), 1–11.

21. "Gesellschaftlich" here implies both a cooperative effort and warm fellowship.

22. Numerous studies of Schubert's cycle address its tonal scheme using one of these approaches. Examples here were drawn from Franz Valentin Damian, *Franz Schuberts Liederkreis Die schöne Müllerin* (Leipzig, 1928); John Reed, "*Die schöne Müllerin* Reconsidered," ML 59 (1978), 411–19; Turchin, "Robert Schumann's Song Cycles," 191–94; Christopher Lewis, "Text, Time, and Tonic: Aspects of Patterning in the Romantic Cycle," *Intégral: The Journal of Applied Musical Thought* 2 (1988), 37–73; and Rita Steblin, *A History of Key Characteristics in the Eighteenth and Early Nineteenth Centuries* (Ann Arbor, 1983).

23. Recently, for example, Ernst-Jürgen Dreyer opened his discussion of a cycle that predates Beethoven's by stating that *An die ferne Geliebte* seemed to have been born "*ex nihilo*" in "Kleine Beiträge: Leopold Schefer und die 'in die Luft schwebende Musik': ein Beitrag zur Frühgeschichte des Liederzyklus," Mf 51 (1998), 438.

24. Louise Eitel Peake, "The Song Cycle: A Preliminary Inquiry into the Beginnings of the Romantic Song Cycle and the Nature of an Art Form" (Ph.D. dissertation, Columbia University, 1968), 253–55. For a recent discussion of Loewe, Fanny Hensel, Liszt, Franz, and Cornelius, see Jürgen Thym's "Crosscurrents in Song: Five Distinctive Voices," in GLNC, 153–85.

25. Arthur Komar, for example, uses this definition in his "The Music of *Dichterliebe*: The Whole and Its Parts," in *Schumann: Dichterliebe: An Authoritative Score* (New York, 1971), 64–66.

26. "Mimesis" here relates to John Neubauer's use in *The Emancipation of Music from Language: Departure from Mimesis in Eighteenth-Century Aesthetics* (New Haven, 1986).

27. Joseph Kerman, "*An die ferne Geliebte*," in *Beethoven Studies*, ed. Alan Tyson (New York,

1973), 123–24, and reprinted in Kerman's *Write All These Down: Essays on Music* (Berkeley, 1994), 173–74.

28. "Der Dichter, mag er nun, wie angegeben, heissen, oder nicht . . . ," AmZ 19 (1817), 73.

29. Turchin, "Robert Schumann's Song Cycles," 67–69.

30. See Rufus Hallmark's "Robert Schumann: The Poet Sings," GLNC, 75–118, for a more thorough discussion of Schumann's cycles of 1840, as well as of his lesser-known later songs and cycles. For a more specialized consideration of Schumann and the song cycle restricted to a single poet, see David Ferris, *Schumann's Eichendorff Liederkreis and the Genre of the Romantic Cycle* (New York, 2000).

31. This is somewhat of an oversimplification. In his "Robert Schumann: The Poet Sings," 77–79, Hallmark points out several possible reasons why Schumann began composing songs, including Clara Wieck's inspiration, stylistic changes, ambitions to compose an opera, and Mendelssohn's encouragement, in addition to economic reasons. Others who have theorized explanations for Schumann's "conversion" to songs include Fritz Feldman, "Zur Frage des 'Liederjahres' bei Robert Schumann," AfM 9 (1952), 246–69; Leon Plantinga, *Schumann as Critic* (New York, 1976); Eric Sams, "Schumann's Year of Song," MT 106 (1965), 105–07; Stephen Walsh, *The Lieder of Schumann* (London, 1971); and Turchin, "Schumann's Conversion to Vocal Music: A Reconsideration," MQ 67 (1981): 392–404. Daverio, "The Song Cycle," 289 and fn. 34, also notes the connection between Schumann's piano and song cycles and cites Eric Sams's *The Songs of Robert Schumann*, 2nd edn. (London, 1975), 36, which examines the inspiration for the Heine *Liederkreis* in sketches for *Davidsbündlertänze*.

32. Schumann reviewed Lieder by Berger, Loewe, Bernhard Klein, Marschner, Ries, and others. Plantinga, *Schumann as Critic*, 164–71, summarizes Schumann's views.

33. See Daverio's section, "After Schumann: Experiments, Dramatic Cycles, and Orchestral Lieder," on the song cycles of Cornelius, Brahms, Wagner, Wolf, Mahler, and Strauss, in GLNC, 293–305.

6 Schumann: reconfiguring the Lied

I should like to thank Ralph Locke for his assistance in reading a draft of this essay and Luca Lombardi and Miriam Meghnagi for their hospitality at the shores of Lago Albano near Rome, where much of this chapter was written during a delightful December visit.

1. Johannes Brahms published three of them in 1893 in a supplement volume to the *Schumann Collected Works Edition* (XIV/1, 34–37). Universal Edition published six more, edited by Karl Geiringer, Robert Schumann: *Sechs Frühe Lieder*, in 1933; another appeared in the same year as a supplement in the centennial issue of the *Neue Zeitschrift für Musik*. Rufus Hallmark saved another from obscurity in 1984; see his "Die handschriftlichen Quellen der Lieder Robert Schumanns," in *Robert Schumann: Ein romantisches Erbe in neuer Forschung* (Mainz, 1984), 99–117, more specifically 101–02. A few others remain manuscripts.

2. The beginnings of *An Anna II* and *Im Herbste* are recycled in the slow movements of the Sonatas in F♯ minor and G minor, respectively, and the melodic substance of *Hirtenknabe* returns in the *Intermezzo*, Op. 4, No. 4.

3. The ubiquity of strophic song within the history of the eighteenth-century German Lied is considered above in chapter 2; see also Heinrich Schwab, *Sangbarkeit, Popularität und Kunstlied* (Regensburg, 1965) and J. W. Smeed, *German Song and its Poetry: 1740–1900* (London, 1987).

4. Cited in Dietrich Fischer-Dieskau, *Robert Schumann: Wort und Musik. Das Vokalwerk* (Stuttgart, 1981), 25.

5. Schumann, *Briefe: Neue Folge*, ed. F. Gustav Jensen (Leipzig, 1904), 143.

6. Quoted from Wolfgang Boetticher, *Robert Schumann in seinen Briefen und Schriften* (Berlin, 1942), 340.

7. Helma Kaldewey, "Die Gedichtabschriften von Robert und Clara Schumann," in *Robert Schumann und die Dichter*, ed. Josef Kruse (1991), 88–99.

8. Rufus Hallmark, "Die Rückert Lieder von Robert and Clara Schumann," 19CM 14 (1990), 3–30.

9. Among others, John Daverio, in chapter 5 of his *Robert Schumann: Herald of a "New Poetic Age"* (Oxford, 1997), 182–96, discusses the difficult circumstances leading up to the Schumann marriage.

10. Schumann, *Briefe: Neue Folge*, 164.

11. Franz Brendel, "Robert Schumann with Reference to Mendelssohn-Bartholdy and the Development of Modern Music in Germany," trans. Jürgen Thym, in *Schumann and His World*, ed. R. Larry Todd (Princeton, 1994), 317–37, especially 328.

12. Wasielewski, *Robert Schumann: Eine Biographie*, 4th edn. (Leipzig, 1906 [first edn., 1858]), 283.

13. Arnfried Edler, *Robert Schumann und seine Zeit* (Laaber, 1982), 212–13 and Daverio, *Robert Schumann*.

14. See further Fritz Feldmann, "Zur Frage des 'Liederjahres' bei Robert Schumann," AfM 9 (1952), 246–69, and Leon Plantinga, *Robert Schumann as Critic* (New Haven, 1967) for an extensive discussion of the biographical and critical issues connected with the *Liederjahr*.

15. Schumann's review of Franz's Lieder first was published in the NZfM 19 (1843), 34–35; it also is found in Robert Schumann, *Gesammelte Schriften über Musik und Musiker*, ed. Martin Kreisig, 5th edn. (1914), II: 147–48; Schumann, *On Music and Musicians*, 241–42; and Plantinga, *Schumann as Critic*, 176–77.

16. Edler, *Robert Schumann*, 215–16.

17. Wasielewski, *Schumann*, 290, cites a letter by Schumann to Karl Koßmaly, which leaves no doubt that Schumann was aware of his accomplishment as a Lieder composer: "In your essay about the Lied I was a little saddened that you position me in second class. I would not request to be placed in the first, but I think I have a right to a category of my own, and least of all I like to be seen next to [Carl Gottlieb] Reissiger, [Karl Friedrich] Curschmann, and others. I know that my striving and my means go far beyond those composers."

18. *The Ring of Words: An Anthology of Song Texts*, ed. Philip L. Miller (New York, 1963), provides poems of songs in their original versions and lists textual variants of settings. Schumann clearly gets most of the annotations. See also Hallmark, "Schumanns Behandlung seiner Liedtexte," in *Schumanns Werke: Texte und Interpretationen*, ed. Akio Mayeda and Klaus Wolfgang Niemöller (Mainz, 1987), 20–42.

19. See Herwig Knaus, *Musiksprache und Werkestruktur in Robert Schumanns Liederkreis* (Munich, 1974), for a facsimile of the autograph. For a transcription and interpretation of the various compositional layers, see Barbara Turchin, "Schumann's Song Cycles: The Cycle within the Song," 19CM 8 (1985), 238–41. See also Hallmark, "Schumann's Revisions of 'In der Fremde,' Op. 39, No. 1," in *Of Poetry and Song: Approaches to the German Lied*, ed. Jürgen Thym (Rochester, forthcoming).

20. Theodor W. Adorno, "Zum Gedächtnis Eichendorff – Coda: Schumanns Lieder," in *Noten zur Literatur I* (Berlin, 1958), 134–45. Fuga XXIV from the first volume of Bach's *Well-Tempered Clavier* seems to have been the model for capturing the eerie atmosphere of deception in *Zwielicht*.

21. See Schumann's review of Theodor Kirchner's Lieder, Op. 1 in NZfM 18 (1843), 120; also in *Gesammelte Schriften*, ed. Kreisig, 123–24.

22. Hallmark, "Rückert Lieder," 3–30.

23. Schumann actually composed twenty poems of Heine's *Lyrisches Intermezzo*: the four settings left out when *Dichterliebe* appeared in 1844 were published later as individual songs. See Arthur Komar, ed., *Robert Schumann: Dichterliebe* (New York, 1971) and Hallmark, "The Sketches for *Dichterliebe*," 19CM 1 (1977), 110–36.

24. Ruth Solie, "Whose Life? The Gendered Self in Schumann's *Frauenliebe* Songs," in *Critical Approaches*, ed. Steven P. Scher (Cambridge, 1992), 219–40. For a different perspective, see Kristina Muxfeldt, "*Frauenliebe und Leben* Now and Then," 19CM 25 (2001), 27–48.

25. Barbara Turchin, "Schumann's Song Cycles," 19CM 8 (1985), 233–34.

26. Edler, *Schumann und seine Zeit*, 220.

27. Barbara Turchin, "The Nineteenth-Century Wanderlieder Cycle," JM 5 (1987), 498–526.

28. Hallmark, "Rückert Lieder," passim.

29. David Ferris, *Schumann's Eichendorff Liederkreis and the Genre of the Romantic Cycle* (Oxford, 2000) and John Daverio, "The Song Cycles: Journey Through a Romantic Landscape," in GLNC, 289–90. See also Anthony Newcomb, "Schumann and Late Eighteenth-Century Narrative Strategies," 19CM 11 (1987), 164–74, and Erika Reiman, "Schumann's Piano Cycles and the Novels of Jean Paul: Analogues in Discursive Strategies" (Ph.D. dissertation, University of Toronto, 1999).

30. *Gesammelte Schriften über Musik und Musiker*, ed. Kreisig, I: 272.

31. Jack Stein, *Poem and Music in the German Lied* (Cambridge: MA, 1971), 89–110.

32. See further Edward T. Cone, *The Composer's Voice* (Berkeley, 1974); also Cone, "Poet's Love or Composer's Love," in *Music and Text: Critical Inquiries*, ed. Steven P. Scher (Cambridge, 1992), 177–92.

33. *Music and Poetry* (Berkeley and Los Angeles, 1994), 146–48.

34. For a sensitive reading of this song see Edward T. Cone, "Words into Music: The Composer's Approach to Text," in *Sound and Poetry*, ed. Northrop Frye (New York, 1956), 3–15.

35. Jonathan Bellman, "*Aus alten Märchen*: The Chivalric Style of Schumann and Brahms," JM 13 (1995), 117–35.

36. Schumann, *Briefe: Neue Folge*, 302.

37. See the table of works in Daverio, *Robert Schumann*, 390–91.

38. *Briefe: Neue Folge*, 302.

39. For instance, Eric Sams, *The Songs of Robert Schumann* (New York, 1969) and Steven Walsh, *The Lieder of Robert Schumann* (New York, 1971).

40. Ulrich Mahlert, *Fortschritt und Kunstlied: Späte Lieder Robert Schumanns im Licht der liedästhetischen Diskussion ab 1848* (Munich and Salzburg, 1983) and Reinhard Kapp, *Studien zum Spätwerk Robert Schumanns* (Tutzing, 1984).

41. Luigi Dallapiccola uses the last poem in the cycle set by Schumann (*Gebet*) in its Latin original as *Preghiera di Maria Stuarda* in his 1941 *Canti di Prigiona.*

42. Hallmark, "The Poet Sings," in GLNC, 104–08.

43. Fischer-Dieskau, *Robert Schumann*, 184.

44. Hallmark, "The Poet Sings," 109.

45. Daverio, *Schumann*, 463–64.

46. Hallmark, "The Poet Sings," 104.

47. Mahlert, *Fortschritt*, 40–82.

48. Ibid., 98–115 and Hallmark, "The Poet Sings," 100–02.

7 A multitude of voices: the Lied at mid century

1. Throughout this essay, I use "Lied" as a generic term for the art song in Germany. See Dahlhaus, NCM, 98, for an all-too-brief differentiation between "Lied" and "Gesang." His contention, based on evidence from the nineteenth century, is that "Gesang" was used for freer compositions. Very few of the pieces under consideration here bear the title "Gesänge."

2. August Reißmann, *Das deutsche Lied in seiner historischen Entwicklung* (Kassel, 1861), 209. My translations, unless otherwise indicated.

3. Reißmann / Mendel, "Deutsches Lied," in *Musikalisches Conversations-Lexicon*, ed. Hermann Mendel (Berlin, 1873) III: 131 and 131–32; here the reference undoubtedly is to Liszt, since his Lieder were then the best-known song products of the New German School.

4. Julius Weiss, "Liederschau," *Neue Berliner Musik-Zeitung* 2 (9 February 1848), 41.

5. Wasielewski, "Zwölf Lieder von Klaus Groth . . . von Carl Banck. Op. 68," *Signale für die musikalische Welt* 16 (February, 1858), 91.

6. Jürgen Thym confirms the diversity of the period in his "Crosscurrents in Song: Five Distinctive Voices," GLNC, 153–85; in so doing, he, too, recognizes no central Lied figure at mid century.

7. Ibid., 153–54. These categories were first identified by Heinrich W. Schwab, *Sangbarkeit, Popularität und Kunstlied* (Regensburg, 1965).

8. Ferdinand Simon Gaßner, *Universal-Lexikon der Tonkunst*, neue Ausgabe (Stuttgart, 1849), 542.

9. Hans Michel Schletterer, "L. Spohr's Liedercompositionen," *Musikalisches Wochenblatt* 1 (28 October 1870), 690.

10. On organicism in nineteenth-century music, see above all Ruth Solie, "The Living Work: Organicism and Musical Analysis," 19CM 4 (1980), 147–56; and David Montgomery, "The Myth of Organicism: From Bad Science to Great Art," MQ 76 (1992), 17–66.

11. Julius Schucht, "Lenau's lyrische Gedichte für Componisten," *Rheinische Musik-Zeitung* 2 (5 June 1852), 804–05.

12. Edouard Schuré, *Geschichte des deutschen Liedes* (Berlin, 1870), 379–91. See also Carl Kossmaly's "Zerstreute Bemerkungen über Liedercompositionen," *Neue Berliner Musik-Zeitung* 14 (18 April 1860), 121, and Eduard Hanslick's "Aesthetische Betrachtung über Composition sogenannter unmusicalischer Texte, veranlasst durch Hoven's Composition der *Heimkehr* von H. Heine," *Rheinische Musik-Zeitung* 2 No. 15 (11 October 1851), 531–34 and No. 16 (18 October), 541–43.

13. Schuré, *Geschichte des deutschen Liedes*, 365.

14. Schucht, "Lenau's lyrische Gedichte für Componisten," 803.

15. NCGL, 84; LMLR, 18.

16. George Kehler, ed., *The Piano in Concert* (Metuchen, NJ, 1982), I: 763.

17. LMLR, 18.

18. See Sanna Pederson, "A. B. Marx, Berlin Concert Life, and German National Identity," 19CM 18 (1994), 87–107; and Celia Applegate, "How German Is It? Nationalism and the Idea of Serious Music in the Early Nineteenth Century," 19CM 21 (1998), 274–96. Even Dahlhaus, NCM, does not mention the political implications of the Lied in his sub-chapter on it (pp. 96–105), despite the fact that he discusses nationhood and national awareness of the folksong (pp. 110–11).

19. Brendel, "Zur Anbahnung einer Verständigung: Vortrag zur Eröffnung der Tonkünstler-Versammlung," NZfM 1 (1859), 265–73.

20. *Dr. Carl Loewe's Selbstbiographie*, ed. Carl Hermann Bitter (Berlin, 1870). The definitive biography is by Henry Joachim Kühn, *Johann Gottfried Carl Loewe: Ein Lesebuch und eine Materialsammlung zu seiner Biographie* (Halle, 1996).

21. *Selbstbiographie*, 10 and 71.

22. Ibid., 71; Thym, "Crosscurrents,"155.

23. Paul Althouse, "Carl Loewe (1796–1869): His Lieder, Ballads, and Their Performance" (Ph.D. dissertation, Yale University, 1971), 48.

24. *Selbstbiographie*, 70–71.

25. Martin Plüddemann, "Karl Loewe," *Bayreuther Blätter* 15 (1892), 328. For a discussion of his literary sources, see Günter Hartung, "Loewes literarische Vorlagen," in *Carl Loewe, 1796–1869: Bericht über die*

wissenschaftliche Konferenz anlässlich seines 200. Geburtstages vom 26. bis 28. September 1996 im Händel-Haus Halle (Halle, 1997).

26. DL, II: 155. According to Thym, "Crosscurrents," 155, Schumann disparaged Loewe "as the cultivator of a remote musical island with little wider influence."

27. Hans Kleemann, *Beiträge zur Ästhetik und Geschichte der Loeweschen Ballade* (Halle, 1913), 32.

28. Walther Dürr, *Das deutsche Sololied im 19. Jahrhundert: Untersuchungen zu Sprache und Music* (Wilhelmshaven, 1984), 204.

29. See Thym, "Crosscurrents," 159–60, for an appraisal of this singular work.

30. Plüddemann (1854–97) was a Wagnerian who attempted to apply the advances of Wagner to the *Lied* in its most dramatic expression, the ballad.

31. James Parakilas, *Ballads Without Words: Chopin and the Tradition of the Instrumental Ballade* (Portland, 1992), considers the nineteenth-century piano ballad.

32. Given the perception of Loewe in the 1850s as a composer who had already made his mark on the Lied, it is not surprising that his later ballads did not receive much attention in the musical press. Em. Klitzsch, "Kammer- und Hausmusik. Lieder und Gesänge," NZfM 33 (13 August 1850), 67.

33. See Marcia Citron, "The Lieder of Fanny Mendelssohn-Hensel," MQ 69 (1983), 570–94; *Fanny Hensel, geb. Mendelssohn Bartholdy: Das Werk*, ed. Martina Helmig (Munich, 1997); and Antje Olivier, *Mendelssohns Schwester Fanny Hensel: Musikerin, Komponistin, Dirigentin* (Düsseldorf, 1997).

34. The letter is dated 9 July 1846. Quoted from *The Letters of Fanny Hensel to Felix Mendelssohn*, trans. Marcia Citron (Stuyvesant, NY, 1987), 349.

35. This support of her husband was not without its darker moments. As Annette Maurer has shown, Fanny's reduced Lieder production from June 1829 through the 1830s and into the 1840s may well have at least partial cause in a dispute with Wilhelm Hensel over her composition of poetry by Gustav Droysen, whom he regarded as a rival. See Maurer's "Biographische Einflüsse auf das Liedschaffen Fanny Hensels," in *Fanny Hensel, geb. Mendelssohn Bartholdy: Das Werk*, 33–36.

36. Nancy Reich, "The Power of Class: Fanny Hensel," *Mendelssohn and his World*, ed. R. Larry Todd (Princeton, 1991), 86.

37. See Marcia Citron, "The Lieder of Fanny Mendelssohn-Hensel," 577, for a listing of poets.

38. Thym, "Crosscurrents," 163–64.

39. There are exceptions: some early songs are through-composed for the purpose of text interpretation, and some late songs are strophic settings.

40. Thym, "Crosscurrents," 166.

41. Reich, "The Power of Class," 92.

42. Thym does not consider Felix Mendelssohn in his survey of mid-century Lied composers. Even Mendelssohn scholars seem reluctant to deal with his songs: the essay collection *Mendelssohn and his World*, ed. R. Larry Todd (Princeton, 1991), makes only one footnote reference to them, despite treatment of virtually every other compositional genre.

43. According to the AmZ, 5 December 1827, Mendelssohn knew Schubert's music by that date.

44. Wulf Konold, *Felix Mendelssohn Bartholdy und seine Zeit* (Laaber, 1984), 251.

45. Konold speculates that Mendelssohn was opposed not to the illustrative element in music, but rather to the purity of the genre, in which drama should play no role (p. 249). See also his letter from July 1831 to his aunt, the Countess Pereira in Vienna, in which Mendelssohn states: "It appears to me totally impossible to compose music for a descriptive poem. The pile of compositions of this type prove my point rather than the contrary, for I know of no successful ones among them." *Reisebriefe aus den Jahren 1830 bis 1832 von Felix Mendelssohn-Bartholdy*, ed. Paul Mendelssohn-Bartholdy, in *Briefe*, vol. I, 7th edn. (Leipzig, 1865), 205.

46. Karl Klingemann, ed., *Felix Mendelssohn Bartholdys Briefwechsel mit Legationsrat Karl Klingemann in London* (Essen, 1909), 86.

47. Gisela A. Müller, "'Leichen-' oder 'Blüthenduft'? Heine-Vertonungen Fanny Hensels und Felix Mendelssohn Bartholdys im Vergleich," in *Fanny Hensel, geb. Mendelssohn-Bartholdy: Das Werk*, 49.

48. Monika Hennemann, "Mendelssohn and Byron: Two Songs Almost without Words," *Mendelssohn-Studien* 10 (1997), 131–56, shows how Mendelssohn mediated English cultural values to the German public through his composition of songs to Byron texts.

49. According to Dürr, Mendelssohn was dissatisfied with the song (perhaps because it was atypical of his work), which may explain why he never published it during his lifetime (p. 150). See also Eric Werner, *Mendelssohn: Leben und Werk in neuer Sicht* (Zurich, 1980), 388 and Luise Leven, *Mendelssohn als Lyriker unter besonderer Berücksichtigung seiner Beziehungen zu Ludwig Berger, Bernhard Klein und Adolf Bernhard Marx* (Krefeld, 1927), 20.

50. *Reisebriefe aus den Jahren 1830 bis 1832*, 236.

51. Reinecke was best known for his children's songs; an anonymous writer in the 1849 *Signale* notes how his other Lieder are Mendelssohnian in their "respectable elegance" and "fine expression of emotion," but lack "passion" and "depth." J. B., "Die Compositionen von Carl Reinecke," *Signale für die musikalische Welt* 7 (1849), 258.

52. The two most important films are *Song of Love* (1947) and *Spring Symphony* (1986), with Katherine Hepburn and Nastassia Kinski respectively playing Clara Schumann. Recent fiction and non-fiction biographies (of varying viewpoints) include Joan Chissell, *Clara Schumann: A Dedicated Spirit* (London, 1983); Nancy Reich, *Clara Schumann: The Artist and the Woman*, revised ed. (Ithaca, 2001); Eva Weissweiler, *Clara Schumann: Eine Biographie* (Hamburg, 1990); Susanna Reich, *Clara Schumann: Piano Virtuoso* (New York, 1999); and James Landis, *Longing* (New York, 2000).

53. One of the better scholarly studies of Clara Schumann's songs is the "Vorwort" by Joachim Draheim and Brigitte Höft to each of the two volumes of *Sämtliche Lieder* (Wiesbaden, 1990 and 1992). See also Janina Klassen, "'Mach' doch ein Lied einmal': Clara Wieck-Schumanns Annäherung an die Liedkomposition," *Schumann-Studien* 6 (1997), 13–25.

54. For provocative examinations of the only joint publication between Clara and Robert, see Rufus Hallmark, "The Rückert Lieder of Robert and Clara Schumann," 19CM 14 (1990), 3–30 and, in the same journal, Melinda Boyd, "Gendered Voices: The *Liebesfrühling* Lieder of Robert and Clara Schumann," 23 (1999), 145–62. The latter study examines the Lied through the prism of feminist and gender theories, especially the notion that in terms of the Lied gender roles are transmutable.

55. Reich, "The Power of Class," 239.

56. Berthold Litzmann, *Clara Schumann. Ein Künstlerleben* (Leipzig, 1902), I: 411–12.

57. *Robert Schumann: Tagebücher*, vol. II: *1836–1854*, ed. Gerd Nauhaus (Leipzig, 1987), 134.

58. Clara copied poems that struck her as well suited for composition, as did Robert. Again, it is difficult to establish a separate identity for Clara on the basis of Lieder texts.

59. Reich, "The Power of Class," 237.

60. See the review "Robert Schumanns Gesangskompositionen" in the 1842 AmZ, in which the anonymous reviewer refuses to attribute individual songs (44 [19 January 1842], col. 61).

61. Draheim and Höft, "Vorwort," 5.

62. "Robert Schumanns Gesangskompositionen," cols. 61–62.

63. See the anonymous review of Op. 13 in vol. 20, 25 March 1844, p. 97.

64. *Robert Schumanns Briefe: Neue Folge*, ed. F. Gustav Jensen, 2nd edn. (Leipzig, 1904), 431, letter of 23 June 1841. One should not be surprised that Robert would write favorably to a potential publisher about this co-production, which primarily consists of his own works.

65. "Clara Schumann," NZfM 41 (1 December 1854), 252.

66. In keeping with the gradual canonization of Clara Schumann, music appreciation texts of the late twentieth century such as *The Enjoyment of Music* and *Music: An Appreciation* have focused on her instrumental music rather than her songs.

67. See Konrad Sasse, *Beiträge zur Forschung über Leben und Werk von Robert Franz 1815–1892* (Halle, 1986), 78–82. The Händel-Haus in Halle also has encouraged performance of Franz's music.

68. *Robert Franz (1815–1892)*, ed. Konstanze Museleta (Halle, 1993). For a recent dissertation, see Bernhard Hartmann, *Das Verhältnis von Sprache und Musik in den Liedern von Robert Franz*, in Europäische Hochschulschriften 36/55 (Frankfurt, 1991).

69. Thym, "Crosscurrents," 173; NCGL, 232.

70. *Robert Franz an Arnold Freiherr Senfft von Pilsach: Ein Briefwechsel 1861–1888*, ed. Wolfgang Golther (Berlin, 1907), 114, letter of 23 October 1871. Franz Liszt observed: "Franz writes Lieder as Schubert did, but [Franz] deviates so significantly from him that the Lied has entered a new phase through his composition." *Robert Franz* (Leipzig, 1872), 10.

71. "Robert Franz: Eine Charakteristik," *Signale für die musikalische Welt* 176 (25 August 1859), 354.

72. Robert Schumann, "Lieder," NZfM 19 (31 July 1843), 33–35. In that year, Franz had solicited commentary about some songs from Schumann, who liked them so much that he recommended the Lieder to one of his own publishers.

73. Alan Walker, *Franz Liszt*, vol. III: *The Final Years, 1861–1886* (New York, 1996), 469. Olga Janina (= Olga Zielinska-Piasecka), an emotionally unsettled Liszt associate, published the first of her antagonistic Liszt memoirs (*Souvenirs d'une cosaque* [Paris, 1874]) under the fictional name "Robert Franz," which caused the infirm composer distress. See Walker, *Liszt*, III: 187–88 for an analysis of her motives behind the pseudonym.

74. *Er ist gekommen in Sturm und Regen* (Op. 4, No. 7) and *12 Lieder* in three volumes:

(1) *Schilflieder*, Op. 2 (complete); (2) *Der Schalk* (Op. 3, No. 1), *Der Bote* (Op. 8, No. 1), *Meeresstille* (Op. 8, No. 2); (3) *Treibt der Sommer* (Op. 8, No. 5), *Gewitternacht* (Op. 8, No. 6), *Das ist ein Brausen und Heulen* (Op. 8, No. 4), *Frühling und Liebe* (Op. 3, No. 3).

75. August Göllerich, *Franz Liszt* (Berlin, 1908), 90.

76. Thym, "Crosscurrents," 173.

77. In a remarkable letter of 23 March 1860 to Joachim, who was trying to collect signatures in early 1860 for a published manifesto against the New German School of Liszt and Wagner, Franz makes clear his difficult position. While he is too indebted to Liszt, who "has always shown himself as noble and unselfish towards me," Franz believed the New German clique deserved the harshest criticism. *Briefe von und an Joseph Joachim*, ed. Joachim and Andreas Moser (Berlin, 1912), II: 82–83.

78. "To my question, whether he considers Liszt to be an important person, totally apart from his compositions, Franz gave a positive response. He has a high opinion of Liszt, and what [Liszt] wrote about him is the best." Wilhelm Waldmann, *Robert Franz: Gespräche aus zehn Jahren* (Leipzig, 1895), 20.

79. Sasse provides an overview of attempts to periodize Franz's output. See his *Beiträge zur Forschung über Leben und Werk von Robert Franz 1815–1892* (Halle, 1986), 30–39.

80. Letter to Arnold Freiherr Senfft von Pilsach, 8 July 1877, in *Robert Franz an Arnold Freiherr Senfft von Pilsach*, 270. This is one of Franz's most informative letters about his perspectives on the Lied.

81. See, respectively, Waldmann, *Franz*, 8 and Thym, "Crosscurrents," 174.

82. W. K. von Jolizza, *Das Lied und seine Geschichte* (Vienna and Leipzig, 1910), 470.

83. Waldmann, *Franz*, 153.

84. Ibid., 109.

85. Letter to Erich Prieger, 29 January 1882, *Über Dichtung und Musik. Drei Briefe von Robert Franz*, ed. Erich Prieger (Berlin, 1901), 7.

86. See Thym, "Crosscurrents," 172–73, for a more detailed discussion of Franz's failure to identify irony, such as the "smiling-through-tears effect" of Schubert's *Trockene Blumen*. See also Hartmann, *Verhältnis*, *passim*; Joachim Draheim, "Robert Franz und Robert Schumann – Aspekte einer schwierigen Beziehung," *Robert Franz (1815–1892)*, ed. Musketa, 163–87; and Gerhard Dietel, "Musikgeschichtliche Aspekte der Liedästhetik bei Robert Schumann and Robert Franz," in the same volume, 188–95.

87. Letter to Erich Prieger, 27 January 1882, in *Über Dichtung und Musik*, ed. Prieger, 5.

88. Letter to Ludwig Meinardus, October 1850, in Richard Tronnier, *Von Musik und Musikern* (Münster, 1930), 189. His concept of "polyphonic melody" enables harmony and melody to work together in organic relationship. See Waldmann, *Franz*, 25–26.

89. Hartmann, *Verhältnis*, 31. This explains why his melodies are generally such that they do not work well independently of their accompaniment.

90. See Markus Waldura, "Lenaus *Schilflieder* in Vertonungen durch Robert Franz, Peter Heise und Wilhelm Claussen: Ein Vergleich," in *Robert Franz (1815–1892): Bericht über die wissenschaftliche Konferenz anläßlich seines 100. Todestages* (Halle, 1993), 78–100 and, in the same collection, Dagmar Brazda, "Die *Schilflieder* op. 2," 302–17.

91. Letter to Arnold Freiherr Senfft von Pilsach, 14 September 1876, in *Robert Franz an Arnold Freiherr Senfft von Pilsach*, 246–47.

92. Waldura, "Lenaus *Schilflieder*," 92.

93. Gustav Engel, "Recensionen. Robert Franz, Sechs Gesänge . . . Op. 22," *Neue Berliner Musik-Zeitung* 10 (14 May 1856), 153.

94. There exists an extensive bibliography about Cornelius as song composer; most recently see Karlheinz Pricken, "Peter Cornelius als Dichter und Musiker in seinem Liedschaffen (eine Stiluntersuchung)" (Ph.D. dissertation, University of Cologne, 1951); and Günter Massenkeil, "Cornelius als Liederkomponist," in *Peter Cornelius als Komponist, Dichter, Kritiker und Essayist*, ed. Hellmut Federhofen and Kurt Oehl (Regensburg, 1977), 159–67.

95. If this tendency in Cornelius calls Wagner to mind, it developed independently from Wagner and before their contact in the 1860s. Cornelius's poems are partially reproduced by Adolf Stern in *Peter Cornelius: Literarische Werke*, vol. IV: *Gedichte* (Leipzig, 1904). Even other composers, such as Hans von Bronsart, Eduard Lassen, and Alexander Ritter, set poetry by Cornelius to music.

96. Massenkeil, "Cornelius als Liederkomponist," 161.

97. Thym, "Crosscurrents," 182.

98. In a letter to Liszt, 7 October 1854, Cornelius summarized the ethos of each song: "The first Lied bespeaks an irreplaceable loss. The second: remembrance. The third: moderation of grief. The fourth: solace in dreams. The fifth: promise of eternal faithfulness. The sixth: elevation to God." *Peter Cornelius: Literarische Werke*, vol. IV: *Ausgewählte Briefe*, ed. Carl Maria Cornelius (Leipzig, 1904), I: 160–61.

99. Thym, "Crosscurrents," 180.
100. Jolizza, *Das Lied*, 478.
101. Gottfried Schweizer, in his dissertation *Das Liedschaffen Adolf Jensens* (Gießen, 1933), provides a useful chronological chart of Jensen's Lieder (pp. 6–7), as well as a complete frequency list for song poets (p. 9).
102. *Hugo Riemanns Musik-Lexikon*, 11th edn., ed. Alfred Einstein (Berlin, 1929), 832.
103. LMLR, 18.

8 The Lieder of Liszt

1. *Drei Lieder aus Schillers "Wilhelm Tell"* (*Der Fischerknabe* ["Es lächelt der See"], *Der Hirt* ["Ihr Matten lebt wohl"], *Der Alpenjäger* ["Es donnern die Höh'n"], orchestrated in the 1840s but only published in 1872; *Jeanne d'Arc au bücher* (A. Dumas, "Mon Dieu! J'étais bergère," "Scène dramatique"; orchestrated late 1840s, revised 1850s and 1874; published 1877); *Die Loreley* (Heine, "Ich weiss nicht, was soll's bedeuten," 1860; published 1863); *Die Vätergruft* (Uhland, "Es schritt wohl auf die Haide," 1859; published 1860); *Mignons Lied* (Goethe, "Kennst du das Land"; 1860; published 1863); *Die drei Zigeuner* (Lenau, "Drei Zigeuner fand ich einmal," 1860; published 1872); *Die Allmacht* (Schubert, "Gross ist Jehovah der Herr," 1871; published 1872); *Zwei Lieder von Francis Korbay* (*Le matin* [Bizet], *Gebet* [Geibel], 1883; unpublished).
2. Liszt turned to the orchestration of his own songs in the late 1850s while completing six Schubert transcriptions for voice and orchestra: *Die junge Nonne, Gretchen am Spinnrade, Lied der Mignon* ("Kennst du das Land"), *Erlkönig, Der Doppelgänger*, and *Abschied*. The last two remain unpublished.
3. For Liszt, in all but a very few cases, once a musical idea engaged him sufficiently to work it out into a full-fledged composition, it rarely lost its viability or continuing interest. Thus we have two, three, and even four distinct settings of a single text. In the case of songs, the act of transposition evidently opened up even further possibilities.
4. Three volumes of Lieder were published by the Franz-Liszt-Stiftung between 1917 and 1922 in *Franz Liszts Musikalische Werke*, edited by Peter Raabe (VII, 1–3). The critical apparatus of these volumes was of a very high standard and can still be used fruitfully, if with care, for information concerning the sources. Breitkopf & Härtel was to have continued the project, bringing out the complete works, but only about one half of Liszt's musical output was ever published, and the edition ceased in 1936. The *Neue Liszt Ausgabe* (Editio Musica Budapest,

1979–) aims to remedy this situation, but thus far only piano music has been issued.
5. The most obvious mistakes are found in the first version of *Mignons Lied* ("Kennst du das Land"), in which the musical/syntactical stress is put on the word "du," and in *Petrarch Sonnet* No. 123 ("I' vidi in terra angelici costumi"), in which the word "soglia" is set as three syllables. It should be noted, however, that in later printed versions these errors are corrected.
6. It should be clear that my view is diametrically opposed to that of Christopher Headington, whose essay on the songs in *Franz Liszt: The Man and His Music*, ed. Alan Walker (New York, 1970), 221–47, remains the only extended tract concerning these works. Headington writes, "Liszt's songs, considered as a whole, could hardly be claimed to rank among his greatest achievements" (p. 221).
7. At this point, Liszt was engaged in transcribing the Beethoven symphonies for solo piano, as well as *An die ferne Geliebte* and the Schubert materials described below. See further Alan Walker, "Liszt and the Schubert Song Transcriptions," MQ 75 (1991), 248–62 and Thomas Kabisch, *Liszt und Schubert* (Munich, 1984).
8. See my *Franz Liszt: The Schubert Song Transcriptions for Solo Piano*, Series I (New York, 1995), ix–xiii.
9. At present there is no thematic catalogue for Liszt's music that addresses the problems associated with determining the sequence of variants, as well as the multiple settings, in the oeuvre; but one is underway, co-authored by this writer and Mária Eckhardt of Budapest, to be published by Henle Verlag in Munich.
10. Blandine was born 18 December 1835 in Geneva; the two other children were Cosima (born 24 December 1837 in Bellaggio), and Daniel (born 9 May 1839 in Rome).
11. The Countess eloped to Switzerland with Liszt in mid-1835, leaving her husband and surviving daughter in their residence at Croissy. Liszt and Marie traveled extensively during the next four years, maintaining a series of residences in Switzerland and Italy through 1840. They separated permanently in 1844.
12. The 1843 *Sechs Lieder* published by Eck of Cologne included *Morgens steh' ich auf und frage* (Heine), *Die tote Nachtigall* (Kauffmann), *Du bist wie eine Blume* (Heine), *Bist du* ("Mild wie ein Lufthauch," Metschersky), *Vergiftet sind meine Lieder* (Heine), and *Dichter, was Liebe sei* (Charlotte von Hagn). The 1848 *Schiller und Goethe Lieder von Franz Liszt* issued by Haslinger in Vienna included the three *Lieder aus Schillers "Wilhelm Tell,"* two versions of *Freudvoll und*

leidvoll (Goethe), *Wer nie sein Brot mit Thränen ass* (Goethe), and *Ueber allen Gipfeln ist Ruh* (Goethe).

13. *Im Rhein, im heiligen Strome* (Heine), *Der du von dem Himmel bist* (Heine), *Die Loreley* ("Ich weiss nicht, was soll's bedeuten"), *Die Zelle in Nonnenwerth* ("Ach nun taucht die Klosterzelle," Lichnowsky), *Mignons Lied* ("Kennst du das Land," Goethe), and *Es war ein König in Thule* (Goethe). Liszt called the piano versions *Buch der Lieder für Piano allein*. For a critical analysis of the very complex Liszt–Heine relationship, see Susan Bernstein, *Virtuosity of the Nineteenth Century: Performing Music and Language in Heine, Liszt, and Baudelaire* (Palo Alto, CA, 1998), 58–151. The tension between the two men was more evident on Heine's side and had existed since their first acquaintance in Paris in the 1830s. It was exacerbated by Heine's series of critical reviews of Liszt's performances, and reached its apogee in the poem entitled *Im August 1849*, one of twenty in the collection *Lazarus*. Here Heine castigated Liszt for apparently having done nothing politically during the August 1849 Hungarian uprising, which had been brutally crushed by the combined Austrian and Russian forces. While Liszt does not appear to have responded to the poem, it is likely that, as usual, he turned inward and to the keyboard to vent his feelings – toward Heine and the Hungarian events – composing the *Funérailles*, No. 7 in the *Harmonies poétiques et religieuses*, which is subtitled "Oktober 1849." In the early 1840s, however, Liszt was quite willing to ignore the vituperative language of Heine's essays and reach beyond for his poetry.

14. The 1840 Rhine Crisis was precipitated by the apparently "expansionist" movement of the French Cabinet, which called into question the Rhine River as France's easternmost boundary – an aggravation of the ancient Gallic–Teutonic border dispute over the Rhineland provinces (Alsace and Lorraine), which had become increasingly negative as a result of the treaties of 1815 ending the Napoleonic Wars. For France, those treaties were unjust, and as the Napoleonic legend once again took hold in their national imagination, a minor Levantine crisis in Egypt was used as the pretext for much chauvinistic posturing. For Germans, the Rhine could never be anything but wholly German, and the nationalistic fervor that arose in the Germanic Confederation when the French seemed once again to be aggressively inclined culminated in a pronouncement by the King of Bavaria that the Germans should reacquire Strasbourg. Heine, an expatriate resident of Paris since 1831, was an outspoken member of the Young Germany

movement, the *Vormärz*. See Cecelia Hopkins Porter, *The Rhine as Musical Metaphor: Cultural Identity in German Romantic Music* (Boston, 1996); see also the same author's "The Rheinlieder Critics: a Case of Musical Nationalism," MQ 63 (1977), 74–98.

15. Piano versions of several songs were also transcribed, but all were individually published later and not conceived within sets.

16. *O! quand je dors, Comment disaient-ils, Enfant, si j'étais roi, S'il est un charmant gazon, La tombe et la rose,* and *Gastibelza*. According to Liszt's letter of 18 March 1843 to Heinrich Schlesinger, in Paris, the Hugo Songs originally had seven or eight numbers; however, only six were published, and the question of what were the missing texts cannot be answered conclusively. It is likely that one of the songs was *Quand tu chantes bercée*, rediscovered in the early 1970s by Istvan Kecskeméti in the autograph album of Mathilde Juva Branca, the famed soprano for whom Rossini had written out aria ornamentation. See Kecskeméti, "Egy ismeretlen Liszt-dal," *Magyar Zene* 15 (1974), 17–25, and "Two Liszt Discoveries: 1. An Unknown Piano Piece; 2. An Unknown Song," MT 115 (1974), 646–48 and 743–44. The piano transcriptions of the six published Hugo Songs, completed at Princess Carolyne Sayn-Wittgenstein's estate in Woronince (Ukraine) in October 1847, remained in manuscript until 1985, when they were published in the *New Liszt Edition*, Series ii, vol. XVIII. See Rena Charnin Mueller, "Liszt's *Tasso* Sketchbook: Studies in Sources and Revisions" (Ph.D. Diss., New York University, 1986), 168 ff.

17. Marie d'Agoult collected texts in all languages for Liszt's use in all genres; her "Poetisches Album" (Weimar, Goethe-und-Schiller Archiv, MS 60/142), contains selections, among many others, from the works of Byron (*Manfred*), Lichnowsky (*Die Zelle in Nonnenwerth*), Strozzi (*Michelangelo's 'La Notte'*), Lenau (*Aus 'Faust'*), and Rellstab (*Beethoven Fest-Kantate*).

18. "J'aurais aimé t'envoyer aussi une chanson de V.H. 'Oh! Quand je dors viens auprès de ma couche, Comme à Petrarque, etc.' . . . [apparaissait Laura.] Merci des volumes de Hugo. Je vais lire." *Correspondance de Liszt et de la comtesse d'Agoult*, ed. Daniel Ollivier, 2 vols. (Paris 1933–34), II: 198.

19. See Mueller, "Liszt's *Tasso* Sketchbook," 144 ff.

20. Haslinger, Vienna. Until recently, it had been thought that the vocal versions came out in 1847. At this point, *Benedetto sia 'l giorno* was

the second sonnet, preceded by *Pace non trovo* in both the sketches in WRgs MS59/N8 and in the published vocal and keyboard sets. Only later in 1858, when Liszt decided to include the Petrarch Sonnets in the *Années de pèlerinage II (Italie)*, did he reverse the order of the sonnets and place *Benedetto* before *Pace non trovo*.

21. "The Unknown Liszt – The World of his Songs with Piano," liner notes for *Franz Liszt – Lieder*, performed by Dietrich Fischer-Dieskau, accompanied by Daniel Barenboim (DGG 2740254; 1981).

22. Hamburg, Universitäts-und-Stadtbibliothek Liszt Nachlass, MSS II/3 and I/6.

23. Even to this day, the two genres are mixed, since accompanists in Lieder performances often appropriate the cadenzas from the solo piano versions in concert, even though they only appear in the piano text.

24. See Rena Charnin Mueller, "Reevaluating the Liszt Chronology: The Case of *Anfangs wollt ich fast verzagen*," 19CM 12 (1988), 132–47.

25. Liszt had written about his own Lieder to his friend and fellow composer Joseph Dessauer, criticizing his early works as being "too inflated and sentimental" and questioning whether he would ever return to song. The letter is undated, but clearly comes from the early 1850s, according to corollary evidence. See *Franz Liszts Briefe*, ed. La Mara, 2 vols. (Leipzig, 1893–1905), II: 403, and *Letters of Franz Liszt*, ed. and trans. Constance Bache, 2 vols. (New York, 1968), II: 502.

26. See Mueller, "Liszt's *Tasso* Sketchbook," 31–97, for a complete overview of the Weimar scriptorium and its documents. This situation pertains to Liszt's music in general, and not simply to that of the Lieder.

27. *Isten veled* (P. Horvath, 1847), *Die drei Zigeuner* ("Drei Zigeuner fand ich einmal," Lenau, 1860; this work contains Hungarian elements, although the poem is in German), *Magyar király-dal* ("Aldott légyen Magyarok királya," 1883); *Go not happy day* (Tennyson, 1879); *Ne brani menya, moy drug* (A. Tolstoy, 1866).

28. "die Retterin meiner 'ersten' und 'letzten' Lieder, für welche Sie keine Zivil-Verdienstmedaille von irgendeinem Konservatorium (noch weniger von der Zunft der Critik) zu erwarten haben!" Otto Goldhammer, *Nonnenwerth*, facsimile edn., Nationale Forschungs- und Gedenkstätten der klassischen deutschen Literatur in Weimar (Weimar, 1961).

29. Liszt contemplated a number of operatic projects in the 1840s, but only the subject of Byron's *Sardanapalus* interested him enough to actually compose music; an incomplete draft is in Weimar, WRgs MS59/N4.

30. The other items include: *Vergiftet sind meine Lieder* (Heine), *Du bist wie eine Blume* (Heine), *Anfangs wollt' ich fast verzagen* (Heine), *Kling leise, mein Lied* (Nordmann), *Morgens steh' ich auf und frage* (Heine), *Ihr Auge* ("Nimm einen Strahl der Sonne," Rellstab), *Dichter, was Liebe sei?* (Charlotte von Hagn), *Comment disaient-ils* (Hugo), *Amaranthe* ("Es muss ein Wunderbares sein," Redwitz), *Es rauschen die Winde* (Rellstab), *Schwebe, schwebe, blaues Auge* (Dingelstedt), *Die Vätergruft* (Uhland), *Wo weilt er* (Rellstab), *O! quand je dors* (Hugo), *S'il est un charmant gazon* (Hugo), *Lasst mich ruhen* (Hoffmann von Fallersleben), *In Liebeslust* (Hoffmann von Fallersleben), and *Ich möchte hingehn* (Herwegh).

31. For instance, the *Harmonies poétiques et religieuses*, *Années de pèlerinage I (Suisse) and II (Italie)*, and the *Hungarian Rhapsodies*. See further, Mueller, "Sketches, Drafts, and Revisions," in *Die Projekte der Liszt-Forschung: Bericht über das internationale Symposion Eisenstadt, 19–21 Oktober 1989*, ed. Detlef Altenburg (Eisenstadt, 1991), 23–34.

32. Liszt credited Louis Köhler's *Melodie der Sprache* (1859) with a substantial influence on his text-setting capabilities, especially his revision of *Ich möchte hingehn* (Herwegh), which he dedicated to Köhler, on the manuscript and in a letter, although it never appeared in print.

33. Kahnt issued a French edition of a number of songs in 1880, and Liszt again revised many, adding ossia lines for both voice and piano.

34. Beilage, *Deutscher Musen-Almanach*, ed. Charles Schaad (Würzburg, 1856).

35. While it is correctly thought that Wagner codified much of the practice concerning the double-tonic complex, we see, again, that Liszt was the pioneer in matching relative key areas as points of repose in the same way composers fifty years earlier had equated parallel tonalities. For an example of this process in the symphonic poems, see Mueller, *Introduction* to the new edition of *Les Préludes*, Editio Musica Budapest (1997). For the primary explanation of Wagner's usage, see Robert Bailey's essay "An Analytical Study of the Sketches and Drafts" in Bailey's edition of *Richard Wagner: Prelude and Transfiguration from Tristan und Isolde* (New York, 1985), 113–46, especially pp. 120–22.

36. Liszt uses a swaying *barcarolle* movement, common to many settings of music dealing with the Rhine.

37. The Henle Urtext Edition of the second *Ballade* in B minor (1996) reproduces all three endings together for the first time.

38. Liszt wrote six melodramas, to texts by Bürger (*Lenore*), F. Halm (*Vor hundert Jahren*), Lenau (*Der traurige Mönch*), Jókai (*Des toten Dichters Liebe*, for which the main theme served as the basis for *Alexander Petofi*, No. 6 of the *Historische ungarische Bildnisse*), A. Tolstoy (*Der blinde Sänger*), and Strachwitz (*Helges Treue*), the latter a substantial revision of a composition by Felix Draeseke.

39. The poem was written June 1840 and first published December 1841 in *La Revue des Deux Mondes*. Musset died in 1857; it is tempting to suggest that Liszt remembered the poem, rather than simply coming across it in the Musset *Oeuvres Complètes* (1866–83).

40. Cosima married Hans von Bülow in 1857; their two daughters, Daniela and Blandine, were born in 1860 and 1863, respectively.

41. Isolde (b. 1865), and Eva (b. 1867); their third child, Siegfried, was born in 1869.

42. His son, Daniel, had died in Berlin in 1859; his eldest daughter, Blandine Ollivier, had died a month after the birth of her only child in 1862.

43. Williams, *Franz Liszt: Selected Letters*, 745.

44. For a study that traces this idea as well as many others through Liszt's late works, see David Butler Cannata, "Perception and Apperception in Liszt's Late Piano Music," JM 15 (1997), 178–208.

45. Schoenberg, "Franz Liszt's Work and Being," in *Style and Idea: Selected Writings of Arnold Schoenberg*, ed. Leonard Stein, trans. Leo Black (London, 1975), 442–47.

9 The Lieder of Brahms

1. Elisabet von Herzogenberg to Brahms on 21–22 May 1885. *Johannes Brahms: The Herzogenberg Correspondence*, trans. Hannah Bryant ([1909], rpt. with an introduction by Walter Frisch [New York, 1987]), 226–27.

2. In addition to the solo songs, Brahms arranged numerous volumes of folk songs. For a complete listing of both Brahms's Lieder and his folk song arrangements, together with dates, poets, and other pertinent details, see Margit L. McCorkle, *Johannes Brahms: Thematisches-Bibliographisches Werkverzeichnis* (Munich, 1984).

3. For a biographical sketch of Jenner, see Richard Schaal, "Jenner," in *Die Musik in Geschichte und Gegenwart* (Kassel, 1957), 6: 1882–83.

4. Gustav Jenner, *Johannes Brahms als Mensch, Lehrer und Künstler: Studien und Erlebnisse* (Marburg in Hessen, 1905; 2nd edn. 1930; rpt. Munich, 1989). Jenner's reminiscences first appeared in the 1903 volume of *Die Musik*. Parts of this essay, including most of the section on

songwriting, recently appeared in English translation by Susan Gillespie. These excerpts are included in *Brahms and His World*, ed. Walter Frisch (Princeton, 1990), 185–204. All Jenner references are taken from this English translation.

5. The non-musical books that have survived from Brahms's library are catalogued in Kurt Hofmann, *Die Bibliothek von Johannes Brahms: Bücher- und Musikalienverzeichnis* (Hamburg, 1974).

6. Together with Andreas Kretzschmer, Zuccalmaglio brought out two volumes entitled *Deutsche Volkslieder mit ihren Original-Weisen* (1838, 1840). Both Kretzschmer and Zuccalmaglio contributed essays on folk-related topics for Schumann's NZfM.

7. Stein, *Poem and Music in the German Lied from Gluck to Hugo Wolf* (Cambridge, MA, 1971), 131.

8. See, for example, Clara Schumann's objections to the text of *Willst du, daß ich geh'?*, Op. 71, No. 4, in a letter dated 2 May 1877. *Letters of Clara Schumann and Johannes Brahms 1853–1896*, ed. Berthold Litzmann (New York, 1927), II: 7.

9. Richard Heuberger, *Erinnerungen an Johannes Brahms*, 2nd edn., ed. Kurt Hofmann (Tutzing, 1976), 38. Max Friedländer, *Brahms's Lieder: An Introduction to the Songs for One and two Voices*, English trans. C. Leonard Leese (London, 1928), 23.

10. Hermann Deiters, *Johannes Brahms: A Biographical Sketch*, trans. Rosa Newmarch, ed. John Alexander Fuller-Maitland (London, 1888; photocopy, Austin, 1995), 92.

11. Through the analysis of sketches and autographs, George Bozarth has demonstrated that Brahms transformed early versions of *Agnes*, Op. 59, No. 5, and the duet *Die Schwestern*, Op. 61, No. 2, from simple to modified strophic settings in order to better match the changing tone of the respective poems. George S. Bozarth, "Brahms's Duets for Soprano and Alto, Op. 61: A Study in Chronology and Compositional Process," *Studia Musicologica Academiae Scientiarum Hungaricae* 25 (1983), 191–210.

12. *Wie Melodien* will not be considered here as its subtleties are described by Austin Clarkson, "Brahms, Song Op. 105 No. 1: A Literary-Historical Approach," and Edward Laufer, "Brahms, Song Op. 105 No. 1: A Schenkerian Approach," in *Readings in Schenker Analysis and Other Approaches*, ed. Maury Yeston (New Haven and London, 1977), 230–53 and 254–72.

13. As reported by Florence May, *The Life of Johannes Brahms* (1905, 2nd edn.; rpt. Neptune City, 1981), 109.

14. Richard Specht, *Johannes Brahms*, trans. Eric Blom (London and Toronto, 1930), 334.

15. The half note falls on the word "bin" and in Brahms's own lifetime this instance of poor declamation attracted much criticism. Jenner mentions this and reports Brahms's dismissal of such criticisms.

16. Letter to Brahms, dated 8 November 1877; quoted in *Billroth und Brahms im Briefwechsel: Mit Einleitung, Anmerkungen und 4 Bildtafeln* (Berlin and Vienna, 1935; rpt. 1991), 248–50.

17. Rudolf Gerber provides the best overview of the forms of Brahms's Lieder, and aside from analyzing modified-strophic pieces, he diagrams various types of expanded ternary forms (see pp. 36–40). Gerber, "Formprobleme im Brahms'schen Lied," *Jahrbuch der Musikbibliothek Peters*, 29 (1932), 23–42.

18. Eric Sams, *The Songs of Hugo Wolf*, 2nd edn. (London, 1983), 81, translates Horace's epigraph as: "You ever in tearful strains dwell on Mystes taken away: your loving laments cease not when the evening star rises, nor when it flees the swift sun." Wolf printed this quotation at the beginning of his setting of the Mörike poem.

19. See August Langen, "Zum Symbol der Aeolsharfe in der deutschen Dichtung," *Zum 70. Geburtstag von Joseph Müller-Blattau*, ed. Christoph Hellmut-Mahling (Kassel, 1966), 160–91.

20. Friedländer, *Brahms's Lieder*, 33.

21. Max Kalbeck, *Johannes Brahms*, 4 vols. (Vienna, Leipzig, and Berlin, 1904–14), II: 141.

22. I explain this effect in greater detail in my article "Unrequited Love and Unrealized Dominants," *Intégral* 7 (1994), 119–48.

23. I discuss the intricacies of the phrase structure of each stanza in this song in fuller detail in "Text-Music Relationships in the Lieder of Johannes Brahms" (Ph.D. dissertation, Graduate Center of the City University of New York, 1992), 150–60.

24. George S. Bozarth, "The 'Lieder' of Johannes Brahms – 1868–1871: Studies in the Chronology and Compositional Process" (Ph.D. dissertation, Princeton University, 1978), 113–14, and Bozarth, "The Musical and Documentary Sources for Brahms's Lieder: Evidence of Compositional Process," booklet to Deutsche Grammophon's *Johannes Brahms Lieder* (Hamburg, 1983), 42–43.

25. Hellmut Federhofer, "Zur Einheit von Wort und Ton im Lied von Johannes Brahms," in *Kongress-Bericht Gesellschaft für Musikforschung Hamburg 1956*, ed. Walter Gerstenberg, Heinrich Husman, and Harald Heckmann (Kassel, 1956), 97–99. Siegfried Kross, "Rhythmik und Sprachbehandlung bei Brahms," in *Bericht über den Internationalen Musikwissenschaftlichen*

Kongress, Kassel 1962, ed. Georg Reichert and Martin Just (Kassel, 1963), 217–19.

26. See Kristina Muxfeldt, "Schubert, Platen, and the Myth of Narcissus," JAMS 49 (1996), 480–527.

27. Brahms has been criticized for introducing word repetitions because they alter the structure of the original poem, and some authors consider that they are inserted purely for the purpose of extending the melody. See, for example, Eric Sams, *Brahms Songs* (London and Seattle, 1972), 8. Nevertheless, Brahms and most other Lied composers (including Wolf) rarely arbitrarily repeat words; word repetitions usually underscore a particularly important moment in a poem. Thus, in the first stanza of *Ruhe, Süßliebchen* Brahms repeats "ewig" an additional time within the repeat of the final line, emphasizing the depth of Peter's commitment. See also Edward T. Cone, "Words into Music: The Composer's Approach to Text," *Sound and Poetry*, ed. Northrop Frye (New York, 1957), 11–13.

28. See Wolf's remarks on Brahms's *Salome*, Op. 69, No. 8. *Hugo Wolf: Letters to Melanie Köchert*, trans. Louise McClelland (New York, 1991), 11.

29. Konrad Giebeler offers perhaps the most sustained exploration of Brahms's declamation, though he seems to consider only the relationship of rhythm and poetic accents, and does not take into account harmonic or melodic emphasis. Giebeler, *Die Lieder von Johannes Brahms: Ein Beitrag zur Musikgeschichte des 19. Jahrhunderts* (Münster, 1959).

30. I explain the influence of the Wagner–Wolf style on the reception of Brahms's Lieder in my essay "The Influence of Hugo Wolf on the Reception of Brahms's Lieder," *Brahms Studies* 2 (Lincoln, NE, 1998), 91–111.

31. Ernst Decsey, *Hugo Wolf*, 2nd edn. (Leipzig, 1903), I: 92. Max Kalbeck, *Johannes Brahms*, III: 335–37.

32. Compare the reports of Brahms's word painting by Elaine Brody and Robert A. Fowkes, *The German Lied and its Poetry* (New York, 1971), 135, with the numerous instances of word painting described by Walter Hammermann, *Johannes Brahms als Liedkomponist: Eine theoretisch-ästhetische Stiluntersuchung* (Leipzig, 1912), 3–4 and 21–27.

33. Ira Braus, "Textual Rhetorical Organization and Harmonic Anomaly in Selected Lieder of Johannes Brahms" (Ph.D. dissertation, Harvard University, 1988), 261–62.

34. Werner Morik, *Johannes Brahms und sein Verhältnis zum deutschen Volkslied* (Tutzing, 1965), 282.

35. The melodic line of this song is full of evocative gestures. The line "Vor Schmerz" is set

off from the surrounding ones and the voice dramatically falls a fifth, forming a rhyme with "ums Herz" of line 1. By contrast, at the beginning of stanza 2 a gently falling melodic line depicts the image of the character laying his head down.

36. See Hermann Deiters's review of Opp. 46–49 in AmZ 4/14 (7 April 1869), 106–08; and Paul Mies, *Stilmomente und Ausdrucksstilformen im Brahms'schen Lied* (Leipzig, 1923). Aside from considering the expressive quality of various chords, Mies considers pedal points, triadic melodies, ornaments, and rhythm. Mies and Erwin Rieger also have discussed the affective role of key characteristics in Brahms's songs. Mies, "Tonmalerei in den Brahmsschen Werken," *Die Musik* 26 (1923–24), 184–88, and Rieger, "Die Tonartencharakteristik im einstimmigen Klavierlied von Johannes Brahms," *Studien zur Musikwissenschaft* 22 (1955), 142–216.

37. George Henschel, *Personal Recollections of Johannes Brahms: Some of His Letters to and Pages from a Journal kept by George Henschel* (1907; rpt. New York, 1978), 22–23. One such analysis of *Mainacht* is by Christian Martin Schmidt, who argues, however, that in Brahms's Lieder the motivic structure is completely independent of the texts. Most other observers refute this conclusion and show that some of the motivic transformations and repetitions are linked to the texts. Schmidt, "Überlegungen zur Liedanalyse bei Brahms' 'Die Mainacht,' Op. 43. 2," in *Brahms-Analysen Referate der Kieler Tagung 1983*, ed. Friedhelm Krummacher and Wolfram Steinbeck (Kassel, 1984), 47–59.

38. Arnold Schoenberg, "Brahms the Progressive" (1947), *Style and Idea: Selected Writings of Arnold Schoenberg*, ed. Leonard Stein, trans. Leo Black (Belmont, 1975; rpt. Berkeley, 1984), 431–35.

39. Walter Frisch, *Brahms and the Principle of Developing Variation* (Berkeley, 1984; rpt. 1990), 151–56.

40. Eduard Hanslick, "Johannes Brahms' Erinnerungen und Briefe" in *Musikalische Kritiken und Schilderungen: Am Ende des Jahrhunderts* (2nd edn. Berlin, 1899), 393.

41. George Bozarth, "Synthesizing Word and Tone: Brahms's Setting of Hebbel's 'Vorüber'," in *Brahms: Biographical, Documentary and Analytical Studies*, ed. Robert Pascall (Cambridge, 1983), 85. Eduard Behm "Studien bei Brahms," *Allgemeine Musikzeitung*, 64/13–14 (26 March 1937), 183–85.

42. Friedländer, *Brahms's Lieder*, 58.

10 Tradition and innovation: the Lieder of Hugo Wolf

1. Marie Lang, "Hugo Wolfs Entwicklungszeit" in *Die Zeit* (Vienna) for 3 January 1904, cited in Frank Walker, *Hugo Wolf: A Biography* (London, 1968, 2nd edn., rpt. Princeton, 1992), 325.

2. See Susan Youens, *Hugo Wolf: The Vocal Music* (Princeton, 1992); Youens, *Hugo Wolf and his Mörike Songs* (Cambridge, 2000); and Amanda Glauert, *Hugo Wolf and the Wagnerian Inheritance* (Cambridge, 1999).

3. Walker, *Hugo Wolf*, 142–43, recounts a delightful anecdote by the writer (and Wolf roommate) Hermann Bahr from the summer of 1883. Wolf was on vacation in Rinnbach and would regale his friends with scornful readings of bad poetry, probably Richard Kralik von Meyrswalden's effusions.

4. Wolf made this statement about Schubert's settings of Goethe's "Prometheus" and "Ganymed" in a letter of 22 December 1890 to Emil Kauffmann. See Hugo Wolf, *Briefe an Emil Kauffmann* (Berlin, 1903), 25.

5. A letter Wolf wrote to his family on 15 March 1876 (two days after his sixteenth birthday) recounts the meeting with Wagner and is cited in Walker, *Hugo Wolf*, 35–36.

6. On 27 March 1888, Wolf told his friend Friedrich ("Fritz") Eckstein, "On Saturday I composed, without having intended to do so, 'Das verlassene Mägdlein', already set to music by Schumann in a heavenly way. If in spite of that I set the same poem to music, it happened almost against my will; but perhaps just because I allowed myself to be captured suddenly by the magic of this poem, something outstanding arose, and I believe that my composition may show itself beside Schumann's." See Walker, *Hugo Wolf*, 205–06.

7. Wolf's exuberant letters to his friends Edmund and Marie Lang, Eckstein, and Josef Strasser are cited in Walker, *Hugo Wolf*, 202–06.

8. Hugo Wolf, *Briefe an Emil Kauffmann*, letter of 5 June 1890, 113–14.

9. See Manfred Koschlig, "Mörikes barocker Grundton und seine verborgenen Quellen: Studien zur Geschichtlichkeit des Dichters," *Zeitschrift für Württembergische Landesgeschichte* 34–35 (1975–76), 231–323.

10. See Jeffrey Adams, ed., *Mörike's Muses: Critical Essays on Eduard Mörike* (Columbia, SC, 1990); Renate von Heydebrand, *Eduard Mörikes Gedichtwerk. Beschreibung und Deutung der Formenvielfalt und ihrer Entwicklung* (Stuttgart, 1972); and Peter Lahnstein, *Eduard Mörike: Leben und Milieu eines Dichters* (Munich, 1986).

11. Mörike does not link the poems together, but Wolf imagined that the young

philanderer-in-the-making ("Der Knabe . . .")
would, at some future date, betray the young
woman who laments in "Ein Stündlein wohl vor
Tag." See Youens, *Hugo Wolf and his Mörike
Songs*, 115–28.
12. For an exemplary discussion of this song, see
Deborah J. Stein, *Hugo Wolf's Lieder and
Extensions of Tonality* (Ann Arbor and London,
1985), 9–10.
13. The tradition continues. Hanns Eisler uses
a very slow dactylic pattern in the piano
throughout his Brecht song, "Über den
Selbstmord."
14. See Edmund von Hellmer, *Hugo Wolf:
Erlebtes und Erlauschtes* (Vienna and Leipzig,
1921), 137.
15. One of Wolf's earliest manuscripts (1875) is
an incomplete setting of Nikolaus Lenau's ballad
"Der Raubschütz," and his first Mörike setting is
also a ballad, "Suschens Vogel."
16. Eduard Hanslick, *Fünf Jahre Musik
(1891–1895). Der "Modernen Oper"* (Berlin,
1896), 270–71.
17. Johann Wolfgang von Goethe, *Gedichte*, ed.
Erich Trunz (Munich, 1981), 146–47.
18. Cited in Walker, *Hugo Wolf*, 323–24.
19. The poems came from Walter-Heinrich
Robert-Tornow, trans., *Die Gedichte des
Michelangelo Buonarroti* (Berlin, 1896). The
statement to Edmund von Hellmer that "the
sculptor must sing bass" is cited in Walker, *Hugo
Wolf*, 428.
20. Eric Sams, *The Songs of Hugo Wolf* (New
York, 1962), 260.
21. This letter to Oskar Grohe of 27 March 1897
is cited in Walker, *Hugo Wolf*, 428–29.
22. This statement appears in the same
letter to Emil Kauffmann of 5 June 1890 cited
in n. 8.
23. This is the final line of one of Goethe's
Venetianische Epigramme: "Werke des Geists und
der Kunst sind für den Pöbel nicht da." See
Goethe, *Gedichte*, ed. Trunz, 176.

11 Beyond song: instrumental transformations and adaptations of the Lied from Schubert to Mahler

1. While the present discussion is limited to
transformations of Lieder, the larger issue of
vocal music's presence within instrumental
works has recently received increasing attention
from musicologists, especially those interested in
narrative strategies; see, for example, Carolyn
Abbate's landmark study *Unsung Voices: Opera
and Musical Narrative in the Nineteenth Century*
(Princeton, 1991).
2. For a brief discussion of Schubert's
representative status with respect to the Lied, see

Christopher H. Gibbs, "The Elusive Schubert,"
in CCS, 8–9.
3. *Wiener Theaterzeitung* (21 May 1838), 447;
the review is excerpted in Otto Brusatti, *Schubert
im Wiener Vormärz* (Graz, 1978), No. 86; all
translations are my own unless otherwise noted.
4. A review from the AmZ, 40 (1838), 795 f.,
describes the extraordinary commercial success
of Liszt's transcriptions.
5. *Wiener Zeitschrift für Kunst, Lituratur,
Theater und Mode* (7 December 1839), 1176;
translation from Klára Hamburger, *Liszt*, trans.
Gyula Gulyás (Budapest, 1980), 46; also cited in
Brusatti, *Schubert im Wiener Vormärz*, No. 107,
cf. No. 115. The historical importance of Liszt's
transcriptions was later acknowledged in Eduard
Hanslick's classic study of Vienna's concert life:
"Liszt's transcriptions of Schubert Lieder were
epoch-making. There was scarcely a concert in
which Liszt did not play one or two of them;
even when they were not listed on the program
they would have to be played. Far be it from me
to praise the artistic value of these transcriptions
or even to see a glorification of Schubert in
them. When one takes away the words and voice
from Schubert Lieder, one has not glorified
them, but rather impoverished them. Still the
fact remains incontestable that Liszt, through
these paraphrases, did a great deal for the
dissemination of Schubert Lieder. Printed
concert programs prove that since the
appearance of Liszt's transcriptions of Schubert
songs, the originals have been publicly sung
more frequently than before: the power of
virtuosity proves itself once again and this time
served a good cause." Quoted from *Geschichte
des Concertwesens in Wien* (Vienna, 1869),
I: 336.
6. Robert Schumann, *Music and Musicians*, ed.
Konrad Wolff, trans. Paul Rosenfeld (New York,
1969), 155.
7. Ibid., 154.
8. Peter Raabe, *Liszts Schaffen* (Tutzing, 1968),
II: 5–9; the most thorough study of Liszt's
relation to Schubert is Thomas Kabisch, *Liszt
und Schubert* (Munich, 1984).
9. See, for example, Brusatti, *Schubert im
Wiener Vormärz*, Nos. 86, 91, 94, 108; and Otto
Erich Deutsch, *Schubert: Memoirs by His Friends*,
trans. Rosamond Ley and John Nowell (London,
1958), 186.
10. The classification of Liszt's Lied reworkings,
not just of Schubert's music, is best discussed by
Diether Presser in "Studien zu den Opern- und
Liedbearbeitungen Franz Liszts" (Ph.D.
dissertation, University of Cologne, 1953), 133
ff. See also Alan Walker, "Liszt and the Schubert
Song Transcriptions," MQ 67 (1981), 50–63;

and Humphrey Searle, *The Music of Liszt* (London, 1966).

11. *Franz Liszt: Unbekannte Presse und Briefe aus Wien 1822–1886*, ed. Dezso Legany (Vienna, 1984), 29.

12. We witness the opposite phenomenon from Liszt, who removed words from actual songs, in that words were sometimes later added to Mendelssohn's *Lieder ohne Worte*.

13. Eric Werner, *Mendelssohn: A New Image of the Composer and His Age*, trans. Dika Newlin (London, 1963), 220; see also Christina Tost, *Mendelssohns Lieder ohne Worte* (Tutzing, 1988).

14. *Music and Musicians*, 210. Schumann's own experimentations with the idea of "songs without words" extend the potential even further, as, for example, in the "unsung" middle voice (innere Stimme) in *Humoresk*, Op. 20; for a discussion of this piece and other influences of song and song cycles on Schumann's piano works, see Charles Rosen, *The Romantic Generation* (Cambridge, MA, 1995), chapters 1–3, 12.

15. *The Schubert Song Companion* (New York and London, 1997), 495.

16. See James Parakilas, *Ballads Without Words: Chopin and the Tradition of the Instrumental Ballade* (Portland, OR, 1992).

17. Arrangements of Schubert Lieder are discussed in Christopher H. Gibbs, "The Presence of Erlkönig: Reception and Reworkings of a Schubert Lied" (Ph.D. dissertation, Columbia University, 1992); there are at least two other solo violin treatments of this song, by August Möser (c. 1843) and Baptist von Hunyady (1844); ibid., 316–27.

18. See Edward Kravitt, "The Orchestral Lied: An Inquiry into its Style and Unexpected Flowering around 1900," MR 37 (1976), 209–26; also Hermann Danuser, "Der Orchestergesang des Fin de siècle: Eine historische und ästhetische Skizze," Mf 30 (1977), 425–52; concerning orchestrations of Schubert Lieder, see Christopher H. Gibbs, "*Haus* to *Konzerthaus*: Orchestrations of Schubert's *Erlkönig* and other Lieder," in *Liber amicorum Isabelle Cazeaux: Symbols, Parallels and Discoveries in Her Honor*, ed. Paul-André Bempéchat (New York, forthcoming). This discussion draws briefly from that article and Gibbs, "The Presence of *Erlkönig*," 327–36.

19. At the behest of the celebrated singer Julius Stockhausen, for example, Brahms orchestrated *An Schwager Kronos, Memnon, Geheimes, Greisengesang, Ellens zweiter Gesang*, and *Gruppe aus dem Tartarus* in the 1860s; see McCorkle, *Johannes Brahms: Thematisch-Bibliographisches Werkverzeichnis*, 636–44; and Robert Pascall, "Brahms and Schubert," MT 124 (1983), 289;

and Pascall, "'My Love of Schubert – No Fleeting Fancy': Brahms's Response to Schubert," *Schubert durch die Brille* 21 (June 1998), 39–60.

20. *The Beethoven Quartets* (New York, 1967), 191–222.

21. *Beethoven*, revised, 2nd edn. (New York, 1998), 387.

22. About the latter see Carl Dahlhaus, NCM, 153; and also Richard Taruskin's persuasive deconstruction of Dahlhaus's argument in *Defining Russia Musically: Historical and Hermeneutical Essays* (Princeton, 1997), 253–60.

23. Reed, *Schubert Song Companion*, 494; Schwind's remark was made in a letter of 14 March 1824 to Franz von Schober; see SDB, 333.

24. See H. C. Robbins Landon, *Haydn: The Years of 'The Creation' 1796–1800*, vol. IV of *Haydn: Chronicle and Works* (Bloomington, 1977/1994), 271–83; 293–97.

25. An appendix to Reed's invaluable *Schubert Song Companion* lists many of the interconnections between songs and other works by Schubert; pp. 494–98.

26. Ibid., 494.

27. In addition to the appendix to Reed's *Schubert Song Companion* cited above, musical connections among Schubert's works are examined by Maurice J. E. Brown, "Schubert: Instrumental Derivations in the Songs," ML 28 (1947), 207–15; Reinhard van Hoorickx, "Schubert's Reminiscences of His Own Works," MQ 60 (1974), 373–88; and Leo Black, "Oaks and Osmosis," MT 138 (June 1997), 4–15. The most detailed study to date is Michael Raab, *Franz Schubert: Instrumentale Bearbeitungen eigener Lieder* (Munich, 1997).

28. This sort of recycling is not uncommon – we might remember, for example, Beethoven's use of the "Prometheus" theme in a Contredanse (WoO 14, No. 7), in his ballet *Die Geschöpfe des Prometheus*, Op. 43, in the 15 Variations for Piano, Op. 35, and in the *Eroica* Symphony, Op. 55.

29. For a fascinating psychoanalytic investigation of this issue see Theodor Reik, *The Haunting Melody: Psychoanalytic Experiences in Life and Music* (New York, 1953).

30. In most editions Liszt requested that the publishers print the words, either at the beginning of the score or, better, directly above the piano part so that the pianist could easily relate the text to the music. Late in his life Liszt reaffirmed his position taken earlier with the Schubert Lied reworkings and wrote to Breitkopf & Härtel to ask that they include the words below the music: "I wish this, for the sake of the poetical delivery in all of the songs" (*Letters of Franz Liszt*, ed. La Mara, trans. Constance

Bache [London, 1894, rpt. New York, 1968],
II: 263–64).

31. Carl Dahlhaus has observed a similar
phenomenon in a reversal in modes of reception
between the nineteenth and twentieth centuries.
Whereas many past audiences sought to add
texts to instrumental music, contemporary
audiences listen to vocal music as if it were
absolute music, often totally oblivious to the
meaning of the words, which may in any case be
in a foreign language; NCM, 5. Arnold
Schoenberg confessed that he realized he had no
idea of what the poems were about in certain
Schubert Lieder and yet "grasped the real
content" of the music in any case; see "The
Relation to the Text," in *Style and Idea: Selected
Writings of Arnold Schoenberg*, ed. Leonard Stein,
trans. Leo Black (Berkeley, 1984), 141–45.

32. For more on this period in Schubert's life see
Elizabeth Norman McKay, *Franz Schubert: A
Biography* (Oxford, 1996), 164–207; Christopher
H. Gibbs, *The Life of Schubert* (Cambridge,
2000), 91–114.

33. Christoph Wolff, "Schubert's *Der Tod und
Das Mädchen*: Analytical and Explanatory Notes
on the Song D531 and the Quartet D 810," in
*Schubert Studies: Problems of Style and
Chronology*, ed. Eva Badura-Skoda and Peter
Branscombe (Cambridge, 1982), 143–71.

34. Maurice Brown, "Schubert and Some
Folksongs," ML 53.2 (1972), 173–78.

35. Manfred Willfort, "Das Urbild des Andante
aus Schuberts Klaviertrio Es-Dur, D929,"
Österreichische Musikzeitung 33 (1978),
277–83.

36. Rufus Hallmark, "Schubert's 'Auf dem
Strom,'" in *Schubert Studies*, 25–46. There is
some debate about the dating of the Trio and its
performance history: see Eva Badura-Skoda,
"The Chronology of Schubert's Piano Trios," in
Schubert Studies, 277–98.

37. These two coded tributes to Beethoven
suggest that Schubert used songs more often
than previously thought, that he did not limit
the raw material to his own Lieder, and that such
devices can offer hermeneutic keys to certain
works and yield important biographical insights.
For more on the "secret program" of the trio, see
Gibbs, *The Life of Schubert*, 146–48; 157–59; an
in-depth study is forthcoming.

38. Greg Vitercik, *The Early Works of Felix
Mendelssohn: A Study in the Romantic Sonata
Style* (Philadelphia, 1992), 235–67.

39. Dillon Parmer, "Brahms, Song Quotation,
and Secret Programs," 19CM 14 (1995), 161–90.

40. George S. Bozarth, "Brahms's *Lieder ohne
Worte*: The 'Poetic' Andantes of the Piano
Sonatas," in *Brahms Studies: Analytical and
Historical Perspectives. Papers Delivered at the
International Brahms Conference, Washington,
D.C., 5–8 May 1983*, ed. George S. Bozarth
(Oxford, 1990), 345–78.

41. R. Larry Todd, "On Quotation in
Schumann's Music," *Schumann and His
World*, ed. R. Larry Todd (Princeton, 1994),
80–112.

42. Parmer, "Brahms and Song Quotation,"
181–90.

43. Nicholas Marston, *Schumann: Fantasie,
Op. 17* (Cambridge, 1992), 34–42; Anthony
Newcomb, "Schumann and the Marketplace:
From Butterflies to *Hausmusik*," in
Nineteenth-Century Piano Music, ed. R. Larry
Todd (New York, 1990), 295–96; Berthold
Hoecker, "Schumann and Romantic Distance,"
JAMS 50 (1997), 109–32; Nicholas Marston,
"Voicing Beethoven's Distant Beloved," in
Beethoven and His World, ed. Scott Burnham and
Michael P. Steinberg (Princeton, 2000), 139–42;
and Rosen, *The Romantic Generation*, 100–12.

44. The *Cypresses* are examined in *Rethinking
Dvořák: Views from Five Countries*, ed. David R.
Beveridge (Oxford, 1996), which contains
contributions by four scholars in a section
entitled "The Unknown Dvořák: A
Mini-Symposium on the Early Song Cycle,
Cypresses" (pp. 31–70).

45. Jan Smaczny, "Cypresses: A Song Cycle and
its Metamorphoses," in *Rethinking Dvořák*,
61–67.

46. See Sigmund Freud, "Remembering,
Repeating, and Working-Through (Further
Recommendations on the Technique of
Psycho-Analysis, II)," in *The Standard Edition
of the Complete Psychological Works of Sigmund
Freud*, ed. James Strachey (London, 1961),
XIV: 147–56.

47. Jan Smaczny speculates on further
quotations in "Cypresses and its
Metamorphoses," 67–70.

48. Jan Smaczny, *Dvořák: Cello Concerto*
(Cambridge, 1999), 83–84; and John Clapham,
Antonin Dvořák: Musician and Craftsman (New
York, 1966), 234.

49. Smaczny, *Dvořák: Cello Concerto*, 54–58,
77–85.

50. *Mahler: His Life, Work and World*, ed. Kurt
Blaukopf and Herta Blaukopf (London, 1991),
204.

51. From the vast Mahler literature, particularly
helpful studies include Monika Tibbe, *Über die
Verwendung von Liedern und Liedelementen in
instrumentalen Symphoniesätzen Gustav Mahlers*
(Munich, 1971); Henry-Louis de La Grange,
"Music about Music in Mahler: Reminiscences,
Allusions, or Quotations?," in *Mahler Studies*,
ed. Stephen E. Hefling (Cambridge, 1977),
122–68; Constantin Floros, *Gustav Mahler: The*

Symphonies, trans. Vernon and Jutta Wicker (Portland, OR, 1993); and the essential multi-volume studies by Donald Mitchell, *Gustav Mahler: The Early Years*, 2nd edn. (Berkeley, 1980); *Gustav Mahler: The Wunderhorn Years* (Berkeley, 1995); and *Gustav Mahler: Songs and Dances of Death* (Berkeley, 1985); and Henry-Louis de La Grange, *Mahler*, vol. I (New York, 1973); *Gustav Mahler*, vol. II: *Vienna: Years of Challenge (1897–1904)*, (Oxford, 1995); and *Gustav Mahler*, vol. III: *Vienna: Triumph and Disillusion (1904–1907)*, (Oxford, 1999).

52. The First Symphony should also be considered under the spell of the *Wunderhorn* poetry, for although Mahler had not yet set any of the collection, his own poems for the cycle *Lieder eines fahrenden Gesellen*, most especially the first song, share the same themes and language.

53. The most thorough study of the symphony is James L. Zychowicz, *Mahler's Fourth Symphony* (Oxford and New York, 2000).

54. Floros, *Gustav Mahler: The Symphonies*, 109.

55. Natalie Bauer-Lechner, *Recollections of Gustav Mahler*, trans. Dika Newlin (Cambridge, 1980), 153.

56. Ibid.

57. Natalie Bauer-Lechner, *Gustav Mahler in den Erinnerungen von Natalie Bauer-Lechner*, 2nd edn., ed. Herbert Killian (Hamburg, 1984), 172; translation adapted from Mark Evan Bonds, *After Beethoven: Imperatives of Originality in the Symphony* (Cambridge, MA, 1996), 183.

58. "Eternity or Nothingness? Mahler's Fifth Symphony," in *The Mahler Companion*, ed. Donald Mitchell and Andrew Nicholson (Oxford, 1999), 236–325.

59. "Mahler's 'Kammerton,'" in *The Mahler Companion*, 217–35.

60. Stephen E. Hefling, *Mahler: Das Lied von der Erde* (Cambridge, 2000); and Donald Mitchell, *Gustav Mahler: Songs and Dances of Death*.

12 The Lieder of Mahler and Richard Strauss

1. Max Kalbeck, *Johannes Brahms*, 4 vols. (Vienna, Leipzig, and Berlin, 1904–14), vol. III, pt. I, p. 109, and vol. I, pp. 171–72; quoted from Mark Evan Bonds, *After Beethoven: Imperatives of Originality in the Symphony* (Cambridge, MA and London, 1996), 1.

2. Kalbeck, *Johannes Brahms*, I: 229.

3. August Reißmann, *Das deutsche Lied in seiner historischen Entwicklung* (Kassel, 1861), 209. James Deaville draws attention to Reißmann's statement at the start of chapter 7. Interestingly, the three composers Reißmann holds up as having perfected the Lied during the century's

first half are Schubert, Mendelssohn, and Schumann. History would seem to have disagreed with him on the inclusion of Mendelssohn.

4. Harold Bloom, *The Anxiety of Influence: A Theory of Poetry* (New York and Oxford, 1973). Bonds, in *After Beethoven* (pp. 3–4), has pointed out that Bloom's theory of influence, in focusing only on the anxiety of influence, disregards a plethora of others. As Bonds (p. 4) states: "While the anxiety of influence may well be manifest in a great many poems [or symphonies or songs], there is nothing to be gained from granting it the status of exclusivity."

5. The five *Wesendonck Lieder* (1857–58), so called because they are settings of texts by Mathilde Wesendonck, are: *Der Engel, Stehe still!, Im Treibhaus, Schmerzen*, and *Träume*. Wagner described two of the songs as "studies for *Tristan und Isolde*"; *Im Treibhaus* adumbrates the prelude to act 3 while *Träume* anticipates the act 2 duet. Wagner's own arrangement of the latter song, for solo violin and chamber orchestra, was performed for Mathilde's birthday under Wagner's direction on 23 December 1857. In addition to Mottl's orchestral version of the other four songs, another exists by Hans Werner Henze (1976).

6. Such was the case when the Munich critic Rudolf Louis, as late as 1909, in his *Die deutsche Musik der Gegenwart* (Munich, 1909), 237, decried "the disturbing incongruity between the intimate content of the text and the demands for intensity made today upon [orchestral] media." For more on the orchestral Lied see Edward Kravitt, "The Orchestral Lied: An Inquiry into its Style and Unexpected Flowering around 1900," MR 37 (1976), 209–26; Hermann Danuser, "Der Orchestergesang des fin de siècle: Eine historische und ästhetische Skizze," Mf 30/4 (1977), 425–52; and Hans-Joachim Bracht, "Nietzsches Theorie der Lyrik und das Orchesterlied: Ästhetische und analytische Studien zu Orchesterliedern von Richard Strauss, Gustav Mahler und Arnold Schönberg" (Ph.D. dissertation, University of Mainz, 1991). Elisabeth Schmierer devotes a study specifically to Mahler's orchestral Lieder in *Die Orchesterlieder Gustav Mahlers* (Kassel, 1991).

7. Georg Göhler, "Gustav Mahlers Lieder," *Die Musik* 10 (1911), 357.

8. *Gustav Mahler Briefe 1879–1911*, ed. Alma Mahler (Vienna, 1924), no. 230, and *Gustav Mahler Briefe*, rev. and enlarged edn., ed. Herta Blaukopf (Vienna, 1983), 341.

9. As noted above, Mahler sometimes took liberties with his poetical sources; in this case, he used two different *Wunderhorn* poems and

conflated them for his own purposes. The two poems in question are: "Wer hat dies Liedlein erdacht?!" and "Wer Lieben erdacht."

10. Analysts who opt for Bb Phrygian follow the lead of Fritz Egon Pamer, author of the first dissertation on Mahler's songs, "Gustav Mahlers Lieder: eine stilkritische Studie" (University of Vienna, 1922). A shorter form of this investigation was posthumously published as "Gustav Mahlers Lieder," *Studien zur Musikwissenschaft* 16 (1929), 116–38 and 17 (1930), 105–27; the reference here derives from this latter source, vol. 16, p. 120. See also William Eastman Lake, "Hermeneutic Musical Structures in *Das irdische Leben* by Gustav Mahler," *In Theory Only* 12 (1994), 1–14.

11. Bonds examines the influence of Beethoven and his Ninth Symphony on subsequent composers in his *After Beethoven*; his discussion of the Ninth's influence on Mahler's Fourth Symphony appears on pp. 175–200. For a discussion of the Lied-like character of the principal theme of the Ninth's Choral Finale, see James Parsons, "'*Deine Zauber binden wieder*': Beethoven, Schiller, and the Joyous Reconciliation of Opposites," *Beethoven Forum* 9 (2002), 1–53, esp. 16–21. For a discussion of Mahler's Fourth Symphony, see James L. Zychowicz, *Mahler's Fourth Symphony* (Oxford and New York, 2000).

12. Natalie Bauer-Lechner, *Gustav Mahler in den Erinnerungen von Natalie Bauer-Lechner*, ed. Herbert Killian (Hamburg, 1984), 35.

13. Of the modern editions of *Des Knaben Wunderhorn*, see the essentially *Urtext* version edited by Willi A. Koch (Munich, 1957; rev. edn., 1984) published in one volume; and also the annotated one edited by Heinz Rölleke (Stuttgart, 1987), published in three volumes, each with a critical commentary.

14. Bethge based his *Die chinesische Flöte* on a work by Hans Heilmann, which in turn is based on two French translations by Le Marquis d'Hervey de Saint-Denys and Judith Gautier; see also Stephen E. Hefling, *Mahler: Das Lied von der Erde* (Cambridge and New York, 2000), 36. For a highly instructive example of the "thrice removed" source Mahler used in *Das Lied von der Erde*, see the table included in Hefling, *Mahler: Das Lied von der Erde*, pp. 38–42.

15. Arthur Wenk, "The Composer as Poet in *Das Lied von der Erde*," 19CM 1 (1977): 33–47 and Hefling, *Das Lied von der Erde*, 36–43.

16. Henry-Louis de La Grange, *Mahler*, vol. I (Garden City, NY, 1973), 741. The two Lieder Mahler planned to compose for the set of six are *Die Sonne spinnt* and *Die Nacht blickt mild*,

which would have used poems by Mahler himself.

17. Susan Youens, "Schubert, Mahler and the Weight of the Past: 'Lieder eines fahrenden Gesellen' and 'Winterreise,'" ML 67 (1986), 256–68.

18. Natalie Bauer-Lechner, *Erinnerungen an Gustav Mahler*, ed. and annotated Knud Martner (Hamburg, 1984), 136; trans. Dika Newlin as *Recollections of Gustav Mahler*, ed. and annotated Peter Franklin (New York, 1980), p. 130.

19. La Grange, *Gustav Mahler*, vol. II: *Vienna: The Years of Challenge (1897–1904)* (Oxford and New York, 1995), 730–31.

20. Quoted after La Grange, *Mahler*, II: 774.

21. Quoted by Hans Moldenhauer and Rosaleen Moldenhauer, *Anton von Webern: A Chronicle of His Life and Work* (New York, 1979), 75.

22. Donald Mitchell, *Gustav Mahler: Songs and Symphonies of Life and Death* (London, 1985), 68.

23. Theodor Wiesengrund Adorno, "Zu einer imaginären Auswahl von Liedern Gustav Mahlers," in *Impromptus, Gesammelte Schriften* (Frankfurt, 1982), XVII: 189.

24. For a thorough examination of this subject, see Christopher Lewis, "On the Chronology of the Kindertotenlieder," *Revue Mahler Review* 1 (1987), 21–45.

25. On Mahler's harmonic usage in the song cycles, see further V. Kofi Agawu, "Mahler's Tonal Strategies: A Study of the Song Cycles," JMR 6 (1986), 1–47.

26. La Grange, *Mahler*, II: 836.

27. V. Kofi Agawu, "The Musical Language of the *Kindertotenlieder* No. 2," JM 2 (1983), 81–93.

28. For a useful discussion of the symphony and song cycle as they helped to inform this work, see Hermann Danuser, *Gustav Mahler: Das Lied von der Erde* (Munich, 1986), 28–36.

29. *Gustav Mahler: Briefe*, ed. Blaukopf, no. 400.

30. While it generally is agreed that the voices are a tenor and a contralto, a case has been made for tenor and baritone. The composer's autograph bears the subtitle "Eine Sinfonie für eine Alt- und eine Tenorstimme und Orchester" (A symphony for tenor and contralto and orchestra). Since Mahler neither saw the work into print nor heard it in performance, questions have been raised about his intentions, especially given that the manuscript for voice and piano appears to leave the matter open-ended in the designation "Singstimme," that is, voice. See also Hefling, "Das Lied von der Erde," 52–53.

31. As Hefling observes, *Mahler: Das Lied von der Erde*, 81, the keys of A and C are "probably not coincidentally . . . also the principal key areas

in the first act of *Tristan und Isolde*, Mahler's
favorite work of musical theatre."
32. Letter from Britten to Henry Boys, June
1937, in *Letters from a Life: The Selected Letters
and Diaries of Benjamin Britten, 1913–1976*,
ed. Donald Mitchell, 2 vols. (Berkeley, 1991),
I: 493.
33. Quoted after La Grange, *Mahler*, II: 769.
34. See E. H. Mueller von Asow, *Richard Strauss:
Thematisches Verzeichnis* (Vienna, 1955–74) and
Franz Trenner, *Richard Strauss Werkverzeichnis*
(Vienna, 1985). See also the valuable discussion
of Strauss the Lied composer by Alan Jefferson,
The Lieder of Richard Strauss (London, 1971)
and Barbara A. Petersen, *"Ton und Wort": The
Lieder of Richard Strauss* (Ann Arbor, 1980); this
last work was updated in Petersen, "Richard
Strauss: A Lifetime of Lied Composition," in
GLNC, 250–78.
35. Suzanne Marie Lodato, "Richard Strauss
and the Modernists: A Contextual Study of
Strauss's fin-de-siècle Song Style" (Ph.D.
dissertation, Columbia University, 1999).
36. This last song, *Malven*, for voice and piano,
came to light only in 1984, after the death in
1982 of its dedicatee, Maria Jeritza, the soprano
who participated in the first performances of
Ariadne auf Naxos (both versions) and *Die Frau
ohne Schatten*.
37. See further Ursula Lienenlüke, "Die
Vertonungen zeitgenössicher Lyrik" (Ph.D.
dissertation, University of Cologne, 1976).
38. Timothy Jackson, "Ruhe, meine Seele! and
the *Letzte Orchesterlieder*," in *Richard Strauss
and His World*, ed. Bryan Gilliam (Princeton,
1992), 90–137.
39. See Marie Rolf and Elizabeth West Marvin,
"Analytical Issues and Interpretive Decisions in
Two Songs by Richard Strauss," *Intégral* 4
(1990), 67–103.
40. A shortlist of nineteenth-century
melodramas includes Schubert's 1820 *Die
Zauberharfe* (D644), six by Liszt, and Wagner's
Melodram Gretchens, from his *Sieben
Kompositionen zu Goethes Faust*, Op. 5, No. 6
(1832); the six by Liszt are provided in fn. 38,
chapter 8.
41. Hellmut Federhofer considers these songs in
fuller detail in "Die musikalische Gestaltung des
'Krämerspiegels' von Richard Strauss," in *Musik
und Verlag: Karl Vötterle zum 65. Geburtstag*, ed.
Richard Baum and Wolfgang Rehm (Kassel and
New York, 1968), 260–67.
42. Timothy Jackson, "Ruhe, meine Seele! and
the *Letzte Orchesterlieder*," 90–131.
43. As Norman Del Mar has commented, III:
167–68, "there seems to have been more than a
little self-identification on Strauss's part with the

Jupiter of these closing pages [of the opera *Die
Liebe der Danae*]."
44. Aubrey S. Garlington, Jr. discusses Strauss's
four final songs in precisely this way, as Strauss's
musical last will and testament to German
Romanticism; see his "Richard Strauss's *Vier
letzte Lieder*: The Ultimate Opus Ultimatum,"
Musical Quarterly 73 (1989), 79–93. Other
studies of the *Vier letzte Lieder* include John
Michael Kissler, "The Four Last Songs by
Richard Strauss: A Formal and Tonal
Perspective," MR 50 (1989), 231–39 and
Timothy L. Jackson, "The Last Strauss: Studies
in the letzte Lieder" (Ph.D. dissertation, City
University of New York, 1988).

13 The Lied in the modern age: to mid century

1. Strauss alters Eichendorff's text at this crucial
moment, substituting "dies" (this) for the more
general "das" (that). Throughout this essay, all
translations are my own unless otherwise noted.
2. The title *Vier letzte Lieder* is not Strauss's.
Timothy Jackson argues that the entire set owes
its existence to a generating idea from the 1894
"Ruhe, meine Seele!," Op. 27, No. 1. From this
Jackson concludes that the early and the four late
songs form a coherent whole. See "Ruhe, meine
Seele! and the *Letzte Orchesterlieder*," in *Richard
Strauss and His World*, ed. Bryan Gilliam
(Princeton, 1992), 90–137.
3. Paul Griffiths, "V. Lieder. The Twentieth
century," *New Grove* 2, XIV: 680.
4. LMLR, 245.
5. As true as this statement is, George Steiner
makes a point equally worth bearing in mind:
"in Romantic pastoralism there is as much of a
flight *from* the devouring city as there is a return
to nature." Quoted from Steiner, *In Bluebeard's
Castle: Some Notes Toward the Redefinition of
Culture* (New Haven, 1971), 20; the emphasis is
Steiner's.
6. The poem is Goethe's "Mailied." Quoted
from Johann Wolfgang von Goethe, *Sämtliche
Werke nach Epochen seines Schaffens*, ed. Karl
Richter (Munich, 1987), IX: 43.
7. Quoted from Robert L. Herbert,
Impressionism: Art, Leisure and Parisian Society
(New Haven, 1988), 4; quoting in turn from
Maxime Du Camp, *Les chants modernes* (Paris,
1855), preface, p. 5.
8. Marx, *The Machine in the Garden: Technology
and the Pastoral Ideal in America* (Oxford and
New York, 2000 [1964]).
9. As a recent exhibition of paintings, prints,
and photographs in Berlin at the
Martin-Gropius-Bau amply document, the
spread of industry into the countryside and
within the city has been a subject of enduring

artistic concern. See the copiously illustrated catalogue, *Die zweite Schöpfung: Bilder der industriellen Welt vom 18. Jahrhundert bis in die Gegenwart*, ed. Sabine Beneke and Hans Ottomeyer (Berlin, 2002).

10. Part II (Scene six), piano vocal score, p. 111; the words are sung by the character of Anita: "Das Leben, das du nicht verstehst, es ist Bewegung, und darin ist das Glück. Darin du selbst sein, das ist alles! In jedem Augenblick du selbst sein, in jedem Augenblick es ganz sein, und jeden Augenblick leben, als ob kein andrer kämem weder vorher, noch nachher, und sich doch nicht verlieferen."

11. See, respectively, Hugh Kenner, *The Pound Era* (Berkeley and Los Angeles, 1971) – the quotation "patterned energies" derives from p. 153 – and "Notes Toward an Anatomy of 'Modernism,'" in *A Starchamber Quiry: A James Joyce Centennial Volume, 1882–1982*, ed. Hugh Kenner and Edmund L. Epstein (London and New York, 1982), quoting from 4–5 and 28.

12. Marshall Berman, *All That is Solid Melts into Air: The Experience of Modernity* (New York, 1982), 16.

13. LMLR, vii–ix; my occasional disagreements with Kravitt notwithstanding, his book is essential reading for anyone wishing to understand how German song from this period relates to that in the century's second half.

14. Dahlhaus, NCM, 330 and 370.

15. From Schoenberg's program notes for the work's first performance, as quoted in Willi Reich, *Schoenberg: A Critical Biography*, trans. Leo Black (New York, 1971), p. 49. The study's original German title is worth citing: *Arnold Schönberg, oder Der konservative Revolutionär* (Vienna, 1968).

16. This last point is derived from Walter Frisch's *The Early Works of Arnold Schoenberg: 1893–1908* (Berkeley, 1993), chapter 10, pp. 258–72.

17. Hermann Kretzschmar, "Das deutsche Lied seit dem Tode Richard Wagners," *Aufsätze aus den Jahrbüchern der Musikbibliothek Peters* (Leipzig, 1911), 285.

18. I discuss the ties of the so-called "Freude tune" in the finale of Beethoven's Ninth Symphony in my "'Deine Zauber binden wieder': Beethoven, Schiller, and the Joyous Reconciliation of Opposites," *Beethoven Forum* 9/1 (2002), 1–53.

19. Franz Waxman (1906–67) fled Berlin in 1935 to settle in Hollywood where later he would go on to compose two Academy Award winning film scores (*Sunset Boulevard* [1950] and *A Place in the Sun* [1951]). In his last composition, he turned to poetry written by

children imprisoned at Theresienstadt. Waxman described the resulting work, the song cycle *Das Lied von Terezín*, as his "most dramatic musical composition."

20. Walter Niemann, *Die Musik der Gegenwart und der letzten Vergangenheit bis zu den Romantikern, Klassizisten und Neudeutschen* (Berlin, 1921), 159.

21. Grete Wehmeyer, *Max Reger als Liederkomponist: Ein Beitrag zum Problem der Wort-Ton-Beziehung* (Regensburg, 1955), 261.

22. Ruldolf Louis, *Die deutsche Musik der Gegenwart*, 2nd edn. (Munich, 1909), 212 and 214 ff. Quoted after LMLR, 3–4; trans. amended.

23. Niemann, *Die Musik der Gegenwart*, 190–91.

24. Ibid.

25. Riemann, *Große Kompositionslehre* (Stuttgart, 1913), III: 236.

26. Fritz Stein, *Max Reger* (Potsdam, 1939), 128.

27. Brinkmann, "The Lyric as Paradigm: Poetry and the Foundation of Arnold Schoenberg's New Music," in *German Literature and Music: An Aesthetic Fusion 1890–1989*, ed. Claus Reschke and Howard Pollack (Fink, 1992), 115. Earlier in the essay Brinkmann explores this concept in greater scope. On p. 112, he writes: "*Die Moderne* is defined as a form of art that forgoes a merely illustrative relationship to a preceding reality and, in fact, seems to abandon completely the mimetic character of poetry; an art that displays a new consciousness of form penetrated by reflection . . . and, above all, an art that reflects itself in itself . . . The work of art of *Die Moderne* is self-referential and culminates in the concept and the realization of the 'absolute poem.'"

28. Schoenberg acknowledges Reger's standing in general and influence on his own music in a number of publications. In his "Criteria for the Evaluation of Music" (1946), he groups Reger with Mahler and himself as pioneers of a "new technique," namely that of "developing variation." In his essay "National Music (2)" (1931), Schoenberg declares that he learned a great deal from Reger, along with Schubert, Mahler, and Strauss. Both essays are included in *Style and Idea: Selected Writings of Arnold Schoenberg*, ed. Leonard Stein, trans. Leo Black (London, 1975), respectively 129–30 and 174.

29. On Reger's admiration for Brahms in general, see Helmut Wirth, "Johannes Brahms und Max Reger," *Brahms-Studien* 1 (1974), 91–112.

30. Werner Diez, *Hans Pfitzners Lieder. Versuch ein Stilbetrachtung* (Regensburg, 1968), 1.

31. Hans Rectanus, "Die musikalischen Zitale in Hans Pfitzners *Palestrina*," in *Festschrift aus Anlaß des 100. Geburtstags . . . von Hans Pfitzner*, ed. Walter Abendroth (Munich, 1969), 23–27.

32. Pfitzner, "Die neue Ästhetik der musikalischen Impotenz," *Gesammelte Schriften* (Augsburg, 1926), II: 212.

33. Alex Ross, "The Devil's Disciple," *The New Yorker*, 21 July 1997, 77.

34. Kretzschmar, "Das deutsche Lied," 201.

35. Quoted in Hugh Frederick Garten, *Modern German Drama* (Fair Lawn, NJ, 1959), 173.

36. For more on this concept see Jost Hermand, "Unity within Diversity? The History of the Concept 'Neue Sachlichkeit,'" in *Culture and Society in the Weimar Republic*, ed. Keith Bullivant (Manchester, 1977), 162–82. See also Fritz Schmalenbach, "The Term *Neue Sachlichkeit*," *The Art Bulletin* 22 (1940), 161–65.

37. *Es liegt in der Luft*, a "Revue in vierundzwanzig Bildern," first performed 15 May 1928. The theme song, first heard in the revue as the act 1 finale, is repeated at the end of the last act, act 2. Quoted here from a typed copy of the stage manuscript in the Stiftung Archiv der Akademie der Künste, Archivabteilung Darstellende Kunst und Film, Berlin, [Spoliansky 65] entitled *Es liegt in der Luft, von Marcellus Schiffer und Max Colpet, Musik: Mischa Spoliansky* (Berlin: Verlag für Bühne Film Funk, n.d.), 41–43. Other sources and indexes at the Akademie der Künste do not list Colpet as a contributor.

38. For a recent examination of both operas, see Frank Mehring, "Welcome to the Machine! The Representation of Technology in *Zeitopern*," *Cambridge Opera Journal* 11 (1999), 159–77. For a broader examination of the subject, see Susan C. Cook, *Opera for a New Republic: The Zeitopern of Krenek, Weill, and Hindemith* (Ann Arbor, 1988).

39. Schmalenbach, "The Term *Neue Sachlichkeit*," 164, fn. 22.

40. *Wilhelm Meister's Apprenticeship*, ed. and trans. Eric A. Blackall, *Goethe's Collected Works*, vol. IX (Princeton, 1995), 175. For the German, see Johann Wolfgang Goethe, *Gedenkausgabe der Werke, Briefe und Gespräche*, ed. Ernst Beutler (Zurich, 1949), VII: 313.

41. Klaus Pringsheim, "Der Zustand heutiger Musik," *Der Querschnitt* 10 (April 1930), 215–19.

42. Ernst Krenek, "Self-Analysis," *The University of New Mexico Quarterly* 23 (Spring 1953), 23.

43. Friedrich Schiller, "Über Bürgers Gedichte" (1791), trans. Timothy J. Chamberlain in *Eighteenth-Century German Criticism: Herder, Lenz, Lessing, and Others*, ed. Timothy J. Chamberlain (New York, 1992), 263; the emphasis is Schiller's.

44. Heinrich Kreissle von Hellborn, *Franz Schubert* (Vienna, 1865).

45. *Schillers Werke: Nationalausgabe*, ed. Lieselotte Blumenthal (Weimar, 1961), XX: 428.

46. Georg Wilhelm Friedrich Hegel, *Phenomenology of Spirit*, trans. A. V. Miller (Oxford, 1977), 15–16.

47. Thomas Mann, in a concluding "Author's Note" to his 1948 novel *Doctor Faustus*, described the twelve-tone technique as Schoenberg's "intellectual property." As Krenek noted in 1934, "perhaps at first one fears that the use of the twelve-tone system would automatically result in the "Schönberg style" . . . But even one's first attempt proves this is not the case. The row-principle is not some sort of 'ideological superstructure' to justify theoretically the expressive habits of a particular master. Instead, it allows each composer his own **individual**, characteristic tone-speech." Quoted from Krenek, "Erfahrungen mit dem "Zwölftonsystem,'" *Vossische Zeitung*, 3 March 1934, Musikblatt. The *Sperrdruck* emphasis is Krenek's.

48. George Steiner, *Errata: An Examined Life* (New Haven and London, 1997), 75.

49. For an excellent overview of Schoeck the song composer, see Derrick Puffett, *The Song Cycles of Othmar Schoeck* (Bern and Stuttgart, 1982). See also Theo Hirsbrunner, "Othmar Schoeck: Zwischen Romantik und Moderne," *Musica* 35 (1981), 246–49.

50. A short list of the most outstanding German-speaking Swiss authors includes Gottfried Keller, Meyer, Hesse, Carl Spitteler, Jeremias Gotthelf (pseudonym of Albert Bitzius), Max Frisch, and Friedrich Dürrenmatt. Meyer is the poet to whom Schoenberg turned for his Op. 13 *Friede auf Erden*, for mixed a cappella chorus, a setting of a Christmas poem Meyer had written in 1886.

51. Quoted from *Sämtliche Werke des Freiherrn Joseph von Eichendorff Historisch-Kritische Ausgabe*, ed. Harry Fröhlich and Ursula Regener (Stuttgart, Berlin, and Cologne, 1993), I: 282.

52. See Hans Corrodi, *Othmar Schoeck: Bild eines Schaffens* (Frauenfeld, 1956); this is an enlarged new edition of the same author's *Othmar Schoeck: eine Monographie* (1st edn. Frauenfeld and Leipzig, 1931 and 2nd edn. 1936).

53. Four years before Schoeck composed his Hesse songs, Rainer Maria Rilke revealed that in his *Duino Elegies* "affirmation of life and affirmation of death are shown to be one." See Rilke, letter of 13 November 1925 in *Briefe*, ed. Karl Altheim (Wiesbaden, 1950), II: 480.

54. Ernst Krenek, "Anton von Webern: A Profile," *Anton von Webern: Perspectives*, ed. Hans Moldenhauer and Demar Irvine (London, 1967), 4.

55. Anton Webern, *The Path to New Music*, ed. Willi Reich, trans. Leo Black (Bryn Mawr, 1963), 44.

56. Julian Johnson, *Webern and the Transformation of Nature* (Cambridge and New York, 1999), 31.

57. Shreffler, "*Mein Weg geht jetzt vorüber:* The Vocal Origins of Webern's Twelve-Tone Composition," JAMS 47 (1994), 279.

58. Johnson, *Webern*, 7.

59. Shreffler "*Mein Weg*," 329.

60. Quoted from Hanns Eisler, *Materialien zu einer Dialektik der Musik* (Leipzig, 1976), 39.

14 The circulation of the Lied

1. Although relatively infrequent within musicology, studies of media and modes of circulation figure significantly in a variety of other disciplines. From a vast literature, see Roger Chartier, "Texts, Printings, Readings," in *The New Cultural History*, ed. Lynn Hunt, Studies on the History of Society and Culture (Berkeley, 1989), 154–75; Chartier, *Forms and Meanings: Texts, Performances, and Audiences from Codex to Computer*, New Cultural Studies (Philadelphia, 1995); Friedrich A. Kittler, *Discourse Networks 1800/1900*, trans. Michael Metteer, with Chris Cullens (Palo Alto, CA, 1990); Kittler, *Gramophone, Film, Typewriter*, trans. Geoffrey Winthrop-Young and Michael Wutz, Writing Science (Palo Alto, CA, 1999). For an overview of attempts (more prevalent for recent and especially for popular music) to consider musicology in this light, see Helmut Rösing and Alenka Barber-Kersovan, "Musikvermittlung in der modernen Mediengesellschaft," in *Musikwissenschaft: Ein Grundkurs*, ed., Herbert Bruhn and Rösing, Rowohlts Enzyklopädie (Reinbek bei Hamburg, 1998), 364–89. The recent appearance of Kate van Orden, ed., *Music and the Cultures of Print* (New York and London, 2000), however, suggests that topics of media and circulation may be beginning to receive attention within historical music as well.

2. John Reed, *Schubert* (London, 1987), 31. For a more recent and nuanced exploration of Schubert's revolutionary creative act, see Lawrence Kramer, *Franz Schubert: Sexuality, Subjectivity, Song* (Cambridge and New York, 1998), especially 9–10.

3. Cited in SDB, 57.

4. Elizabeth Norman McKay, *Franz Schubert: A Biography* (Oxford, 1996), 58.

5. SDB, 62–63.

6. Maurice J. E. Brown, for instance, wrote that Schubert's letter was "another example of his inability to estimate fully the merits of his own work, for this song, an extremely long one, is an unequal piece of writing with 'two grains of corn hid in two bushels of chaff.'" Brown, *Schubert: A Critical Biography* (London, 1958; rpt. New York, 1988), 91.

7. *Erlafsee*, D586, had appeared in the *Mahlerisches Taschenbuch für Freunde interessanter Gegenden, Natur- und Kunst-Merkwürdigkeiten der Österreichischen Monarchie* (Vienna, 1818).

8. SDB, 155. Deutsch notes that the appearance of two of Schubert's Lieder in periodicals by that time rendered the author's statement inaccurate in the strictest terms, but this differentiation merely highlights the distinction between the publication of ephemera and the appearance of the *works* (opera) that established a composer's identity.

9. Review of *Franz Schuberts nachgelassene musikalische Dichtungen für Gesang und Pianoforte. Ossians Gesänge*, V Hefte, *Iris im Gebiete der Tonkunst* 1/39–40 (12 November 1830) (no pagination in original): "kein einziges der Stücke eine Gestalt hat; wir haben einige Zeilen Recitativ, dann einige Takte Arioso, endlich einen Satz, der fast durchaus melodisch genannt werden kann, sich aber dennoch nicht zu einer bestimmten Form gestaltet, kurz eine Häufung von Gedanken und Einzelheiten, ohne ein Ganzes daraus zu Gestalten."

10. For a consideration of Schubert's poets, see Susan Youens's "Schubert and his Poets: Issues and Conundrums," in CCS, 99–117, and her SPML.

11. Joseph Kerman, "A Romantic Detail in Schubert's *Schwanengesang*," MQ 48 (1962), 36–49; revised in SCAS, 48–64.

12. Ibid., 50.

13. Even Schubert's earliest independent publications show awareness of this process. Opp. 1 and 2, *Erlkönig* and *Gretchen am Spinnrade*, are each introduced (albeit the latter very briefly), and although each of the subsequent three works includes songs lacking introductions, after Op. 3 they occupy the later positions within the opus; the first two songs of Opp. 4 and 5 each begin with introductions. After Op. 5, songs without introductions no longer occur at all, but even before, the work as a whole is given the weight and separation provided by an introduction.

14. This formulation draws on Foucault's concept of an "author function." See Michel Foucault, "What Is an Author?" in *The Foucault Reader*, ed. Paul Rabinow (New York, 1984), 101–20, esp. 107–09.

15. Richard Kramer also has thematized the transformation of Schubert's songs through publication, although he views it rather as a process through which their original significance was lost. Although this perspective conflicts with the one presented here, it does recognize the crucial role of changing media. See Kramer, *Distant Cycles: Schubert and the Conceiving of Song* (Chicago, 1994), esp. chapter 1, "In Search of Song," 3–21.

16. Rolf Wilhelm Brednich, "Das Lied als Ware," *Jahrbuch für Volksliedforschung* 19 (1974), 11–20.

17. Ann Le Bar, "The Domestication of Vocal Music in Enlightenment Hamburg," JMR 19 (2000), 97–134. Quotations from 126.

18. Benedict Anderson, *Imagined Communities: Reflections on the Origin and Spread of Nationalism*, revised edn. (London, 1991), 37–46. Quotation from 44.

19. See David Gramit, *Cultivating Music: The Aspirations, Interests, and Limits of German Musical Culture, 1770–1848* (Berkeley, 2002), 65–73. The quotation is from Schulz's preface to the second edition of his *Lieder im Volkston* (Berlin, 1785): "mehr *volksmäßig* als *kunstmäßig.*" Schulz outlined his ideals for music education in his *Gedanken über den Einfluß der Musik auf die Bildung eines Volks, und über deren Einführung in den Schulen der königl. Dänischen Staaten* (Copenhagen, 1790).

20. Schulz, *Lieder im Volkston*, Vorrede: "Der Beyfall, womit das Publikum meine bisherigen Liederkompositionen aufgenommen hat, muntert mich auf eine angenehme Art auf, dieser neuen Ausgabe meiner sämtlichen **Lieder im Volkston** alle diejenige Vollkommenheit zu geben, die von meinen Fähigkeiten abhängt. Sie wird demnach aus mehreren Theilen bestehen. . . . Die ausgelassenen Theater-Gesänge werden nebst den besten Volksliedern aus meinen **Gesängen am Klavier** einen mit manchen neuen Liedern vermehrten zweyten Theil ausmachen, auf den ich, so bald eine hinlängliche Anzahl guter Liedertexte mich in den Stand setzen wird, sie mit solchen Melodien, die ich dem Publiko anbieten zu können glaube, zu versehen, nach und nach mehrere Theile von gleicher Stärke folgen zu lassen gesonnen." The unfamiliarity of this passage is due not only to its contents, but also to its appearing only in summary form in Max Friedlaender, DL, while the rest of the preface appears in full (I: 256–57).

21. On the separation of producers and consumers brought about through the development of impersonal modes of commodity circulation, see Ingeborg Cleve, *Geschmack, Kunst und Konsum: Kulturpolitik als Wirtschaftspolitik in Frankreich und Württemberg (1805–1845)*, Kritische Studien zur Geschichtswissenschaft 111 (Göttingen, 1996), esp. 10.

22. Reichardt, "An junge Künstler," *Musikalisches Kunstmagazin* 1 (1782), 6: "Ein geschrieben Blatt was mir mancher wahre Künstler auf meinen Reisen aus seinem verborgnen Schatze gab, war oft unendlich mehr werth als zwanzig gestochene und gedruckte Werke desselben Mannes, zubereitet für das enge Herz seiner gnädigen Käufer und den Eisenkrämereien seines Notenverlegers."

23. From Schubert's letter to Leopold Kupelwieser of 31 March 1824, cited in SDB, 339.

24. See Franz Lachner's account of a violinist who dismissed Schubert's variations on *Der Tod und das Mädchen* in the String Quartet, D810: "My dear fellow, this is no good, leave it alone; you stick to your songs!" Cited in Deutsch, ed., *Schubert: Memoirs by His Friends* (London, 1958), 289. For attempts to defend Schubert against a superficial public, see the statements of Josef Kenner and Josef von Spaun, 82, 86, and 140. On Schubert as too focused on song to rank as a truly great composer, see Leopold von Sonnleithner (112) and Josef Hüttenbrenner's account of the singer Ludwig Tietze (191).

25. *Robert Schumanns Briefe: Neue Folge*, ed. Gustav Jansen (Leipzig, 1886), 143: "sind Sie vielleicht wie ich, der ich Gesangskomposition . . . nie für eine grosse Kunst gehalten?" Rufus Hallmark, "Robert Schumann: The Poet Sings," in GLNC, 78–79, discusses possible reasons for Schumann's turn to a genre he had so recently resisted, including the possibility of economic gain from song composition.

26. See, for instance, Rudolf Schenda, *Volk ohne Buch: Studien zur Sozialgeschichte der populären Lesestoffe, 1770–1910*, Studien zur Philosophie und Literatur des neunzehnten Jahrhunderts 5 (Frankfurt am Main, 1970); Rolf Engelsing, *Der Bürger als Leser: Lesergeschichte in Deutschland 1500–1800* (Stuttgart, 1974); and Martha Woodmansee, *The Author, Art, and the Market: Rereading the History of Aesthetics* (New York, 1994).

27. Dahlhaus, NCM, 102–04; quotation from 102.

28. Wilhelm von Humboldt, document of 8 July 1809, cited in Wilhelm Dilthey and Alfred Heubaum, "Ein Gutachten Wilhelm von Humboldts über die Staatsprüfung des höheren Verwaltungsbeamten," *Jahrbuch für Gesetzgebung, Verwaltung und Volkswirtschaft im Deutschen Reich* 23 (1899), 253. Cited and trans. in Kittler, *Discourse Networks*, 59.

29. For a more detailed discussion of the role of the Lied in *Bildung*, see David Gramit, "Schubert's Wanderers and the Autonomous Lied," JMR 14 (1995), 147–68. Lawrence Kramer (see especially *Franz Schubert*) considers the Lied's construction of bourgeois subjectivity with emphasis on its potential to express socially deviant rather than normative subjectivity. My account stresses rather the ability of normative culture to recuperate those potentially disruptive meanings.

30. For a discussion of the *volkstümliches Lied* as a compositional genre, see LMLR, 113–23. Popular collections of Lieder including folksongs as well as simpler songs by composers ranging from Reichardt and Zelter through Lortzing and Silcher to Beethoven, Schubert, and Mendelssohn went through numerous often quite large editions throughout the later nineteenth and early twentieth centuries. See, for example, Ludwig Erk, ed., *Erk's Deutscher Liederschatz* (Leipzig, n.d.); and Kurt Thiele, ed., *Deutschlands Liederschatz* (Halle, n.d.), the eighteenth printing of which (after 1924) consisted of the 105,000th through 108,000th exemplars of the collection.

31. Deutsch, ed., *Memoirs*, 297–98.

32. For more on this point, see Gramit, "Schubert's Wanderers," and, more generally, Kittler, *Discourse Networks*.

33. From an 1868 essay on Robert Volkmann, cited and trans. in Margaret Notley, "Late-Nineteenth-Century Chamber Music and the Cult of the Classical Adagio," 19CM 23 (1999), 59.

34. For an overview of women as composers of Lieder, see Marcia J. Citron, "Women and the Lied, 1775–1850," in *Women Making Music: The Western Art Tradition 1150–1950*, ed. Jane Bowers and Judith Tick (Urbana, 1986), 224–48.

35. On concert performance of Lieder in the late nineteenth century, see Kravitt, LMLR, 18–26.

36. Arnold Schoenberg, "The Relationship to the Text," in *Style and Idea: Selected Writings*, ed. Leonard Stein, trans. Leo Black (London, 1975), 141–46; quotation from 144.

37. For a consideration of Schoenberg's relationship to bourgeois culture and its view of art, see Carl E. Schorske, "Explosion in the Garden: Kokoschka and Schoenberg," in *Fin-de-Siècle Vienna: Politics and Culture* (New York, 1981), 322–66.

38. On cabaret in relation to *Pierrot lunaire*, see Jonathan Dunsby, *Schoenberg: Pierrot lunaire* (Cambridge, 1992), 4–5.

39. For instance, in J. B. Steane, *The Grand Tradition: Seventy Years of Singing on Record* (London, 1974), only a single chapter of twenty considering pre-LP recordings treats Lieder; the remainder is almost entirely devoted to opera. Similarly, "Opera recordings" and "Orchestra recordings" both have extended entries in Guy A. Marco, ed., *Encyclopedia of Recorded Sound in the United States* (New York, 1993), while the Lied has none (Dietrich Fischer-Dieskau's entry does mention his Lied recordings, but Gerald Moore, for instance, has no entry).

40. On the Hugo Wolf Society recordings, see Timothy Day, *A Century of Recorded Music: Listening to Music History* (New Haven, 2000), 69–70.

41. On the early history of attempts to disseminate classical music, see Mark Katz, "Making America More Musical through the Phonograph, 1900–1930," *American Music* 16 (1998), 448–75.

42. London, 1936. The performer's priority also further minimizes the generic distinction between Lied and operatic aria, which are marketed in essentially similar ways.

43. Roland Barthes, "The Grain of the Voice" (1972), in *The Responsibility of Forms: Critical Essays on Music, Art, and Representation*, trans. Richard Howard (New York, 1985), 267–77.

44. "The Romantic Song" (1976), in ibid., 286–92; quotations from 289 and 292.

45. Robert Fink, "Elvis Everywhere: Musicology and Popular Music Studies at the Twilight of the Canon," *American Music* 16 (1998), 135–79; quotation from 139. For a sociological study of musical taste that supports this conclusion, see Richard A. Peterson and Albert Simkus, "How Musical Tastes Mark Occupational Status Groups," in Marcel Fournier and Michèle Lamont, *Cultivating Differences: Symbolic Boundaries and the Making of Inequality* (Chicago, 1992), 152–86. On the broadening of available classical works, see Michael Chanan, *Repeated Takes: A Short History of Recording and Its Effects on Music* (London, 1995), 12–14.

46. Simon Frith, "Art versus Technology: The Strange Case of Popular Music," *Media, Culture, and Society* 8 (1986), 269.

47. This is by no means to suggest, however, that composers have not continued to find the Lied a genre worth cultivating, or that twentieth-century Lieder are of less musical or aesthetic interest than their predecessors. Indeed, as chapter 13 shows, this is far from the case. My argument concerns rather the visibility and impact of those Lieder within society.

48. Fink, "Going Flat: Post-Hierarchical Music Theory and the Musical Surface," in *Rethinking Music*, ed. Nicholas Cook and Mark Everist (Oxford, 1999), 121. Jameson's position is

developed at length in his *Postmodernism, or the Cultural Logic of Late Capitalism* (Durham, NC, 1991).

49. See Chanan, *Repeated Takes*, 116–21, for a survey of commentators who have stressed the tendency of recordings to privilege the musical surface. The retrospective (and socially privileged) character of Barthes's musical writings is discussed in Pierre Bourdieu, *Distinction: A Social Critique of the Judgement of Taste*, trans. Richard Nice (Cambridge, 1984), 76.

50. Dietrich Fischer-Dieskau, "German Song," in *The Fischer-Dieskau Book of Lieder*, trans. George Bird and Richard Stokes (New York, 1984), 27.

A guide to suggested further reading

This bibliography, although wide-ranging, makes no claim to completeness. That goal, in any event, would be impractical as a perusal of the on-line version of *RILM Abstracts of Music Literature* (*Répertoire International de Littérature Musicale*), an annotated index of music titles from 1967 to the present, quickly confirms. In December 2002, for example, one would have discovered slightly more than 3,500 individual bibliographic citations using the words "Lied" and "Lieder" as search parameters. Although many of the studies cited here reflect the richness and diversity of Lied research in recent decades, older studies, where significant, have been included, as have biographies of focal Lied composers and poets, as well as works devoted to Lied performance. In a handful of instances, song anthologies are referenced, especially those relating to important poets or heretofore previously neglected repertories.

Agawu, Victor Kofi. "Perspectives on Schubert's Songs." MA 16 (1997), 107–22. "Theory and Practice in the Analysis of the Nineteenth-Century Lied." MA 11 (1992), 3–36.

Albert, Claudia. *Das schwierige Handwerk des Hoffens: Hanns Eislers "Hollywooder Liederbuch."* Stuttgart, 1991.

Albert, Hermann. *Goethe und die Musik.* Stuttgart, 1922.

Alberti-Radanowicz, Editha. "Das Wiener Lied von 1789–1815." *Studien zur Musikwissenschaft.* Beihefte zu Denkmäler der Tonkunst in Deutschland 10 (1923), 37–76.

Althouse, Paul Leinbach, Jr. "Carl Loewe (1796–1869): His Lieder, Ballads, and their Performance". Ph.D. dissertation, Yale University, 1971.

Angermann, Klaus, ed. *Paul Dessau: von Geschichte gezeichnet. Symposion Paul Dessau, Hamburg 1994.* Hofheim, 1994.

Bailey, Kathryn. *The Life of Webern.* Cambridge and New York, 1998.

Ballin, Ernst August. *Das Wort-Ton-Verhältnis in den klavierbegleiteten Liedern Mozarts.* Schriften der Hochschule Mozarteum Salzburg 8. Kassel, 1984.

Barr, Raymond Arthur. "Carl Friedrich Zelter: A Study of the Lied in Berlin during the Late Eighteenth and Early Nineteenth Centuries." Ph.D. dissertation, University of Wisconsin, 1968.

Beaufils, Marcel. *Le lied romantique allemand*, 2nd edn. Paris, 1956.

Beaumont, Antony. *Zemlinsky.* Ithaca, 2000.

Becker, Peter. "'Nicht nur lesen! Immer singen! Und ein jedes Blatt ist dein!': Versuch über ein liederliches Goethewort." *Musik und Bildung* 18 (1986), 224–26.

Bennett, Benjamin. *Goethe's Theory of Poetry: Faust and the Regeneration of Language.* Ithaca, 1986.

Betz, Albrecht. *Hanns Eisler: Political Musician*, trans. Bill Hopkins. Cambridge and New York, 1982.

Bie, Oskar. *Das deutsche Lied*. Berlin, 1926.

Bingham, Ruth O. "The Song Cycle in German-Speaking Countries 1790–1840: Approaches to a Changing Genre." Ph.D. dissertation, Cornell University, 1993.

Blackall, Eric A. *The Emergence of German as a Literary Language, 1700–1775*, 2nd edn. Ithaca, 1978.

Blake, David, ed. *Hanns Eisler: A Miscellany*. New York, 1995.

Boettcher, Hans. *Beethoven als Liederkomponist*. Augsburg, 1928.

Boyd, Melinda. "Gendered Voices: The *Liebesfrühling* Lieder of Robert and Clara Schumann." 19CM 23 (1999): 145–62.

Boyle, Nicholas. *Goethe: The Poet and the Age*. Vol. I, *The Poetry of Desire, 1749–1790*; vol. II, *Revolution and Renunciation*. Oxford and New York, 1991 and 2000.

Bozarth, George Severs, Jr. "The Lieder of Johannes Brahms – 1868–1871: Studies in Chronology and Compositional Process." Ph.D. dissertation, Princeton University, 1978.

Bracht, Hans-Joachim. "Lied und Autonomie: Ein Beitrag zur Ästhetik des Liedes im Übergang vom Aufklärungszeitalter zur Romantik." AfM 49 (1992): 110–21.

"Nietzsches Theorie der Lyrik und das Orchesterlied: Ästhetische und analytische Studien zu Orchesterliedern von Richard Strauss, Gustav Mahler und Arnold Schönberg." Ph.D. dissertation, University of Mainz, 1991.

Brinkmann, Reinhold. "Lied als individuelle Struktur: Ausgewählte Kommentare zu Schumanns Zwielicht." In *Analysen: Beiträge zu einer Problemgeschichte des Komponierens. Festschrift für Hans Heinrich Eggebrecht zum 65. Geburtstag*, ed. Werner Breig, Reinhold Brinkmann, and Elmar Budde, 257–75. Wiesbaden, 1984.

"The Lyric as Paradigm: Poetry and the Foundation of Arnold Schoenberg's New Music." In *German Literature and Music: An Aesthetic Fusion 1890–1989*, ed. Claus Reschke and Howard Pollack, 95–129. Munich, 1992.

"Schönberg und George. Interpretation eines Liedes." AfM 26 (1969), 1–28.

Schumann and Eichendorff: Studien zum Liederkreis Opus 39. Munich, 1997.

Brody, Elaine, and Robert Fowkes. *The German Lied and Its Poetry*. New York, 1971.

Brown, A. Peter. "Joseph Haydn and Leopold Hofmann's 'Street Songs.'" JAMS 33 (1980), 356–83.

"Musical Settings of Anne Hunter's Poetry: From National Song to Canzonetta," JAMS 47 (1994), 39–89.

Brown, Marshall. *The Shape of German Romanticism*. Ithaca, 1979.

Brown, Maurice J. E. "Schubert: Discoveries of the Last Decade." MQ 47 (1961), 293–314.

Browning, Robert M., ed. *German Poetry from 1750 to 1900*. New York, 1984.

German Poetry in the Age of the Enlightenment: From Brockes to Klopstock. University Park, PA, 1978.

Bruford, W. H. *Culture and Society in Classical Weimar 1775–1806.* Cambridge, 1962.

　German in the Eighteenth Century: The Social Background of the Literary Revival. London, 1971.

Bücken, Ernst. *Das deutsche Lied; Probleme und Gestalten.* Hamburg, 1939.

Bührig, Dieter. "Der morgige Tag ist mein: Lied und politische Verführung-Szenische Interpretation eines Liedes aus dem Musical *Cabaret.*" *Musik und Unterricht* 8 (1997), 6–22.

Busse, Eckart. *Die Eichendorff-Rezeption im Kunstlied: Versuch einer Typologie anhand von Kompositionen Schumanns, Wolfs und Pfitzners.* Würzburg, 1975.

Cadenbach, Rainer. *Max Reger und seine Zeit.* Laaber, 1991.

Capell, Richard. *Schubert's Songs.* London, 1928; reprint New York, 1977.

Chadwick, Nicholas. "A Survey of the Early Songs of Alban Berg." Ph.D. dissertation, University of Oxford, 1972.

Challier, Ernst. *Grosser Lieder-Katalog. Ein alphabetisch geordnetes Verzeichnis sämmtlicher einstimmiger Lieder: mit Begleitung des Pianoforte sowie mit Begleitung des Pianoforte und eines oder mehrerer anderer Instrumente.* Berlin, 1885–1914; reprint, Wiesbaden, 1979.

Chapple, Gerald, Albert Frederick, and Hans Schulte, eds. *The Romantic Tradition: German Literature and Music in the Nineteenth Century,* McMaster Colloquium on German Studies 4. Lanham, 1992.

Chusid, Martin, ed. *A Companion to Schubert's "Schwanengesang": History, Poets, Analysis, Performance.* New Haven and London, 2000.

Citron, Marcia. "The Lieder of Fanny Mendelssohn Hensel." MQ 69 (1983), 570–94.

　"Women and the Lied, 1775–1850." In *Women Making Music: The Western Art Tradition, 1150–1950,* ed. Jane Bowers and Judith Tick, 224–48. Urbana, IL, 1986.

Clive, Peter. *Schubert and His World: A Biographical Dictionary.* Oxford, 1997.

Cone, Edward T. "'Am Meer' Reconsidered: Strophic, Binary, or Ternary?" In *Schubert Studies,* ed. Brian Newbould, 112–26. Aldershot, 1998.

　The Composer's Voice. Berkeley, 1974.

　"Words into Music: The Composer's Approach to the Text." In *Sound and Poetry: English Institute Essays,* ed. Northrop Frye, 3–15. New York, 1957; also in Cone, *Music: A View from Delft,* 115–23. Chicago, 1989.

Conrady, Karl Otto. *Das große deutsche Gedichtbuch.* Munich, 1991.

Cooper, Barry. *Beethoven's Folksong Settings: Chronology, Sources, Style.* Oxford and New York, 1994.

Danuser, Hermann. *Gustav Mahler: Das Lied von der Erde.* Munich, 1986.

　"Der Orchestergesang des fin de siècle: Eine historische und ästhetische Skizze". Mf 30 (1977), 425–52.

Daverio, John. *Nineteenth-Century Music and the German Romantic Ideology.* New York, 1993.

　Robert Schumann: Herald of a "New Poetic Age." Oxford, 1997.

Del Mar, Norman. *Richard Strauss: A Critical Commentary on His Life and Works,* 3 vols. London, 1972.

Deutsch, Otto Erich. *Mozart: A Documentary Biography*, trans. Eric Blom, Peter Branscombe, and Jeremy Noble. Stanford, 1965.

Diez, Werner. *Hans Pfitzners Lieder: Versuch einer Stilbetrachtung.* Regensburg, 1968.

"Sehnsucht nach der Vergangenheit: Bermerkungen zum deutschen Kunstlied am Ende der Romantik." *Neue Zeitschrift für Musik* 80 (1969): 239–44.

Dittrich, Marie-Agnes. "Ein 'Blick in das gelobte Land des späteren Schubertschen Liedes'? Zur Harmonik in Mozarts Liedern." *Bericht Internationaler Musikwissenschaftlicher Kongress zum Mozartjahr 1991, Baden-Wien*, ed. Ingrid Fuchs, 537–54. Tutzing, 1993.

Harmonik und Sprachvertonung in Schuberts Liedern, Hamburger Beiträge zur Musikwissenschaft 38, Hamburg, 1991 [Ph.D. dissertation, University of Hamburg, 1989].

Dümling, Albrecht. "'Wir sehen jetzt durch einen Spiegel': Zu den Gottfried Keller-Vertonungen von Johannes Brahms." In *Johannes Brahms oder die Relativierung der "absoluten" Musik*, ed. Hanns-Werner Heister, 91–120. Hamburg, 1997.

Dunsby, Jonathan. *Schoenberg: Pierrot lunaire.* Cambridge, 1992.

Düring, Werner-Joachim. *Erlkönig-Vertonungen: Eine historische und systematische Untersuchung.* Regensburg, 1972.

Dürr, Albrecht. "Josephine Caroline Lang: 'Meine Lieder sind mein Tagebuch . . .'" In *Annäherung an sieben Komponistinnen*, ed. Brunhilde Sonntag (Kassel, 1999), X: 125–36.

Dürr, Walther. *Das deutsche Sololied im 19. Jahrhundert: Untersuchungen zur Sprache und Musik*, 2nd edn. Wilhelmshaven, 2002.

"Schubert and Johann Michael Vogl: A Reappraisal." 19CM 3 (1979), 126–40.

"Schubert's Songs and their Poetry: Reflections on Poetic Aspects of Song Composition." In *Schubert Studies: Problems of Style and Chronology*, ed. Eva Badura-Skoda and Peter Branscombe, 1–24. Cambridge, 1982.

Dürr, Walther, and Andreas Krause, eds. *Schubert Handbuch.* Kassel and Stuttgart, 1997.

Eggebrecht, Hans Heinrich. "Prinzipien des Schubert-Liedes." AfM 27 (1970), 89–109.

Einstein, Alfred. *Mozart: His Character, His Work*, trans. Arthur Mendel and Nathan Broder. London and New York, 1945.

Erwe, Hans-Joachim. "Musik nach Eduard Mörike." Ph.D. dissertation, University of Hamburg, 1987.

Fehn, Ann Clark. "Who is Speaking? Edward T. Cone's Concept of Persona and Wolfgang von Schweinitz's Settings of Poems by Sarah Kirsch." JMR 11 (1991), 1–31.

Fehn, Ann Clark, and Rufus Hallmark. "Text and Music in Schubert's Pentameter Lieder: A Consideration of Declamation." In *Studies in the History of Music*, vol. I: *Music and Language*, ed. Ronald Broude, 204–46. New York, 1983.

Fehn, Ann Clark, and Jürgen Thym. "Repetition as Structure in the German Lied: the Ghazal." *Comparative Literature* 41 (1989), 33–52.

Feil, Arnold. *Franz Schubert: Die schöne Müllerin, Winterreise,* trans. Ann C. Sherwin. Portland, 1988.

Ferris, David. *Schumann's Eichendorff Liederkreis and the Genre of the Romantic Cycle.* New York, 2000.

Feurzeig, Lisa. "Heroines in Perversity: Marie Schmith, Animal Magnetism, and the Schubert Circle." 19CM 21 (1997), 223–43.

"Idea in Song: Schubert's Settings of Friedrich Schlegel." Ph.D. dissertation, University of Chicago, 1997.

Filler, Susan. "A Composer's Wife as Composer: the Songs of Alma Mahler." JRM 4 (1983), 427–41.

Finson, Jon. "The Intentional Tourist: Romantic Irony in the Eichendorff *Liederkreis* of Robert Schumann." In *Schumann and His World,* ed. R. Larry Todd, 156–70. Princeton, 1994.

Fisch, Samuel. *Goethe und die Musik.* Frauenfeld, 1949.

Fischer-Dieskau, Dietrich. *The Fischer-Dieskau Book of Lieder,* trans. George Bird and Richard Stokes. New York, 1984.

Robert Schumann: Wort und Musik. Das Vokalwerk. Stuttgart, 1981.

Schubert's Songs: A Biographical Study. New York, 1977.

Flores, Angel, ed. *An Anthology of German Poetry from Hoelderlin to Rilke.* New York, 1960.

Freund, Volker. *Hans Pfitzners Eichendorff-Lieder: Studien zum Verhältnis von Sprache und Musik.* Hamburg, 1986.

Fricke, Harald. "Rückert und das Kunstlied." *Rückert-Studien* 5 (1990), 14–37.

Friedländer, Max. *Das deutsche Lied im 18. Jahrhundert: Quellen und Studien.* 2 vols. Stuttgart and Berlin, 1902.

Frisch, Walter. *The Early Works of Arnold Schoenberg, 1893–1908.* Berkeley, 1993.

"Schubert's Nähe des Geliebten (D. 162): Transformation of the *Volkston.*" In SCAS, 175–99.

Garland, Henry and Mary. *The Oxford Companion to German Literature.* Oxford, 1976.

Garlington, Aubrey S., Jr. "Richard Strauss's *Vier letzte Lieder:* The Ultimate *Opus Ultimatum.*" MQ 73 (1989), 79–93.

Georgiades, Thrasybulos. *Schubert: Musik und Lyrik.* Göttingen, 1967.

Gerhardt, Elena. "Strauss and His Lieder: A Personal Reminiscence." *Tempo* 12 (1949), 9–11.

Geyer, Hans-Herwig. *Hugo Wolfs Mörike-Vertonungen: Mannigfaltigung in lyrischer Konzentration.* Kassel, 1991.

Gibbs, Christopher H., ed. *The Cambridge Companion to Schubert.* Cambridge, 1997.

The Life of Schubert. Cambridge, 2000.

"The Presence of Erlkönig: Reception and Reworkings of a Schubert Lied." Ph.D. dissertation, Columbia University, 1992.

Glauert, Amanda. " 'Ich singe, wie der Vogel singt': Reflections on Nature and Genre in Wolf's Setting of Goethe's *Der Sänger.*" JRMA 125 (2000), 271–86.

Hugo Wolf and the Wagnerian Inheritance. Cambridge, 1999.

Gorrell, Lorraine. *The Nineteenth-Century German Lied*. Portland, OR, 1993.

Gramit, David. "The Intellectual and Aesthetic Tenets of Franz Schubert's Circle." Ph.D. dissertation, Duke University, 1987.

"Lied, Listeners, and Ideology: Schubert's 'Alinde' and Opus 81." CM 58 (1995), 28–60.

"Schubert and the Biedermeier: The Aesthetics of Johann Mayrhofer's *Heliopolis*." ML 74 (1993), 355–82.

"Schubert's Wanderers and the Autonomous Lied." JMR 14 (1995), 147–68.

Green, Richard D., ed. *Anthology of Goethe Songs*. Madison, WI, 1994.

Gülke, Peter. *Franz Schubert und seine Zeit*. Laaber, 1991.

Hallmark, Rufus, ed. *German Lieder in the Nineteenth Century*. New York, 1996.

"The Rückert Lieder of Robert and Clara Schumann." 19CM 14 (1990), 3–30.

"The Sketches for Dichterliebe." 19CM (1977), 110–36.

Hartmann, Bernhard. *Das Verhältnis von Sprache und Musik in den Liedern von Robert Franz*. Frankfurt, 1991.

Hefling, Stephen E. *Das Lied von der Erde (The Song of the Earth)*. Cambridge, 2000.

Hennenberg, Fritz. *Brecht-Liederbuch*. Frankfurt am Main, 1984.

Paul Dessau: Eine Biographie. Leipzig, 1965.

Hindenlang, Karen A. "Eichendorff's *Auf einer Burg* and Schumann's *Liederkreis, opus 39*." JM 8 (1990): 569–87.

Hirsch, Marjorie Wing. *Schubert's Dramatic Lieder*. New York and Cambridge, 1993.

Höhn, Gerhard. *Heine-Handbuch: Zeit, Person, Werk*. Stuttgart, 1997.

Hollaender, Friedrich. *Von Kopf bis Fuss: Mein Leben in Text und Musik*. Weidle, 1996.

Holländer, Hans. "Franz Schubert's Repeated Settings of the Same Song Text." MQ 14 (1928), 563–74.

Hosler, Bellamy. *Changing Aesthetic Views of Instrumental Music in 18th-Century Germany*. Ann Arbor, 1981.

Huschke, Wolfram. "Liszts Goethe-Lieder: Liszt contra Goethe?" In *Liszt und die Weimarer Klassik*, ed. Detlef Altenburg, 59–67. Laaber, 1997.

Ivey, Donald. *Song: Anatomy, Imagery, and Styles*. New York, 1970.

Jackson, Timothy. "The Last Strauss: Studies of the letzte Lieder." Ph.D. dissertation, City University of New York, 1988.

"Ruhe, meine Seele! and the *Letzte Orchesterlieder*." In *Richard Strauss and His World*, ed. Bryan Gilliam, 90–137. Princeton, 1992.

"Schubert's Revisions of 'Der Jüngling und der Tod,' D. 545a–b, and 'Meeresstille,' D. 216a–b." MQ 75 (1991), 336–61.

Jefferson, Alan. *The Lieder of Richard Strauss*. London, 1971.

Jelavich, Peter. *Berlin Cabaret*. Cambridge, MA, 1993.

Johnson, Graham. Liner notes for *The Hyperion Schubert Edition*, 37 CDs. 1987–99.

Johnson, Julian. *Webern and the Transformation of Nature*. Cambridge, 2000.

Jolizza, W. K. von. *Das Lied und seine Geschichte*. Vienna and Leipzig, 1910.

Jost, Christa. "Hans Pfitzner und das romantische Lied." *Mitteilungen der Hans Pfitzner-Gesellschaft* 57 (1997), 5–37.

Kabisch, Thomas. *Liszt und Schubert*. Berlin, 1984.

Kerman, Joseph. "A Romantic Detail in Schubert's *Schwanengesang*." MQ 48 (1962), 36–49; also in SCAS, 48–64.

"An die ferne Geliebte." In *Beethoven Studies*, ed. Alan Tyson, 123–57. New York, 1973; also in Kerman, *Write All These Down: Essays on Music*, 173–206. Berkeley, 1994.

Kinderman, William. *Beethoven*. Berkeley, 1995.

Klassen, Janina. "'Mach' doch ein Lied einmal': Clara Wieck-Schumanns Annäherung an die Liedkomposition." *Schumann-Studien* 6 (1997), 13–25.

Klusen, Ernst, ed. *Deutsche Lieder: Texte und Melodien*. Frankfurt am Main, 1980.

Knaus, Herwig. "Im Reich der Nacht: Wort und Ton im bürgerlichen romantischen Lied um 1870." *Musikerziehung* 42 (1988), 19–26.

Musiksprache und Werkstruktur in Robert Schumanns "Liederkreis." Mit dem Faksimile des Autographs. Munich, 1974.

Köster, Maren, ed. *Hanns Eisler: 's müsst dem Himmel Höllenangst werden.* Hofheim, 1998.

Kramer, Lawrence. "Beyond Words and Music: An Essay on Songfulness." In *Musical Meaning: Towards a Critical History* [Lawrence Kramer], 51–67. Berkeley, 2002.

Franz Schubert: Sexuality, Subjectivity, Song. Cambridge and New York, 1998.

Music and Poetry: the Nineteenth Century and After. Berkeley and Los Angeles, 1984.

"The Schubert Lied: Romantic Form and Romantic Consciousness." In SCAS, 200–36.

Kramer, Richard. *Distant Cycles: Schubert and the Conceiving of Song.* Chicago, 1994.

"Distant Cycles: Schubert, Goethe and the Entfernte." JM 6 (1988), 3–26.

"Schubert's Heine." 19CM 8 (1985), 213–25.

Kravitt, Edward F. *The Lied: Mirror of Late Romanticism.* New Haven and London, 1996.

"The Lieder of Alma Maria Schindler Mahler." MR 49 (1988), 190–204.

"The Orchestral Lied: An Inquiry into its Style and Unexpected Flowering around 1900." MR 37 (1976), 209–26.

Kretzschmar, Hermann. *Geschichte des neuen deutschen Liedes.* Leipzig, 1911.

Kross, Siegfried. *Geschichte des deutschen Liedes.* Darmstadt, 1989.

Kühn, Henry Joachim. *Johann Gottfried Carl Loewe: Ein Lesebuch und eine Materialsammlung zu seiner Biographie.* Halle, 1996.

Kurth, Richard. "Music and Poetry, a Wilderness of Doubles: Heine – Schubert – Nietzsche – Derrida." 19CM 21 (1997), 3–37.

Lafite, Carl Johann Sigismund. *Das Schubertlied und seine Sänger.* Vienna, Prague, and Leipzig, 1928.

Landau, Anneliese. *The Lied. The Unfolding of Its Style.* Washington, DC, 1980.

Lehmann, Lotte. *More than Singing.* New York, 1945.

Lemke, Ann Willison, ed. *Von Goethe inspiriert: Lieder von Komponistinnen des 18. und 19. Jahrhunderts.* Kassel, 1999.

Lessem, Alan. "Sound and Sense: The Search for a Unified Expression in the Early Songs of Arnold Schoenberg." In *German Literature and Music: An Aesthetic Fusion: 1890–1989*, ed. Claus Reschke and Howard Pollack, 85–94. Munich, 1992.

Lewin, David. "*Auf dem Flusse*: Image and Background in a Schubert Song." In SCAS, 126–52; also 19CM 6 (1982), 47–59.

Lewis, Christopher. "Text, Time, and Tonic: Aspects of Patterning in the Romantic Cycle." *Intégral* 2 (1988), 37–73.

Liess, Andreas. *Johann Michael Vogl: Hofoperist und Schubert-Sänger*. Graz and Cologne, 1954.

Lindner, Ernst Otto Timotheus. *Geschichte des deutschen Liedes im XVIII. Jahrhundert*, ed. Ludwig Erk. Wiesbaden, 1968; reprint, Leipzig, 1871.

Liszt, Franz. *The Schubert Song Transcriptions for Solo Piano*, 3 vols. New York, 1996–99.

Lodato, Suzanne Marie. "Richard Strauss and the Modernists: A Contextual Study of Strauss's Fin-de-siècle Song Style." Ph.D. dissertation, Columbia University, 1999.

Loewe, Carl. *Dr. Carl Loewe's Selbstbiographie*, ed. Carl Hermann Bitter. Berlin, 1870.

MacDonald, Malcolm. *Brahms*. New York, 1990.

Maier, Gunter. *Die Lieder Johann Rudolf Zumsteegs und ihr Verhältnis zu Schubert*, Göppinger akademische Beiträge 28. Göppingen, 1971.

Marston, Nicholas. "Voicing Beethoven's Distant Beloved." In *Beethoven and His World*, ed. Scott Burnham and Michael P. Steinberg, 124–47. Princeton, 2000.
  "*Wie aus der Ferne*: Pastness and Presentness in the Lieder of Beethoven, Schubert, and Schumann." *Schubert durch die Brille* 21 (1998), 126–42.

Mayer, Birgit. *Eduard Mörike*. Stuttgart, 1987.

Mayer, Günter, ed. *Hanns Eisler der Zeitgenosse. Positionen, Perspektiven: Materialien zu den Eisler-Festen, 1994/95 im Auftrag der Internationalen Hanns Eisler Gesellschaft*. Leipzig, 1997.

McCreless, Patrick. "Song Order in the Song Cycle: Schumann's Liederkreis, Op. 39." MA 5 (1986), 5–40.

McKay, Elizabeth Norman. *Franz Schubert: A Biography*. Oxford, 1996.

Mercier, Richard. *The Songs of Hans Pfitzner: A Guide and Study*. Greenwood, CT, 1998.

Mews, Siegfried, and James Hardin, eds. *Nineteenth-Century German Writers, 1841–1900*, vol. CXXIX, *Dictionary of Literary Biography*. Detroit, 1993.
  Nineteenth-Century German Writers to 1840, vol. CXXXIII, *Dictionary of Literary Biography*. Detroit, 1993.

Miller, Philip, ed. and trans. *The Ring of Words: An Anthology of Song Texts*. New York, 1973.

Miller, Richard. *Singing Schumann: An Interpretive Guide for Performers*. New York and Oxford, 1999.

Mitchell, Donald. *Gustav Mahler: Songs and Symphonies of Life and Death*. Berkeley, 1985.

Moore, Gerald. *Am I too Loud?: Memoirs of an Accompanist.* London, 1962.
　Poet's Love: the Songs and Cycles of Schumann. New York, 1981.
　Singer and Accompanist. New York, 1953.
　The Unashamed Accompanist. London, 1959.
Moser, Hans Joachim. *Die Ballade.* Wolfenbüttel, 1959.
　Das deutsche Lied seit Mozart. Tutzing, 1968.
　The German Solo Song and the Ballad. New York, 1958.
Mosley, David L. *Gesture, Sign and Song: An Interdisciplinary Approach to
　Schumann's Liederkreis, Op. 39.* New York, 1990.
Mueller, Rena Charnin. "Reevaluating the Liszt Chronology: The Case of *Anfangs
　wollt ich fast verzagen.*" 19CM 12 (1988), 132–47.
Müller, Günther. *Geschichte des deutschen Liedes vom Zeitalter des Barock bis zur
　Gegenwart.* Homburg, 1959; reprint of 1925 1st edn.
Müller-Blattau, Joseph. *Das Verhältnis von Wort und Ton in der Geschichte der
　Musik.* Stuttgart, 1952.
　Deutsche Volkslieder: Wort und Weise, Wesen und Werden, Dokumente. Königstein
　im Taunus, 1959.
Musgrave, Michael. *A Brahms Reader.* New Haven and London, 2000.
Mustard, Helen. *The Lyric Cycle in German Literature,* Columbia University
　Germanic Studies No. 17. Morningside Heights, 1946.
Muxfeldt, Kristina. "*Frauenliebe und Leben* Now and Then." 19CM 25 (2001),
　27–48.
　"Schubert, Platen, and the Myth of Narcissus." JAMS 49 (1996), 480–527.
Neubauer, John. *The Emancipation of Music from Language: Departure from Mimesis
　in Eighteenth-Century Aesthetics.* New Haven, 1986.
Oehlmann, Werner. *Reclams Liedführer.* Stuttgart, 1973; 4th edn., Stuttgart, 1993.
Olivier, Antje. *Mendelssohns Schwester Fanny Hensel: Musikerin, Komponistin,
　Dirigentin.* Düsseldorf, 1997.
Orrey, Leslie. "The Songs." In *The Beethoven Reader,* ed. Denis Arnold and Nigel
　Fortune, 411–39. New York: W. W. Norton, 1971.
Ossenkop, David. *Hugo Wolf: A Guide to Research.* New York, 1988.
Osthoff, Wolfgang. *Hans Pfitzner und die musikalische Lyrik seiner Zeit: Bericht über
　das Symposion Hamburg 1989.* Tutzing, 1994.
Ottenberg, Hans-Günter. *Carl Philipp Emanuel Bach,* trans. Philip J. Whitmore.
　Oxford and New York, 1987.
Otto, Uli and Eginhard König, eds. "*Ich hatt einen Kameraden*": *Militär und Kriege
　in historisch-politischen Liedern in den Jahren von 1740 bis 1914.* Regensburg,
　1999.
Parsons, James. "'*Deine Zauber binden wieder*': Beethoven, Schiller, and the Joyous
　Reconciliation of Opposites." *Beethoven Forum* 9 (2002), 1–53.
　"Lied. § III. c. 1740 – c. 1800." *The New Grove Dictionary of Music and Musicians,*
　2nd edn., ed. Stanley Sadie, XIV: 668–71. London and New York, 2001.
　"Ode to the Ninth: The Poetic and Musical Tradition Behind the Finale of
　Beethoven's Choral Symphony." Ph.D. dissertation, University of North Texas,
　1992.

Paulin, Roger. *Ludwig Tieck: A Literary Biography*. Oxford and New York, 1985.

Perrey, Beate Julia. *Schumann's Dichterliebe and Early Romantic Poetics: Fragments of Desire*. Cambridge, 2002.

Petersen, Barbara A. *Ton und Wort: The Lieder of Richard Strauss*. Ann Arbor, 1980.

Phleps, Thomas. "'Das wird ein Winter, mein Junge!' Anmerkungen zu Hanns Eislers Ballade von den Säckeschmeissern." *Beiträge zur Musikwissenschaft* 31 (1989), 118–30.

"... ich kann mir gar nicht vorstellen etwas Schöneres": Das Exilschaffen Hanns Eislers." In *Musik im Exil: Folgen des Nazismus für die internationale Musikkultur*, ed. Hanns-Werner Heister, Claudia Maurer-Zenck, and Peter Petersen, 475–511. Frankfurt am Main, 1993.

Platt, Heather. "Dramatic Turning Points in Brahms Lieder." *Indiana Theory Review* 15 (1994), 69–104.

"Hugo Wolf and the Reception of Brahms's Lieder." *Brahms Studies* 2 (1998), 91–112.

"Jenner versus Wolf: The Critical Reception of Brahms's Songs." JM 13 (1995), 377–403.

"Text–Music Relationships in the Lieder of Johannes Brahms." Ph.D. dissertation, City University of New York, 1992.

Pollak-Schlaffenberg, Irene. "Die Wiener Liedmusik von 1778–1789." *Studien zur Musikwissenschaft: Beihefte zu Denkmäler der Tonkunst in Deutschland* 5 (1918), 97–139.

Porter, Cecelia Hopkins. *The Rhine as Musical Metaphor: Cultural Identity in German Romantic Music*. Boston, 1996.

Prawer, Siegbert S., ed. *The Penguin Book of Lieder*. Baltimore, 1964.

Reed, John. *The Schubert Song Companion*. Manchester, 1985.

Reeves, Nigel. *Heinrich Heine: Poetry and Politics*. London, 1974.

Rehm, Ludger. "'Es ist eine Art Symbolik für das Ohr ...': Carl Friedrich Zelters Gedichtvertonung Ruhe nach Goethes Lied *Über allen Wipfeln ist Ruh*." *Berliner Beiträge zur Musikwissenschaft: Beihefte zur Neuen Berlinischen Musikzeitung* 11 (1996), 46–62.

Reich, Nancy B. "Die Lieder von Clara Schumann." *Brahms-Studien* 11 (1997), 97–105.

Clara Schumann: The Artist and the Woman, rev. edn. Ithaca, 2001.

Reich, Willi. *Schoenberg: A Critical Biography*, trans. Leo Black. London, 1971.

Reichardt, Luise. *Songs*, compiled and with an introduction by Nancy B. Reich. New York, 1981.

Reißmann, August. *Das deutsche Lied in seiner historischen Entwicklung*. Kassel, 1861.

Revers, Peter. *Mahlers Lieder: Ein musikalischer Werkführer*. Munich, 2000.

Reynolds, Christopher. "Liederkreis 'An die ferne Geliebte' Op. 98." *Beethoven: Interpretationen seiner Werke*, ed. Albrecht Riethmüller, Carl Dahlhaus, and Alexander L. Ringer, II: 99–108. Laaber, 1994.

Riha, Karl. *Moritat, Bänkelsang, Protestballade. Kabarett-Lyrik und engagiertes Lied in Deutschland*, 2nd edn. Königstein, 1979.

Rose, Ernst. *A History of German Literature*. New York, 1960.

Rosen, Charles. *The Classical Style.* New York, 1972.

    The Romantic Generation. Cambridge, MA, 1995.

Rosselli, John. *The Life of Mozart.* Cambridge and New York, 1998.

Salmen, Walter. *Johann Friedrich Reichardt; Komponist, Schriftsteller, Kapellmeister und Verwaltungsbeamter der Goethezeit.* Freiburg and Zurich, 1963.

Sammons, Jeffrey L. *Heinrich Heine: A Modern Biography.* Princeton, 1979.

    Heinrich Heine: The Elusive Poet. New Haven, 1969.

Sams, Eric. *The Songs of Hugo Wolf,* 2nd edn. London, 1983.

    The Songs of Robert Schumann. London, 1969.

Schachter, Carl. "Motive and Text in Four Schubert Songs." In *Aspects of Schenkerian Theory,* ed. David Beach, 61–76. New Haven, 1983.

Schebera, Jürgen. " 'Da darf man sich auf keinen Fall gehenlassen, wenn die Luft schön milde ist.' Kalifornien 1942–43: Hanns Eislers *Hollywooder Liederbuch* als musikalische Meisterleistung und politisches Zeitdokument." In *Exil: Literatur und die Künste nach 1933,* ed. Stephan Alexander, 93–103. Bonn, 1990.

    Hanns Eisler: eine Biographie in Texten, Bildern und Dokumenten. Mainz and New York, 1998.

    Hanns Eisler im USA-Exil: zu den politischen, ästhetischen und kompositorischen Positionen des Komponisten 1938 bis 1948. Meisenheim am Glan, 1978.

Schenker, Heinrich. "Franz Schubert: Gretchen am Spinnrade." *Der Tonwille* 6 (1923): 3–8.

Scher, Steven Paul. "Musicopoetics or Melomania: Is There a Theory behind Music in German Literature?" In *Music and German Literature: Their Relationship Since the Middle Ages,* ed. James M. McGlathery, 328–37. Columbia, SC, 1992.

Schiwy, Günther. *Eichendorff: Der Dichter in seiner Zeit: eine Biographie.* Munich, 2000.

Schmierer, Elisabeth. *Die Orchesterlieder Gustav Mahlers.* Kassel, 1991.

Schroeder, David P. "Alban Berg and Peter Altenberg: Intimate Art and the Aesthetics of Life." JAMS 46 (1993), 61–294.

    "Haydn and Gellert: Parallels in Eighteenth-Century Music and Literature." CM 35 (1983): 7–18.

Schuh, Willi. *Goethe-Vertonungen: Ein Verzeichnis.* Zurich, 1952.

Schumann, Elisabeth. *German Song.* London, 1948.

Schumann, Robert, *Dichterliebe,* ed. Arthur Komar. *Norton Critical Score.* New York, 1971.

Schuré, Edouard. *Geschichte des deutschen Liedes.* Berlin, 1870; 3rd edn, 1884.

    Histoire du lied, ou, La chanson populaire en Allemagne. Paris, 1903.

Schwab, Heinrich W. *Sangbarkeit, Popularität und Kunstlied: Studien zu Lied und Liedästhetik der mittleren Goethezeit 1770–1814.* Regensburg, 1965.

Seebass, Tilman. "Classical and Romantic Principles in Schubert's Lieder: *Auf dem See* and *Des Fischers Liebesglück.*" In *Studies in Musical Sources and Style: Essays in Honor of Jan LaRue,* ed. Eugene K. Wolf and Edward H. Roesner, 481–504. Madison, WI, 1990.

Seidlin, Oskar. *Versuch über Eichendorff.* Göttingen, 1978.

Sengle, Friedrich. *Biedermeierzeit: Deutsche Literatur im Spannungsfeld zwischen Restauration und Revolution, 1815–1848,* 3 vols. Stuttgart, 1971.

Sharpe, Lesley. *Friedrich Schiller: Drama, Thought and Politics*. Cambridge, 1991.

Shawn, Allen. *Arnold Schoenberg's Journey*. New York, 2002.

Shreffler, Anne Chatoney. "*Mein Weg geht jetzt vorüber*: The Vocal Origins of Webern's Twelve-Tone Composition." JAMS 47 (1994), 275–339.

   Webern and the Lyric Impulse: Songs and Fragments on Poems of Georg Trakl. Oxford, 1994.

Simms, Bryan R. *The Atonal Music of Arnold Schoenberg, 1908–1923*. Oxford and New York, 2000.

Simms, Bryan R., ed. *Schoenberg, Berg, and Webern: A Companion to the Second Viennese School*. Westport, CT, 1999.

Sinkovicz, Wilhelm. "Paul Hindemiths Liederzyklus Marienleben und seine beiden Fassungen als Beispiel für den Stilwandel der Musik in der ersten Hälfte des 20. Jahrhunderts." Ph.D. dissertation, University of Vienna, 1993.

Smeed, John William. *German Song and Its Poetry 1740–1900*. London and New York, 1987.

   "*Süssertönendes Klavier*: Tributes to the Early Piano in Poetry and Song." ML 66 (1985), 228–40.

Snyder, Lawrence D. *German Poetry in Song: An Index of Lieder*. Berkeley, 1995.

Solie, Ruth. "Whose Life? The Gendered Self in Schumann's *Frauenliebe* Songs." In *Music and Text: Critical Inquiries*, ed. Steven Paul Scherr, 219–40. Cambridge, 1992.

Solomon, Maynard. *Beethoven*, 2nd, rev. edn. New York and London, 1998.

   Mozart: A Life. New York, 1995.

   "Schubert and Beethoven." 19CM 3 (1979), 114–25.

Spann, Meno. *Heine*. New York, 1966.

Spillman, Robert. *The Art of Accompanying*. New York, 1985.

Stark, Lucien. *A Guide to the Solo Songs of Johannes Brahms*. Bloomington, IN, 1995.

Stein, Deborah J. *Hugo Wolf's Lieder and Extensions of Tonality*. Ann Arbor, MI, 1985.

Stein, Deborah, and Robert Spillman. *Poetry into Song: Performance and Analysis of Lieder*. New York and Oxford, 1996.

Stein, Franz A. *Verzeichnis deutscher Lieder seit Haydn*. Bern and Munich, 1967.

Stein, Jack M. "Musical Settings of the Songs from *Wilhelm Meister*." *Comparative Literature* 22 (1970), 125–46.

   Poem and Music in the German Lied from Gluck to Hugo Wolf. Cambridge, MA, 1971.

Sternfeld, Frederick W. *Goethe and Music*. New York, 1979.

Stevens, Denis, ed. *A History of Song*, rev. edn. New York, 1970.

Stockhausen, Julius. *Der Sänger des deutschen Liedes*. Frankfurt, 1927.

Stoljar, Margaret. *Poetry and Song in Late Eighteenth-Century Germany: A Study in the Musical Sturm und Drang*. London, 1985.

Swafford, Jan. *Johannes Brahms: A Biography*. New York, 1998.

Thayer, Alexander Wheelock. *Thayer's Life of Beethoven*, rev. and ed. Elliot Forbes. Princeton, 1973.

Thomas, R. Hinton. *Poetry and Song in the German Baroque*. Oxford, 1963.

Thym, Jürgen. *100 Years of Eichendorff Songs.* Madison, WI, 1983.

"The Solo Song Settings of Eichendorff's Poems by Schumann and Wolf." Ph.D. dissertation, Case Western Reserve University, 1974.

"Text–Music Relationships in Schumann's *Frühlingsfahrt.*" *Theory and Practice* 5 (1980), 7–25.

Thym, Jürgen, and Ann Clark Fehn. "Sonnet Structure and the German Lied: Shackles or Spurs?" *American Liszt Society Journal* 32 (1992): 3–15.

Trembath, Shirley. "Joseph Haydn's XII *Lieder für das Clavier* (Erster Teil) of 1781: Song Cycle or Collection?" *Studien zur Musikwissenschaft: Beihefte der Denkmäler der Tonkunst in Österreich* 43 (1994), 145–57.

Tubeuf, André. *Le lied allemand: Poètes et paysages.* Paris, 1993.

Turchin, Barbara P. "The Nineteenth-Century Wanderlieder Cycle." JM 5 (1987), 498–526.

"Robert Schumann's Song Cycles in the Context of the Early Nineteenth-Century Liederkreis." Ph.D. dissertation, Columbia University, 1981.

"Schumann's Song Cycles: The Cycle within the Song." 19CM 8 (1985), 238–41.

Unger, Hermann. *Max Reger.* Bielefeld, 1924.

Utz, Helga. *Untersuchungen zur Syntax der Lieder Franz Schuberts.* Munich, 1989.

Van Tassel, Eric. " 'Something Utterly New': Listening to Schubert Lieder: I: Vogl and the Declamatory Style." *Early Music* 25 (1997), 702–14.

Velten, Klaus, ed. *Musik über Worte: Studien zum lyrischen Gesang in Romantik und Moderne.* Saarbrücken, 1999.

Vetter, Walther. *Der Klassiker Schubert,* 2 vols. Leipzig, 1953.

Vogel, Johann Peter. *Hans Pfitzner: Leben, Werke, Dokumente.* Zurich, 1999.

Vogel, Werner. *Othmar Schoeck.* Zurich, 1976.

Vyslouzilova, Vera. "Bei den Anfängen des Wiener Kunstliedes: Josef Antonin Stepan und seine Sammlung deutscher Lieder." In *Wort und Ton im europäischen Raum: Gedenkschrift für Robert Schollum,* ed. Hartmut Krones, 69–77. Vienna, 1989.

Walker, Alan. "Liszt and the Schubert Song Transcriptions." MQ 75 (1991), 248–62.

Walker, Frank. *Hugo Wolf: A Biography.* London, 1968; 2nd edn., reprint Princeton, 1992.

Webster, James, and Georg Feder. *The New Grove Haydn.* London and New York, 2002.

Wehmeyer, Grete. *Max Reger als Liederkomponist.* Regensburg, 1955.

Weiner, Marc A. *Undertones of Insurrection: Music, Politics and the Social Sphere in Modern German Narrative.* Lincoln, NE, and London, 1993.

Wellbery, David E. *The Specular Moment: Goethe's Early Lyric and the Beginnings of Romanticism.* Palo Alto, 1996.

Wellesz, Egon. *Arnold Schönberg.* New York, 1969.

Wendt, Matthias, ed. *Schumann und seine Dichter: Bericht über das 4. Internationale Schumann-Symposion am 13. und 14. Juni 1991 im Rahmen des 4. Schumann-Festes, Düsseldorf.* Mainz and New York, 1993.

Wenk, Arthur. "The Composer as Poet in *Das Lied von der Erde.*" 19CM 1 (1977), 33–47.

West, Ewan Donald. "Schubert's Lieder in Context: Aspects of Song in Vienna 1778–1828." Ph.D. dissertation, Oxford University, 1989.

Wigmore, Richard. *Schubert: The Complete Song Texts*. New York, 1988.

Williamson, John. *The Music of Hans Pfitzner*. Oxford and New York, 1992.

Winn, James. *Unsuspected Eloquence: A History of the Relations between Poetry and Music*. New Haven, 1981.

Wiora, Walter. *Das deutsche Lied: Zur Geschichte und Ästhetik einer musikalischen Gattung*. Wolfenbüttel and Zurich, 1971.

Wolf, Werner, and Walter Bernhart, eds. *Word and Music Studies: Essays on the Song Cycle and on Defining the Field. Proceedings of the Second International Conference on Word and Music Studies at Ann Arbor, Michigan, 1999*. Amsterdam, 2001.

Youens, Susan. "Behind the Scenes: *Die schöne Müllerin* before Schubert." 19CM (1991), 3–22.

Franz Schubert: Die schöne Müllerin. Cambridge, 1992.

Hugo Wolf and his Mörike Songs. Cambridge, 2000.

Hugo Wolf: The Vocal Music. Princeton, 1992.

Retracing a Winter's Journey: Franz Schubert's Winterreise. Ithaca and London, 1991.

Schubert, Müller, and Die schöne Müllerin. Cambridge, 1997.

Schubert's Late Lieder: Beyond the Song Cycles. Cambridge, 2002

Schubert's Poets and the Making of Lieder. Cambridge, 1996.

Zbikowski, Lawrence. "The Blossoms of *Trockne Blumen*: Music and Text in the Early Nineteenth Century." MA 18 (1999), 307–45.

Index